Lecture Notes in Computer Science 8510

Commenced Publication in 1973
Founding and Former Series Editors:
Gerhard Goos, Juris Hartmanis, and Jan van Leeuwen

T0190059

Masaaki Kurosu (Ed.)

Human-Computer Interaction

Theories, Methods, and Tools

16th International Conference
HCI International 2014
Heraklion, Crete, Greece, June 22-27, 2014
Proceedings, Part I

 Springer

Volume Editor

Masaaki Kurosu
The Open University of Japan
2-11 Wakaba, Mihama-ku, Chiba-shi
Chiba 261-8586, Japan
E-mail: masaakikurosu@spa.nifty.com

ISSN 0302-9743   e-ISSN 1611-3349
ISBN 978-3-319-07232-6   e-ISBN 978-3-319-07233-3
DOI 10.1007/978-3-319-07233-3
Springer Cham Heidelberg New York Dordrecht London

Library of Congress Control Number: 2014938357

LNCS Sublibrary: SL 3 – Information Systems and Application, incl. Internet/Web
and HCI

Typesetting: Camera-ready by author, data conversion by Scientific Publishing Services, Chennai, India

Printed on acid-free paper

Springer is part of Springer Science+Business Media (www.springer.com)

Foreword

The 16th International Conference on Human–Computer Interaction, HCI International 2014, was held in Heraklion, Crete, Greece, during June 22–27, 2014, incorporating 14 conferences/thematic areas:

Thematic areas:

- Human–Computer Interaction
- Human Interface and the Management of Information

Affiliated conferences:

- 11th International Conference on Engineering Psychology and Cognitive Ergonomics
- 8th International Conference on Universal Access in Human–Computer Interaction
- 6th International Conference on Virtual, Augmented and Mixed Reality
- 6th International Conference on Cross-Cultural Design
- 6th International Conference on Social Computing and Social Media
- 8th International Conference on Augmented Cognition
- 5th International Conference on Digital Human Modeling and Applications in Health, Safety, Ergonomics and Risk Management
- Third International Conference on Design, User Experience and Usability
- Second International Conference on Distributed, Ambient and Pervasive Interactions
- Second International Conference on Human Aspects of Information Security, Privacy and Trust
- First International Conference on HCI in Business
- First International Conference on Learning and Collaboration Technologies

A total of 4,766 individuals from academia, research institutes, industry, and governmental agencies from 78 countries submitted contributions, and 1,476 papers and 225 posters were included in the proceedings. These papers address the latest research and development efforts and highlight the human aspects of design and use of computing systems. The papers thoroughly cover the entire field of human–computer interaction, addressing major advances in knowledge and effective use of computers in a variety of application areas.

This volume, edited by Masaaki Kurosu, contains papers focusing on the thematic area of human–computer interaction (HCI), addressing the following major topics:

- Design theories, methods and tools
- HCI and design education

- Models, patterns and tools for UI development
- Adaptive and personalized interfaces
- Evaluation methods, techniques and case studies Visualization methods and techniques

The remaining volumes of the HCI International 2014 proceedings are:

- Volume 2, LNCS 8511, Human–Computer Interaction: Advanced Interaction Modalities and Techniques (Part II), edited by Masaaki Kurosu
- Volume 3, LNCS 8512, Human–Computer Interaction: Applications and Services (Part III), edited by Masaaki Kurosu
- Volume 4, LNCS 8513, Universal Access in Human–Computer Interaction: Design and Development Methods for Universal Access (Part I), edited by Constantine Stephanidis and Margherita Antona
- Volume 5, LNCS 8514, Universal Access in Human–Computer Interaction: Universal Access to Information and Knowledge (Part II), edited by Constantine Stephanidis and Margherita Antona
- Volume 6, LNCS 8515, Universal Access in Human–Computer Interaction: Aging and Assistive Environments (Part III), edited by Constantine Stephanidis and Margherita Antona
- Volume 7, LNCS 8516, Universal Access in Human–Computer Interaction: Design for All and Accessibility Practice (Part IV), edited by Constantine Stephanidis and Margherita Antona
- Volume 8, LNCS 8517, Design, User Experience, and Usability: Theories, Methods and Tools for Designing the User Experience (Part I), edited by Aaron Marcus
- Volume 9, LNCS 8518, Design, User Experience, and Usability: User Experience Design for Diverse Interaction Platforms and Environments (Part II), edited by Aaron Marcus
- Volume 10, LNCS 8519, Design, User Experience, and Usability: User Experience Design for Everyday Life Applications and Services (Part III), edited by Aaron Marcus
- Volume 11, LNCS 8520, Design, User Experience, and Usability: User Experience Design Practice (Part IV), edited by Aaron Marcus
- Volume 12, LNCS 8521, Human Interface and the Management of Information: Information and Knowledge Design and Evaluation (Part I), edited by Sakae Yamamoto
- Volume 13, LNCS 8522, Human Interface and the Management of Information: Information and Knowledge in Applications and Services (Part II), edited by Sakae Yamamoto
- Volume 14, LNCS 8523, Learning and Collaboration Technologies: Designing and Developing Novel Learning Experiences (Part I), edited by Panayiotis Zaphiris and Andri Ioannou
- Volume 15, LNCS 8524, Learning and Collaboration Technologies: Technology-rich Environments for Learning and Collaboration (Part II), edited by Panayiotis Zaphiris and Andri Ioannou

- Volume 16, LNCS 8525, Virtual, Augmented and Mixed Reality: Designing and Developing Virtual and Augmented Environments (Part I), edited by Randall Shumaker and Stephanie Lackey
- Volume 17, LNCS 8526, Virtual, Augmented and Mixed Reality: Applications of Virtual and Augmented Reality (Part II), edited by Randall Shumaker and Stephanie Lackey
- Volume 18, LNCS 8527, HCI in Business, edited by Fiona Fui-Hoon Nah
- Volume 19, LNCS 8528, Cross-Cultural Design, edited by P.L. Patrick Rau
- Volume 20, LNCS 8529, Digital Human Modeling and Applications in Health, Safety, Ergonomics and Risk Management, edited by Vincent G. Duffy
- Volume 21, LNCS 8530, Distributed, Ambient, and Pervasive Interactions, edited by Norbert Streitz and Panos Markopoulos
- Volume 22, LNCS 8531, Social Computing and Social Media, edited by Gabriele Meiselwitz
- Volume 23, LNAI 8532, Engineering Psychology and Cognitive Ergonomics, edited by Don Harris
- Volume 24, LNCS 8533, Human Aspects of Information Security, Privacy and Trust, edited by Theo Tryfonas and Ioannis Askoxylakis
- Volume 25, LNAI 8534, Foundations of Augmented Cognition, edited by Dylan D. Schmorrow and Cali M. Fidopiastis
- Volume 26, CCIS 434, HCI International 2014 Posters Proceedings (Part I), edited by Constantine Stephanidis
- Volume 27, CCIS 435, HCI International 2014 Posters Proceedings (Part II), edited by Constantine Stephanidis

I would like to thank the Program Chairs and the members of the Program Boards of all affiliated conferences and thematic areas, listed below, for their contribution to the highest scientific quality and the overall success of the HCI International 2014 Conference.

This conference could not have been possible without the continuous support and advice of the founding chair and conference scientific advisor, Prof. Gavriel Salvendy, as well as the dedicated work and outstanding efforts of the communications chair and editor of *HCI International News*, Dr. Abbas Moallem.

I would also like to thank for their contribution towards the smooth organization of the HCI International 2014 Conference the members of the Human–Computer Interaction Laboratory of ICS-FORTH, and in particular George Paparoulis, Maria Pitsoulaki, Maria Bouhli, and George Kapnas.

April 2014   Constantine Stephanidis
                                         General Chair, HCI International 2014

Organization

Human–Computer Interaction

Program Chair: Masaaki Kurosu, Japan

Jose Abdelnour-Nocera, UK
Sebastiano Bagnara, Italy
Simone Barbosa, Brazil
Adriana Betiol, Brazil
Simone Borsci, UK
Henry Duh, Australia
Xiaowen Fang, USA
Vicki Hanson, UK
Wonil Hwang, Korea
Minna Isomursu, Finland
Yong Gu Ji, Korea
Anirudha Joshi, India
Esther Jun, USA
Kyungdoh Kim, Korea

Heidi Krömker, Germany
Chen Ling, USA
Chang S. Nam, USA
Naoko Okuizumi, Japan
Philippe Palanque, France
Ling Rothrock, USA
Naoki Sakakibara, Japan
Dominique Scapin, France
Guangfeng Song, USA
Sanjay Tripathi, India
Chui Yin Wong, Malaysia
Toshiki Yamaoka, Japan
Kazuhiko Yamazaki, Japan
Ryoji Yoshitake, Japan

Human Interface and the Management of Information

Program Chair: Sakae Yamamoto, Japan

Alan Chan, Hong Kong
Denis A. Coelho, Portugal
Linda Elliott, USA
Shin'ichi Fukuzumi, Japan
Michitaka Hirose, Japan
Makoto Itoh, Japan
Yen-Yu Kang, Taiwan
Koji Kimita, Japan
Daiji Kobayashi, Japan

Hiroyuki Miki, Japan
Shogo Nishida, Japan
Robert Proctor, USA
Youngho Rhee, Korea
Ryosuke Saga, Japan
Katsunori Shimohara, Japan
Kim-Phuong Vu, USA
Tomio Watanabe, Japan

Engineering Psychology and Cognitive Ergonomics

Program Chair: Don Harris, UK

Guy Andre Boy, USA
Shan Fu, P.R. China
Hung-Sying Jing, Taiwan
Wen-Chin Li, Taiwan
Mark Neerincx, The Netherlands
Jan Noyes, UK
Paul Salmon, Australia

Axel Schulte, Germany
Siraj Shaikh, UK
Sarah Sharples, UK
Anthony Smoker, UK
Neville Stanton, UK
Alex Stedmon, UK
Andrew Thatcher, South Africa

Universal Access in Human–Computer Interaction

Program Chairs: Constantine Stephanidis, Greece, and Margherita Antona, Greece

Julio Abascal, Spain
Gisela Susanne Bahr, USA
João Barroso, Portugal
Margrit Betke, USA
Anthony Brooks, Denmark
Christian Bühler, Germany
Stefan Carmien, Spain
Hua Dong, P.R. China
Carlos Duarte, Portugal
Pier Luigi Emiliani, Italy
Qin Gao, P.R. China
Andrina Granić, Croatia
Andreas Holzinger, Austria
Josette Jones, USA
Simeon Keates, UK

Georgios Kouroupetroglou, Greece
Patrick Langdon, UK
Barbara Leporini, Italy
Eugene Loos, The Netherlands
Ana Isabel Paraguay, Brazil
Helen Petrie, UK
Michael Pieper, Germany
Enrico Pontelli, USA
Jaime Sanchez, Chile
Alberto Sanna, Italy
Anthony Savidis, Greece
Christian Stary, Austria
Hirotada Ueda, Japan
Gerhard Weber, Germany
Harald Weber, Germany

Virtual, Augmented and Mixed Reality

Program Chairs: Randall Shumaker, USA, and Stephanie Lackey, USA

Roland Blach, Germany
Sheryl Brahnam, USA
Juan Cendan, USA
Jessie Chen, USA
Panagiotis D. Kaklis, UK

Hirokazu Kato, Japan
Denis Laurendeau, Canada
Fotis Liarokapis, UK
Michael Macedonia, USA
Gordon Mair, UK

Jose San Martin, Spain
Tabitha Peck, USA
Christian Sandor, Australia

Christopher Stapleton, USA
Gregory Welch, USA

Cross-Cultural Design

Program Chair: P.L. Patrick Rau, P.R. China

Yee-Yin Choong, USA
Paul Fu, USA
Zhiyong Fu, P.R. China
Pin-Chao Liao, P.R. China
Dyi-Yih Michael Lin, Taiwan
Rungtai Lin, Taiwan
Ta-Ping (Robert) Lu, Taiwan
Liang Ma, P.R. China
Alexander Mädche, Germany

Sheau-Farn Max Liang, Taiwan
Katsuhiko Ogawa, Japan
Tom Plocher, USA
Huatong Sun, USA
Emil Tso, P.R. China
Hsiu-Ping Yueh, Taiwan
Liang (Leon) Zeng, USA
Jia Zhou, P.R. China

Online Communities and Social Media

Program Chair: Gabriele Meiselwitz, USA

Leonelo Almeida, Brazil
Chee Siang Ang, UK
Aneesha Bakharia, Australia
Ania Bobrowicz, UK
James Braman, USA
Farzin Deravi, UK
Carsten Kleiner, Germany
Niki Lambropoulos, Greece
Soo Ling Lim, UK

Anthony Norcio, USA
Portia Pusey, USA
Panote Siriaraya, UK
Stefan Stieglitz, Germany
Giovanni Vincenti, USA
Yuanqiong (Kathy) Wang, USA
June Wei, USA
Brian Wentz, USA

Augmented Cognition

Program Chairs: Dylan D. Schmorrow, USA, and Cali M. Fidopiastis, USA

Ahmed Abdelkhalek, USA
Robert Atkinson, USA
Monique Beaudoin, USA
John Blitch, USA
Alenka Brown, USA

Rosario Cannavò, Italy
Joseph Cohn, USA
Andrew J. Cowell, USA
Martha Crosby, USA
Wai-Tat Fu, USA

Rodolphe Gentili, USA
Frederick Gregory, USA
Michael W. Hail, USA
Monte Hancock, USA
Fei Hu, USA
Ion Juvina, USA
Joe Keebler, USA
Philip Mangos, USA
Rao Mannepalli, USA
David Martinez, USA
Yvonne R. Masakowski, USA
Santosh Mathan, USA
Ranjeev Mittu, USA

Keith Niall, USA
Tatana Olson, USA
Debra Patton, USA
June Pilcher, USA
Robinson Pino, USA
Tiffany Poeppelman, USA
Victoria Romero, USA
Amela Sadagic, USA
Anna Skinner, USA
Ann Speed, USA
Robert Sottilare, USA
Peter Walker, USA

Digital Human Modeling and Applications in Health, Safety, Ergonomics and Risk Management

Program Chair: Vincent G. Duffy, USA

Giuseppe Andreoni, Italy
Daniel Carruth, USA
Elsbeth De Korte, The Netherlands
Afzal A. Godil, USA
Ravindra Goonetilleke, Hong Kong
Noriaki Kuwahara, Japan
Kang Li, USA
Zhizhong Li, P.R. China

Tim Marler, USA
Jianwei Niu, P.R. China
Michelle Robertson, USA
Matthias Rötting, Germany
Mao-Jiun Wang, Taiwan
Xuguang Wang, France
James Yang, USA

Design, User Experience, and Usability

Program Chair: Aaron Marcus, USA

Sisira Adikari, Australia
Claire Ancient, USA
Arne Berger, Germany
Jamie Blustein, Canada
Ana Boa-Ventura, USA
Jan Brejcha, Czech Republic
Lorenzo Cantoni, Switzerland
Marc Fabri, UK
Luciane Maria Fadel, Brazil
Tricia Flanagan, Hong Kong
Jorge Frascara, Mexico

Federico Gobbo, Italy
Emilie Gould, USA
Rüdiger Heimgärtner, Germany
Brigitte Herrmann, Germany
Steffen Hess, Germany
Nouf Khashman, Canada
Fabiola Guillermina Noël, Mexico
Francisco Rebelo, Portugal
Kerem Rızvanoğlu, Turkey
Marcelo Soares, Brazil
Carla Spinillo, Brazil

Distributed, Ambient and Pervasive Interactions

Program Chairs: Norbert Streitz, Germany, and Panos Markopoulos, The Netherlands

Juan Carlos Augusto, UK
Jose Bravo, Spain
Adrian Cheok, UK
Boris de Ruyter, The Netherlands
Anind Dey, USA
Dimitris Grammenos, Greece
Nuno Guimaraes, Portugal
Achilles Kameas, Greece
Javed Vassilis Khan, The Netherlands
Shin'ichi Konomi, Japan
Carsten Magerkurth, Switzerland

Ingrid Mulder, The Netherlands
Anton Nijholt, The Netherlands
Fabio Paternó, Italy
Carsten Röcker, Germany
Teresa Romao, Portugal
Albert Ali Salah, Turkey
Manfred Tscheligi, Austria
Reiner Wichert, Germany
Woontack Woo, Korea
Xenophon Zabulis, Greece

Human Aspects of Information Security, Privacy and Trust

Program Chairs: Theo Tryfonas, UK, and Ioannis Askoxylakis, Greece

Claudio Agostino Ardagna, Italy
Zinaida Benenson, Germany
Daniele Catteddu, Italy
Raoul Chiesa, Italy
Bryan Cline, USA
Sadie Creese, UK
Jorge Cuellar, Germany
Marc Dacier, USA
Dieter Gollmann, Germany
Kirstie Hawkey, Canada
Jaap-Henk Hoepman, The Netherlands
Cagatay Karabat, Turkey
Angelos Keromytis, USA
Ayako Komatsu, Japan
Ronald Leenes, The Netherlands
Javier Lopez, Spain
Steve Marsh, Canada

Gregorio Martinez, Spain
Emilio Mordini, Italy
Yuko Murayama, Japan
Masakatsu Nishigaki, Japan
Aljosa Pasic, Spain
Milan Petković, The Netherlands
Joachim Posegga, Germany
Jean-Jacques Quisquater, Belgium
Damien Sauveron, France
George Spanoudakis, UK
Kerry-Lynn Thomson, South Africa
Julien Touzeau, France
Theo Tryfonas, UK
João Vilela, Portugal
Claire Vishik, UK
Melanie Volkamer, Germany

HCI in Business

Program Chair: Fiona Fui-Hoon Nah, USA

Andreas Auinger, Austria
Michel Avital, Denmark
Traci Carte, USA
Hock Chuan Chan, Singapore
Constantinos Coursaris, USA
Soussan Djamasbi, USA
Brenda Eschenbrenner, USA
Nobuyuki Fukawa, USA
Khaled Hassanein, Canada
Milena Head, Canada
Susanna (Shuk Ying) Ho, Australia
Jack Zhenhui Jiang, Singapore
Jinwoo Kim, Korea
Zoonky Lee, Korea
Honglei Li, UK
Nicholas Lockwood, USA
Eleanor T. Loiacono, USA
Mei Lu, USA

Scott McCoy, USA
Brian Mennecke, USA
Robin Poston, USA
Lingyun Qiu, P.R. China
Rene Riedl, Austria
Matti Rossi, Finland
April Savoy, USA
Shu Schiller, USA
Hong Sheng, USA
Choon Ling Sia, Hong Kong
Chee-Wee Tan, Denmark
Chuan Hoo Tan, Hong Kong
Noam Tractinsky, Israel
Horst Treiblmaier, Austria
Virpi Tuunainen, Finland
Dezhi Wu, USA
I-Chin Wu, Taiwan

Learning and Collaboration Technologies

Program Chairs: Panayiotis Zaphiris, Cyprus, and Andri Ioannou, Cyprus

Ruthi Aladjem, Israel
Abdulaziz Aldaej, UK
John M. Carroll, USA
Maka Eradze, Estonia
Mikhail Fominykh, Norway
Denis Gillet, Switzerland
Mustafa Murat Inceoglu, Turkey
Pernilla Josefsson, Sweden
Marie Joubert, UK
Sauli Kiviranta, Finland
Tomaž Klobučar, Slovenia
Elena Kyza, Cyprus
Maarten de Laat, The Netherlands
David Lamas, Estonia

Edmund Laugasson, Estonia
Ana Loureiro, Portugal
Katherine Maillet, France
Nadia Pantidi, UK
Antigoni Parmaxi, Cyprus
Borzoo Pourabdollahian, Italy
Janet C. Read, UK
Christophe Reffay, France
Nicos Souleles, Cyprus
Ana Luísa Torres, Portugal
Stefan Trausan-Matu, Romania
Aimilia Tzanavari, Cyprus
Johnny Yuen, Hong Kong
Carmen Zahn, Switzerland

External Reviewers

Ilia Adami, Greece
Iosif Klironomos, Greece
Maria Korozi, Greece
Vassilis Kouroumalis, Greece

Asterios Leonidis, Greece
George Margetis, Greece
Stavroula Ntoa, Greece
Nikolaos Partarakis, Greece

HCI International 2015

The 15th International Conference on Human–Computer Interaction, HCI International 2015, will be held jointly with the affiliated conferences in Los Angeles, CA, USA, in the Westin Bonaventure Hotel, August 2–7, 2015. It will cover a broad spectrum of themes related to HCI, including theoretical issues, methods, tools, processes, and case studies in HCI design, as well as novel interaction techniques, interfaces, and applications. The proceedings will be published by Springer. More information will be available on the conference website:
http://www.hcii2015.org/

General Chair
Professor Constantine Stephanidis
University of Crete and ICS-FORTH
Heraklion, Crete, Greece
E-mail: cs@ics.forth.gr

Table of Contents – Part I

Design Theories, Methods and Tools

HCI and Design Education

Models, Patterns and Tools for UI Development

Adaptive and Personalized Interfaces

Evaluation Methods, Techniques and Case Studies

Visualisation Methods and Techniques

Table of Contents – Part II

Gesture-Based Interaction

Gesture, Gaze and Activity Recognition

Speech, Natural Language and Conversational Interfaces

Natural and Multimodal Interfaces

Human-Robot Interaction

Emotions Recognition

Table of Contents – Part III

Interacting with the Web

Mobile Interaction

HCI for Health, Well-Being and Sport

Mobility, Transport and Environment

Interacting with Games

Business, Sustainability and Technology Adoption

Design Theories, Methods and Tools

Psychological Personas for Universal User Modeling in Human-Computer Interaction

Caio Felix de Araujo and Plinio Thomaz Aquino Junior

Centro Universitário da FEI, Department of Computer Science, Brazil
caio.felix.de.araujo@gmail.com, plinio.aquino@fei.edu.br

Abstract. Applying techniques to understand the user needs and expectation in product development is important practices for find consistent strategies. However, available techniques need human interaction, is a psychologist examining a profile or usability expert capturing information about user's group. In this situation, data collection and analysis require a large effort and cost to make the purpose of knowing the user needs. This paper aims to create a set of personas from psychological profiles theory that define a generic model, clustering information about knowledge, skills, impulses and concerns, outlining action patterns of users diversity that exist today. This set of personas can be used in global solutions, considering universal usability aspects. Finally, the worldwide acceptance of psychological profiles allows updated and consistent personas, decreasing cost and increasing quality.

Keywords: Personas-Psychological Profiles-User Modeling-User Profile.

1   Introduction

Personas are a support technique to identify users profile in product development. They provide easily and directly communication about who are the users in a particular product. Based on the concept of user-centered development, this technique provides necessary information to designers for make decisions.

Are several methods to do effective personas, like: target groups interview, mining database, subjective observation. These methods give a set of personas that represents only the profiles considered, personas created within a particular context based on project domain. Theoretical definition [1] and lifecycle [2] of personas say that the set of created personas is particular to the project, a reuse requires additional effort about evolution or mutation of each persona.

With time, electronic devices and systems will be used for everyone requiring development based on different profiles. In this purpose, universal usability becomes a critical requirement in a product design [3], considering diversity of global projects, without race discrimination color or national origin, adding value to universal design and accessibility [4]. To reach universal usability, designers need to consider that a lot of people will use the product in practical applications [5].

Therefore, this paper aims to contribute to a set of personas that represent diversity of existing users nowadays, and create a general model for product development.

M. Kurosu (Ed.): Human-Computer Interaction, Part I, HCII 2014, LNCS 8510, pp. 3–13, 2014.
© Springer International Publishing Switzerland 2014

Applying established theories in a field of psychology and administration, defining people based on their behavior [6] with personas theory, set up inputs for creation of psychological personas, and applied field research validating the hypotheses of this work.

The paper is structured as follows: state of the art presentation of personas and psychological types. Methodology used in development and results. Beyond that is presented the result of the application of Psychological Personas into a project of Research and Statistic based on Digital Collection of Patient Medical Record in Center User Telemedicine (PEAP-PMPT, in Portuguese) which Personas are created by the use for Universal User Modeling in Human-Computer Interaction. The entire research field used to confirm the hypothesis, conclusions and proposals for a future work.

2   Personas

The persona concept was first cited by Carl Jung [6], with define that humans tend to act differently in each social environment. Was subsequently proposed by Alan Cooper [1], applying personas as a practical tool for interaction design [2].

Robert Barlow-Busch [2] compared traditional methods between personas with marketing area applied to industry highlighting those that were considered remarkable advantages. Personas do not solve problems of designers, but they are additions to the toolbox of any person who seek a better experience for the end user of a product or service [2]. Personas are a descriptive model of users who represent a real group of people and their characteristics [1]. These models focus information about knowledge, skills, motivations and concerns, describing action patterns that a user group has on a particular project [7][8], allowing the information exchange between user profile and the project team [9]. This general representation of involved users enables the development of projects that respond diversity [3].

Bagnall [10] describes the personas technique as powerful design tools in order to exchange information assisting the creative team for develop interactive systems. Calde, Goodwin and Reimann [11] highlighted that the successful use of personas depends not only from the experts who created them, but the quality of resources and sources chosen for data. Other applications scenarios of personas technique generating satisfactory results can be analyzed in McGinn e Kptamraju [7], Thoma and Williams [12], Khalayli et al [13], Adlin et al [14] and Pruitt and Grudin [15]. The combination of the Personas technique with other techniques of product development has shown promising results, the emphasis on the process of user-centered design can be considered a bridge between organizations, user requirements and system [16]. In summary, the composition of Personas can be formulated based on creating information or sources, thus shaping the personality of Personas [3].

The presented papers serve as validation both on validity of personas technique to assist in product development, and in constant need to collect data for personas composition. This research considers the personas as a method that supports the creation of new products with the knowledge of the user profile in a target project.

Considering projects that respond to diverse populations (e.g., interfaces for e-gov), it is necessary to be able identifying the target audience with help of additional techniques that increase information about user behavior. For this, the acknowledgment of the user psychological type can help to identify it as a persona and consider your needs and preferences in the interactive process.

3   Psychological Types

Proposed by Jung [6], the psychological types are models of attitudes that explain the process by which people see themselves and the world, a basic guideline that indicates the direction of the interests. Briefly are thought patterns in the execution of an action. These thought patterns are based on two activities: Capture information or organize information and reach conclusions.

With these assumptions, Jung [6] classifies every individual in four opposite pairs, each pair shows a set of personal characteristics: [E Extraversion/ I Introversion, S Sensation / N Intuition, T Thought / F Feeling, J Judgment / P Perception]. Finally these opposite pairs characterize, as a person will act in situations of preferences, decision-making, attention and experience.

Katharine Cook Briggs and Isabel Briggs Myers [17][18] concludes that the typology can represent a method to describe the difference between personalities and can be used in practice. In this way, the MBTI (Myers and Briggs Type Indicator) indicator was built to prove the psychological preferences through Jung's typology [6][19].

Davis [20], Ludford and Tervenn [21] investigate and check the effects of Jung's psychological types next to information on the performance of users within the context of information systems. As a result the authors had determined some connections between typology of each person to the organization and decision-making.

The authors of the articles cited above, as well Rosati [22], Bannerot [23], Chois and Deek [24][25], Harrington and Loffredo [26], Per and Beyoglu [27],Yan [28], Wang, Jing and Xue [29], Nichols, McPeek and Breiner [30], Li et al [31], Rosati, Russell and Rodman [32], Bell et al [33] and Yu [34] use MBTI as a tool to identify profiles from each group involved in their studies, proving that even in different scenarios, with different purposes, the indicator is considered effective.

People's values differ fundamentally from one another, Keirsey [35] developed a classifier of temperaments, based on Jung's [6] and Myers [17][18]. The new classifier called Temperament Sorter (KTS-II) is an instrument that uses the answer of 70 questions to decide the user's psychological type [36][37] and was used as a tool to characterize temperaments in some papers. Authors as Cha-Hwa and Mcleod [38] and Herman [39], use KTS-II to classify profiles in different scenarios, proving its validity, also confirming diversity proposal in psychological type's theory.

The presented papers with different purposes and different people of distinct pieces of world have the same human behavior, following patterns, actions sequence based on the structure of personality, allowing us to say that psychological types can describe, explain and interpret these patterns.

This paper presents a method that supports the process of identifying the user profile based on their activities and behaviors with the use of psychological types, making the information in the user's personality, completely characterize the contents of the user profile declared as persona.

The objective was to create a set of personas that can express any type of user, based on a theory proven in environments of psychology, psychoanalysis and administration, such as psychological types.

4   Psychological Persona Methodology

For the definition of Psychological Persona was used as a principle the four basic psychological functions identified by Jung [6]: thinking, feeling, sensation and intuition.

For each basic psychological function (mentioned in psychological type's session) is a set of psychological types related. The set of psychological types of each function is shown below: [Sensation (ISTJ / ISFJ / ESTP / ESFP), Intuition (INTJ / INFJ / ENTP / ENFP), Thinking (ISTP / INTP / ESTJ / ENTJ), Feeling (ISFP / INFP / ESFJ / ENFJ)].

In addition to the definitions made by Jung [6], was used terms and descriptions provided in the work of Keirsey [35] and Myers [17], [18]. The personas are created and declared in a standard format according to each approach. Table 1 represents the structure of psychological personas declaration.

Table 1. Structure of Psychological Personas Declaration

Item	Description
(N) Name	Used as communication facilitator between professionals.
(Pf) Psychological function	Personas were created from each basic psychological function, and this function is a direct relationship between the persona and the psychological types.
(Pt) Psychological set of types	Each basic psychological function comprises four psychological types.
(T) Temperament	Portrays personality of the individual, used to decision-making.
(Pfe) Professional features	Some professional features can be defined for each basic psychological function, featuring a more detailed look at the persona. Allowing the designer to understand the motivations and ways of each basic psychological function relating with other people and the project itself.
(Gc) General characteristics	This attribute is composed of the most important aspects of the declared persona

5   Results

From structure of declaration mentioned in Table 1, it was possible create four psychological personas displayed on Table 2, Table 3, Table 4 and Table 5.

Table 2. Persona Defined from Psychological Function Sensation

Item	Description
N(Pf)	Helen (Sensation)
	She has strong preference for information through the five senses and understands what is real. Is a person with a focus on direct experience, the perception of details and facts. Cares about the actual experience and always has priority over the discussion or the analysis of experience.
Pt	ISTJ / ISFJ / ESTP / ESFP
T	Its most remarkable characteristic is to be observant.
Pfe	Is a person who tends to respond to any situation in your life immediately, deals effectively with all types of crises and emergencies. Works very well with tools, equipment, vehicles and tools in general. Rarely trusts in insights and rarely makes mistakes of fact. Tends to be good at precision work. Finally, it is too impatient when details lead to complications, however values the conclusion.
Gc	Have a greater preference for using skills already learned, instead of learning new ones. It is a concrete person, realistic, practical and traditional.

Table 3. Persona Defined from Psychological Function Intuition

Item	Description
N(Pf)	Jessica (Intuition)
	Prefers information through a "sixth sense", which seems to perceive. She's very good at processing information in terms of past experience, future goals and unconscious processes. Things like that can happen, or what is possible, are more important to her than the experience of life itself. And because of his speed in the correlation between intuitive information with detailed information, it has great difficulty in separating their conscious interpretations of raw sensory data.
Pt	INTJ / INFJ / ENTP / ENFP
T	Introspective is the most remarkable characteristic of her, their beliefs and associations of ideas are always present in your daily lives.

Table 3. (*continued*)

Pfe	Is a person who processes information very quickly and very easily relates to, automatically, past experience with the relevant information. Like enough to solve problems, and hates routine. It has great hurry about learning new skills, much more than use them and often jump to conclusions. Works with lots of energy, fueled by enthusiasm, with slack periods between activities. It is very patient with complicated situations and always follows your inspirations. Finally, do not like to spend time with little things.
Gc	Do not like to do the same thing repeatedly. It is an imaginative person, who loves working with the original theoretical concepts to develop new ideas.

Table 4. Persona Defined from Psychological Function Thinking

Item	Description
N(Pf)	Rafael (Thinking)
	He has strong preference for organizing and structuring information to make decisions logically and objectively, a great sense of truth, with judgments derived from impersonal criteria, logical and objective.
Pt	ISTP / INTP / ESTJ / ENTJ
T	Its most remarkable characteristic is to be firm in their projects.
Pfe	He's a thoughtful and a great planner. Your decisions are taken impersonally, ignoring the wishes of the people. He needs to be treated with honesty and is able to relate to other people more rational. Like analysis and use logical for everything, often tends to hurt people's feelings without noticing.
Gc	He's extremely logical and critical, often considered difficult to handle.

Table 5. Persona Defined from Psychological Function Feeling

Item	Description
N(Pf)	Airton (Feeling)
	He prefers to organize and structure information at the time of decision making and personally oriented values. He has great advice for the emotional aspects of experience and prefers strong and intense emotions even negative, apathetic and warm experience.
Pt	ISFP / INFP / ESFJ / ENFJ
T	Its most remarkable characteristic is his charisma.
Pfe	Standards such as good or bad, right or wrong, define how it makes decisions. Always looking to be close to others and respect their feelings. Loves to please others even when things are not important, prefers harmony. Usually leaves their decisions be influenced by desires and preferences of others.
Gc	Always take their decisions based on what is right.

This set of psychological personas can be used within development lifecycle of any product, for this research, psychological personas were confronted with a case study.

6   Psychological Personas in Action

The case study identifies the patterns of attitude, behavior and temperament presented in Jung's theory. These patterns are validated in a dynamic group with people from different professions and in different positions.

The dynamic group aimed to identify the similarity of actions and comparison of data according to the model presented in personas based on psychological types. Was performed to monitor the implementation of the dynamic group for several days with different members, for only thus obtain the diversity needed to validate the model. Five days of group activities, totaling sixteen hours of work.

The dynamic consisted of a description of an image pre-selected by the psychologist who uses the dominant role of psychological type of each person as a criterion for group division. After the division of the profiles, all groups of people receive an image. It is requested that the group describe the image as best as possible, in order to describe it to other members. Thus, it was possible to identify the characteristics of people, allowing their subsequent analysis.

Table 6. Analysis Result of Similarity Between the Dynamics and Psychological Personas

Group	Users	Sensation	Intuition	Thinking	Feeling	Hit Rating
01	20	6	3	5	6	90,9%
02	18	5	4	6	4	95,0%
03	38	11	9	8	10	91,5%
04	48	12	10	17	9	86,5%
Total	124	34	26	36	29	90,9%

In dynamics execution, the behavior of each participant from each group, was observed and analyzed in contrast to psychological personas. Table 6 presents a summary of analyzed data, first column identifies analyzes performed on different days, second column identifies the number of people participating on dynamics, third, fourth, fifth and sixth columns identify the division of each group according to the psychological function. Finally, seventh column indicates the hit rating of each group in contrast to the psychological personas. This hit rating was calculated according to a threshold between 0 and 10 related to each existing items in personas description, in contrast to actions performed for each participants of the case study.

The results showed that 90,9% of the cases, psychological personas were satisfactory in its description, proving the hypotheses proposed in this paper.

7   Application Method

The application method to identify personas in a user group is composed of steps:

Step 1 – Questionnaire application: Apply KTS-II [35]. The KTS-II was chosen for a couple of reasons: (a) is the result of a published book (b) is quoted in numerous papers (c) use this methodology explained clearly in his book (d) is available for free on the internet [36].

Step 2 – Evaluation and definition of psychological types: Analyze the questionnaire and determine the psychological type.

Step 3 – Validation of the framework and personas: From the topic 'set of psychological types' presented in each of the personas defined in this work, with the definition of the user-defined type in step 2, it is necessary to frame this user among one of the personas that have been created.

Step 4 – Application of personas in the project: With the questionnaires of the user groups and their respective personas, you can define the most relevant to the project, personas and thus use them to better define the scope for the development since interfaces until the necessary processes.

In this step you will need, according to each project, define a percentage of cut to the personas used as the basis of the project. This step is exemplified in the table below.

Table 7. Sample Project

Number of users who answered the KTS-II questionnaire	200	
Personas that represent each user	Users	%
Helen	60	30%
Jessica	45	23%
Airton	65	33%
Rafael	30	15%
Percentage cutoff for this project	30%	
Personas used in this project	Helen and Airton	

In the project sample 200 users were used to define personas after they answer the KTS-II questionnaire, and each user was fit in a persona defined in the model. After defining a percentage cut, only the personas those are above this percentage fall to the project.

8   Conclusions

The personas theory contributes to bring users together, those responsible for the development of a product, whether for interface or system development. However, for a set of personas can insert value within the development group, these personas should be well developed and in connection with all aspects related to users.

The psychological personas were identified and implemented in PEAP-PMPT project. These personas were used to characterize the behavior of a group of 10 doctor's hospital participating in the project. The psychological personas helped identify new doctors to validate results of usability tests. These personas were used to document the profile of physicians and suggest improvements in the interface.

With a set of personas based on an already established theory in Psychology, descriptions and characteristics of this theory has been proven and validated, giving personas confidence necessary in relation to the users.

In this work, a personas work-related review exemplifies the above statement, with the psychological type's work-related review, which shows that it is possible to determine how personality dimensions, how to make decisions and the way people see the world, regardless of their location or culture. Thus, with the personas generated in this work, together with the case study, it is possible to characterize the personas concept of universal usability.

The method described is intended contribute to a support user profile identifying, through a set of personas that serves as data source for creative teams and product development. For future works, from psychological types theory is possible to create personas more specific or more generic than the proposed personas, thus creating greater comprehensiveness for new projects.

9   Future Work

From the theory of psychological types, you can create more specific or generic personas in comparison of those proposed in this paper, thus creating greater control to the professionals who have used personas. The identification of this new set of personas is through the same method proposed in this paper, also allowing simply a breadth of information to be handled in the most profitable.

Along with this work, it is also possible to validate a possible correlation between the personas created and habits in the use of technology, I can infer that there may be a consensus among most types who like technology and others less, or even get to the point of defining what some types use more communication vehicles such as e-mails and social networks and not others.

With the addition of these two future work, we can create personas with enough information to compose a Framework personas oriented psychology covering the population in order to facilitate both the collection of information in the analysis of target audience, as the user-centered development creating a repository of information where the developer can create a whole interaction between the system and the user.

And finally, with all the information from this framework, that may services to other areas such as marketing, to characterize target public campaigns, for teaching students to characterize and develop best in class activities, among many other applications.

Acknowledgment. This work is supported by FINEP: PEAP-PMPT project (Research and Statistic based on Digital Collection of Patient Medical Record in Center User Telemedicine), ref. 1465/10, Institutional Process number 01.10.0765.00, MCT/FINEP/SAUDE TELESAUDEE TELEMEDICINA No - 1/2010. Special thanks to the project coordinators: Dr. Otávio Curioni e Prof. Ricardo de Carvalho Destro.

References

1. Cooper, A.: The inmates are running the asylum: Why high-tech products drive us crazy and how to restore the sanity. Macmillan, New York (1999)
2. Pruitt, J., Adlin, T.: The Persona Lifecycle: Keeping People in Mind Throughout Product Design. Morgan-Kaufmann, San Francisco (2006)
3. Aquino, Jr., P.T.: PICaP Padrões e Personas para Expressão da Diversidade de Usuário no Projeto de Interação. Tese de doutorado, Escola Politécnica da USP (2008)
4. Aquino Jr., P., Filgueiras, L.V.L.: The Multiple Identity of Universality. In: Interfaces and Human Computer Interaction 2007 - IADIS International Conference 2007, Proceedings of the IADIS Multi Conference on Computer Science and Information Systems (MCCSIS 2007), Lisboa (2007)
5. Vanderheiden, G.: Fundamental Principles and Priority Setting for Universal Usability. In: Proceedings of Conference on Universal Usability (CUU), pp. 32–38. Association for Computing Machinery (2000)
6. Jung, C.G.: Psychological Types. Princeton University Press, Princeton (1971)
7. Mcginn, J., Kotamraju, N.: Data-Driven Persona Development. In: CHI (2008)
8. Miller, G., Williams, L.: Personas: Moving Beyond Role-Based Requirements Engineering, Microsoft and North Carolina State University (2006)
9. Pruitt, J., Grudin, J.: Personas, Participatory Design and Product Development: An Infrastructure for Engagement. In: Proceedings of the Participartory Design Conference, PDC 2002, pp. 144–161 (2002)
10. Bagnall, P.: Using Personas Effectively. In: Proceedings of the 21st BCS HCI Group Conference, vol. 2. British Computer Society (2007)
11. Calde, S., Goodwin, K., Reimann, R.: SHS Orcas: The first integrated information system for long-term healthcare facility management. In: Conference on Human Factors and Computing Systems. ACM Press, New York (2002)
12. Thoma, V., Williams, B.: Developing and Validating Personas in e-Commerce: A Heuristic Approach. In: Gross, T., Gulliksen, J., Kotzé, P., Oestreicher, L., Palanque, P., Prates, R.O., Winckler, M. (eds.) INTERACT 2009, part II. LNCS, vol. 5727, pp. 524–527. Springer, Heidelberg (2009)
13. Khalayli, N., et al.: Persona Based Rapid Usability Kick-Off. In: CHI (2007)
14. Adlin, T., et al.: Panel: Putting Personas to Work. In: CHI (2006)
15. Pruitt, J., Grudin, J.: Personas: Practice and Theory. In: Proceedings of the 2003 Conference on Designing for User Experiences, pp. 1–15. ACM Press (2003)
16. Markensten, E., Artman, H.: Procuring a Usable System Using Unemployed Personas. In: NordiCHI (2004)
17. Myers, I.B.: The Myers-Briggs Type Indicator. Consulting Psychologist Press (1962)
18. Myers, I.B.: Introduction to Type: A Description of the Theory and Applications of the Myers–Briggs Type Indicator. Consulting Psychologist Press (1987)
19. Quenk, N.L.: Essentials of Myers-Briggs Type Indicator Assessment. John Wiley & Sons, Inc. (1999)

20. Davis, L.D.: An Experimental Investigation of the Form of Information Presentation, Psychological Type of the User, and Performance within the context of a Management Information System. Gainesville, University of Florida: Doctoral Dissertation (1981)
21. Ludford, J.P., Terveen, G.L.: Does an Individual's Myers-Briggs Type Indicator Preference Influence Task-Oriented Technology Use? In: Proceedings of Interact, Zurique (2003)
22. Rosati, P.: Students' Psychological Type and Success in Different Engineering Programs. In: Proceedings of Frontiers in Education Conference, Pittsburgh, vol. 2, pp. 781–784 (1997)
23. Bannerot, R.: Who Graduates in Mechanical Engineering? In: Frontiers in Education Conference (FIE), pp. 11–16 (2007)
24. Choi, S.K., Deek, P.F.: Exploring the underlying aspects of pair programming: The impact of personality. Information and Software Technology 50, 1114–1126 (2008)
25. Choi, S.K., Deek, P.F.: Pair dynamics in team collaboration. Computers in Human Behavior 25, 844–852 (2009)
26. Harrington, R., Loffredo, D.A.: MBTI personality type and other factors that relate to preference for online vs. face-to-face instruction. Internet and Higher Education 13, 89–95 (2010)
27. Per, M., Beyoglu, A.: Personality types of students who study at the departments of numeric, verbal and fine arts in education faculties. Procedia – Social and Behavioral Sciences 12, 242–247 (2010)
28. Yan, S.: Successful Implementation of E-Learning from the Situated Cognition and MBTI Perspective. In: Computer Design an Applications (ICCDA), vol. 2, pp. 123–125 (2010)
29. Wang, Y., Jing, L., Xue, Y.: University-Industry Cooperation Game Research Based on Different Psychological Types and Demands. In: Proceedings of Information Management, Innovation Management and Industrial Engineering, Kunming, vol. 1, pp. 583–587 (2010)
30. Nichols, A.L., McPeek, R.W., Breiner, J.F.: Personality as a Predictor of Older Driver Performance. Traffic Psychology and Behavior 14, 381–389 (2011)
31. Li, S.Y., et al.: An exploratory study of the relationship between age and learning styles among students in Taiwan. Nurse Education Today 31, 18–23 (2011)
32. Rosati, P., Russell, K.D., Rodman, M.S.: A Study of the Relationship Between Students' Learning Styles and Instructors. IEEE Transactions on Education, 208–212 (1988)
33. Bell, A.M., et al.: Do Personality Differences Between Teachers and Learners Impact Students? Journal of Surgical Education 68, 190–193 (2011)
34. Yu, C.: The Relationship Between MBTI and Career Success for Chinese Example. In: Management and Service Science (MASS), pp. 1–6 (2011)
35. Keirsey, D.: Please Understand Me II. Prometheus Nemesis Book, Del (mar 1998)
36. The Keirsey temperament Sorter II, http://www.keirsey.com/aboutkts2.aspx
37. The KTSII – Personality Test, http://www.keirsey.com/sorter/instruments2.aspx
38. Cha-Hwa, L., McLeod, D.: Temperament-Based Information Filtering. In: ICME 2000, vol. 2, pp. 941–944. Univ. of Southern California, Los Angeles (2000)
39. Herman, S.: Career HOPES: An Internet-delivered career development. Journal Computer in Human Behavior (2010)

Immediacy in User Interfaces:
An Activity Theoretical Approach

Sturla Bakke

The Norwegian School of Information Technology, Oslo, Norway
sb@nith.no

Abstract. In this paper the relation between the [new] concept of *immediacy* in user interfaces is discussed by taking an activity theoretical approach. When discussing so-called 'user-friendly' technical artefacts, the term intuitive often turns up in the human-computer interaction (HCI) discourse, as a kind of buzzword. The problem with the term *intuition* is that it lacks a sufficient level of precision, and could very well mean different things to different people. This paper discusses how familiar HCI concepts such as *intuition* and *affordances* in combination can form the basis of the new concept of *immediacy*, and how it can be justified on the basis of activity theory.

Keywords: immediacy, user-interfaces, activity theory, action.

1   Introduction

The very basic foundation for interaction is, besides having an idea of what to do, the activity itself, and the "what"-part is increasingly done with the help of some kind of computerized artifact - through a human-technology interface. We could ask what is the character or quality elements in an user-interface which makes it a good tool? This paper employs the *mediated action perspective* on affordances presented by Kaptelinin and Nardi which states that "the most characteristic feature of humans, differentiating them from other animals, is that their activities and minds are mediated by culturally developed tools, including technology." [1].

Intuitive user-interfaces has been a central term or term in HCI-research as something to strive for in many instances of socio-technical practice. However, we believe that it is not sufficiently precise, and means different things to different people, which makes it a clear candidate for abolishment. In this paper we present *immediacy* as a contextual activity-related concept, and as a framework for discussing the quality and character of socio-technical interdependent work and play. This paper discusses *immediacy* as a new conceptual term within the HCI discourse with the activity theoretical approach that has increasingly dominated the field from the 90's to the present. We propose a definition of the term *immediacy* in user-interfaces as: *an immediate UI, is immediately understandable and actionable, not to all users regardless of education, experience or what they wish to achieve, but to users within a specific context, with a specific goal, based on defined conceptual models. It relies on the user's experience-based intuitive approach to the task at hand, combined with the contextually relevant affordances in the UI.* It is presented here as a part of the activity theoretical HCI discourse.

M. Kurosu (Ed.): Human-Computer Interaction, Part I, HCII 2014, LNCS 8510, pp. 14–22, 2014.
© Springer International Publishing Switzerland 2014

The paper continues with a brief presentation of activity theory connected with HCI-discourse, related to the topic of this paper, followed by an empirical example from a case study within the shipping industry regarding software support for the process of stowing chemical tankers, and leading to the discussion of activity theory and immediacy. The paper ends with the concluding remarks.

2   Current Theory and Literature

We draw from the body of literature, emphasizing, although not exclusively, on Nardi's focus on contextual practice [2]p. 7], Kuuti's underlining of object dependent transformative activity *structure* [3], while including Bödker's mediation and transparency perspective [4], and also Kaptelinin and Nardi's foundational activity theoretical HCI-approach [5] among others.

2.1   Activity Theoretical HCI: Context, Structure and Mediation

Nardi states that activity theory «focuses on practice, which obviates the need to distinguish 'applied' from 'pure' science—understanding everyday practice in the real world is the very objective of scientific practice. [...] The object of activity theory is to understand the unity of consciousness and activity.» Also activity takes place within a context of the group and the group's goal [2]p. 7].

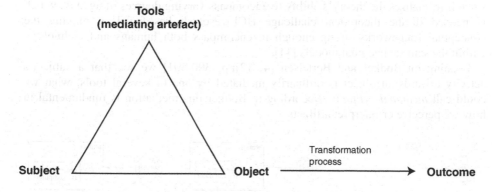

Fig. 1. The structure of activity [6]p. 29

Kuutti, concurs with Nardi's descriptive theory approach, but is focusing on the structure of activity . "An activity is a form of doing directed to an object, and activities are distinguished from each other according to their objects. Transforming the object into an outcome motivates the existence of an activity. An object can be a material thing, but it can also be less tangible." [3]

Kuuti [3; 6], Engeström [7] and Miettinen [8] shows that activity is primarily goal-directed, and mediated by artefacts in addition to being contextual and social. On an individual level the relationship between subject and object is mediated through tools. In Nardi and Kaptelinin these are coined as mediated affordances[1]. In an activity system, where we can analyze the complex structure of human activity, we might, in addition, see that the relationship between a subject and the community is mediated by rules (of conduct), the relationship between the community and the object of activity is mediated by division of labor [9].

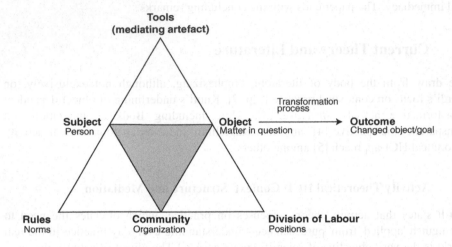

Fig. 2. The structure of an activity system. Based on Engeström [10].

This is an important aspect of the discussion about the structure of activity theory since it formalizes the theory's ability to encompass varying degrees of agency, which is needed in the theoretical challenge HCI research has faced in making the conceptual frameworks strong enough to encompass both humans and technology within the same conceptual models [11].

Leaning on Bødker and Bertelsen [4; 12]pp. 300-301] we see that a subject's activity towards an object is ordinarily mediated by one or several tools, what we could call *mediated artifacts*. According to Bødker this mediation is fundamental in how we perceive or interpret artifacts.

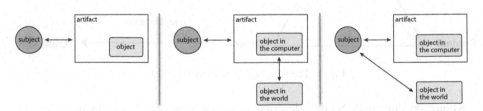

Fig. 3. Mediating aspects of different activity situations [4]pp. 38-39]

The figure to the left shows a situation in which the object exists only in the artifact, while the figure in the middle shows a situation where the object exists as a physical object, but is only present in the activity as an UI-abstraction in the software. The figure to the right shows a situation where the object exists physically outside the artifact and might be accessed without going through a user-interface. We'll apply this model from Bødker on the empirical example in the discussion section.

3   Empiric Example from a Case Study

To convey some concepts of the activity theoretical HCI-approach to *immediacy*. We'll present a part of a related case study, regarding the development and implementation of a client/server software for the control of stowing chemical tankers. A chemical tanker differs from an oil tanker in almost all aspects of being a tanker. An oil tanker transports one type of cargo, crude oil, in five or six huge tanks, from the point of extraction to a refinery. A chemical tanker is significantly smaller, and transports chemicals in a multitude of smaller, specialized tanks, between various port terminals, in a multi-point to multi-point pattern. Also, a chemical tanker must adhere to international rules and regulations that requires chemical tankers to follow the International Bulk Chemical Code (IBC Code)[1] regarding transport of hazardous liquids at sea like eg. SOLAS ch. VII[2] and MARPOL Annex II[3]. One example could be that we must, for instance, transport phosphoric acid in a stainless steel tank and not in a tank with coating. Likewise, there are rules for the filling of adjacent tanks - which chemical liquid that may be transport alongside each other. This is an operational practice associated with a significant degree of complexity, sometimes critical complexity.

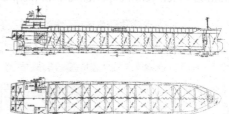

Fig. 4. Users planning stowage <u>through</u> the   **Fig. 5.** Technical drawing of physical object
mediating artifact

There is an adamant need for a software that can handle this kind of complexity in a fashion that is as easily understandable as possible, due to the context and environment that it will be operating. The software is used both on land, in the company HQ (operations), and on the bridge on all ships loading and unloading cargo (fleet). This means that there will be a rather heterogenous group of users, as well.

---

[1] http://www.imo.org/OurWork/Environment/PollutionPrevention/
ChemicalPollution/Pages/IGCCode.aspx. Accessed: Sept. 5th 2013.
[2] International Convention for the Safety of Life at Sea (SOLAS). Chapter VII - Carriage of dangerous goods.
[3] International Convention for the Prevention of Marine Pollution from Ships (MARPOL). Annex II - Regulations for the Control of Pollution by Noxious Liquid Substances in Bulk.

Fig. 6. Physical objects - tanks on chemical tanker, as seen from the bridge

The new stowage software utilizes abstractions in the user interface that, in short, are based entirely on previous activity – *vocational practice*. User participants have been involved from the very beginning, drawing on experience from a very specific work practice and environment, and also with an established division of work tasks, in addition to ten years experience with the previous software.

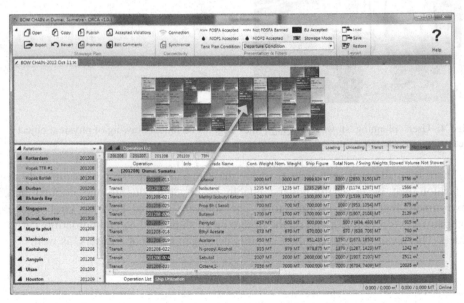

Fig. 7. Tank plan in the new stowage system. <u>Mediation</u>: Abstracted representation of vessel, with interaction directly unto the tank representations which provide direct system feedback. The Operation list beneath the tank plan has direct drag and drop functionality, both related to the Rotation list to the left and to the tank plan above. This is simple activity based HCI development. The yellow arrow is not part of the UI, but a marking made by the author to visualize drag and drop activity.

This resulted in a set of specifications that relied solely on former practice - *intention and action*. On top of the user requirements list was «Good user experience/friendliness». The next important points on the list of requirements were: 2. Support ease of communication between Vessel-Operator 3. Support ease of communication between Operator-Broker 4. Emphasis on an intuitive Graphical User Interface (GUI).

4 Discussion

Bødker's mediation perspective, that people are not working *on* the interface but *through* it, as in employing the UI as a tool that eventually, by the users' active engagement becomes *transparent*, is thus an essential aspect of explaining the importance of *immediacy*. *Immediacy* arises when the combination of mediated affordances and user's level of intuitive skills, and subsequent active engagement with the user-interface, makes it transparent, ie. when the users don't consciously think of interacting through it, but just do.

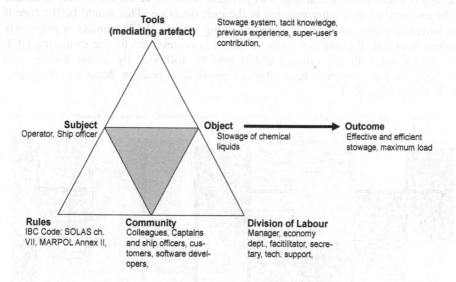

Fig. 8. Activity system linked to the empirical example

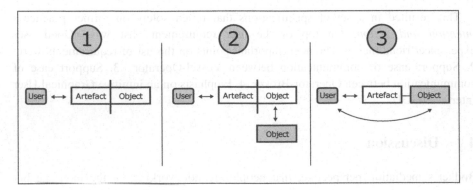

Fig. 9. Activity as a hierarchical system related to the stowage software [12]p. 307

In the depiction in Figure 9, of activity as a hierarchical system, we would, by linking it to the empirical example of stowing chemical tankers, see three distinctly different types of situations: **1.** The object, in which in this case is a tank, is present only <u>through</u> the mediating artefact (GUI). This would have been the occasion if this situation had been eg. a simulator session for training captains and ship officers. **2.** The object exists as an actual object as physical tanks on vessel but is only available in the use-activity as a representation in the user interface. This would be the case if this situation shows an actual stowage planning session. **3.** The object is physically co-present outside the artefact. Tank on vessel is represented by the mediating GUI. The interaction with the artefact (GUI) will be followed by actual loading and unloading of tank, which is accessible for physical inspection. Model by Bertelsen and Bødker [12]p. 307].

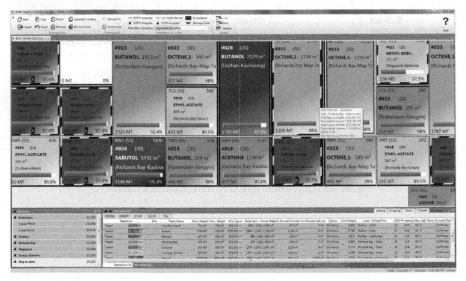

Fig. 10. Details of tank plan in the new stowage system. Observe how the system provides direct feedback on each abstracted element: recipient port, weight, grade of filling, warning border for adjacent hazard, and so on.

The tank plan gives us, through the user-interface, ie. the mediating artifact, an abstracted representation of the vessel, with interaction directly unto the tank representations which provide direct system feedback. The Operation list beneath the tank plan has direct drag and drop functionality, both related to the Rotation list to the left and to the tank plan above. This is simple activity based HCI development, and immediacy in a user-interface. The operator intuitively knows, by vocational experience, what is shown on the screen. The functional elements in the user-interface then affords, based also on the previous experience the required/possible/best practice actions that collectively constitute the stowage activity, in junction with the experiential intuition. By leaning on these two elements of the user-experience we rely on making it a good one, not on intuition alone, but combined with the mediated affordances in the user-interface, giving us an added level of precision, by the possibility of adjusting or designing one more parameter or element within the mediated artifact.

This activity based approach, follows what Kaptelinin and Nardi calls "second wave"-HCI, with its user activity centric focus. They argue that human agency through mediation is an important aspect of activity theory, and therefore, it provides the conceptual tools in order to analyze how people relate to ie. new software, and also how, through adherence to 'rules' and participating in the 'community', a 'subjects's knowledge becomes extended [13]p. 190]. Mediation in an activity-theoretical HCI perspective is goal- and artifact-oriented' and therefore rather suitable as an analytical framework for the activity theoretical *immediacy* concept. How might we situate the *immediacy* term within the activity theoretical discourse? One argument, mentioned previously in this paper, which is based on Dreyfus and Dreyfus [14], is that intuition is based on skills. Skills originate from experience. While experience, according to Rubinshtein ([15], cited in [5]p. 47]) should not be separated from action. This situates the term experience and the term derived from it, intuition, within an activity theoretical discourse. Then by turning to affordances in an HCI context, we might follow Kaptelinin and Nardi in situating affordances on the top of the activity structure triangle, see figure 1, defining «technology affordances» as possibilities for acting through the technology in question on a certain object [5]p. 6], thus adopting what they frame as a *mediated action perspective* [1].

5   Concluding Remarks

As the main method of measuring the character of *immediacy* in a HCI setting is through human activity - action, it follows that an important aspect of *immediacy* is human agency. How much control, in terms of customization, mimicking real life work flow, possibility of overriding software guidance and suggestions based on field discourse and rules, does the software allow? We would argue that the number, or absence, of user errors could say something about the perceived *immediacy* of a piece of software. The character of a user-experience, measured by the the outcome of the activity, will determine the degree of *immediacy* with which a user perceives a program. As of its epistemological connection, this paper, then, argues that, as *immediacy* emerges from a combination of empirical, skill based intuition and mediated affordances in the user-interface, and since both intuition and affordances are grounded within the activity theoretical discourse, *immediacy* will inherit this theoretical relation.

References

1. Kaptelinin, V., Nardi, B.: Affordances in HCI: toward a mediated action perspective. In: Proceedings of the 2012 ACM Annual Conference on Human Factors in Computing Systems, pp. 967–976. ACM (2012)
2. Nardi, B.A.: Context and Consciousness: Activity Theory and Human-Computer Interaction. The MIT Press (1996)
3. Kuutti, K.: Activity theory, transformation of work, and information systems design. In: Engeström, Y., Miettinen, R., Punamäki, R.-L. (eds.) Perspectives on Activity Theory (Learning in Doing: Social, Cognitive and Computational Perspectives). Cambridge University Press (1999)
4. Bødker, S.: Through the interface. CRC Press (1990)
5. Kaptelinin, V., Nardi, B.: Activity Theory in HCI: Fundamentals and Reflections. Synthesis Lectures Human-Centered Informatics 5(1), 1–105 (2012)
6. Kuutti, K.: Activity Theory as a Potential Framework for Human-Computer Interaction Research. In: Nardi, B.A. (ed.) Context and Consciousness: Activity Theory and Human-Computer Interaction. The MIT Press (1995)
7. Engeström, Y.: Expansive Learning at Work: Toward an activity theoretical reconceptualization. Journal of Education and Work 14(1), 133–156 (2001), doi:10.1080/13639080020028747
8. Miettinen, R., Hasu, M.: Articulating User Needs in Collaborative Design: Towards an Activity-Theoretical Approach. Computer Supported Cooperative Work 11, 129–151 (2002)
9. Miettinen, R.: The riddle of things: Activity theory and actor-network theory as approaches to studying innovations. Mind, Culture, and Activity 6(3), 170–195 (1999), doi:10.1080/10749039909524725
10. Engeström, Y.: Learning by expanding. An activity-theoretical approach to developmental research (1987)
11. Kaptelinin, V.: Computer-mediated activity: Functional organs in social and developmental contexts. In: Nardi, B.A. (ed.) Context and Consciousness: Activity Theory and Human-Computer Interaction. MIT Press, Cambridge (1996)
12. Bertelsen, O.W., Bødker, S.: Activity theory. In: Carroll, J.M. (ed.), Morgan Kaufmann, San Francisco (2003)
13. Kaptelinin, V., Kuutti, K., Bannon, L.: Activity theory: Basic concepts and applications. In: Blumenthal, B., Gornostaev, J., Unger, C. (eds.) EWHCI 1995. LNCS, vol. 1015, pp. 189–201. Springer, Heidelberg (1995)
14. Dreyfus, H.L., Dreyfus, S.E.: Mind over machine: The power of human intuition and expertise in the era of the computer. Free Press (1986)
15. Rubinshtein, S.L.: Foundations of general psychology. Academic Pedagogical Science, Moscow (1946)

The Resilience of Analog Tools in Creative Work Practices: A Case Study of LEGO Future Lab's Team in Billund

Nanna Borum, Eva Petersson Brooks, and Søren R. Frimodt-Møller

Department of Architecture, Design and Media Technology
Aalborg University Esbjerg, Denmark
{nb,ep,sfm}@create.aau.dk

Abstract. This paper discusses the use of digital and analog tools, respectively, in a creative industry. The research was done within the EU-funded research project IdeaGarden, which explores digital platforms for creative collaboration. The findings in a case study of LEGO® Future Lab, one of LEGO Group's largest innovation departments, show a preference for analog tools over digital in the creative process. This points towards a general need for tangible tools in the creative work process, a need that has consequences for the development of new digital tools for creative collaboration.

Keywords: digital tools, collaboration technology, creative work practices.

1 Introduction

This paper discusses to which extent work practices in the creative industries to day have gone digital, and to which extent they still rely on analog tools.

The research in this paper is a product of the EU-funded, international research project IdeaGarden, comprised of institutions from Austria, Germany, Switzerland, Greece and Denmark, and exploring the possibilities of digital platforms designated for creative collaboration. The main focus of IdeaGarden is collaborations on visual or tangible designs, because these collaborations highlight the need for other digital tools than those currently available for collaborating on text-based information (e.g. Google Docs, Evernote etc.) IdeaGarden includes three case studies that have been chosen in order to exemplify different environments in which such creative processes can take place: EOOS, a small Viennese design company, Muthesius Academy of Fine Arts and Design in Kiel, Germany, and finally, LEGO® Future Lab, which is, in comparison, a fairly large work unit that collaborates on generating new concepts for LEGO products, and due to the size of the unit has to put this creative process into very clear (infra)structures in order to keep the work of individual team members integrated in one big process. The present paper focuses on the LEGO Future Lab case study, because it shows a very clear tendency regarding the use of analog tools vs. digital, given that LEGO Future Lab is a work unit one would expect to be even more dependent on digitalized workflows than the other two cases, due to its size and international scope.

M. Kurosu (Ed.): Human-Computer Interaction, Part I, HCII 2014, LNCS 8510, pp. 23–34, 2014.
© Springer International Publishing Switzerland 2014

In the first sections of the paper, the method and set-up of the case study are described. After this, the work processes that are practically limited to either analog or digital tools are discussed first. After this discussion, the paper addresses the different areas of LEGO Future Lab's workflow that include both digital and analog tools. Finally, the paper concludes with a short discussion of what the interplay between digital and analog tools in the creative working environment means for the development and success of new technologies that facilitate creative work.

2   Related Work

The notion of the 'paperless office', i.e. a workplace that is not dependent on any kind of analog tool, was first coined in 1980 by XEROX PARC, but in fact, the basic thought can be traced back to the mid 1800's when the telegraph was invented [1]. Sellen and Harper explain that through the years the 'paperless office' has been a goal for many companies as it is regarded to support a more efficient workflow, decrease costs and in addition improve the ecological profile of the company . Still there is a resilience of going from analog, in other words, paper documents to digital documents. Gaver [2] argues that the tangibility of paper affords different interactions that digital documents do. Especially, Gaver highlights that paper supports both formal and informal situations and, in addition, the format of the notes works as a memory-trigger regarding the level of formality of the situation for the designer afterwards. Similarly, Brereton and McGarry [3] also point to how physical objects function as an episodic memory trigger.

Other qualities are that paper is considered free of boundaries and that it is transformable in a different way than a regular text file.

For physical object in general e.g. Geyer & Reiterer [4] point to the importance of spatial representation of artifacts, in order to facilitate collaborative design.

Some researchers have conceptualized design as a reflective conversation with physical materials in the situation [5], but more recent work has drawn attention to the way design artifacts can be catalysts for the (further) design process [6], [7], [3], as well as have an impact on the design situation in virtue of their material qualities [8]. Dorta et al. [7] argue that it is simply a necessity for designers to exteriorize their mental models, not only as physical but also sometimes as digital representations in order to engage in a discussion of these models. This process of exteriorization furthermore needs to be on going, i.e. reiterated as models develop, and be accessible for the designers wherever they work, such that design decisions can be revisited and reviewed.

In addition, due to their tangibility, physical objects simply afford interpersonal communication in a different way than digital ones, and therefore make different types of idea generation possible. Some studies on the use of physical models in the field of engineering do, however, suggest that a design process might stagnate, once a physical model of a design is built, given that only few changes are made to a model, once its physical representation is introduced [9].

3   Case Description and Research Questions

LEGO® Future Lab is a recent fusion between LEGO Concept Lab and LEGO New Business Group. LEGO Future Lab works with frontend innovation, more specifically, development of new toy product lines and concepts in close correspondence with the market.

This study focuses on the approximately 30 persons large office in Billund but also addresses how this office collaborates with the other international branches of the same department.

Already before the case study was carried out, a tendency presented itself in conversations with the creative practitioners at the three test beds involved in IdeaGarden, especially the practitioners from LEGO Future Lab: The relatively high dependence on analog tools throughout the creative process, in spite of the ready availability of digital tools at many stages of the creative process as well as for communication between co-workers. This is of particular interest when looking at LEGO Future Lab, given that LEGO Future Lab is a work unit one would, as hinted at earlier, expect to be even more dependent on digitalized workflows than the other two test beds, due to its size and international scope.

Consequently, the main research question that has guided the questions for the interviews at LEGO Future Lab is related to this tension between the dependence on digital tools on one hand, and the individual team member's preference for analog tools on the other. This question splits into the sub questions of how analog and digital tools, respectively, are being used in parts of the work processes. In the sections that follow, the documented interplay between analog and digital tools has been grouped into aspects related to (in random order) sharing information with others, note-taking, collaboration, communication with external collaborators, tools for presentation and working with physical models.

When the interviews were carried out, LEGO Future Lab was divided into three "streams", namely Insights and Early Innovation, Pipeline, and Launch. (Today, the two latter streams have been merged into one, but the different functions and roles the respective streams took up in the work process described in the following, are still carried out by different people.) The distribution of tasks were, in slightly simplified form as follows:

The Insights and Early Innovation reacts to a "brief" from a selection of LEGO's stakeholders invited to a so-called "gate meeting". A brief can be a request to develop something that will address a particular market or target group, or make use of a particular technology. Insights and Early Innovation then undertakes field research on the possible market, target groups or technologies in question. This research can involve interviews with target groups, presenting the group with early mock-ups and loosely formulated suggestions for play concepts, or simply document typical patterns of playing in a particular group. From the insights gathered via field research, the stream comes up with ideas for directions the new products could take. The design directions from the Insights and Early Innovation stream are handed over to the Pipeline stream, which develops a number of actual product ideas based on these directions. The selected stakeholders choose one or more of the product ideas to be developed for a product launch, a process carried out by the Launch stream. In addition, the Launch stream tests the almost-finished products together with children, working closely together with the market in order to get the packaging and model designs as fitting as possible.

All three streams work with both marketing and design, as the way the product is shaped is dependent on its possible market and vice versa. The IdeaGarden partners from Aalborg University Esbjerg interviewed two employees from each of the three streams – for each stream, one person who worked with design, and one person who worked with marketing or project management.

4   Method

In order to investigate the work practices at LEGO® Future Lab, five semi-structured situated interview sessions [10] were conducted over a three-day period. In total six participants were interviewed, the individual interviews lasting between 60-96 minutes (mean= 77,8 min). The sessions were carried out with an ethnographic approach (Pink, 2007) [11] putting an emphasis on observing the participants' work practices in their working environment. The interviews were audio recorded, and combined with photos and field notes, the data is detailed, thick and hence applicable for a case study analysis [12]. In the analysis process the interviews were transcribed and main themes were identified [13] and elaborately described.

The unit of analysis focused on five topics: (a) digital and analog tools in relation to specific work practices, (b) tools for internal collaboration, (c) tools for remote and external communication, (d) tools for presentations, and (e) working with physical models. The results of the case study shows that even though the creative team strives to keep their workflow digital, they still rely heavily on analog, paper-based tools and physical models, as well as regular face-to-face communication.

5   Results

5.1   Digital and Analog Tools in LEGO® Future Lab

The following sections will discuss digital and analog tools in relation to specific work practices of LEGO® Future Lab. Certain work practices are, however, almost entirely carried out using one specific group of tools, digital for some practices, analog for others.

The processes that are practically only carried out in the digital realm include different means of sharing larger or more formal pieces of information with other team members. Interviews indicate that file-sharing via LEGO Group's internal servers is the preferred option of the administrative personnel, while many of the creative workers prefer sending attachments via e-mail:

"I prefer the folder system, because outdated files fly around through e-mails and dead links rule. The problem with the folder system is that I read 60-70% of my mails on the phone, and from there I can not access the system so often, so it is actually nice that people attach the file, but it is problematical when people start to work on attached files since it results in multiple different copies." Michael, Project Leader of new products, Launch.

"[Speaking of the problem with multiple versions and the difficulties arising from files getting misplaced:] the designers have a bit of a mess going on. [...] it gets a bit confusing, or actually not confusing, but tiring." Sidd, Creative Lead, Launch.

Another aspect of the working process, which is primarily digital, is exploration of existing ideas or technological and design tendencies, which a member of Launch explained is typically done via the Internet, e.g. by looking at trending sites. If a team member stumbles on anything of interest he or she usually shares the information with the other team members via e-mail. LEGO Future Lab is currently developing an online platform where the whole of LEGO Future Lab can share information on inspirational trends, technologies and toys. In parallel, a similar platform is being developed, that allows digital access to several inspirational resources such as methodological tool kits and guidelines previously developed and utilized in connection with idea generation and design cycles in LEGO Future Lab. Until now these resources have mainly been stored in tangible, primarily paper and cardboard-based forms. Some resources are available in the shared office space in the form of e.g. a board with a set of guidelines. Each guideline, presented on a 15 cm x15 cm piece of thick cardboard, are velcroed to the board, enabling a co-worker to remove the tile temporarily and bring the information to their table for inspiration. Other resources such as a pocketsize Moleskin archive containing sets of guidelines have been distributed to all co-workers to bring with them when working off-location.

Also on the analog end of the digital-analog spectrum, one finds the personal notes taken by the individual team member. For this purpose, practically everyone uses post-its or other paper-based media:

"I use post-its. I do not like digital notes. Physical notes 'scream for attention' when they are present. It helps me remember, and I can add on to them, delete tasks and so on as the day goes by. I can easily sort the post-its by relevance and by urgency [...]

[Speaking of idea development:] In general, I sketch! If I need to get a hold on things, I take notes and try to find new connections. I could also partner up with a colleague and storyboard on the theme." Maiken, Digital Product Designer, Pipeline.

"I prefer to have things in print. Let us just say that I am not the one who saves the rainforest. I print a lot. I cannot really take it in if it is on a screen, I need to be able to write directly on things, and doodle and so on. [...] Also, I do not misplace it when I have it physically, and I remember things easier." Mette, Insights Manager, Insights and Early Innovation.

Only one interviewee expressed preference for digital note taking: "I use this [tablet] for personal notes because it is easy to carry around and you can quickly share the notes afterwards." Michael, Project Leader of new products, Launch.

Fig. 1. Typical desktop of a member of the Insights and Early Innovation stream at LEGO Future Lab. Note the stacked post-its on the right side; and in the middle, to the left of the coffee mug, printed out snapshots of a billboard, with the stream member's hand-written notes added.

In general, observations and interviews at the Billund office showed that all employees used post-its for note taking, both privately and at meetings. Many working desks were almost completely covered by post-its, and some employees even had written post-it notes stacked in layers (see Figure 1). Post-its are also used to present ideas for and discuss ideas with others, using the movable billboards as space for sticking – and later moving around with – the post-its. One employee from Insights and Early Innovation described how she would write notes on post-its, because it made the transition from her private work sphere to the sphere of discussing with others easier: she could simply bring the post-its with her personal notes and stick them directly on the billboard at which the discussion was taking place. Another employee from Launch expressed that the small, portable format of the post-it block made it easy to bring to a meeting. It is also the interpretation of the authors of this paper that the sizes of the post-its force the employees to think in a very concise 'to-the-point' format. For visual ideas, drawings on larger paper are also used.

Recently, the team has started utilizing an app called 'Prototype on Paper' for rapid paper prototyping when discussing possible ideas for the design of an app. The basic idea of this tool is that it allows you to sketch the different screens of the app on paper, take snapshots of them with a smart device, and then quickly define links between the different screens by simple finger gestures. It is the impression of the authors that while this is still very new to the employees, they have welcomed the intuitive interface and the spontaneity supported by the system, which hence could prove to be a valued tool further on.

5.2   Tools for Collaboration

Collaborative work within LEGO® Future Lab as a whole (international divisions included) includes both digital and analog tools.

The Billund division of LEGO Future Lab collaborates externally with their counterpart in Los Angeles. These collaborations are conducted via e-mail, infrequent videoconferences and phone calls (due to the time difference), but also via shipping of e.g. physical models from one country to another. Otherwise, the majority of the employees work together within the context of the office. All of the interviewees agreed that they preferred face-to-face contact to electronic communication. In other words, if the employees need input from their colleagues, they usually shout or walk over to the colleague's desk. The employees who do not want to be disturbed, work with their headphones on. Of course, whether the team members go for analog or digital means of collaboration is also dependent on the specific context:

"A prioritized list of the tools I use would be: e-mail, face-to-face, phone/Skype. Actually, I [would prefer not to use] e-mails, but the primary reason for me using them is that we spend much time separated from each other. A lot of our communication happens at nighttime and across distances. It is really a poor form of communication since A) we receive loads of e-mails, hence people tend to not read every single one of them, B) communication is often 'lost in translation'. [...] In general, it is just more beneficial to handle things face-to-face." Michael, Project Leader of new products, Launch.

"I could work from home everyday. It is actually a possibility for me, but I decide not to. Something just happens in that informal communication you have with your colleagues on an everyday basis." Maiken, Digital Product Designer, Pipeline.

"I like meeting face-to-face when communicating with the designers. They prefer to express themselves visually and physically so it just enables communication. Of course they could also just add it to a PowerPoint and send it to me, but it is just easier to do it face-to-face." Louise, Project Leader, Pipeline.

5.3   Communication with External Collaborators

Communication in itself, especially with collaborators outside the Billund office, provides a lot of specific problems, many of which stem directly from the geographic dislocation of the collaborators:

"The downside to video communication is that we all need to be online at the same time and that is usually not possible in our case. Another disadvantage is that you do not have the communication in writing as a reference afterwards." Michael, Project Leader of new products, Launch.

Some problems have to do with the same need for face-to-face interaction as described in section 5.2:

"We [the Billund office and external partners in a different time zone] do not communicate on a daily basis and try not to be dependent on each other because communication can be tiresome. It's a bad match time zone wise. In general, just the fact that you are not located the same place is really problematic since you miss out on the informal interaction with your colleagues that occurs during the day and that is of great importance. [...]

"[On video communication:] It definitely comes with a barrier. Things are more easily misunderstood or perceived 'stringently' via video. Reading body language is not as easily possible in video communication. The sound is not stable, and delays in connection are also common. It's just not the same as being situated together, and it never will be." Maiken, Digital Product Designer, Pipeline.

"We try to meet up with our Los Angeles team at least once a month to ensure that we are on the same track, but it is a long trip." Louise, Project Leader, Pipeline.

Another issue with respect to the choice of digital vs. analog tools for collaborative work is language barriers between collaborators of different nationalities.

"The language barrier is equally big in writing and video communication, however in some cases people have more time to formulate their wording in writing and hence e-mails come across as a more clear tool for communication. In other cases, video is better since you can better explain your opinion." Michael, Project Leader of new products, Launch.

For collaborators actively working on visual or tangible designs, communicating ideas for such designs over a physical distance also provides special problems:

"We use a lot of e-mails, because a lot of the stuff we see is visuals, drawings, images, and so on. So we usually use attachments in e-mails." Sidd, Creative Lead, Launch.

"It is difficult to convey physical objects via video communication. Sometimes we show the model in front of the camera, but when the receiver does not have an opportunity to feel and touch the model, it is complicated. Other times we build the models in pairs and ship one off to the receiver." Maiken, Digital Product Designer, Pipeline.

The preference for sharing physical models with external collaborators is something that will be dealt with further in section 5.5 below.

5.4   Tools for Presentation

With regular intervals, one or more members of LEGO® Future Lab have to present their work either to members from a different stream of LEGO Future Lab, to external partners or to their superiors. Again, the choice of presentation tools depends on the context. For demonstrating e.g. a particular process involving a physical product to a remote collaborator in a different time zone, video logs are often used:

"Recently we have started to use video logs to convey our creative thoughts to our external companies. We send one once a week to keep each other updated." Michael, Project Leader of new products, Launch.

For internal presentations within the specific office, or with external collaborators via video link, physical foam boards and models may be employed in a "show and tell"-like manner, sometimes taking an individual team member's workspace as the starting point. For many purposes, however, PowerPoint seems to be a preferred tool:

"PowerPoint is the one software that everybody uses. It is stupid really, because it is used for tasks that it is not designed for. People use it to do visual work. The reason for that is that everyone has access to it. As a designer, I would prefer to use Illustrator to do visual design, but the project managers do not have access to it." Maiken, Digital Product Designer, Pipeline.

Other interviewees have different reasons for seeking supplements to PowerPoint: "[on plans for new office interior decor:] we want to have more digital screens for several reasons. We would like to have more dynamic content such as videos and loops with info. From a hypothetical standpoint, we hope it will be used more frequently. Then I can take my PowerPoint or Excel sheet, that I already use, and 'shoot' it onto the shared screen for presentations." Michael, Project Leader of new products, Launch.

5.5 Working with Physical Models

As much as two-dimensional images are an integral part of the workflow, the interviewees at LEGO® Future Lab all expressed a need for tangible models as part of the displays for discussion of which the billboards are the center. Consequently, practically all billboards are supplemented with tangible models directly in front of them on small desks. Tangible models can include both LEGO prototypes and competitor products. The latter are sometimes supplemented with QR codes that make it possible to quickly access web links related to these products.

"We display competitor products in the office space. We buy a lot and make an effort to have them physically represented. It is not enough to look at things online when you can touch, feel and play with them instead, try them out and see how they work." Maiken, Digital Product Designer, Pipeline.

"I prefer to work with physical models. If I use LDD [= Lego Digital Designer, see below] it is only to replicate something I already built physically. I always have bricks ready at hand at my desk, just to play around with." Maiken, Digital Product Designer, Pipeline.

LEGO bricks are, as mentioned earlier, also a tool used by the employees in their daily workflow, both for prototyping and for playing during pauses (or, as an employee from Insights and Early Innovation confided, during telephone meetings.) Even though the designers have access to the software LEGO Digital Designer (LDD) that allows the user to build any LEGO model in a virtual environment, brick by brick (and easily generate assembly instructions), none of the interviewed designers preferred working in LDD before the stage of finalizing an idea for presentation, or a final product. In fact, when sharing early prototypes with foreign partners, the Billund office prefers to build an extra version of the prototype and send this to the foreign office, rather than sending a digital version constructed in LDD.

"When we travel we often have boxes of bricks shipped to our destination. People need to work with tangibles. [...]

[On sharing models:] We do not use digital software [LDD]. It takes extra time to do it, you have to do it step by step and construct a building instruction. It is complex, and takes a lot longer than just building an extra copy of the model." Maiken, Digital Product Designer, Pipeline.

"I use a lot of physical models as you can see on my desk. I can have 6-7 versions of the same model standing while I try to figure out how it should be. [...]

When the models are done, I make them in 3D so it is there and people can always use that file to build again. It is fairly easy to build a model brick by brick. [...]

[Responding to the question of why he does not work from scratch in the digital environment:] It is easier for me to build it [physically], and to change things around, and a lot of the design happens by looking at the pieces – in the digital one you need to go through menus to see them. When you see all the bricks in real life, you are inspired to use certain bricks. That does not happen digitally. Also a lot of troubleshooting happens when you do it physically, in digital it is not as easy as with your hands." Sidd, Creative Lead, Launch.

The need for tangible, physical models in the creative process is evident by the fact that even environments that are intended to be only virtual, e.g. environments visualized as if built in LEGO in one of LEGO's computer games, are sometimes created as full physical models:

"[Explaining the idea behind a large landscape model on the floor:] It is a 'blueprint' model from one of the workshops with our external company, where we tried to make decisions on sizes and dimensions in a digital game. It is a way of making it tangible so instead of spending time on discussing these matters, discussions that could have an academic approach, we just build it instead. Then everybody understands across professional backgrounds and language barriers. We feel that it is easier, and it saves time and development loops." Michael, Project Leader of new products, Launch.

6   Conclusion

In general, the case study of LEGO® Future Lab shows that even in a working unit where the use of digital tools is important and mandatory due to a rigidly organized workflow involving many, often geographically dislocated people, individual team members are still dependent on, and prefer using analog tools throughout the larger part of the creative process.

One explanation is the individual's preference for working with something tactile. This goes for post-it notes and pencils as well as working with LEGO bricks. Another explanation is the need to have different objects readily 'at hand', so as to be more easily inspired by the objects (e.g. LEGO bricks, models, images etc.) than one would do when having to look in digital folders for information. In relation to collaboration, the preference for analog communication, in the sense of face-to-face meetings indicates the failure of existing digital communication tools to sufficiently reduce the distance between the communicating partners: Even video-based conversations lack the possibility of direct or even simulated eye contact. Finally, an important factor in the choice of tools is the dependence of multiple types of artifacts in the workspace, i.e. artifacts for presentation, note-taking and physical modeling, items for inspiration etc., and the absence of one overarching digital system to bind all these artifacts together. Rather than using many digital tools for different parts of the process, the user typically limits her to a few digital tools (e.g. e-mail, PowerPoint) and takes care of other parts of the process via analog tools.

Especially two aspects in connection with the suggested explanations above have direct implications for the development of digital tools for creative collaboration, such as the ones, which are indeed the focus of the IdeaGarden research project:

1) The need to bridge the gap between the dependence on digital tools and the creative worker's preference for analog ones point towards the integration of tangible tools in the digital environment, e.g. digital pens for use on an interactive whiteboard, or the ability to quickly scan or otherwise identify physical objects and paper notes for use in a collaborative digital environment

2) The LEGO Future Lab team member's dependence on multiple types of artifacts in the daily workflow suggests that a new digital system for creative collaboration either should be simple enough to easily interact or integrate with existing tools in the workplace, or have to provide team members with a myriad of functions, preferably with tangible counterparts, that cover the same bases as their existing tools.

A third aspect, which is of particular importance for the work processes of LEGO Future Lab, but might not be a general problem for creative professionals, is the wish to remove distance between digital collaborators, or to put it differently, bring the online communication situation closer to resembling a physical meeting between the communicating parties.

In the future work of the researchers within the IdeaGarden project, the two aforementioned aspects play a central role in the development of prototypes and software that can facilitate creative collaborative processes. The aforementioned aspect related to removing distance, will, however, not be addressed to the same extent, given that this aspect has less importance in relation to the two other test beds involved in IdeaGarden. [Footnote: For more information on future developments within this research project, please visit www.idea-garden.org]

References

1. Sellen, A., Harper, R.: Paper as an Analytic Resource for the Design of New Technologies. In: Proceedings of the ACM SIGCHI Conference on Human Factors in Computing Systems, pp. 319–326. ACM (1997)
2. Gaver, W.W.: Situating Action II: Affordances for Interaction: The Social is Material for Design. Ecological Psychology 8, 111–129 (1996)
3. Brereton, M., McGarry, B.: An Observational Study of How Objects Support Engineering Design Thinking and Communication: Implications for the Design of Tangible Media. In: Proceedings of the SIGCHI Conference on Human Factors in Computing Systems, pp. 217–224. ACM (2000)
4. Geyer, F., Reiterer, H.: A Cross-Device Spatial Workspace Supporting Artifact-Mediated Collaboration in Interaction Design. In: Proceedings of the 28th International Conference Extended Abstracts on Human Factors in Computing Systems, pp. 3787–3792. ACM (2010)
5. Schön, D.: The Reflective Practitioner: How Professionals Think in Action. Basic Books, New York (1983)

6. Fish, J.: Cognitive catalysis: Sketches for a Time-Lagged Brain. In: Goldschmidt, G., Porter, W. (eds.) Design Representation, pp. 151–185. Springer, London (2004)
7. Dorta, T., Pérez, E., Lesage, A.: The Ideation Gap: Hybrid Tools, Design Flow and Practice. Design Studies 29, 121–141 (2008)
8. Jacucci, G., Wagner, I.: Performative Roles of Materiality for Collective Creativity. In: Proceedings of the 6th ACM SIGCHI Conference on Creativity & Cognition, pp. 73–82. ACM (2007)
9. Christensen, B.T., Schunn, C.D.: The Relationship of Analogical Distance to Analogical Function and Pre-Inventive Structure: The Case of Engineering Design. Memory and Cognition 35, 29–38 (2007)
10. Buur, J., Ylirisku, S.: Designing with Video: Focusing the User-Centred Design Process. Springer, London (2007)
11. Pink, S.: Doing Visual Ethnography, 2nd edn. Sage, Thousand Oaks (2007)
12. Yin, R.K.: Case Study Research - Design and Methods, 4th edn. Sage, Thousand Oaks (2009)
13. Kumar, R.: Research Methodology: A Step-by-Step Guide for Beginners. Sage, London (1999)

Using Cultural Probes to Inform the Design of Assistive Technologies

Michael Brown, Allen Tsai, Sharon Baurley, Therese Koppe, Glyn Lawson,
Jennifer Martin, Tim Coughlan, Meretta Elliott, Stephen Green,
and Unna Arunachalam

School of Engineering and Design, Brunel University, Uxbridge, Middlesex, UK
Horizon Digital Economy Research, University of Nottingham, Nottingham, UK
Michael.Brown@nottingham.ac.uk,
{Allen.Tsai,sharon.baurley,Therese.Koppe,
Meretta Elliott,Stephen.Green}@brunel.ac.uk,
{glyn.lawson,Jennifer.Martin,
tim.coughlan,Unna.Arunachalam}@nottingham.ac.uk

Abstract. This paper discusses the practical implications of applying cultural probes to drive the design of assistive technologies. Specifically we describe a study in which a probe was deployed with home-based carers of people with dementia in order to capture critical data and gain insights of integrating the technologies into this sensitive and socially complex design space. To represent and utilise the insights gained from the cultural probes, we created narratives based on the probe data to enhance the design of assistive technologies.

Keywords: Cultural probes, Assistive technology, Dementia, Design.

1 Introduction

'Cultural Probes' were first developed by Gaver et al [2] as a research method to design technologies for the home. It is a technique that is used to inspire ideas in a design process and serves as a means of gathering inspirational data about people's lives, values and thoughts. There are several ways in which cultural probes can be implemented and interpreted. In the case of design teams, they can be seen as a tool to help build a rich picture of the lives and experiences of potential users of products.

Cultural Probe investigations involve giving participants a package of artefacts (such as a map, postcard, camera or diary) along with instructions to perform tasks such as recording specific events, feelings or interactions. The packages are designed to provoke responses to help designers better understand participants' culture, thoughts and values. There are several common features in cultural probes [1]: The process is inherently participatory as participants are the active data contributors, rather than passive study subjects; probes can make details of familiar events noticeable by capturing the significant aspects of everyday actions, places, objects and people; the artefacts which can be used, such as cameras, maps, diagrams and postcards, are engaging tools that allow participants to capture image-rich responses;

M. Kurosu (Ed.): Human-Computer Interaction, Part I, HCII 2014, LNCS 8510, pp. 35–46, 2014.
© Springer International Publishing Switzerland 2014

probes document people's lives by merging diary narratives with photographs to elaborate stories of people's lives and daily routines in an autobiographical format; wishes, desires, emotions and motives can be aggregated as personal meaning and connotation to the data; probes can facilitate dialogues between researcher and participant by reducing the power imbalance between them [3].

Cultural probes can be effective as they elicit evocative responses from participants during the data gathering phase. Traditional approaches of data gathering that rely on methods such as observations, focus groups, interviews and questionnaires contribute meaningful knowledge only focused on the design team's perspectives, which do not always adequately reflect participants' concerns. This informational gap can be resolved by utilising cultural probes as a research method to allow participants to determine the focus of some of the elicitation activities, and help designers gain a deeper insight into people's lives that may not otherwise be considered [2].

When carrying out an investigation using cultural probes, it is imperative to keep the focus open to encourage participants to highlight issues from their own viewpoints without being directed by the objectives of researchers. It is an approach that values uncertainty and ambiguity, and detects inconspicuous data in the studies. Furthermore, the collected stories can often lead to unexpected insights, which can inspire designers to think differently about the problem and drive new ways to design.

While they generally share the characteristics described above, cultural probes have been appropriated and reformulated in HCI research [7]. This adaptability is a strength, as an exploratory method that can be widely applied to different concerns, but it also brings with it a need to describe and reflect upon the detailed use of the method in different contexts. Therefore, this paper describes and reflects upon the details of our application of cultural probes, the insights that resulted, and how these insights can be utilised.

Assistive Technology can be defined as any piece of equipment, object, or product system to help individuals with disabilities improve and maintain functional capabilities. Through the appropriate use of Assistive Technologies, people with disabilities can have better control over themselves and their environment, resulting in greater freedom of movement, exploration, and participation alongside their peers at home and workplaces, thereby improving their quality of life [4].

Assistive Technology has been increasingly adapted to enhance the facilitation of healthcare services for many years [8]. The revolution of Smart Homes, equipped with responsive sensor networks and monitoring solution is also making an impact on the development of Assistive Technology. It is now greatly evolved and has the expediency to provide effective support to people with cognitive impairment, such as dementia, so that they can remain independent in their own home. However, while the importance of Assistive Technology is increasingly recognised across the world, the biggest challenge is how to find ways to adjust the context of the technology properly in order to obtain sufficient outcomes for the end users.

2   Project Background

This paper reports on the development and use of cultural probes in the AHRC-funded project Stories of User Appropriation, where they have been applied to support the development of design-drama techniques for use in the process of designing assistive technologies for people with Dementia and their carers. The aim of the project is to transfer knowledge about creative innovation processes from the creative economy to a wider economy, healthcare domain in particular, by combining design-drama techniques with digital-enabled open innovation platforms to engage users in the design process. The project was devised to tackle barriers that healthcare manufacturers face when considering how, where, and why their products will be used. In particular, the following issues have been identified:

1. Without overcoming significant practical and ethical difficulties, the current research methods used by the medical device manufactures were inappropriate and unlikely to collect the type of data that is needed to inform design.
2. A number of barriers show the results of user research cannot be fully integrated into the development of new medical devices. User data that fed back to manufacturers was not effective in conveying the range, depth and importance of the information.

In this project, we focus on the healthcare domain as a particularly appropriate area for innovation in knowledge exchange practices, to be achieved through the co-development of digital platforms that make user-centred design techniques accessible. Through this process, information exchange can be stimulated between research from user-centred design, human-computer interaction, drama and film, and small-medium sized medical device manufacturers. These SMEs do not generally have the resources to conduct user-centred research, and as such they lack a grounded understanding of their potential customers, and other stakeholders, that could be key to effective innovation and success.

The key challenges in new medical device development will underpin the development of our digital platforms, framed by a specific case study: the range and variety of the obstacles that face people living with dementia, and the opportunities for assistive technology intervention to support independent living at home. In the context of this project cultural probes were deployed to create exemplar narratives describing issues faced by people with dementia and the people that care for them in the home. Examples from seven research investigations are presented in this paper to showcase how cultural probes support data collection in the home environment with people who take care of family members with dementia in different stages.

3   Methodology

3.1   Design of the Probes

The content of the cultural probes was based on a series of rich and engaging tasks that people could partake by choice and over time. Cultural probes should be designed to ensure the process is intuitive, and open to interpretation. The open-ended activities included in the probes allow the participants to spend their own time producing narratives to illustrate their lives for researchers and designers. By implementing this uncontrolled approach, data in the opposite direction of the researcher's knowledge and patterns might be discovered.

The creation process of a probe needs to be carefully evaluated to avoid bias and subjective expectations and it usually involves many hours of preparation. Since this research is dealing with vulnerable people, the probe is also implemented at a level of sensitivity which allows data to be collected on participants which provides an understanding of their lives through a typical day without being intrusive.

3.2   Objectives of the Probe

Currently, there is no cure for dementia. It is a complex medical condition, and for those who have been diagnosed, it involves a life-long process fighting with the illness. There is no one way to care for someone with dementia; however, it's important to know that the key to care is to help the person maintain mental function, manage behaviour symptoms and sustain his/her independence in life.

There are a variety of factors that can influence the quality of dementia care as well as the condition changes of the person with dementia. The design of our probe was based on this notion and intentionally structured to capture as many of these variables as possible. To look after someone with dementia it is imperative to perform a Person-Centred Care approach since no two are the same, and different things mean different context to different people. Therefore, before investigating one's living space and finding opportunities for assistive technology interventions, one's identity, personhood and his/her relation with the specific items and elements in the space will need to be examined first.

The content of our probe is focussing on several subjects about the life of the person with dementia from the perspectives of psychological, physical and social. In order to help researchers and designers dissect the inherent causes of issues and phenomenon, the probes were deployed to the family carers to record, observe and help us build a realistic picture of the user. Our cultural probes contain two parts:

3.3   Activity Booklet 1 – Life Background Narratives

Several short interviews with the participants who expressed interest in taking part in the research project were conducted before the cultural probe content was formulated. From the interviews we learned that individuals' conditions are relatively diverse and often attributed by the changes of personhood development and situation of care to a certain degree. We took this into account and structured questionnaires in a way to learn about everyone better as individuals. The first booklet from the cultural probe pack is designed to gain an overview of the carer's role, the illness progression of the person with dementia as well as the condition of care in the home. Scale charts and diagrams were frequently used in this booklet as a prompt to encourage participants to evaluate the questionnaire items subjectively. They were asked to mark the scale charts related to the subjects and given further detail about the decision of their selections. Information such as family carer's care management plans and support channels as well as symptoms of cognitive/mental impairment of the person with dementia is acquired here.

Because personhood is critical to the progression of dementia, important aspects from the life, background and social network of the person with dementia were also comprised to encourage the participants to reflect their own experience whether or not it is positive or negative, in which help build a preliminary picture about their lives for researchers and designers during the cultural probe investigation process.

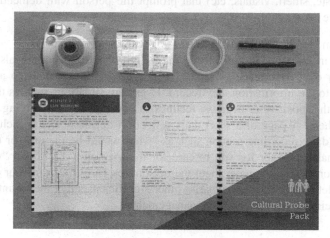

Fig. 1. A cultural probe pack

3.4   Polaroid Camera + Activity Booklet 2 – Life and Daily Recording

Many items and commodities that a person would use and keep around the living space have profound meanings to his/her life background history and personhood development. For people with dementia, these things represent an important part of their remained memory in the world, and constantly remind them who they are. The second part of the cultural probe was designed to document this unique aspect of one's life, from the owned items, favourite tastes in music and sound.

A life recording and a daily recording activity were formulated with the use of another booklet and a Polaroid camera. In the beginning of booklet 2, the family carer is asked to point out key activities that the person with dementia does in typical weekdays to allow the researchers and designers to gain some acquaintance with critical dimensions of the life of the person with dementia and see an even more completed picture about that individual's daily routine.

Entering the life recording activity in booklet 2, participants are invited to use the provided Polaroid camera from the probe pack to capture events and commodities from the living space of the person with dementia and double-sided tape the developed photographs in the booklet with writing description on each one of them. This activity was included to encourage family carers to think about aspects of living space that are important to the persons that they are looking after. It was specified that the participants could take any pictures they wanted but not directly to the sufferers' faces in order to protect their identities. The participants were given the choice of taking photographs related to the following themes:

- Living space of the person with dementia
- Objects that the person with dementia frequently uses in his/her living space
- Objects that have been around the longest in the living space of the person with dementia
- Things (taste, smell, visuals, etc) that prompt the person with dementia from the living space

In addition to performing the tasks of capturing photographs and adding descriptions, in booklet 2's daily recording activity, participants are also asked to evaluate their own experience by using the provided emotion scale to add another layer of data to the information they record. Everyday situations such as the moment that brings either positive or negative feelings to participants' care giving experience are reported here. A page of a short daily reflection questionnaire is included in the end of every daily recording section such as "what would be the one (or two) things that would make it easier for you to care for this person today?" and "what is the biggest (or worry) that you have about the person you care for, or in your care giving process?" to let family carers summarise other significances that they want to address relevant to their everyday care giving management.

3.5   Recruitment of Participants

A group of participants were recruited at a "Carers's Circle" meeting held at Brunel University, UK as well as through the recruitment posting on the university's intranet system. This group of participants were all family carers who are caring for loved ones who have been diagnosed with a form of dementia or have acquired syndromes that are similar to dementia. We received responses from ten university staffs that were interested in taking part, and seven of them were willing to participate after meeting with our researchers for more information about the project.

The majority of the caring subjects that this group of family carers are looking after are women in their 80's, who are in the mid stage of dementia, and are situated in either care homes or in senior housing near the homes of the family carers. The criteria of our recruitment were fairly open, aspects such as social-economic and cultural backgrounds are not strictly considered. However, the recruited participants' situations presented a range of health conditions and care needs, including mobile-disability, memory loss, cognitive impairment, mental health problems and social engagement issues to allow us to discover a greater spectrum of design opportunity.

3.6   Delivery of the Probe Packs

We gave the probes to the family carers of the people with dementia in a series of short, casual meetings in the university, and show them how to operate a Polaroid camera for the tasks that they need to perform in the research. Ethical concerns were explained to them during the meetings and the participant signed a sheet of ethical agreement form after he/she has agreed to take part in the program. The original intention for the probe deployment was to let the participants bring it home and doing the recording for one week then returning to us. However, it became apparent that there were a variety of caring relationships, and as such, contact could be irregular. In response we decided to extend the timeframe and let the participants to take as much time as they need to complete the probe pack.

4   Insights into Living with Dementia

4.1   Content Analysis

Content analysis provides an established and systematic research methodology, looking at quantitative and qualitative materials gathered by research participants through a variety of data collecting methods [5]. It presumes that repeating keywords and groups of words can refer to underlying themes and allows the researcher to reflect people's cognitive schema [6]. Combining qualitative probe data generated by questionnaires with a life recording activity (inviting participants to use a Polaroid camera to document daily life), content analysis provides a tool to systematically describe written and visual material. Using a deductive approach, categories have been formulated prior to analysis deriving from the project's theoretical framework. The aim of the research project is to 1) generate findings for design guideline to integrate articulations of smart home sensors and 2) to generate findings to address key points for constructing re-enact scenarios for co-design purpose.

Four main categories were identified: two categories focusing on the family carers experiences; and the condition of care and emotion. On the other hand, two categories observed the effects of dementia on patients' daily life. They include observations of daily patterns and condition changes due to dementia.

4.2   Results and Analysis

The qualitative research approach using cultural probes has provided a rich data set, giving insight into both of the challenges of living with the illness and day-to-day experiences of dementia care. The family carers filled in the probe packs with a different range of accuracy. Some chose to use the Polaroid camera to visualise the living environment of the person in care, others preferred to fill in the diary with writings only instead, following daily routines and providing information about the conditions of care. In relation to the objectives formulated in the probe design.

5   Life Background Narratives

5.1   Carer's Role

The probes highlighted, that for people who care for family members with dementia, time management and organisation of care resources are imperative for them to maintain the balance between the quality of care and their personal wellbeing. Most family carers are employed, at least on a part-time basis. Therefore, care arrangements can be an additional and quite stressful responsibility to be taken on top of the daily or weekly agenda. Participants usually visit their loved-ones after work, or on weekends. In rare cases they are taking on a full-time care responsibility.

Our first recruited participant is in her late 50s and cares for her father. Working in a full-time position, she visits her father twice a week for a few hours in his care home. She is worried about the care home situation, as her father gets anxious with the staff and had to change already three care homes due to her father's "unacceptable behaviours". She said to have visited 60 care homes in the past three years, which illustrates how difficult it can be to find an appropriate care home for a relative with significant character changes during the progression of the illness.

• *Illness progression of the person with dementia*

As conditions of dementia start to differ, emotional instability of people with dementia will increase. For people with dementia, the ability to express themselves and reasoning can affect the quality of their social relations, whereas their family carers can significantly experience more difficulties engaging interaction with them. From one of our most significant cases in the probe data collection, the increasing impairments of reasoning pose a threat to the participant's love one's wellbeing. During a regular visit, the participant found that her mother had diligently gone around the house switching all the sockets off, including the storage heater. To guarantee independence of people living with dementia and to enable them to stay in their homes alone safe, aids need to be intervened i.e. in situations as the example mentioned above. Nevertheless, even though family carers try to integrate social activities into the weekly schedule, interaction with others is worsening as the illness progresses for the person with dementia, and the person with dementia will become less responsive to the surround situation.

• *Condition of care in the home space*

The cultural probes identified how the emotional condition of family carers is strongly connected to the situation of care. It is important to ensure that the family carers are comfortable with a care plan through good cooperation within their support network is necessary in order to alleviate the stress of their duty. The support from family members, friends and other healthcare professionals plays an important role during a care responsibility. Knowledge exchange among carers is critical to prevent the feeling of being left alone or isolated in the situation of care. Our research participants have also addressed that shared visiting responsibilities among family members as a way to reduce stress. In addition, professional healthcare authorities dealing with questions of dementia providing information and knowledge play an important role in training and supporting family carers.

Concerning the condition of care, one of the participants was very fearful about the care approach performed in the care home. According to her observations, staff do not follow the recommendations of the physiotherapist in handling seat transfers. The photographs she has taken for the activity booklet 2 help to visualise her father's daily life activity and his living environment. Photographs are an insightful tool to understand and highlight commodities, as well as D.I.Y. solutions family carers develop to adapt to certain needs in a care situation. For example, to alleviate struggles during the transfer from his main chair to the wheelchair, the legs of the chair have been raised.

Good communication between other carers involved, or the care home staff, is crucial to the personal wellbeing and stress-reduction of the family carer. Many participants pointed out their worries about their loved ones while not being with them in their home, or care home. Especially the decline of cognitive and physical abilities, i.e. handling of devices such as a mobile phone, has challenging implications. Carers describe the situation of not being able to reach their relative, as a very stressful and worrying experience.

6   Life and Daily Recording

6.1   -Living Space of the Person with Dementia

Most family carers point out, that they would prefer to enable their relatives to stay in their homes for as long as possible. Available care time and the ability of the person with dementia to live independently, are determining factors. Especially, older generations have often lived in their homes for decades and the home environment is strongly connected with memories and family history. With increasing symptoms of dementia, the living space of the patient has to be adapted accordingly. As for example long ways in the home can start to be a challenge for the person with dementia and orientation abilities decrease, new arrangements in the house have to be made. One participant, for instance, moved her mother's bedroom to the ground floor to shorten her routes within the home. Some interventions do not succeed unfortunately, as her mother still had difficulties to find the rooms even though they have been labelled with descriptions.

Another family carer described how her mother started to forget how to handle commodities that are part of her daily routine. With the increasing progress of dementia, she was not able to use the microwave anymore without burning her food, even though her daughter attached instructions to the front of the microwave. Assistive technologies play an important role to enable people with dementia to stay longer in their homes. Responsive sensor networks could provide technical interventions to maintain functional capabilities and to create a safe living environment.

- *Objects that the person with dementia frequently use in his/her living space*

People with dementia have different capacities of independence. In order to maintain personal identity and wellbeing, their motivation to keep up daily routines is essential; this can provide cognitive stimulation and help sustain their self-management ability. Daily routines that have been part of the patient's life for decades have been pointed out as being crucial to the wellbeing of the person with dementia, e.g., fixed hours for enjoying a cup of tea, the morning programme on the radio, as well as reading the newspaper. With the progression of the illness, there is an increasing need for assistance in the handling of commodities in daily life of the person with dementia, i.e., remote control, mobile phone, lighting, heating system, etc.

Referring back to the father of the first recruited participant, to fight the increasing memory loss the family created a family tree with photographs and attached it to the wall in his room. Whenever they talk about a family member he cannot remember; they point at the image to stimulate his memory. Other visual stimulations, such as family photographs, birthday cards and paintings from his old house are placed within his field of vision. Participants also mention activities such as Sudoku and crosswords as a way to keep their relatives active and thereby avoiding a quicker deterioration of cognitive abilities.

- *Objects that have been around the longest in the living space of the person with dementia*

Objects mentioned to have been around for a long time in the living space, are often referred to as paintings and photographs. They are main reference points to the person's private life and memories. Paintings of places were the person has been born, or lived for a long time of his/her life, as well as travel souvenirs and pictures taken with loved ones. As physical performance is often very limited, items connected with intimate memories seem to play an important role in the person with dementia's life. Family carers point out an increasing limitation of the perceptual field of the person they are caring for. Therefore, they arrange items close to the person's field of action, such as the table in front of the chair (where most patients spent their day, especially in later stages of dementia).

- *Things (taste, smell, visuals, etc) that prompt the person with dementia from the living space*

As mentioned previously, people often stick rigidly to daily routines that have been part of their lives for years. Things that prompt people with dementia are for instance the radio, TV, crosswords and Sudoku, newspaper and books. Family carers are been very creative to position stimulating items in the main living areas. As said before, photographs play a crucial role and one carer created a family tree to stimulate her father's memory. Calendars have been placed in the side of field to prompt the patient's time awareness and to memorise for instance weekly appointments, or activities. Crosswords and Soduku seem to be popular, especially among patients in the early stage of dementia. A carer refers to her mother saying, that it might help her to slow down the decline of her cognitive ability. Some carers recommended the people they are looking after to use To-Do lists, to structure their days and minimise the chance of forgetting things. Overall, family carers are very creative to adjust the patient's house and to respond to the needs of people living with dementia, often based on their own observations and care experience.

7   Building Design Narratives

While the data created from these probes is interesting and insightful, it can also be unwieldy and difficult to interpret, thus we used the information from them to create a series of design narratives, providing a set of accessible, rich and grounded design resources to inspire design implications of assistive technologies.

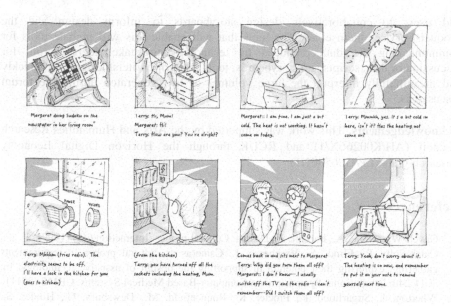

Fig. 2. Example storyboard developed from Probe Data

There's a unique aspect to this project, using design narratives to bring picture and the understanding of dementia. This approach was selected as it can avoid the ethical difficulties by using scripts and storyboards to represent the living condition of the vulnerable populations in order to present the data to a wider audience. Design narratives has the advantage of supporting collaborative design to drive creativity and dialogue among different groups of stakeholders, as it can be an open and accessible medium. The scripts and storyboards are informed by the cultural probes and therefore able to point out different challenges people living with dementia can face. It can serve as an inspiration and profound research information for designers, healthcare professionals and family carers. This approach supports the project's ultimate focus on developing co-design methods for producing assistive technologies for people with dementia.

8   Implications

This work has provided specific insight to support the design of assistive technology - specifically to build a social-media based co-design digital platform that will enable users to be engaged in the design process with SMEs in the healthcare sector. We envisage producing re-enactments of narratives from the probes using actors that will serve as a repository of user experiences. We envisage that our platform will comprise: 1. A system for delivering scripted narratives in the home which will deliver and collect user responses, in order to understand patients' requirements in context, and evaluate future technologies though the use of narratives. 2. A prototype platform for web based co-design, which will bring together script-writers, designers and users to collaboratively design storyboards to inform design and the products/services themselves. The tools that will enable this will include tools for communicating the data produced by technology to stakeholders; forum for discussion of data, scripts and storyboards; tools for scriptwriters/designers to quickly and meaningfully interpret the large volumes of text generated during the forum discussions.

Acknowledgements. This work was supported by the Arts and Humanities Research Council (AH/K00266X/1) and RCUK through the Horizon Digital Economy Research grant (EP/G065802/1).

References

1. Gaver, W., Dunne, A., Pacenti, E.: Design: Cultural probes. Interaction 6(1) (1999)
2. Caleb-Solly, P., Flind, A., Vargheese, J.: Cameras as cultural probes in requirements gathering: exploring their potentia in supporting the design of assistive technology. In: 2011 24th International Symposium on Computer-Based Medical Systems, CBMS (2011)
3. Wherton, J., Sugarhood, P., Procter, R., Rouncefield, M., Dewsbury, G., Hinder, S., Greehalgh, T.: Designing assisted living technologies 'in the wild': preliminary experiences with cultural probe methodology. BMC Medical Research Methodology 2012 12, 188 (2012)
4. Bain, B.K., Leger, D.: Assistive Technology: an interdisciplinary approach, 5th edn., Churchill Livingston Inc., US (1997)
5. Hanington, B., Martin, B.: Universal Methods of Design. Rockport Publishers (February 2012)
6. Weber, R.: Basis Content Analysis, 2nd edn. Sage Publications, Thousand Oaks (1990); Huff, A.S.: Mapping strategic thought. John Wiley and Sons, Chichester (1990)
7. Boehner, K., Vertesi, J., Sengers, P., Dourish, P.: How HCI interprets the probes. In: Proceedings of the SIGCHI Conference on Human Factors in Computing Systems, pp. 1077–1086. ACM, New York (2007)
8. Greenhalgh, T., Robert, G., Macfarlane, F., Bate, P., Kyriakidou, O.: Diffusion of innovations in service organizations: systematic review and recommendations. Milbank Quarterly 82(4), 581–629 (2004)

Is There HCI in IDTV?

An Exploratory Study on Their Words

Samuel B. Buchdid and Maria Cecília Calani Baranauskas

Institute of Computing, University of Campinas, Av. Albert Einstein N1251,
Campinas-SP, Brazil
{buchdid,cecilia}@.ic.unicamp.br

Abstract. Interactive Digital TV (iDTV) is an emerging technology that faces problems that are inherent to it; for example the lack of users' experience interacting with television content. The knowledge constructed from the Human Computer Interaction (HCI) field could be an ally for dealing with interaction design for the iDTV context. This work sought to map out the main issues that have been addressed in the iDTV and HCI fields in recent years, aiming at finding ways of bringing HCI to typical iDTV interaction issues. A data collection and analysis of tag clouds created from titles found in the full programs of two major conferences in the field of HCI (ACM CHI and IFIP Interact), and the major conference in the field of iDTV (EuroITV), complemented with other ACM-DL iDTV publications revealed the individual characteristics of HCI and iDTV publications, as well as their similarities and differences. Thus, this study offers a view of iDTV relative to the HCI field as revealed by the publications words.

Keywords: Interactive Digital TV, Human Computer Interaction, Analysis, Conferences, Publications, Tag Clouds.

1   Introduction

Technology is increasingly being used in the public and private spheres as computers and hyperconnectivity are being incorporated into objects (e.g., toys, appliances, cars, books, clothes and furniture) and also into everyday environments (e.g., airports, garages, malls, houses and offices) [4]. This phenomenon redefines our relationship with technology, brings people together as citizens and members of global communities, and changes the way we live, by continually increasing the digital presence in our daily lives [19]. Bannon [3] argues that sophisticated and complex technologies have problems that go beyond simple human-machine adjustment and ergonomic corrections. Instead of increasing our ability to choose, the new devices are confusing and sometimes disabling us. Thus, when designing some interactive artifact, it is necessary to rethink the place of technology in our values frame, how we live with and through technology, and give priority to human beings, their values, their activities, tools and environments.

M. Kurosu (Ed.): Human-Computer Interaction, Part I, HCII 2014, LNCS 8510, pp. 47–57, 2014.
© Springer International Publishing Switzerland 2014

To meet this demand, some authors discuss the possibility of reimagining HCI as a new way to think about the human-technology relationship. Bødker [4] has drawn attention to a new wave in the HCI field, Harrison et al. [10] suggest the creation of a third paradigm, and Bannon [3] suggests a possible replacement for the term "HCI", which would be "human-centered computing" or "human-centered design". These new perspectives address new subjects (e.g., ethnography and arts) and multiple theories (e.g., user-centered design), which should be incorporated into the traditional HCI field, in light of their understanding, culture, values, concerns, beliefs and activities.

Developing applications for an emerging medium such as the iDTV is challenged by the lack of references to processes for clarifying solutions, evaluating mechanisms, and specific guides for the technology design [12]. In addition, it presents issues inherent to this technology: some problems are relative to the interaction limited by the remote control, the viewer's lack of experience interacting with television content, the physical distance between the user and the television, the usual presence of other viewers in the same physical space, etc. [8, 12]. In many countries, the iDTV did not offer anything new, and disappointed most viewers who were invited by the government, broadcasters, commerce and industry to use it [5].

Within the iDTV field, the HCI corpus of knowledge can be useful to shed light on problems that are inherent to it, including its usability and accessibility [12]. Considerations about daily, emotional, and contextual issues have been necessary for HCI professionals in their development of a design thinking that is suitable for contemporary devices and uses, and also for an increasingly diversified audience [4]. Some lines of research, among which are those published by Cesar et al. [8]; Rice and Alm [17], also show the importance of bringing the end user and his/her viewpoint into the discussions of the project in order to incorporate system features that go beyond technical issues, to identify conflicts, to understand the impact, and shape the system to satisfy the audience.

In this sense, this study sought to identify the relationship between the iDTV issues in the scope of the HCI field, complementing preliminary studies conducted to identify gaps in HCI [6] and iDTV fields [7], separately. Thus, this paper proposes an analysis of publications of the two major conferences in the HCI field (ACM CHI [2] and IFIP Interact [11]), the major conference of iDTV (EuroITV [9]) and other iDTV publications found in the ACM Digital Library (ACM-DL [1]), based on the works titles. The discussion is illustrated with the creation and analysis of tag clouds generated from the available titles of papers. As a contribution, this paper reveals characteristics of iDTV publications, how they relate to the HCI conferences, similarities and differences between the two fields, and gaps for further research in iDTV relative to the HCI field.

The paper is organized as follows: the second section briefly presents the analyzed conferences from the fields of HCI and iDTV, and the ACM-DL repository; we also introduce related concepts and rationale for the use of tag clouds as data representation. The third section describes the method for data extraction that was used to create tag clouds and to conduct the analysis. The fourth section presents and discusses the findings. The last section presents the final considerations about the study and directions for further research.

2   Study Context

The analysis in this work considered two major conferences with tradition in the HCI field: i) The **Conference on Human-Computer Interaction (IFIP Interact)**, which is promoted by the International Federation for Information Processing (IFIP) and its Technical Committee on Human-Computer Interaction (TC13). The first Interact was held in 1984 in the city of London in the UK, and since then has taken place in countries on several continents. From 1995 on, it was held every two years [11]. This study analyzes the editions held in South Africa, Portugal and Sweden, in the years of 2013, 2011 and 2009, respectively; and ii) The **Conference on Human Factors in Computing Systems (ACM CHI)**, since created in 1982, it has been held annually, more frequently in certain countries, including the United States and Canada. Sporadically, the conferences are held in other countries, including Italy (2008) and Holland (1993). The CHI is promoted by the Association for Computer Machinery (ACM) [2]. In this paper, the five editions of the CHI conferences held between 2009 and 2013 were chosen for analysis. For the sake of simplicity, in this paper, the ACM CHI and IFIP Interact conferences are called just "CHI" and "Interact", respectively.

The proposed roadmap in the field of iDTV and related issues was drawn with data from two sources: i) The **European Interactive TV Conference (EuroITV)**, which began in 2003 in the city of Brighton in the UK, where it took place for another year. Since then, it has been held in many countries in Europe. It is the main conference held on the field of iDTV, and it held annually in countries such as Austria (2008), the Netherlands (2007), Greece (2006) and Denmark (2005). This study analyzes the conferences held in Belgium, Finland, Portugal, Germany, and Italy between 2009 and 2013, respectively [9]; and ii) The **ACM Digital Library (ACM-DL)**, which is a comprehensive collection of full-text articles and bibliographic records that cover the fields of computing and information technology. The full-text database, with more than 2 million items, includes the complete collection of ACM publications and index for publications of others ACM's affiliated organizations (e.g., ALGOL Bulletin, Evolutionary Computation, Journal of Usability Studies, Personal and Ubiquitous Computing and The International Journal on Very Large Data Bases), including journals, conference proceedings, magazines, newsletters, and multimedia titles [1]. In this study, ACM-DL iDTV publications were used as additional references.

2.1   Tag Cloud Representations and Tools

A tag cloud is a visual representation of a set of words, which are typically tag words (labels). Each word is highlighted within the cloud according to its frequency within the word set, and it is enhanced through the manipulation of visual features, such as font size, color, weight, etc. This term gained notoriety when it was used on social software websites (e.g., "*Flickr®*"). For Rivadeneira et al. [18], this format is useful for quickly revealing the most prominent terms and relative importance of a specific word within the analyzed set. Also, it provides a general impression of all words and the "essence" of the represented data set. For instance, on social media websites, tag clouds can provide an impression of the person's interests or/and expertise. In addition to first impression formation, Rivadeneira et al. [18] suggest three different tasks that can be supported by tag clouds: i) **Searches:** to locate a specific term in a set; ii) **Browsing:** as a means to browse, where one can access details if interested; and iii) **Recognition/Matching:** to recognize information through visual characteristics linked to each tag cloud generated, which creates a visual identity.

In some specific cases, the tag clouds are less accurate and less efficient if compared to other visualization forms such as tables (e.g., to determine the presence or absence of a specific word) [15] or wordlists (e.g., to identify relationships among concepts) [13]. However, they are advantageous when capturing the essence, and they present a succinctly large amount of descriptive information, which improves user satisfaction [13]. This success scenario and the need for a summarized presentation of a large amount of data (first impression formation or Gisting) are some of the reasons we chose tag clouds as one of the resources in the analysis conducted in this study.

The tool used in this study was *Wordle®*. The occurrence of each word in the source text is grouped together and the most recurring words stand out more. The word size proportionally reflects the number of times it appears in the input text. The tool does not group ("stem") words. "Stemming" means understanding different words as variations of some root or stem (e.g., the words "teach" and "teaching" are combined into a single representation of the word). One way to prevent similar words from appearing separately is to apply the Porter Stemming Algorithm [16] to the source text, which groups similar words by recurrence, in order to organize the words in wordlist by the weight (frequency), as defined in *Wordle®*'s advanced options to create tag clouds.

3   The Study Method

Considering the fact that the title of a text must reflect its content and "indicates the general subject," [14] we based the analysis on information from the paper titles. This method involved word quantification from data collection and then the tag clouds generation and comparison of word sets. The method of this study involved 3 phases and 9 steps, as shown in Figure 1.

In the "Data Refinement" phase, the goal was to gather information from the data available in the ACM-DL (item "A" in Figure 1) and in the conferences websites (item "B" in Figure 1). To start, the titles were extracted (part manually and part automatically) from the full programs of CHI, Interact, and EuroITV conferences between 2009 and 2013 (item "2" in Figure 1). As each conference has a different structure of its sections, we sought articles that were in similar sections. Thus, we gathered: i) from **CHI:** Papers and Works In Progress; ii) from **Interact:** Full, Short and Industrial papers, Posters and Demos; and iii) from **EuroITV:** Full, Short and Industrial papers, Posters and Demos. As additional reference to the iDTV, the **ACM-DL** data source was used to get other iDTV publications. We refined the search with the "Interactive" and "Digital TV" keywords, considering the period between 2009 and 2013 (item "1" in Figure 1). The search was expanded to "The ACM Guide to Computing Literature" (where there are more than 2,000,000 records of bibliographic citations). For all publications, an extra refinement was also necessary to remove duplications and irrelevant items (e.g., proceedings names, authors' names, presentation times, affiliations). As a result of "Data Refinement", text files containing the titles were organized by conference/year.

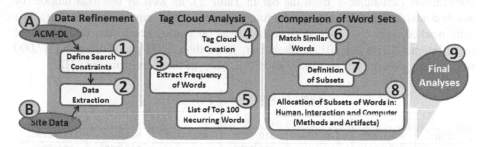

Fig. 1. Steps in the Method

In the "Tag Cloud Analysis" phase, we generated tag clouds from the refined data. The Porter Stemming Algorithm [16] was applied to extract the frequency of words (item "3" in Figure 1). Different images were created with *Wordle®* from the data set and compared (item "4" in Figure 1). The advanced features were used in order to generate the tag clouds. It also was possible to extract a list of the top 100 most recurring words in each tag cloud (item "5" in Figure 1). In this paper, we illustrate tag clouds from the data of all years between 2009 and 2013 representing: i) the HCI scenario (made from titles of CHI and Interact); and ii) the iDTV scenario (made from titles of EuroITV and ACM-DL iDTV publications).

In the "Comparison of Word Sets" phase, the relationships among the lists of the top 100 most recurring words of each scenario (iDTV and HCI) were analyzed (item "6" in Figure 1). For this, the words were automatically classified into 3 groups: one with common words that appear in the two tag clouds, and two groups with words that appear exclusively in each tag cloud. To refine the analysis (items "7" and "8" in Figure 1), the words were allocated into four sets of words addressing HCI sub-areas ("Interaction", "Human" and also "Computer", which was divided into "Methods" and "Artifacts"). Table 1 describes the criteria used to classify the words into the sub-areas, inspired by literature [3, 4, 8, 10, 17, 19]; this classification suggests trends in the iDTV and HCI field.

Table 1. HCI sub-areas

Sub-area	Criteria
Interaction	User interface and features, types of interaction, experiences, and other user-computer relationships.
Human	Users, activities and behaviors, cultural, social, and work-related issues that directly or indirectly involve users.
Methods	Methods and other formal issues related to technology.
Artifacts	Devices, documents, software applications, studies.

The analysis of the tag clouds and sub-sets of words are the basis of the discussion (item "9" in Figure 1) presented in the following sections.

4   Synthesis of Results and Discussion

During the "Data Refinement" stage it was possible to count the number of publications (left number from the bar in Table 2), as well as the total number of words contained in all titles for each group of papers (right number from the bar). The cells marked with "---" indicate that there was no conference in the year indicated (e.g., Interact 2010 and 2012). Altogether, more than 3700 paper titles and 37,000 words were gathered between 2009 and 2013. Most of them are from the CHI.

Table 2. Number of titles per set

	2009	2010	2011	2012	2013	Total
CHI	396/3723	320/3202	510/4885	486/4772	631/6280	2343/22862
Interact	188/1829	—	236/2475	—	240/2505	664/6809
EuroITV	69/656	86/879	65/579	67/653	47/454	334/3221
ACM-DL	123/1261	80/837	75/807	69/715	54/537	401/4157
Total	776/7469	486/4918	886/8746	622/6140	972/9776	3742/37049

The tag clouds shown in Figures 2 and 3, were generated from words represented in the last column of Table 2.

Fig. 2. HCI Tag cloud

Fig. 3. iDTV Tag cloud

Figure 2 was created from title words from the HCI data, and it includes more than 29,000 words. The tag cloud shows that: i) "Design" and "Interaction" are the most frequent words; ii) "User" and "Mobile" appear at the second salient level; iii) "Social" appears at the third salient level, followed by "Support", "Evaluation", "Interface", "Study", "Visual" and "System"; iv) "Experience", "Games", "Information" and "Exploring" appear at the fourth salient level, followed by "Devices", "Communication", "Displays", "Effects", "Web" and "Collaborative"; and v) "Usability", "Gesture", "Online", and "Technology" appear at the fifth salient level.

Figure 3 shows the tag cloud created from tittle words of EuroITV and ACM-DL. Altogether, more than 7,300 words were used to create the image. The tag cloud shows that: i) "TV", "Interactive" and "Digital" are the most frequent words. In this case, the words gained prominence because EuroITV is focused on iDTV, and keywords used in the search from ACM-DL were "Interactive" and "Digital TV"; ii) "Television", "User" and "Video" appear at the second salient level, followed by "Applications" and "System"; iii) "Services", "Content" and "Personalized" are the third most frequent words, followed by "Mobile", "Based", "Media", "Social", and "Design"; and iv) "Experience", "Approach", "Recommendation" and "Web" appear at the fourth salient level, followed by "Networks" and "Study".

Table 3. Diferences and similariuties between HCI and iDTV tag clouds

	Explanation
Similarities	• "Interaction", which is the most frequent word in HCI, appears in the first groups of words more frequently as "Interactive" in the iDTV tag cloud.
	• "User", which appears at the second salient level in the HCI tag cloud, is also among the second most frequent words in the iDTV tag cloud.
	• "Web" appears at the fourth salient level in both HCI and iDTV tag clouds.
Differences	• "Design" appears in the two tag clouds. In the HCI set, it appears in the first group of more frequent words. In the iDTV tag cloud, the word appears with less emphasis.
	• "Mobile" appears in the HCI tag cloud more frequently than in the iDTV tag cloud.
	• "Evaluation" and "Interface", which are at the third salient level in the HCI tag cloud, they appear with low emphasis in the iDTV tag cloud.
	• "Social" appears with relative emphasis in the two tag clouds, but it appears more frequently in the HCI tag cloud than in the iDTV tag cloud.
	• "Study" appears with less emphasis in iDTV publications. The same thing happens with the word "Information".
	• "Visual" are in the group of the most frequent words in the HCI tag cloud, but the word does not appear in the iDTV tag cloud.
	• "TV" and "Television" are in the group of the most frequent words in the iDTV tag cloud. The words do not appear in the HCI tag cloud.
	• "Digital" and "System" appear with more emphasis in the iDTV tag cloud than in HCI tag cloud. The same thing happens with the word "Application" which appears at the second salient level in the iDTV tag cloud.
	• "Video" appears more frequently in iDTV publications than in the HCI tag cloud. Similar results were found in the case of the word "Media", but with less emphasis.
	• "Personalized" and "Recommendation" appear in the groups of third and fourth most frequent words in iDTV tag cloud, respectably, but it does not appear in HCI tag cloud. Words that refer to similar concepts, such as "Adaptive" appear with lowest emphasis in both the HCI and iDTV tag cloud.
	• "Content", which appears in the groups of third most common words in iDTV tag cloud, does not appear as emphatically in the HCI tag cloud.

Table 3 highlights a comparative analysis between HCI (Figure 2) and iDTV (Figure 3) tag clouds, in order to find whether the most frequent HCI words are been discussed in iDTV publications, and the inverse.

In summary, Table 3 suggests that the iDTV publications seem to put more emphasis on technical elements as medium (e.g., "Video", "Media" and "Digital") and system references (e.g., "Applications" and "System"). The HCI tag cloud seems to be more focused on processes (e.g., "Design"), type of devices (e.g., "Mobile"), evaluation as process (e.g., "Evaluation"), category of usage (e.g., "Social") and attributes of the user interface (e.g., "Usability") issues.

As a result of the "Comparison of Word Sets", it shows the relationships from lists of the 100 most frequent words from both HCI and iDTV groups. As a result of match the words between the two groups (item "6" in Figure 1), there are coincidentally 50% of words in common in both HCI and iDTV tag clouds, and 50% different words that appear exclusively in each tag cloud.

Table 4. Word classification from words in common in both HCI and iDTV tag clouds

Words in Common (iDTV and HCI)			Total = 50 words
Human	Interaction	Artifacts	Methods
user, social, behavior, people, environment, home, information	experience, interface, exploring, navigation, collaborative, gesture, communication, adaptive	applications, games, mobile, video, web, devices, media, control, online, digital, tool, network, system, technology, text	design, approach, study, analysis, model, practices, management, case, method, evaluation, learning, development, research
16.3% (7 words)	18.6% (8 words)	34.9% (15 words)	30.2% (13 words)
7 unclassified words: support, towards, performance, enhancing, dynamic, based and content			

Table 5. Word classification from exclusive HCI words

Exclusive HCI words			Total = 50 words
Human	Interaction	Artifacts	Methods
understanding, children, perception, human, personal, public, privacy, work, group, affect, cognitive, emotional, engagement, activity, space	interaction, visual, effects, usability, accessibility, search, touch, sharing, feedback, multi-touch, pointing, tangible, comparing, tactile	displays, computer, phone, input, tabletop, surface, virtual, energy, physical, remote, objects	techniques, measuring, investigating, task
34.1% (15 words)	31.8% (14 words)	25.0% (11 words)	9.1% (4 words)
6 unclassified words: improving, data, large, hci, augmented and influence			

Table 6. Word classification from exclusive iDTV words

Exclusive iDTV words			Total = 50 words
Human	Interaction	Artifacts	Methods
live, advertising, brazilian, recommendation, marketing, aware, elderly, production, context, audience	interactive, personalized, viewing	tv, television, iptv, itv, multimedia, screen, platform, idtv , dtv, internet, program, smart, multimodal, integrated	framework, architecture, broadcast, implementation, guide, processing, annotation, ncl, semantic, streaming, standard, coding, authoring
25.0% (10 words)	7.5% (3 words)	35.0% (14 words)	32.5% (13 words)
10 unclassified words: services, convergence, generation, concept, access, documents, structure, multiple, news and presentation			

Tables 4, 5 and 6 present the 3 subsets of HCI and IDTV common and specific words classified in the HCI sub-areas (Table 1) – see item "8" in Figure 1. The tables' last row shows the unclassified words, which were disregarded in the total number of words when the percentage was calculated. These disregarded words were usually adjectives, and some verbs, or function words that did not fit into the classification.

In summary: i) Table 4 shows that most of the common words between iDTV and HCI sets are associated with "Artifacts" (over 34%) and "Methods" (over 30%). This suggests that word sets in common largely involve the area of technology; ii) Table 5 shows that exclusive data of the HCI set are in both "Human" (over 34%) and "Interaction" (over 31%) columns; and iii) Table 6 (words appearing exclusively in iDTV publications) shows words were distributed mainly in "Artifacts" (with 35%) and "Methods" (over 32%) classes, which also suggest its focus on the area of technology.

4.1   Discussion

The findings of "Tag Cloud Analysis" show that important issues in the HCI field that should have being taken into account in any interactive device are not being included in iDTV publications yet. For example, "Design" and "Evaluation" issues, which are so important to any interactive device, are hardly visible in the iDTV tag cloud. "Usability" issues should also have being considered in applications and devices of iDTV. Nevertheless, some important interaction solutions regarding audience diversity (e.g., "Personalized", "Recommendation" and "Social") emerge in a relevant way in the iDTV tag cloud. Considering the wide reach of television and the population diversity (e.g., cognitive, social, cultural and economic issues), ignoring the design issues means imposing barriers to access and to the culture of interactivity on TV.

Another point to consider is that, on the other hand, by searching for words genuinely related to TV in the HCI tag clouds, we note that they are not being addressed in the HCI field. The main examples are the words "TV" or "Television", which are not commonly seen in HCI conferences. Even new types of interaction that could be applied to TV (e.g., "Gestures") appear with low frequency. The lack of research in the HCI issues within iDTV can be related to the demotivated audience and difficult interaction for the viewers. Only "Mobile" devices, which can be collaboratively used with the TV, appear in both HCI and iDTV tag clouds.

Words direct or indirectly quoted by HCI and iDTV studies (e.g., [3], [4], [8], [10], [17], [19]), and that refer to emergent devices and their use (e.g., emotion, motivation, cultural, affective, etc.), so important to iDTV, appear modestly or do not appear in any tag cloud. For instance, "Emotional" and "Affect" words appear at the lowest salient level of the HCI tag cloud. Words as "Cultural" and "Motivation" did not appear in the tag clouds. Considering the complex social context in which people live and the TV is inserted, these words would be essential in contextual studies to understand the place of TV in an individual and social context, in order to propose devices, services and applications that make sense for people.

The results of "Comparison of Word Sets" analysis suggest that, despite the fact that the HCI conferences and iDTV publications converge in 50% of the most recurrent words, most of the words were predominantly related to technological issues, a result which is represented by the "Artifacts" column (e.g., "Applications", "Mobile", "Web" and "Devices") and the "Methods" column (e.g., "Design", "Approach", "Study" and "Evaluation"). If we compare the iDTV and HCI data, the iDTV data emphasized "Artifacts" (e.g., "Screen", "Multimedia" and "IPTV") while the HCI emphasized "Human" (e.g., "Children", "Personal" and "Cognitive") and "Interaction" (e.g., "Accessibility", "Touch" and "Tactile"). In this sense, it seems that more studies that consider the TV within a digital and social ecosystem, recognizing and addressing technical and social issues as well are needed.

In summary, the findings suggest that, despite some common interests, there is still a gap between the HCI conferences and the iDTV field. Discussions about technological issues and new artifacts, which support the interaction between users and the television, may be important for the iDTV field, which itself has striking technical restrictions over interaction. But working on human and interaction issues can be a way for making television as an active medium of interaction, which might also help users to overcome barriers of digital inclusion.

5   Conclusion

The new devices incorporated into the modern world are changing the way we interact and communicate. iDTV can be considered an emerging technology that has not yet been explored to its full potential. The HCI field has accumulated knowledge regarding the design of interactive devices. Getting an overview of the main issues that have been addressed in recent years in the field is a way to identify both unresolved issues and new opportunities. This paper shed light on the main focuses of research addressed in iDTV publications compared to HCI conferences; tag clouds created from words of contribution titles, are discussed as a way to illustrate the main differences and similarities between the research focuses.

Among the highlights, the results obtained from the analyses also indicate that the use of tag clouds provided a quick and effective overview of the data that was considered. For instance, although the conferences have approximately 50% of their most frequent words in common, there is a marked visual difference between the tag clouds generated for each data set.

Words from the HCI data set that are important for iDTV, are still rarely discussed in iDTV publications. The opposite also occurs: words that are important for user interaction with the TV are also rarely discussed at HCI conferences. The clearest example of this is that "TV" does not appear at all in the HCI data. These results suggest opportunities for iDTV studies in the HCI field, since words (and therefore, perhaps, topics) involving the "human" and the "interaction" classes discussed herein are not yet as frequently addressed as the "computer"-related topics.

Finally, attention to aspects such as e.g., emotion, motivation, cultural, affection, values, etc., pointed out by both iDTV [8, 17] and HCI [3, 4, 10, 19] authors, are still absent. In a further study, we intend to explore these gaps in the "H" and the "I" aspects of iDTV concepts in order to bring subjects such as social context, user motivation and affective aspects into the design of situated iDTV applications.

Acknowledgments. This research is partially funded by CNPq (#165430/2013-3).

References

1. ACM Digital Library, http://dl.acm.org
2. ACM SIGCHI, http://www.sigchi.org
3. Bannon, L.: Reimagining HCI: Toward a More Human-Centered Perspective. Interactions 18(4), 50–57 (2011)
4. Bødker, S.: When second wave HCI meets third wave challenges. In: 4th Nordic Conference on Human-computer Interaction, pp. 1–8. ACM Press, New York (2006)
5. Broeck, W.V.D., Bauwens, J.: The promises of iDTV: between push marketing and consumer needs. In: 7th European Conference on Interactive Television, pp. 41–48. ACM Press, New York (2009)
6. Buchdid, S.B., Baranauskas, M.C.C.: HCI in context: What the Words Reveal About It. In: 15th International Conference on Enterprise Information Systems, pp. 167–175. SciTePress, Lisboa (2013)
7. Buchdid, S.B., Baranauskas, M.C.C.: Interactive Digital TV as revealed through Words: Focuses and Research Sources. In: 19th Brazilian Symposium on Multimedia and the Web, pp. 289–296. ACM Press, New York (2013)
8. Cesar, P., Chorianopoulos, K., Jensen, J.F.: Social Television and User Interaction. Computers in Entertainment-Social Television and User Interaction 6(1), 1–10 (2008)
9. European Interactive TV Conference, http://www.euro-itv.org
10. Harrison, S., Tatar, D., Sengers, P.: The three paradigms of HCI. In: Alt.CHI 2007, pp. 1–18. ACM Press, New York (2007)
11. IFIP Technical Committee on Human-Computer Interaction, http://www.tc13.org
12. Kunert, T.: User-Centered Interaction Design Patterns for Interactive Digital Television Applications. Springer, Berlin (2009)
13. Kuo, B.Y.-L., Hentrich, T., Good, B.M., Wilkinson, M.D.: Tag clouds for summarizing web search results. In: 16th International Conference on World Wide Web, pp. 1203–1204. ACM Press, New York (2007)
14. Merriam-WebsterDictionary, http://www.merriam-webster.com
15. Oosterman, J., Cockburn, A.: An Empirical Comparison of Tag Clouds and Tables. In: 22nd Conference of the Computer-Human Interaction Special Interest Group of Australia on Computer-Human Interaction, pp. 288–295. ACM Press, New York (2010)
16. Porter, M.F.: An algorithm for suffix stripping. Program 14(3), 130–137 (1980)
17. Rice, M., Alm, N.: Designing new interfaces for digital interactive television usable by older adults. Computers in Entertainment-Social Television and User Interaction 6(1), article 6, 1–20 (2008)
18. Rivadeneira, A.W., Gruen, D.M., Muller, M.J., Millen, D.R.: Getting our head in the clouds: toward evaluation studies of tagclouds. In: Proceeding of the SIGCHI Conference on Human Factors in Computing Systems, pp. 995–998. ACM Press, New York (2007)
19. Sellen, A., Rogers, Y., Harper, R., Rodden, T.: Reflecting Human Values in the Digital Age. Communications 52(3), 58–66 (2009)

A Knowledge-Construction Perspective on Human Computing, Collaborative Behavior and New Trends in System Interactions

Isabel Cafezeiro[1,2], Carmem Gadelha[3], Virginia Chaitin[2], and Ivan da Costa Marques[2]

[1] Computing Institute, Vocational Masters Course in Diversity and Inclusion
Fluminense Federal University
[2] Graduate Program of History of Science and Techniques and Epistemology
Federal University of Rio de Janeiro
[3] School of Communication
Federal University of Rio de Janeiro
isabel@dcc.ic.uff.br, carmem@gadelha.com.br,
virginia.mfgc@gmail.com, imarques@ufrj.br

Abstract. This article presents an analysis of collaborative behavior within the historical process of the construction of scientific thought. We start from evidence that the origin of computing was immersed in a conceptual background heavily dominated by structuring thought, resulting in a mode of thinking organized around a centralized unit, strengthening categorization, disciplinarity and a predominant dichotomous logic. However, the new settings in which computer systems are involved, such as collaborative behavior and human computation, reveal a mode of thought and organization within an acentered model of realization. Sociology of knowledge helps us to understand this dynamic, allowing us to verify that the rhizomatic model of realization embraces not only what is traditionally viewed as the setting of computer systems, but also extends to the way of thinking, organization and operation of collective relations around computer systems.

Keywords: human computing, collaborative behavior, sociology of knowledge, hybrids, rhizome.

1 Aims and Organization of This Paper

This paper proposes an analysis, from a historical perspective, of the current settings of computational systems based on collaborative behavior and human computation. This approach operates outside of the usual disciplinary boundaries, since it borrows from the sociology of knowledge the practice of traduction (traduction<>trahison) [1] and adopts, from philosophy, the concept of rhizome [2] to address not only the collective relationships that are established around collaborative systems, but also the actual construction of these systems. Multiplicities, flux, materialities, heterogeneities and co-construction are features that are becoming increasingly evident within new configurations of computing. However, not only the mode of thought that supports the

M. Kurosu (Ed.): Human-Computer Interaction, Part I, HCII 2014, LNCS 8510, pp. 58–68, 2014.
© Springer International Publishing Switzerland 2014

construction of computer systems, but also the usual ways of analyzing the relationships of these systems within the collective to which they belong are tied to structures and their centered organization, and thus, do not favor a broad understanding of this dynamic. We thus propose a traduction of the concept of rhizome [2], expanding a proposal already suggested by Deleuze and Guattari. We show how computation fits a rhizomatic model of realization and how this model goes beyond what is traditionally thought to be the setting of computer systems, extending this setting to include the mode of thought, organization and operation of collective relations.

We argue in this paper that the rhizomatic approach can contribute to our understanding of computation in at least three different ways. First, it provides a better understanding of situations that appear to be paradoxical. Paradoxes occur within a dichotomous mode of thinking when two visions that are understood as irreconcilable are put in confrontation. The adoption of a mode of thought supported by a network of relationships highlights the negotiation process among heterogeneous agents, consisting of a dynamic that leaves no room for the paralyzing feeling that stems from an apparent impossibility of reconciliation. Secondly, it brings a new comprehension of power configurations involving this scenario of multiplicities, flux, materialities, heterogeneities and co-construction. This new comprehension results from the shift from a structured conception where a single unit - under which everything is ruled - represents a mark of power and authority, to an acentered configuration where authority is negotiated. Thirdly, it helps to undermine the strict separation that takes place still today between what is said to be "technical", "exact", "objective", "computable" and what is called "social", "humanistic", "subjective", "non-computable", or "not computable in an acceptable amount of time". This forces a revision in the understanding of knowledge construction. By highlighting the participation of computer systems in this negotiation network in which programs, machines, mathematics, humans, feelings, spontaneous actions and a variety of heterogeneous agents also take part, the three above-mentioned contributions directly affect the conception and construction of computer systems, as well as the comprehension of their (co)operation with/in the collectivity.

This paper is organized as follows. We start, in Section 2, from evidence that the origin of computing was immersed in a conceptual background heavily dominated by structuring thought, resulting in a mode of thinking organized around a centralized unit, strengthening categorization, disciplinarity and a predominant dichotomous logic. Section 3 argues that this model of realization no longer accounts for the new settings that computer systems have come to assume, such as collaborative behavior and human computation, which demand a way of thinking and organization in an acentered model of realization. In light of this, we analyze in Section 4 the evolutionary pathway from CAPTCHAs to reCAPTCHAs, which are current manifestations of collaborative behavior and human computation. We conclude in section 5 commenting some contributions of this approach for computer science.

2   The Primacy of Structures and the Emergence of Computation

Mathematicians, who embrace the idea of abstract theories, define abstract objects that are understood and thought of as forming *a shared body of knowledge*. They refer to these abstract objects as autonomous entities, and communicate and build new abstractions from them, which are increasingly disconnected from the entities in the world in which we live that initially served as inspiration for these objects. Fleck, a sociologist of knowledge in the 1930's, referring to knowledge in general, not specifically to mathematics, explained that when these links with the world in which we live are not perceived, one achieves so-called "objectivity", giving the impression of universality, neutrality and accuracy, exempt from any personal judgment [4].

In the first decades of the twentieth century, the scientific research conducted in Europe and the United States showed a strong tendency toward the quest for objectivity and categorization of knowledge. In mathematics, this trend became evident in the expression of mathematical thinking by representing relationships between entities in an abstract manner (as schemata or structures) with the aim of hiding the connections between such entities and any trace of "concrete reality". Rudolf Carnap was one of the philosophers of mathematics who strongly argued in favor of this approach. According to Daston and Galison [3], "[o]bjectivity, for Carnap, was deeply associated with this very particular way of abstaining from particularity while maintaining a commitment to the structural integrity of *shared knowledge*". Bertrand Russell, a British philosopher of mathematics, also argued in favor of structures which he saw as emerging from abstract representations of relations between entities. Once the structures are identified, the mathematician should abandon any correlation with the things in life that served as inspiration: "We may say, of two similar relations, that they have the same 'structure'. For mathematical purposes (though not for those of pure philosophy) the only thing of importance about a relation is the cases in which it holds, not its intrinsic nature." [5]

This was not, however, a consensus. The impatient resistance of the pragmatist William James is an example of the intense debate provoked by the proposal to decouple abstract representations from the world in which we live. William James defended maintaining the ties with the things in the world for the sake of clarity in the knowledge construction process: "Mr. Russell, and also Mr. Hawtrey, of whom I shall speak presently, seem to think that in our mouth also such terms as 'meaning,' 'truth,' 'belief,' 'object,' 'definition,' are self-sufficient with no context of varying relation that might be further asked about. What a word means is expressed by its definition, isn't it? The definition claims to be exact and adequate, doesn't it? Then it can be substituted for the word - since the two are identical - can't it? Then two words with the same definition can be substituted for one another, *n'est-ce pas*? Likewise two definitions of the same word, *nicht wahr*, etc., etc., 'till it will be indeed strange if you can't convict some one of self-contradiction and absurdity." [6]

Despite objections, in the mid-twentieth century the search for structural objectivity gained strength through the initiatives of the Vienna Circle: "(...) the search for a neutral system of formulae, for a symbolism freed from the slag of historical languages; and also the search for a total system of concepts. Neatness and clarity are striven for, and dark distances and unfathomable depths rejected."[7] A respectable group of scientists, amongst whom was Carnap, published the manifesto "The Scientific Conception of the World", which provided basic guidelines of what would be identified as "scientific practice". The Vienna Circle entered the scene with a double composition that placed logical analysis as a privileged component of scientific practice: a strict linguistic approach, combined with a formal logical system, whose accuracy would clarify the statements, eliminating ambiguities and inaccuracies of speech, and precisely determining their meaning. Logical analysis would then be combined with a decisive mechanism to ensure truth: empirical evidence obtained by breaking statements into their constituent parts until those parts are simple enough that they can be directly compared with concrete reality.

The Scientific Conception of the World settled comfortably on a foundation which has been strengthened in European culture since the seventeenth century in an effort to establish boundaries and disciplinarity as expressed in the four precepts of cartesian logic: evidence, analysis, order, classification [8]. Those percepts were respectable enough to minimize the echo of arguments against them, such as those proposed by William James. In this manner, mathematics, while suffering from a mistaken abstract, structured conception, was strengthened by appearing to be objective, neutral and universal.

As the second half of the twentieth century began, structure dominated thinking was still in vogue; within this milieu computers emerged. In 1936, mathematician Alan Turing imagined an abstract device, later to be named the Turing machine [9]. Attempting to mimic the processes that a human performs when computing a number, the Turing machine constitutes a formal counterpart to the intuitive notion of "computation". Turing's purpose at the time was to understand the extent of Hilbert's proposal, which consisted of a system (a structure) within which any statement would have a formal proof of its truth or falsity. The Turing machine, conceived using arborescent rationality, later came to be materialized in what are currently named computers.

As devices designed from formal systems, from structured symbolic representations, computers show in various different aspects the dynamic of control departing from a centralized unit. This is a consequence of the arborescent (structured) model in which they were conceived: languages grammatically organized from the start symbol, and whose operation is derived by repetition of rules forming the syntactic tree that has the start symbol as its root; automata correspondingly to grammars, also with a designated initial state, from which the process unfolds remaking patterns in repetition; and memory, a system unit on which all processing is done from successive storage retrievals and updates with new values. Computers are therefore systems organized around a strong central unit that dominates everything, a marker of power: "Regenerations, reproductions, returns, hydras, and medusas do not get us any further. Arborescent systems are hierarchical systems with centers of significance and subjectification, central automata like organized memories. In the corresponding models, an element only receives information from a higher unit, and only receives a subjective affection along preestablished paths. This is evident in current problems in information science and computer science, which still cling to the oldest modes of thought in that they grant all power to a memory or central organ." [2]

3   Computation, Dichotomies and the Rhizome

One of the legacies of the formation process of modern thought is a tendency to categorize knowledge into two distinct ontological zones. This dichotomy is a direct consequence of the totalizing (centralized) unit of the arborescent model, since it gives rise to characterizations of the kind "what is inside" and "what is outside", "what is generated from the root" and "what is not generated from the root", "the correct" and "the wrong", "humans" and "nonhumans" [10], resulting in a conception of pure entities, that is, entities that fit comfortably in its structure.

Alongside with this goes the division between social and technical knowledge, a demarcation strongly supported on the assumption that a certain kind of knowledge (which is said to be technical) is objective, that is, independent from the fluctuations of human subjectivity. For many years, the field of sociology of knowledge reinforced this dichotomy by considering mathematics (the core of objective reasoning) as a kind of thinking that demanded a specific mode of understanding. Since the process of construction of mathematical entities was not adequately understood it was not uncommon to admit that these entities existed on their own, independently from human thought, a view shared by sociologists of knowledge as well as philosophers of mathematics. Therefore, mathematics remained outside the realm of study of the sociology of knowledge, protected from its key postulate: *the impossibility of properly understanding modes of thought without taking into account the corresponding context of collective action, or separately from their social origins* [11]. Only in the 1970s with the adoption of the principles proposed in the Strong Programme in Sociology of Science at the University of Edinburgh, did the sociology of knowledge community resolutely begin to consider that mathematics belongs to their field of study, providing evidence that mathematics - as well as all technical knowledge and, in fact, any other kind of knowledge - does not depend solely on what is considered to be "objective". Indeed, all kinds of knowledge require the collaboration of multiple heterogeneous agents [12]. As argued by Lévi-Strauss in his writings on anthropology: "Any system which treats individuation as classification (and I have tried to show that this is always so) risks having its structure called in question every time a new member is admitted." [13]

We see then that certain situations in life force us to deal with entities for which we cannot find a comfortable place in the usual classifications. For example, in the case of computers, the *rapprochement* between the logic of 0's and 1's and the materiality of digital circuits reduces the gap between abstraction and matter, between the idea and the thing. The computer combines mathematical rationality with materiality. Computers function the tension that results from the assemblage between rationality and materiality. As a result of this tension, computers and computation, as well as the mathematics which provides their conceptual foundation, are in a constant state of flux. Hence, even if this flux occasionally acquires a certain stability, such stability can only be provisional. Perhaps for this reason, the publication of Gödel's theorem in the 1930's [14] was a severe surprise for those who advocated an approach to mathematics based solely on an arborescent mode of thought. Contrary to Hilbert's expectations, sufficiently strong formal systems are capable of expressing statements about themselves, giving rise to the incompleteness theorem which demonstrates the existence of true statements that can be formulated within the system but cannot be proved. This exposed the inability of a formal system, even though it may be consistent, to decide every question that can be expressed mathematically within the system. The incompleteness theorem explicitly signals the impotence of totalizing systems for both mathematics and computing: formal systems require externalities in order to have some semblance of consistency and completeness. But these externalities come in a tensioned negotiation. Although incompleteness was exposed within the mathematical machinery itself, it was difficult for mathematicians to avoid extensions of these results outside of mathematics; even today most mathematicians reject with antipathy any associations between Gödel's results and other fields of knowledge. For accepting such associations would undermine the demarcation of borders between mathematics and other fields and consequently the unique prestige of mathematics as a form of purified thought: "Many references to the incompleteness theorem outside of the field of formal logic are rather obviously nonsensical and appear to be based on gross misunderstandings or some process of free associations." [15] Gödel's theorems are a deleuzian "line of flight" enabling mathematics to escape from itself. As a consequence mathematics is renewed and strengthened. Therefore, incompleteness shows the flux in which mathematics, computers and computing are immersed by their constant need to reconstruct and to rebuild themselves.

However, computers as well as computer networks are also totalizing entities, arborescent systems, and therefore sometimes give a feeling of phagocytosis, as if machines were engulfing the world. Furthermore, just as mathematics is not completely captured by formal systems, the world escapes the machine, evidencing a kind of incompleteness of techniques for completely capturing the world. Computer and computer networks (as well as formal systems) require exteriorities, demanding human participation at some level. These human actions lead to a historical re-insertion of technical knowledge since they impose a link between the application of a technique and an individual situation where it is applied, possibly not the same situation for which this technique was designed. Hence, a rhizome arises in the line of flight of the collaboration between machines and humans. We are then forced to find explanations that cope with multiplicity, flux, materialities, heterogeneity and co-construction. In opposition to - but not excluding - the arborescent model, Deleuze and Guatarri [2] suggest a conception of a net of relationships, the rhizome, that helps us to see how this human-machine encounter both separates as it approximates humans and machines, at the same time undoing and redoing the human-machine dichotomy: "[U]nlike trees or their roots, the rhizome connects any point to any other point, and its traits are not necessarily linked to traits of the same nature; [...] It is composed not of units but of dimensions, or rather directions in motion. It has neither beginning nor end, but always a middle (*milieu*) from which it grows and which it overspills. [...] Unlike a structure [...] the rhizome is made only of lines: lines of segmentarity and stratification as its dimensions, and the line of flight or deterritorialization as the maximum dimension after which the multiplicity undergoes metamorphosis, changes in nature. [...] Unlike the tree, the rhizome is not the object of reproduction: neither external reproduction as image-tree nor internal reproduction as tree-structure. The rhizome is an antigenealogy. It is a short-term memory, or antimemory. The rhizome operates by variation, expansion, conquest, capture, offshoots. [...] In contrast to centered (even polycentric) systems with hierarchical modes of communication and preestablished paths, the rhizome is an acentered, nonhierarchical, nonsignifying system without a General and without an organizing memory or central automaton, defined solely by a circulation of states." [2]

In the following section we discuss a case involving computers, human computing, and collaborative behavior. The multiplicity, flux, heterogeneity, materiality and co-construction that become apparent in this case reject an analysis in terms of totality (unity), and therefore show the arborescent approach is incapable of providing, by itself, an adequate understanding of the configurations involved. This example shows the rhizome as a model of realization of the tensioned meeting between humans and computer networks. It also shows that the rhizome embraces the tree structures as it is remade from them. In other words the opposition with respect to the tree does not imply the exclusion of the tree model of realization from the rhizome, which would then amount to a tree-rhizome dichotomy.

4 Human Computing, Collaborative Behavior and New Trends in Systems Interaction

In this text "collaborative behavior" denotes an activity where individual human action, supported by information sharing and collective knowledge, contributes to the realization of a task in a process that may involve computers for the purpose of coordinating man-machine cooperation. Collaborative behavior appears to be an essentially human activity, but a more careful look at it reveals heterogeneity, the alignment of humans with machines, rationalities as well as emotions and subjectivities. It is a collective assemblage that involves negotiation and mutual trust among a diversity of agents that materializes, provides a body to, a hybrid entity. Apparently a negotiation is a binary link, but again a more careful look reveals multiplicity. Each agent is several, since it carries with it a history of previous negotiations. Even the machine carries in its architecture a multitude of agents and negotiations, as Latour [16] shows us in his analysis of Tom West's incursion in the DEC laboratory, a story told by T. Kidder [17]: "Looking into the VAX, West had imagined he saw a diagram of DEC's corporate organization. He felt that VAX was too complicated. He did not like, for instance, the system by which various parts of the machine communicated with each other, for his taste, there was too much protocol involved. *He decided that VAX embodied flaws in DEC's corporate organization.* The machine expressed that phenomenally successful company's cautious, bureaucratic style." Furthermore, negotiation takes place in many directions, weaving a network of encounters, and therefore tending to an acentered configuration. This moves us away from structures in which connectivities start at a point and then proceed by dichotomy. However, structures recur insistently. They emerge unexpectedly from the network in a movement of reterritorialization of the network. Collaborative behavior takes place in a rhizome in which arborescent thought deterritorializes and reterritorializes.

The case study that we now consider starts on a strict separation between humans and machines, supported by an arborescent mode of thought. We consider the analysis of L. Ahn, who refers to a task involving induction which humans are capable of easily performing but which computers are either unable to perform or are unable to perform in a reasonable amount of time [18]. Thus the ability to perform such inductions is considered to be an essentially human trait. In addition to the enormous amount of time that is "wasted" by people in computational activities such as playing games (nine billion human-hours of solitaire in 2003, as reports L. Ahn[1]), the fact that the ability to perform certain inductive tasks is an essentially human trait has led to a new area of computer science research called "Human Computation". This emerging field seeks to harness human tasks involved in spontaneous activities such as playing games, for the purpose of benefiting society [19]. The following is an example given by L. Ahn: in search engines for images on the Internet it is currently very difficult to relate an image to the typed keyword. However, at a quick glance, a human being is able to suggest a word that permits the identification of the image and which thus could be used as a caption. In this manner, associating the action of inferring captions for images to a game-playing activity, a large number of images could be captioned, contributing not only to web searches, but also providing access for the visually impaired. Thus, the field of Human Computation proposes outsourcing to humans only those sub-tasks which machines cannot carry out on their own. Humans cooperate with the machine by performing a sub-task that the machine cannot do (or cannot do in a feasible amount of time). This joint, collaborative work creates a half human, half machine hybrid entity that can carry out the desired computational task.

In proposing a deleuzian analysis of the emergence of this new field of research in computing, this paper focuses on the evolutionary pathway from CAPTCHAs to reCAPTCHAS. The "Completely Automated Public Turing test to tell Computers and Humans Apart" (CAPTCHA) was proposed in an article published in the *Communications of the ACM* in February 2004 to describe a solution for a pressing contemporary problem: how to stop bots from invading websites. In other words, how can we control unauthorized access to computers or web pages by invasive computer programs. The proposal of Ahn *et al.* consists in displaying distorted characters so that in order to access a web page, the user must decipher and retype them, a demonstration that the accessing agent is human and not a robot. The use of this technique is now widespread in many popular websites such as Yahoo, Hotmail and PayPal, among others.

The dichotomous mode of thought, strictly separating as it does what it assumes to be opposites, has the effect of hindering the realization that entities act in co-construction, and consequently generates situations that seem to be paradoxical. Ahn remarks: "Notice the paradox: a CAPTCHA is a program that can generate and grade tests that it itself cannot pass (much like some professors)." [19]. There are other aspects which may also seem paradoxical when a dichotomous logic is maintained: although CAPTCHAS are based on a clear, sharp distinction between humans and machines, they were inspired by the Turing Test, which was intended to show the indistinguishability of machines and humans, as Turing claims in his 1950 paper where he presents the test: "I believe that at the end of the century the use of words

---

[1] http://www.youtube.com/watch?v=tx082gDwGcM

and general educated opinion will have altered so much that one will be able to speak of machines thinking without expecting to be contradicted." [20] Ahn does not comment on this strange turn of events. Instead, he claims that his proposal and the Turing test both distinguish humans from computers. Even though CAPTCHAs arose from a context dominated by a structuring mode of thought, paradoxically this proposal leads to a hybridization between humans and machines, interweaving an engine that offers a solution to a task that machine seems not able to perform by itself. Building upon this hybridization, we are then led to reCAPTCHAS, which are proposed as a mechanism for leveraging human action in collaboration with machines for the purpose of digitizing printed works with expired copyrights in order to make them freely available: "Although CAPTCHAs are effective at preventing large scale abuse of online services, the mental effort each person spends solving them is otherwise wasted. This mental effort is invaluable, because deciphering CAPTCHAs requires people to perform a task that computers cannot. We show how it is possible to use CAPTCHAs to help digitize typeset texts in nondigital form by enlisting humans to decipher the words that computers cannot recognize." [19]. Thus, CAPTCHAs and their subsequent evolution to reCAPTCHAs, simultaneously unmakes and remakes the distinction between humans and machines. Collaborative behavior deterritorializes and reterritorializes the arborescent thought processes throughout the human-machine dichotomy.

5   New Trends of System Interactions, the Need for Different Understandings of Collective Configurations

The rhizome allows us to perceive this movement of (de/re)territorialization. The endeavor to reestablish structures on acentered networks manifests itself, as we have seen, in paradoxes, unfolds in the reinstatement of the rhizome itself. As the rhizome slips and remakes itself, the structure deterritorializes and the acentered network restates itself. It no longer has the static image of a paradox, a typical paralyzing incompatibility which arises from a binary conception within the dichotomous mode of thought. It is the motion of reconstruction, the flux of a new conformation that results from a co-constructive negotiation.

This development also brings a new comprehension of the power of different configurations involving this scenario. These configurations result from the shift from a structured conception - where a single unit under which everything is ruled represents a mark of power and authority - to an acentered configuration where authority is negotiated. ReCAPTCHAS put in evidence a new scenario in which a multitude of human brains cooperate with the machine performing that part of the task of text decryption which scanners cannot. This creates a framework in which people perform a certain task but in most cases do not know the purpose of this action. Even when they know that it is to offer free digitalization, they certainly do not know of which text, nor which phrase they are helping to disseminate. When employing dichotomous modes of thought, people function like the pieces of a big engine. These pieces provide the machine with the ability to perform what is clearly recognized to be an exclusively human capability: namely, induction. This new configuration reverses the usual understanding that humans employ machines to solve their problems and not vice-versa - for example, a man with an artificial heart. It creates a situation in which machines employ humans to solve their problems, which makes humans confused about "Who is in command? Who owns the control?". The control no longer emanates from a unit of power, the root of a structure, but results from the continuous negotiation among of heterogeneous agents that participate in the network.

In addition, this configures a situation where social mechanisms act in a conformation which would normally be considered purely technical, placing humans and machines side by side in a symbiotic interaction. Computers changed the terms of the debate on the hybridization of knowledge to its current form. The directions that computing took in the 1980's, the widespread use of computers, and later the new forms of interaction provided by the Internet and by human computing and collaborative behavior, are forcing us to revise our understanding of knowledge construction. Computing is now seen to be a hybrid phenomenon, an area in which the human and the non-human are juxtaposed; hence the hybridization between "technical" and "social" becomes more readily visible, thus undermining the rigid and severely disciplined hierarchical, arborescent organization of modern thought.

Acknowledgments. We thank Prof. Gregory Chaitin for explaining to us some of the subtitles of the English language.

References

1. Law, J.: Traduction/Trahison: Notes on ANT. Department of Sociology Lancaster University, http://www.lancaster.ac.uk/sociology/stslaw2.html
2. Deleuze, G., Guatttari, F.: A thousand plateaus: capitalism and schizophrenia. University of Minnesota Press (1987)
3. Daston, L., Galison, P.: Objectivity. Zone Books, New York (2007)
4. Fleck, L.: Genesis and Development of a Scientific Fact. University of Chicago Press (1935, 1981)
5. Russell, B.: Introduction to Mathematical Philosophy. George Allen & Unwin, Ltd., London (1919)
6. James, W.: The Meaning of Truth (1907), http://ebooks.adelaide.edu.au/j/james/william/meaning/
7. Hahn, H., Neurath, O., Carnap, R.: The Scientific Conception of the World. The Vienna Circle, PhilPapers http://philpapers.org/rec/HAHTSC
8. Decartes, R.: Discourse on the Method of Rightly Conducting One's Reason and of Seeking Truth (1637) GutemberProject, http://www.gutenberg.org/ebooks/59
9. Turing, A.: On computable numbers, with an application to the Entscheidungsproblem. Proceedings of the London Mathematical Society, Series 2, (42), 230–265 (1936)
10. Latour, B.: Nous n'avons jamais été modernes. Editions La Decouverte, Paris (1991)
11. Mannheim, K.: Ideology and Utopia, An Introduction to the Sociology of Knowledge. Harcourt, Brace & Co., New York (1954)
12. Bloor, D.: Knowledge and social imagery. University of Chicago Press, Chicago (1991)
13. Lévi-Strauss, C.: The savage mind. Weidenfeld and Nicolson Inc., London (1966)
14. Gödel, K.: Über Formal Unentscheidbare Sätze der Principia Mathematica und verwandter Systeme. I, Monatsch. Math. Phys. 38, 173–178 (1931)

15. Franzén, T.: Gödel's theorem, an incomplete guide to its use and abuse. Lulea University of technology Sweden (2005)
16. Latour, B.: Science in Action: How to Follow Scientists and Engineers through Society. Harvard University Press, Cambridge (1987)
17. Kidder, T.: The soul of a new Machine. Aller Laner, London (1981)
18. Ahn, L., Blum, M., Langford, J.: Telling Human and Computers apart. Communications of the ACM 47(2), 58–60 (2004)
19. Ahn, L., Maurer, B., McMiller, C., AbrAhn, D., Blum, M.: reCAPTCHA: Human-Based Character Recognition via Web Security Measure. Science 321 (September 12, 2008)
20. Turing, A.: Computing machinery and intelligence. Mind 59, 433–460 (1950)

A Revised Lexical Approach for Analyzing Online Reviews

Xiaowen Fang[1] and Fan Zhao[2]

[1] School of Computing, DePaul University, Chicago, IL, U.S.
xfang@cdm.depaul.edu
[2] Lutgert College of Business, Florida Gulf Coast University, Fort Myers, FL, U.S.
fzhao@fgcu.edu

Abstract. Inspired by the lexical approach used by psychologists to study personality traits, this paper proposes a revised version of this approach for analyzing online reviews. The lexical approach is based on a lexical hypothesis stating that personality traits are reflected in the adjectives invented by people to describe them. The revised lexical approach contains five steps: collecting online reviews, parsing adjectives, extracting consumer/user observations, factor analysis, and exploring factors/patterns. The paper elaborates each of these steps. It further discusses implications of this new approach.

Keywords: lexical approach, content analysis, qualitative research, online reviews.

1   Introduction

Web 2.0 technologies such as blogs, wikis, and forums have created a perfect environment for content sharing. Consumers can share their opinions about a product or service with large audiences with minimal efforts (such as a few mouse clicks). These online reviews often contain critical information for both practitioners and researchers in an unprecedented scale. There have been numerous reports suggesting the increased use of online content for both academic research and business decision-making [7].

Content analysis, a class of methods at the intersection of the qualitative and quantitative traditions, has been commonly applied for rigorous exploration of many important but difficult-to-study issues of interest to management researchers [4]. When applying the content analysis method to online reviews, there are two major problems that may jeopardize the quality of the analysis results.

- The analysis of texts and interpretation of results are subjective. Researchers who specialize in content analysis research have expressed major concerns of this method about a disconnect between what the content analysis results can tell readers legitimately versus how the findings are actually being interpreted by the authors [2, 4]. This disconnect is caused by not only researchers' subjective interpretation of results, but also by extensive human coding of texts.

M. Kurosu (Ed.): Human-Computer Interaction, Part I, HCII 2014, LNCS 8510, pp. 69–76, 2014.

- The sheer volume of online reviews poses a major problem in content analysis. For example, Simmons et al. [7] report a computer aided content analysis of over 20,000 movie reviews. The number of online reviews can easily rise up to a million or more in some contexts. It is impractical to use human judges to code comments presented in online reviews.

Researchers have attempted to apply natural language processing technologies to improve the efficiency and effectiveness of content analysis [4, 7]. While to some extent, the efficiency of content analysis can be improved to deal with a large number of reviews, quality of the analysis can be compromised by the fact that most online reviews tend to be informal and do not adhere to accurate grammar rules. Any attempt to accurately parse semantics in online reviews will be proved counter-productive. It is argued that the real essence of content analysis is to explore consumers' language and discover its true meanings. Super-imposing formal grammar rules to a consumer language that one tries to investigate is no doubt very dangerous and may likely skew the results.

Inspired by the lexical approach adopted by psychologists to study personality traits [1], this paper proposes a revised lexical approach aiming at addressing the aforementioned limitations of current content analysis method: namely subjective judgments, large number of online reviews, and inappropriate use of natural language processing technologies. This revised lexical approach is promising and will likely contribute to both research and practice in any area concerning human behaviors such as human computer interaction, information systems, management, and psychology by substantially improving the rigor of content analysis of online reviews.

The rest of the paper is organized as follows: it first introduces the lexical approach used by psychologists to study human personality. After the following section proposes the lexical hypothesis, Section "A Revised Lexical Approach" elaborates details of the revised lexical approach for analyzing online reviews.

Then the paper presents discussions about the strengths and potential weaknesses of the revised lexical approach.

Finally, the last section discusses how this revised lexical approach can be applied in research and practice, and its profound implications.

2   The Lexical Approach Used in Personality Study

The idea of using a lexical approach to obtain personality traits stems from the lexical hypothesis for personality research. The lexical hypothesis states that people will want to talk about personality traits that they view as having important consequences in their lives [1]. As a result, people will inevitably invent some words to describe those who exhibit high or low levels of these essential traits. Over long periods of time, words that describe important traits should become established in every language [1]. In applying a lexical approach to personality research, a researcher first systematically searches the dictionary of the language to be examined in order to obtain a list of personality–descriptive adjectives [1]. After establishing this list of adjectives, the researcher excludes terms that are rarely used. The resulting list is then administered to a large sample of participants who are asked to provide self-ratings on these adjectives, indicating the extent to which each adjective describes their own personalities. A factor analysis is then performed on the ratings collected through the survey. Each factor discovered in this factor analysis constitutes a unique personality trait. The list of words converging on a factor suggests the nature of this personality trait and how to describe this trait.

Cattell [3] was the first researcher to conduct a factor analysis of ratings on personality-descriptive adjectives in the English language. His analysis revealed 12 factors. However, when other researchers later re-analyzed Cattell's data, they found only a consistent set of five personality factors[8]. These five personality factors later became the well-received Big Five personality factors to describe personality traits – openness, conscientiousness, extraversion, agreeableness, and neuroticism [5].

This paper argues that the lexical approach used in personality research can be an invaluable method in content analysis of online reviews for two reasons: 1) this approach effectively reduces the unit of analysis to a single word without necessarily interpreting its meaning beforehand. 2) The factor analysis in this approach leads to the discovery of any significant patterns that may exist in the language used by reviewers. Overall, this approach provides a possible solution to avoid potential pitfalls of subjective judgments by researchers in content analysis while leading to the findings of patterns in reviewer language.

However, the lexical approach cannot be applied in content analysis of online reviews before the following three issues are addressed:

1. The lexical hypothesis must reasonably stand for the text content to be analyzed. The lexical approach hinges on this hypothesis. If it doesn't hold true, an attempt to apply the lexical approach will be futile.
2. The lexical approach requires the use of a list of adjectives that describe a research object such as a product or service. Unlike human personality, researchers usually do not have full knowledge about the language used by consumers about a product or service. No dictionary of adjectives is available for online reviews.
3. The survey conducted towards the end of the lexical approach may become an unconquerable barrier for many studies. In order to achieve reliable and robust results in the factor analysis, this survey may require thousands of responses. The survey is clearly too time-consuming and inefficient.

To move forward with the lexical approach, the next section addresses the essentiality of the lexical approach and Section "A Revised Lexical Approach" proposes a revised lexical approach applicable to content analysis of online reviews.

3   The Lexical Hypothesis

The lexical hypothesis states that a finite set of traits of a product or service are consistently perceived by its consumers and these traits can be expressed by consumer language. This hypothesis is the premise of applying the lexical approach in content analysis of online reviews. In general, this hypothesis likely holds true if an online community focusing on a product or service where consumers can share their opinions have been formed for an extended period of time and the amount of online reviews is substantial. For example, lexical hypothesis may likely hold true for computer games because game players have posted reviews and formed online communities for years.

4   A Revised Lexical Approach

Attempting to address the issues associated with content analysis and the original lexical approach in personality research, this paper proposes a revised lexical approach. This approach has five major steps: 1) Collecting online reviews, 2) Parsing adjectives, 3) Extracting consumer/user observations, 4) Factor analysis, and 5) Exploring factors/patterns. Details about each step are discussed in the following subsections.

4.1   Collecting Online Reviews

The goal of this step is to gather user-generated content from the Internet. Most of online reviews are available for downloading on the Internet. To ensure a good quality of the downloaded reviews, one has to attend to the following details:

1)   The downloaded reviews should be representative. The reviews must include views and opinions expressed by different stakeholders such as vendor/manufacturer, retailer, and users, and different product types.
2)   Only the reviews posted by users will be included. Any texts appearing on a website as standard elements such as headers and footers should be excluded.
3)   Repetitive content must be removed. Many users post their reviews in response to others'. The repetitive content may skew the results.
4)   Reviews must be separated by both reviewer and product. Each review should have been posted by one reviewer about one product/service.
5)   A database needs to be designed to store structural information such as product name, reviewer information, and time of the review.

Each review has to be stored as one record in a database. The meta-information about each review is vital for interpreting the results from factor analysis in a latter stage.

4.2   Parsing Adjectives

Since no known dictionary of adjectives likely exists for a regular consumer product or service, it is imperative to identify such adjectives from online reviews. A computer program that applies the most basic Natural Language Processing (NLP) techniques can be used/developed to perform the following tasks:

1) Parsing words. The NLP application first breaks texts into words. Any special characters or white spaces are removed.
2) Checking the part of speech. The NLP application then connects to a lexical database for the English language such as WordNet[6], to check the type of part of speech of each word.
3) Detecting adjectives that describe the target product or service. These adjectives will then be saved as the candidate words to be further analyzed.

In this step, it is critical NOT to apply any sophisticated NLP techniques attempting to shorten the list of adjectives or interpret semantic meanings of those words. The assumption is that consumers or users have their own language that is not necessarily the same as the standard English. Researchers ought to keep the adjectives used by consumers/users intact and free from external interference. If there are any prominent patterns in the consumer/user language such as phrases and synonyms, they will surface in later analyses.

4.3   Extracting Consumer/User Observations

As discussed in Section 2, one of the challenges to directly apply the lexical approach in the analysis of online reviews is the difficulty of conducting a large-scale survey. Fortunately, the online reviews themselves represent invaluable consumer/user observations that can be used to substitute the survey in the original lexical approach. Each online review can be treated as an individual observation made in a natural environment. Only the most important and most appropriate adjectives would have been chosen in these reviews. Consumers/users voluntarily contributed these reviews without any external pressure. Even though the online reviewers weren't given the opportunity to choose their words from the complete list of adjectives used by their peers, this paper argues that the online reviews constitute a huge dataset with higher quality than the responses from a hypothetical survey conducted in a later stage. The size of such a dataset is unprecedented and could have never been achieved in a regular survey. Arguable, selecting words from a long list can be tedious, time-consuming, and inaccurate. Ultimately, the quality of a hypothetical survey can be at risk due to the fatigue factor. The huge amount of online reviews also helps find patterns that may never be found through other means.

To prepare for the upcoming factor analysis, the online reviews must be converted to a dataset by a computer program as follows: 1) Each word on the list of adjectives produced in the second step, "Parsing Adjectives", is treated as an individual item. The list of adjectives can be saved as the field names of a database table. 2) Retrieve all online reviews one at a time. Each review about one product/service is treated an individual record. Adjectives used in the same review must be somehow related because they describe the same product/service. If an adjective appears in this review, the value for this adjective (field) shall be 1. Otherwise, a zero value should be registered.

The end product of this step is a table of values "0" and "1". "1" indicates the appearance of an adjective in a particular online review while "0" suggests absence of the word. This table is used as the dataset for the upcoming factor analysis.

4.4   Factor Analysis

An exploratory factor analysis is conducted to discover the patterns of adjectives used by consumers. Each of the factors surfaced in this analysis represents a small list of adjectives that share some commonalities because they have been used together for some reason. These commonalities may provide critical information to researchers regarding different perspectives of the target product or service. Although they are subject to further interpretation, there is no doubt that the existence of these commonalities is factual.

4.5   Exploring Factors/Patterns

The purpose of this step is to interpret the meanings and implications of each factor discovered in the previous factor analysis. Qualitative methods such as interviews can be used to help understand each factor. Although there is still a subjective component in this process, the patterns of adjectives are derived from actual data. These patterns are robust and can reasonably withstand biases from human judgments. These factors represent common issues or concerns expressed by the majority of consumers or users. The spectrum of these factors will likely cover all perspectives of a product/service. This information is invaluable to all stakeholders that are involved in the entire life cycle of a product/service.

5   Discussions

This paper proposes a revised lexical approach for analyzing online reviews. This promising approach will benefit both researchers and practitioners in any subject area that concerns about human behavior. The strengths of this revised lexical approach are summarized as follows:

- It significantly improves the rigor of content analysis of online reviews by introducing a well-established statistical analysis into a subjective and qualitative process of content analysis. The results from the factor analysis should clear any doubts about whether or not a pattern observed from the analysis is factual or not. The data speaks for itself.
- The proposed approach makes it possible to use an unprecedentedly large sample that has never been achieved before. Due to the benefits of a large sample, the thoroughness and validity of this analysis can reach a higher level than what researchers have ever attempted to achieve.
- Data collection is naturalistic and non-intrusive. Most online reviews posted by ordinary customers are typically written in a natural environment that is free of

external influence such as financial incentive, time pressure, biased instructions from the experimenter, fatigue, and the like. The quality of the collected data may be higher than that of the data collected in most empirical studies we have seen so far.

- The proposed approach is economic. The guiding principle of this approach is to let the data speak for itself. No interpretation of any word, sentence, or review written by consumers or users will be necessary. No sophisticated natural language processing techniques are ever used. All computer programs involved in the analysis can be programmed by a student who possess a Bachelor's degree in computer science or a graduate student majoring in any IT field.

However, as any research method in general, the revised lexical approach is not perfect either. There are two main constraints of this method:

- By analyzing only adjectives in online reviews, the revised lexical approach might have overlooked some useful information expressed through other parts of the languages such as nouns. Additional analyses of other parts of speech such as nouns can be conducted to complement the analysis of adjectives.
- The environment where an online review is written cannot be controlled. A reviewer doesn't have an opportunity to assess the applicability of all possible words from a complete dictionary in an online review. A score of 0 or 1 might have oversimplified a reviewer's evaluation of a word.

6   Conclusions

The revised lexical approach proposed in this paper may have profound implications in both academia and industry. It provides a rigorous quantitative solution to a problem that used to be solved only by subjective and qualitative methods. It is conceivable that this method can be applied in a wide spectrum of research disciplines.

References

1. Ashton, M.C.: Individual Differences and Personality. Academic Press, San Diego (2007)
2. Carlson, L.: Use, Misuse, and Abuse of Content Analysis for Research on the Consumer Interest. The Journal of Consumer Affairs 42(1), 100–105 (2008)
3. Cattell, R.B.: Confirmation and clarification of primary personality factors. Psychometrika 12, 197–220 (1947)
4. Duriau, V.J., Reger, R.K., Pfarrer, M.D.: A Content Analysis of the Content Analysis Literature in Organization studies-research themes, data sources, and methodological refinements. Organizational Research Methods 10(1), 5–34 (2007)
5. Goldberg, L.R.: An alternative 'description of personality': The Big-Five factor structure. Journal of Personality and Social Psychology 59(6), 1216–1229 (1990)

6. Miller, G.A., Beckwith, R., Fellbaum, C., Gross, D., Miller, K.J.: Introduction to WordNet: an on-line lexical database. International Journal of Lexicography 3(4), 235–244 (1990)
7. Simmons, L.L., Conlon, S., Mukhopadhyay, S., Yang, J.: A computer aided content analysis of online reviews. The Journal of Computer Information Systems 52(1), 43–55 (2011)
8. Tupes, E.C., Christal, R.E.: Recurrent personality factors based on trait ratings. Journal of Personality 60, 225–251 (1992)

Ergonomics in the Practice of Project Architect on Selected Examples

Klaudiusz Fross

Silesian University of Technology, Faculty of Architecture
ul. Akademicka 7, 44-100 Gliwice, Poland
klaudiusz.fross@wp.pl

Abstract. Ergonomics is present in everyday design practice. Designers use it consciously or intuitively. They also do not take into account the realization of its principles. The paper presents a variety of examples of the application of ergonomic principles in the design. It shows the various aspects of ergonomic design selected examples of projects and the implementation of the author. It discusses ergonomics in kitchen technology, medical technology hospital facilities, hotels projects, industrial plants, water parks, playgrounds, etc. The purpose of this paper is to show the diversity of ergonomic issues occurring in daily practice. Demonstration of the need to start the design of the initial findings of ergonomic parameters, modules and optimization of technological systems. Ergonomics as a vital and necessary part of the initial phase of design - programming, which not only simplifies the design but also ensures optimum and safe use. Ergonomic design gives a measurable and tangible benefits for developers, investors and users. The paper is the author's statement, presents his point of view, ergonomic in design.

Keywords: architectural design, ergonomics in the design, building quality evaluation.

1   Theory

Ergonomics is one of the most important elements of architectural design. Ergonomics is part of the preliminary stage of design - programming. A large part of the principles of ergonomics ensure building regulations applicable in a given country. For example, the dimensions of the stairs, toilet cubicles, door width, the minimum amount of space, the minimum size for the data types of premises, the mandatory functional systems. In addition, the principles of ergonomics include provisions for such categorization of hotels, pharmaceutical design of pharmacies, health rules concerning back-kitchen, cloakroom workplaces, etc.

Ergonomics can be learned from the guides and the observations of the built environment - with observations designed space, methods of use and user behavior.

These functions where ergonomics is almost mandatory. These include for example: hotel rooms and hospital, kitchen facilities, operating theaters, pharmacies, etc. In these cases the application of ergonomics in the field of optimal functional

M. Kurosu (Ed.): Human-Computer Interaction, Part I, HCII 2014, LNCS 8510, pp. 77–85, 2014.

relations cannot be discretionary. But there are many features which the system depends on the creativity of the designer, his talent, skills, knowledge, experience, needs, investor, customer expectations, etc. The application of ergonomics is voluntary, so the built environment operate in both spaces ergonomically designed and unergonomic.

In the theory of qualitative research are noteworthy references: Preiser W., Rabinowitz H., White E. [1988]: Post-Occupancy Evaluation; Preiser W. [1989]: Building Evaluation; Preiser W., Vischer J.C. (red.) [2005]: Assessing building performance, Nasar J.L., Preiser W., Fisher T. [2007]: Designing for Designers: Lessons Learned from Schools of Architecture; Lang J. [1997]: Creating architectural architectural Theory. The role of the Behavioral Science in Environmental Design; Groat L., Wang D. [2002]: Architectural Research Methods; Zeisel J. [1990]: Inquiry by design, Tools for environment-behavior research; Johnson P.A. [1994]: The Theory of Architecture. Concepts, Themes & Practice; Anderzhon J., Fraley I.L., M. Green M. [2007]: Design for Aging Post-Occupancy Evaluations. Lessons learned from Senior Living Environments featured in the AIA's Design for Aging Review; Kernohan D., Gray J., Daish J., Joiner D. [1992]: User participation in building design and management. Architecture; Baird G., Gray J., Isaacs N., Kernohan D., McIndoe G. [1996]: Building Evaluation techniques; Duerk D.P. [1993]: Architectural programming. Information management for design; Foqué R. [2010]: Knowledge in architecture; van der Voordt T.J.M., van Wegen H.B.R. [2005]: Architecture in use. An introduction to the programming, design and evaluation of building; de Jong T.M. i van der Voordt D.J.M. [2005]: Ways to study and research. Urban, Architectural and Technical Design [1].

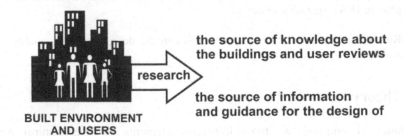

Fig. 1. Flow chart describing additional sources of knowledge and information derived from studies of the built environment and its users (the author's elaboration)

2   Own Research - Observations and Professional Practice

According to the author one of the effective methods of knowledge of good and bad practices of ergonomic solutions are qualitative study of existing objects. The entire built environment is a database of information. It is a database and a record of success and design errors. Reaching for the information you can get to know a good solution - worthy of attention and avoid mistakes.

There are many methods for assessing and obtaining information from the built environment as: POE (Post Occupancy Evaluation), REN (Real Estate Norm), BQM (Building Quality Assessment), FSA (Functional Suitability Assessment), STM (Serviceability Tools and Methods), PBAP&MM (Physical Building Audit Procedures and Maintenance Management), LCA&LCCA (Life Cycle Analysis & Life Cycle Costs Anlysis), BIU (Building-in-Use), BPE (Building Performance Evaluation), BREEAM (Building Research Establishment Environmental Assessment Method), EPIQR, TOBUS, INVESTIMMO, LIFECON, EUROLIFEFORM, SUREURO, ECB&CS (Energy Conservation in Buildings and Community System Programme), EIA (Environmental Impact Assessment), GBC (Green Biulding Tool), LSA (Land Suitability Analysis), LEED (Leadership in Energy and Environmental Design), LCA (Life Cycle Assessment), LCC (Life Cycle Cost), LCCA (Life Cycle Costs Analysis), MSDG (Minnesota Sustainable Design Guide), SBE (Scenic Beauty Estimation), SIA (Scenic Beauty Estimatio), MSBG (The State of Minnesota Sustainable Building Guidelines), VIA (Visual Impact Assessment) [1].

It is necessary to fit research methods and techniques to meet the needs of design, evaluation criteria, the specifics of the country. According to the author gives good results at the same time the use of several techniques such as observational studies, interviews-interviews and questionnaires. In his own practice as the most effective author acknowledges interview with the users in the form of a loose spontaneous conversation and interview with the manager object.

The author has developed its own simplified test methods: pre-design objects with similar functions, and after a period of use in order to verify design decisions.

It should be emphasized that qualitative research design are not widely used in all environments, architectural and countries. Leading are the United States, United Kingdom, Netherlands, Australia, also Sweden, Germany. In Poland, are rare. Built environment is divided into two groups: designers using traditional and modern methods of programming in this study. The traditional approach to design is based on the artistic vision of the architect. In contrast, the second research approach is based on the scientific method of qualitative research.

The author has developed its own simplified, rapid and effective method of research:

— Pre-project "in the 8-steps" of objects with similar functions. These studies are helpful in gaining knowledge of programming and design.
— Assessment object realized "in the 7-steps" when using the designed object. They provide a verification of the design decisions taken and the source of knowledge to new projects [1].

The methods are described in the book Fross K. [2012]: Quality evaluation in architectural design on selected examples, Publisher Silesian University of Technology, Gliwice, Poland. Additional information and diagrams copyright research methods can be obtained by writing to the author at: klaudiusz.fross@wp.pl.

We own professional practice, the author applied the principles of ergonomics in projects: the hotel (module and layout of the hotel room), a water park (changing rooms, water attractions system), hospital (hospital functional layout, arrangement of rooms, single, double bed ward, operating theater, the individual functional units), restaurant (kitchen back system), pharmacy (functional layout), factory (land development, production technology, social facilities staff), external recreation park (playground equipment safety zone), single-family house (layout of the rooms), an adaptation of an ancient palace in the new commercial functions (system function), the office of the city (optimal functional relationships departments).

An interesting example is the object hospital. When the design was used to optimize the ergonomics of functional relations, optimizing the dimensions and area of the house, character strings communications, supplies, maintenance and evacuation. First important was the optimal arrangement of a whole hospital in the major areas: admissions, individual wards and the operating theater and childbirth. Then the optimal (ergonomic) layout of the rooms of a single branch. At the same time he was an important model system in bed room (2-seater with a private bathroom). Optimally ergonomic and economical layout of the room with equipment imposed dimensions of the building and wheel design. The structural arrangement strictly the result of the adopted module (width) of the room. Next solved optimal systems of individual functional units as operating theater, pharmacy, hospital auxiliary functions, etc.

Fig. 2. Scheme line hospital in Siemianowice, Scheme of a typical floors (chamber receptions) and typical floors (branch bed). Project team: J. Kaminski NDN, Euro Project Dr. Fross, K. Fross, M. Jurkiewicz, visualization B. Braksator, 2013, an investor Nefrolux, Silbud Property Ltd., contractor Skanska construction work. (the author' s elaboration).

Fig. 3. Hospital in Siemianowice (Poland) under construction, 2013/2014. Photo: K. Fross 2013

3   Summary and Conclusions

— Noticeable is the universality of the application of ergonomics.
— Clearly ergonomics is one of the most important elements of architectural design.
— Ergonomics is part of the pre-design stage - programming.
— One of the most effective methods of knowledge of good and bad practices of ergonomic solutions are qualitative study of existing objects.
— The entire built environment is a database of information.
— It is a database and record the successes and mistakes of design also in terms of ergonomics.
— Reaching for the information you can get to know the good, ergonomic design - worthy of attention and avoid mistakes.
— Qualitative research has a direct impact on improving the quality of design and the objects themselves.
— There are many effective techniques to acquire information from the environment (methods developed by the author may be obtained by writing to the following address: klaudiusz.fross@wp.pl).

The summary diagrams are included for research quality and ergonomic solutions in projects.

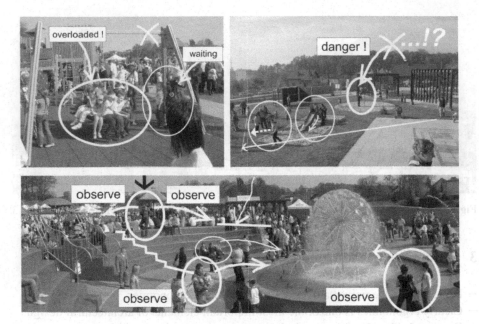

Fig. 4. Examples of observational studies. "Tropical Island" - recreation park in Marklowice and "Rafa" – recreation park in Rydultowy (Poland). Photo: K. Fross, 2008.

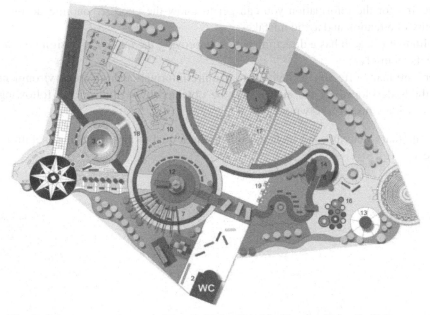

Fig. 5. Scheme recreation park "Tropical Island" in Marklowice (Poland), K. Fross project

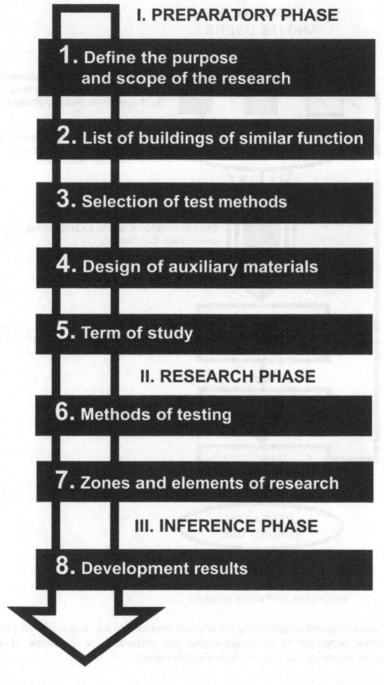

I. PREPARATORY PHASE

1. Define the purpose and scope of the research

2. List of buildings of similar function

3. Selection of test methods

4. Design of auxiliary materials

5. Term of study

II. RESEARCH PHASE

6. Methods of testing

7. Zones and elements of research

III. INFERENCE PHASE

8. Development results

Fig. 6. Diagramofthe author's method of pre-design studies in "the 8 steps" supporting the acquisition of knowledge required for programming and designing (the author's elaboration)

84   K. Fross

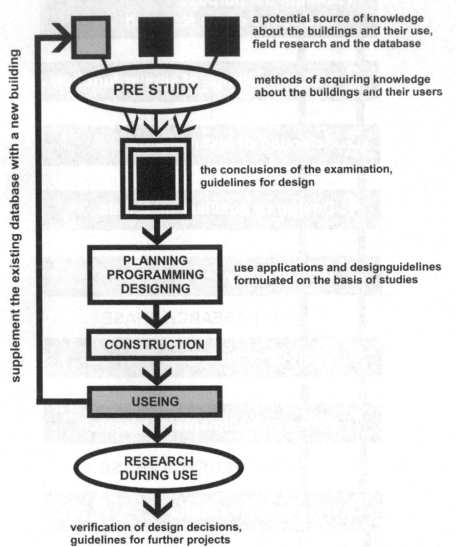

Fig. 7. General diagram recapitulating the research approach to the design process propagated by the author, supported by pre-design studies and verification in the course of using or occupying the constructed facility (the author's elaboration)

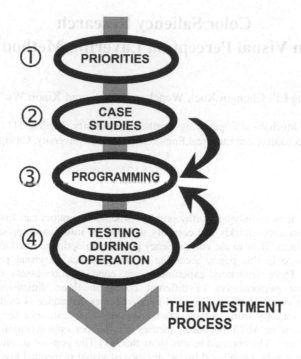

Fig. 8. Essential sources of knowledge in the investment process (the author's elaboration, 2010)

Reference

1. Fross, K.: Quality evaluation in architectural design on selected examples. Silesian University of Technology, Gliwice (2012)

Color Saliency Research
on Visual Perceptual Layering Method[*]

Jing Li[1], Chengqi Xue[1], Wencheng Tang[1], and Xiaoli Wu[1,2]

[1] School of Mechanical Engineering, Southeast University, Nanjing 211189, China
[2] College of Mechanical and Electrical Engineering, Hohai University, Changzhou 213022,
China
lijing7736@126.com

Abstract. It is a studying worthy problem whether operators can find targets among distractors quickly and correctly with lots of information presented on user interfaces. How to use color saliency properly to optimize interface design is dis-cussed in this paper, according to the guidance of visual perceptual layering. Three laboratory experiments are conducted to assess the anti-interference performances of different colors in three dimensions (hue, brightness and saturation). The an-ti-interference performance is evaluated in reaction time by using a non-parametric statistical test, and the unit of measurement is $\Delta E76$ Euclidean metrics on the perceptually uniform CIE L*a*b* space. The obtained results show that, (1) The pop-out of information effectively can be established by the distance of visual perceptual layering. (2) Visual saliencies of warm colors are different from those of cool colors, and the formers are more salient. High saturated warm colors are more salient than low saturated warm colors, and high bright cool colors are more salient than low bright cool colors. Furthermore, high bright cool colors are less salient than high saturated cool colors. (3) In the hue-contrast condition, with the color difference is more than 20 $\Delta E76$, the visual saliency of target may not change with the change in color differences. Target's saliency is more effected by distractor brightness than by background brightness, whereas it is more effected by back-ground saturation than by distractor saturation.

Keywords: Color Saliency, Visual Perceptual Layering, Anti-interference Performance, Color Difference.

1 Introduction

With numerous data and complex structures in the integrated display interface, people are easily to be distracted by irrelevant items when searching for target items, which caused clutter, confusion, and even more human error[1-2]. As a stage of information processing, hierarchy processing of visual perception influences the cognitive order of information. Designing basis can be offered for searching targets quickly and correctly, using cognition rules which are of high reliability and validity to build relationships between perceptual layers and design elements. With color as one such

---

[*] Corresponding author.

M. Kurosu (Ed.): Human-Computer Interaction, Part I, HCII 2014, LNCS 8510, pp. 86–97, 2014.

design ele-ment[3], Theeuwes[4-6] proposed that irrelevant singleton color captured attention faster when it is more salient than the target color. For the selection of objects is guided by pre-attentively acquired information about a limited set of attributes[7], color has effects on cognitive performance and also can help to guide visual perceptual layering[8].

2   Background

During the early research, there were two main approaches to study the perceptual distance among colors. One was the color segmentation using perceptual attributes (hue, brightness and saturation), such as perceived colors from the Munsell color solid. The other was the proposed color difference with which the obtained result of the difference or distance between two colors is consistent with that of the human eye[9]. With the rapid development of visual display interface, color can be used to highlight goals and weaken interference terms, guiding users' eye gaze. In the relevant fields, Darren Van Laar[10-11] strengthened the display segmentation by colors to provide visual clues. Jen-Her Wu and his partners[12] used different color combinations for textual display, finding the visual preference was not consistent with the reading speed. Peter B[13] suggested to put colored display items on several "conspicuity levels" and constructed a formula and some guidelines for the algorithm. Ulf Ahlstrom[14] dis-cussed the use of luminance contrast to manipulate salience and presented a prototype color palette that uses color-coding to maintain good legibility. Dennis[15] provided that intrinsic color structures can be formulated objectively and represented a visual hierarchy. Iztok Humar[16] studied the legibility of a web page text on displays ac-cording to the impacts of color combination and luminance contrast. Some other documents gave the order of cognitive performance for color combinations [17-19]. As the studies mentioned above, more and more studies have begun taking the problem of attaining efficient color coding for large numbers of data and information seriously. Few scholars have set foot in visual perceptual layering method through color saliency.

In the present article, we first give a qualitative discussion of visual perceptual layering in the information design field. Then with the stimulus-driven selection and attentional capture mechanism, a mapping relation between color saliency and perceptual distance is presented. A systematic experimental study based on the three color attributes is investigated. Combining non-parametric statistical method with color difference formula, color saliency is judged with the anti-interference performance of target color, and effect factors are analyzed with multiple linear regression equation method. Finally, propose design optimization methods according to the results.

3   Visual Perceptual Layering Method

In the brain of human being, the visualizing information entered the recoding phase of cognition through the visual sense (in Fig.1). With a large amount of information presented on the display interface, a reasonable visual information space can be established by using appropriate priorities and hierarchical rhythmic structures. Visual perceptual layering refers to guide users to recognize information in sequence according to different visual saliency. It gives a control of information classification and management through the mapping relationship between information encoding and its cognition, basing on the mechanism of attentional capture.

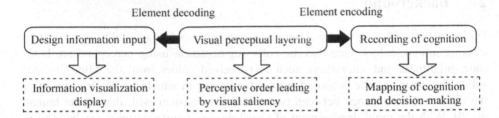

Fig. 1. The Transfer Process of Design Information

There are two hierarchical and two mapping relationships connected with it (in Fig.2). Information layering is a hierarchical management structure of information, basing on structures and attributes of information elements. With prior knowledge, memory structure and schema, cognition layering manages to regulate cognitive processing activities according to the order and important degree of information. By analyzing the semantic mapping relation between information attribute and design style, design elements (i.e. color, shape, direction, position) and visualization structures (i.e. list structure, coordinate structure, space position structure, net or tree shaped structure, time flow structure and composite structure)[20] can be used to create design feature model and array mode, which afford the mapping relationship between information elements and visual perception. The mapping relationship between visual perception and brain cognition has effects on reconstruction rules of information processing, which refers to that perceptive order guides cognitive order.

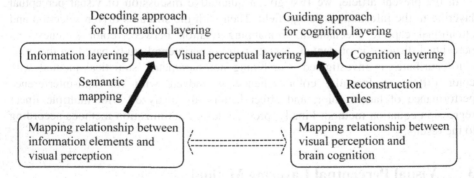

Fig. 2. The Relationships of Visual Perceptual Layering

As one of the design elements, colors have the most effective guiding function. In the digital interface with multicolor encoding, the more possibility of one color being disturbed by others, the worse its saliency value performed. Colors with strong visual saliency become the foreground colors on the psychological recognition, which have close distances to users on the visual perception of space (in Fig.3). As seen in Fig.4, directions of arrows are guidelines for visual flows according to layered color perception. It is likely to make for a better cognitive performance with visual flows toward the same direction, whereas it may be harmful to the performance with visual flows have opposite directions.

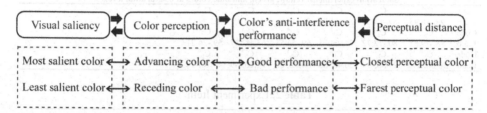

Fig. 3. Relation between color's visual saliency and perceptual distance

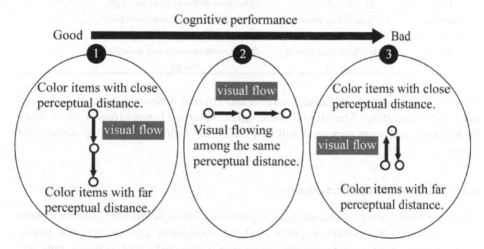

Fig. 4. Visual flowing lines based on perceptual distance

4   Visual Search Experiments

4.1   Materials

Taking the perceptual distance in the Munsell color solid into consideration, 55 colors given in Table 1 were chosen as experimental stimuli, using CIELAB color notation system. On search trials the target was presented with 11 white and 11 colored homogeneous distractors. All visual stimuli were presented on a uniform black

Table 1. Experimental stimuli

	Hue experiment: 10 colors of different hue									
Code	A_1	A_2	A_3	A_4	A_5	A_6	A_7	A_8	A_9	A_{10}
L,a,b	60,29,10	60,22,29	60,6,37	60,-14,35	60,-32,16	60,-30,-3	60,-14,-28	60,13,-37	60,21,-21	60,30,-13

	Brightness experiment: yellow, green, and blue colors at 9 brightness levels								
Code	B_y^1	B_y^2	B_y^3	B_y^4	B_y^5	B_y^6	B_y^7	B_y^8	B_y^9
L,a,b	99,-6,25	98, -10,49	98,-14,71	98,-15,87	98,-16,93	80,-13,79	62,-11,64	42,-8,48	20,-5,28
Code	B_g^1	B_g^2	B_g^3	B_g^4	B_g^5	B_g^6	B_g^7	B_g^8	B_g^9
L,a,b	95,-24,19	92,-46,39	90,-64,59	88,-75,74	88,-79,81	72,-67,68	55,-54,55	37,-40,41	17,-25,24
Code	B_b^1	B_b^2	B_b^3	B_b^4	B_b^5	B_b^6	B_b^7	B_b^8	B_b^9
L,a,b	83,8,-25	67,19, -51	50,35,-78	36,55,-101	30,68,-112	23,58,-95	15,47,-77	7,35,-57	2,11,-30

	Saturation experiment: yellow, green, and blue colors at 6 saturation levels					
Code	C_y^1	C_y^2	C_y^3	C_y^4	C_y^5	C_y^6
L,a,b	98,-16,93	89,-14,84	83,-13,74	76,-11,61	69,-9,45	62,-6,27
Code	C_g^1	C_g^2	C_g^3	C_g^4	C_g^5	C_g^6
L,a,b	88,-79,81	80,-72,72	74,-64,63	69,-54,51	63,-42,37	59,-26,21
Code	C_b^1	C_b^2	C_b^3	C_b^4	C_b^5	C_b^6
L,a,b	30,68,-112	29,58,-99	30,46,-86	34,32,-68	39,20,-49	45,10,-28

Table 2. Experiment Item

Item	Target sets	Colored distractor sets	Number of trials
Hue	A_1、A_3、A_5、A_7	Other hues different from the target	36
Brightness	All levels of lightness in table 1	Other lightness different from the target	216
Saturation	All levels of saturation in table 1	Other saturations different from the target	90

background. As shown in Table 2, targets and colored distractors were chosen from color sets separately. The stimuli were small squares (16mm×16mm) on a black background, and were presented within a 8.2°×6.2° region at a viewing distance of 0.5 m.

4.2   Equipment and Participants

The experiments were conducted in an ergonomics lab of Southeast University under the normal lighting condition (40W daylight continuous current tungsten lamp). Stimulus presentation and response collection were performed using a purpose-written E-Prime script (Psychology Software Tools). The display of visual stimuli was presented on a CRT monitor whose CPU main frequency was 3.0 GHZ and display size was 17 inch (1280 by 1024 pixels).

The participants consisted of 10 students (5 male, 5 female), ranging in age from 22 to 26 years. All participants had normal or corrected vision without color blindness or color weakness.

4.3   Procedure

The nature of the test was to search for the color-singleton target among white and colored distractors, and to identify which side of the rectangle field (right or left) does the target lay on. Buttons "a" and "l" were used to response the left and right side separately. During the test phase, participants completed two sets of practice trials and test trials in each experiment. Each trial began with a fixation cross in the center of the screen, displayed for 1000ms. Then, a black screen displayed for 500ms, followed by the search display. Each trial terminated if the participant pressed one of the response buttons (a or l) , or no response was made within 5s (in Fig.5).

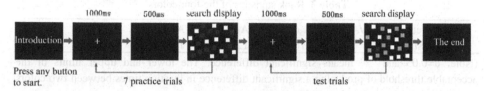

Fig. 5. The experimental procedure

5   Data Collection and Analysis

A color's anti-interference performance refers to the reaction time and accu-racy when searching for it among distractor colors. Excluding the errors, the faster the reaction time is obtained, the better the anti-interference performance per-formed. Color saliency is evaluated by the anti-interference performance which can be calculated through the non-parametric statistical method. It is transformed to be

$$C_a = \left\{ t_{aj} \middle| a \in S_{11} / S_2 / S_3 ; j \in S_{12} / S_2 / S_3 ; a \neq j \right\} \tag{1}$$

where S11 is the target set of the hue experiment, S11={A1、A3、A5、A7 }, S2 ={different levels of lightness in table 1}, S3 ={different levels of saturations in table 1}, a is the target, j is the distractor, is the reaction time, t_{aj} and C_a is the color saliency.

5.1   Saliency Comparison Among different Hue Targets

The relationship between reaction time and color difference between target and colored distractor is described in Fig.6. Differences in anti-interference performances between any two hues were assessed with the Wilcoxon rank-sum test (in Table 3). The visual saliencies of red and yellow were significant different from those of green and blue. Moreover, according to the Wilcoxon-Mann-Whitney rank sum test, red and yellow targets were more salient than green and blue targets (U=308,α=0.05), which confirmed the previous research results[21-22].

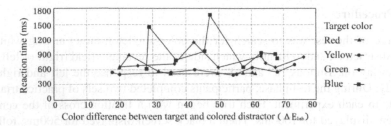

Fig. 6. Reaction time as a function of the color difference between target and distractor colors

Table 3. Rank statistics of the four colors

target/target	A_3/A_1	A_5/A_1	A_5/A_3	A_7/A_1	A_7/A_3	A_7/A_5
Rank statistic	77	116*	122*	122*	125*	105

(Note: $\alpha=0.05$ and "*" means significant difference. The lower and upper limits of the acceptable threshold of producing a significant difference in reaction times between two colors are calculated that $r_1=63$ and $r_2=108$)

5.2   Saliency Comparison among different Saturation Targets

The comparison of saliency for any two saturations levels of the same hue (yellow, green and blue) was calculated by using the Wilcoxon rank-sum test (in Table 4). The anti-interference performances of Cy1, Cy2, and Cy3 were significant different from those of Cy4, Cy5, and Cy6, and the formers were better. No difference was found among different saturation levels of green and blue.

Table 4. Rank statistics of the saturation levels

Target/Target	C_y^1/C_y^2	C_y^1/C_y^3	C_y^1/C_y^4	C_y^1/C_y^5	C_y^1/C_y^6	C_y^2/C_y^3	C_y^2/C_y^4	C_y^2/C_y^5	C_y^2/C_y^6
Rank statistic	28	32	19*	19*	15*	30	19*	19*	15*
target/target	C_y^3/C_y^4	C_y^3/C_y^5	C_y^3/C_y^6	C_y^4/C_y^5	C_y^4/C_y^6	C_y^5/C_y^6	C_b^1/C_b^2	C_b^1/C_b^3	C_b^1/C_b^4
Rank statistic	19*	19*	15*	26	21	25	23	23	21
target/target	C_b^1/C_b^5	C_b^1/C_b^6	C_b^2/C_b^3	C_b^2/C_b^4	C_b^2/C_b^5	C_b^2/C_b^6	C_b^3/C_b^4	C_b^3/C_b^5	C_b^3/C_b^6
Rank statistic	23	24	28	26	26	28	26	27	28
target/target	C_b^4/C_b^5	C_b^4/C_b^6	C_b^5/C_b^6	C_g^1/C_g^2	C_g^1/C_g^3	C_g^1/C_g^4	C_g^1/C_g^5	C_g^1/C_g^6	C_g^2/C_g^3
Rank statistic	26	27	29	25	24	21	21	21	25
target/target	C_g^2/C_g^4	C_g^2/C_g^5	C_g^2/C_g^6	C_g^3/C_g^4	C_g^3/C_g^5	C_g^3/C_g^6	C_g^4/C_g^5	C_g^4/C_g^6	C_g^5/C_g^6
Rank statistic	20	20	23	24	26	29	31	21	29

(Note: $\alpha=0.05$ and "*" means significant difference. The lower and upper limits of the acceptable threshold of producing a significant difference in reaction times between two colors are calculated that $r_3=19$ and $r_4=36$)

5.3 Saliency Comparison among different Brightness Targets

With the Wilcoxon rank-sum test, there was no significant difference among different brightness levels of yellow, green or blue. The variance analysis was used to test the difference between searching for high bright colors among low bright ones and searching for low bright colors among high bright ones. According to Table 5, it shows that no difference was found between the two conditions in yellow encoding ($F=2.145$, $P=0.162$, $P>0.05$), whereas the significant differences appeared in green ($F=12.82$, $P=0.002$, $P<0.05$) and blue ($F=6.957$, $P=0.018$, $P<0.05$) encodings. Moreover, the anti-interference performances of high bright colors were better than those of low bright colors in green and blue encodings.

Table 5. One-way analysis of variance table

Source		Sum of Squares	df	Mean Square	F	Sig.
Yellow	Inter-group	147098.880	1	147098.880	2.145	0.162
	Intra-group	1097371.880	16	68585.742		
	Total	1244470.760	17			
Blue	Inter-group	2040873.389	1	2040873.389	6.957	0.018*
	Intra-group	4693777.669	16	293361.104		
	Total	6734651.058	17			
Green	Inter-group	3304934.801	1	3304934.801	12.82	0.002*
	Intra-group	4123843.436	16	257740.215		
	Total	7428778.236	17			

(Note: $\alpha=0.05$, and "*" means significant difference.)

5.4 Saliency Comparison Between High Bright Colors and High Saturated Colors

Since both the high bright color and the high saturated color had good an-ti-interference performances, which one of them is more salient? According to the brightness experiment, reaction times of high bright colors and high saturated colors shown in Table 6 were analyzed by using the variance analysis. Results showed that there was no significant difference between the two conditions in yellow encoding ($F=0.374$, $P=0.549$ $P>0.05$), whereas anti-interference performances of high saturated colors were better than those of high bright colors in green ($F=10.897$, $P=0.005$, $P<0.05$) and blue ($F=9.519$, $P=0.007$, $P<0.05$) encodings.

Table 6. High bright colors and high saturated colors

Target color	Yellow	Green	Blue
High saturated colors	B_y^1, B_y^2, B_y^3	B_g^1, B_g^2, B_g^3	B_b^1, B_b^2, B_b^3
High bright colors	B_y^4, B_y^5, B_y^6	B_g^4, B_g^5, B_g^6	B_b^4, B_b^5, B_b^6

5.5 Interference Factors of Target's Salient Degree

According to the design of the former experiments, target's salient degree was effected by the background color and distractor colors. With multiple linear regression equation, the interference degrees of background, white distractor and colored distractor were analyzed. According to Table 7, the established regression equation in the hue experiment is invalid (F=0.6, P=0.618, P>0.05). By combining Fig 6 and earlier researches[23], it is known that with two colors have different hue values, the search speed of one color is fast enough if the color difference of them is greater than 20 $\Delta E76$. Furthermore, it did not have significant change with the increase in color difference. As in the brightness and saturation experiments (in Table 8), following regression equations were obtained:

$$RT_{brightness}=648.304-4,537\Delta E(T-D)+3.501\Delta E(T-B)+4.234\Delta E(T-W) \qquad (2)$$

$$RT_{saturation}=2441.124-5.548\Delta E(T-D)-18.091\Delta E(T-B)+14.136\Delta E(T-W) \qquad (2)$$

Where $\Delta E(T-B)$ is the color difference between target and background, $\Delta E(T-D)$ is the color difference between target and colored distractor, $\Delta E(T-W)$ is the color difference between target and white distractor. For color difference is inversely linked to reaction time[24], by the formulas above, target color was more effected by colored distractor brightness than background brightness, and it was more effected by background saturation than colored distractor saturation.

Table 7. ANOVA in regression equation

Model		Sum of Squares	df	Mean Square	F	Sig.
Hue experiment	Regression	148251.435	3	49417.145	0.600	0.618[a]
	Residual	4115800.214	50	82316.004		
	Total	4264051.648	53			
Brightness experiment	Regression	8646255.669	3	2882085.223	8.375	0.000[a]
	Residual	7.296E7	212	344148.075		
	Total	8.161E7	215			
Saturation experiment	Regression	3768425.779	3	1256141.926	3.429	0.021[a]
	Residual	3.151E7	86	366366.974		
	Total	3.528E7	89			

a. Predictors: (Constant), $\Delta E(T-D)$, $\Delta E(T-B)$, $\Delta E(T-W)$
b. Dependent Variable: RT

Table 8. The regression equation coefficient

Model		Unstandardized Coefficients		Standardized Coefficients	t	Sig.
		B	Std. Error	Beta		
Brightness Experiment	(Constant)	648.304	239.865		2.703	0.007
	$\Delta E(T-D)$	-4.537	1.732	-0.181	-2.620	0.009
	$\Delta E(T-B)$	3.501	1.358	0.179	2.579	0.011
	$\Delta E(T-W)$	4.234	1.797	0.153	2.356	0.019
Saturation Experiment	(Constant)	2441.124	331.735		7.359	0.000
	$\Delta E(T-D)$	-5.548	3.094	-0.190	-1.793	0.077
	$\Delta E(T-B)$	-18.091	10.116	-0.708	-1.788	0.077
	$\Delta E(T-W)$	14.136	12.577	0.443	1.124	0.264

a. Dependent Variable: RT

6 Conclusion

As the effective "pop out" of information may be established by the distance of visual perceptual laying, some design points can be clarified by the current study:

(1) The visual saliency of the warm color is different from that of the cool color, and the former is more salient.

(2) The influences of saturation levels and brightness levels on saliency are different between warm colors and cool colors. High saturated colors are more salient than low saturated colors in warm colors, whereas there was no significant difference between the two conditions in cool colors. High bright colors are more salient than low bright colors in cool colors, whereas no difference is found be-tween the two conditions in warm colors.

(3) High bright colors are less salient than high saturated colors in cool colors, whereas both of the conditions are equal in warm colors.

(4) As presented in Fig 7, the order of visual saliency may be concluded.

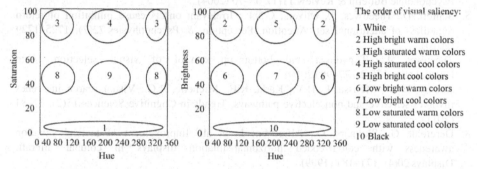

The order of visual saliency:

1 White
2 High bright warm colors
3 High saturated warm colors
4 High saturated cool colors
5 High bright cool colors
6 Low bright warm colors
7 Low bright cool colors
8 Low saturated warm colors
9 Low saturated cool colors
10 Black

Fig. 7. The distribution of visual saliency in HSB color plane

(5) In the hue-contrast condition, with the color difference is more than 20 $\Delta E76$, the visual saliency of target may not change with the change in color differences. Target's saliency is more effected by distractor brightness than by background brightness in the brightness-contrast condition, whereas it is more effected by background saturation than distractor saturation in the saturation-contrast condition.

7 Application

As color coding of complex information on controller displays is still new, a palette that achieves good margins of legibility and color identification for different information is needed. According to the experimental conclusion, it is possible that cognitive performance of display interface could be optimized with standard settings of visual perceptual layering by using color contrast. This study was not conduced for all colors, so the data is not an exact science but represents a trend.

Acknowledgments. This work was supported by the National Nature Science Foundation of Chi-na (Grant No.71071032,71271053), and the Social Science Fund for Young Scholar of the Ministry of Education of China(Grant No. 12YJC760092).

References

1. Li, P., Zhang, L., Dai, L., Huang, W.: Effects of Digital Human-Machine Interface Characteristics on Human Error in Nuclear Power Plants. Nuclear Power Engineering 32(1), 48–51 (2011) (in Chinese)
2. Roman, S., Klaus, M.: Coping with information overload in email communication: Evaluation of a training intervention. Computers in Human Behavior 26(6), 1458–1466 (2010)
3. Wolfe, J.M., Horowitz, T.: What attributes guide the deployment of visual attention and how do they do it? Nature Reviews Neuroscience 5, 495–501 (2004)
4. Theeuwes, J.: Top-down search strategies cannot override attentional capture. Psychonomic Bulletin & Review 11(1), 65–70 (2004)
5. Schreij, D., Theeuwes, J., Olivers, C.N.L.: Irrelevant onsets cause inhibition of return regardless of attentional set. Attention, Perception, & Psychophysics 72(7), 1725–1729 (2010)
6. Theeuwes, J.: Top–down and bottom–up control of visual selection. Acta Psychologica 135(2), 77–99 (2010)
7. Jeremy, M.W., Melissa, L.-H.V., Karla, K.E., Michelle, R.G.: Visual search in scenes involves selective and nonselective pathways. Trends in Cognitive Sciences 15(2), 77–84 (2011)
8. Derefeldt, G., Skinnars, O., Alfredson, J., et al.: Improvement of tactical situation awareness with colour-coded horizontal-situation displays in combat aircraft. Displays 20(4), 171–184 (1999)
9. Tseng, D.-C.: Color segmentation using perceptual attributes. In: Proceedings of 11th IAPR International Conference on Image, Speed and Signal Analysis, pp. 228–231 (1992)
10. Laar, D.L.V.: Psychological and cartographic principles for the production of visual layering effects in computer displays. Displays 22(4), 125–135 (2001)
11. Laar, D.L.V.: Color coding with visual layers can provide performance enhancements in control room displays. In: Proceedings of People in Control. International Conference on Human Interfaces in Control Rooms, Cockpits and Command Centres, Manchester, United kingdom, p. 481 (2001)
12. Wu, J.-H., Yuan, Y.: Improving searching and reading performance: the effect of highlighting and text color coding. Informaiton and Management 40(7), 617–637 (2003)
13. Peter, B.: Chromaticity contrast in visual search on the multi-colour user interface. Displays 24(1), 39–48 (2003)
14. Ulf, A., Arend, L.: Color usability on air traffic control displays. In: Proceedings of the Human Factors and Ergonomics Society 49th Annual Meeting, Oriando, FL, United States, pp. 93–97 (2005)
15. Dennis, M.P.: Perceiving hierarchy through intrinsic color structure. Visual Communication 7(2), 199–228 (2008)
16. Humar, I., Gradišar, M., Turk, T.: The impact of color combinations on the legibility of a Web page text presented on CRT displays. International Journal of Industrial Ergonomics 38(11-12), 885–899 (2008)

17. Lei, Z., Damin, Z.: Color matching of aircraft interface design. Journal of Beijing University of Aeronautics and Astronautics 35(8), 1001–1004 (2009) (in Chinese)
18. Guo, Z., Li, Y., Ma, G., et al.: Influence of Color-matching of EMU Control Interface on Recognition Efficiency. Journal of The China Railway Society 34(2), 27–31 (2012) (in Chinese)
19. Jie, Z.: The Cognitive Ergonomical study of color-coded character, Fourth Military Medical University, Xi'an (2012) (in Chinese)
20. Li, J., Xue, C., Shi, M., et al.: Information visual structure based on multidimensional attributes of information. Journal of Southeast University (Natural Science Edition) 42(6), 1094–1099 (2012) (in Chinese)
21. Alvin, G.W., Delwin, T.L., Kathryn, M.S., et al.: Use of a porcelain color discrimination test to evaluate color difference formulas. The Journal of Prosthetic Dentistry 98(2), 101–109 (2007)
22. Wu, J.-H., Yuan, Y.: Improving searching and reading performance the effect of highlighting and text color coding. Information & Management 40(7), 617–637 (2003)
23. Carter, R., Huertas, R.: Ultra-Large Color Difference and Small Subtense. Color Research and Application 35(1), 4–17 (2010)
24. Healey, C.G.: Choosing effective colours for data visualization. In: Proceedings of Visualization 1996, pp. 263–270 (1996)

Generating Human-Computer Micro-task Workflows from Domain Ontologies

Nuno Luz[1], Nuno Silva[1], and Paulo Novais[2]

[1] GECAD (Knowledge Engineering and Decision Support Group),
Polytechnic of Porto, Portugal
{nmalu,nps}@isep.ipp.pt
[2] CCTC (Computer Science and Technology Center), University of Minho, Portugal
pjon@di.uminho.pt

Abstract. With the growing popularity of micro-task crowdsourcing platforms, a renewed interest in the resolution of complex tasks that require the cooperation of human and machine participants has emerged. This interest has led to workflow approaches that present new challenges at different dimensions of the human-machine computation process, namely in micro-task specification and human-computer interaction due to the unstructured nature of micro-tasks in terms of domain representation. In this sense, a semi-automatic generation environment for human-computer micro-task workflows from domain ontologies is proposed. The structure and semantics of the domain ontology provides a common ground for understanding and enhances human-computer cooperation.

Keywords: Human-Machine Computation, Micro-Task Workflows, Ontologies.

1 Introduction

With the emergence of micro-task crowdsourcing platforms such as CrowdFlower and Mechanical Turk, human computation has gained renewed interest in the resolution of complex tasks that require the cooperation of human and machine participants [1–6]. This interest has led to several approaches built upon workflows of micro-tasks.

Micro-task workflows present new challenges at different dimensions of the human-machine computation process, namely in micro-task specification and human-computer interaction [1, 2]. The unstructured nature of micro-tasks in terms of domain representation makes it difficult (i) for task requesters not familiar with the crowdsourcing platform to build complex micro-task workflows and (ii) to include machine workers in the workflow execution process [7]. Furthermore, it is seldom explicitly defined that while some of the micro-tasks in the workflow are better performed by humans, others are better performed by a machine.

Obrst et al. [8] state that ontologies "represent the best answer to the demand for intelligent systems that operate closer to the human conceptual level". Considering this, this paper presents a semi-automatic generation environment for human-computer

M. Kurosu (Ed.): Human-Computer Interaction, Part I, HCII 2014, LNCS 8510, pp. 98–109, 2014.

micro-task workflows from domain ontologies. The inherent process relies in the domain expertise of the requester to supervise the automatic interpretation of the domain ontology. The structure and semantics of the domain ontology enhances human-computer cooperation and allows the automatic generation (with included contextual information) of preliminary micro-task worker interfaces using a markup language.

This paper is organized as follows. Section 2 provides some background knowledge on micro-task workflow approaches and ontologies. It is followed by, in section 3, the presentation of the overall architecture behind the proposed micro-task workflow generation approach. Section 4 presents the generation process through a running example. Finally, the conclusions are given along with some remarks on the future directions of this work.

2 Background Knowledge

2.1 Human Computation and Micro-task Workflows

Several experiments in different domains have shown that human computation (in particular micro-task crowdsourcing) has great potential for solving large scale problems that are often difficult for computers to solve automatically, on their own [9]. These problems usually require a degree of creativity or just common sense plus some background knowledge [10, 11]. The interpretation and recognition of images and natural language are two examples of these kinds of problems.

Crowdsourcing platforms like Mechanical Turk, CloudCrowd, ShortTask and CrowdFlower are widely used for tasks such as (i) categorization and classification, (ii) data collection (e.g., finding a website address), (iii) moderation and tagging of images, (iv) surveys, (v) transcription from multimedia content (e.g., audio, video and images), and (vi) text translation.

In particular, micro-task workflow approaches like CrowdForge, Jabberwocky and Turkomatic employ divide and conquer and map reduce strategies to build workflows. This usually involves workflows that include tasks for (i) the partitioning of the complex task (partition tasks), (ii) the execution of the partitioned tasks (map tasks), and (iii) the aggregation of results (reduce tasks).

However, the input given by workers, in several cases, is unstructured and in natural language. Furthermore, micro-task interfaces are built using markup languages that contain little if no meta-data, making it difficult for machine micro-tasks to be included in the workflow.

The terminology employed in the crowdsourcing domain often varies from platform to platform. In the context of this paper, the following terms and entities are considered:

- Worker – a person that solves tasks;
- Community – a set of workers;
- Job – a complex task or workflow of tasks;
- Task (or micro-task) – a definition of a concrete computation or operation that may be performed by workers;
- Requester – an entity (typically a person) that submits jobs;

- Unit – an input of a task;
- Reference Unit – an input of a task for which the output is already known;
- Assignment – an assignment of a unit to a single worker;
- Answer – the given solution of a worker to a specific assignment;
- Workflow – the continuity of work by passing the output of one task as the input of another.

2.2   From Domain Ontologies to Micro-task Workflows

In this work, Description Logics (DL) knowledge bases and ontologies are considered. A DL knowledge base is defined as containing both a TBox (terminological box) and an ABox (assertion box), where the TBox contains all the concepts and relationships that define a specific domain, and the ABox contains the instances or individuals defined according to the elements in the TBox [12]. It is assumed that ontology is synonym of TBox.

In the TBox, a set of concepts (or classes) and properties exist. Each concept has associated property restrictions that define the necessary, and necessary and sufficient conditions for an individual to be an instance of the concept. These conditions may be enforced according to two main types of properties: object properties and data-type properties. While object properties relate instances (or individuals) with other instances, data-type properties relate instances with "primitive" type values (e.g., string, integer, double, date, time).

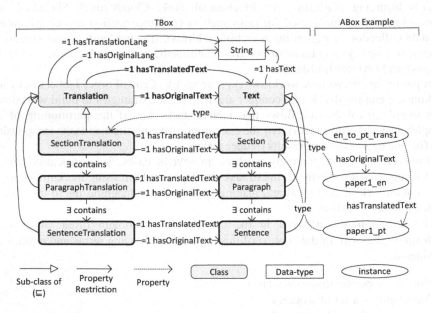

Fig. 1. The article translation ontology (TBox only) with ABox example

Consider the translation ontology presented in Fig 1, where each rectangle represents an instance and each ellipse represents a class. Arrows in the TBox represent property restrictions and dashed arrows are actual property relationships in the ABox.

3   Three-Layered Workflow Generation

Micro-tasks, whether they involve physical actions or not, can be seen as a process that, in a specific context, results in the emergence of new data (answers) from the presentation of other particular pieces of data (units) to a worker. Analogously, a workflow of micro-tasks is the continuous ordered increment of new (different types of) data, in a specific context or domain.

The context (or domain) can be defined and delimited through domain ontologies, modelling all input and output data. Thereafter, a micro-task can be considered to be *the instantiation of classes and specification of new relationships between instances* according to the domain ontology. A workflow of micro-tasks is then considered as *the incremental instantiation of the domain ontology according to its structure and semantics.*

In order to harness the power of ontologies in micro-task workflows, an iterative semi-automatic workflow generation process is proposed. This process is based in a layered architecture that defines the set of operations that can be performed by micro-tasks on top of the ontology data (see Fig 2).

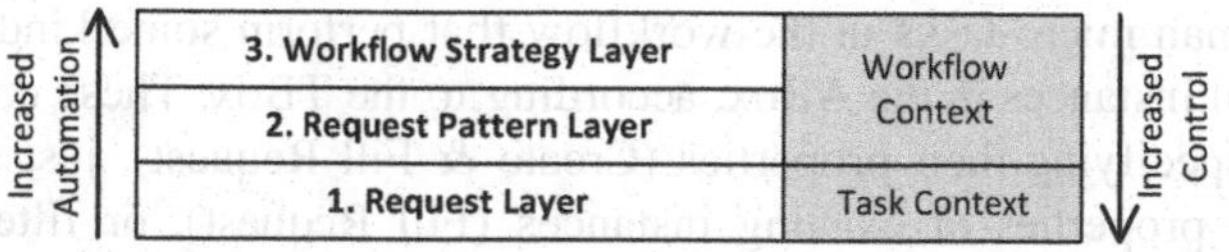

Increased Automation	3. Workflow Strategy Layer	Workflow Context	Increased Control
	2. Request Pattern Layer		
	1. Request Layer	Task Context	

Fig. 2. The layered architecture of the generation process

The request layer defines the set of possible atomic operations that can be performed over the ontology and workflow data. In this layer, a low-level structural analysis of the ontology is performed.

A request pattern, in the request pattern layer, is a set of requests associated to a specific ontological pattern [13, 14]. Request patterns often depend on the employed ontology construction methodology [15]. In some cases, though, they may also depend on the domain of the ontology. In the request pattern layer, mostly high-level structural and low-level semantic analyses of the ontology are performed.

The workflow strategy layer is an abstraction over the previous base layers. Each workflow strategy represents a subset of requests and request patterns, often found in specific workflow domains. They automate the process by restricting the set of possible choices presented to the requester during the workflow extraction process. For instance, a workflow strategy for recommendation workflows could restrict the possible choices of the requester through its set of possible request patterns and requests. Through the workflow strategy layer, a high-level semantic analysis of the ontology is performed.

3.1   The Request Layer

A request is always associated with a workflow step and defines the operation to be performed. Multiple types of requests can be performed. They can be classified according to their operation (see Fig 3) and structure. A request can be of multiple non-disjoint types.

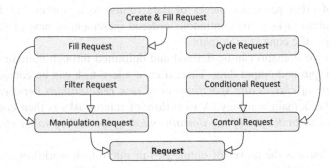

Fig. 3. Classification of requests according to their operation

In terms of operation, there are two main request types: (i) manipulation requests and (ii) control requests. On the one hand, manipulation requests (i) represent explicit machine or human micro-tasks in the workflow that perform some kind of operation over ontological instances in the ABox, according to the TBox. These can be creating instances and specifying their properties (Create & Fill Request), just specifying or completing the properties of existing instances (Fill Request), or filtering existing instances (Filter Request). On the other hand, control requests (ii) (e.g., conditional blocks, cycles) establish flow control components in the workflow.

Table 1. Structure of a request and corresponding classification

Symbol	Component (Structure)	Classification
C	An ontology class (or concept)	Concept Request
Rest	A set with at least one restriction	Restricted Request
P	A path of relations (property restrictions)	Path Request
NPRel	A non-built relation in the path	Relation Request
LP	At least one link path	Link Path Request
I	A cycle	Cycle Request
Cond	A condition	Conditional Request

A request is a tuple $RQ(C, Rest, P, NPRel, LP, I, Cond)$ as presented in Table 1. The existence of each of the presented components is directly related to the classification in Table 1. The ontology class defines the object of the operation. For example, new instances of a specific class can be requested through a Create & Fill Concept Request.

In some situations, the ontology class is not expressive enough to restrict the set of instances to be affected or created by the operation. A Restricted Request specifies property values that must be present for instances of the ontology class. If an instantiation is performed, these property values will automatically be set and enforced. Otherwise, if instances are already present, those that do not contain these property values will be filtered from the operation.

Often, the target of a request is not the whole set of instances of an ontology class, but only those related to instances of other classes and so on. These relations form a path of relationships between named classes that represent the context in which the operation will be performed. Requests that include a path from the ontology graph, typically ending in the requested ontology class, are Path Requests.

Path Requests contain relations that are either missing (one, at most) or present in the built graph. If a new relation (not in the built graph) is requested, the request is classified as a Relation Request (see Fig 4).

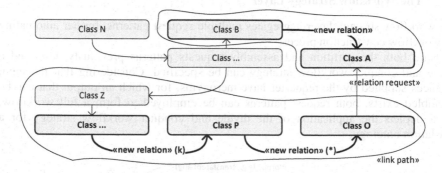

Fig. 4. Structure of a Relation Link Path Request (k and * are fixed and multiple cardinality values, respectively)

While Path Requests and Restriction Requests capture operations upon all related entities surrounding the ontology class (or its context), it may also be useful to instantiate secondary paths in order to establish relationships that, otherwise, would be lost. These secondary paths are called link paths, as depicted by the link path area in Fig 4.

Link paths may contain the instantiation of at most one class, and the specification of at most two new relations. If two new relations are required, at least one must have a known fixed exact cardinality. If this is not verified, a combinatorial explosion of relationships problem, which falls outside the context of an atomic operation, occurs.

Without link paths, additional secondary paths to instances generated by a specific request would not be possible, since it is not possible to select only instances generated by a previous request.

3.2   The Request Pattern Layer

The request pattern layer establishes a correspondence between an ontology pattern and a set of requests. These correspondences are called request patterns and provide automation over the direct usage of requests.

Ontology patterns can be found in several different ontologies describing a variety of domains. In the case of micro-task workflows, several approaches exist that try to employ divide and conquer or map-reduce strategies. These strategies focus on dividing the task at hand, executing the resulting units, and assembling the results. Such strategies can also be employed through the definition of partition and assembly request patterns.

Both partition and assembly request patterns can be defined through meronymic (part-of relation) ontology patterns. While the partition request pattern picks requests using a top-down search following meronymic relationships, the assembly request pattern picks requests using a bottom-up search.

3.3   The Workflow Strategy Layer

The workflow strategy layer aggregates multiple request patterns, further automating the workflow construction process.

Using both the partition and assembly requests patterns previously described a divide and conquer workflow strategy can be specified. Considering that the input instances supplied by the requester have meronyms, for which an output that can be assembled exists, both request patterns can be employed to form a full workflow. Fig 5 depicts the application of the divide and conquer workflow strategy for a translation ontology.

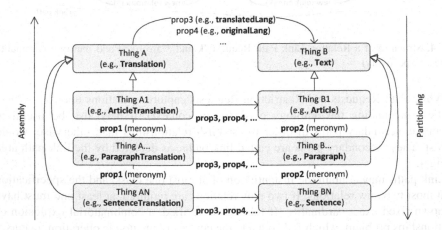

Fig. 5. Application of the divide and conquer workflow strategy with both partition and assembly request patterns

4   The Generation Process

The workflow generation process consists in four steps: (i) ontology and input specification, (ii) input pre-processing, (iii) iterative construction and (iv) post-processing. Each of these steps will be described through a running example, which consists in the construction of a workflow for translating articles or papers.

During both the iterative construction step (iii), a task pattern detection algorithm, which acts according to the defined strategy, is triggered. If a pattern (or sequence of patterns) is detected, the requester may choose to apply the pattern, automatically adding several micro-tasks to the workflow.

4.1   Input Specification and Pre-processing

The process starts with the ontology and input specification (i) by the requester. The input includes the initial ABox (instances and relationships) fed to the workflow and the ontology describing the domain (e.g., the translation ontology in Fig 1). Typically, input instances contain data describing the initial task that will be supplied to workers.

From these data, two graphs are extracted in the input pre-processing step (ii): the ontology graph and the built graph. The ontology graph is fully instantiated during this step and contains nodes that represent named classes in the ontology. Each edge represents a property restriction that relates two named classes and contains relevant information about the relationship such as the type of restriction (e.g., existential quantification, universal quantification, cardinality) and corresponding cardinality. The built graph will contain all classes and relations requested during the iterative construction step (iii). The built graph is partially instantiated during this step with the classes and properties found in the input data.

For instance, the input in table 2 will result in a built graph containing the classes Article and ArticleTranslation, and the object property restriction originalText relating ArticleTranslation with Article.

Table 2. Input statements/triples for the translation ontology use case

Instance	Property	Value
onto:paperTranslation1	rdf:type	onto:ArticleTranslation
onto:paperTranslation1	onto:originalLang	"Portuguese"
onto:paperTranslation1	onto:translatedLang	"English"
onto:paperTranslation1	onto:originalText	onto:paper1
onto:paper1	rdf:type	onto:Article
onto:paper1	onto:lang	"Portuguese"

4.2   Iterative Construction

Using both built and ontology graphs, the iterative construction step (iii) presents the requester with a set of possible choices (requests, request patterns or workflow strategies). As the requester iteratively picks one of these choices, new classes and relations (present in the chosen requests) are added to the built graph. Ultimately, the built graph becomes a clone of the ontology graph.

As requests are picked by the requester, they are added to the request graph. Edges in this graph define the dependencies between requests.

During the first iteration of the article translation example, the requester can opt to either request the entire translation of the article (using only the top-level classes Translation and Text, or ArticleTranslation and Article), or to partition the article before requesting translations. This partitioning of the task may be useful for articles with many paragraphs.

For the entire translation of the articles given as input, one request would suffice, that is, a Create & Fill request for Article instances related to ArticleTranslation through the onto:translatedText property. Notice that, during the workflow construction, the requester deals only with the TBox (ontology classes and properties). The ABox (instances) will only be handled during the execution of the workflow. The initial input ABox is an exception to this rule, with the purpose of facilitating the specification of the input TBox.

If the requester opts to partition the article into paragraphs, two possible request choices are presented (see Table 3).

Table 3. Possible requests for the ontology class Paragraph in the translation example - first iteration of the iterative construction step (new relation in path in bold)

#	Operation	Path
1	Create & Fill	-
2	Create & Fill	ArticleTranslation - originalText - **Article - part - Paragraph**

Request 1 is always presented for any ontology class. It results in instances of Paragraph, completely unrelated to already existent instances. Request 2 is only possible because the path ArticleTranslation - originalText - Article already exists in the built graph (added during the input specification step).

For a specific Path request, a set of possible link paths is usually presented. In the case of request 2, the following possible link paths exist (notice how the start and end in classes present in the request path):

1. ArticleTranslation - translatedText - Article - part - Paragraph
2. ArticleTranslation - part - ParagraphTranslation - originalText - Paragraph
3. ArticleTranslation - part - ParagraphTranslation - translatedText - Paragraph

Picking one of these link paths will result in a connection from onto:paperTranslation1 to all instantiated Paragraphs through an intermediary "empty" (no other properties will be specified) instance. As instances of ParagraphTranslation are required in order to request the actual translation of paragraphs in future iterations, all link paths will be excluded except for link path 2.

Up to this point, the requester has built a workflow (with only one micro-task) that partitions articles into paragraphs. Further partitioning of paragraphs into sentences is also possible by repeating the previous choice pattern.

In the second iteration, the requester can finally request translations of paragraphs. The possible request choices for this iteration are presented in Table 4.

Table 4. Possible requests for the ontology class Paragraph in the translation example - second iteration of the iterative construction step (new relation in path in bold)

#	Operation	Path
1	Create & Fill	-
2	Create & Fill	ArticleTranslation - part - **ParagraphTranslation - translatedText - Paragraph**
3	Filter	ArticleTranslation - part - ParagraphTranslation - originalText - Paragraph

As the requester picks the request 2, only one possible link path is presented: ArticleTranslation - translatedText - Article - part - Paragraph. This link path must be selected, otherwise no relation between the translated Article and its corresponding Paragraphs will be set.

After requesting paragraph translations, the requester can finally request the translation of the article (third iteration). Table 5 contains the possible requests of this iteration.

Table 5. Possible requests for the ontology class Article in the translation example - third and final iteration of the iterative construction step

#	Operation	Path
1	Create & Fill	-
2	Fill	ArticleTranslation - translatedText - Article
3	Filter	ArticleTranslation - translatedText - Article
4	Fill	ArticleTranslation - originalText - Article
5	Filter	ArticleTranslation - originalText - Article

Picking request 2 will add a micro-task to the workflow, requesting workers to fill the translated article data-type property data, which includes the actual translated text. All related instances are given as contextual information, meaning that workers will have access to all related translated paragraphs and properties of the Translation instance.

4.3   Post-processing

The post-processing step (iv) is executed after the requester decides to conclude the iterative construction step. It outputs the workflow structure after applying a transitive reduction algorithm over the edges of the request graph.

For the given running example, it results in a sequential workflow with three micro-tasks (see Fig 6).

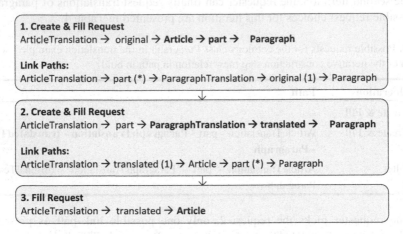

Fig. 6. Request workflow generated from the translation ontology

5   Conclusions and Future Work

The proposed process tackles the challenge of assisting requesters in building complex micro-task workflows while promoting human-machine cooperation through high-level, declarative and semantically explicit domain ontology models. This is achieved through a semi-automatic micro-task workflow generation process that filters and proposes the following steps in a workflow according to pattern analysis and the context given by previous tasks.

The current prototype of this process possesses a simple command line interface and allows the implementation of different adapters that interact with different crowdsourcing platforms such as CrowdFlower.

Future work includes the continuous analysis of several ontologies, which may result in the identification of new relevant task patterns and strategies. Also, a focus to the automatic generation of micro-task worker interfaces from the domain ontology and context must be given. Evolving the prototype implementation and providing a friendly and efficient graphical user interface implementation, instead of the current command line interface, is also part of the future work.

Acknowledgements. This work is partially funded by FEDER Funds and by the ERDF (European Regional Development Fund) through the COMPETE Programme (operational programme for competitiveness) and by National Funds through the FCT (Portuguese Foundation for Science and Technology) under the projects AAL4ALL (QREN13852) and FCOMP-01-0124-FEDER-028980 (PTDC/EEI-SII/1386/2012).

References

1. Ahmad, S., Battle, A., Malkani, Z., Kamvar, S.: The jabberwocky programming environment for structured social computing. In: Proc. 24th Annu. ACM Symp. User Interface Softw. Technol., pp. 53–64 (2011)
2. Kittur, A., Smus, B., Khamkar, S., Kraut, R.E.: Crowdforge: Crowdsourcing complex work. In: Proc. 24th Annu. ACM Symp. User Interface Softw. Technol., pp. 43–52 (2011)
3. Kulkarni, A.P., Can, M., Hartmann, B.: Turkomatic: automatic recursive task and workflow design for mechanical turk. In: Proc. 2011 Annu. Conf. Ext. Abstr. Hum. Factors Comput. Syst., pp. 2053–2058 (2011)
4. Little, G., Chilton, L.B., Goldman, M., Miller, R.C.: Turkit: human computation algorithms on mechanical turk. In: Proc. 23rd Annu. ACM Symp. User Interface Softw. Technol., pp. 57–66 (2010)
5. Luz, N., Silva, N., Maio, P., Novais, P.: Ontology Alignment through Argumentation. In: 2012 AAAI Spring Symp. Ser. (2012)
6. Sarasua, C., Simperl, E., Noy, N.F.: CROWDMAP: Crowdsourcing ontology alignment with microtasks. In: Cudré-Mauroux, P., Heflin, J., Sirin, E., Tudorache, T., Euzenat, J., Hauswirth, M., Parreira, J.X., Hendler, J., Schreiber, G., Bernstein, A., Blomqvist, E. (eds.) ISWC 2012, Part I. LNCS, vol. 7649, pp. 525–541. Springer, Heidelberg (2012)
7. Quinn, A.J., Bederson, B.B.: Human computation: a survey and taxonomy of a growing field. In: Proc. 2011 Annu. Conf. Hum. Factors Comput. Syst., pp. 1403–1412 (2011)
8. Obrst, L., Liu, H., Wray, R.: Ontologies for corporate web applications. AI Mag. 24, 49 (2003)
9. Von Ahn, L.: Human computation. In: 46th ACM/IEEE Des. Autom. Conf., pp. 418–419 (2009)
10. Chklovski, T.: Learner: A System for Acquiring Commonsense Knowledge by Analogy. In: Proc. 2nd ACM Int. Conf. Knowl. Capture, Sanibel Island, FL, USA, pp. 4–12 (2003)
11. Singh, P., Lin, T., Mueller, E.T., Lim, G., Perkins, T., Zhu, W.L.: Open Mind Common Sense: Knowledge Acquisition from the General Public. In: Meersman, R., Tari, Z. (eds.) CoopIS 2002, DOA 2002, and ODBASE 2002. LNCS, vol. 2519, pp. 1223–1237. Springer, Heidelberg (2002)
12. Baader, F.: The Description Logic Handbook: Theory, Implementation, and Applications. Cambridge University Press (2003)
13. Hammar, K., Sandkuhl, K.: The State of Ontology Pattern Research: A Systematic Review of ISWC, ESWC and ASWC 2005-2009. In: Workshop Ontol. Patterns Pap. Patterns ISWC Workshop, Shangai, China, pp. 5–17 (2010)
14. Gangemi, A.: Ontology Design Patterns for Semantic Web Content. In: Gil, Y., Motta, E., Benjamins, V.R., Musen, M.A. (eds.) ISWC 2005. LNCS, vol. 3729, pp. 262–276. Springer, Heidelberg (2005)
15. Blomqvist, E.: OntoCase - A Pattern-Based Ontology Construction Approach. In: Meersman, R., Tari, Z. (eds.) OTM 2007, Part I. LNCS, vol. 4803, pp. 971–988. Springer, Heidelberg (2007)

Methodological Capabilities for Emergent Design

Carl M. Olsson and Jeanette Eriksson

Department of Computer Science, Malmo University, Sweden
{carl.magnus.olsson,jeanette.eriksson}@mah.se

Abstract. In this paper we revisit emergent design and review five design oriented methodologies; action research, design research, controlled experiments, participatory design and ethnographic based approaches. Based on this review, we outline implications for the use of these methodologies in conjunction with an emergent design stance. Adopting such a stance is in line with both the exploratory way in which users embrace technology and the strong acceptance that agile software development approaches have had. It is therefore, we argue, appropriate that our research methodologies are adapted to embrace this change.

Keywords: Emergent design, opportunism, methodological review, abduction.

1 Introduction

In this paper, we re-visit the notion of emergent design that surfaced during the eighties and nineties [1-3] and consider if popular design oriented research methodologies actually embrace this notion. The discourse on emergent design is based on emergent strategy [4] and the argument that design goals emerge from engaging in design activity [5] rather than as a part of planning.

Rooted in the desire to develop software support for problem situations of increasing complexity – despite reports of breakdowns between users' and developers' mental models of the problem and designed solution [6] – the opportunistic nature of emergent design implies accepting the need for continuous re-negotiation of design goals based on emerging and discarded requirements during the entire design process [1] as well as during use [7]. The past decade's diffusion of agile software development approaches that rely on similar emerging and constantly changing requirements [8-10] provides additional support for the continued relevance for emergent design today.

Our working hypothesis is that a nuanced review of presently popular research methods related to the design of information technology, in terms of emergent design, is relevant as such design oriented research represents a growing trend both within HCI and outside (e.g. in software engineering, information systems, and computer science). The reviewed streams of research include action research [11], design research [12], controlled experiments [13], participatory design [14], and ethnography based approaches [15-16].

M. Kurosu (Ed.): Human-Computer Interaction, Part I, HCII 2014, LNCS 8510, pp. 110–121, 2014.
© Springer International Publishing Switzerland 2014

At the center of our findings lies the argument that none of the reviewed methodologies embrace an emergent design stance despite the impact that this notion has had over the last decades. Using Lanzara [17] as a classification system for the approach to design taken, we can see that (1) controlled experiments tend to view design as functional analysis and verification of this analysis, (2) action research and design research view design as a problem-solving exercise, while (3) participatory design and the ethnography based approaches primarily view design as an exercise in understanding the problem-setting.

Based on this argument, we initiate a discussion of the fundamental aspects that adapting current design oriented research methodologies may rely on in order to embrace emergent design. We also provide de facto examples of studies that – explicitly or implicitly – rely on emergent design already, despite the limited methodological capabilities in our current view of the research methods. These examples, together with our fundamental aspects of emergent design, represent a contribution towards development of design oriented research methodologies.

2   Design and Sensemaking

The use of agile methods in software development has become popular for many organizations (and their customers) in the last decade. These methods are characterized by incremental refinement of requirements and functionality with a high emphasis on small and frequent deliveries to capture the true problem or potential of a system, as well as on the creative abilities of designers to respond to change [8-10]. Such gradual refinement of goals, requirements, and design is neither new, however, nor restricted to software engineering research. For instance, Gasson [1] provides a useful model for the situated and evolutionary learning activity that design entails (Fig 1).

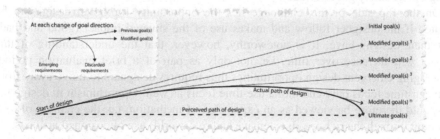

Fig. 1. The emergent design process. Adapted from [1].

The implications of such emergent design, as [1] refers to it, is that goals constantly evolve as the understanding of the design improves. The actual path of the design holds more complexity — and is much longer — than it is perceived by actors external to the design process. Her model is founded on fusing the concept of emergent strategy [4] with the argument that design problems and goals emerge from actively engaging in design activity [5], rather than as a part of planning. This view of design goals and problems as emerging aspects recognizes that designers (as all human beings) are guided by what makes sense in the specific context of activity, and use partial plans to justify action-taking, given the specific resources available [18].

The inherent subjectivity in design problem investigation, Gasson [1] argues, is linked with the notion of 'opportunism' in design [2-3]. Such opportunistic design aligns well with prototype and evolutionary systems development through the open stance towards 'learning-by-doing' [19]. This is further developed by [20] using the concept of 'reflection-in-action', signifying such reflection-in-action as purposeful and relying on tacit knowledge for execution. Gasson [1, p. 132] concludes (emphasis provided by the original text): *"The critical processes of design thus become the exploration, representation, sharing and **evolution** of partial, emergent design goals and the inductive assessment of when a satisficing solution has been reached."*

As a result of the opportunistic view on design, emergent design is in contrast with the three archetypical views that Lanzara [18] identifies where design is viewed as inherently rational. This matches well with current literature such as Bannon [21], Bødker [22], and Yoo [23], who discuss the implications of information technology increasingly blending into everyday life. This blending of use situations results in constantly changing interactions with designs, where the user focus goes beyond a single artifact (or even just a few artifacts at a time). As a result, users re-negotiate the use pattern and usefulness of an artifact beyond the capability for designers to control [24].

Our designs subsequently become tools for sensemaking of the world itself as well as the artifacts we interact with within this world. This exploratory stance towards designs and their situated meaning in the world means that designers hold a great responsibility towards the impact of their designs, despite their lack of control over end user sensemaking and use patterns [24]. In simpler terms: designing is coupled with responsibility for the end user impact as designs over time inevitably will be used beyond the intentions of the designer. It is subsequently naïve to expect any design to be solely good (or bad).

On the flip side of this challenge lies the opportunity for novel designs to be created if the designer follow and makes use of the situated impact (good and bad) that their designs have. It is noteworthy, however, that the understanding of this impact will increase over time, i.e. not only as part of a brief evaluation period. Leveraging emergent design opportunities thus requires designers to move away from a design-time focus only and into a use-time focus as well. Opportunism in design [2-3] should therefore be viewed as an expression of mediation, i.e. the creation of new meaning through the rich (read: extensive and real-world) use of designed artifacts.

We therefore arrive at two components of emergent design. First, during design-time, we have the process of continuous re-negotiation of the design path based on emerging and – depending on the situational relevance – discarded requirements that leads to gradual changes in terms of the design goal. Second, during the use-time of the artifact, we note that embracing an emergent design stance implies viewing opportunism as an expression of mediation, and that this mediation is better understood over time rather than as part of a brief (in relation to the lifetime of the design) evaluation time.

3   Design Oriented Research Methodologies

In this section, we present a summary of five streams of research that are commonly used to guide and assess designed artifacts: action research), design research, controlled experiments, participatory design, and ethnography based approaches. These will later be discussed in relation to Lanzara [17] and the capabilities for supporting emergent design from a process and mediation perspective.

3.1   Action Research

Rapoport [25] describes that the sociology and psychology roots of action research come from a post World War II era of multi-disciplinary motivation for collaboration. This explains the fundamental desire of action research to leverage cross-disciplinary skills and contribute to both practitioners and researchers in their respective problem situations [25-26].

Action research is characterized by the use of multiple iterations as a mechanism to combat the challenges of serving two masters – practice and research – and the careful negotiation of interests this implies [11][27]. Through iteration, cumulative research data about specific units of analysis in different contexts is collected, which means that findings are strengthened by building on the results of previous iterations. Using multiple iterations thus allows the scope to gradually increase, so that results may be tested in additional organizations to improve validity of findings [27]. Beyond the cyclical process, action research is also recognized by its rigorous structure, collaborative researcher involvement, and primary goals of organizational development together with scientific knowledge [28]. Within what today is known as canonical action research [11], practice and research goals are furthermore considered of equal value.

Canonical action research uses five phases and is executed in one or more cycles, where each cycle contains all five phases: diagnosing, action planning, action taking, evaluating, and specifying learning [11][28]. Diagnosing refers to the joint (researcher and practitioner) identification of situated problems and their underlying causes. As an outcome of this phase, theoretical assumptions are developed about the practice situation and problem domain. Action planning refers to the process of identifying interventions that can help resolve the problem situation, while action taking is the implementation of these interventions as change actions or system changes. In the evaluation phase, the interventions are jointly assessed by researchers and practitioners in relation to the problem that was originally specified. Finally, specifying learning refers to the ongoing process of documenting and synthesizing learning outcomes of the entire action research cycle.

3.2   Design Research

Design research been recognized within information system research as means to increase the effectiveness of IT systems and to solve existing business problems [29]. Design science research has been discussed and evolved in other domains, however, e.g. the natural science domain [30]. The iterative flow of design science research involve getting to know the problem – where the problem may originate from practice but must add knowledge to the research community through a solution proposal – a tentative design based on this proposal, development, evaluation, and conclusions that are then fed into the next iteration of design.

Seven guidelines for design science research have been proposed [12]: (1) design as an artifact, e.g. a construct, model, method or instantiation, (2) problem relevance, e.g. development of relevant solutions to important business problems, (3) design evaluation, e.g. definition of rigorous evaluation methods, (4) research contributions of a verifiable nature, (5) research rigor, e.g. rigorous methods for construction and evaluation, (6) design as a search process utilizing available means, and (7) communication of re-search in a way that speaks to technology as well as management oriented audiences.

Peffers et al. [31] outline six activities as part of the research process to follow when conducting design science research: (A1) identify problem and motivate the importance, (A2) define objectives of a solution, (A3) design and develop the artifact, (A4) demonstrate in suitable context that the artefact solves the problem, (A5) observe how effective and efficient the artefact is, (A6) communicate the result in scholarly publications as well as in professional publications. Research can start from one of the four first activities, while evaluation (A5) and communication (A6) iterates back to either aA2 or A3.

3.3   Controlled Experiments

Controlled experiments recognize that the ability to solve problems evolves over time. The evolution is based on experiences and knowledge that are built into models. These models are validated and verified by experiments, empirical evidence, and critical reflection with the goal of applying the models on new problems and solutions [32]. It has since played a large role in for instance software engineering [33-34]. However, controlled experiments are also widely used within HCI, particularly to evaluate interface designs and interaction styles, in order to understand the cognitive processes when the user interacts with a design [35].

Simplified, the general idea of controlled experiment is to be able to answer what happens with variable Y if variable X is changed. Controlled experiments in software engineering can be of four different types [36-37]: (1) experiments, i.e. the introduction of an intervention to observe its effects, (2) randomized experiment, i.e. the experiment units are used in a randomized order or the condition of the experiment is randomized, (3) quasi-experiments, i.e. where conditions are not randomized, and (4) correlations studies, i.e. observations of the direction and strength of relationships between variables. A core principle of controlled experiments is that they must be replicable, either in a very similar context or in a slightly different setting to expose if the results are valid for other contexts than the original.

To conduct a controlled experiment there are four activities to perform: (1) define the objectives of the experiment, (2) make experiment design, (3) execute the experiment and (4) analyze the data from the experiment. The experiment design is a detailed plan of states and conditions that dictate the parameters of experiment execution, as well as the variables to explore and which roles these variables have. The objective of the experiment design is to allow as much data and knowledge as possible to be generated from the experiment with as few experiment repetitions (instances) as possible [38].

3.4 Participatory Design

Participatory design is an approach where stakeholders are actively involved in the design process. That is, those individuals that have to adapt to the introduced change should be a part of the decision making [39]. The core principles of participatory design are [40]: (1) participants are experts in their own field, (2) all participants must be able to express their opinions, (3) groups composed of a diversity of people guarantee good design solutions, (4) democracy in decision making, and (5) participants are engaged in changing their own work environment. It is rooted in the democratic movement in Scandinavia during the seventies.

Tools and techniques are an essential part of participatory design projects. The techniques provide ways of revealing the relationship between work and technology, and mediate the descriptions of current and future work scenarios [39]. These tools and techniques can be used in different phases of the development cycle. Examples of tools and techniques are ethnographic methods [41-42] where the purpose is to understand users' work activities. Ethnographic methods involve visits to the workplace to make researcher understand the rich context of the actors in the workplace. For instance, contextual inquiry [43] is applied to help the users articulate their work practices. So called card games [41] may be used to analyze tasks and designs. The cards represent events within a system, a work-place event, or a user action. To make the users elaborate on problems and create visions of the future, Löwgren and Stolterman [44] outline 'future workshops'. This technique has three phases: critique, fantasy and implementation. Finally, a well-known technique is the use of mock-ups [45] that give users a way to explore and visualize the future by experimenting with new design proposals. These mock-ups may then be combined with other forms of prototyping that involve users and developers to collaboratively achieve familiarity with possible future artifact designs.

3.5 Ethnography Based Approaches

Ethnography based approaches have researchers enter the work environment with a probing and explorative attitude instead of trying to find quick answers to predefined and detailed questions [44]. Ethnography is founded in anthropology and with further roots in sociology. The approach is based on first-hand experience of the researcher who is directly involved in the studied setting [46]. The principles of ethnography are [15]: One, that the study must be conducted in a natural setting as people have restricted capabilities to express how they do their work; what you do often differs from what you think you do. The researcher therefore must study how the people actually do their work. Two, the researcher must try to get a holistic view of the setting to be able to see how things fit together and to ensure a complete understanding of what is going on. Three, the approach is mainly descriptive, but the researcher my point out problems and suggest potentials for change. Four, the situation is described in a way that is relevant and understandable to the people in the work place, i.e. the researcher must advocate the perspective of the actors within the problem-setting.

To execute ethnography based studies there are several techniques to use [15]: observations, interviews, self-reporting techniques (such as the use of diaries), remote data collection, video, observations, and researcher analysis of artifacts that the actors interact with. Such artifacts are studied to understand the role of the material to the actor.

4   Implications

After the summary presentation of the five popular design oriented methodologies above, we will in this section classify them use the Lanzara [17] archetypes of design. This allows us to make two types of reflections: One, what design stance that each research process promotes, and two, what the implications are in terms of emergent design support within the reviewed methodologies.

4.1   Design Stance Promoted

The first type of design that Lanzara [17] describes is when design is used as a vehicle for functional analysis. This implies that the design is the result of a rational process for achieving specific known goals. The second type of design, Lanzara argues, is when the act of designing and artifact produced acts as a catalyst in a problem-solving process. The design of an appropriate solution is in this case formed by identifying context cues from the problem situation that show the inherent structure and external dependencies of this problem, in order to guide the design of the artifact (or system). In the third type of design, where the design is coupled with the problem-setting, Lanzara argues that a rich understanding of mixed interests that actors have of the problem-setting may form a strong foundation for the design. This implies that once all actors' interests are well known, an appropriate design will emerge through this rich understanding of the problem-setting.

Using Lanzara [17] as a classification system for design approach analysis, the reviewed methodologies may be categorized as follows. Controlled experiments tend to view design as functional analysis and verification of this analysis, i.e. in accordance with the first of Lanzara's design views. This is visible as controlled experiments focuses on the testing and verification of hypotheses embedded in the design, rather than the design process to use in order to reach the final design. In this regard, controlled experiments – from a methodological perspective – have an uncontrolled development process where the functional analysis and rational deductive reasoning guides the design, rather than methodological principles for designing.

Meanwhile, action research and design research view design as a problem-solving exercise, and thus matches the second of Lanzara's design view. These methodologies both start from a well-known problem and mapping designed solutions to the effects that this problem has in the context where it appears, and the external dependencies that this problem is bound by. To achieve this, they both promote use of iterations to form guiding principles for the design that may be implemented in practice and inductively evaluated.

Finally, participatory design and the ethnography based approaches primarily view design as an exercise in understanding the problem-setting, i.e. the third viewpoint on design that Lanzara outlines. Closely related, participatory design and ethnographic based approaches place a particular value on understanding the mixed interests of actors within the problem-setting. Through elaborate studies of these – with a more involved researcher in the case of participatory design – both methodologies strive towards making sense of the interaction patterns first and foremost. Once this is achieved, potential design opportunities that emerge from this understanding may be considered. Due to the focus on a rich researcher/designer understanding of the mixed interests and complex interaction patterns within the problem setting, both ethnographic and participatory design research tends towards a rational approach to the design process, where designers are cautious with introducing changes that may upsetting the mixed interests of the actors in the problem-setting.

4.2   Emergent Design Support

As argued by Gasson [1], an emergent design stance rests on different foundations than the three types of design that Lanzara [17] outlines. An implication of our reviewed methodologies support Lanzara's design types is that the design oriented methodologies that are popular to use do not – as they are presently described – support an emergent design approach. In other words, this is the case despite the early recognition of emergent design and the present day examples of practice and research embracing agile software development which bears considerable resemblance to emergent design. A relevant question to ask then, is if there are examples of de facto use of emergent design in studies that adopt the reviewed research methodologies, despite the lack of formal adaptation and clear recognitioning of the fundamental change in the view of design that this implies?

To answer this question, we must first consider where this fundamental difference between emergent design and Lanzara's design types lies. Gasson [1] stresses emergent design as situated and evolutionary learning – two aspects that could be interpreted as in line with the second and third view of design that Lanzara [17] presents. In action research and design research, the learning process is part of the iterative and gradual extension of the research focus, continuously situated in the problem-situation they are addressing. Additionally, in ethnographic and participatory design research, the situated learning is the context in which the actors of mixed interest interact and that the researchers strive to promote and improve. The similarity between these may be the reason why we see examples of research that implicitly have adopted emergent design. However, the core difference that separates them from emergent design is the context in which Gasson [1] argues, relying on Guindon [2] and Khushalani et al. [3] as she frames emergent design as rooted in *opportunism*. This opportunistic framing embraces that the design path and goal will change as part of the process, contrary to the rigorously planned approaches of action and design research that invite such change only under carefully controlled circumstances. It also implies that action-taking (i.e. designing and re-designing) is continuously coupled with the changing world and the impact this change has on the problem structure itself and the problem-setting, rather than viewed as stable enough to first develop a rich understanding and then develop a design as in ethnographic and participatory design research. We therefore see control stand against flexibility in design path and goal, as well as rich insight against opportunistic tinkering.

In a similar fashion, controlled experiments could be argued – through repetition of experiments – as a process of evolutionary learning and thus similar to emerging design. However, here the obvious difference lies in controlled experiments not being situated in the very world that the testing is trying to predict the impact of. Certainly, a key element in good controlled experiments is the relevance of the experiment setting, but it is inevitably an approximation and the very nature of the 'controlled' element is that a number of variables are assumed to be stable. This explains why controlled experiments hold a deductive – rather than an inductive (the other four research methodologies) inference style as results are extrapolated and analyzed. The very nature of controlled experiments therefore deals with snapshots of time and the impact that designs have under the specific parameters that the experiment assumes, rather than extended real-world use.

This leads us to answering the question we posed above – are there examples with de facto use of emerging design using these methodologies already? While it was outside the scope of this paper to conduct an exhaustive review of all five research methodologies, we are comfortable to answer 'certainly' although perhaps not for all our reviewed methodologies and with varied levels of intentional use. For instance in controlled experiments, we could not find any studies that embraced emerging design – possibly as a result of the greater focus on evaluation rather than the design process itself. In action research, however, the work by McKay and Marshall [47] suggests smaller and continuous iterations within the canonical process, while Olsson [7] actually includes an emergent design perspective as he develops exploratory action research as an extension of the canonical action research process. Other examples include the persistent 'living labs' (cf. [48]) where the process of participatory design no longer ends with the deployment of the new information system. Instead, the user involvement and participation goes beyond that point [16][49] to be able to keep the software tuned with the context over time.

Rather than rejecting currently favored design methodologies, we argue for them to be formally adapted to embrace emerging design instead – in particular as several studies implicitly and de facto are doing this already and could be used to guide such adaptation. It is, after all, not a surprise that our research environment faces changes as part of the also changing use-patterns of designs.

As part of an opportunistic stance comes the willingness to make abductive inferences, rather than only inductively or deductively test what we already know exists. Based on what Apellicon erroneously translated from Aristotle, and Peirce [50] later corrected, abductive inference is an important complement to inductive and deductive inference [50, p. 171]: *"Abduction is the process of forming an explanatory hypothesis. It is the only logical operation which introduces any new idea; for induction does nothing but determine a value, and deduction merely evolves the necessary consequences of a pure hypothesis."* However, Peirce [50] recognizes that there is still a distinct role for all three types of inferences. Deduction proves something that *must* be, while induction shows something that *actually is*, and abduction suggests what *may* be. This leads us to our final argument that emerging design should welcome abductive inferences as a natural part of the opportunistic stance it holds. Without exploration of what may be, new and novel design paradigms are likely to be few and far apart.

5   Conclusions

In this paper, we set out to revisit emergent design and consider if current design oriented research methodologies actually embrace this notion. Emerging design is by nature opportunistic and addresses the need for continuous re-negotiation of design goals based on emerging and discarded requirements during the entire design process. Our contribution of this paper lies in the recognition that current research methodologies do not embrace emergent design, and a discussion of the implications that adding such a perspective would have.

References

1. Gasson, S.: Co-operative information system design how multi-domain information system design takes place in UK organisations. PhD thesis, University of Warwick, Warwick Business School (1997)
2. Guindon, R.: Knowledge exploited by experts during software system design. International Journal of Man-Machine Studies 33, 279–304 (1990)
3. Khushalani, A., Smith, R., Howard, S.: What happens when designers don't play by the rules: Towards a model of opportunistic behaviour in design. Australasian Journal of Information Systems 1(2), 13–31 (1994)
4. Mintzberg, H., Waters, J.H.: Of strategies, deliberate and emergent. Strategic Management Journal 6, 257–272 (1985)
5. Hutchins, E.: Cognition in the wild. MIT Press, Bradford (1995)
6. Orlikowski, W.J.: Evolving with Notes: Organizational change around groupware technology. Working paper 186, MIT Center for Coordination Science (1995)
7. Olsson, C.M.: Developing a mediation framework for context-aware applications: An exploratory action research approach. PhD thesis. Department of Computer Science and Information Systems, University of Limerick, Limerick, Ireland (2011)
8. Poppendiek, M., Poppendiek, T.: Lean software development: An agile toolkit. Addison-Wesley Professional, Boston (2007)
9. Schwaber, K., Beedle, M.: Agile software development with Scrum. Prentice Hall, NJ (2002)

10. Suscheck, C.A., Ford, R.: Jazz improvisation as a learning metaphor for the Scrum software development methodology. Software Process Improvement and Practice 13, 439–450 (2008)
11. Susman, G., Evered, R.: An assessment of the scientific merits of action research. Administrative Science Quarterly 23, 582–603 (1978)
12. Hevner, A.R., March, S.T., Park, J., Ram, S.: Design science in information systems research. MIS Quarterly 28(1), 75–105 (2004)
13. Wohlin, C.: An Evidence Profile for Software Engineering Research and Practice. In: Münch, J., Schmid, K. (eds.) Perspectives on the Future of Software Engineering - Essays in Honor of Dieter Rombach, pp. 145–158. Springer (2013)
14. Simonsen, J., Robertson, T.: Handbook of participatory design. Routledge Ltd., NY (2012)
15. Blomberg, J., Burrell, M., Guest, G.: An ethnographic approach to design. In: Jacko, J.A., Sears, A. (eds.) The Human-Computer Interaction Handbook, Mahwah, New, pp. 964–986 (2002)
16. Dittrich, Y., Eriksèn, S., Hansson, C.: PD in the wild; Evolving practices of design in use. In: Proceedings of PDC 2002, Malmo, Sweden, pp. 124–134. CPSR (2002)
17. Lanzara, G.F.: The design process: Frames, metaphors and games. In: Briefs, U., Ciborra, C., Schneider, L. (eds.) Proceedings of IFIP WG 9.1: Systems Design For, With and By The Users. North-Holland Publishing Company, Italy (1983)
18. Suchman, L.A.: Plans and situated actions: The problem of human-machine communication. Cambridge University Press, New York (1987)
19. Jeffries, R., Turner, A.A., Polson, P.G., Atwood, M.E.: The processes involved in designing software. In: Anderson, J.R. (ed.) Cognitive Skills and Their Acquisition. Lawrence Erlbaum Associates, Hillsdale (1981)
20. Schön, D.A.: The reflective practitioner: How professionals think in action. Basic Books, New York (1983)
21. Bannon, L.: Reimagining HCI Towards a more human-centered perspective. Interactions 18(4), 50–57 (2011)
22. Bødker, S.: When second wave HCI meets third wave challenges. In: Proceedings of the 4th Nordic Conference on Human-Computer Interaction: Changing Roles, Oslo (2006)
23. Yoo, Y.: Computing in everyday life: A call for research on experiential computing. MIS Quarterly 34(2), 213–231 (2010)
24. Dourish, P.: Where the action is: The foundations of embodied interaction. MIT Press, Cambridge (2001)
25. Rapoport, R.: Three dilemmas in action research. Human Relations 23(3), 499–513 (1970)
26. Lewin, K.: Action research and minority problems. Journal of Social Issues 2, 34–46 (1946)
27. Kock, N.: Information systems action research: an applied view of emerging concepts and methods. Springer, New York (2007)
28. Baskerville, R., Wood-Harper, T.: Diversity in information systems action research methods. European Journal of Information Systems 7(2), 90–107 (1998)
29. Nunamaker, J., Chen, M., Purdin, T.: System Development in Information Systems Research. Journal of Management Information Systems 7(3), 89–106 (1991)
30. March, S.T., Smith, G.F.: Design and natural science research on information technology. Decision Support Systems 15(1), 251–266 (1995)
31. Peffers, K., Tuunanen, T., Rothenberger, M.A., Chatterjee, S.: A design science research methodology for information systems research. Journal of Management Information Systems 24(3), 45–77 (2008)

32. Basili, V.R.: The role of experimentation in software engineering: past, current, and future. In: Proceedings of the 18th International Conference on Software Engineering, Berlin, pp. 442–449 (1996)
33. Basili, V.R., Reiter Jr., R.: A controlled experiment quantitatively comparing software development approaches. IEEE Trans. Software Eng. SE-7(5), 299–320 (1981)
34. Ko, A., LaToza, T., Burnett, M.: A practical guide to controlled experiments of software engineering tools with human participants. Empirical Software Engineering, 1–32 (September 2013)
35. Blandford, A., Cox, A.L., Cairns, P.A.: Controlled Experiments. In: Cairns, P.A., Cox, A.L. (eds.) Research Methods for Human Computer Interaction, pp. 1–16. CUP (2008)
36. Sjøberg, D.I.K., Hannay, J.E., Hansen, O., Kampenes, V.B.: A survey of controlled experiments in software engineering. IEEE Trans. Software Engineering 31(9), 733–753 (2005)
37. Shadish, W.R., Cook, T.D., Campbell, D.T.: Experimental and Quasi-Experimental Designs for Generalized Causal Inference. HoughtonMifflin (2002)
38. Juristo, N., Moreno, A.M.: Basics of Software Engineering Experimentation. Springer Publishing Company, Incorporated (2010)
39. Kensing, F.: Methods and Practices in Participatory Design, Doctoral Thesis. ITU University, ITU Press, Copenhagen (2003)
40. Sanoff, H.: Editorial - special issue on participatory design. Design Studies 28(3), 213–215 (2007)
41. Muller, M.J., Wildman, D.M., White, E.A.: Participatory Design. Communication of ACM 36(4), 23–28 (1993)
42. Kensing, F., Blomberg, J.: Participatory Design - issues and concerns. Computer Supported Cooperative Work (CSCW) 7, 167–185 (1998)
43. Kuniacsky, M.: Observing the User Experience - A Practitioner's Guide to User Research, 1st edn. Morgan Kaufmann Publishers, San Fransisco (2003)
44. Löwgren, J., Stolterman, E.: Design av Informationsteknik, 2nd edn., Studentlitteratur, Lund (2004) (in Swedish)
45. Ehn, P., Kyng, M.: Cardboard computers: mocking-it-up or hands on the future. In: Greenbaum, J., Kyng, M. (eds.) Design at Work - Cooperative Design of Computer System, 1st edn., pp. 139–154. Lawrence Erlbaum Associates, Hillsdale (1991)
46. Rönkkö, K.: Ethnography. In: Laplante, P. (ed.), Engineering. Taylor and Francis Group, New York (2010)
47. McKay, J., Marshall, P.: Driven by two masters, serving both: The interplay of problem solving and research in information systems action research projects. In: Kock, N. (ed.) Information Systems Action Research: An Applied View of Emerging Concepts and Methods, pp. 131–158. Springer, New York (2007)
48. Björgvinsson, E., Ehn, P., Hillgren, P.-A.: Participatory design and "democratizing innovation". In: Proceedings of the 11th Biennial Participatory Design Conference, Sydney, Australia, November 29-December 03 (2010)
49. Marcolin, M., D'Andrea, V., Hakken, D.: Participatory maintenance-in-use: users' role in keeping systems alive. In: Proceedings of the 12th Participatory Design Conference, vol. 2, pp. 57–60 (2012)
50. Peirce, C.S.: Harvard lectures on pragmatism. In: Hartshorne, C., Weiss, P. (eds.) Collected Papers of Charles Saunders Peirce, vol. 5(of 8). Harvard University Press, Cambridge (1903)

Value Pie: A Culturally Informed Conceptual Scheme for Understanding Values in Design

Roberto Pereira and Maria Cecília Calani Baranauskas

Institute of Computing – UNICAMP, Av. Albert Einstein,1251, 13084-722, Campinas, Brazil
{rpereira,cecilia}@ic.unicamp.br

Abstract. Interactive technologies have spread from the context of the workplace to our homes and everyday lives, and people use them for different purposes, through different devices, and in quite different and complex contexts. In the last years, the HCI research community has devoting attention to the subject of values, pointing out to the need for placing values in the core of technology design, and for studies that support researchers, designers and practitioners in doing so. In this paper, we introduce the Value Pie: a theoretically grounded artifact created to support the understanding and involvement of values in design. The paper presents the grounds used to create the artifact and discusses on how it can favor a comprehensive and informed understanding of values and their cultural context.

Keywords: Organizational Semiotics, HCI, Culture.

1   Introduction

In the mid 50s, Sharp [1] analyzed how the introduction of the steel axe by a group of missionaries undermined the stone axe and triggered destructive changes in the Yir Yoront Aboriginal tribe. It was expected the steel axe to improve natives' productivity and quality of life, but what was perceived was an inevitable collapse of the tribe traditional culture and values.

The Yir Yoront example draws attention to the impact that technology causes on the environment it is inserted and on the people that live in it (even in those who do not use the technology). This impact may be caused by the technology itself, the way it is introduced, the way it is used, the interests behind it, and so on. Therefore, thinking of the values and the culture of the different stakeholders involved in a design context is an ethical commitment we must assume as researchers and practitioners in the technological field.

Interactive technologies are a growing reality worldwide and people use them for different purposes, through different devices, and in quite different and complex contexts. As Bødker [2] asserts, technology has spread from the context of the workplace to our homes, everyday lives, and culture.

Sellen et al. [3] recognize values as a critical issue when designing technologies for the digital age. In this context, as Winograd [4] had already argued, the designer's role goes beyond the construction of an interface to encompass all the interspace in which people live, requiring a shift from seeing the machinery to see the lives of the

M. Kurosu (Ed.): Human-Computer Interaction, Part I, HCII 2014, LNCS 8510, pp. 122–133, 2014.

people using it. This shift demands attention to relevant factors that become hard to quantify and even identify: values and culture are surely among them.

A value cannot be understood outside its cultural context. While a value indicates something that is important and needs to be taken into account, the cultural context explains why such value is important. In the Yir Yoront example, the missionaries offered some western goods for the natives as a gift/payment for their services: the steel axe was the most disseminated and accepted one. The missionaries, however, ignored the fact that the stone axe was a central tool in the tribe culture: it was used for producing food, constructing shelter, heating their homes; it represented power and defined the hierarchical position in the tribe; different rituals and celebrations were conducted involving the stone axe; only the old men had the right to possess a stone axe, etc. When the missionaries distributed steal axes equally for men, women and even children, they broke this entire structure. Elders, once high respected, become a burden to the tribe; rituals lost their meaning and importance for the younger; trading activities involving the stone axe produced by the tribe disappeared, and so on. The destructive consequences of the steal axe were triggered more by the way it was introduced in the tribe than by the technology itself. Because the missionaries ignored the tribe culture and values, they had no strategy, no plan, no knowledge about the environment, and no means to know the possible consequences of their actions.

In fact, the implications of values (or their lack of consideration) in the design of technologies are usually too subtle and only noticed when a social rule is violated, a behavioral pattern is broken, or a conflict of interest arises. Friedman [5] argues that, because designers necessarily communicate values through the technology they produce, values emerge from the tools designers build, and how people choose to use them. As the author highlights, although the neglect of moral values in any organization is disturbing, it is particularly damaging in the design of computer technology because, unlike people with whom we can disagree and negotiate values and their meanings, we can hardly do so with technology.

In this sense, although there are some initiatives that contemplate values in technology design, some authors [6] claim that the existing models and approaches usually restrict the analysis to a set of preconceived values, rather than encouraging designers to inquire about other values that may appear and that are relevant to a particular context. As [6] suggests, models which consider global values and do not account for their cultural nature, if followed strictly, may prevent the identification and understanding of some important and culturally specific values.

The Value Pie (VP) is a culturally informed conceptual scheme we proposed in [7] for organizing values identified in the context of social software. The VP was built on the grounds of Organization Semiotics [8] and the Building Blocks of Culture [9], organizing values according to their formality and areas of culture — see Fig. 1. To our knowledge, the VP is pioneer in supporting the consideration of both culture and values in an explicit, informed, and integrated way.

In addition to support the organization of values, we have used the VP for supporting and grounding discussions on specific values (e.g., emotion and affection, privacy, identity). For instance, in [10] the VP was used to ground discussions about reputation on web communities from the perspective of values, allowing us to approach reputation according to three dimensions: formality (informal, formal, technical), culture (the "Classification" slice of VP) and interplay — the relationship of reputation with other values and VP's slices. In that work, the VP allowed us to understand reputation as a cultural value for a given community of users, informing the design of computing features for reputation in a social software designed with representatives from the community. It also encouraged the analysis and inquiring about other values that emerged from and were relevant to the design context, such as Identity, Privacy, Security and Collaboration. Understanding reputation as a value for that community and discussing it from different perspectives grounded the design of features for supporting this value in a social network system.

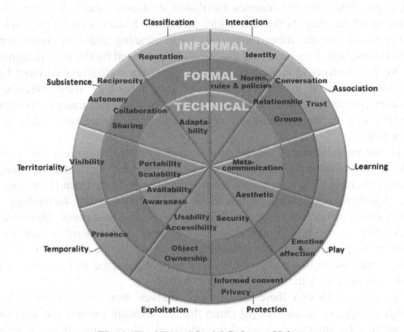

Fig. 1. The VP and Social Software Values

The VP has shown to be able to inform and support the work with values in design activities. It articulates different theoretical and methodological theories, favoring a comprehensive, informed and situated understanding of values and their cultural context. In this paper, we present the VP as a comprehensive and useful artifact for guiding discussions on values in design. We claim for a culturally informed view for understanding values in HCI, approaching key issues (e.g., usability, accessibility, privacy) from the perspective of values. Therefore, this paper: i) presents the theoretical bases articulated to create the VP; ii) introduces the VP as a conceptual basis for supporting the understanding and discussion of values in the design of interactive systems, and iii) presents examples and discussions of its application.

2   Value Pie's Foundation

The natural act of thinking is strongly modified by culture [11]. Authors such as Hall [9] and Schwartz [12] assert that values, their importance and roles,vary strongly according to the culture being analyzed. According to Hall [9], culture refers to people's attitudes, material things, learned behavioral patterns, and values; it represents the very different ways of organizing life, thinking, and understanding basic assumptions about the family, the economic system, and even the mankind.

When talking about culture, Hall [11] believes it is more important to look at the way things are put together than at specific theories. In fact, although it is useful to enquiry about specific situations, understanding the cultural context in which people live can offer more information than looking at pre-defined hypothesis. In this sense, aiming to formalize and structure the characterization, analysis and comparison between different cultures, Hall [9] proposed 10 Primary Messages Systems (PMS), or areas, named the basic building blocks of culture: Interaction, Association, Learning, Play, Protection, Exploitation, Temporality, Territoriality, Classification and Subsistence, suggesting that cultures develop values with regard to them. These areas are the ten slices in VP (Fig. 1) and can be understood as follows:

Interaction: to be alive means to interact with the environment, and everything people do involves interaction with something/someone else: people, systems, objects, animals, etc. All the other following areas have interaction in their nature: as Hall [9] asserts, interaction is at the centre of the universe of culture and everything grows from it. Values in interaction are related to the preferred forms of communication between people, behavioral patterns and social protocols, the importance of other living things and the concern with them, etc. The identity of a people is the sum of their characteristics, including all its values.

Association: all living things organize their life in some pattern of association. Governmental and social structures may vary strongly according to the culture, not only in nature, form and function, but also in importance. Values in association are usually related to the way society structure itself, its groups, public and private organizations/entities, the role and importance of family and other social relationships (e.g., friendship, partnership, marriage), and so on.

Learning: learning has an important role in the course of man evolution, being one of the basic activities present since the beginning of life. Education and educational systems are strongly tied to emotion and as characteristic of a culture as its language. Values in this area are related to the preferred styles of learning (e.g., informal, formal), the importance given to different forms of knowledge, the valued abilities, knowledge and professions, as well as the relative importance of experience, expertise, meritocracy, and so on.

Play: funny, emotion and pleasure are terms related to it. Although the role of this area in the evolution of species is not well understood yet, it is clearly linked to the other areas — e.g., in learning it is considered a catalyst; in relationships a desirable characteristic, the notions of beauty and attractiveness are influenced by culture, etc. Values in this area are clearly linked to emotional and affective aspects. As Hall [9] asserts, if one controls the humor of a people, s/he is able to control almost everything else.

Protection: originally named "defense", we adopted the modification proposed in the OS theory [8]. Cultures have different mechanisms and strategies of protection (e.g., medicine, military strategy, religion). Defense is a specialized activity of vital importance, and people must defend themselves against not only hostile forces in nature, but also internal forces and those within human society. Values in protection are related to the rules, strategies and mechanisms developed in order to protect the space (physical, digital, personal), the objects used to guarantee protection, the medical therapy adopted/preferred, etc.

Exploitation: this area refers to the use of materials in order to explore the world. Materials in an environment are strongly related to the other aspects of a culture: there are specific tools and artifacts for cooking, protecting, playing, learning, etc. It is impossible to think about a culture with no language and no materials. Values in exploitation are related to the preferred tools, objects, instruments, and procedures for working, playing, learning, protecting, eating, etc., and their importance.

Temporality: time is related to life in several ways: from cycles, periods and rhythms (e.g., breath rate, heartbeat) to measures (e.g., hours, days) and other aspects in society (e.g., mealtime, vacations). There is specific time for different activities, expected time for marrying, reasonable time to forget an offense, pre-defined time to pay for a debt/crime, and so on. Values in this area are related to the ways people deal with time, its importance and roles in society.

Territoriality: while having a territory is essential to life, the lack of a territory is one of the most precarious conditions. This area refers to the possession, use and defense of space: there are physical (e.g., country, house, bedroom) as well as social (e.g., social position, hierarchy, position in a line) and personal spaces (e.g., personal data and stuffs, office desk). Values in this area are related to the ways space is understood, used, distributed and valued in the society.

Classification: originally named "bisexuality", this area is related to the differences in terms of form and function related to gender. Cultures have different forms of distinction and classification, and give different importance to each one. We preferred to use the name "classification", suggested by the OS theory [8], in order to encompass, beyond differences in gender, the ones related to socio-economic conditions, age, abilities, etc. Values in classification refer to preferred style of dressing, jobs, sports, and so on, of men and women; the importance given to different social statuses and classes; the rights/obligations of people according to pre-defined classifications, etc.

Subsistence: this area includes from people's food habits and jobs to the economy of a country. Professions, supply chains, deals, natural resources are all aspects related to this area, being influenced not only by the other areas but also by geographical and climatic conditions. Values in subsistence are related to the importance and conditions of working and retirement; foods, nourishment and sanitation preferences/habits; the way the society understands and deals with inequalities, social policies, public interests, etc.

Hall [9] also introduced the notions of informal, formal and technical levels in which humans operate and understand the world: the VP's three layers (see Fig. 1). These levels are simultaneously present in everything, although one always dominates, and we deal with them separately. For instance, during elections, people talk about their preferences and candidates, proving/recommending a certain candidate, criticizing, and so on: this is the informal in action. People may also join a political party, and participate in interviews and prospection pools; there are specific dates and requirements for voting, and so on: the formal is dominating here. Finally, there are solutions developed in order to receive and compute votes, such as electronic voting or paper ballot: here, the technical aspect is emphasized. When a level is dominating, the other two are underlying it. For Hall, understanding the shifts between these levels is the basic requirement to understand the process of change.

Stamper [13] proposed a structure represented by the Semiotic Onion that explains how these levels exist in the context of organizations and information systems (see Fig. 2). The informal represents the organizational culture, customs and values that are reflected as beliefs, habits and individual behavior patterns of its members. The formal corresponds to aspects that are well established and accepted, becoming social conventions, norms or laws; in this level, rules and procedures are created to replace meanings and intentions. Finally, the technical situated in the core of the onion represents aspects that are so formalized that can be technically approached and supported. Therefore, the semiotic onion illustrates that any technological artifact is embedded in a formal system that, in turn, is embedded in an informal one.

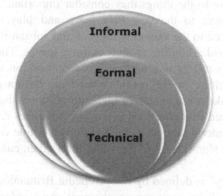

Fig. 2. The Semiotic Onion

Baranauskas [14] argues that the three levels must be considered for a socially aware design of computing systems. In fact, we must consider the three levels in which values may be manifested in society and understood by its members. Otherwise, important values may go unnoticed, being identified only when some problem arises (e.g., the need for adaptability), and important aspects of values may be misunderstood, or neglected, making no sense to users (e.g., a reputation feature that causes embarrassment instead of motivation).

3   Value Pie's Dimensions

The VP was built on the grounds of Organization Semiotics theory [8] and the Building Blocks of Culture [9]. It is formed by three layers that organize values according to their formality, and is divided into ten slices that recognize the cultural nature of values — see Fig. 1. The three layers (informal, formal and technical) represent the different levels in which humans operate and understand the world proposed by Hall [9], and are structured according to the Semiotic Onion to reflect the way they are perceived in the context of information systems [13]. The ten slices represent cultural patterns of behavior in which values are developed, and that allow the mapping and comparison between different cultures [9][11].

The VP artifact supports the understanding and discussion about values from three different perspectives: Culture, Formality, and Interplay. These perspectives bring quite different aspects of values that must be considered in order to have a comprehensive and consistent view of them. Following, we explain each dimension.

3.1   Culture

Values are developed in different cultures according to basic behavioral patterns: from the tools people use to the things they consider important in life, from the way they associate and protect to the way they learn and play, from the way they understand time and space to the way they interact and subsist in the world. Humans tend to interpret the world according to their cultural lenses. Therefore, ignoring the cultural nature of values results in a narrowed comprehension about them and their role in stakeholders' culture; it may even mislead the design process, resulting in solutions that do not make sense to stakeholders, do not meet their demands and that, possibly, trigger undesired side effects on them. The VP slices represent the ten areas of culture because considering the areas related to each value contributes to a better understanding about the significance of the value for a given culture, as well as about the culture itself.

For instance, "Privacy" is defined by Encyclopedia Britannica [15] as *"the quality or state of being apart from company or observation; freedom from unauthorized intrusion (one's right to); a private matter"*. Understanding privacy as a value in a situated contexts requires understanding the cultural roots of this value. Considering the definition of privacy and the explanations for each are of culture, we can understand privacy as a value developed in the Protection area, reflecting importance of protecting personal information, things, ideas etc. What is necessary and/or expected to protect and why, what are the means to protect it, the extension and limits of privacy, and the importance given to it are examples of aspects that differ strongly according to the culture being analyzed.

3.2   Formality

Values have different facets that are situational, varying not only according to the cultural context, but also across time and space. Discussions on values usually represent a snapshot in which some aspects are visible and some are not. To see other relevant aspects, one must take another snapshot, from a different angle. Therefore, when discussing values, it is necessary to pay attention not only to the culture areas in which they are manifested, but also in the different levels of formality. Values are manifested in one of the three levels (informal, formal, technical layers in the VP), but have aspects to be considered in all the three simultaneously.

Values manifested in the informal level usually have a personal or ethical nature; values manifested in the formal level are collective or social values where there is a social rule or system of norms; and values placed in the technical level can be understood as quality attributes or special features related to technological artifacts. For instance, considering the examples of privacy, people from different cultures have their own informal understanding of what privacy is, its meaning and importance. There are social protocols, conventions, rules and laws that are formally established to define the limits and guarantees of an individual's privacy and that varies according to the culture being analyzed. There are also some facets of privacy that are so formally accepted that can be technically supported, such as a curtain to cover a window, the wall for restricting the visibility of a house, secrete voting for elections, and the privacy of medical examinations.

According to Stamper [13], norms stand for a field of force that governs how members think, behave, make judgments and perceive the world. Norms are present in the formal aspect of each value and are the bridge between the informal and the technical levels. They regulate and influence people's behavior, specify rules and policies, and determine the way technical features work. Therefore, if social norms are not understood in their cultural settings, they tend to be automated by technical features that do not make sense to users and do not afford the behaviors they are used to in their social world.

3.3   Interplay

The VP is not a classification scheme in which the elements are assigned to one and only one class within a system of mutually exclusive and non-overlapping classes. Values may be developed at the intersection of multiple areas, and they may interact with each other. In fact, although values have a clear relationship to an area, they usually illustrate some aspect in which the area interacts with other area, and reveals other values that influences/are influenced by it. Using the example of privacy again, it is a value developed in the protection area, but it has a clear intersection with "Territoriality": privacy is the protection of the space (personal, social, physical).

Schwartz [12] draws attention to the interactive nature of values according to their underlying motivational principles. The VP reinforces the interactive nature of values, but considering the relationships according to values' cultural nature: it assumes that values developed in the same area of culture, i.e., values placed in the same slice in VP, have a natural relationship to each other. Because all the ten areas interact with each other and values may be developed in the intersection of them, designers must also pay attention to the values developed in related areas. There are at least three kinds of relationships: dependence, congruence, and conflict.

Dependence means that a value is so strongly related to other values that it cannot be approached in a direct way; i.e., it depends on others values to be considered.

Congruence means that a value has compatibility with other values, extending to them the positive/negative effects it suffers; i.e., when promoting a specific value other related values are endorsed. This relation is bidirectional: the promotion of related values triggers positive effects on it. In the same way, the lack of attention to the value triggers negative impacts on the related ones.

Conflict means that a value competes with other values; i.e., promoting a specific value compromises the related ones. This is also a bidirectional relation: the promotion of related values may trigger negative effects on it.

4   Using the Lenses of Values: Practical Steps

From the core areas in Computer Science listed by ACM, HCI is the area that must both to deal with issues that are universal and transversal to other areas and to consider specific aspects (e.g., social, cultural, political, economic, geographic) of the environment in which its application occurs. These characteristics confer to HCI a key role in the design of solutions for a society mediated by information and communication technologies and a strong responsibility regarding the impact caused by these technologies.

The subject of values, therefore, is not only a matter of research, but also a matter of practice and posture in our academic and practical fields. It is a matter of seeing the world through the lenses of cultural values, revisiting well-known concepts, methods and theories, rethinking our tools and practices, redefining the focus of our teaching disciplines.

Bannon [16] provides interesting examples that show the need for understanding values in their socio-cultural context when designing technologies. Talking about "Ambient Assisted Living", he mentions how often designers and even researchers conduct their researches and develop their products hoping they will support elderly people living independently, having a better quality of life at home instead in an institution, and not becoming a burden on other people or on the state as they grow older. However, he highlights that, although much of this work is justified by the need of "empowering older people through independent living", on closer examination they are more engaged in providing fulltime remote monitoring of these people than in adding to their dignity or empowering themselves to remain autonomous.

The development of educational technologies, especially for disable students, usually falls into the same trap. Researchers and teachers are often interested in promoting students learning, developing their abilities, capacitating them to use technology, etc. However, although these studies present a sounding theoretical and methodological foundation, applying user-centered design, and defending social inclusion, on closer examination some of them end up: only automating activities and procedures conducted at the classrooms; expecting students to achieve a "normal performance"; and evaluating students according to pre-defined parameters. It means that, in both the examples, the concern with the central people (elderly, students), their real needs, concerns and values is not primary as it would be expected, but secondary.

In Bannon's example [16], thinking on technology development or medical assistance before understanding the stakeholders and their values may prevent the understanding of more basic issues, such as elderly people's need to be in contact with their family, friends and neighbors in a natural way; the need to manage their privacy and keep control over themselves, etc. In our example, thinking on technology development and pedagogical goals before understanding the students and their values prevent the development of technologies that make sense to them, add to their quality of life and promote their welfare. It may even prevent the design of new teaching strategies that consider students and their particularities, developing the abilities necessary for the students' context of life, evaluating them according to their own progress.

The VP is able to support the reasoning and discussion of existing concepts through the lenses of values, regardless the design process, techniques and tools adopted. The simple act of mapping a concept into VP's different dimensions provides a values-oriented and culturally informed view of the concept and related issues. Some practical steps for using the VP are:

- Select a concept to be discussed: try to look for critical/important concepts involved in the design context. For instance: accessibility.
- Identify the slice (area of culture) it is related to: considering the explanations presented for each VP's slice, identify the one that the chosen concept is clearly related to (if more than an slice is suitable, see which one is the dominating and consider the other as a related area). According to the VP and the values suggested by [7], accessibility may be related to the "Exploitation" area, i.e., it is as a value related to the exploration of the world.
- Investigate the informal, formal and technical aspects related to the selected concept: remember that each value has aspects to be simultaneous discussed at these three levels. For instance:
  - *Informal*: the first thing to recognize is that people have different needs, views, understandings and expectations regarding accessibility. Different stakeholders will value and react to accessibility in a different way. Therefore, it is important to clarify the role and importance of accessibility for the situated context of design.
  - *Formal*: there are rules, laws and norms related to accessibility that must be understood and followed. There are accessibility standards and certifications, requirements for accessibility, formal training and education, etc. Even in cases where there is no formal regulation, there will be well-defined social protocols that explains how a society deals with a given value.
  - *Technical*: there are physical structures, tools and technical devices for providing accessibility (e.g., assistive technologies), or that require accessibility. There are public and private services related to accessibility, technical procedures, frameworks, and so on. Technical features communicate and disseminate values, causing impact on them.

- Analyze the possible relationships with other:
  - Areas (VP's slices): the value may have aspects manifested in other areas, being influenced by them. For instance, accessibility has a clear relationship with the interaction area and is commonly approached according to pre-defined criteria/types (classification) — e.g., kinds of impairments, aging, education. Physical accessibility is related to territoriality and may depend on the time (e.g., having something available); the (lack of) accessibility may affect values related to subsistence, etc. Each area may offer a different perspective to the value being considered, favoring a wider perception regarding its impact on the design context.
  - Values: as we pointed out, a value interacts with other values in different ways. For instance, promoting accessibility is a basic requirement for supporting autonomy, guaranteeing that people will find no barriers for living and acting regardless their limitations and specificities. The lack of accessibility impacts negatively on peoples' autonomy, as well as on other values such as privacy (e.g., a person has to depend on others to conduct basic activities), emotion (e.g., motivation, welfare, self-esteem) and identity (e.g., who the person think s/he is in the world, the things s/he can do, the aspirations s/he may have).

Approaching a concept like accessibility from the perspective of values favors a deeper understanding regarding the concept and the complex social context in which it is being considered. It contributes not only for a social responsible design of technologies as a process, but also as a product, favoring the design of solutions suitable to the target audience, its needs and expectations. In fact, values should be used as lens through which we look at the design context. The interested reader may consult [7] and [10] for further examples and discussions on the VP and other artifacts to support design activities.

5   Conclusion

Although recognized as important, there are few initiatives relating values to technology. In fact, there is even a lack of theoretically grounded approaches for investigating values and practical artifacts for supporting designers in their activities.

In this paper, we introduced the Value Pie as a comprehensive and useful artifact for guiding discussions on values in design. The Value Pie articulates different theoretical and methodological theories, favoring a comprehensive, informed and situated understanding of values and their cultural context. The theoretical and methodological grounds of the artifact are presented, and discussions and examples are presented in order to show how de artifact can contribute to a value-oriented perspective in HCI.

The Value Pie draws attention to the diversity of values, their cultural and interactive nature, allowing the discussion of values according to three different dimensions: culture, formality and interplay. The artifact may be helpful for guiding researchers, designers, analysts, and practitioners to understand values and dealing with them in the design of interactive technologies.

Acknowledgements. This research is partially funded by FAPESP (#2013/02821-1) and Proesp/CAPES (#23038.01457/2009-11).

References

1. Sharp, L.: Steel Axes for Stone–Age Australians. Human Organization 11(1) (1952)
2. Bødker, S.: When second wave HCI meets third wave challenges. In: Proceedings of 4th Nordic Conference on Human-computer Interaction: Changing Roles, Oslo, Norway, pp. 1–8. ACM Press (2006)
3. Sellen, A., Rogers, Y., Harper, R., Rodden, T.: Reflecting human values in the digital age. Communications of the ACM 52, 58–66 (2009)
4. Winograd, T.: The design of interaction. In: Beyond Calculation: The Next Fifty Years of Computing, pp. 149–161. Springer (1997)
5. Friedman, B.: Value-Sensitive Design. Interactions 3(6), 16–23 (1996)
6. Isomursu, M., Ervasti, M., Kinnula, M., Isomursu, P.: Understanding human values in adopting new technology – A case study and methodological discussion. International Journal of Human-Computer Studies 69, 183–200 (2011)
7. Pereira, R., Baranauskas, M.C.C., da Silva, S.R.P.: Social Software and Educational Technology: Informal, Formal and Technical Values. Educational Technology & Society 16(1), 4–14 (2013)
8. Liu, K.: Semiotics in information systems engineering. Cambridge University Press (2000)
9. Hall, E.T.: The Silent Language. Anchoor Books (1959)
10. Pereira, R., Hornung, H., Baranauskas, M.C.C.: Cognitive Authority revisited in Web Social Interaction. In: Frameworks of IT Prosumption for Business System Development, pp. 142–157. IGI Global (2012)
11. Hall, E.T.: Beyond culture. Anchor Books (1977)
12. Schwartz, S.H.: Basic human values: Their content and structure across countries. In: Values and Behaviors in Organizations, Vozes, Rio de Janeiro, pp. 21–55 (2005)
13. Stamper, R., Liu, K., Hafkamp, M., Ades, Y.: Understanding the Role of Signs and Norms in Organisations – a semiotic approach to information systems design. Journal of Behaviour and Information Technology 19(1), 15–27 (2000)
14. Baranauskas, M.C.C.: Socially Aware Computing. In: Proceedings of VI International Conference on Engineering and Computer Education (ICECE 2009), pp. 1–5 (2009)
15. http://www.britannica.com/bps/dictionary?query=privacy (last access: March 1, 2014)
16. Bannon, L.: Reimagining HCI: toward a more human-centered perspective. Interactions 18(4), 50–57 (2011)

The Formulation and Visualization of 3D Avatar Design, Including Three Basic Theoretical Elements: Aesthetic, User Experience and Psychology

Thomas Photiadis and Panayiotis Zaphiris

Department of Multimedia and Graphic Arts, Cyprus Interaction Lab,
Cyprus University of Technology
{Thomas.Photiadis,Panayiotis.Zaphiris}@cut.ac.cy

Abstract. This paper presents a different, until now, perspective of aesthetic experience during the process of designing 3D avatars, formulating and visualizing the combination of user-experience and psychology. The present research aims to define 3D aesthetic experience and the relation of HCI (Human-Computer Interaction) through a theoretical model delivering new insights on the process of 3D avatars' design.

There is limited research about the procedure and the influences (emotions, mood and external factors) during the process of users designing their three-dimensional (3D) depictions otherwise known as avatars. The provided theoretical model is a combination of the three subjective factors (aesthetics, psychology and user experience) which are interrelated, and are present during such design procedures. The common element that connects all of these areas is Human Computer Interaction (HCI).

In each area of interest, on its own, there is relevant and sufficient research. But, to a large extent their common relation to 3D environments has not been explored yet. It is the objective of this paper to explore the aesthetic experience from the designer view, in other words, is defined the 3D aesthetic experience of the user but from the side of the designer.

An additional reason of the formulation and the focus on 3D visualization is to simplify the procedure of 3D avatar design while simultaneously embracing the influence of aesthetics, user experience and psychology; which are provided via an overview of existing research, concentrating on the procedure for 3D avatar design.

Keywords: Human – Computer Interaction, Aesthetics, User Experience, Avatars, Psychology.

1 Introduction

In the last two decades 3D environments are utilized extensively and this popularity with their broad acceptability arise from the feeling of freedom that users have for their first 3D interaction-moment. The meaning of this opinion (freedom) is that users can interact in a social environment without any rules, and with a profile that often

M. Kurosu (Ed.): Human-Computer Interaction, Part I, HCII 2014, LNCS 8510, pp. 134–144, 2014.
© Springer International Publishing Switzerland 2014

seeks to reflect the real life, while providing for additional user benefits [Castronova, 2003]. The initial notion of freedom is derived from the user's depiction, called "3D character" or "avatar". This contains several illustrations of the user, which are applied to make their selves through 3D worlds, the avatar is the vehicle to navigate and interact. As Ducheneaut, Wen, Yee & Wadley [2009] pinpoint, users have the possibility through their avatars to socialize, communicate, collaborate, learn, and work with other participants in the 3D world. In addition, we also need to consider that there are 3D environments (e.g. games) which provide standard characters that users are required to select, without flexibility to make any changes. This is in contrast with other virtual spaces like Second Life that allows users to design their 3D external appearance. Subsequently, the main aspect that plays significant role in designing the external appearance is the subjectiveness of aesthetic experience, the experience that users have influencing the aesthetic estimation.

Aesthetics is an aspect that mediates to the creation of a 3D avatar connected directly with perception influencing. The individual's judgment about aesthetics, beauty, or what is pleasing is based upon personal, social and cultural background (user – experience).

At this point, is noteworthy to say that the behavior (role) of the avatar by extension of the user is directly affected from his/her 3D self-depiction [Ducheneaut, 2009].

Another major factor in the procedure of customizing a 3D character as a body image is physical appearance. This is tied directly with aesthetic and psychology, and is influenced by the user-experience. External appearance determines the three-dimensional interaction, affected alongside from individual's social and cultural background, a phenomenon that occurs in all kinds of interactions. It is worthy to mention that the 3D design and interaction influence not only avatar but the user-owner respectively.

As mentioned above the central level, which determines the individual's belief about themselves and their physical appearance is the user-experience. The user experience may be conceptualized as the moment-sense of how someone perceives and interprets something that they are surrounded by, and determining the next interaction. Therefore, user experience places emphasis on how someone feels expresses and modifies his emotions, mood and the effects that are derived; associated with the definition of usability and user satisfaction. User experience encompasses more than just satisfaction.

As all theoretical models, this one also needs to be tested further so we will conclude the paper by proposing a set of future research questions and evaluation approaches.

2   Related Work

2.1   Aesthetics

Aesthetics is a notion that has its origins of ancient times and is emerged and evolved through the six great civilizations: Greece, Egypt, Mesopotamia, Rome, India and

China, associated with beauty and subjectivity. Plato, Greek philosopher, was the first originator of aesthetics using the Greek word "aisthanomai" which was defined as an object's beauty, arising from its proportions, harmony and unity [Hoffmann, & Krauss, 2004]. Plato also contened that, traditionally aesthetic correlate directly with arts, architecture, natural landscapes, and with beauty. Aristotle from the other side argued that aesthetics was an object's beauty but he believed that beauty came from order, symmetry and definiteness. Based on Greek philosophers definitions the word "aisthanomai" was enlarged and enriched with several English terms such as sensations, perception, appearance, mind and knowledge, which enabled philosophers to describe the notion of aesthetics [Theuma, 2007]. In 1750, the German philosopher Alexander Gottlieb noted about aesthetics that people discover the world through perception and thus through their senses [Hoffmann, & Krauss; 2004, Theuma, 2007]. Similarly, Cawthon and Moere [2006] also proposed that, aesthetics is seen as something that rekindles the body and the mind, awakening the senses and as a result of user's personal, social and cultural background.

However, Huxley, in his book, had included all the definitions of aesthetics as a list [Hjelle & Ziegler, 1976]:

- A beauty in appearance
- Visual appeal
- An experience
- An attitude
- A property of objects
- A response or judgment
- A process

Against this background the study of aesthetics is split into two components: philosophy of arts and aesthetic experience of non art entities [Hassenzahl, & Tractinsky, 2006; Cawthon & Moere, 2006]. From the part of philosophy of arts, according to Postrel 2004, aesthetics pleases and liberates the masses [Postrel, 2004]. Therefore aesthetics is defined as an artistically beautiful or pleasing appearance [America Heritage Dictionary of the English Language], as well, in accordance with Merriam – Websters Collegiate dictionary, a pleasing appearance or effect: beauty [Merriam – Websters Collegiate Dictionary]. From the sight now of non art entities, the term which is associated directly with aesthetics is the visual sense, occupying almost half of the brain [Ware, 2008].

The first opinion about aesthetics is the salient expression of what is beautiful which shows the hidden qualities of a person via their physical appearance. This consensus indicates the argument of people to gain benefits or to avoid sanctions via their appearance [Tractinsky, 2013].

Visual aesthetics can be viewed from three perspectives, design perspective, psychological perspective and practical perspective.

- Design perspective: Through this perspective, aesthetic is derived through the integration of the artifact (virtual world) and the affected individual. Visual aesthetics is considered as a dimension that increases other aspects of the design and the overall user experience.

- Psychological Perspective: Visual aesthetic research in HCI is directly related to positive psychology. This positive influence regards emotional and cognitive processes, improving satisfaction and well being.
- Practical Perspective: There are two aspects of this perspective. The first describes aesthetics as the factor which differentiates the similar products and the second is about the interrelation between aesthetics and information technology.

As notice before, the common term that is associated with aesthetics is beauty; many people believe that if something aesthetically is accepted, it is therefore beautiful [Filonik & Baur, 2009]. Beauty, according to Tractinsky [2004], may be conceptualized as the quality of use of an object and virtuosity. However, in Renaissance, beauty was considered a result of nature [Tractinsky, 2004]. Based on this, Kant, suggested that "beauty is in the eye of the beholder" identifying two types of beauty, pure and conditional beauty [Udsen & Jørgensen, 2005, Mbipom & Harper, 2009]. Pure beauty means the true nature, a person from birth learns some standard things about beauty and as grows up all these standards are enriched or changed depending on life's experiences [Hassenzahl & Tractinsky 2006]. Conditional beauty is according to an ideal, what humans are expected to look like. Objects can be arranged into these two categories depending on the mental ideal picture of the person [Mbipom & Harper, 2009]. Beauty is an end (not a means) which satisfies a general human need [Norman, 2004].

Physical Appearance – Characteristics. The first thought when someone reads the word beauty is the appearance and more parturarly the external/physical appearance of a subject. Physical appearance is defined as self perspectives; including self perception and self attitudes. It involves thoughts, beliefs, feelings and behaviors. The subjective experience of physical appearance is often more psychosocially powerful from social appearance [Cash, 2004; Forrester, 2000]. Physical appearance of people influences the social interaction, specifically attractiveness, but they are not affected, only from beauty of others, but from aesthetics of nature, of architecture and of artifacts.

Focusing on the physical appearance, the realization of self –perception, beauty and social interaction, is worthy to refer about the avatars and how are perceived and depicted from their owners.

2.2   Avatars

The higher level of immersion in 3D worlds is facilitated through advanced users' interfaces which provide better performance and experience which can be enhanced with 3D avatars [Blascovich, 2002]. The word Avatar comes from Hindu avatara, the descent of god or incarnation. The incarnation is an internal representation or the ideal identity of the user [Martin, 2005]. An avatar is not only a label or a name of a participant; it is a digital depiction (graphical and textual) that is controlled by his creator and its role is represented by the responses to others' actions. Avatars are like user-controlled puppets [Bell, 2008].

Blascovich [2002] stated that avatars are a controllable 3D embodiment of the user [Blascovich, 2002]. The outfit and the role of an avatar in the virtual environment indicate the behavior and some characteristics of the user. The design of an avatar as mentioned above, demonstrates how a user realizes their self and their intentions [Schultze & Leahy, 2009].

In a similar manner Boberg, Piipo and Ollila [2008], argued that an avatar can reflect the role of a person in the virtual world but they suggested that if an avatar is realistic, but not enough, is a zombie [Boberg, Piipo & Ollila, 2008]. A similar argument comes from Danzico in 2010 who said that the more realistic an avatar looked the less confrontation, it is, so many users change their avatars in four ways: for events (seasons, holidays), affiliations (sports team, company), social causes (awareness, national causes, elections) and status (points, color, demonstrations of beauty or wealth) [Danzico, 2010].

Avatars mediate users in the virtual world, receiving all the sensory information from the environment [Castronova, 2003], associating with online role-play, and most users learn from their daily interaction with their avatar. There used the term avatar following technological features in 3D environment [Schultze, Leahy in 2009]:

- A body which has a form (human, animal, and machine) and features such as shape, skin, eyes, hair and are available to be customized.
- Existing objects like clothes, furniture, weapons and currency.
- Things that interact with avatar and vice versa.
- A personality profile which includes name, group affiliations and interest.
- An additional camera besides the virtual eyes of avatar.
- Voice, open and private chat, note card and textures.

Finally, Vasalou, Joinson, and Pitt [2007], suggest different aspects of avatars classifying them into the private facet of self and the public facet of self. Private facet-self originates from the interpersonal consciously communication, enhancing the revelation of the self. Public facet-self represents the knowledge of the experience and user perceives as a social entity. Usually these people (who publish their selves) are attracted and affected from the other's opinion [Vasalou, Joinson & Pitt, 2007; Vasalou & Joinson, 2002].

2.3   User Experience

The individual's judgment about aesthetics, beauty, or what is pleasing is based upon personal, social and cultural background (individual-experience). Experience arises from the integration of perception, action, motivation and cognition in an inseparable meaningful ensemble. Otherwise, the experience is like an episode emerging from the dialogue of a person with her or his world through action; a track of time via sights and sounds, feelings and thoughts, motives and actions. All these are interrelated, stored in memory labeled, relived and communicated to others [Hassenzahl, 2013]. Another definition states that experience is determined before, during and after interacting with a product, system, service or an object. Feelings and experience are set up individually representing each member of a group and are assessed during the interaction [Law, Roto, Hassenzahl, Vermeeren & Kort, 2009]. Essential experience is a totality, engaging self in a relationship with an object in a situation.

User experience consists of various meanings from traditional usability to beauty hedonic affecting technology use [Norman, 2004]. People control their outcome emotions, tending to portray positive experiences to others [Koskinen, et. Al., 2002], and this positive depiction of the experience is noticeable through technology, which is the tool that creates the experience. The positive emotions and meanings are caused to coverage the universal psychological need. The way of designing an experience noted by Buxton [2007], is based on how someone feels acting through a product, the moment it is used, the moment – by-moment experience. The notion of experience focuses on how something is used and the aesthetics of interaction [Buxton, 2007]. There are three types of experience:

- Experience: Happens under the conscious flow of self talk. Assessing goals relative to the people, products and environment that surrounds them at any time.
- An experience: Is characterized from interaction through products and emotions, has a beginning and an end, with integral formation in one's memory. Also, it inspires emotional and behavioral changes in the experiencer.
- Co-experience: Has to do with user experience in social context, which is created together or shared with others. People find certain experiences worth sharing and lift them up to share attention (interpretations by others). Reveals the individual experiences and the interpretations which, influenced by the physical or virtual presence of others.

The designing experience is applied on three levels: What, How and Why. What, is reflected by the products functionality, the things people can do via an interactive product. How is tied to the product and its context of use, presenting the action through an object. Therefore user experience depends on the designer who is responsible in providing a usable way with aesthetic pleasure. It makes the interaction with the product experiential through sensual aesthetic and novel arrangement. Why, clarifies the needs and emotions involved in an activity, the meaning, and the experience. The sequence of these levels starts firstly from the why to set the tone, after that is the product's functionality (What) and last the act of the functionality [Hassenzahl, 2013].

Hassenzahl and Tractinsky [2006] refer to two ways of handling emotions in user experience: one line of research emphasizes that emotions are derived as effects of product use. The second way focuses on the previous product use and evaluative judgments. Aesthetic experiences consist of the user's idiosyncrasies and taste to object's. Therefore is the common objective point between individuals and designers [Leder, Belke, Oeberst & Augustin, 2004]. Designing aesthetic is directly associated with affective responses and reflective thoughts [Hassenzahl, 2013].

2.4   Psychology

Emotions and mood are the two components that are directly connected with the avatar design and in extension with aesthetic judgment and experience. How aesthetically beautiful is something, is subjective and depends on the moment-feelings/emotions which are generated from the individual's experience. According to aesthetics psychology is the key point of how a person should perceive something and how an image will be positioned in the user's mind, generates an experience [Tranctinsky, 1997]. The essence of this psychology's aspect relies on feelings that arc considered to be the main factor on how a person should accept something positive or negative and consequently the proportional experience. It also examines the aesthetic behavior of humans through a given stimulus of interest [Raja, Bowman, Lucas & North, 2004)]

Hassenzahl and Tractinsky [2006] argued that psychological aesthetics originate from the human behavior. According to them, users who were exposed to a visual stimulus, the aesthetic pleasure was increased. When the participant was mentally overloaded and the complexity of stimulus increased, the aesthetic pleasure was reduced.

Jacobsen [2006] suggested an illustration of a framework for the psychology of aesthetics which consists of seven different aspects: diachronia, ipsichronia, mind, body, content, person and situation:

* Diachronia: The aesthetic choices depend on time.
* Ipsichronia: The cultural, and social life of a person affect the person's aesthetic opinions.
* Mind: Aesthetic judgments influenced from the mental model of the visual stimulus / emotions.
* Body: Brain activities could have an effect on evaluation processes.
* Content: The aesthetic assessment of a stimulus can be influenced by convenience of use.
* Person: The background of a person may play a role in aesthetic preference.
* Situation: The time, the place and in general the surrounding conditions are factors which influence the aesthetic choices.

The aforementioned aspects of the psychology of aesthetics are not mutually exclusive, but they should be considered as guides whilst determining aesthetics [Jacobsen, Schubotz, Hofel & Cramon, 2006].Therefore, emotions are generated in social contexts and determine how someone feels, expresses and modifies his emotions and the effects which are derived [Forlizzi & Battarbee, 2004].

2.5   Human – Computer Interaction

The common key of the three analyzed areas (aesthetics, user experience and psychology) is human – computer interaction. Traditionally, Human-Computer Interaction (HCI) and aesthetics are the areas that enhance the positive or negative feelings through user experience on technology. Researchers have explored aesthetics, providing definition from their standpoint [Karvonen, 2000].

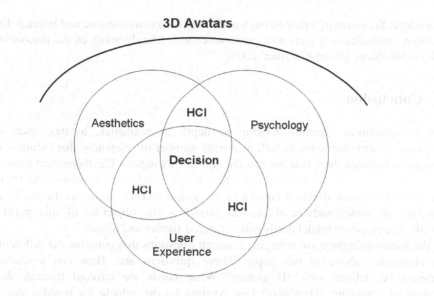

Fig. 1. The theoretical model of the designing process of *3D Avatars*

Nielsen also suggested that satisfaction is one of the five attributes of usability that is associated with aesthetics. He stated that satisfaction has to do with emotions, a common quality between aesthetics and user satisfaction. He argued that the preferences of people follow some general principles of styles, trends or fashions according to what they believe about the definition of beauty [Nielsen, 2000; Karvonen, 2000].

People in general love to experience something beautiful. Nature of beauty increases the attempt of HCI being more user-oriented. Hassenzahl and Tractinsky's study revealed that if users perceive an interface as "good looking", then it's easy for them to navigate and get what they want [Hassenzahl & Tractinsky, 2006].

Jordan [1998] argued that aesthetics is the main aspect during the interaction that enhances the pleasure of user experience [Jordan, 1998]. Following the same pathway, Hassenzhal and Tractinskys' [2005] work had a profound influence on the user experience and it's composed of the interaction between a user's mental state (expectations, needs and mood), attributes of the technology (complexity, functionality, and usability), and the context in which the technology is being used (social gathering, in the workplace, everyday use).

Human appearance is affected aesthetically according to Transctinsky and Hassenhal between human-human interactions. Thus, they demonstrated that people base their opinion about someone on someone's physical appearance; thereafter if someone is perceived as good looking then their attitude towards that person will be positive [Lavie & Tractinsky, 2004]; [Hassenzahl & Tractinsky, 2006].

Moreover human thinking according to aesthetics as essentials and functional. Anyone who is aesthetically essentialist is undisclosed and seen as a unit. The functional thinking person is like a receiver and reference point, so is ready to communicate [Raja, Bowman, Lucas & North, 2004].

Therefore, the intent of a user through aesthetics is to communicate and interact. In conclusion aesthetics is a section of communication, 'the dilemma of the discourse which is speechless' [Filonik & Baur, 2009].

3   Conclusion

There is substantial literature looking in depth at aesthetics, avatars, user – experience, 3D environments, as well as a wide number of references that mention a combination between them that informs the aim of this paper. The theoretical nature of the above areas, and the different research multidisciplinary perspectives that they entail, as well as their overlaps (shown in the graph below), points to the need of developing an understandable theoretical model – the objective of this paper. Naturally, the proposed model needs to be explored further and tested.

In the meanwhile,there are emerging research questions that combine the different areas elaborated above in this paper. These questions are: How can aesthetic experience be defined with 3D avatars? What needs are covered through the procedure of designing 3D avatars? Can Avatars be the vehicle for positive user-experience? It is hoped that the proposed model contributes to further elaboration on the subject.

References

1. Altheide, D.L.: Identity and the Definition of the Situation in a MassMediated Context. Symbolic Interaction 23(1), 1–27 (2000)
2. American Heritage Dictionary of the English Language
3. Bell, M.W.: Virtual Worlds Research: Past, Present & Future (July 2008)
4. Blascovich, J.: Social influence within immersive virtual environments. In: The Social Life of Avatars, pp. 127–145 (2002)
5. Boberg, M., Piippo, P., Ollila, E.: Designing avatars. In: Proceedings of the 3rd International Conference on Digital Interactive Media in Entertainment and Arts, pp. 232–239. ACM (September 2008)
6. Buxton, B.: Sketching User Experiences: getting the design rights and right design. Bedford, Massachusetts (2007)
7. Cash, T.F.: Body image: Past, present, and future. Body Image 1(1) (2004)
8. Castronova, E.: Theory of the Avatar (2003)
9. Cawthon, N., Moere, A.V.: A conceptual model for evaluating aesthetic effect within the user experience of information visualization. In: Tenth International Conference on Information Visualization, IV 2006, pp. 374–382. IEEE (2006)
10. Danzico, L.: Making face: practices and interpretations of avatars in everyday media. Interactions 17(3), 11–14 (2010)
11. Ducheneaut, N., Wen, M.H., Yee, N., Wadley, G.: Body and mind: a study of avatar personalization in three virtual worlds. In: Proceedings of the 27th International Conference on Human Factors in Computing Systems, pp. 1151–1160. ACM (2009)
12. Filonik, D., Baur, D.: Measuring aesthetics for information visualization. In: 2009 13th International Conference on Information Visualisation, pp. 579–584. IEEE (2009)

13. Forlizzi, J., Battarbee, K.: Understanding experience in interactive systems. In: Proceedings of the 5th Conference on Designing Interactive Systems: Processes, Practices, Methods, and Techniques, pp. 261–268. ACM (2004)
14. Forrester, M.: Psychology of the Image. Routledge (2000)
15. Fox, K.R.: The physical self: From motivation to well-being. Human Kinetics (1997)
16. Hassenzahl, M.: User Experience and Experience Design. In: Soegaard, M., Dam, R.F. (eds.) The Encyclopedia of Human-Computer Interaction, 2nd edn., The Interaction Design Foundation, Aarhus (2013), http://www.interactiondesign.org/encyclopedia/user_experience_and_experience_design.html
17. Hassenzahl, M., Tractinsky, N.: User experience-a research agenda. Behaviour & Information Technology 25(2), 91–97 (2006)
18. Hjelle, L., Ziegler, D.: The phenomenological perspective in personality theory: Carl Rogers, ch. 11, New York (1976)
19. Hoffmann, R., Krauss, K.: A critical evaluation of literature on visual aesthetics for the web. In: Proceedings of the 2004 Annual Research Conference of the South African Institute of Computer Scientists and Information Technologists on IT Research in Developing Countries, pp. 205–209, South African Institute for Computer Scientists and Information Technologists (2004)
20. Huxley, A., Bradshaw, D.: The art of seeing. Harper (1942)
21. Huxley: The Art of seeing. In: Chatto & Windus, London, pp. 1–79 (1974)
22. Jacob Nielsen, D.W.: Usability. The Practice of Simplicity (2000)
23. Jacobsen, T., Schubotz, R.I., Höfel, L., Cramon, D.Y.V.: Brain correlates of aesthetic judgment of beauty. Neuroimage 29(1), 276–285 (2006)
24. Jordan, P.W.: Human factors for pleasure in product use. Applied Ergonomics 29(1), 25–33 (1998)
25. Karvonen, K.: The beauty of simplicity. In: Proceedings on the 2000 Conference on Universal Usability, pp. 85–90. ACM (2000)
26. Koskinen, I., Kurvinen, E., Lehtonen, T.K., Kaski, J., Keinänen, N., Absetz, K.: Mobile image. Edita, IT Press (2002)
27. Law, E.L.C., Roto, V., Hassenzahl, M., Vermeeren, A.P., Kort, J.: Understanding, scoping and defining user experience: a survey approach. In: Proceedings of the 27th International Conference on Human Factors in Computing Systems, pp. 719–728. ACM (2009)
28. Leder, H., Belke, B., Oeberst, A., Augustin, D.: A model of aesthetic appreciation and aesthetic judgments. British Journal of Psychology 95(4), 489–508 (2004)
29. Markus, H., Nurius, P.: Possible selves. American Psychologist 41(9), 954–969 (1986)
30. Martin, J.: Virtually visual: the effects of visual technologies on online identification. In: Anais do DiGRA 2005 Conference: University of British Columbia (2005)
31. Mbipom, G., Harper, S.: Visual Aesthetics and Accessibility. HCW—EIVAA Technical Report 2, 1–48 (2009)
32. Mc Dough, J.P.: Designer Selves: Construction of Technologically Mediated Identity within Graphical Multi user Environments. University of California (1999)
33. Norman, D.A.: Introduction to this special section on beauty, goodness, and usability. Human–Computer Interaction 19(4), 311–318 (2004), Merriam – Websters Collegiate dictionary
34. Postrel, V.: The substance of style: How the rise of aesthetic value is remaking commerce, and consciousness. Harper Perennial (2004)
35. Raja, R., Bowman, A., Lucas, J., North, C.: Exploring the Benefits of Immersion in Abstract Information Visualization, Department of Computer Science, pp. 1–7 (2004)
36. Santayana, G.: What is Aesthetics? The Philosophical Review, 13(3), 320–327 (1904)

37. Schultze, U., Leahy, M.M.: The avatar-self relationship: Enacting presence in second life. In: Internat. Conf. Inform. Systems, Association of Information Systems, Phoenix, AZ (2009)
38. Stone, G.P.: Appearance and the self: A slightly revised version. In: Life as Theater: A Dramaturgical Sourcebook, pp. 141–162 (1990)
39. Theuma: Evaluating the Aesthetics of Websites, Using materials analysis and visual design heuristics. University College London, pp.1–43 (2007)
40. Tractinsky, N.: Toward the study of aesthetics in information technology. In: 25th Annual International Conference on Information Systems, Washington, DC, pp. 771–780 (2004)
41. Tractinsky, N.: Visual Aesthetics. In: Soegaard, M., Dam, R.F. (eds.) The Encyclopedia of Human-Computer Interaction, 2nd edn. The Interaction Design Foundation, Aarhus (2013), http://www.interaction-design.org/encyclopedia/visual_aesthetics.html
42. Tractinsky, N.: Aesthetics and apparent usability: empirically assessing cultural and methodological issues. In: Proceedings of the SIGCHI Conference on Human Factors in Computing Systems, pp. 115–122. ACM (1997)
43. Tractinsky, N., Hassenzahl, M.: Arguing for aesthetics in human-computer interaction. I-com 4(3/2005), 66–68 (2005)
44. Udsen, L.E., Jørgensen, A.H.: The aesthetic turn: unravelling recent aesthetic approaches to human-computer interaction. Digital Creativity 16(04), 205–216 (2005)
45. Vasalou, A., Joinson, A.N., Pitt, J.: Constructing my online self: avatars that increase self-focused attention. In: Proceedings of the SIGCHI Conference on Human Factors in Computing Systems, pp. 445–448. ACM (2007)
46. Vasalou, A., Joinson, A.N.: Me, myself and I: The role of interactional context on self-presentation through avatars. Computers in Human Behavior 25(2), 510–520 (2009); Taylor, T.L.: Living digitally: Embodiment in virtual worlds. In: The Social Life of Avatars: Presence and Interaction in Shared Virtual Environments, pp. 40–62 (2002)
47. Wallace, P., Maryott, J.: The impact of avatar self-representation on collaboration in virtual worlds. Innovate: Journal of Online Education 5(5) (2009)
48. Ware, L.: Worlds remade: inclusion through engagement with disability art. International Journal of Inclusive Education 12(5-6), 563–583 (2008)

Augmentation and the Visual Mind

Hendrik Wahl

American University in Dubai, UAE
hendrik@optio-n.com

Abstract. This paper discusses the User Interfaces of digital technology as locations where two different fractions of human thinking and being meet each other. A survey on either side of the boundary between logical and bodily domain reveals interdependencies, contradictions, ideological positions and approaches towards a creative process of user interaction. Based on considerations about creation, relevance and appreciation of visual expression regarding to digital graphics, User Interface and Interaction Design a perspective will proposed; focusing the unpredictability of human creativity as the Key-Element in Interaction.

Keywords: augmentation, democratization of digital technology, digital graphics, Logical-bodily-Boundary, sensomotoric interaction, sublime dispatching, Multimodal-Interface, visual demands.

1   Preface

Computers are only possible due to the existence of formal logic. Everything what can be made with computers is result of formal logic. Therefore interfaces between computer and human being are imperative to consider as formal logic.

Starting from this rigid position, this paper will describe a journey along the skin, where two fundamentally different fractions of thinking and being meet each other. On one side we will have a look at the clear and incorruptible manners of truth, deducted by the use of formal logic. Here everything is either 100% precise or does not exist. Fuzziness is not allowed and therefore we become aware of an extreme powerful and sophisticated cognitive tool. Opposite of this, we can find things in disarray. We face fuzziness, excitation, passion and vehemence, here we face one of the most unpredictable subjects in this world, the human being. And this human being is using digital technology - not to answer the question about the ultimate truth [1] or to construct valid statements based on any given propositions, but to listen to music, to send tweets around the globe, to create graphics consisting of shades from gray or to do any kind bizarre non logic things.

In this paper we want to adopt various positions on either side of the Logical-Bodily-Boundary, to conduct a dialogue in between those two concepts.

M. Kurosu (Ed.): Human-Computer Interaction, Part I, HCII 2014, LNCS 8510, pp. 145–156, 2014.
© Springer International Publishing Switzerland 2014

2   The Context Becomes Fuzzy

To consider the use of digital technology as an iconic activity in contemporary societies, not only in developed countries but worldwide, is nowadays not breaking news. Within a timespan of a few years [2] digital technology has become subject to unprecedented democratization. All of us are well familiar with digital user interfaces. The playful interaction, wiping on a surface of a smart phone, a tablet or the touchscreen of an ATM gives the user, the Inter-Agent, a feeling of sovereignty, of control, of mastership upon the tasks, arising from his/her social network activities, ubiquitous online communication, mobile businesses and so on. Facing this playful confidence and considering the human interaction with digital technology not too long ago, renders typing a Command-Line similar to cave painting. Considering this dramatic change urges a closer look to the manners and regions where interaction takes place.

On one hand, the logic inside the machine needs an unambiguous diction, which the person in front is, of course unable to deliver by ordinary language. One of the first attempts to deal with this has been introducing artificial languages, which were to be learned by humans in order to formulate proper tasks to be understood by the machine. Despite of their precious work in the heart of the machine, the artificial languages got more and more dispelled from the surface by manifestations from the pictorial domain. The One-dimensional function of the text, which ruled the early terminals undisputedly and which could order a window to open now was banished in to a window, which quite seldom shows up on most computers today. The Two-dimensional visual representation of the desktop metaphor, proved its superiority in formulation of instructions accessible from the inner core with ease. Visual concepts such as proximity, contrast, color, balance, resemblance, empty space, consistency and typography took over. Considering the demand of discrete input by digital technology, it is remarkable that particularly visual concepts, which are anything but logical, proved to be an alternative to a text in a command line. None of the concepts mentioned above can be derived from logic. In any case, the opinion of a human being is required to tell what resembles what [3] or when a visual balance of objects in an Image-Space is achieved or where empty space contributes to the overall appearance of a graphic. These functions cannot be done in by any kind of formal logical or mathematical equation.

A view from the "inner side" of the machine can give us the idea of insufficiencies of the human Inter-Agent. Therefore User Interfaces can be considered as a layer enveloping the core, as operating to guide the users perception, to limit his options, to stagger his requests and to schedule his interaction - in short, to "optimize" ordinary human behavior in to binary relevant expressions. Form this point of view, the core; the logical domain obtains primacy over human weaknesses. To justify this standpoint we may recall, that the interface with all its procedures and visual appearances to the last pixel in an Anti-aliased line, is 100% determined by binary logic.

On the other hand, it becomes clear that Graphic User Interfaces relive the user form dramatic "logical overload", which is unconditionally necessary to keep the machine operating, but which is absolutely meaningless from the user´s point of view.

For him e.g. the position and extent of a window on his screen in numbers is absolutely not relevant. To change size and position he also does not need to know any value. He just clicks, moves and releases the mouse button. If he is not just a beginner in using computer, he will probably not even notice this interaction. Moreover, he will get the impression of stickiness in case that GPU delivers not enough performance to draw smoothly and with steady movement. This unconscious interaction and the impressions, moods and feelings during the interaction, are making an important point in deliberations about augmentation related to User Interaction Design. If we use a hammer, if we drive a car in rush hour, if we create a drawing on paper or on a screen, the fact and process of holding, of moving, of using the tool is usually not part of our perception and consciousness - again, if we are not just beginners in using the specific interface. In the case that a person is trained in driving a car or creating digital graphics or using a smartphone, the "what" question quite likely can be answered from a standpoint within the logical domain - the "how" question in contrast obviously not. But if we are focusing on the process of interaction between the digital and the humanoid world and not on statistical surveys about clicks on a certain button within a defined target population, the "what" question tends to become meaningless. The "how" question on the other hand, does not need to be answered in words or numbers. Usually the "how to do" question gets best answered directly by the interaction. If a person is using a hammer, he is not required to calculate mass and force and acceleration to bang in a nail, which answers with some luck the "what" question. But if this person is a skilled mechanic, he gets not only the task done, but due to his experiences in working with metal, he feels the deformation of the material, he gets an intuitive awareness when rusted bolting start to loosen under the applied pressure, he gets an instant Non-Formal information about the process he is doing while he is doing it. This gives him the ability to achieve probably more exiting results in metalwork than just hammering a nail. If this person is an illustrator or a Graphic-Designer he or she will have similar experiences. People who are working professionals in this sector know about their tools intuitively very well. They are able to feel the rigidness of graphite and the friction of certain papers; they know how to shade a gradient to make the spectator believe in Three-dimensionality. They are usually very Well-Trained in perception and embodied movement, creating astonishingly visual expressions using the pictorial concepts mentioned above. But asked how to do this, they will be unable to formulate anything that is even close to a formal description or an equation. One reason is, that during the creative process the person, the Inter-Agent, is fully engaged, is spectator and creator in one All he/she wants is a continuous flow, a non interrupted process, a bilateral iteration between the visible and the imagined, whereby the imagined should not consider to be something predefined. If the human body and brain would work perfectly logically, nothing of this would be possible. We would be unable to create, unable to learn or to perceive, we would be, in the best, case a sort of logical zombies. Back again to the place where the interaction takes place and seen from the user point of view, we get aware of major changes, which have occurred in conjunction with the appearance and the vanishing of mouse on our desktops. In reference to the replacement of the Command-Line by a Tow-dimensional face, the direct finger access indicates a transition from the point to the line. Due to enhanced graphic performance Touch-Sensitive Interfaces providing a more direct response and if the interaction is fluent, the act of interacting disappears form the awareness and gives space to processes which are closer to the sub consciousness and more oriented to answer "how" questions. This interaction is not formal, not verbal, not noticeable and therefore inaccessible to anything from the logical domain. Nevertheless, due to the human Inter-Agent, a synthesis of these both concepts, leads to something new in computer generated output, but also in a metaphorical sense to a significant expression, with is comparable to the introduction of the typewriter, with all its connotations.

Up to here we have been conducting a historical analysis. Before we are going to make an attempt to extrapolate, an initial summary should be done. This characterizes the Human Computer Interface to be a boundary and a bridge in same time. To formulate reasonable statements, it is necessary to adopt a distinct point of view. Either from the perspective of the formal logic, where any solution is correct as long the process leading to is formally right, regardless of the input - or, from a Common Sense perspective, where the processes inside, behind the graphical surface, are not relevant at all. A third perspective seems to be not possible, which suggests understanding the interface between the two concepts as a skin with Zero-Dimension in thickness. Characterizing the two concepts meeting here, a distinction between the "what" and the "how" question might be helpful. The "what" question is much more likely to produce answers, suiting the digital domain. It can easily be answered by single expression (he is using a hammer). By a small tweak this can be transformed in the "if" expression (if he is using a hammer, this sentence is true) and this is already digital logic because of tertium non datur, no third answer is permitted. To get logic to work in a computer, millions of these expressions need to get executed, some with other conjunctions (else, or, nor…) but always producing valid values. For a digital interpreter this is the way it works and it is the only way it works. If the tasks to process get more complex, the only answer can be to increase the number of logical operations in shorter time spans to keep the output fluent. This characterizes the digital technologies as mechanical and extensive.

If we are talking with human interpreters about e.g. Digital User Interfaces, the "what" question and the following "if" expression are less important because normally easy to answer by evaluation of perceivable situations (yes, he is using a hammer). But answers on this level are not able to give us the impression focusing the essence of the actual situation. If we want to get satisfactory answers the "how" question provides a much boarder access. The answers to this question are infinite in numbers and not limited to be binary. From a logical point of view, this is a nightmare, but strange enough not for an ordinary human being. For us this means freedom [4], means to be able to think totally new, to be creative in any way. Moreover, the answer we are able to give on the "how" questions do not need to be formal nor necessarily manifest. A dance, a gesture or look can be a valid answer to "how" questions. This ability to give sufficient but not necessarily true answers marks the advantage of human beings in relation to any kind of digital technology. As already mentioned above, a human Inter-Agent who is engaged with a task on a digital interface loses consciousness, not in a way as LSD may provide, but about the fact using a device and interacting via an interface. Under this aspect the process of learning plays an important role. As mentioned above the skill level of the Inter-Agent can be seen as a decisive parameter. People who are about to learn something practical, e.g. to use a certain interface, need more time to fulfill a task then a Well-Trained professional. This is obvious - but why? What its actual difference? Sure, on the first level the knowledge about specific facts, but why do people fail e.g. the practical test in a driven school despite their success in the written examination? No question, because of their insufficient experience: in distributing attention while in crowded Traffic-Situations, in handling the pedals and gear stick, in staying cool also in tense situations. Sure, a beginner has no idea where to put the attention first. He has no idea how to intact fluently. Therefore practical training exists, not only in driving schools, but also in drawing classes, computer courses and everywhere wherever pure unextended knowledge is not enough to master the task. What becomes clear from these reflections, at first looks extreme trivial. We need to practice to make perfect difficult tasks. But looking further there is something more. Driving a car, using certain software, creating a drawing from a given set, is for people who do this frequently anything but difficult - also their appreciation about the difficulty of the task changes. The important thing here is, they are able to forget and they are able to do the specific task without thinking, without cognitive processing, without any logic. They shift the gears without being aware of it, they scroll through the interfaces as if blind, they create outstanding graphics by recognizing sublime differences in visual perception, sensomotoric interaction [5] and respond to non verbal expressible visual demands. The reason why a human being, despite of their insufficiencies in formal diction, is still standing out of any computer is because we are able to forget things which become autonomous from thinking due to practical training. We don't need to think about where the clutch is, how to shade a sphere or to draw a cube in convincing perspective, or which button does what - after being trained we are free while the computer needs to calculate everything always anew, with the same perfect result. Knowing this, it becomes time to turn our attention to the future of User Interface Design and to try an extrapolation. In means of technology, this appears not to be very difficult. There is no reason to believe in a change with regard to the constant dematerialization. The extent of the devices will further shrink as has happened in the past, from the levers of the Hollerith to direct finger access of the mobile phone. But this is only half of the story. It is quite likely that the functionality of mobile devices will also decrease. Due to faster networks, resources intensive tasks might be outsourced from the personal piece of technology to some backbone technology, which is cloudy and therefore less in public focus. Due to the fact that Logic-Based technology is an extensive enterprise this sector still expands in extent and performance, bringing along also social implications about the question of further democratization.

From an Interface Design related position, predictions are more difficult to make. Reviewing the past reveals a continuous reduction of distinct haptic interactions. From typing a clear and unambiguous expression, to the mouse click, to a fuzzy gesture at a track pad or a glass covered Graphic User Interface, the interaction gets faster and less precise. To predict something in this diction we may consider that the development has been less stringent then in the technical sector. So e.g. the attempts in creating spatial distributed User Interfaces can comprehend to be less convincing. Being optimistic, the adoption of a more human like behavior, of a design which takes the human being more seriously, which can solve the learning problem mentioned above can point in the right direction. Thinking of technology and design together and considering the past as a more or less straight development, a more Long-Term prediction can be the disappearance of hardware and also of Two-dimensional User Interfaces through a process called augmentation. Adopting a the position of a strong believer in digital technology and a bright digital future, a sentence such as: "Due to augmentation, using a Multimodal-Interface, Two-dimensional visualization of objects become obsolete." can be an program for User Interaction Design - to follow or better to think about. The latter will be done in the next section.

3   Picture 2D

Considering the claim form above, we may have a closer look at the concept called picture. There are lots of definitions, for what a picture is. A representation of something absent, a conglomerate consisting of a symbols pointing to certain meanings, a source of imaginative force making the spectator speechless, a non verbal expression, a piece of wood or just an ephemeral Two-dimensional manifestation on a screen. In terms of User Interface Design, the Two-dimensionality seems to be an important characteristic, not at least because of the attempts and the less convincing outcomes in creating Three-dimensional, spatial extended User Interfaces. Considering the Two-dimensionality as prominent feature of the picture, the visualization, the result of what Paul Klee called making visible, several approaches can be done to analyze this concept. From a syntactic point of view, the denial of the picture's Z dimension appears to be helpful in reducing complexity, towards something more essential. A Two-dimensional picture seems to be more handy in reality, but also in mind. Ignoring the wood, the paper, the layered paint does not really limit our perception or border our concepts or compromise the use of the term picture. Moreover, the omnipotence of the featureless Media-Interfaces even enhance the impression of the picture as something Material-less, which needs to be in Two-dimensions just to be perceivable. A Two-dimensional thing is more easily framed and stored in folders as a hardcopy and at the desktop metaphor. From a semantic perspective, the Two-dimensionally of a picture also has something charming too. So, the position and the extent of something that is considered to be a sign, of something seen to be the origin for a perceived meaning, can be easily described in discrete values. The distinction between picture, frame and non picture in Two-dimensionally can easily be done, just by a ruler and the idea of the picture as an insubstantial Image-Program, consisting of meaningless elements, combined in a certain manner, able to express anything, also does not depend on the third or any higher dimension. A confrontation with the Two-dimensional picture seems to be also more convenient, because there is already a flat front. Also, from a pragmatic position a Two-dimensional picture is most attractive in handling, hanging it on a flat wall (gallery), putting it in front of the audience (cinema), setting up a clear spatial situation (signage). Not at least, in means of user interaction, Two-dimensionally is an indispensable prerequisite for any kind of wipe.

Actually, the Two-dimensional picture/Picture-Program is a nice, smooth concept, everything is in a single layer, clear to distinguish, close to something essential … and most obsolete, if we talk about augmentation. The reason for this is: regarding to interaction, the pictures Two-dimensionality is in the same way relevant, as the well known (never seen) back of rice somewhere in China. Seeing a picture as a picture is something totally different from seeing (interacting with) Leonardo´s Mona Lisa, Klee´s Highway and Byways, a motion picture, or a Graphic User Interface. Slicing a picture into discrete portions of information, as e.g. size, format, color, semiotic references and so on, might contribute to the amount of formal knowledge in this world, but will also dissolve the picture itself. Who would consider a black painted 79 by 79 cm square of canvas as something meaningful: if it would not be known as the "Black Square" by Kazimir Malevich? To understand something about a picture - interaction matters. The manner of interaction, the duration, the spatial relations, the knowledge base, and also the spectator's mood making the picture become reality and relevant. This cannot take place in a Two-dimensional world. Considering the Human-Picture interaction shows, there is not difference from ordinary Human-World interaction. It is dynamic, highly movement and body related and quite less a matter of pure logic. Pictures are able to generate pleasure, fear, excitement, sadness, …but only during the interaction. Pictures are neither Space-Wise nor Time-Wise stable things. A static view focusing on a picture would fail to see anything. Only a moving eye is able to recognize, and movement is already defined to be function of space and time. Pictures are unable to exist independent from the human mind. Considering this, a picture can be understood as something between the reality of things and the reality of mind as an in between reality, also known as Interface.

4   Augmentation

After interrogating the term "picture" now augmentation comes into focus. If the context is given by the framework of User Interaction Design, Augmented Reality and all the connotations coming from this side - augmentation seems to be an idea, aiming to render itself unperceivable. Considering the story of Human Interface Design, and extrapolating the idea of a tendency in dematerialization and obliteration of discrete boundaries, a vector the Command-Line, over to the distinguished double click on a well framed icon, to the whip on an iPad - towards something multimodal, like an iPlug on one's head's backside or to 802.11.ac iFi can be drawn. This process can be understood as an ongoing augmentation, in which the interface itself, together with its Two-dimensional visualization becomes obsolete. Thinking through "augmentation" to the very end, not only the interface will disappear in Multi-modality. In a totally augmented world, which is the actual promise of this term, everything is not on your fingertips anymore, but on your synapses´endings. There would be no visual overlay, showing a building's name or the best deal within a radius of 150 m. We would know the building's name (if we want to or not), we would have already submitted our credit card number (regardless of the deal) and we would be unable to know what is caused by augmentation and what is the Un-augmented reality. Moreover, we would not be able to know about the Un-augmented world - and because of the in distinguishability, augmentation also would not exist.

5   Sublime Dispatching

Just before we get lost in an ideology of augmentation - we may consider Roland Barthes idea of sublime dispatching [6] in front of this backdrop. Doing this unbiased and with conviction that human being and augmentation are not alternatives, it becomes clear that an augmented world does not need necessarily to be weird, dark and controlled by an evil mastermind. Because: if someone is the subject of sublime dispatching, perception must be possible. And if perception exists, total augmentation is impossible. Reviewing the idea of sublime dispatching critically reveals it is nothing that comes from above by superior authority as the reading of "The Rhetoric of the Image" might suggest. Despite this, sublime dispatching is an essential factor not only in visual but also other forms of communication. It is an inevitable and deeply interwoven part of our (in the context discussed here) visual perception. It is actually a decisive part of our methods in making and understanding the visible. Everything we perceive and create pictorially appeals sublimely to pre- and sub consciousness [7]. Considering time base media at first gives us an approach to deeper insights. If we are watching a movie we are deceived in many ways. First we are convinced of seeing motion, literally a motion picture. Despite this we should know and certainly outside of the cinema we actually know, that a movie consists of 24 single frames projected within a second. Back in the cinema hall when the film starts we forget this fact immediately. We develop passion, empathy, anger upon light projections, upon seen personalities and characters we feel familiar with, again outside the cinema we know these are actors shielded by bodyguards or digital created illusions. We get scared and frighten if Godzilla does weird things or if someone is posing with a kitchen knife behind a shower curtain, moreover, also upon just imaginary imaginations such as the Blair Witch - and this in not just an ephemeral or a subsidiary deception of the mind. This leads to actual physical reaction while the mind is in a total denial of the real world, of anything outside the current imagination. We know, when creating a move several techniques and technologies (more and more digital) are in use. We know a movie consist of acts, scenes, takes and shots. We know about shooting angles and picture composition and some of us know how to use this to create suspense, to evoke and to satisfy visual demands, to put the audience under charm, to make them forget the real world - to dispatch their attention and to a certain degree their physical reaction in a sublime manner. Yes, cinema is not the ordinary life and under circumstances, which a more harsh then sitting in a soft cinema chair, the tendency of losing consciousness and become sublime dispatched seems to be less likely. But if we use another example this conviction may chance. To be in a foreign airport, changing planes, maybe under time pressure is a situation requiring one´s full attention. There is not much room for failure but there is still sublime dispatching. Modern airports are designed to handle huge amounts of traffic. Vast numbers of unpredictable, sometimes tired or easy to distract people, need to find their way from the arrival gate to the departure, immigration, transfer, baggage claim and so on, whereby they are unlikely to speak the same language. The way to organize this in an effective way is to establish a system, which guides and supports the passenger´s movement unconsciously in the right direction. By organizing a consistent spatial situation, providing "to go" perspectives, by redundancy and placing of signage on positions where it gets perceived at first glance an information setup gets create. This leads the human Inter-Agent on a sublime level of attention to the right location. Whoever has been in a similar situation, tired from a delayed transcontinental flight, surrounded by a gabbling crowd, supposed to proceed immediately to gate number 211, threatened for unloading his baggage, knows that he or she is hardly able to find the way by formal deliberations and is happy for any sublime dispatching, which helps on an unconscious level. There are quite likely much more examples to find, rendering vast areas of the interaction humans are engaged with as determined by unconscious, sublime processes. On one hand this limits the chances to become overwhelmed by augmentation staged by some interest groups and aiming to change ones behavior in a certain direction. Despite of the capabilities of Big-Data-Domain the human perception, the human mind, the human consciousness appears still complex enough to prevent a total coverage of sublime dispatching or remote control by a subordinated mastermind. A brief look in the history ideological interference shows that state of the art technology was always used to distribute a particular ideology, to survey its impact, to reward or to sanction the related behavior of target populations - and that always enough people could stay independent from these attempts, being the seed of the changes to come. Another brief look in my kitchen reveals Roland Barth´s to pessimistic perspective; there is no indication that Panziani could convince me to fill up my shelves with their products - neither on intellectual nor on a sublime level.

On the other hand, despite of the dark hunch and convinced to be independent enough in mind and thinking to conduct a widely self-determined life, the idea of sublime dispatching can mark an interesting position in understanding and creating User Interaction Design.

6   How to (Inter)act

From a digital artist´s point of view, interaction consists at first, in a similar way as for the person at the airport and in the cinema, of sublime and subconscious procedures and only to a minor part of logical rationality. The computer does not exist while generating a graphic, an animation, but also while doing logical tasks as writing an expression. Everything unifies in a continuing process, which is only describable in retrospect. The creative work is characterized by immense inner tensions, not at fist because of external parameters, but because of an intense interaction between the, let's say imagination (despite of this is less than the have of what is actual meant) and the perceived changes on or in the medium where the manifestation takes place. In this process nothing is sure, the idea, the intention, the actual situation in the mind is anything else than stable. It is under constant influences by the topic (if we talk about a work in an given contest), by the perception of the traces arising from the movement of one´s own hand, the underlying mood and a lot more much more fuzzy parameters. This situation has much more to do with the idea of iteration, then with the myth of an artist, who gets an inspiration from divine in fusion or from another unverifiable source and consequently starts to form this on a canvas, a video or in an installation to make it perceivable. In reality, the creation of anything is already something new. But this is not a translation of a more or less sophisticated concept, but a struggle on relations, curves, composition and colors to reach a level of inner satisfaction upon one´s own visual demands. If we are trying to organize this Visual Picture Interaction Process we can use four terms interwoven with each other: Perceptive analysis (1), perceptive synthesis (2), productive synthesis (3), productive analysis (4). Since this process is considered to be circular, it actually does not matter where to begin, but in terms of a narrative, the perceptive analysis (1) should be first. In this part the human being perceives the overall situation guided by the intension to achieve a overview of the spatial situation, the properties of the material, the subject if there one in case of nature study. This information will next be correlated to the experiences, the "traditions" this particular person has developed in his everyday life and due to the successful solving of visual problems. This can considered to be a perceptive synthesis (2). The result of this is not, or very, very seldom, a distinct pictorial idea but a mental state, which establishes the tension in between the imagination and the perceived actual situation on or in the medium. This is the basic force driving the artist forward, making him use his hands to create, to synthesize something within the image space in front of him. This is the productive synthesis (3). During this process the action on the medium - the canvas, the paper, the Computer-Screen - is under constant surveillance by the creator. Not only by visual evaluation, but also through a feedback of the whole body, the muscle tension in the arm, the nerves in the fingertips, the balance of standing... This is what is meant by productive analysis (4). Now some one may think: if a sufficient state formalization of the Sub-Processes can be achieved, cycling the whole thing on sufficient computing power might be the way to teach a robot drawing. Apart from the question, why robots should be able to produce drawings - there are some more difficulties. The formalization of the Sub-processes is already a highly ambitious enterprise, but thing are getting worse if we realize that this is not a strict circular process, which if repeated in sufficient numbers delivers a more and more accurate outcome. The perception of a professional in pictorial expression is so sensitive, that a tiny, hardly notable change in terms of visibility, vision and constitution, in the perception and thinking can cause major changes in the whole project. This is less serious than it sounds at first, because visual questions have always more than one, commonly infinite solutions, and in opposition to statistics and the Gaussian Normal Distribution, the less common, the most unconventional solution gets usually admired and considered to be extraordinary creative.

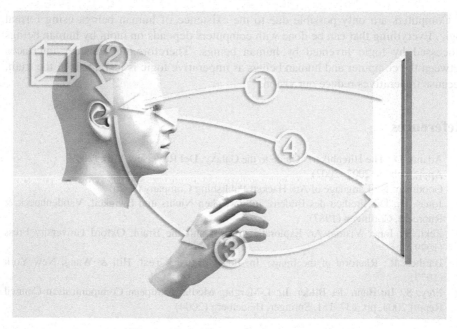

Fig. 1. Visual Picture Interaction Process

7   Conclusion

Everyone expecting to get Bite-sized findings, ready-made procedures or recipes how to augment the visual mind will either be disappointed or have already given up. But, considering the last sentence of the section above, gives less reason to believe in existence of this. Therefore it was neither the intention nor the purpose of this essay to deliver a certain amount of formal knowledge or to execute logical arrays, processing given input into formalized output. Instead of this, the attempt has been made to proceed in a way, which resembles an interaction with the visual. There is no start, no In-between, no loop caused by false or idle and no final finding. But there are infinite possible answers, there are hopefully Access-Points to think further and there is confidence. Confidence that interaction is always fuzzy, that interaction needs be fuzzy to be meaningful, because interaction is our only way to gain input, which may become subject of the logical thinking. Only due to interaction distinct outside the box, we can sustain our critical thinking. Only this helps to understand how reasoning works, that reason is just a part of every human's abilities, how reason can become ideology and how ideologies substitute each other. Interaction matters only while doing, then formal knowledge can be transformed into experience, can be forgotten and can become embodied. Then the Inter-Agent can get relived form formal task and becomes able to pay attention to answers given by feeling, moods and sensation to "how" questions. Interaction cannot be design by an "intelligent designer", by a Super-ordinated authority claiming to be an endless growing function. Only human beings are able to interact meaning fully - because, and not despite of, formal logic.

Computers are only possible due to the existence of human beings using formal logic. Everything that can be done with computers depends on input by human beings processed by logic invented by human beings. Therefore, to consider interfaces between the computer and human beings as imperative logic is just a half of the truth, because imperatives reduce our vision.

References

1. Adams, D.: The Hitchhiker's Guide to the Galaxy. Del Rey, New York (2009)
2. Apple I phone 2007 (2007)
3. Goodman, N.: Language of Art. Hackett Publishing Company (1976)
4. Jonas, H.: Die Freiheit des Bildens. In: Zwischen Nichts und Ewigkeit, Vandenhoeck & Ruprecht, Göttingen (1987)
5. Zeki, S.: Inner Vision: An Exploration of Art and the Brain. Oxford University Press (1999)
6. Barthes, R.: Rhetoric of the Image. In: Image- Music- Text. Hill & Wang, New York (1977)
7. Frey, S.: Im Bann der Bilder. In: E-Merging Media, European Communication Council Report 2004, pp. 137–151. Springer, Heidelberg (2004)

Scripting Interactive Art Installations in Public Spaces

Yu Zhang, Joep Frens, Mathias Funk, Jun Hu, and Matthias Rauterberg

Department of Industrial Design, Eindhoven University of Technology
Eindhoven, The Netherlands
{yu.zhang,j.w.frens,m.funk,j.hu,g.w.m.rauterberg}@tue.nl

Abstract. Traditional dynamic arts have much to offer and it is time to explore how the elements and techniques from stage performances could contribute to interaction design. We try to apply performance techniques and elements from dynamic art forms in the design process of interactive art installations for public spaces. Currently we try not to identify new technologies; instead we investigate how the installation would blossom when approached from a performance art perspective that essentially includes the users as well as a broader physical or social context. This paper introduces the role and function of script in the field of interactive art installation in public spaces. Script inspired from traditional dynamic art forms opens up new design opportunities. This paper discusses these opportunities, followed by an example how this approach can be applied in the design of a public art installation.

Keywords: Interactive Art Installations, Public Spaces, Script, Traditional Dynamic Art Forms.

1   Introduction

There are a variety of different forms of dynamic performance events, including theatre, and opera. These performance events use production equipment and techniques such as staging, scenery, mechanicals, sounds, lighting, video, special visual effects, communications, costume and makeup to convey an experience that are often scripted in advance to the live audience. This is similar to interaction design, the goal of which is in many cases, if not all, to convey a creative experience that is designed in advance to the users.

The main objective of this paper is to explore new opportunities in the context of interactive experience design in public spaces. We first list series of interesting elements from dynamic arts that could be inspiring for interaction design, and then focus on script, followed by an example of scripting interactive art installation. The example shows how script can be applied in the interaction design.

2   Elements Inspired from Traditional Dynamic Art Forms

In earlier publications [1] we have identified a few key elements inspired from traditional dynamic art forms that could contribute to the design of interactive public media art installations [2].

M. Kurosu (Ed.): Human-Computer Interaction, Part I, HCII 2014, LNCS 8510, pp. 157–166, 2014.
© Springer International Publishing Switzerland 2014

2.1   Stagecraft

Stagecraft in traditional dynamic arts includes lighting (e.g. different lighting effects used to change or enhance mood), costumes, makeup (e.g. in Beijing Opera, different colors of facial makeup identify different personalities of roles), props, stage management (e.g. on the stage how to set the positions of props and actors) and recording and mixing of sound. However, in the actual interactive process there might not be any clear boundary between stage space and audience space. The space could include the spread of stage and the combination installation itself and its surroundings, as well as the participants. For the interactive public media arts, stagecraft is reflected by not only arrangement on the installation itself, but also management about whole environment and all possible participants. In interactive design, stagecraft is added technological elements, for instance designers use new multimedia tool, like photographs, video, or projector to make media art installations.

2.2   Different Roles in Performance Arts: Operators, Performers and Spectators

The participant of an interactive public art installation is more than a passive user. For example, participation comes to an interactive experience happened in public spaces, is about: what one does is experienced by someone else, and that the others are seeing and experiencing that one is experiencing something[3]. One of ways of participating in creating and interacting[4] with a public art installation is to transform roles among operator, performer, and spectator at designated or preferred time [1]. On many occasions, participants are both operating and performing, and also are spectators. On some occasions, operators (designers or artists) could be performers.

2.3   Different Attention Spaces: Foreground, Mid-ground and Background

Getting the attention of the public is usually a challenging task especially when the art installation is in an open space, surrounded by buildings, lights, plants and busy people. Dividing the space of the interactive public art installation into foreground, mid-ground and background could help get attention from people in random surroundings [1].

2.4   Front Stage and Back Stage in Time and in Space

Every public space could be seen as a stage. We defined the space of interactive art installation which is on front stage and other invisible components on back stage (like organization, supervision, mechanical devices, managers, etc.) When a participant on the front stage, she does not know what happened, is happening or will happen on the backstage. Sometimes interactive designers deliberately blur the difference between these two stages. That's sometimes why we can see mechanical devices be moved to the interactive space and opened to the public. On this kind of occasions, the meta-level of the "making" also plays a role, and this might even deliver a completely new experience.

Talking about interaction design in public spaces, what is possible in a given environment? "It can be an experience of two folds: the first is the stimulation to imagination and emotion that is created by carefully crafted uncertainty. The second is the satisfaction provided by closure when the play is completed, if the plot has been successfully constructed. The experience unfolds over time" [1].

Next, based on these elements learned from traditional dynamic arts, we also find how to script well above-mentioned elements and how to make a "script" in the process of designing installation could shape the user's experience.

3 Scripting Interactive Art Installations in Public Spaces

3.1 Script and Scenario

If we look through passing thousand years of history of traditional dynamic arts, like drama, script is the base of traditional dynamic arts, which mainly composed of lines and stage directions. Scripts use dialogue, monologue, narrations or librettos as first-person narrators to represent the development of stories. Furthermore, in drama, the stage directions in the script are a kind of narrative text which is based on the tone of the writers. These directions include the story of the time and the place, the arrangement of image characteristics, body movements and activities in the real scene, description of the atmosphere, as well as the stagecraft and other requirements. In the history of drama, the script appears roughly officially formed and mature drama. For script writing, the most important aim is to be performed on the stage, not just as literature text. It could become only half finished until after the stage performances (e.g. "show text") is the ultimate artistic rendering. Yet the actors can perform on stage based on the original script, with necessary changes or modifications according to every different stage, and different understanding of the actors themselves as well. Therefore, script has an important function that allows modification, and during the process these modifications would produce detailed annotation, and mark a passage in the script how to work with the real show script.

A script often falls into a theme. The most common contemporary understanding of the theme for a script is an idea or concept that is central to a story, which can often be summarized in the "path of life" [5] (e.g. for "birth", for "communion", and for "passing on"). "In all religions and cultures there was this understanding that life happens in distinctive eras with each a specific content, that there are thresholds that give entrance to it and that it is important to cross them consciously and with the right effort. When the time was right the community prepared together with that person, symbolized the transition to procure conscious life." [5] An example of this would be in Harry Potter film series. The theme of script for *Harry Potter and the Philosopher's Stone* is death while *Harry Potter and the Goblet of Fire* is prejudice. Every show-work always has a theme even when it is just a script. Motif and expression are two parts for one script, including "What the work says about the subject" and "what the audiences think the work is about". One of these two parts can sometimes overwhelm the other one depending on interpretation and performance.

Scenario is a close concept to script which is the description of one piece or one possibility of series of actions and events depending on the story context. It is used in different kinds of areas (like military, politics, design). A scenario is often developed initially to indicate how the original source, if any, is to be adapted and to summarize the aspects of character that can be expanded later. To some extent, scenario could be look as the outline of scripts.

In interaction design, an interaction scenario is "a fully specified design vision: the users and task(s) being supported, the information needed to carry out the task, the actions the users take to interact with the task information, and the responses the system provided to users actions" [6]. Scenarios often play an important role in the process of concretization of a design concept by specifying a story to construct and illustrate the design concept or design solution [7]. Scenarios may be related to use cases and help focus design efforts on the user's requirements. Scenarios can be understood by people who do not have any technical background. They are therefore suitable for being used during participatory design activities.

Nevertheless scenario planning has several notable limitations [8]:

> "1: One criticism of scenario commonly used is that resulting results in somewhat arbitrary scenario themes.
> 2: Apart from some inherent subjectivity in scenario design, the technique can suffer from various process and content traps.
> 3: A third limitation of scenario planning in organizational settings is its weak integration into other planning and forecasting techniques."

According to the comparison, we can find that scripting interactive art installations in public spaces can make up for the limitations of scenario. That's the reason for us to introduce script instead of scenario in designing interactive art installations in public spaces. Designers sometimes need to predict all possibilities before the design process and confront with traps during the design process, at this point, script could help designers push concepts much deeper and make the concepts to be fulfilled as closer as their purpose. This kind of sketching technique can be helpful in pitching the idea to a prospective producer, director or composer.

3.2   Script in Traditional Dynamic Art Forms

In traditional dynamic arts, script is the instructions for actors to perform a play. It includes the lines each of the actors must say, some indications of stage actions (also called stage directions) and the description of surroundings. While script for traditional dynamic arts specifies normal lines or stage directions, interpretation and performance techniques can vary. How to attract attention is one part of script. In ancient time for both eastern opera and western drama, theatrical performance always took place in a noisy and crowded open and public space with a rudimentary stage, which is different from the situation nowadays in quiet and well organized theaters. Ancient troupes also found effective approaches to attract audiences and you also can find this kind of instructions in the script. They would repeatedly remind the audience of the happened plot in latter scenes. An actor would wear a plate with the name of the character, so that the audience could easily find the character relationship at any given time. Also, at the beginning, they would use the long lines to introduce the development of whole story. A unique technique often used in Beijing Opera is that, before the opening, the protagonist would always sing shortly on the back stage before appearing on the front stage, to prepare the audience, raise the expectation and set the mood. In traditional dynamic arts, these aforementioned performance techniques are one important part of script, which also is the main reason for us to introduce script to design of interactive art installation

3.3 How to Transform Script into Interactive Art Installations in Public Spaces

We have tried to apply performance techniques and elements from dynamic art forms in the design process of interactive art installations for public spaces [1]. As a stage play needs a script, do we also need a script when we design an interactive art installation for a public space? What is the role and function of such a script in the design process and in the designed installation? And how much space we shall leave in the script for the interpretation and performance?

3.4 Opportunities and Challenges

For interactive art installations in public spaces, we are facing the same problem of noisy environments and often crowed audience. Scripting interactive art installation can be a possible solution to tell participants something will happen or something already happened to the audience that joins and leaves at any time. To a certain extent, script helps extend the time. Extending the time here, not just extending the time for interaction process, also about extending the time for expectation and time for traces after interaction.   For a dynamic audience, we would also expect the scripting, interpretation and performance techniques could help to extend the experience from one audience to the other. For example, interaction with the installation by one audience would leave trace to the audience later. Traces could be the non-verbal and emotional information [9] left by people. Traces can also mean the full sensorium of experiences felt by people as they encounter smells, footprints, shadows, coughing sounds, talking, and so on, left behind by people who have previously pass through the installation space. It's also called "experience of involuntary memory". This also could be one part of script designed at beginning.

Next we show a concrete example of applying these scripting, interpretation and performance techniques in the design of one interactive public art installation named "Consistency". This installation is the result of a three-week international workshop joined by 9 teams of Dutch and Chinese design students, in the concept of "interactive patina of culture" [10].

4 Concept and Implementation

4.1 Concept

"Consistency" is an interactive art installation that is based on the principle of YinYang and acts as a reminder to this ancient philosophy. It is one of projects from the 3-week international workshop in Taicang, China, during 21Oct. and 8 Nov. in 2013. The place for this installation is chose in the center of Taicang, which is a public square and located next to a river, surrounding by green trees. Even it is in the city center, it is still a peaceful and quite location. In the center of this square, there is a circular platform a bit higher than the ground which makes the whole square looks exactly like an opening stage.

YinYang is an ancient Chinese philosophy that is deeply rooted in the Chinese culture and acted as a guide in people lives. YinYang is about finding the balance through breaking the balance. In Daoist philosophy, "All things submit to Yin and embrace Yang. They soften their energy to achieve harmony." as stated in the Dàodéjīng at chapter 42. And in chapter 2, it also said, "Presence and absence produce each other. Difficulty and ease bring about each other. Long and short delimit each other. Highness and lowness rest on each other. Sound and voice harmonize each other. Front and back follow each other." Light and dark, high and low, hot and cold, fire and water, life and death, etc. can be defined as Yin and Yang here. Yin and Yang, both of them transform each other, they also exist together. Hence the installation is named "Consistency".

Based on this understanding, in our project, Yang is treated as solid matter and Yin as liquid, which are hard and soft, being two opposite elements. We continued to consider about the surroundings, connecting this abstract philosophy to the exact public square, using the overlap circle sculpture on this square and the river next to the square, pushing this concept into an interaction in which one can leave traces in the sand (Yang and also solid) and over time the water (Yin and also liquid) will erase the traces you left behind (Fig.1).

As we mentioned before, script has an important function that allows modification, and during the process these modifications would produce detailed annotation. After the theme of our project (Consistency) was made clear, we used a step-by-step script to build up a construction for this installation and combined different implementations.

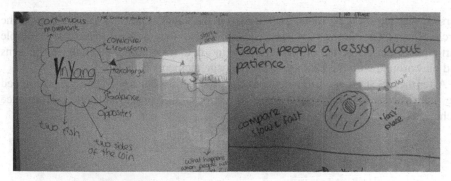

Fig. 1. Outlines of concept about YinYang

Script step1. The installation is triggered by the implicit and explicit behavior of people. As someone walks alongside the circle, water ripples appear on the water as if they are triggered by the steps of the person (Fig.2).

Fig. 2. Script step1

Script step2. Step 2 is based on the script step 1. After someone walks alongside the circle, water ripples appear on the water. This person enters the circle, the water retreats to the opposite direction and the sand becomes visible. By the person walking around footsteps appear on the sand (Fig.3).

Fig. 3. Script step2

Script step3. Step 3 is based on the story of script step 2. As someone walks alongside the circle, water retreats appear on the water. As a person enters the circle the water retreats to the opposite direction and the sand becomes visible. By the person walking around, footsteps appear on the sand. After the person leaves the circle, the water comes back and slowly erases the created footsteps. Multiple participants can cooperate on the circle to find new ways to create footprint patterns and play around with the balance of the opposite elements (Fig.4).

After these 3 steps, we had a detailed construction for concept. Then we prototyped the construction, adding vary stage directions, interpretation and performance techniques.

Fig. 4. Script step3

4.2   Implementation

During the 3-week workshop, we did a small-scale prototype to realize our concept. This small-scale prototype implements the interaction between people and installation on the square, and the effect of movement. Infrared distance sensors are used to detect the speed and direction of the movement. In this prototype, viewpoints of sand and water, footprint left on the sand and movement of water are all visualized by projection mapping (Fig.5). We also made gravity mechanisms on the bottom of this prototype, the whole central circle part would be slightly tilted depending on the number of audiences and positions of audiences.

Fig. 5. Final prototype

5   Conclusion

Based on the previous research on interactive art installations in public spaces inspired from elements of traditional dynamic arts, in this paper, we tried to introduce script as a new element to the design process. The design of example project highlights how this element could introduce new perceptive and new possibilities into the expression and forms, by giving detailed story, considering implementation, bringing in different results and controlling the tension and theme of the whole interaction process, and trying to offer different experiences for participants.

The script in the example is minimalistic. We have not yet tried whether the script shall be formulated in the similar forms of lines and stage directions. More work needs to be done to identify more of script for the design of interactive art installations in public spaces and organize it into a clearer structure, and to investigate not only how it could be applied in an interactive design, but also how the creation process of script in the traditional dynamic arts could be applied deeply in the process of creating ideas and concepts for interaction design of public media arts.

Acknowledgements. We would like to thank the support from China Scholarship Council for this research. We also acknowledge Sino-Dutch Design Center for Social and Cultural Computing (www.desis.id.tue.nl), Jiangnan University (www.sytu.edu.cn) and Eindhoven University of Technology (www.tue.nl).We thank the fund from Science and Education New Town of Taicang. The group No.1 at workshop, conducted the original creative concept, used the final video in their design process and made working programming code in software V4, providing valuable interactive prototype, experience and comments. We thank Kang Kai, Sara Wang, Danny Wu and Yasemin Arslan who made up their project, for their participation in this research.

References

1. Zhang, Y., Gu, J., Hu, J., Frens, J., Funk, M., Kang, K., et al.: Learning from Traditional Dynamic Arts: Elements for Interaction Design. In: International Conference on Culture and Computing, Kyoto, Japan, pp. 165–166 (2013)
2. Hu, J., Wang, F., Funk, M., Frens, J., Zhang, Y., Boheemen, T.V., et al.: Participatory Public Media Arts for Social Creativity. In: International Conference on Culture and Computing, Kyoto, Japan, pp. 179–180 (2013)
3. Dalsgaard, P., Hansen, L.K.: Performing perception—staging aesthetics of interaction. ACM Transactions on Computer-Human Interaction (TOCHI) 15, 13 (2008)
4. Le, D., Funk, M., Hu, J.: Blobulous: Computers As Social Actors. In: Experiencing Interactivity in Public Spaces (EIPS), CHI 2013, Paris, pp. 62–66 (2013)
5. Vissers, M., Wang, F., Baha, E., Hu, J., Rauterberg, M.: Path of Life in Mixed Reality. In: Culture and Computing, Hangzhou, China, pp. 216–227 (2012)

6. Rosson, M., Carroll, J.: Usability engineering: scenario-based development of human–computer interaction. Information Research 8 (2003)
7. Cooper, A., Reimann, R., Cronin, D.: About face 3: the essentials of interaction design. John Wiley & Sons (2012)
8. Sadri, S., Sadri, J.: Case Writing and Scenario Planning as Instruments of Corporate Training: An Exposition. BVIMSR's Journal of Management Research, 16–17 (2009)
9. Nakatsu, R., Rauterberg, M., Salem, B.: Forms and theories of communication: from multimedia to Kansei mediation. Multimedia Systems 11, 304–312 (2006)
10. Frens, J., Funk, M., Hu, J., Zhang, S., Kang, K., Wang, F.: Exploring the Concept of Interactive Patina of Culture. In: 8th International Conference on Design and Semantics of Form and Movement (DeSForM 2013), Wuxi, China, pp. 211–124 (2013)

Design-Neuroscience: Interactions between the Creative and Cognitive Processes of the Brain and Design

Rachel Zuanon

Sense Design Lab, PhD and Master Design Program,
Anhembi Morumbi University, Sao Paulo, Brazil
rzuanon@anhembi.br

Abstract. This paper discusses the rapprochement between Design and Neuroscience at the approach to the interaction between the creative and cognitive processes of the brain and design. Presents the importance of mental images in mediating these processes. Articulates the parallels between instances of design: imaging, presenting and testing and brain: interpreter, actor and comparator. Proposes the relationship between the spiral development of the brain and of the design as an interactive action beyond the iterative condition, able to support innovative and open perspectives for projective methodologies in design.

Keywords: Design, Neuroscience, Creative Process, and Cognitive Process.

1 Introduction

The rapprochement between the areas of research design and neuroscience is still underexplored by researchers in these fields of knowledge. Neuroscience as a relatively new science that deals with the development, chemistry, structure, function and pathology of the nervous system [12] may open perspectives for research in design, since in this context cognition is investigated from the properties of the brain, or by assigning specific brain structures to all forms of behavior and experience, even if only approximately. In other words, changes in brain structure imply changes in behavior and experience, and therefore the interaction with products designed by design.

In turn, the design field as "essentially hybrid that operates the junction between body and information artefact, user and system" [4] can bring significant contributions to the neuroscientific questions, especially those directed to the understanding of brain functions, including memory, learning, perception and spatial orientation. At this meeting, on the one hand, it is assumed the combination of the biobased properties to the cognition, on the other biological phenomena and mental are considered products of the cognitive structure of the system itself [18] in co-evolution with the environment in which it is inserted.

Researches in neuroscience [5]; [6]; [9]; [10]; [16] indicate that the human brain is particularly suited to design things - concepts, tools, languages and places. Thus the

M. Kurosu (Ed.): Human-Computer Interaction, Part I, HCII 2014, LNCS 8510, pp. 167–174, 2014.

human brain may have evolved to be creative - to imagine new ideas, put into practice what they invent and to critically analyze the results of human actions. In other words, the brain creatively builds senses to its context, as well as designers create products that reconfigure these contexts and stimulate the brain to reconstruct the senses existing or build new.

The natural urgency to investigate and resolve problems that designers have dedicated is rooted in problem-solving brain circuits. The brain, to promote reflection and action, subsidizes the desire for organization to attribute meaning to things in their respective contexts, as well as underpinning the planning and taking decisions intrinsic to the design. This interaction and coherence also corroborate the definition of our self, of who we are in relation to the context.

Thus this paper aims to focus on how the creative and cognitive process of the brain interacts with the creative and cognitive process of design, since the understanding of the structure and neuronal processes in the brain by the design, can lead to a more favorable environment for the creation and development of projectual proposals.

2   Mental Images: Mediation between Creative and Cognitive Process

The construction of images consists in a fundamental brain process, at the base of the formation of thoughts, perceptions, memories and plans. The factual knowledge required for reasoning and decision-making comes to the mind in the form of images [7].

It is possible to identify three different types of images that form in the brain associated with the time of the action: images that represent the present; images that represent the past and those related to the projection of a possible future.

The images that represent the present, also known as perceptual, are those formed in the brain resulting from actions taken and felt at that moment, for example, when contemplating a landscape, touching the surface of an object, smell a flower, tasting a wine.

In contrast, those associated with the past, as recalled images, invoke thoughts and memories related to actions that have already occurred. In other words, shapes, colors, movements, sounds, smells and flavors experienced in the past return to the brain by the present stimuli.

And finally, the images that emerge in the brain as the result of plans designed such actions in the future be it near or far. They are also referred by Damasio as "memory of a possible future". Just like when a desired trip is planned, for which consolidates the "memorize of this fiction" [7] in mind which may or may not occur.

By its very nature, these images formed during the planning of actions to be implemented in the future, they have become closer than we understand as the design process. However, this instance is not dissociated from perceptual images and recalled images. Rather, the images constructed as potential future existence invoke and articulate with the constituted at present and those recovered from past acts and revived in present.

Thus, the images formed in the mind are the result of interactions between individuals and between them and the objects in their contexts. Such interactions are mapped into neural patterns and constructed in accordance with the organism [6] being under the control of sensory receptors driven to the outside of the brain - the retina -, or under the control of dispositional representations - arrangements - contained in within the brain in cortical and subcortical regions [7]. Therefore, the images are based directly on neural representations, and only those that occur in early sensory cortices and are topographically organized [7].

However, images are more than figures internalized in the minds of individuals. They represent subjective knowledge, used to develop and organize ideas in such areas as architecture and design [20], visual perception and learning [3], language [15], child development [13], and economics and politics [2].

In the design's field, mental images represent not only the starting point of the creative process that guides the development projectual but a recurring instance that supports and permeates the whole cognitive process in a repetitive cycle in which each return adds complexity to the previous moment.

Like an engine, the use of mental images impels the designer thinking about objects in space, allowing the solution to the given problem is "viewed" in your mind. As the scientists Faraday and Maxwell that mentally viewed electromagnetic fields as tiny tubes filled with fluid. Kekule who saw the benzene ring as mental image projected from the reference of snakes biting their tails. Watson and Crick turned mentally models of what would be the double helix of DNA.

Mental simulations that allow relive many experiments simultaneously, from which new images emerge. Einstein summarized the importance of mental images for creative and cognitive processes when he says "my specific skill lies not in the mathematical calculation, but in visualizing effects, possibilities and consequences" [14]. A parallel with the work of the designer is identified here and it'll be explained below.

3   The Parallels among Imaging | Interpreter, Presenting | Actors and Testing | Comparator

Imaging, presenting and testing consists of the instances that are articulated to configure what is known as the creative process in any individual. Such instances are also seen as elementary activities analytically distinct and intrinsic to the design field. And for which corresponding instances are identified within the brain processing: interpreter, actors and comparator, respectively.

Imaging is the ability to go beyond the information presented. The process of see something where nothing seemed to exist before [3] or the ability to construct mental images of a fragment of the world. In design, these images provide a broad experimental framework in which is possible to engage and disengage specific parts to problem solving, yet internalized in mind.

The designers apply those mental images to better define the problem they are working on and guide their search for answers. This process reveals a cooperative scenario where the design is improved, as the images will be more elaborate.

Such activity in design - imaging - finds its parallel in brain processing in the action of the interpreter [20], dedicated to manufacture, fantasize, and create ideas and concepts. Concentrated in the left hemisphere of the brain, that mental function - interpreter - is dedicated to inventing stories, myths and concepts to explain the experience through the development of explanatory models, either descriptive or fanciful.

These pre-mental representations play a key role in the creative process and design as it provide creative leaps in identifying new connections between existing elements, in the unfettered realm of ideas, preceding what will be, and therefore still disconnected from any liens that may cause their physical feasibility.

Presenting refers to the ways in which designers externalize and communicate their mental images. Besides the presentation of ideas and concepts, this implies in choosing the best medium for this representation, considering the moment in which the design process lies.

Not restricted only to this that choice also extends to the selection of imagery that will gain visibility in the eyes of the designer himself and other individuals. A paradoxical process because while it reduces the field of imagined possibilities of design - with increasingly specific projectual detailing - expands the scope of new problems related to the new projectual delimitation. "Designers present not images themselves but the implications of images" [17], resulting in representation of a problem with the simple purpose of achieving transparency necessary for obtaining a solution.

Within the brain processing, this function - presenting - is played by the actor [20], involving several brain areas such as the occipital, parietal and frontal lobes, in a process of continuous adaptation to the stimuli received from the environment. Such stimuli are perceived by sensory organs, decoded and interpreted by the brain, giving them meaning, as recognized information (perception) and / or performed action (motor response). Thus, external representations assume their meanings - their intentions and extensions - from the inner meaning, mental states and actions of the people who built and use them [8].

And finally, testing relates to the various ways and means used and applied by designers to verify consistency between the proposals, which were presented as a result of the interaction between the imaging and presenting instances, and objectives intended as a product.

Such activity requires an analytical and critical posture of the designer in front of the object outlined until then aiming to confront it with the different factors involved in the whole design process for the achievement of its purposes - the first ideas proposed by the designer from formulated mental images; needs, desires and expectations of the client, the relationship between the projective elements, social, cultural, economic and even political issues, beyond those directly related to the user experience in their relationship with the product delivered by design, such as their emotional, sensory, ergonomic, neurophysiological aspects, among others.

Considering the cerebral perspective, this activity - testing - finds its parallel in the action of the comparator, concentrated in the frontal lobe, and dedicated to compare the hypotheses raised by the interpreter with the perceptions and motor responses conducted by the actor in order to identify possible disconnections so enhance the development of the emerging image.

The continues relationship among these pairs - Imaging | Interpreter, Presenting | Actor, Testing | Comparator - and among their instances that comprise the activities of design - Imaging, Presenting, Testing - as well as among those that make up the brain functions - Interpreter, Actor, Comparator - resulting in what we call a interaction between creative and cognitive processes of the brain and the design, as explained below.

4   Brain's Designer and Design: Interactions between Creative and Cognitive Processes

"The Brain's Creative Development Spiral" diagram, as proposed by John Zeisel, understands that when one has a perception, develops a plan, or reacts to the environment, the mind uses the same iterative process that designers use in their design process, as detailed previously. In other words, the brain uses an iterative process of repeated cycles of imaging, presenting, and testing to make sense of the world and ourselves in it [20].

The "Design Development Spiral" presents the metaphor of design as a spiral process and it can be applied to model how various design elements connect. A spiral process reflects the following design features: (a) backtracking, (b) repeating, and (c) combining that permeates all the design elementary activities.

(a) The designers backtrack at certain times instead of moving forward, aiming to foster problem solving [20]. In other words, over a design project, a designer returns to the problem already studied to revise or adjust earlier decisions [1]. Every decision made by the designer, even though he considers being his final decision, generates consequences for future stages of the process, as well as the previous steps, as new problems arise as the previous decisions are reviewed [11].

(b) By repeating the same series of activities successive times, designers solve new problems, since each repetition relates to a different problem [20]. In each cycle of a design project, designers conceive, present, test and redesign answers to a set of related problems. And the time devoted by the designer to each one varies, as each activity in these cycles has not its beginning and ending at a specific point. Each contains remnants of the previous action and roots the next.

(c) Such seemingly multidirectional movements together result in a movement directed to a single action [20]. In other words, the combination among return movements, repetitions at different levels and cycles progressively connected result in a single motion directed to the goal of an acceptable projectual response.

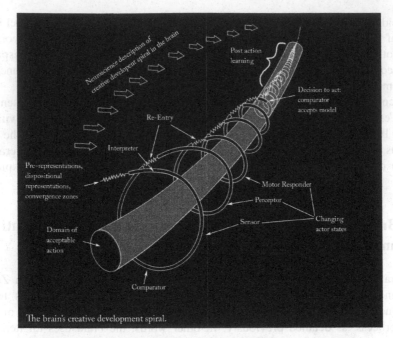

Fig. 1. Diagram "The Brain's Creative Development Spiral"[20]

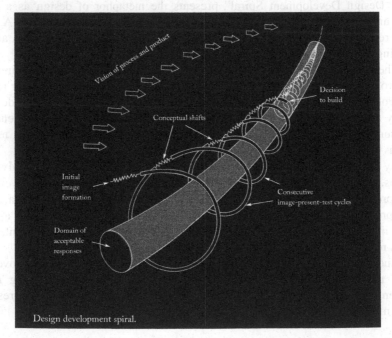

Fig. 2. Diagram "Design Development Spiral"[20]

Such brain and design development spiral as well as iterative they are also inherently interactive, since they change mutually in a process of continuous communication between the creative and cognitive spheres, which both have influence on one another. An organism forms neural representations which can become images, be manipulated in a process called thought, and influence behavior by helping predict the future, plan accordingly, and choose the next action [7], as a need to create a sense of coherence and continuity allowing the emergence of a unified belief system [16].

5   Conclusion

The design-neuroscience relationship proves to be a fruitful field of research, especially in relation to the creative and cognitive processes. In this context, the mental images play a key role in the formation of perceptions, thoughts, memories and plans, as well as in mediating between the creative and cognitive spheres of the brain and design.

From the perspective of design, three instances are outlined as basic activities that permeate the states of creation and cognition present in the design practice: imaging, presenting and testing.

As part of brain processing, these same three instances find their parallels in the mental functions of the interpreter, actor and comparator, respectively.

Such instances of design and their brain pairs articulated in a spiral flow in continuous adaptation to the stimuli from the surrounding environment in which the designer and product design are modeled each other in the actions of backtracking, repeating, and combining.

This understanding broadens the role and responsibility of the designer in front of the products designed by him, since the brain activity involved in creative and cognitive processes of design are understood as the underlying basis and at the same time, the reflection of their actions. This implies one similarity between the structure of activity of work (exterior) and the structure of mental processes (inside) [19].

Thus identifies the existence of a neuroscientific basis able to support and open innovative perspectives for projective methodologies in design, contemplating the association between creative and cognitive processes of the brain and design in the project and development of products.

References

1. Archer, L.B.: The structure of design process. In: Broadbent, Geoffrey, Ward (eds.) Design Methods in Architecture. Lund Humphries for the Architectural Association, London (1969)
2. Boulding, K.E.: The Image: Knowledge in Life and Society. Ann Arbor, University of Michigan Press, Michigan (1956)
3. Bruner, J.S.: Beyond the Information Given: Studies in the Psychology of Knowing. Norton, New York (1973); Anglin, J. M. (ed.)
4. Cardoso, R.: Design para um mundo complexo. Cosac Naify, São Paulo (2012)

5. Changeux, J.P.: Neuronal Man. Princeton University Press, Princeton (1985)
6. Damasio, A.R.: Em busca de Espinosa: prazer e dor na ciência dos sentimentos. Companhia das Letras, São Paulo (2004)
7. Damasio, A.R.: O Erro de Descartes. Companhia das Letras, São Paulo (1996)
8. Dennett, D.C.: Tipos de mentes: rumo a uma compreensão da consciência. Rocco, Rio de Janeiro (1997)
9. Eberhard, J., Patoine, B.: Architecture with the Brain in Mind. Cerebrum 6(2), 71–84 (2004)
10. Gazzaniga, M.S.: The Mind's Past. University of California Press, Berkeley (1998)
11. Jones, J.C.: Design methods: seeds of human futures. Wiley, London (1970)
12. Lundy-Ekman, L.: Neurociência: Fundamentos para Reabilitação. Elsevier, Rio de Janeiro (2004)
13. Piaget, J., Inhelder, B.: The Gaps in Empiricism. In: Koestler, A., Smythies, J.R. (eds.) Beyond Reductionism: The Alpbach Symposium. Hutchinson, London (1969)
14. Pinker, S.: Como a Mente Funciona. Companhia das Letras, São Paulo (1998)
15. Polanyi, M.: Personal Knowledge: Towards a Post-Critical Philosophy. University of Chicago Press, Chicago (1958)
16. Ramachandran, V.S., Blakeslee, S.: Phantoms in the Brain: Probing the Mysteries of the Human Mind. William Morrow and Company, New York (1998)
17. Simon, H.A.: The Sciences of the Artificial. MIT Press, Cambridge (1969)
18. Varela, F.J., Thompson, E., Rosch, E.: A mente incorporada: ciências cognitivas e a experiência humana. Artmed, Porto Alegre (2003)
19. Frawley, W.: Vygotsky e a Ciência Cognitiva: linguagem e integração das mentes social e computacional. Artes Médicas Sul, Porto Alegre (2000)
20. Zeisel, J.: Inquiry by Design: Environment/Behavior/Neuroscience in Architecture, Interiors, Landscape, and Planning. Norton, New York (2006)

HCI and Design Education

Charting the Landscape of HCI Education in Brazil

Clodis Boscarioli[1], Milene S. Silveira[2], Raquel Oliveira Prates[3],
Sílvia Amélia Bim[4], and Simone Diniz Junqueira Barbosa[5]

[1] Departamento de Ciência da Computação, UNIOESTE, Cascavel, PR, Brazil
clodis.boscarioli@unioeste.br
[2] Faculdade de Informática, PUCRS, Porto Alegre, RS, Brazil
milene.silveira@pucrs.br
[3] Departamento de Ciência da Computação, UFMG, Belo Horizonte, MG, Brazil
rprates@dcc.ufmg.br
[4] Departamento de Informática, UTFPR, Curitiba, PR, Brazil
sabim@utfpr.edu.br
[5] Departamento de Informática, PUC-Rio, Rio de Janeiro, RJ, Brazil
simone@inf.puc-rio.br

Abstract. One of the issues the Brazilian HCI community has paid great attention to is HCI education in the country. One of the efforts has been to understand, through the use of surveys, how HCI has been taught in Brazil. So far, two reports on HCI education profile in Brazil have been presented: one from 2009 that described HCI courses being taught, and another from 2012 that was in response to a SIGCHI demand and targeted a broader audience, not taking into account specificities of the Brazilian context. Therefore, the need for an updated analysis of HCI education in Brazil was identified and a new survey applied. In this paper we present the initial analysis of the results of this survey and delineate what HCI courses have been offered at undergraduate or graduate levels around the country and their topics they cover.

Keywords: HCI Education, Brazilian HCI community.

1 Introduction

Fifteen years have passed since the recommendation of HCI courses to the Brazilian Computing programs by the Brazilian Computer Society (SBC).[1] During this time, the HCI community in Brazil has deepened discussions about its education matters, reporting different approaches HCI courses or modules [3]. Such discussions took place in working groups and, in recent years (since 2010), mainly at a permanent workshop during the national HCI conference.

Besides the discussions, the community has been trying to collect data about the way these courses that have been taught in Brazil. Two surveys have already been applied in the community: the first one, in 2009, which collected data about HCI

---

[1] http://www.sbc.org.br/en/

M. Kurosu (Ed.): Human-Computer Interaction, Part I, HCII 2014, LNCS 8510, pp. 177–186, 2014.
© Springer International Publishing Switzerland 2014

courses being taught countrywide [37], and the second one, in 2012, in response to a SIGCHI demand, aimed at identifying the opportunities and challenges of HCI teaching [3]. The 2012 survey brought us interesting results, but since the survey initially targeted a broader audience – it did not take into account Brazilian specificities – some important points were left out. Then, in order to broaden our work, in 2013 a new survey – specific for the Brazilian HCI Community – was designed and applied.

In the next sections, we present the applied survey and its results, as well as a comparison between the new results and the older ones, in order to better chart the landscape of HCI Education in Brazil.

2 2013 Landscape of HCI Education in Brazil

The 2013 survey was open for the community to answer from April to July. It consisted of an online questionnaire, which was distributed to several HCI email lists in Brazil, in an attempt to reach not only Computer Science faculty, but also designers and related professionals who teach HCI in Brazil.

2.1 Respondents' Profile

Overall, 114 people answered the survey, but only 75 of them were considered valid (since filling out information on at least one taught class was required).

Respondents consisted of HCI-related professors, whose degrees and majors varied, though most of them (67%) are directly related to Computing. Nineteen percent (19%) claimed to have a Master's degree or Doctorate specifically in HCI, and 48% claimed to have other Computing-related degrees. The remaining respondents belong to such fields as Graphic Design, Business, Anthropology, Arts, Psychology, Education, Marketing and Electrical Engineering. Such variety thus points to a multidisciplinary feature observable in customary HCI teaching. Respondents' HCI teaching experience averaged 4.7 years, but 37% of respondents reported between 6-7 years of HCI teaching. This last piece of information strengthens the fact that HCI is a new field in Brazil, still inexistent in many universities' curricula.

The graphic displayed in Fig. 1 shows respondents' geographical distribution throughout Brazil. Teachers who responded to the survey are affiliated with both public and private universities, totaling 26 federal universities, 11 state universities, and 15 private universities.

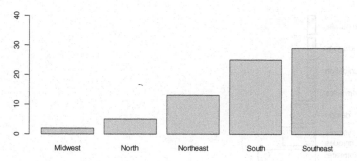

Fig. 1. Nationwide respondents' distribution

2.2   Undergraduate HCI-related Courses

We investigated undergraduate courses fully dedicated to HCI and only related to HCI. Among the dedicated ones, the fact that they were similarly named in different universities stood out. In addition, the emphasis each course gave to HCI did not differ greatly.

HCI-related contents showed up in such courses named as 'Software Engineering II', 'Graphic Design: Webdesign', 'Languages for Structuring and Presenting Content', 'Graphical and Multimedia Environments', 'Cooperative Systems' and 'Education and Novel Technologies'.

As for Bachelor's Degrees, the course load for specific HCI courses varies from 60 to 90 hours, and there was a single 40-hour course mentioned in reference to a vocational education training course. When it comes to HCI-related courses, informants reported that work hours allocated to teaching HCI varies from 4 to 40 hours. The number of students in these courses averages 31 – the smallest group consisted of 10 students and the largest one had 60 students.

The number of HCI courses reported by different programs can be seen in Fig. 2. There was a total amount of 70 courses; many of them are linked to more than one program at the same University and were taught by more than one professor.

None of the mentioned HCI courses requires prerequisites, and not all of them are mandatory. They are offered in different semesters, and most of them belong to Computing majors, which correlates to the degrees teachers who answered the survey. Among the mentioned major programs, Computer Science (CS), Computer Engineering (CE) and Information Systems (IS) are the ones that offer most HCI courses.[2]

---

[2] Systems analysis and development was not considered because it is a technical course and not a major program.

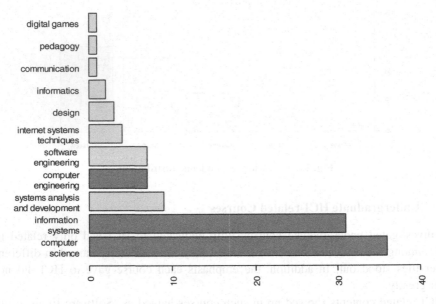

Fig. 2. Number of HCI courses per major

By focusing on the three high-frequency HCI course majors, we can further observe the number of HCI courses per major in Fig. 3 below, which also shows whether they are mandatory or not.

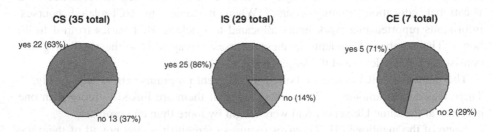

Fig. 3. HCI mandatory ratio on CS, IS and CE curricula, as reported in the survey

When analyzing all courses and their corresponding curriculum study load at the universities, we can classify the main topics in the following groups: (i) Basic Concepts; (ii) HCI Analysis; (iii) HCI Design; (iv) HCI Evaluation; (v) Other Topics, which chiefly include Assistive Technology and Accessibility, Information Visualization, Information Architecture, Websites and Multimedia Content and, lastly, Mobile Devices Interaction.

Fig. 4 shows the course load distribution in hours assigned to each topic mentioned in all curricula study loads for Computer Science, Information Systems and Computer Engineering. It enables us to picture the variations among the emphases each major gives to each topic, which define the commitment each of them hold in shaping future professionals.

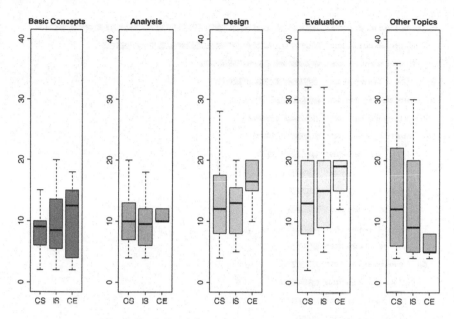

Fig. 4. Study load for each topic and course, in hours

The graphic in Fig. 5 demonstrates the bibliography mentioned in course descriptions. Notice that half of the entire textbook list corresponds to titles in Brazilian Portuguese (represented by an asterisk next to the authors' names). It is also interesting to notice that the top three most often used books are in Portuguese and that the top two textbooks are used twice as much as the ones following in the list. The top book on the list is a Portuguese version of the 1st edition of the book, which is already on its 3rd edition in English. The high preference for books in Portuguese indicates that it is much easier for students to use a book in their native language, and not all Brazilian students read English well.

2.3   HCI Courses in Graduate Programs

Sixteen HCI-specific and HCI-related courses were mentioned, all of which are offered in Masters' and doctorate programs in the computing field, except for one course, which is offered in a multidisciplinary program. The list below displays the course names.

- Alternative Techniques on Interaction and Virtual Reality
- Design and User interface evaluation
- Human Computer Interaction (2 instances)
- Information Architecture
- Intelligent Interfaces
- Interaction Design
- Interactive Systems Quality
- Interface Projects

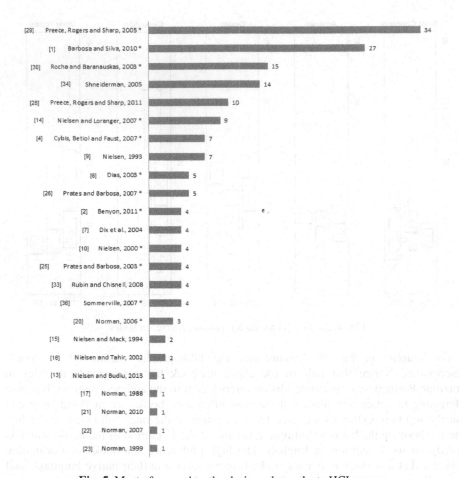

Fig. 5. Most often used textbooks in undergraduate HCI courses

- Introduction to Human Computer Interaction
- Research Design and Academic Writing
- Semiotic Engineering
- Special Topics on HCI and SE
- Topics on HCI
- User-centered Design
- Visualization of Information

Considering that many undergraduate programs lack either HCI courses or prerequisites to them, when we analyzed specific graduate HCI courses and their syllabi, we noticed that their topics end up being similar to the topics grouped in Section 2.2, though they may differ in emphasis and depth. However, at the graduate level, courses on more specific or advanced topics were listed: 'Cooperative Interface', 'Ergonomics', 'Semiotic Engineering', 'Natural and Artificial Interface Languages', 'HCI interactions with Software Engineering and HCI Research Methods'.

When observing the course syllabi – corresponding to both undergraduate and graduate levels –, a variety of topics stand out in all Brazilian HCI courses, which further points to concerns with Information Visualization and Data Manipulation. Besides illustrating that, Fig. 6 also portraits a nationwide multidisciplinary approach to this field.

Fig. 6. Word frequency counter for HCI disciplines course topics in Brazil

At the graduate level, the list of adopted textbooks shows that not only is the number of books smaller, but many of them are Brazilian Portuguese versions of textbooks in English (Fig. 7). Most books deal with general topics such as HCI Concepts, Analysis, HCI Design and Evaluation.

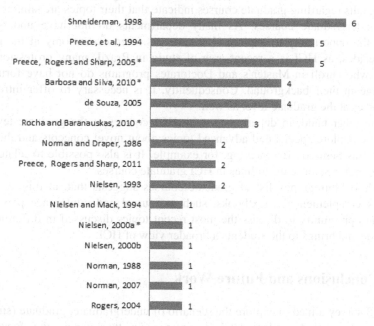

Fig. 7. Most often used textbooks in graduate HCI courses

The workload of such disciplines adds up to 42 hours, with an average of 10 enrolled students.

3 Exploring This Landscape

Although the majority of HCI courses are mandatory in CS (63%), IS (86%), and CE (71%) majors, their study load is still low, 75 hours on average, which means one course during the entire undergraduate program. The results show that the focus of the course for each program varies according to the course. CE courses, for example, emphasize basic concepts, design and evaluation. On the other hand, CS and IS courses, in general, make a more balanced distribution of the topics, dedicating more hours to other topics than CE does. Thus, although courses in different programs cover many of the same topics, they explore them differently. As a result, they form computer professionals with different HCI knowledge profiles, which could be interesting to fulfill industry needs.

Concerning the undergraduate HCI programs, we noticed that half the books adopted were in Portuguese, and that those included the three most often used books. This indicates that HCI education material in Portuguese is a better resource for our students. Looking closer at Portuguese titles, we notice that half of them are national productions and the other half translations to Portuguese. The advantage of also having books written by our HCI community members is that they could include in the text issues that are relevant to the Brazilian society and culture, as well as HCI perspectives and approaches broadly researched in Brazil.

The results regarding graduate courses indicate that their topics are similar to those of the undergraduate courses. As many departments do not have undergraduate courses, the opportunity to explore HCI concepts often occurs only at the graduate level. Besides, as HCI is a recent area of study in Brazil, many professionals and students who enroll in Master´s and Doctorates programs do not have formal HCI knowledge in their background. Consequently, it is necessary to offer introductory HCI courses at the graduate level as well.

On the other hand, in departments with HCI courses at the graduate level, it is possible to explore special and advanced topics about novel concepts and theories of HCI, such as Semiotic Engineering, for example. It is also possible to relate HCI to other Computer Science disciplines in HCI graduate courses.

The short bibliography list of graduate courses suggests that, at this level, other resources complement the textbooks, such as journal and conference papers. This offers the opportunity to discuss the most recent topics discussed in different events worldwide and brings to the students a broader view of HCI.

4 Conclusions and Future Work

The 2013 survey aimed to explore the scenario of undergraduate, graduate (stricto and lato sensu) and independent HCI disciplines. In this paper, the focus is on undergraduate and stricto sensu graduate programs. The data about lato sensu and independent HCI courses will be discussed in future works.

Although this survey was widely distributed, the response rate was low. We believe this may have occurred because the survey required participants to enter detailed information on the courses taught, which was quite time consuming. Thus, although the survey included participants from all Brazilian geographical regions and allowed for an interesting analysis of what is being taught, we cannot make any claims regarding its statistical validity. Furthermore, most of the respondents were from Computer–related fields. Thus, one of the challenges we face is to succeed in collecting more data about HCI courses in other areas, such as Design and Communications, for example. Most of the job offers for HCI position in Brazil require a Design background, but the knowledge requirements are the same that are taught in HCI courses within Computer Science departments.

This paper presents an initial analysis of the data collected. A more thorough analysis of the courses' programs and how they relate to diverse aspects such as geographic region and number of students will be further explored in the next steps of our research.

To complement this survey, we would also like to investigate the students' perspective on the courses they take and how they use the acquired knowledge professionally.

Acknowledgements. Clodis Boscarioli thanks Fundação Araucária for the support to his research work. Raquel Prates thanks Fapemig for the partial support to this work. Simone Barbosa thanks CNPq (process #308490/2012-6) for the support to her research work.

References

1. Barbosa, S.D.J., Silva, B.S.: Interação Humano-Computador. Editora Campus – Elsevier (2010)
2. Benyon, D.: Interação Humano-Computador, 2ª Edição. Pearson, São Paulo (2011)
3. Boscarioli, C., Bim, S.A., Silveira, M.S., Prates, R.O., Barbosa, S.D.J.: HCI Education in Brazil: Challenges and Opportunities. In: Kurosu, M. (ed.) HCII/HCI 2013, Part I. LNCS, vol. 8004, pp. 3–12. Springer, Heidelberg (2013)
4. Cybis, W., Betiol, A.H., Faust, R.: Ergonomia e Usabilidade: conhecimentos, métodos e aplicações. Novatec Editora, 334 p. (2007)
5. de Souza, C.S.: The Semiotic Engineering of Human-Computer Interaction. The MIT Press, Cambridge (2005)
6. Dias, C.: Usabilidade na Web - Criando Portais Mais Acessíveis. AltaBooks (2003)
7. Dix, A., Finlay, J., Abowd, G., Beale, R.: Human-Computer Interaction, 3rd edn. Prentice Hall (2004)
8. Nielsen, J., Mack, R.L. (eds.): Usability Inspection Methods. John Wiley & Sons, New York (1994) ISBN 0-471-01877-5
9. Nielsen, J.: Usability Engineering. Academic Press, Boston (1993)
10. Nielsen, J.: Projetando Websites. Editora Campus, Rio de Janeiro

11. Nielsen, J.: Designing Web usability: the practice of simplicity, 419 p. New Riders (2000) ISBN 1-56205-810-X
12. Nielsen, J.: Usability Engineering. Academic Press, Chestnut Hill (1993)
13. Nielsen, J., Budiu, R.: Mobile Usability. New Riders (2013)
14. Nielsen, J., Loranger, H.: Usabilidade na Web – Projetando Websites com Qualidade. Campus, Rio de Janeiro (2007)
15. Nielsen, J., Mack, R.L.: Usability Inspection Methods. John Wiley & Sons, New York (1994) ISBN 0-471-01877-5
16. Nielsen, J., Tahir, M.: Homepage: Usabilidade 50 sites descontruídos. Campus (2002)
17. Norman, D.A.: The Psychology of Everyday Things. Basic Books, New York (1988)
18. Norman, D.A.: The Design of Future Things. Basic Books, New York (2007)
19. Norman, D.A., Draper, S.W.: User Centered System Design. Lawrence Erlbaum Associates, Hillsdale (1986)
20. Norman, D.A.: O design do dia a dia. Rocco, Rio de Janeiro (2006)
21. Norman, D.A.: O design do futuro, 192 p. Rocco (2010)
22. Norman, D.A.: The design of future things. Basic Books, New York (2007)
23. Norman, D.A.: The Invisible Computer. MIT Press, Massachusetts (1999)
24. Norman, D.A.: The Psychology of Everyday Things. Basic Books, New York (1988)
25. Prates, R.O., Barbosa, S.D.J.: Avaliação de Interfaces de Usuário - Conceitos e Métodos. Jornada de Atualização em Informática, SBC (2003)
26. Prates, R.O., Barbosa, S.D.J.: Introdução à Teoria e Prática da Interação Humano Computador fundamentada na Engenharia Semiótica. In: Kowaltowski, T., Breitman, K.K. (Org.) Jornada de Atualização em Informática do Congresso da Sociedade Brasileira de Computação (2007)
27. Preece, J., et al.: Human-Computer Interaction. Addison-Wesley, Harlow (1994)
28. Preece, J., Rogers, Y., Sharp, H.: Interaction design: beyond human-computer interaction. Willey, EUA (2011)
29. Preece, J., Rogers, Y., Sharp, H.: Design de Interação. RS. Bookman, Porto Alegre (2005)
30. Rocha, H.V., Baranauskas, M.C.C.: Design e Avaliação de Interfaces Humano-Computador. Nied/Unicamp Campinas (2003), Free Download: http://pan.nied.unicamp.br/publicacoes/publicacao_detalhes.php?id=40
31. Rogers, Y., Sharp, H., Preece, J.: Interaction Design: Beyond Human-Computer Interaction, 3rd edn. John Wiley & Sons, Inc. (2011) ISBN 0-470-66576-9, 978-0-470-66576-3
32. Rogers, Y.: New theoretical approaches for human-computer interaction. Annual Review of Information Science and Technology 38(1), 87–143 (2004)
33. Rubin, J., Chisnell, D.: Handbook of Usability Testing: How to Plan, Design, and Conduct Effective Tests. Wiley (2008)
34. Shneiderman, B.: Designing the user interface, 4th edn. Addison Wesley (2005)
35. Shneiderman, B.: Designing the User Interface: strategies for effective human-computer interaction, 3rd edn. Addison-Wesley, Reading (1998)
36. Sommerville, I.: Engenharia de Software, 4th edn. Pearson Addison-Wesley, São Paulo (2007)
37. Prates, R.O., Filgueiras, L.: Usability in Brazil. In: Douglas, I., Zhengjie, L. (Org.) Global Usability, 1st edn., vol. 1, pp. 91–110. Springer, London (2011)

Human-Computer Interaction Education and Diversity

Tom Gross

Human-Computer Interaction Group, University of Bamberg, Germany
tom.gross@uni-bamberg.de

Abstract. Human-Computer Interaction has evolved into an established field of teaching and research. Its multidisciplinary and cross-continental roots combined with its broad scope and multiplicity of paradigms, methods, tools, and application areas have led to a huge diversity. In the community there are currently debates about the pros and cons of this diversity and some voices claim for unifying theory and practice and standardising teaching curricula. In this paper I discuss HCI education, and analyse the past, present, and future of HCI in order to derive implications for HCI education.

Keywords: Human-Computer Interaction, Diversity.

1 Introduction

Human-Computer Interaction (HCI) has over the last decades evolved into an established field of teaching and research that marks an important paradigm shift. Wegner [31, p. 81] writes: 'interactive systems are more powerful problem-solving engines than algorithms.'. Yet, the field of HCI is multidisciplinary, which to some authors seem challenging. Grudin [14, p. 59] writes: 'different views of human-computer interaction are presented ... and differences will remain'. Researchers and teachers in HCI have reacted to multidisciplinarity by elaborating on shared understandings in HCI education. Claims for unification have been raised. For instance, Churchill et al. have compiled an informative report on 'Teaching and Learning Human-Computer Interaction: Past, Present, and Future' [5]. It analyses one of the big challenges of teaching HCI: the rapid evolution of the field. The authors write: 'during the past 15 years, the speed of change has been particularly dramatic' and they continue 'in response to these technological changes, user populations have diversified and grown' [5, p. 44]. The authors point out that in their interviews 'a common refrain we hear is "We need a mission statement or a value proposition that people can hang their hats on." Our survey respondents and interviewees call for some form of unity or consensus; there is a desire for "a unified theoretical perspective" and "a common curriculum."'.

In this paper I examine the field of HCI and HCI education with respect to their diversity. For this purpose, I analyse HCI education today and study HCI curricula and books. I then characterise trends in HCI. I draw conclusions for HCI education. Finally, I summarise the paper.

M. Kurosu (Ed.): Human-Computer Interaction, Part I, HCII 2014, LNCS 8510, pp. 187–198, 2014.
© Springer International Publishing Switzerland 2014

2   HCI Education Today

HCI education needs to reflect multidisciplinary origins in computer and human science and beyond, respect the complexity in theories, methods, and tools, for the design, implementation, and evaluation of interactive systems. Several authors have emphasised this *multidisciplinary* and have also identified disciplines and areas of HCI that are relevant for HCI research and teaching. Carroll [4, p. 1] emphasises the combination of the human and the computer side: 'human-computer interaction (HCI) lies at the intersection between the social and behavioural sciences on the one hand, and computer and information technology on the other.' Yet, to add even more complexity, HCI should not only be seen from a research perspective, but also an engineering and design perspective, and they are rather distinct. MacKenzie [21, p. 126f] points out: 'there are many ways to distinguish research from engineering and design. ... Engineers and designers are in the business of building things. ... Research tends to be narrowly focused. Small ideas are conceived of, prototyped, tested, then advanced or discarded.'

Teaching HCI from the perspective of designing *artefacts* that are easy to understand and use, sometimes seemed quite easy. There the focus was primarily on the artefacts that are designed and their capability to communicated their handling to users (e.g., for doors it should be immediately clear if users need to push or pull). For instance, Norman [22, p. 188f] suggested 'seven principles for transforming difficult tasks into simple ones' such as: 'simplify the structure of tasks'. Beyond the artefact, design is always about the *users* who interact with the artefact. In his later publications Norman points out that [23, p. 8]: 'in the 1980s, in writing The Design of Everyday Things, I didn't take emotions into account. I addressed utility and usability, function and form, all in a logical, dispassionate way.'. Norman in this book identifies three different aspects of design [23, p. 5f]: 'visceral design concerns itself with appearances. ... behavioural design has to do with the pleasure and effectiveness of use. ... finally, reflective design considers the rationalisation and intellectualisation of a product.'. Draper and Norman [8, p. 1] already in the 1980ies identified the need to deal with humans and computers, but also *interaction*: 'to understand successful design requires an understanding of the technology, the person, and their mutual interaction.'.

Since then, the field of HCI has grown considerably and with that also the *body of knowledge* of potential interest for students of HCI. Carroll [4, p. 6] writes that in the 1980s 'it was reasonable to expect HCI professionals, particularly researchers, to have a fairly comprehensive understanding of the concepts and methods in use. Today, there are too many theories, too many methods, too many application domains, too many systems.'. Subsequently I analyse HCI curricula and HCI reference books and textbooks with respect to their contents, and structure. I will particularly reflect the disciplines and areas identified in the quotes above: the role of computer and information technology versus social and behavioural sciences; the role of research versus design and engineering; the role of users' goals and tasks; the role of visceral, behavioural, and reflective aspects; as well as the role of theories and methods versus application domains and systems.

2.1   HCI Curricula

In this section I introduce three curricular suggestions for teaching HCI: the Curricula for Human-Computer Interaction of the Association of Computing Machinery's Special Interest Group on Computer-Human Interaction of (ACM SIGCHI), the Computing Curricula 2001 - Computer Science of the Joint Task Force on Computing Curricula of the Institute of Electrical and Electronics Engineers Computer Society (IEEE CS) and the Association for Computing Machinery (ACM), and the Recommendations for Software Ergonomics Education of the German Informatics Society (Gesellschaft für Informatik e.V., GI).

In the *Curricula for Human-Computer Interaction* Hewitt et al. [17] list the following 'contents of HCI': the nature of HCI: meta-models, and models for HCI; use and context of computers: human social organisation and work; application areas; human-machine fit and adaptation; human characteristics: human information processing; language, communication, interaction; ergonomics: computer system and interface architecture; input and output devices; dialogue techniques; dialogue genre; computer graphics; dialogue architecture; development process: design approaches; implementation techniques; evaluation techniques; example systems and case studies; as well as project presentations and examinations. The authors suggest that this content can be tailored to different courses. For instance, in a computer science department the content could be presented in two courses of 14 weeks and 42 contact hours each with a broad and even distribution of topics in the first course, and a special focus on human social organisation and work; human information processing; and language, communication, and interaction in the second. While the nature of the first course is practical, the one of the second is scientific. Alternatively, a psychology, human factors, or industrial engineering department could offer a course on the psychology of HCI with 14 weeks and 42 contact hours emphasising the theoretical and empirical foundation of the above contents. This course could offer a broad overview of all topics. Finally, in an information systems department a course on human aspects of information systems with also 14 weeks and 42 contact hours could deepen a non-technical understanding of user needs and system capabilities for users and managers.

In the case of fewer resources for HCI, Hewitt et al. suggest to include HCI courses 'into all technology-oriented courses'. And the authors claim that 'iterative design, usability testing, and user productivity be at least mentioned as issues of concern in courses at all levels'. While these suggestions are two decades old and details have changed, the content is from a conceptual perspective still relevant. The *Computing Curricula* [18] outlines important changes that influence the computer science discipline. It names technical changes through technological advancements in areas such as the World-Wide Web, networking technologies, graphics and multimedia, embedded systems, but also HCI; and cultural changes in the 'cultural and sociological context' such as changes in pedagogy enabled by new technologies, growth of computing through the world, but also a broadening of the discipline. This curriculum lists the computer science body of knowledge with 14 main areas, one of them being HCI. Within HCI the curriculum names the two core topics: foundations of HCI; and building a simple graphical user interface. It lists six further topics: human-centred software evaluation; human-centred software development; graphical user-interface design; graphical user-interface programming; HCI aspects of multimedia systems; and HCI aspects of collaboration and communication. Beyond these topics the curriculum also suggests various advanced courses 'whose content is substantially beyond the material of the core'. For HCI the following advanced courses are suggested: human-centred design and evaluation; graphical user interfaces; multimedia systems development; interactive systems development; and computer-supported cooperative work.

The *Recommendations for Software Ergonomics Education* [20] names the following nine desired qualifications of HCI experts: understanding of software development as a part of work and organisation design; ability to recognise the requirements of work situations and to take these into account in system design; ability to analyse and describe work and tasks; ability to determine an appropriate human-computer functional separation; ability to design HCI; ability to judge software products with respect to their functionality for task-adequate functionality and user-adequate handling; ability to organise the system development process while taking user requirements into account; ability to organise the cooperation process between users and developers; and ability to introduce systems in such a way that hindrances or pressures for those affected are kept to a minimum and that no-one's rights are reduced. The curriculum recommends an introduction with software-ergonomic design of human-computer systems; theoretical, psychological, ergonomic basics; and design with design of computer-supported work systems, dialogue systems, input and output design, ergonomics-oriented system development, system introduction and use, and system evaluation.

A *later curriculum of the GI* has updates compared to the original recommendation, but is only availably in German [29]. Being published 13 years later, it emphasises differences compared to the original recommendation with respect to application areas of HCI (i.e., e-business, e-learning, e-government, edutainment, infotainment, and games), with respect to new forms of devices and interaction (i.e., mobile devices, mobile phones, wearable), and with respect to new usability engineering methods. The suggested basic module for HCI should have a minimum of 15 weeks of two weekly hours. The contents includes three blocks: introduction with chapters on human, task, software, on the development of software-ergonomics, and on standards and legal foundation; basics of HCI with chapters on human information processing and activities, on input and output devices, on interaction techniques, and work and task design; and user-centred development processes with chapters on user-centred process models, on analysis of needs and requirements, on specification and prototyping, and on evaluation. Analysing these curricula it becomes clear that the core topics of HCI education have witnessed some evolution, but at the same time they have kept a balance between technical (computer and information technology) and human (social and behavioural sciences). Users' goals and tasks as well as theories and methods play a major role. They have a stronger focus on research and engineering over design, and visceral, behavioural, and reflective aspects play a minor role. Application domains and systems are primarily addressed in additional courses beyond the core topics.

2.2   HCI Reference Books and Textbooks

Books for students of HCI have proliferated recently. Reference books have been followed by textbooks for various levels of teaching and studying HCI. Comprehensive reference books with great collections of publications on HCI topics have early been published in [16] and in [1], and later in [25]. The two most prominent early and comprehensive *reference books* are the Handbook of Human-Computer Interaction by Helander et al. with over 1500 pages and the Readings in Human-Computer Interaction by Baecker et al. with over 900 pages. Both have been updated to a second edition [cf. 1, 16], but have not further. While both are still of great use as reference books, they do not provide details on teaching or studying HCI; in fact, Baecker et al. suggest to follow the ACM SIGCHI Curricula and explain how their book covers topics of the four courses described above (two for computer science, one for psychology, one for management information systems).

The reference book by Sears and Jacko on The Human-Computer Interaction Handbook has been updated to a second edition [25] and is a follow up of the two reference books above. In his foreword Shneiderman suggests the book to readers with various backgrounds [25, p. xix]: 'practitioners … newcomers to HCI … outsiders … visionary readers'. The parts of the book are: humans, computers, designing human-computer interactions, application and domain specific design, designing for diversity, development process, and managing HCI and emerging issues. So, a correspondence to the above curricula is obvious (esp. with respect to the later curriculum of the GI mentioned above). *Textbooks* homogeneously present HCI material, often in the form of monographs, to teachers and students of HCI. There are introductory textbooks that either provide a broad and general overview of the field [e.g., 24], or primarily focus on methods and the doing [e.g., 28], or primarily focus on basic concepts of HCI [e.g., 7]. Intermediate level textbooks aim at combining breadth and depth of these matters [e.g., 2]. Advanced books provide advanced-level material [e.g., 4].

The *introductory textbook* entitled Interaction Design by Preece et al. [24] provides an up-to-date basic introduction to HCI. It is in its 3rd edition and can be used by undergraduate students and beyond. It is a balanced combination of traditional HCI topics (e.g., understanding and conceptualising interaction, cognitive aspects) and current topics (e.g., social interaction, emotional interaction) as well as of theoretical concepts (e.g., interfaces, evaluation studies) and practical methods (e.g., data gathering, data analysis). Stone et al.'s textbook on User Interface Design and Evaluation [28] has a focus is on practical and professional skills, knowledge and understanding, and cognitive skills rather than on history and broad theory of HCI. The textbook Human-Computer Interaction by Dix et al. is—like the book by Preece et al.—well balanced, but at the same time 'is also rooted in strong principles and models' [7, p. xix]. It provides four parts: part one with chapters on foundations (i.e., the human, the computer, the interaction, paradigms) and part two with chapters on the design process (i.e., interaction design basics, HCI in the software process, design rules, implementation support, evaluation techniques, universal design, user support). The next part goes has chapters on models and theories (i.e., cognitive models, socio-organisational issues and stakeholder requirements, communication and collaboration models, task analysis, dialogue notations and design, models of the system, modelling rich interaction). Finally, despite the fact that this 3rd edition was already published in 2004 a fourth part has chapters with recent trends in HCI (i.e., groupware, ubiquitous computing and augmented realities, hypertext, multimedia and the World-Wide Web).

The *intermediate textbook* entitled Designing Interactive Systems by Benyon et al. [2] does not only provide a good combination of HCI in the parts: essential interactive systems design, people and technologies, activities and contexts of interactive systems design, psychological foundations for interactive systems design, techniques for interactive systems design and evaluation as well as information spaces, and computer-supported cooperative working, but also contributes recommendations on how to teach HCI. Through permutations of chapters several courses can be configured, some examples of which are, with 15 credits each: introduction to HCI; interaction design; user-centred design; future and emerging issues in HCI; advanced interactive systems design; designing for cooperation; web design; psychological foundations of HCI. This is possible, because the textbook not only contains traditional HCI knowledge, but also more recent lessons on methods and techniques (e.g., contextual design) as well as on information spaces (e.g., information architecture, information design, navigation of information space, agent-based interaction, ubiquitous computing and distributed information) and computer-supported cooperative work (e.g., supporting communication, understanding cooperative working, technology to support cooperation).

The *advanced-level book* on HCI Models, Theories, and Frameworks: Towards a Multidisciplinary Science edited by Carroll [4] is a profound presentation of the theoretical and scientific basis of HCI and is used for teaching higher level students. It provides a deep insight into HCI with the following chapters: applied perception; behavioural models for HCI; information processing and skilled behaviour; notational systems; users' mental models; exploring and finding information; distributed cognition; cognitive work analysis; common ground in electronically mediated communication; activity theory; applying social psychological theory to the problems of group work; studies of work in HCI; computational formalisms and theory; and design rational as theory. There are more books available, but those here constitute prominent representatives of different complexity. They show that the topics of the curricula are covered, but also new topics have been added. Both human and technical factors are presented, yet for most books human factors are more detailed than technical factors. This is due to the fact that most books are designed to complement other courses, mainly computer science courses that already cover technological factors in great detail. Visceral, behavioural, and reflective aspects play an increasingly important role, especially in more recent books. And overall, theories and models are included as much as application domains and systems. Research and engineering are covered to a great extent, and design is covered with knowledge on designing interactive systems (esp. about users and their context) as well as methods to develop prototypes. Design from the perspective of aesthetics and artistic skills and craftsmanship is not part of standard HCI literature. Yet, books from disciplines overlapping with or at the fringe of HCI have been published that provide great introductions to these matters for readers without artistic knowledge and skills [e.g., 9].

3   Trends in HCI

In the above section I have already pointed at some developments in HCI curricula and books. In this section I look more closely to such developments in HCI from the past to the present in order to identify trends in HCI into the future.

3.1   The Emergence of HCI

The *emergence and evolution of HCI* was very often leveraged by the emergence of new technologies. Benyon et al. bring this to the point [2, p. ixx]:

In the early 1990s the 'world wide' Web appeared, opening up website design as a new area. … By the late 1990s mobile phones had become a fashion statement for many people; style was as important as function. … User interfaces became tangible, graspable and immediate and software systems had to be engaging as well as functional. … All this has brought us to where we are today: a dynamic mix of ideas, approaches and technologies being used … in different contexts.

As has been pointed out above HCI has *a human and a technical* side. Carroll [4, p. 2] explains: 'HCI was originally a joining of software engineering and human-factors engineering.'. Both sides—the human and the technological—are evolving. Yet, as Grudin writes, the pace of development can be different [15, p. 2]: 'aspects of the human side of HCI change more slowly if at all. Much of what was learned about perceptual, cognitive, social, and emotional processes in interacting with older technologies applies to emerging technologies'. Looking at the evolution of the *technological factors* it is interesting to start at the origins. MacKenzie [21] characterises a trajectory from the early seminal work of Vannevar Bush [3] who claimed that we should build systems that support the creation, maintenance, and following of associations between documents—just like hypertext systems and links in the World-Wide Web today. Another milestone was Ivan Sutherland's SketchPad, which provided interactive graphics that users could grasp and move. It was already published in 1963, and reprinted in 2003 [30]. And, as a last example, Doulas Engelbarts and William English's [10] NLS system was presented and live demonstrated in 1968 and offered users an interactive text processor application to write texts, including figures and tables, and featured an integrated audio and video conferencing tool to communicate with remote colleagues. Part of the NLS was the computer mouse—as we know it today—that the authors invented at the same time. The technical progress then continued, and can be characterised with an evolution from single-user systems that were based on graphical user interfaces and windows, mice, menus, and pointing devices; to cooperative systems that supported the communication and collaboration over distance; to ubiquitous computing with technology to sense users' presence and activities, infer their needs, and adapt the environment accordingly; and finally to ambient intelligence that 'adapts to the presence of people and objects and assists users smartly while preserving security and privacy' [12, p. 274]. While these technologies follow each other chronologically, they do not necessarily replace, but rather complement each other, and have been used in parallel until today (e.g., most users still use windows-based systems such as Mac OS X or Windows).

With respect to *human factors* used in HCI Draper and Norman point out that technology is important, yet a focus on users and their needs should prevail [8, p. 2f]: 'the emphasis is on people, rather than technology, although the powers and limits of contemporary machines are considered in order to know how to take that next step from today's limited machines toward more user-centred ones.'. And technological progress does not happen in isolation of the human aspects and methods in HCI. Gross analysed the consequences of the evolution of technology on the process and methods to design, implement, and evaluate the respective technology [13]. According to the author, for instance, the waterfall model was adequate for the time when mainframe hardware was dominant and development cycles very long. Later, with a stronger focus on users and the advent of HCI, more iterative models were used. And, more recently, human-centred models focus on users, tasks, contexts, and ambient adaptations and their iterative design, development, and evaluation. Carroll emphasises the evolution and diversification of the human factors and methods in HCI in his book in a chapter entitled Let 100 Flowers Blossom with a 'differentiation within the original cognitive-science community of HCI' [4, p. 4f]. In the 1980s computer technology was new to most users and so the focus was on 'learning and comprehension problems of novice users … It addressed issues such as abductive reasoning, learning by exploration, external representations, and the development of analogies and mental models.'. Furthermore, at that time cognitive science also became more diverse and multidisciplinary per se. As Carroll [4, p. 4f] puts it:

Social psychologists, anthropologists, and sociologists entered the cognitive-science discourse, sometimes taking HCI as their empirical touchstone. Suchman's study of photocopier use described a variety of usability problems with advanced photocopier-user interfaces. She considered the interaction between the person and the machine as a sort of conversation that frequently fails because the participants do not understand one another.

And another driving force for diversification was the internationalisation of HCI, which according to Carroll [4, p. 4f] was 'facilitated by several International Federation for Information Processing (IFIP) conferences held in Europe, and by initiatives within major computer companies'. Combining technological and human factors into an overall focus on *HCI as a discipline* Shackel published a seminal paper in 1997 with a reprint in 2009 [26], where he characterises the technological, human, and methodological progress, but also the evolution of the field with research centres, conferences and journals, and a body of knowledge that has been growing rapidly. In a similar vein Grudin [15] characterised the overall evolution of HCI, as well as human factors and ergonomics, and information systems. He—like Carroll—also points out the increasing diversity, which in his opinion is related to the divergence of HCI and human factors.

Overall, HCI has evolved, yet many seminal works and theories, and models do not outdate. For instance, Erickson and McDonald [11, p. 3] write that there is 'valuable older work fading from our discipline's working memory. We are interested in bringing back that work in a way that reflects the diversity of the field's influences, and the idiosyncrasies of the individuals who constitute the discipline.'.

3.2   The Present and the Future of HCI

HCI as a field has been developing at great speed and is integrating new disciplines as well as by expanding into other disciplines. Sears and Jacko are *positive* about this development and write [25, p. xxi]: 'HCI is no longer just an area of specialisation within more traditional academic disciplines, but has developed such that both undergraduate and graduate degrees are available that focus explicitly on the subject.'. In an article with the title Is HCI Homeless? Grudin is *less optimistic*. He discusses distinguishes HCI from human factors and ergonomics, and from information systems along various dimensions: for instance, discretionary use of technology in HCI versus non-discretionary use of technology in human factors and ergonomics as well as in information systems.

Liu et al. [19] analysed all papers of the ACM CHI conference of *two decades* with a total of 3152 papers and 16035 keywords and did a co-word analysis. The first decade of 1994 to 2003—compared to the second of 2004 to 2013—had a fixed focus. In the second decade the field and the number of publications had grown tremendously (i.e., 702 vs. 2450 papers) and spread into directions such as mobile and social interaction, with novel scenarios such as crowdsourcing and privacy in the online world. The authors identify *major research themes* for the first decade such as computer-supported cooperative work, interaction design, computer-mediated communication; World-Wide Web, empirical study, email; ubiquitous computing, augmented reality, tangible user interface; etc. For the second decade similarities and differences in the most prominent topics could be identified, with topics such as: mobile phone, sustainability, ethnography; ubiquitous computing, privacy, mobile; visualisation, collaboration, user interface; etc. Looking closer into recent trends of the second decade emerging changes can be identified that give an impression on how the publication topics of the ACM CHI conference might evolve in the future. For instance, sustainability and ethnography are popular topics, and education, learning, communication, and awareness are backbone topics, and according to the authors need special attention since they are vital for the field. The authors conclude that HCI is a diverse and dynamic field with a fast pace of technological development, and a slower but still important pace of theories and models in HCI. This corroborates above findings. Topics emerge, topics merge, topics interact with each other, and the overall network of keywords has been polycentric. Thus the HCI community had been and should remain adaptive in the future.

So, over the last 70+ years HCI has witnessed a development with technological progress, conceptual insight, and new theories and methods. The emergence of the field can be characterised by gigantic monolithic projects with project teams of hundreds of members. Over the last two decades the growth and diversification has increased—especially in the last decade. There is agreement among authors that HCI has definitely become bigger and more diverse, but there are different opinions whether this development is positive or negative and whether it is possible to stop it or even turn it back by unifying research strands. Looking at the very detailed analysis of Liu et al. it seems that growth and diversification in the flagship conference of the field—the ACM CHI conference—and beyond is positive and irreversible.

4   Lessons Learned for HCI Education

HCI is *distinct* from other fields such as computer and information science and software engineering, despite the fact that it emerged from such fields. This is partly due to the fact that users with their goals and tasks, needs and requirements, tools and contexts will always remain in the centre of the focus of HCI, but not necessarily the focus of other related disciplines. Because of the growth, diversification, and uniqueness new HCI study programmes only partly fit into old structures and are therefore in many institutions separate from existing programmes. Shneiderman writes [27, p. 71]:

Universities ... sprout successful new units such as the Human-Computer Interaction Institute at Carnegie Mellon University or the Media Lab at the Massachusetts Institute of Technology. Interdisciplinary groups, such as those at Stanford University or the University of Maryland, bring together faculty and students from multiple departments.

Those universities that early on embarked on teaching HCI in traditional face-to-face classroom courses are now also the ones that early produced material that can be taught in *online courses* with remote students. In recent years, Massive Open Online Courses (MOOCs) have become popular, also in HCI [6]. Despite the changes of technological and human factors as well as theories and models, it is important for HCI education to not only run after the most recent trends, but also stay focused and also teach practical skills. HCI thinking emerges through a balance of theoretical knowledge and practical experience. Shneiderman points out [27, p. 112]: 'memorable educational experiences ... enrich students with increased knowledge and skills, provide them with a satisfying sense of accomplishment.'.

And, although the field of HCI is growing fast and becoming increasingly diverse, it is still important to keep the overall picture, which has over centuries been a virtue that has never changed. Shneiderman analysed Renaissance thinking and takes Leonardo da Vinci as a role model and writes [27, p. 2]:

This modern Renaissance would unify thinking about technology by promoting multidisciplinary education and a sympathy for diversity. ... Leonardo integrated engineering with human values. ... Leonardo-like thinking could help users and technology developers to envision the next generation of information and communication technologies.

So, it is quite likely that in the future HCI will further grow and get rather get more diverse, and so will HCI education with respect to both contents and formats of teaching. Recommendations for curricula can give guidance and help avoiding misunderstandings, frame expectations with respect to qualifications of students, and provide a shared reference and orientation. At the same time it is a great strength of HCI that it is diverse in paradigms, theories, principles, methods, tools and conceptual and technological results. HCI education should reflect that and adapt the structure, contents, and format to the respective situation and needs. Since any HCI education, no matter how small it may be, is better than no HCI education, it is also important to scale down HCI education. Scaling up education and providing complete study programmes in the form of Bachelor, Master, or PhD programmes is possible, since over the decades the body of knowledge developed have become so vast.

5   Conclusions

HCI has over the last decades matured to an exciting field of research and teaching. The community is growing, the number and size of scientific and industrial venues is growing, and the body of knowledge is almost exploding. HCI should always have an early focus on users, tasks, and their contexts. Since user populations, tasks, contexts and application scenarios are getting increasingly divers, it is adequate that also the means to deal with them—in terms of theory, paradigms, methods, tools—are also expanding their range. In this paper I have analysed HCI education today. I have characterised the past, present, and future of the field of HCI. I have discussed the consequences for teaching HCI face-to-face and online. Overall, I am very optimistic that the growth and diversification of HCI research and education is positive for the development of the field into the future. As has been pointed out in the introduction at the very beginning of this paper with the quote of Wegner—in his words of the title of the quoted publication 'interaction is more powerful than algorithms. Powerful and complex interaction should be handled with diverse approaches.

Acknowledgments. I would like to thank all colleagues whom I had invaluable discussions; especially my colleagues from the TC.13 on Human-Computer Interaction of the International Federation for Information Processing IFIP, and from the Steering Committee of Human-Computer Interaction and of Computer-Supported Cooperative Work of the Germany Informatics Society (Gesellschaft für Informatik, GI).

References

1. Baecker, R.M., Grudin, J., Buxton, W.A.S., Greenberg, S. (eds.): Readings in Human-Computer Interaction, 2nd edn. Morgan Kaufmann Publishers, San Francisco (1995)
2. Benyon, D., Turner, P., Turner, S.: Designing Interactive Systems. Addison-Wesley, Reading (2005)
3. Bush, V.: As we think. The Atlantic Monthly 176(1), 101–108 (1945)
4. Carroll, J.M. (ed.): HCI Models, Theories, and Frameworks. The Morgan Kaufmann Series in Interactive Technologies. Morgan Kaufmann Publishers, San Mateo (2003)
5. Churchill, E.F., Bowser, A., Preece, J.: Teaching and Learning Human-Computer Interaction: Past, Present, and Future. ACM Interactions, 44–53 (March/April 2013)
6. Cooper, S., Sahami, M.: Education - Reflections on Stanford's MOOCs. Communications of the ACM 56(2), 28–30 (2013)
7. Dix, A., Finlay, J., Abowd, G.D., Beale, R.: Human-Computer Interaction. Pearson, Englewood Cliffs (2004)
8. Draper, S.W., Norman, D.A.: Introduction. In: Norman, D.A., Draper, S.W. (eds.) User Centred System Design, pp. 1–5. Lawrence Erlbaum, Hillsdale (1986)
9. Edwards, B.: The New Drawing on the Right Side of the Brain: A Course in Enhancing Creativity and Artistic Confidence. Penguin Putnam Inc., N.Y. (1999)
10. Engelbart, D., English, W.K.: A Research Centre for Augmenting Human Intellect. In: Proc. of the Fall Joint Computing Conference - FJCC 1968, Montvale, NY, pp. 395–410. AFIPS Press, Washington (December 1968)

11. Erickson, T., McDonald, D.W. (eds.): HCI Remixed. MIT Press, Cambridge (2008)
12. Gross, T.: Cooperative Ambient Intelligence: Towards Autonomous and Adaptive Cooperative Ubiquitous Environments. Int. J. of Autonomous and Adaptive Communications Systems (IJAACS) 1(2), 270–278 (2008)
13. Gross, T.: Towards a New Human-Centred Computing Methodology for Cooperative Ambient Intelligence. J. of Ambient Intelligence and Humanised Computing (JAIHC) 1(1), 31–42 (2010)
14. Grudin, J.: Is HCI Homeless? In Search of Inter-Disciplinary Status. ACM Interactions 13(1), 54–59 (2006)
15. Grudin, J.: A Moving Target: The Evolution of HCI. In: Sears, A., Jacko, J.A. (eds.) Human-Computer Interaction Handbook, 2nd edn., pp. 1–24. Lawrence Erlbaum, Hillsdale (2008)
16. Helander, M.G., Landauer, T.K., Prabhu, P.V.: Handbook of Human-Computer Interaction. Elsevier, Amsterdam (1997)
17. Hewett, T.T., Baecker, R.M., Card, S.K., Carey, T., Gasen, J., Mantei, M.M., Perlman, G., Strong, G., Verplank, W.: ACM SIGCHI Curricula for Human-Computer Interaction. ACM (1992), http://old.sigchi.org/cdg/index.html (accessed January 31, 2014)
18. IEEE & ACM. Computer Curricula 2001. IEEE CS & ACM (2001), http://www.acm.org/education/curric_vols/cc2001.pdf (accessed January 31, 2014)
19. Liu, Y., Goncalves, J., Ferreira, D., Xiao, B., Hosio, S., Kostakos, V.: CHI 1994-2013: Mapping Two Decades of Intellectual Progress through Co-Word Analysis. In: Proc. of the Conference on Human Factors in Computing Systems - CHI 2014 (to appear, 2014)
20. Maass, S., Ackermann, D., Dzida, W., Gorny, P., Oberquelle, H., Roediger, K.-H., Rupietta, W., Streitz, N.: Recommendations for Software Ergonomics Education. GI e.V. (1994), http://www-cg-hci.informatik.uni-oldenburg.de/GI-Recommendations/ (accessed January 31, 2014)
21. MacKenzie, I.S.: Human-Computer Interaction. Morgan Kaufmann Publishers, San Mateo (2013)
22. Norman, D.A.: The Design of Everyday Things, Doubleday/Currency, N.Y. (1988)
23. Norman, D.A.: Emotional Design. Basic Books, N.Y. (2004)
24. Preece, J., Rogers, Y., Sharp, H.: Interaction Design. Wiley, N.Y. (2011)
25. Sears, A., Jacko, J.A. (eds.): Human-Computer Interaction Handbook, 2nd edn. Lawrence Erlbaum, Hillsdale (2008)
26. Shackel, B.: Human-Computer Interaction - Whence and Whither? Interacting with Computers 21, 353–366 (2009)
27. Shneiderman, B.: Leonardo's Laptop. MIT Press, Cambridge (2002)
28. Stone, D., Jarrett, C., Woodroffe, M., Minocha, S.: User Interface Design and Evaluation. Morgan Kaufmann Publishers, San Francisco (2005)
29. Strauss, F., Beck, A., Dahm, M., Hamborg, K.-C., Heers, R., Heinecke, A.M.: Curriculum for a Base Module for Human-Computer Interaction. GI e.V. (2006), http://www.gi-ev.de/fileadmin/redaktion/empfehlungen/GI-Empfehlung_MCI-Basismodul2006.pdf (accessed February 5, 2014)
30. Sutherland, I.E.: Sketchpad: A Man-Machine Graphical Communication System (2003), https://design.osu.edu/carlson/history/PDFs/UCAM-CL-TR-574.pdf (accessed October 10, 2011)
31. Wegner, P.: Why Interaction Is More Powerful Than Algorithms. Communications of the ACM 40(5), 81–91 (1997)

Tangible Disparity - Different Notions of the Material as Catalyst of Interdisciplinary Communication

Michael Heidt[1], Linda Pfeiffer[2], Andreas Bischof[1], and Paul Rosenthal[2]

[1] Chemnitz University of Technology, Research Training Group crossWorlds,
Thüringer Weg 5, Chemnitz 09126, Germany
[2] Chemnitz University of Technology, Visual Computing Group,
Straße der Nationen 62, Chemnitz 09111, Germany
{michael.heidt,paul.rosenthal}@informatik.tu-chemnitz.de,
andreas.bischof@phil.tu-chemnitz.de,
linda.pfeiffer@s2011.tu-chemnitz.de

Abstract. Communicating tangible technology designs hinges on an adequate notion of materiality. However, academic disciplines involved employ wildly differing notions of the material. This issue effects communicative boundaries within interdisciplinary teams tasked with development of tangible digital artefacts. In order to address this problem, we provide an analysis of differing disciplinary modes of conceptualisation and theorisation. Following these considerations, we discuss theoretical artefacts able to serve as communicative interfaces between the disciplines in question.

Keywords: materiality, interdisciplinarity, cultural informatics, critical technical practice.

1 Introduction

Any meaningful deployment of tangible technology finds itself embedded into a heterogeneous array of materials and social practices. While production of physical artefacts calls for practitioners versed in design or possessing skills as artisans, the digital side of tangible technology production usually is addressed by computer professionals. Inevitably tangible technology production takes places in interdisciplinary networks, while each discipline possesses its own theories, intellectual heritage and modes of problem solving.

Recently, the notion of materiality has gained special attention within the community of interaction design [13,1]. Within the field of cultural studies interest in materiality of artefacts has reached a level where scholars proclaim a "material turn"[6]. While different scientific and intellectual trajectories are at work here, tangible interaction projects have to account for these academic developments in order to make use of the intellectual artefacts produced.

M. Kurosu (Ed.): Human-Computer Interaction, Part I, HCII 2014, LNCS 8510, pp. 199–206, 2014.

2   Different Materialities

Most often the term 'tangible' is used in a literal way within tangible interaction projects, denoting artefacts one can touch with one's hand, exhibiting haptic qualities.

While dealing with this type of materiality does not seem to pose greater problems for engineers, accustomed to dealing with artefacts anchored within the realm of the physical, the same cannot be said for computer-scientists. The main mode of production for the computer scientist is the production of source code or other formal or semi-formal types of communication. Floyd describes software as consisting of 'a uniform, abstract building material [. . .] not amenable to sensory perception' [3]. Consequently, those educated mainly in computer science do not find themselves equipped with rich vocabularies for dealing with the tangible or with sensory phenomena in general. At the same time what computer professionals are dealing with, code, exhibits some qualities of a material, rendering it comparable to building materials occuring in disciplines such as architecture.

Accordingly, we found the concept of digital materiality to constitute an ample conceptual bridge, allowing for notions and communications to be translated between researchers and practitioners. Leonardi provides a comprehensive discussion of digital materialities within the context of organisation theory [10].

Furthermore, conceptual integration between computer science and social science already has been achieved by virtue of Paul Dourish's stance of Embodied Interaction (EI) [2]. What embodied interaction achieves is to provide a cogent argumentation for a common conceptual model, encompassing both social as well as tangible computing. Both have to be understood on the basis of situated social actions, in both cases meaning must be conceptualised as being essentially context-bound. EI however does neither want to provide a wealth of concrete design guidelines, furthermore it does not account for the theory-making processes accompanying the practice of software construction. In consequence, we believe it worthwhile to embrace the conceptual devices introduced by EI, while complementing it with theorisations of the material as outlined above.

3   Past Discussions

In the following, we will retrace the discussion process within the HCI community.

Jung and Stolterman [7] employ the classical distinction between material and form. They provide an in depth discussion on the relationship between digital form and materiality. Explicitly aimed at introducing perspectives from disciplines like art, design, social science and humanities they try to reconceptualise key concepts within HCI discourse. They propose a new approach towards development of interactive artefacts dubbed *form-driven interaction design*. Within the digital materiality discourse they hereby claim that construals of the digital as material can be brought to fruition. A key metaphor introduced is that of *material ecologies* aligning itself with discourse on the topic of design and interface ecologies [8,9,5].

In his seminal articles [10,11] Leonardi analyses the problem of material from the perspective of organisational theory. Leonardi gives a semantic analysis centered on language use within legal and institutional domains. He first examines the predicate 'material' within the domain of law. Material evidence is that which pertains to the matters at hand, to the current case, to inquiries that 'matter'. Material provides substance and enforces restrictions. In doing so, the text does not try to extract a unified semantic kernel. Leonardi's efforts center on the question of explaining how digital artefacts can make a difference. In the course of his discussion Leonardi does not lose the distinction material/formal. He does however relegate it to the position of a single dichotomy within a broader conceptual ensemble.

Positions like this explicitly or implicitly relate to positions within the history of ideas. Form/Material is a very old distinction in the history of thought, reaching back to the times of antiquity. Aristotle provides for an analysis of the conceptual division between hyle and morphe. The form being the organising principle, hyle denotes that which is being formed. He applies these categories recursively: Aristotle's thought still remains to be extremely influential. For example categories like such as shape reappear in Jung and Stolterman's text [7] while there is no explicit mention of Aristotle.

What generally tends to be repressed is Aristotle's theory of causation. Not many authors talk of *material causes* though this could constitute an interesting candidate for introduction into the digital materiality discourse.

Leibniz is one of the first authors dealing explicitly with the digital. However, his monadic perspective differs fundamentally from modern conceptions of the material. His position is special, for it marks a radicalisation of Aristotle's conception of the world as a *teleological* structure. There is no 'pure' or 'empty' material for Leibniz, everything is causally integrated. Furthermore, substances represent the wholeness of the world, however imperfectly. While remaining important as thinker of the digital, Leibniz' positions are notoriously hard to incorporate into contemporary discourse of the material. This, of course, ensures his role as potential conceptual irritant. His theories are extremely well structured and formal themselves, appealing to formal scientists' aesthetics.

There is a vast array of literature on the problem of material within the domain of *architecture*. Truth to materials being an ideal of modernist architecture.

Vallgaarda and Redström [14] argue that digital material is not substance. They thus criticise notions of the digital as material as brought forth by Jung and Stolterman [7]. For Vallgaarda and Redström the digital needs to be combined with other elements in order to become material. They thus argue for conceptualising interactive artefacts as being made of a *composite material*. Only when the digital is combined with non-digital material is it able to make a difference. It does not possess substance of its own, nor is it a structuring principle opposed to mere material. By doing so, Vallgaarda and Redström sidestep the implicit judgements of value often attached to distinctions such as form/material. The digital is not seen as more 'pure', instead it is part of a composite. Thus both sides are described by language evoking conceptions of physical material. Neither is there pure material, nor are there pure forms. The authors try to transcend what is perceived as functionalistic restriction within HCI discourses. The approaches they formulate do not revolve around questions of function. Instead they can be construed as evolving relationships between materials.

Loos invokes the material in his seminal essay "Ornament and Crime" [12]. Ornament is seen as a device causing objects 'to go out of style', while their functionality remains intact. It can thus be read in context with contemporary discussions on digital obsolescence as well as the general planned obsolescence discourse.

4   Functions

As seen, invoking the concept of the material can serve a wide array of purposes within interdisciplinary discourse. Analysing the Invoking the concept of material can serve purposes of:

- allowing for new ways of conceptualising systems incorporating both physical and digital material
- contribute towards clarifications of differences in perspective within interdisciplinary design settings
- provide conceptual bridges towards discourse in other disciplines e.g. architecture

5   Application

In order to demonstrate the utility of concepts discussed, we will briefly outline a set of prototypical design artefacts. Their creation process was informed by the theoretical interfaces covered. They are situated within the domain of museum and exhibition contexts.

5.1   Project Context

Observations made as well as concrete discussions conducted took place within the interdisciplinary research training group crossWorlds. Situated within an academic context, researchers with backgrounds in engineering, computer-science, philosophy, cultural theory, design, sociology, media psychology, rhetoric and neuroscience all contributed to the project.

5.2   Requirements

Informed by the notions discussed, the following requirements drove the prototyping process:

- Installations should feature the materiality of the exhibits, not distract from them by providing additional gadgets.
- Installations should facilitate direct social interaction. They should not mesmerise users by capturing their attention within spectacular technological displays.

5.3   Dimensions of Materiality

Within the interface ecology outlined, we deal with different types of materials. These relate to and affect each other throughout the whole setting:

physical materials At first there are historical materials, the exhibits, the objects of interest, whose materiality should be featured. On the other hand there are contemporary materials, which have to align themselves with design requirements. They form the material basis of interaction artefacts such as cards, displays, stamps, smart phones, etc. . Their material characteristics are crucial with respect to interaction processes. Human bodies have also to be considered as physical materials that allow for and constrain interaction due to their material characteristics.

social materials - peoples minds, their comprehension of the world - social and cultural contexts

digital materials could be representations of information about the object of interest, in the form of texts, pictures, videos or structures. Another digital artefact to be considered is software, as an element structuring the interaction process and presentation of information.

5.4   Prototypes

Following the requirements given, we outline two of the prototypes developed, describing how they relate to theories presented:

An *interactive table* installation was developed, allowing visitors to collaboratively access exhibit related information 1. Instead of using digital representations within a traditional multi-touch layout, actual exhibits or physical reproductions are employed as *tangibles*. Placed on the table surface, they act as proxies into the underlying information space, allowing for interactions to be triggered. Thus, the turn towards materiality is reflected within the design artefact produced. Whenever possible, direct tangible interactions with exhibits are employed instead of having users deal with digital representations. In order to remain true to historical materialities, touching actual exhibits is infeasible, reproductions should mimic the original's sensual qualities as closely as possible.

A recommender system is used to guide visitors within the museum space. It embodies the idea that digital material ought to be used to equip other entities with affordances. In its concrete form, it is constructed as a *social recommender* (such as described in [4]) supposed to facilitate direct face-to-face interactions among visitors. The historical materiality of the exhibits is embedded into modes of interaction inherently contemporary. Touching and interacting with exhibits and reproductions triggers events which are part of an UI-design inspired by social networking websites.

6   Discussion

New physical materials are introduced into HCI oriented making practices, causing an increased level of interest in questions of materiality. There has not yet

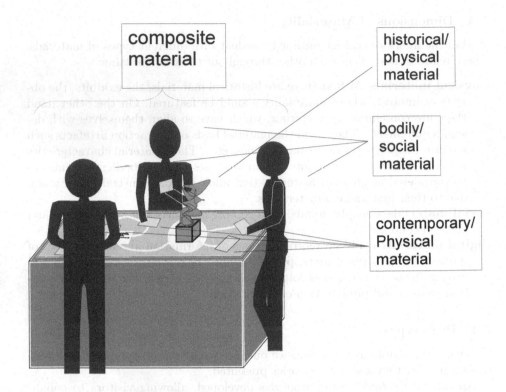

composite
material

historical/
physical
material

bodily/
social
material

contemporary/
Physical
material

Fig. 1. Dimensions of the material with respect to tangible user interfaces

been convergence either between disciplines or within the field of HCI regarding conceptions of digital material. What can be observed however, are new waves of interest in questions regarding materials.

The proposed set of installations presents a blend of contemporary and historical materials. The former are employed in order to highlight the qualities of the latter. They were produced in an interdisciplinary context, paying special attention to differing conceptualisations of the material.

It was shown how the notion of materiality can be employed as a conceptual lens for providing fresh perspectives on interdisciplinary technology design. Tangible technology production calls for highly interdisciplinary design processes. Within these communicative problems can arise regarding different modes of conceptualising the material. At the same time, there are points of convergence in the form of a common "material-turn" among the disciplines. Possible conceptual interfaces were discussed with a focus on the notion of digital materialities. The discussion provided delineates a starting point for exploring these concepts within design contexts.

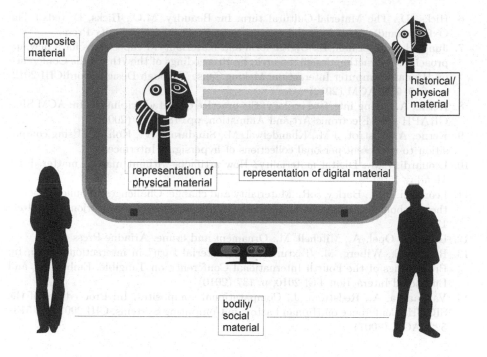

Fig. 2. Different dimensions of the material with respect to a wall-mounted display

Within project contexts, discussions focussing on the notion of the material can further awareness of the conditions of interdisciplinary cooperation. Within these discussion processes different notions of the material designate different disciplinary perspectives.

References

1. Doering, T.: Material-centered design and evaluation of tangible user interfaces. In: Proceedings of the Fifth International Conference on Tangible, Embedded, and Embodied Interaction - TEI 2011, p. 437 (2011)
2. Dourish, P.: Where the Action is: The Foundations of Embodied Interaction. MIT Press
3. Floyd, C.: Software development as reality construction. In: Floyd, C., Züllighoven, H., Budde, R., Keil-Slawik, R. (eds.) Software Development and Reality Construction SE - 10, pp. 86–100. Springer, Heidelberg
4. Heidt, M.: Examining interdisciplinary prototyping in the context of cultural communication. In: Marcus, A. (ed.) DUXU/HCII 2013, Part II. LNCS, vol. 8013, pp. 54–61. Springer, Heidelberg (2013)
5. Heidt, M., Kanellopoulos, K., Pfeiffer, L., Rosenthal, P.: Diverse ecologies – interdisciplinary development for cultural education. In: Kotzé, P., Marsden, G., Lindgaard, G., Wesson, J., Winckler, M. (eds.) INTERACT 2013, Part IV. LNCS, vol. 8120, pp. 539–546. Springer, Heidelberg (2013)

6. Hicks, D.: The Material-Cultural turn. In: Beaudry, M.C., Hicks, D. (eds.) The Oxford Handbook of Material Culture Studies. Oxford University Press,
7. Jung, H., Stolterman, E.: Digital form and materiality: Propositions for a new approach to interaction design research. In: Proceedings of the 7th Nordic Conference on Human-Computer Interaction: Making Sense Through Design, NordiCHI 2012, pp. 645–654. ACM (2012)
8. Kerne, A.: Doing interface ecology: the practice of metadisciplinary. In: ACM SIGGRAPH 2005 Electronic Art and Animation, pp. 181–185 (2005)
9. Kerne, A., Mistrot, J.M., Khandelwal, M., Sundaram, V., Koh, E.: Using composition to re-present personal collections of hypersigns. Interfaces
10. Leonardi, P.M.: Digital materiality? How artifacts without matter, matter. First Monday 15(6)
11. Leonardi, P.M., Barley, S.R.: Materiality and change: Challenges to building better theory about technology and organizing. Information and Organization 18(3), 159–176
12. Loos, A., Opel, A., Mitchell, M.: Ornament and crime. Ariadne Press
13. Robles, E., Wiberg, M.: Texturing the "material turn" in interaction design. In: Proceedings of the Fourth International Conference on Tangible, Embedded, and Embodied Interaction TEI 2010, p. 137 (2010)
14. Vallgaarda, A., Redström, J.: Computational composites. In: Proceedings of the SIGCHI Conference on Human Factors in Computing Systems, CHI 2007, pp. 513–522. ACM (2007)

Improvement of Novice Software Developers' Understanding about Usability: The Role of Empathy Toward Users as a Case of Emotional Contagion

Fulvio Lizano and Jan Stage

Aalborg University, Department of Computer Science, Aalborg, Denmark
{fulvio,jans}@cs.aau.dk

Abstract. There are several obstacles when it comes to integrating Human-Computer Interaction (HCI) activities into software development projects. In particular, a lack of understanding on the part of novice software developers regarding usability is one of the most cited problems related to this integration. Observation of usability evaluation by these developers has been cited in the literature as an alternative to improve their understanding about usability due to the fact that, among other things, this improves the level of empathy with users. In this paper we present the results of a quasi-experiment which explores the origin of this improvement. Our study suggests that the empathy of novice developers towards users could be originated by Emotional Contagion (EC) of these developers. This EC occurs unconsciously in activities where these developers can observe users working with the software. The present research is an initial approximation as to the relation which EC and empathy have in order to improve the novice software developers' understanding of usability.

Keywords: Software development, usability, understanding of usability, empathy towards users, emotional contagion.

1 Introduction

The lack of understanding on the part of novice software developer regarding usability, is one of the most cited problems about to integration of HCI activities (specially usability evaluations), into software development projects. [2, 3], [15], [18]. This problem suggests a low priority of software developers on the user. Developers' motivators confirm their focus on personal matters [9], [14].

According some studies, observation of usability evaluations by developers improves their understanding of usability and also their empathy with users [10], [21]. Other researchers confirm this increasing of empathy in contexts with close interaction with users [6, 7], [12, 13]. Causes of such phenomenon in developers have not been studied yet.

The empathy [5], [20] has its origin in an Emotional Contagion (EC) process [8], [17]. This process occurs between two actors: the observer and the observed. In the pro-cess, the observer unconsciously acquires the emotions of the observed after

M. Kurosu (Ed.): Human-Computer Interaction, Part I, HCII 2014, LNCS 8510, pp. 207–218, 2014.
© Springer International Publishing Switzerland 2014

seeing and interacting with him for some time [4], [20]. The observer assumes a submissive role in her/his interaction with the observed who, in turn, assumes a dominant role. The particular circumstances or personalities of each are decisive in establishing who assumes a particular role [17]. The EC-Process could be fundamental to explain why developers experiment an increasing in the empathy with users and also in the under-standing of usability, during their observation of usability evaluations.

Considering this, we conducted a quasi-experiment [23] which aimed to explore the improvement of the understanding of usability and also the empathy with users by novice software developers, into a usability evaluation context. Our study attempts to fill the gap in the literature by explaining this situation since a perspective of an EC-Process.

In the first section of this paper we present the introduction and a brief literature review. Next, the method is presented in the section 2. Following this, we present the results of our study. After the results have been summarized, the paper presents the discussion section before concluding with suggestions for future work.

2   Method

We conducted a quasi-experiment [19], [23] where nine developers (SE/CS students), grouped in two teams, conducted a usability evaluation with users [16]. Usability evaluations were used to set an interactive environment with users; our focus was on the improvement process of the understanding of usability, more than in the results of the tests.

We collected data related to the students' understanding of usability two weeks before the test (1DC) and immediately after (2DC) the test. Additionally, we held interviews with students. The aim of these interviews was to allow the authors to elaborate on or clarify some findings of the study.

In every DC we used two forms. The first form (F1) was used in order to allow the students to express their opinions related to the main strengths and weaknesses presented in their software. The second form (F2) was used to measure the relative importance given by the students to certain software/usability concepts. In this form, we used 5 pairs of concepts or sentences which could illustrate normal activities for SE or HCI practitioners.

The concepts related to SE were:

- Modelling software requirements.
- Understanding how a system is designed.
- Realizing how the Unified Modelling Language (UML) could be applied to a software project.
- Knowing about software modelling patterns.
- Understanding the main concepts of Object-Oriented modelling.

The concepts related to HCI were:

- Designing an interface both physically and conceptually correct.
- Understanding how a user interface could be designed.
- Realizing how the Gestalt Laws could be applied to a software project
- Knowing about visual design principles.
- Understanding the main concepts of Human-Computer Interaction.

The analysis of the data collected was focused on the identifying the improvement in the understanding of usability by analyzing differences (between 1DC and 2DC) in F1. In addition, we identified the understanding pattern of usability based on [1]. Results were triangulated with F2 and the interviews. As part of the analysis, we identified the origin of such improvement and the implications for the empathy toward users.

3   Results

In this section we present the results of the study. We felt that in order to better understand the mechanism(s) of generation of empathy towards users, we first needed to establish in a general and detailed way, beyond doubt, a real improvement in the understanding of usability. Following this, we could identify and understand better the patterns which characterized this improvement. This explains why we first focused on describing the variations in the understanding of usability after applying the corrective action (conduction of usability evaluation by the students); these results are presented in Sections 3.1, 3.2 and 3.3. Next, in Section 3.4 we will present the patterns which characterized the improvement of the novice software developers' understanding of usability. In this part of the results, we also included some of the students' personal opinions given during the interviews, in order to complete the picture.

3.1   Overall Understanding of Usability

We were interested in gauging the perceptions of students before and after their participation in the usability evaluation Table 1 presents the general results obtained when we enquired about the strengths (S) and the weaknesses (W) of their software (form F1).

Table 1. Strengths (S) and weaknesses (W) related to usability before and after conducting usability evaluation

Facts	F1				Variance	
	1 DC		2 DC			
	S	W	S	W	S	W
Total opinions (software + usability)	40	37	37	48	-3	+11
Opinions related to usability	16	12	11	37	-5	+25
Percentage	40%	32%	30%	77%	-10%	+45%

During 1DC the students provided 40 strengths and 37 weaknesses. 16 strengths were related to usability issues (40%). In addition, they provided 12 weaknesses (32%). In the 2DC the students provided 37 strengths and 48 weaknesses. In this case, 11 strengths were related to usability issues (30%) and 37 weaknesses were related to usability (30%). After the conduction of the usability evaluation the strengths related to usability decreased 10% whilst the weaknesses increased 45%.

The results of the relative importance given by the participants to software or usability matters (form F2) confirmed their perception about strengths and weaknesses. After the usability evaluation, the students' opinions changed in order to consider the usability as more important. It seems that usability becomes more relevant for students after they conduct the usability evaluation. These results are presented in Table 2.

Table 2. Strengths (S) and weaknesses (W) related to usability before and after conducting usability evaluation

Facts	F2			
	1 DC		2 DC	
	Related to software	Related to usability	Related to software	Related to usability
Favorable opinions	37	8	30	15
Percentage	82%	18%	67%	33%

3.2   Detailed Understanding of Usability

In Table 3, we present the strengths and weaknesses provided by students in 1DC and 2DC, which are related to usability. This table also includes the variation presented in these aspects after the usability evaluation.

Table 3. Strengths (S) and weaknesses (W) related to usability before and after conducting usability evaluation

Student	F1				Variance	
	1 DC		2 DC			
	S	W	S	W	S	W
A1	1	2	1	6	0	+4
A2	1	1	0	6	-1	+5
A3	1	2	2	6	1	+4
A4	3	4	0	4	-3	0
B1	2	1	1	4	-1	+3
B2	4	0	3	3	-1	+3
B3	2	1	2	3	0	+2
B4	1	1	1	2	0	+1
B5	1	0	1	3	0	+3
Total	16	12	11	37	-5	+25

The change in the students' opinions between the 1DC and the 2DC, can be grouped into three categories: reduction in the number of strengths and an increase in the number of weaknesses (we identified this category as 'expected change'), no change in the number of strengths and weaknesses (identified as 'no change') and increase in the number of strengths (we identified this category as 'unexpected change').

In the first case, an increase of weaknesses and a reduction of strengths related to usability, present a clear pattern in the change of opinion. After the evaluation, the students changed their opinions in order to report more weaknesses and a lower level of strengths related to usability in their software. The most representative change was given in the high number of weaknesses related to usability reported after the evaluation. For instance, in 1DC the student A-2 provided only one weakness related to usability: "looks awful", although in 2DC, the same student provided six new ones, e.g. "some counterintuitive stuff", "not enough buttons in specific windows", "same labels names – different actions", "confusing interface", "not enough label information" and "not enough indication of selected stuff". Other students also changed their opinions in an important way. This was the case for student A-3 who provided 2 weaknesses in 1DC, but after the usability evaluation, gave 6 weaknesses, e.g. "not consistent in all menus", "dropdown menu blocks buttons", "search function hard to find", "button names can be misleading", "some buttons are missing" and "windows too small". In 2DC, the same student also repeated this last weakness ("windows too small"). A lower variation in weaknesses was presented when it came to the change of opinion of student B-3. First, during 1DC, this student gave only one weakness: "slow UI between normal & full screen". Following this, in 2DC, the student provided three new weaknesses, e.g. "the learning curve", "full screen design flawed" and "bad keyboard navigation".

There were some cases where the students did not change the number of strength and weaknesses related to usability in their software. For example, student B-3 provided two strengths during 1DC such as "non-distracting design" and "intuitive design". In 2DC this student seemed to maintain his emphasis on the design matter; at that moment he reported two strengths, e.g. "smooth playback" and "nice design in normal mode (not full screen)".

Finally, there was an unexpected change in strengths. Student A-3 provided an additional strength after 2DC. In 1DC this student provided only one strength related to usability: "detailed overview for each entry". In 2DC the student maintained the same strength and gave another: "easy to learn". This student has broken the pattern related to reducing the strengths and increasing the weaknesses associated with usability.

3.3   Detailed Results on the Relative Importance of Usability

Our study also collected data relating to the relative importance which the students gave to software and usability matters, before and after their conduction of usability evaluation. These data were collected using the form designed to measure the relative importance given by the students to software/usability concepts (form coded as F2).

These results allow us to see the change in the understanding of usability from another perspective. Our interest was to identify whether or not the students placed more importance on usability matters after conducting the usability evaluation, and if there was a change, how this change occurred.

In this part of our study, we identified two main changes. The first change occurred when the students changed their opinion in order to prefer more usability matters. This change was coded as 'X->U'. On the other hand, the second change occurred when the students had selected software matters such as more important. This alternative change was coded as 'X->S'. Finally, our study also identified one case where no change occurred. We triangulated these results with the students' opinions related to their strengths and weaknesses of their software in order to verify consistency in the results. In Table 4 we present details of these changes.

Table 4. Detailed changes in the relative importance given by the students to software/usability matters, after conducting usability evaluation. (P# Pair of concepts)

Student	P1	P2	P3	P4	P5
A1					
A2	X->U		X->U		
A3			X->U		X->S
A4					X->S
B1	X->U				
B2	X->U				
B3			X->U		
B4	X->U			X->U	
B5		X->S		X->U	X->U

After conducting usability evaluation the students changed their opinion with the aim of considering usability matters as more important. These changes were particularly evident in Group B (students of computer science). Conversely, the group with more change of opinions towards technical aspects of the software, was Group A (students of software engineering). Finally, the common changes of opinion made to place more importance on the usability matter, were oriented to aspects related to designing GUIs and how to apply paradigms which could help this design.

3.4   Patterns in the Understanding of Usability

After identifying and understanding the improvement in the students' understanding of usability, we focused on exploring whether or not it would be possible to identify the detailed characteristics of this improvement process. In order to systematize the identification of the patterns presented in this process, we proceeded to classify the opinions given by students in both 1DC and 2DC. We focused on those opinions which were related to usability, ignoring the opinions coded as technical aspects related to software. Here, both the strengths and the weaknesses are treated together as a unified group of opinions; our interest was to identify the characteristics of the opinions in general, regardless of their nature. The approach of taxonomy of usability proposed in [1], provided us with the framework for the classification. This taxonomy defined six attributes presented in the concept of usability: Knowability (K), Operability (O), Efficiency (E), Robustness (R), Safety (S) and Subjective satisfaction (SS).

In the case of Group A, the opinions are related to the attributes which are more oriented to users (K, O and SS). It is remarkable that the emphasis from students is placed on aspects connected to the "knowability" attribute, especially after the usability evaluation.   The "knowability" attribute is defined as "the property by means of which the user can understand, learn, and remember how to use the system" [1]. For example, two weaknesses reported by the students were "Some counterintuitive stuff" and "Not enough indication of selected stuff". In the same way, one of the strengths was "Easy to learn".

This apparent concern of students for the user needs seems to be produced after the usability evaluation rather than at the same time. During the interviews that we held with two members of this group, their opinions seemed not to show a special affinity by the user during the evaluation. When we asked the students what they were thinking when they saw the users during the tests, one student said "... it can be quite funny to see users operate your program, especially when you make some easy task like finding a button, something that they may find difficult because your program may have some design issues". Another student, reflecting on a specific mistake that all the users found, reported that he "felt embarrassed because in the case of the mistake, it was an obvious mistake, never mind that the users found others mistakes too." More specifically, when we inquired about some special feeling of students toward the users during the tests, the first student responded: "Not really, just found it a bit hilarious, because our design was flawed". The second student reported: "I don't remember to have any specific feeling for the users; I just tried to be as objective as I could. I just focused taking notes all the time".

Next, we showed the students the information provided by them during 1DC and 2DC. We also showed them the change presented in their opinions between those DCs. At this time we asked them if they had realized, at the time of the 2DC, that their change of opinion was more oriented to usability. The first student stated: "Not sure if I was aware of it or not. Might have been since we've put a decent amount of effort in correcting our design mistakes afterwards". The other student reported that "Yes, I thought that I was more usability oriented, when I filled this form because I had my eyes open for the usability part of our software. I really notice which things the users felt using our software". Finally, we wanted to know if the students thought that their feelings toward users had been changed after observing the usability evaluations; their answers were categorical. The first student stated "Well yes, I did not take the user into account before, well of course a little bit but not as much. Lesson learned overall, that the user knows how the users want the design, the designer does not". The second one said "Well, I felt thanked for the users for point out the mistakes we made in our software". These partial results confirm that the students recognize the importance of users, that they express a genuine interest in those usability issues more connected to users' needs, and finally, that these feelings seem to be generated after the evaluation.

On the other hand, in the case of Group B again here it is possible to see a clear orientation to "knowability" attributes, e.g. the weakness "Relevant help information on every form" and the strength "Buttons have size compared to how often they are used". In addition, these students also chose opinions related with the attribute "operability", defined at the taxonomy as "the capacity of the system to provide users with the necessary functionalities and to permit users with different needs to adapt and use the system". For example, one of the weaknesses was "The learning curve" whilst one of the strengths was "Easy to use when have been used once". Finally, the students also selected opinions connected to the attribute "Subjective satisfaction" (e.i. "the capacity of the system to produce feelings of pleasure and interest in users"). In this case, one of the weaknesses and one of the strengths reported by students was, respectively, "Could have had a prettier GUI" and "It looks nice".

Contrary to the previous group, the students of the Group B distributed their opinions in those attributes more oriented to users (K, O and SS). It could be possible to explain this difference based on the conditions in which students of Group B made their usability evaluation. These students worked with more users who developed more tasks, something that allowed these students find more usability problems.

We also held an interview with one student of this group in order to try to identify when this affinity by users' needs occurred. The results were quite similar to those obtained in the previous interviews.

In general, all the students' opinions show two characteristics. First, their opinions are oriented toward usability attributes and fully oriented to users' needs. Second, after conducting usability evaluations, this phenomenon increases, specifically with regards to the concern of the students for aspects related to the needs of the users when it comes to understanding, learning, and remembering how to use the software. In Figure 1 we present these results.

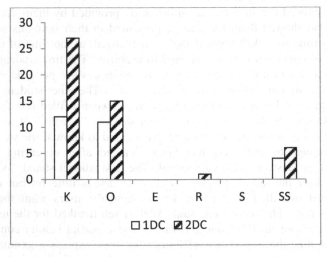

Fig. 1. Distribution of all students' opinions regarding the usability of their software, before and after conducting usability evaluation

4   Discussion

The lack of understanding regarding usability is a factor which limits the application of usability activities as, for example the application of usability evaluations in software development [2, 3]. In our study, the lack of understanding regarding usability is represented in those initial perceptions of students about usability in their software. Before the usability evaluation, this perception was characterized by a lower number of weaknesses related to usability (32%). However, after the usability evaluation, developers changed dramatically this opinion and have reported numerous weaknesses (77%). There is also a change in strengths after the usability evaluation. This initial measurement of the status of the students' understanding of usability, is another example of the low level of relevance that developers normally give to usability matters due, among other things, to their different aims, motivations, or mindset [3], [11], [22]. However, after conducting the usability evaluation, the new measurement of the status of the understanding allowed us to identify a new different perspective held by the students. The corrective action used (usability evaluation) allowed students to gain a different perspective of their software: the users' perspective. At that moment, they could identify new problems in their software (i.e. usability problems or even other functional problems). More important is the fact that their perspective changed in order to realize the relevance of other usability matters. Additional evidence of this change in students' perspective is presented in the analysis of the importance which students gave to usability matters. After conducting the usability evaluation the students changed their opinion, placing more importance on usability matters. These changes were particularly evident in Group B (students of computer science).

This increase in the students' understanding of usability is connected to their empathy toward users, which was increased during the usability evaluation [10]. This is something that we also found in our study when we saw students focusing more on usability issues, after the usability evaluation. This general predilection for usability more than for other technical issues, allows us to infer more attention on users' needs. In addition, analysing the pattern in the understanding of usability allows us to identify that the students certainly had, but more important yet, have increased their attention to usability matters which are strictly connected with users' needs (i.e. knowability, operability, and subjective satisfaction).

Some students (Group A) emphasized their opinions in the knowability attribute. Others spread their opinions on all the attributes connected with users' needs. This could be explained in the characteristics of each usability evaluation. Students of Group B interacted with more users who made more tasks; more usability problems were found during this process. These students worked more time with the users consequently, this higher level of interaction with them allowed students to have a wider vision of users' needs.

The reinforcement in the pattern of the understanding about usability, generated after conducting usability evaluation, suggest some affectation of the students as a result of the observation of the users interacting with their software. This does not occur simultaneously at the same time as the interaction with the users.

The interviews with some of the students clearly allowed us to identify that during the moment of the evaluation, they were not focused on the users. Their concerns at that moment were more of a personal nature. This is the case for one student, who was in charge of conducting the evaluation and expressed his concern because the users had problems thinking out loud. Other student found it funny that users could not use the software system well due to some design flaws, or finally the case of the user who felt embarrassed. All these feelings are strictly personal. Furthermore, all students were conclusive in affirming that during the process they had no special feeling toward the users. However, evidence of empathy is clear when we see the improvement in the students' understanding of usability and the pattern of this understanding. In actual fact, analysing the feelings of students toward users, at the moment of the interviews, we see only positive thoughts towards them.

This unconscious acquisition of empathy by students is crucial in order to gauge whether the process behind the generation of empathy of the students is the contagion of users' emotions that they experimented with in their interaction with the users. Indeed, this unconscious process is the cornerstone of basic conceptualization of the EC theory [8], [17]. In actual fact, our study confirmed that the students acquired the users' feelings or emotions before generating an emotional empathy and, later the cognitive empathy which is reflected in their opinions during the 2DC and the interviews. These opinions are an example of the eventual affective response identified by [5].

This is not trivial, nor is it an elaborate explanation of a process which may seem very logical. Identifying EC as the source of empathy of students, allows us to realize that there are corrective actions which are more effective than other traditional options (e.g. regular training), in order to improve the understanding of usability. This is the case with the observation or conduction of usability evaluations by software developers. In our experiment we detected a level of understanding about usability at 1DC obtained by students, mainly as a result of the training received, including topics related to HCI. After the usability evaluation, the understanding of usability changed radically. This new level of understanding, and empathy toward the users, was generated by EC as a result of the interaction with the users in more real conditions.

5   Conclusion

In this paper we presented the results of a quasi-experiment conducted in order to explore the origin of novice software developers' empathy toward users and its relation to the improvement process in understanding usability. We explored the status of the understanding of usability before and after a corrective action (conduction of a usability evaluation) made in order to enhance the understanding. The corrective action allowed the participants in our study to interact with users while they were working with a software system. In our study we explored in detail the improvement in understanding usability, in order to identify clues to help us trace the origin of the empathy toward users, produced as a result of this improvement process.

We found a clear enhancement in the understanding of usability after applying the corrective action; we detected a new student perspective when it came to their software and also about the relative importance that they gave to usability matters over other software technical aspects. This change in the students' perspective reflects an impact on what Sohaib & Khan, as well as Lee, have identified as the aims and motivations of developers which are normally present in their mindset. A better understanding of usability should involve a higher level of empathy toward users; something which we explored by studying the patterns presented in the understanding.

Patterns presented in the understanding regarding usability before and after the corrective action draw a picture and thus make it possible to find a clear and generalized preference for those usability attributes fully connected with users' needs, i.e. knowability, operability and subjective satisfaction.

More relevant for us was the confirmation that this empathy towards users was acquired in an unconscious process of contagion generated during the interaction with users; something which is consonant with EC theory.

Our study attempts to fill the gap in the literature by explaining the origin of novice software developers' empathy toward users. Additionally, our research suggests that in any corrective action to improve the understanding of usability, there is something behind the scenes. EC plays a relevant role in these processes. EC theory explains why those actions which involve more interaction with real users, in real conditions, could have better results that other more traditional actions, such as training.

Considering that our results could only be generalized to novice software developers, it is necessary to conduct more longitudinal studies in order to explore how EC interacts with other kinds of software developers.

Acknowledgments. The research behind this paper was partly financed by National University (Costa Rica), Ministery of Science and Technology – MICIT (Costa Rica), National Council for Scientific and Technological Research - CONICIT (Costa Rica), and the Danish Research Councils (grant number 09-065143).

References

1. Alonso-Ríos, D., Vázquez-García, A., Mosqueira-Rey, E., Moret-Bonillo, V.: Usability: a critical analysis and a taxonomy. International Journal of Human-Computer Interaction 26(1), 53–74 (2009)
2. Ardito, C., Buono, P., Caivano, D., Costabile, M.F., Lanzilotti, R., Bruun, A., Stage, J.: Usability Evaluation: A Survey of Software Development Organizations. In: Proceedings of 33rd International Conference on Software Engineering & Knowledge Engineering, Miami, FL, USA (2011)
3. Bak, J.O., Nguyen, K., Risgaard, P., Stage, J.: Obstacles to usability evaluation in practice: A survey of software development organizations. In: Proceedings of the 5th Nordic Conference on Human-Computer Interaction: Building Bridges, pp. 23–32. ACM (2008)
4. De Vignemont, F.: The co-consciousness hypothesis. Phenomenology and the Cognitive Sciences 3(1), 97–114 (2004)

5. Decety, J., Jackson, P.L.: A social-neuroscience perspective on empathy. Current Directions in Psychological Science 15(2), 54–58 (2006)
6. Gilmore, D.J., Velázquez, V.L.: Design in harmony with human life. In: CHI 2000 Extended Abstracts on Human Factors in Computing Systems, pp. 235–236. ACM (2000)
7. Grudin, J.: Obstacles to user involvement in software product development, with implications for CSCW. International Journal of Man-Machine Studies 34(3), 435–452 (1991)
8. Hatfield, E., Cacioppo, J.T., Rapson, R.L.: Emotional contagion. Cambridge Univ. Pr. (1994)
9. Hertel, G., Niedner, S., Herrmann, S.: Motivation of software developers in Open Source projects: an Internet-based survey of contributors to the Linux kernel. Research Policy 32(7), 1159–1177 (2003)
10. Hoegh, R.T., Nielsen, C.M., Overgaard, M., Pedersen, M.B., Stage, J.: The impact of usability reports and user test observations on developers' understanding of usability data: An exploratory study. International Journal of Human-Computer Interaction 21(2), 173–196 (2006)
11. Lee, J.C.: Embracing agile development of usable software systems. In: CHI 2006 Extended Abstracts on Human Factors in Computing Systems, pp. 1767–1770. ACM (2006)
12. Newell, A.F., Morgan, M.E., Gregor, P., Carmichael, A.: Theatre as an intermediary between users and CHI designers. In: CHI 2006 Extended Abstracts on Human Factors in Computing Systems, pp. 111–116. ACM (2006)
13. Patton, J.: Hitting the target: adding interaction design to agile software development. In: OOPSLA 2002 Practitioners Reports, p. 1–ff. ACM (November 2002)
14. Rasch, R.H., Tosi, H.L.: Factors affecting software developers' performance: an integrated approach. MIS Quarterly, 395-413 (1992)
15. Rosenbaum, S., Rohn, J.A., Humburg, J.: A toolkit for strategic usability: results from workshops, panels, and surveys. In: Proceedings of the SIGCHI Conference on Human Factors in Computing Systems, pp. 337–344. ACM (2000)
16. Rubin, J., Chisnell, D.: Handbook of usability testing: how to plan, design and conduct effective tests. John Wiley & Sons (2008)
17. Schoenewolf, G.: Emotional contagion: Behavioral induction in individuals and groups. Modern Psychoanalysis 15(1), 49–61 (1990)
18. Seffah, A., Metzker, E.: The obstacles and myths of usability and software engineering. Communications of the ACM 47(12), 71–76 (2004)
19. Shadish, W.R., Clark, M.H., Steiner, P.M.: Can nonrandomized experiments yield accurate answers? A randomized experiment comparing random and nonrandom assignments. Journal of the American Statistical Association 103(484), 1334–1344 (2008)
20. Singer, T., Lamm, C.: The social neuroscience of empathy. Annals of the New York Academy of Sciences 1156(1), 81–96 (2009)
21. Skov, M.B., Stage, J.: Training software developers and designers to conduct usability evaluations. Behaviour & Information Technology 31(4), 425–435 (2012)
22. Sohaib, O., Khan, K.: Integrating usability engineering and agile software development: A literature review. In: 2010 International Conference on Computer Design and Applications (ICCDA), vol. 2, pp. V2–32. IEEE (2010)
23. Shadish, W.R., Cook, T.D., Campbell, D.T.: Experimental and quasi-experimental designs for generalized causal inference. Wadsworth Cengage learning (2002)

Fast and Not Furious

Luiz Lopes Lemos Junior[1], Fábio Evangelista Santana[2], Fernando Antonio Forcellini[3],
Luiz Fernando Vaseak Machado[4], and João Paulo Castilho[5]

[1,4,5] IFSC, Rua Euclides Hack 1603, 89820-000, Xanxerê, SC, Brazil
[2] IFSC, Avenida XV de Novembro 61, Araranguá, 88900-000, SC, Brazil
[3] EMC-UFSC, Caixa Postal 476, Campus Universitário, 88040-900 - Florianópolis, SC, Brazil
luiz.lemos@ifsc.edu.br, fsantana@gmx.de, forcellini@emc.ufsc.br,
{nandinhu_tb,joaocastilhoo}@hotmail.com

Abstract. Two projects sequentially made planed and constructed of a
wheelchair-low-cost and a car to run at the academic Gravity Racing
Championship. The intention of them is provide to the Brazilian market a more
durable and cheaper standard manual wheelchair and a racing car to access for a
wheelchair and its driver. They were designed in CAD program for product
engineering (modeling in 3 axis). The mechanical elements of movements were
bought and retrofitted to the innovative structures. As the racing car was a 4
wheels model, the steering was inspired in the same used in kart models and the
breaks and wheels were cycling components. The loading and unloading system
was made by the driver without assistance of anyone (a ramp helps the person
to load the wheelchair in the car and the person set the ramp up for safety). The
car was not equipped with any propulsion equipment because the championship
rules admit only the influence of gravity.

Keywords: Wheelchair, Mechanical Construction, Racing Car for Wheelchair,
Vehicle for Wheelchair, Mechanical Manufacturing, Paraplegia.

1   Introduction

The project shows the construction of a standard manual wheelchair and the
construction of a racing car to access for a wheelchair and its driver, which original
idea started from Fábio Evangelista Santana. Two groups worked sequentially: the
first group intended to provide the Brazilian market with a more durable and cheaper
standard manual wheelchair; the other, designed and built a car to support the
wheelchair-low-cost to participate of a Gravity Racing Championship.

The wheelchair metallic structure prototype was designed in CAD program for
product engineering (modeling in 3 axis) obeying the standard dimensions of the most
popular wheelchair model of reference of ABNT NBR 9050 (the Brazilian
Organization for Standardization). To achieve the main objective, the wheelchair
should have a few custom parts, focusing on the design and construction of the

M. Kurosu (Ed.): Human-Computer Interaction, Part I, HCII 2014, LNCS 8510, pp. 219–229, 2014.
© Springer International Publishing Switzerland 2014

structure to receive these parts and how assembling the set easily and fast. The mechanical elements of movements, the seat and the backrest were bought and retrofitted to the innovative structure.

Using the three-dimensional model of the wheelchair developed before, the racing car for the academic championship "Gravity Racing", which occurs annually in Araranguá, Brazil, was designed in the CAD program which run dimensional and stress–strain analysis. As the vehicle was a 4 wheels model, the steering was inspired in the same used in kart models and the breaks and wheels were cycling components. There is a locking system to couple the wheelchair in the car. It works locking at 6 positions simultaneously: the two smaller wheels, the two larger (rear) and the two armrests. The loading and unloading system is made by the driver without assistance of anyone (a ramp helps the person to load the wheelchair in the car and the person set the ramp up for safety). The car was not equipped with any propulsion equipment because the championship rules admit only the influence of gravity.

So much for one as for the other project, the roll cage was built with AISI 1010 carbon steel tubes of 22mm outside diameter and 3 mm wall thickness. The most of the fixed parts were welded by MAG process to offer better finish or screwed into internal threads machined in the structure in order to provide greater security to the user avoiding protruding parts.

The wheelchair prototype would be used in the IFSC, Campus Xanxerê, in case of emergency and the racing car would be adapted for donation as a vehicle of transportation to a wheelchair user in need.

2   Theoretical Framework

2.1   Wheelchair-low-cost

According to the Instituto Brasileiro de Geografia e Estatística (IBGE), 2002, there are around 2.5% of the Brazilian population has mobility disabilities, which are temporary or permanent. So, the choice of both projects for the final course project is related to the promotion of accessibility, which is a subject of great importance to the reality of the community.

Despite being a standard for accessibility, ABNT NBR 9050 is free and easily accessible option to search in the Internet for students in undergraduate research technical standard. Another advantage is that it contains the basic dimensions for the construction of the wheelchairs as the ergonomic aspects of the Brazilian population, as shown in Figure 1.

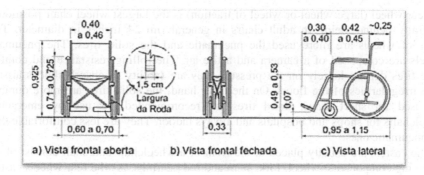

Fig. 1. Wheelchair standard dimensions NBR 9050, 2004

CAD Software. Using these known dimensions, the firsts prototypes in computer began to be created in 3D CAD using SolidWorks® software. This program was chosen because it is currently popular among mechanical manufacturing enterprises for its easy learning because its multilingual interface is highly intuitive (it includes Portuguese language, as in Figure 2). In addition, SolidWorks® contains a huge library of parts available for free by users throughout Internet access in file format of the program and the software is also able to import other formats too. The software is not free, but the IFSC own licenses to use it in professional courses.

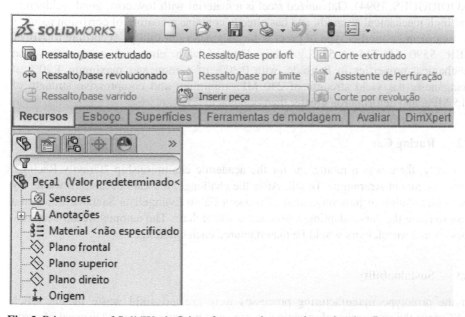

Fig. 2. Print screen of SolidWorks® interface: ease icons and translated to Portuguese Property of the authors

Rear wheel (large wheel or wheel of traction) is the largest wheel chair positioned generally behind, being in adult chairs in general rim 24 inches in diameter. Two kinds of wheels are more used the pneumatic and the solid tires. The pneumatic wheels are composed of a camera and a tire air. The rolling resistance and comfort these tires depend largely on the pressure they are (ability to absorb shocks arising from irregularities of the floor). On the other hand, the solid tires are more durable, but used for short ways. Solid tires are recommended for use by emergency wheelchairs for shops and hospitals and always indoor. They are less comfortable then the pneumatic ones.

The casters are usually placed at the front of a wheelchair and shall consist of the following components: wheel, fork, stem and rod bearings. As the rear wheels casters may have pneumatic or solid wheels too. The casters may vary between 3 and 8 inches. (RODRIGUES, 1994).

The back rest and cushion are very import for many people who use wheelchair spend more than 20 hours per day in the sitting and lying positions, thereby causing various problems in the muscles and the gluteal region, such as skin necrosis and ulcer formation, also causing serious problems of posture (GILSDORF, 1990). The selection of the appropriate seat padding and should take into account the following factors (COOPER, 1998), stability of support for arms, pressure distribution, maintenance of posture to prevent deformities, weight and ease of cleaning and durability.

The frame is part of the wheelchair that supports the weight of the user, the own weight and which are linked wheels, casters, the footrests and armrests, seat and back (RODRIGUES, 1994). Galvanized steel is a material with low cost, good weldability and high mechanical strength, and has already contains a coating of corrosion requires no treatment or another type of process for its greater durability. According to ABNT NBR 5590 (ASTM A-53), galvanized tubes with chemical composition and mechanical properties in B grade, with 0.30% of carbon and maximum 1.20% of manganese, has yield strength of 240 MPa minimum and compressive strength of 415 MPa, and deformation greater than or equal to 23%.

2.2   Racing Car

Annually, there was a racing car for the academic championship "Gravity Racing", which occurs in Araranguá, Brazil. After the challenge, the cars became in waste. By the accumulation of junk on campus, Professor Fábio Evangelista Santana proposed a way to reuse the cars, adapting a structure a wheelchair. The campus would keep few cars on and wheelchairs would be manufactured each challenge.

2.3   Sustainability

In the prototype manufacturing processes were created solid waste metals which IFSC gave the appropriate destination as expected by national laws. Disposal of waste was done according to the ABNT NBR 10.004:2004. Residues class II-A is not inert, such as residues of class II-B is. These two types of waste were produced and them can be recycled or disposed in standard landfills or landfills for recyclable waste.

3   Methodology

3.1   Wheelchair-low-cost

After completion of the design phase in CAD, it was prepared a list of materials to be machined and another for purchasing parts. It was difficult to buy parts to a compatible price for the project, because parts for wheelchairs are rarely marketed in the country. From the same supplier were purchased: 24' rear wheels and front casters. Of cycling shops were bought push handles. The back rest, the cushion, and the arm rest, were built for an expert of restorations of sofas. The frame and the rest of the structure as the foot plate were machined in the campus. The wheelchair type chosen involved a low-grade technological complexity in its manufacture, for the rigid frame (unibody) for internal use and the material used to machine: AISI 1010 carbon steel tubes of 22mm outside diameter and 3 mm wall thickness.

A good option to weld a AISI 1010 carbon steel tube is the MAG process because it offers better finish, low chances of weld bead defects, and increased productivity compared to other methods.

Manufacturing Processes. For the wheelchair, were used these manufacturing processes (see Table 1):

Table 1. Manufacturing process for wheelchair-low-cost (property of the authors)

Manufacturing process	Tool	Function
Cutting	Bandsaw	To cut round tubes and sheets for assembly the structure
Bending	Bending machine	To bend the tubes to create the frame;
Milling	Milling machine	To mill the tubes
Turning	Metalworking lathes	To machine the tips axle
Drilling	Electric drill	To drill for screws bodies pass through
Welding	MIG/MAG equipment	To weld the tubes and the plates of the structure
Surface finishing	Sander and spray painting	To finish to improve the look of it and decrease the oxidation of metals in contact with the atmosphere
Assembling	---	To assembly the parts of the structure with the other steering components and moving parts

To develop the prototype, mechanical manufacturing processes, such as it was planned:

- Machining: the frame were machined in a conventional mechanical around the axis of the rear wheels, with SAE 1020 steel, for fixing the bearings, then cut manually with M12 thread screw. Conventional milling machine was used to machine the tubes, thus preparing the welding and improved design.
- Bend: to bend the tubes was used an automatic hydraulic bending machine for tube. The folds have been made for a specific tool with the diameter of the tube used. This tool was produced in SAE1045 steel and the heat treatment temperature and tempering for the best hit of bend angles. The smooth operation of the tool and the machine depend on the tolerance being obeyed (+0.05mm to 0) as calculated to avoid manufacturing defects, for example, stretch and rupture. The machinery and tooling was donated by the local company CM Cunha Machines LTDA.
- Cutting: to cut the tubes to the structural steel and details were executed using electric hand saw, sander and poly cutting machine with straight cuts and 45 degrees cuts.
- Welding: to weld, the type chosen for the mounting of the chair was MAG welding: using CO^2 active gas and 0.8mm steel wire.
- Assembling: the use of brackets is mounted all the parts of the chair and soldered one by one to make them in symmetry. With grinders with finishing disc was removed the exceeded weld bead. Imperfections that remained were filled with plastic mass, was removed after the excess dough with sandpaper and apply the background paint for metal protection improving the painting. The rear and front wheels were purchased ready-made and only assembled in the structure.

3.2   Racing Car

The first idea was not possible to put in action because the car were so unstable (see Fig. 3). Then, the solution was design an independent car to carry the wheelchair on.

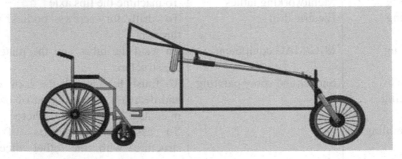

Fig. 3. First conceptual prototype (property of the authors)

Some models with three wheels were tested for the racing car nevertheless the results of analysis showed instability running in curves. The four wheels model was the best solution, as shown in Figure 4.

Fig. 4. Racing car prototype (property of the authors)

The method to create the prototype was similar the method used for the wheelchair-low-price. The three-dimensional assembly model of the wheelchair developed before, was used to design in the CAD program SolidWorks® which run dimensional and stress–strain analysis.

The materials used to machined were, the most part, bought when the first project was made.

As the vehicle was a four wheels model, the steering was inspired in the same used in kart models and the breaks and wheels were cycling components. There is a locking system to couple the wheelchair in the car. It works locking at 6 positions simultaneously: the two smaller wheels, the two larger (rear) and the two armrests. The loading and unloading system is made by the driver without assistance of anyone (a ramp helps the person to load the wheelchair in the car and the person set the ramp up for safety).

The car was not equipped with any propulsion equipment because the championship rules admit only the influence of gravity.

Manufacturing Processes. For the racing car, were used these manufacturing processes (see Table 2):

Table 2. Manufacturing process for racing car (property of the authors)

Manufacturing process	Tool	Function
Cutting	Bandsaw	To cut round tubes and sheets for assembly the structure
Turning	Metalworking lathes	To machine the tips axle
Drilling	Electric drill	To drill of coupling parts to the chair
Welding	MIG/MAG equipment	To weld the tubes and the plates of the structure
Surface finishing	Sander and spray painting	To finish to improve the look of it and decrease the oxidation of metals in contact with the atmosphere
Assembling	---	To assembly the parts of the structure with the other steering components and moving parts

So much for one as for the other project, the roll cage was built with AISI 1010 carbon steel tubes of 22mm outside diameter and 3 mm wall thickness and the mechanical processes were the same also: welded by MAG process to offer better finish or screwed into internal threads machined in the structure in order to provide greater security to the user avoiding protruding parts.

4 Results

Both projects were planned and executed within the period of one year each: the hours of study in the discipline of Design in the Professional Course in Mechanical Manufacture. The areas of education, research and project of extension of the Federal Institute of Santa Catarina (IFSC) were involved.

4.1 Wheelchair-low-cost

Upon three months to completion of the development and assembly of the wheelchair-low-cost project, there were difficulties for the purchase the specific parts of the wheelchair and to project the machinery for machining bends in tube materials. However, it was possible to complete the project within the stipulated time. The project had its chief merit in the dissemination of know-how to manufacture an assistive technology for the IFSC. The entire project was systematically writing and filed at the campus library and made available for the next groups begin their studies from this.

The course proved to be economically viable. The wheelchair designed were compared with the cheapest standard manual wheelchair for sale: the designed wheelchair got selling price of R$246.55 (US$103.72 [1]), and the industrial

---

1 Date of exchange rates: Jan 5th, 2014.

wheelchair (without shipping) cost R$ 261.19 (US$109.89), the designed one had up to 200kg of capacity weight and the industrial wheelchair had up to 80kg. Considering a profit margin of 5 percent, the project will be around R$259.00 (US$109.00) of sale price.

4.2   Racing Car

Initially, the group considered to design of the racing car a very low complexity project; however, the innovative character was challenging at last months. That is because innovation proved a positive difference but an obstacle in some respects, because there is no reference for discussion. The model had to find solutions outside the area of Assistive Technology and inspiration in other technological areas to solve problems. The major problems to be overcome were the steering system and closing the ramp after loading the driver. The cost of the racing car prototype materials was R$428.00 (US$180.07[2]).

The car is capable of carrying 160 kg (352.75 pounds) safely. Therefore it was able to carry the wheelchair and the driver by computing simulation results (see Fig. 5).

Fig. 5. Racing car with wheelchair-low-cost loaded Photographer: authors

---

2 Date of exchange rates: Jan 5th, 2014.

4.3   Sustainability

For the environment, we had a huge gain on disposal of scrap generated by projects without proper allocation of use aimed at the simple practice of acquired knowledge or a temporary use of designed objects. The gravity racing cars that had no destination after the competition, from now will be reaped by future groups because the next develop new chairs to compete. Wheelchairs and racing cars can be used by people with disabilities during the intervals of competitions as for leisure as for conventional utility.

5   Discussions

The projects aligned the plane of access of the Instituto Federal de Santa Catarina (IFSC) to motivate disabled people to study for the professional qualification of them, highlighting the differences between people with and without disabilities. Then, the social impacts are intangible because some students had their first contact with people with disabilities for the first time. As shown in Figure 6, students visited institutions of support people with disabilities, their homes or received visits from people with disabilities in the IFSC. People with disabilities also had the opportunity to attend the campus and to meet new people and technologies.

Fig. 6. People who use wheelchair discussing about technologies for disable Photographer: authors

Technologically, the project made room for future projects. It is possible to motorize the wheelchair or the race car, because its structure was designed for this overweight. When these adjustments are completed, both projects can be donated to people who are unable to pay it.

New projects wheelchair can be made in order to produce customized chairs, because they are much more expensive than conventional. Custom wheelchairs are built for people with non-standard anatomies, such as children and obese people.

References

1. Associação Brasileira De Normas Técnicas. NBR 9050: Acessibilidade a edificações, mobiliário, espaços e equipamentos urbanos, Rio de Janeiro (2004)
2. ABNT. Associação Brasileira De Normas Técnicas. NBR 10004. Resíduos sólidos – Classificação, Rio de Janeiro (2004)
3. Brasil. Coletânca da Legislação sobre os Direitos da Pessoa Portadora de Deficiência. 2. ed. revisada e atualizada, 240 p. SETASS, Campo Grande-MS (2005)
4. Brasil. Constituição Da República. Capítulo III. Da educação, da cultura e do desporto. Seção I. Da educação Art. 205. Art. 206. Art. 208
5. Brasil. IBGE. Censo demográfico (2010)
6. Cooper, R.A.: Wheelchair Selection and Configuration. Demos Medical Publishing, New York (1998)
7. Gilsdorf, P., et al.: Sitting forces and wheelchair mechanics. Journal of Rehabilitation 27(3), 239–246 (1990)
8. Ribeiro, F.L.B.: Introdução ao Método dos Elementos Finitos. COPPE/UFRJ, Rio de Janeiro (2004)
9. Rodrigues, P.B., Silva, A.F.: Cadeiras de rodas manuais–Factores que influenciam a performance de uma cadeira de rodas, Lisboa (1994), http://www.inr.pt/download.php?filename=29+-+Cadeiras+de+rodas+manuais&file=%2Fuploads%2Fdocs%2FEdicoes%2FFolhetos%2FFolheto029.rtf (accessed in: December 19, 2013)

Teaching and Learning HCI Online

Enric Mor[1], Muriel Garreta-Domingo[2], Enosha Hettiarachchi[3], and Nuria Ferran[4]

[1] Computer Science, Multimedia and Telecommunication Studies,
Universitat Oberta de Catalunya, Barcelona, Spain
emor@uoc.edu
[2] Office of Learning Technologies, Universitat Oberta de Catalunya, Barcelona, Spain
murielgd@uoc.edu
[3] Internet Interdisciplinary Institute, Universitat Oberta de Catalunya, Barcelona, Spain
khettiarachchi@uoc.edu
[4] Information and Communication Sciences Studies, Universitat Oberta de Catalunya,
Barcelona, Spain
nferranf@uoc.edu

Abstract. This paper presents the experience of designing and launching an online HCI certificate program. The program was opened in March 2011 and it is currently in its fourth edition. It is a one-year certificate program addressed to practitioners and people working in user experience related fields. The data collected about our students confirm that there is a need for formal HCI education in these sectors and that students enroll in the program to formalize their knowledge acquired on the ground and to deepen it. Taking into account the two main user profiles of online learners (executives and hobby), the program only has "executives". Student satisfaction level on previous editions are very positive and we are currently applying an informal user-centered design approach to the design of the program that helps to refine it iteratively.

Keywords: Education, training, curriculum, online education, teaching, learning, user-centered design.

1   Introduction

Human Computer Interaction (HCI), User-Centered Design (UCD) and User eXperience (UX) are growing both in terms of educational offer and professional demands. Universities and other educational institutions perceive HCI, UCD and UX as critical disciplines [1] and therefore in the last ten years, HCI curriculum [2] is present in the portfolio of an increasing number of educational institutions. At the same time, the education arena is being pushed by audiences, technology and innovation into online environments. In 2013, more than 30% of enrollments in higher education were in online formats and almost 90% of public four-year universities and colleges offer online courses. Furthermore, most education institutions (65%) now say that online learning is a critical part of their long-term strategy [3]. Besides, the disruption of the MOOCs has placed them as players in the future of online learning, with big name key institutions, accreditation programs in the works, and increasing popularity among online learners.

M. Kurosu (Ed.): Human-Computer Interaction, Part I, HCII 2014, LNCS 8510, pp. 230–241, 2014.
© Springer International Publishing Switzerland 2014

Human-Computer Interaction (HCI) is becoming ever more important as a means of achieving competitive designs, and as a growing field of employment for IT graduates and others; such as psychologists, graphic designers and other professionals with a background in humanities or liberal arts. HCI focuses upon how to best design interactive systems that are both productive and as pleasurable to use as possible by their intended end-users, and is the study of how users interact with computer technology [4 -5]. This paper mainly refers to HCI but the term is used widely, including User-Centered Design (UCD), User eXperience (UX), interaction design, usability and other related terms of the field. Currently HCI is commonly used in the context of academic research, however, UX is being used increasingly in the professional practice and on the job market.

HCI is facing many challenges. On the one hand, as a discipline, must be up-to-date with technological advances and with methodologies. On the other hand, more professionals and practitioners are needed to meet the increasing pace of technological products. Also, HCI practitioners should be kept up-to-date as the field is increasingly becoming more multidisciplinary. Consequently, HCI education community and educational institutions should be in a position to offer up-to-date education and training that include state-of-the-art design processes, tools and methodologies for students and professionals with different backgrounds [6].

The following sections present a deeper insight on the aspects of HCI education and the main contribution of this work: the process of design and launch a full online HCI program. The paper is organized as follows: Section 2 provides an overview of HCI education. Section 3 describes the design process of a HCI Certificate Program in a fully online university. Section 4 presents the experience of launching the program and the lessons learnt. Finally, the conclusions drawn from the work and the discussion are summarized in Section 5.

2   HCI Education

The HCI community has always been very committed with the challenges of teaching and learning HCI. Therefore, a lot of work has been done through conferences, workshops, papers and reports. From the beginning of its activities, ACM SIGCHI [2] took HCI education as one of its priorities. A working group on education was created and it has been working on the challenges of HCI education that emerged over time. Thus, through mailing lists, papers, meetings and workshops, the community has been working on topics such as: the need to teach and learn HCI, the need for a shared curricula, the need to incorporate the disciplines to HCI field, and the need to update and adapt processes and methodologies to technological advances and interaction styles.

The ACM Curricula for HCI [2] was the result of a working group sponsored by ACM SIGCHI that set out the basis of the field and became the reference for HCI courses in following years. It had a big impact that affected not only education, but the field since it included one of the most used HCI definitions.

Many experts, practitioners, teachers and researchers were committed to HCI education. Thus, names like Donald Norman, Terry Winograd, Ben Shneiderman, Jenny Preece, Alan Dix, Jonathan Lazar, Yvonne Rogers, Julie Jacko, Elizabeth Churchill and many others are closely linked to the state-of-the-art of HCI teaching and learning. Also, other international and local associations, as well as practitioners, researchers and educators have also worked with a special focus around HCI education. As an overview, below we highlight some of its milestones, achievements and contributions.

The first academic books on HCI to highlight were "Designing the User Interface" [7] by Ben Shneiderman and "User Centered System Design: New Perspectives on Human-Computer Interaction" [8] by Norman and Draper, published before the SIGCHI Curricula. In 1994, Jenny Preece et al [9] published "Human-Computer Interaction" which is considered as the first textbook in HCI. In the new edition, the authors updated the content and the title as "Interaction Design: Beyond Human-Computer Interaction" [10]. Also, Alan Dix et al. [11] wrote one of the classic books, "Human-Computer Interaction".

There are several important contributions and projects related to HCI education. Recently, Churchill et al. [5] presented the results an ongoing project to identify the elements that shape todays HCI education and the challenges for the future. One interesting aspect of the work is that it takes as its starting point the need for a comprehensive global study. So far, the field of HCI had been very U.S./English-speaking centric. The study also shows that HCI field is global and should take into account cultural differences everywhere and analyses one of the biggest challenges of teaching HCI: the rapid evolution of the field. In the report, they have stated that according to their survey participants and interviewees call for some form of unity or consensus; there is a desire for "a unified theoretical perspective" and "a common curriculum".

Another research by Lazar et.al [12] addressed the challenges of keeping the HCI education up-to-date and mentioned the approaches that they have successfully used. Under this, they mentioned the four major areas of HCI education as rapidly changing technology, new design methodologies and student involvement with users, and balance of theory and practice. For rapidly changing technology, it is important to teach students about the HCI issues for handheld and wireless devices. Also, being up to date with governmental laws, guidelines, and rulings that affect usability and appropriate evaluation methods for distributed systems. For new design methodologies, it is needed to adapt established methods of user-centered design and evaluation to new products. Also, it is important to understand social interaction issues, apply new approaches for participatory design, use appropriate techniques for students to experience a design process and structuring of team projects for maximal learning. They also highlighted the importance of student involvement with users, as it gives students the experience of working with real users, understanding the challenges, needs of users and service-learning approaches to HCI courses. Finally, balance and theory of practice relates to the different courses that should be followed by students in order to maintain a balance between theory and practice in HCI education.

According to Thimbleby [13], HCI subject needs to be successful in the world: it needs practitioners who understand, apply and contribute to the subject. Therefore, the focus should be on pedagogy as a proper part of the discipline. HCI is concerned with how people learn to use complex systems effectively. He also mentioned that a lot of HCI is fun, but a lot of it is crucial, both for manufacturers to stay competitive, and for users to stay safe. Many issues in HCI can also be presented as reflections on how it is taught. When it comes to the way of teaching HCI, students could be engaged with the enormous impact that HCI can make to the quality of life around them and to teach them about learning. HCI itself is well-suited to this "metateaching," as one of its core concerns is user learning.

Digital and network technologies create new opportunities and challenges for teaching and learning. However, less attention has focused on teachers' experiences of and attitudes towards teaching HCI online. Preece and Abras [14] have mentioned several challenges of teaching HCI online such as (i) developing relationships; (ii) showing enthusiasm; (iii) balancing time versus activities; (iv) and creating and managing meaningful design projects. They have identified the solutions to the above which points in the direction of the need for creating an online community of learners. At the same time, teachers have to contend with students' motivation and satisfaction. In this case, feedback plays an utmost important role.

Another proof of the growing relevance of HCI is that Massive Open Online Courses (MOOCs) related to this discipline are also available. However, online education in HCI started way before the commencement of MOOCs. According to Daniel [15], the first MOOC was arranged in 2008, and contrary to most current instances, it was based on the philosophy of connectivism and networking, lifelong learning and distributed content [16]. Some of the popular HCI courses offered online can be noted as the Stanford HCI Course, arranged by Scott Klemmer [17] in Coursera launched its third instance in April, 2013 and the course opened to the public by Alan Dix [18] in early 2013. Both of these are open access courses, but with different focus and methods.

The work presented in this paper takes place in Spain, therefore it is interesting to present the situation in relation to HCI. The field was mostly promoted from higher education institutions and from local associations such as AIPO [19] and the local chapter of ACM SIGCHI and UPA [20]. The development of educational resources, the organization of conferences to build community and stimulate scientific research and dissemination were important initial work. AIPO also promoted the first master's program in Spanish-speaking language. Currently, there are several universities and educational institutions that offer HCI and UX programs and courses, conferences and meetings have increased in number and frequency, leading to the creation of an active community.

3   Certificate Program Design

This work takes place at the Universitat Oberta de Catalunya (UOC, Open University of Catalonia)1. It is a fully online higher education institution with a community of more than 50,000 students and more than 3,000 teachers. Teaching and learning mainly take place in a virtual learning environment that integrates independence (asynchronous communication) with interaction (connectivity) to overcome time and space constraints.

There is a team of HCI researchers and lecturers at UOC with previous experience in teaching specific courses in HCI, usability, information architecture and interaction design on undergraduate and graduate programs. Also, some open initiatives have been designed and launched such as ucdgame.org [21]. Overall, the purpose of the activity was to promote a better understanding of a good design process by demonstrating the importance of understanding and focusing on the end user. Taking into account this background, in 2009, the Open University of Catalonia decided to include a one year certificate program in HCI in its program portfolio.

3.1   Design Process: Using UCD to Teach UCD

To conceptualize the program, a process was launched to determine how the program should be and who should be the audience addressed. To do this, a user-centered design process was followed. As a first step, an investigation was planned involving the "users" of the program: students, teachers and employers. Some initial requirements were given by the university's educational model: the program had to be fully online and asynchronous. Also, there was a time requirement: the program should be completed in an academic year.

The research was conducted with the aim to discover relevant information about the program in terms of user needs, wants and expectations. The research activities included a focus group with 8 participants that covered teachers, UX practitioners and national and international students. Also, 11 interviews were conducted with experts from both academia and companies. In addition to that, a benchmarking study was elaborated to include the existing HCI education and training programs at that time. Finally, the job market and job offers were studied in order to identify the competencies deemed important by employers and companies.

The analysis of the data collected in the research activities provided important insights: the program should prepare students for a professional orientation, the goal was to form practitioners and the focus had to be on user-centered design (the full process as opposed, for example, to just usability). This was a common finding where the three actors involved agreed (students, teachers and business employers). Also, it was found that there was a strong need for online HCI education since it allows for current professionals to acquire new knowledge and the HCI job market is growing fast. The program needs to be aligned with industry market and professional practice. It is interesting to mention that, at that time, there were not many higher education

---

[1] http://www.uoc.edu

institutions offering HCI online programs and neither were specific courses such as current MOOC initiatives. Taking all these into account, an HCI online program was an opportunity, but it also posed unique challenges: there was the need to identify and define online teaching and learning strategies that took into account the intrinsic characteristics of HCI and UCD education. Also, based on the research the program should include, integrated along with UCD, the three main elements of HCI: technology, people (human factors) and design. The courses on the program should be skill oriented rather than content oriented because some contents change over time, mainly due to technology advancements, but basic competences and skills needed for UCD projects keep effective over time. Therefore, one of the goal was to provide skills for learners so they can keep up-to-date after graduating. Related to student engagement, some elements need to be taken into consideration: promote knowledge exchange among peers and with teachers with ongoing engagement with course content and activities that take advantage of the multidisciplinary approach of the field.

3.2   Program Definition

The academic design of the program was carried out iteratively, evaluating and discussing the structure of courses and its contents with employers and experts. Both companies and teachers from other universities participated in the discussion and evaluation. In the last stage of the design process of the program a visiting professor from Georgia Tech [22], with experience in the design of HCI educational programs, was invited to work for three months with the UOC team. The work during the visiting position was useful to validate the proposal in terms of definition and design.

From the educational perspective, the definition of the program considered especially: competence skills, contents, activities and assignments. Student engagement in activities and assignments is key to avoid dropout. From the HCI perspective, state-of-the-art methodologies and techniques were important elements to include. However, we wanted to avoid a frequent mistake: putting all the attention on methodologies losing view of the big picture. To avoid this, we decided to explicitly include the concept of process. Thus, each methodology has a context and must be used within a process that provides meaning and a more general perspective, taking the user and his experience as the ultimate goal.

As a result, the program structure follows the main stages of the user-centered design process and is set around four main sections: introduction (fundamentals), user research and requirements, design (including information architecture, interaction design and prototyping) and usability evaluation. Six courses were defined: two including the fundamentals, one for each UCD phase and a final project: 1) Introduction to HCI, 2) Design. People. Technology, 3) User Requirements: Research and Analysis, 4) Interaction Design, 5) Usability Evaluation, and 6) Project.

"Introduction to Human-Computer Interaction" provides a general view of UCD process and its associated with the phases and main methodologies. Also provides the main and basic concepts of HCI as well as an overview of the different terms and concepts. "Design. People. Technology" takes into account the three main elements of

HCI (design, people, technology), and provides recognition and facilities for participants with previous experience or knowledge in any of them. On the one hand, specific content and activities are provided to students with a previous knowledge level. On the other hand, collaboration and mutual criticism are encouraged in order to develop skills related to teamwork and HCI multidisciplinarity. "User Requirements: Research and Analysis" is a course that provides competences to understand and learn about users from a 360 degree perspective, so the user requirements are gathered, analyzed, documented and communicated effectively to other members of a multidisciplinary team. The main goal of "Interaction Design" course is to introduce students to the principles and methods of information architecture and interaction design including, labeling, navigation definition, card sorting, wireframing, prototyping and interaction design paradigms. "Usability Evaluation" course was conceived to provide professional-level knowledge about usability evaluation and show the importance of evaluating and measuring the usability of interactive systems, taking into account the advantages and disadvantages of the different methods. The final project makes students work on a real case project through a user centered design process. The project takes into account all the activities done on the other courses and providing a common goal for all the small parts. This is a way for students to personalize the program through a personal project.

In most programs (such as the HCI Master's offered by Carnegie Mellon [23]) are required as set of pre-requisites to ensure that they have all the knowledge required for an HCI practitioner. Being an interdisciplinary field, students should also have a basic knowledge of the other disciplines - mostly, psychology, technology and design. In order to include this important knowledge, we decided to include the course on "Design. People. Technology". It is a course in which students learn about the 2 disciplines they are less familiar with.

These courses are organized in two specializations that are offered as a whole and individually. The first specialization includes the introduction to UCD and user research. The second covers design and usability. The project is only done by students that are enrolled in the whole program.

4   Data from the Students

The program was launched in March 2011. Since then, 103 students have been enrolled in the certificate program courses: 50 have completed the full program and 53 have completed the specialization about design and usability evaluation. This enrollment data has proved us that design and usability are much more well-known concepts that user research and user-centered design. Our goal when designing the program was to offer students a holistic view of the UCD process and how the methods and phases intertwined. Although specializations can be taken separately, we actively convey the importance of doing the full program.

The average age of the program participants is set around 33 years old, being the oldest one 44 years old and the youngest one 23 years old. In relation to gender, 42%

of students are women and 58% are men. This data about the age and genre of our students is consistent with the average UOC student. As part of the user-centered design tasks undertaken by the Learning Technologies Office at the UOC, we have applied qualitative and quantitative methods to develop our students' personas [24]. We started user research studies in 2005 and since then we have consistently found that our students can be classified into two groups: the "executives" and the "hobby". Our "executive" profile is the persona we call Jordi; a man in its 30s that usually is enrolled in Computer Science or Business programs and that wants to advance in his professional career. Our "hobby" profile is a woman - we called her Martina - around her 40s, married with children. She studies, Humanities or Psychology and enjoys learning. Her main motivation is to learn and to enjoy the process. Despite these two different motivations, we also know that all our students, in the end, want to pass the courses and get a certificate. Lately we have seen an increase in younger and older students that enroll in our programs. We have also carried out user studies with them and the results were that the younger students behave like the "executives" and the older students like the "hobby" profile.

To learn about our students and better adapt the learning activities of the HCI program, we designed an online survey to be responded at the beginning of the program. We have gathered a total of 48 responses and besides the element of the age (the youngest is 23 years old and the oldest is 44 years old), their responses to the question about motivation to study the program place them all in the "executive" profile. None of them replied that they were enrolled in the program for learning as a hobby (Table 1). This means that we have attracted the type of audience we had envisioned when designing the program. That is of professionals that wanted to increase their knowledge in the HCI field. It is surprising however that the most of them are already working in the field with occupations such as: product manager, UX analyst, art director, web designer, web developer, graphic designer, etc. It is also proof that most UX practitioners are self-taught since it is a new field and also HCI education is fairly recent; specially outside of the United States.

Another aspect that was important to us is the background knowledge of our students. We wanted to reach out to a multidisciplinary audience to also show how several disciplines and knowledge is required for the practice of HCI. The main background of the respondents was designed but there is also a mix of previous studies (Table 2)

Table 1. Learners' motivation on the program

32,6%	I have a UX related job and I want to get a diploma
10,2%	I am interested in UX and want to learn more about it
16,3%	I want to expand my knowledge and improve my resume.
0%	Learning is a hobby and I found this program interesting.
26,5%	I have long been interested in usability, accessibility, interaction design, etc. and want to learn more
14,2%	Other

Table 2. Learners' previous background

49%	Design
24%	Technology
8%	Psychology/Human Factors
18%	Other

The background of the students also shows that HCI and the program attracts professionals from different fields (mostly technology, psychology and design) and is, as it should be, a multidisciplinary field. An interesting element that we still need to include in the program is the teamwork with students from different profiles. However, being a one-year online program it is not an easy task since most of our students work full-time and choose our program because it does not have constraints of time and place. Making them work in groups implicitly places some of these constraints.

We also wanted to know their knowledge and experience on HCI (Table 3). Coherent with their backgrounds and current job positions, most of the respondents are experts on "graphic design"; they are confident with "programming/coding" and "user experience" and are learning the most common HCI concepts and methods: "usability test", "contextual inquiry", "user experience", "focus groups", "quantitative methods". Our students also express several levels of confidence on the most well-know concepts of HCI: "usability test", "heuristic evaluation" and "focus groups" for example. The answers regarding "quantitative methods" and "statistics" show a lack of knowledge in this field that should be addressed either prior or during the program. This is an aspect still pending to be resolved. On the other hand, our students are not familiar with newer terms in the field (design thinking or Internet of things).

Table 3. Students with previous experience with HCI/UX elements and methods

	None	Heard about it	Learning	Confident	Expert
Usability test	2	**29**	**49**	14	6
Heuristic evaluation	31	18	24	25	2
Contextual Inquiry	31	24	**35**	6	4
Focus groups	22	**39**	**29**	6	2
Quantitative methods	24	**39**	**29**	6	2
Graphic Design	2	24	20	14	**39**
Human Factors	22	**39**	24	6	8
Statistics	4	**49**	22	20	4
Programming / Coding	18	27	18	**29**	8
Design thinking	**33**	29	20	16	2
Internet of Things	**39**	43	18	0	0

Table 4. Preferred UX areas, ordered by interest

1st	Interaction Design
2nd	Usability
3rd	UCD Project Management
4th	HCI Fundamentals
5th	User Research

Table 5. Preferred application areas, ordered by interest

1st	Mobile devices
2nd	Personal Computer
3rd	Cross-Device Interaction
4th	Experience Design
5th	Product Design

In the survey, we asked the themes that were of most interest. Overall, all 5 elements are relevant to our students with Design and Usability being the most attractive; which is consistent with the enrollment data we showed previously (Table 4).

The survey also included two questions to provide feedback on the design problem the program would focus on. One question was open-ended and the other provided a few options of interest (Table 5).

Most students mentioned that they did not know yet in which design problem to focus for their individual projects and the second most common response was to design taking into account the ecosystem of a service/product; that is web and mobile and physical aspects. Taking that into account and also the orientation towards a practitioner's approach, we decided to use the design problem of the CHI Conference Student Design Competition. Although the timings of the CHI project and our project do not match, it is still an interesting experience for our students to work on problems that the HCI community considers relevant. It also allowed us to provide a focus on a theme as opposed to a device; giving our students a broader space to work with.

As a complement to the online courses of the certificate and also as a dissemination activity, we annually organize a face-to-face User Experience half-day conference. This conference is a way of promoting networking among HCI professionals in Barcelona, a space to acquire new knowledge and be aware of new tendencies and also all the videos of the talks generate content for the program. Tying the program to outside activities that do not require much extra time for our students - the CHI Student Design Competition and the UX conference - is important to ensure that the program is up-to-date but also feasible for our "executive" student profile. For this purpose, we carefully select the theme of each year and the audience is growing annually:

- 2010: The User-Centered Design Process - talks focused on the different steps of a UCD project - 66 participants
- 2011: The relationship between Innovation and UCD - talks from these two approaches - 102 participants

- 2012: Tangible interaction - talks about the internet of things and large interactive devices - 110 participants
- 2013: Designing for mobile apps - 160 participants

Students also complete a satisfaction survey sent to all students enrolled in any of the university programs. This survey aims to collect information and measure five key areas through 45 questions. These areas are: program design, learning materials and resources, tutoring and teaching, virtual learning environment, and the university in general. The overall satisfaction around the HCI program is very positive, and evolved from 4, reaching a 4.4 out of 5. Students, especially value the knowledge and skills that they develop along the program and the learning resources provided. In addition to that, they like the educational model and teaching style. However, student satisfaction varies slightly depending on the edition of the program and therefore some data is biased towards one area or another. Also, it is interesting to notice that satisfaction with the virtual learning environment (virtual campus) has a lower value if compared to other programs in the survey. This is because the subject field students learn in the HCI program makes them more demanding about the design and interaction of digital tools and environments.

5   Conclusions and Discussion

The program was launched in 2011 and the experience has been positive in terms of student and teacher satisfaction. Like we did for the initial design of the program, we try to apply a user-centered design philosophy to the evolution of the program. Therefore, getting feedback from tutors and students as well as being up-to-date with the evolution in technology and the HCI field and education is key to improve the program. In this sense, at each edition we update the focus and theme of the learning activities. For the last edition students worked on the design of apps. We need to find a balance between the newness of the focus and its place on the job market. It cannot be too innovative, that is too far from our students' current work environment.

We have also identified an important element to reconsider that is the terminology used to name the program and some courses. Currently, employers and prospective students do not use the academic term "HCI" but the term UX and its variations. Also, because we would like for our students to enroll in the full program to get the best of it and learn about the whole UCD process. The title of the program is a small but important element because one of the main aims of the program is to prepare participants to professional practice and, consequently, the terminology used should match what is used in job offers. This change of name for the program also goes with a reassignation of the credits for each course. With the goal of providing our students with the main UCD/HCI knowledge, at some point we have crammed too much information and being too ambitious in the amount of knowledge that a one-year online program for professionals can include. As a result, we have decided to place the focus on the theoretical foundations as well as getting practice with the main methods. We would like to address the missing skills and competences through crash courses - for example, in prototyping or statistics.

References

1. Strong, G.W.: New directions in human-computer interaction: education, research, and practice. Interactions 2(1), 69–81 (1995)
2. Chairman-Hewett, T.T.: ACM SIGCHI curricula for human-computer interaction. ACM (1992)
3. Lepi, K.: The Past, Present, and Future of Online Education. In: Edudemic (2013)
4. Goodwin, K.: Designing for the digital age: How to create human-centered products and services. Wiley (2011)
5. Churchill, E.F., Bowser, A., Preece, J.: Teaching and Learning Human-Computer Interaction: Past, Present and Future. Interactions XX(2), 44–53 (2013)
6. Obrenović, Ž.: Rethinking HCI education: teaching interactive computing concepts based on the experiential learning paradigm. Interactions 19(3), 66–70 (2012)
7. Shneiderman, B.: Designing the User Interface: Strategies for Effective Human-Computer Interaction. Addison Wesley, Reading (1987)
8. Norman, D.A., Draper, S.W.: User Centered System Design: New Perspectives on Human-computer Interaction. Lawrence Erlbaum Assoc., Hillsdale (1986)
9. Preece, J., Carey, T., Rogers, Y., Holland, S., Sharp, H., Benyon, D.: Human-Computer Interaction. Addison-Wesley Publishing Company (1994)
10. Sharp, H., Rogers, Y., Preece, J.: Interaction design: beyond human-computer interaction. John Wiley & Sons, West Sussex (2007)
11. Dix, A., Finlay, J.E., Abowd, G.D., Beale, R.: Human-Computer Interaction. Prentice Hall (1993)
12. Lazar, J., Preece, J., Gasen, J., Winograd, T.: New issues in teaching HCI: Pinning a tail on a moving donkey. In: CHI 2002 Extended Abstracts on Human Factors in Computing Systems, pp. 696–697. ACM (2002)
13. Thimbleby, H.: Teaching and learning HCI. In: Stephanidis, C. (ed.) Universal Access in HCI, Part I, HCII 2009. LNCS, vol. 5614, pp. 625–635. Springer, Heidelberg (2009)
14. Preece, J., Abras, C.: The Challenges of Teaching HCI Online: It's Mostly About Creating Community. In: Human-computer Interaction: Theory and Practice, Part I, vol. 1, p. 391 (2003)
15. Daniel, J.: Making sense of MOOCs: Musings in a maze of myth, paradox and possibility. Journal of Interactive Media in Education 3 (2012)
16. Ovaska, S.: User Experience and Learning Experience in Online HCI Courses. In: Kotzé, P., Marsden, G., Lindgaard, G., Wesson, J., Winckler, M. (eds.) INTERACT 2013, Part IV. LNCS, vol. 8120, pp. 447–454. Springer, Heidelberg (2013)
17. Klemmer, S.: Stanford Course "Human Computer Interaction" in Coursera (2013), https://class.coursera.org/hci
18. Dix, A.: HCI Course (2013), http://hcicourse.com
19. AIPO, http://www.aipo.org
20. Usability Professionals Association, http://www.usabilityprofessionals.org
21. Garreta-Domingo, M., Almirall-Hill, M., Mor, E.: User-Centered Design Gymkhana. In: Extended Abstracts of the SIGCHI Conference on Human Factors in Computing Systems, CHI 2007, San Jose, USA (2007)
22. Badre, A.N.: http://www.cc.gatech.edu/gvu/people/faculty/badre.html
23. Carnegie Mellon University: Masters of HCI Curriculum, http://www.hcii.cmu.edu/masters-program-curriculum
24. UOC Personas: http://www.youtube.com/watch?v=DF57IywQCWk

Comparison of Creativity Enhancement and Idea Generation Methods in Engineering Design Training

Barbara Motyl and Stefano Filippi

University of Udine - DIEGM – Department of Electrical,
Management and Mechanical Engineering, Udine -Italy
{barbara.motyl,filippi}@uniud.it

Abstract. The research presented in this paper aims at evaluating how simple and intuitive are the learning, understanding, and application of some creativity enhancement methods by non-expert users in an engineering design context. The three methods under investigation are TRIZ, C-K theory and SCAMPER. To evaluate the training experience the authors set an evaluation framework based on Kirkpatrick's Four Levels of Evaluation and used a questionnaire to collect students' experiences. The results show that the understanding and the consequent application of the three creativity enhancement and idea generation methods are judged positively by the participants. In particular, TRIZ method represents the most appreciated at all, while SCAMPER stands out for its intuitiveness and easiness of use. Finally, C-K theory is revealed as the newest one and very promising for future developments.

Keywords: TRIZ, C-K theory, SCAMPER, training evaluation, engineering education.

1   Introduction

The research presented in this paper aims at evaluating how simple and intuitive are the learning, understanding and use of some creativity enhancement and idea generation methods by non-expert users in an engineering design context.

Product design and development methods are composed by techniques and tools that help engineers and designers in carrying out their task. These methods usually belong to design theories with a proper ontology that describes the rationale of design thinking that characterizes the designers during all the phases of product development.

There are many methods to be used for these purposes. Among the best known there are brainstorming, lateral thinking, six hats, analogies, functional analysis, morphological analysis and SCAMPER. Among design theories that stimulate creativity, C-K theory and TRIZ represent the most structured ones, with dedicated tools to help designers in the development of their work [1-3].

This research aims at investigating how simple is to teach and to learn enhancement creativity methods which are mostly used in the first phases of the product development for concept and idea generation. To test the teachability and learnability of these methods, three of them were selected to assess these skills, considering the experience of involving users with any knowledge of these methods.

M. Kurosu (Ed.): Human-Computer Interaction, Part I, HCII 2014, LNCS 8510, pp. 242–250, 2014.

In particular, the selected methods were TRIZ, C-K theory and SCAMPER. The choice fell on these methods because although they are known, literature lacks of studies concerning their ease of learning and use. In addition, in literature a great variety of examples belonging to the application of TRIZ and C-K theory and their relative tools are present. On the other hand, SCAMPER method was chosen because it represents an intuitive methodology for the development of creative thinking skills a little less widespread than brainstorming but also well-structured and intuitive [1-3].

The paper is outlined as follows. After the introduction section that motivates the research, in the second section, the background, the three methods under investigation are presented. Third section explains the development of the experiment with the description of the activities done and of the measured characteristics. In the fourth section, data collected by a questionnaire survey are analyzed and results are reported. Finally, conclusions and future development are set.

2   Background

The methods considered are TRIZ, C-K theory, and SCAMPER. These methods have been chosen because of their application in a wide range of literature publications and for their emerging interest by companies, including SME's. Moreover, knowledge and use of these methods represent an interesting addition to engineering design education and training for new graduates and for their introduction in the world of work. For this reason, the research has been developed during a post-graduate engineering course for mechanical engineers.

2.1   TRIZ

TRIZ - the theory of inventive problem solving - was developed by G. Altshuller to support engineers and scientists in solving problems using the knowledge of former inventors [4]. TRIZ offers a large set of tools to analyze and solve problems in different perspectives. For the purpose of this research, the students were only introduced to the use of the Inventive Principles - IP. This tool is a set of forty rules, recommendations or suggestions that describe how a product or a system can be modified in order to improve it [5-6]. The IP and their use are relatively easy to explain and to employ, even if the users have never seen them before.

2.2   C-K Theory

C-K theory - or Concept-Knowledge theory - is a unified design theory introduced by Hatchuel et al. [7]. The name reflects the assumption that design can be modelled and analyzed as the interplay between two interdependent spaces, the space of concepts (C) and the space of knowledge (K). C-K theory models the design process through interactions and expansions of the concept space C and the knowledge space K. A fundamental tool of this theory is represented by the C-K map. It models the space C as a tree structure and reflects the concept partitioning while the K space assumes an "archipelagic" structure where each knowledge base contains propositions with logical status for designers. Four kinds of operators can be used to model these two spaces expansions and interactions: K→C, C →K, C→C, and K→K [7-9].

2.3   SCAMPER

Finally, SCAMPER - the acronym for Substitute-Combine-Adapt-Modify-Put_to_other_uses-Eliminate-Rearrange - refers to a problem solving method developed by Eberle for generating creative concepts. It uses a general-purpose checklist with direct and idea-spurring questions to suggest some addition to, or modification of, something that already exists. The stimulus comes from being asked for answering questions that one would not normally pose [10-11].

3   Activities

In order to compare the methods, the authors have set up the following approach. The methods have been presented to the audience, consisting of students, master thesis students and Ph.D. fellows. Then, after the definition of some evaluation metrics, data about the user experiences have been collected and analyzed.

3.1   Introduction of the Methods

The three methods under investigation have been introduced during the lectures of the course "Representation methods and product development" of the MS in mechanical engineering. The participants have been introduced to the fundamentals of the three methods by classroom lessons with the use of slides and selected papers to read. Then, some relevant examples of application, selected form literature, have been presented, without any particular comment on their development [4-11].

Specifically, TRIZ theory was presented focusing only on one of its tools: the Inventive Principles. C-K theory fundamentals were introduced, together with some C-K mapping examples; finally, SCAMPER method was described, focusing the attention on the list of questions to follow for its application in an ordered way.

3.2   Methods Application/Experiences

After a few days, participants were invited to apply the three methods to some practical engineering design problems and design situations extracted from literature or suggested by the instructors' experience.

These design situations focused on: 1) the design of a new office table for alternating standing and sitting positions [1-2]; 2) the design of a novel kind of nut for long threaded shafts [12]; and 3) the design of a novel kind of gym towel. The first two problems were chosen because they appear in some literature examples that the authors consider of future interest for making further comparisons. The third problem was suggested by the instructors because it was used in another experience during previous editions of the course.

A design of experiments with twenty participants was planned. The participants were fifteen students of the MS course, three MS thesis students and two PhD students.

The participants were divided into five teams of four members each: three graduated students plus one MS thesis or a PhD student. Each team was asked to work in a two-hour session and to apply all the method to solve the three different problems in a random order. The experience was developed in three weeks.

During the experiences, teams were supervised by the instructors but they do not receive any suggestion from them; anyway, each team was allowed to consult course materials (slide, lectures and examples) but they are not provided with internet connection.

3.3   Evaluation Framework

In order to evaluate how effective the training was, authors adopted a revised version of the Kirkpatrick's Four Levels of Evaluation [13-16]. This model is considered as a standard in professional training evaluation. It describes four levels of outcomes: learners' Reactions, Learning, Behavior, and Results.

Table 2 reports the revised version of the Kirkpatrick's Four Levels used in this work, with the description of the evaluation metrics and references to the questions for data collection reported in the next section.

Table 1. The revised Kirkpatrick's Four Levels of Evaluation used in this study

Level	Metrics	Questions
Reaction: participants' view on the learning experience	Interest: how participants consider the course arguments as interesting and pertinent to their needs.	Q1
	Materials: completeness and quality of course materials regarding organization and structure.	Q2 Q3
	Usefulness: perceived utility value, or usefulness, of the training for subsequent study/job performance.	Q4
	Difficulty: reactions that cover the cognitive effort required to perform well in training.	Q5
Learning: changes in attitudes, knowledge and skills	Understanding: the trainee knowledge and the processes of knowledge acquisition, organization and application.	Q6
	Skill outcomes: the trainee development of technical skills.	Q7 Q8 Q9
	Attitudinal outcomes: attitudes, motivation, and goals relevant to the objectives of the training program.	Q10

Table 1. (*continued*)

Behavior: changes in practice and application of learning to practice	Behavior: the degree of transfer from what was learned to how the trainee behaves on the job, which in turn determines how much organizational impact the training can have.	Q11
	Motivation to transfer: the extent to which trainees are motivated to apply the material they have learned.	Q12
Results: changes at learners' and organizational levels	Results: the organizational and business impacts of the training.	Q13

3.4   Data Collection

A questionnaire was set to collect information from all the participants. The questions were designed referring to the metrics described in table 2. Participants were asked to answer the questions using a one-to-five scale where one represents the lowest value and five the highest value as explained in the questionnaire. Each question evaluates all the three methods singularly.

At the end of the survey, one open question collects possible participants' opinion to consider for future improvements of course contents and organization. Questions are reported in table 2.

Table 2. Questions of the survey

#	Questions text
Q1	How do you consider the creativity methods introduced by the course? (1 = Not pertinent, 5 = Very interesting) SCAMPER 1 2 3 4 5 C-K theory 1 2 3 4 5 TRIZ 1 2 3 4 5
Q2	How do you judge the completeness of the materials supplied? (1 = incomplete, 5 = complete) SCAMPER 1 2 3 4 5 C-K theory 1 2 3 4 5 TRIZ 1 2 3 4 5
Q3	How well was the training structured (e.g., manageable chunks, logical order, linked to objectives)? (1 = Not structured, 5 = Very structured) SCAMPER 1 2 3 4 5 C-K theory 1 2 3 4 5 TRIZ 1 2 3 4 5
Q4	How effective were the materials in helping you to learn? (1 = Not effective, 5 = Very effective) SCAMPER 1 2 3 4 5 C-K theory 1 2 3 4 5 TRIZ 1 2 3 4 5

Table 2. (*continued*)

Q5   How did you find the content of the training, e.g. amount and difficulty?
(1 = Very poor, 5 = Very good)
SCAMPER   1 2 3 4 5
C-K theory   1 2 3 4 5
TRIZ   1 2 3 4 5

Q6   Did you need to clarify some basics concepts during the application of the three methods?
(1 = Quite always, 5 =Not at all)
SCAMPER   1 2 3 4 5
C-K theory   1 2 3 4 5
TRIZ   1 2 3 4 5

Q7   Please rate your ability to generate new concepts
(1 = No skills, 5 = Very good skills)
SCAMPER   1 2 3 4 5
C-K theory   1 2 3 4 5
TRIZ   1 2 3 4 5

Q8   Please rate your ability to problem-solving
(1 = No skills, 5 = Very good skills)
SCAMPER   1 2 3 4 5
C-K theory   1 2 3 4 5
TRIZ   1 2 3 4 5

Q9   Please rate your ability to creativity method management
(1 = No skills, 5 = Very good skills)
SCAMPER   1 2 3 4 5
C-K theory   1 2 3 4 5
TRIZ   1 2 3 4 5

Q10   Overall, how effective do you believe the training was in improving your job performance?
(1 = Not effective, 5 = Very effective)
SCAMPER   1 2 3 4 5
C-K theory   1 2 3 4 5
TRIZ   1 2 3 4 5

Q11   Did you perceive an improvement of your skills during the course?
(1 = Not at all, 5 = Very much)
SCAMPER   1 2 3 4 5
C-K theory   1 2 3 4 5
TRIZ   1 2 3 4 5

Q12   Do you think you will be motivated to use and apply the learned creative methods in the future?
(1= not motivated, 5 very motivated)
SCAMPER   1 2 3 4 5
C-K theory   1 2 3 4 5
TRIZ   1 2 3 4 5

Q13   Do you think that the creativity contents you have learnt will improve your professional background in product design?
(1= No improvement, 5= Several improvements)
SCAMPER   1 2 3 4 5
C-K theory   1 2 3 4 5
TRIZ   1 2 3 4 5

Q14   How do you think the training materials and course could be improved?

3.5   Analysis and Synthesis of Collected Data

The collected data from the survey have been analyzed using the metrics defined previously and grouped considering the Kirkpatrick's Four Levels of Evaluation: Reaction, Learning, Behavior and Results.

The synthesis of the collected data, subdivided for the three creativity methods is reported in figure 1. The values for each method are calculated, level by level, as the arithmetical average of the averages values calculated based on the values obtained for each group of questions and in function of the students' answers.

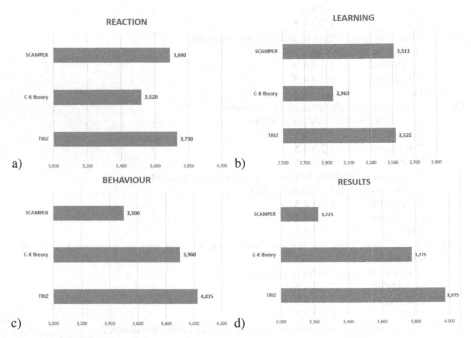

Fig. 1. Cumulative results for the three methods: a) Reaction level; b) Learning level; c) Behavior level and d) Results level

4   Results and Discussion

The results of the investigation show that the three methods have been differently experienced by the participants. The main observations, related to the characteristics highlighted thanks to the questionnaire, are reported, level by level, in the following.

At Reaction level, information on participants' view on learning experience, such as the interest in the topics of the training, in the completeness and usefulness of supplied materials, in the training structure and in encountered difficulties, were collected. For this level, TRIZ and SCAMPER methods report similar evaluations with a slight prevalence of TRIZ.

The cumulative data of the Learning level, which evaluates the changes in attitudes, knowledge and skills, such as the ability to generate new concepts, the problem-solving skill or the creativity method management, highlighted a prevalence of the TRIZ and SCAMPER methods in respect to C-K theory. In particular, regarding the acquisition or the improvement of new skills as the ability of generating new concepts, the SCAMPER method has reached the highest evaluation, followed by TRIZ and C-K theory. Regarding the problem solving expertise TRIZ, with is well-structured framework, gained the highest evaluation. Finally, considering the skills in managing creativity methods, TRIZ and C-K theory collect the same highest score. For the Behavior level, which considers changes in practice and the application of learning to practice, the collected answers highlighted a prevalence of TRIZ followed by C-K theory on SCAMPER method. Finally, in the Results level, where the changes at the level of the learner and of the organization are investigated, TRIZ and C-K theory are slightly ahead on SCAMPER as well.

The three methods show different levels of easiness of use perceived by the participants. The training organization and materials such the use of frontal lessons, slides and their direct application to some real cases of study are positively judged by all the participants. The need of further in-depth study has been highlighted by only few of them in the case of C-K theory that is also the youngest of the three method, as it has benne formulated quite recently and it has a limited series of examples and case studies available in literature.

The overall results of the analysis highlight the advantage of using structured methods by non-expert users since they guide the user during creativity and idea generation processes. In particular, TRIZ has been highlighted by the majority of the participants because of its structured form. Then SCAMPER and C-K theory follow. SCAMPER has been indicated as the most intuitive and it represent a method that can be learned easily in comparison to C-K theory.

5   Conclusions

This paper describes the comparison of three different creativity and idea generation methods, TRIZ, C-K theory and SCAMPER, against their learnability, use and easiness of understanding.

For this evaluation, the authors set an evaluation framework using a revised version of the Kirkpatrick's Four Levels of Evaluation and designed a specific questionnaire.

The results show that the understanding and the consequent application of the structured and intuitive methods for creativity enhancement and idea generation are judged positively by non-expert users. Regarding the four levels of evaluation considered, TRIZ represents the most rated method, while SCAMEPER was appreciated mostly for its intuitiveness and easiness of use. Finally, C-K theory has proved to be the newest and most promising for future developments.

As a result, the training experience proposed by the course with the introduction of the three methods was judged very positive.

Moreover, this course represents a valid tool for engineering design training and also for self-training if adequately structured and supplied with materials containing relevant examples of application.

Further developments may concern the quantitative evaluation of the characteristics used in the research or the introduction of other adequate metrics. Moreover, the evaluation framework may be extended to other creativity and idea generation methods focused on product/process or service innovation and improvement.

References

1. Chulvi, V., Mulet, E., Chakrabarti, A., Lopez-Mesa, B., González-Cruz, C.: Comparison of the degree of creativity in the design outcomes using different design methods. J. Eng. Des. 23, 241–269 (2012)
2. Chulvi, V., González-Cruz, M.C., Mulet, E., Aguilar-Zambrano, J.: Influence of the type of idea-generation method on the creativity of solutions. Res. Eng. Des. 24, 33–41 (2013)
3. Shah, J.J., Kulkarni, S.V., Vargas-Hernandez, N.: Evaluation of idea generation methods for conceptual design: effectiveness metrics and design of experiments. J. Mech. Des. 122, 377–384 (2000)
4. Altshuller, G.: And suddenly the inventor appears. Appeared-TRIZ, the Theory of Inventive Problem Solving. Technical Innovation Center, INC., Worcester, MA (1996)
5. Gadd, K.: TRIZ for engineers. In: Enabling Inventive Problem Solving. John Wiley & Sons, Ltd., Chichester (2011)
6. Rantanen, K., Domb, E.: Simplified TRIZ: New Problem Solving Applications for Engineers and Manufacturing Professionals. St Lucie Press, Boca Raton (2002)
7. Hatchuel, A., Le Masson, P., Weil, B.: C-K theory in practice: lessons from industrial applications. In: Proceedings of International Design Conference - DESIGN 2004, Dubrovnik, May 18-21 (2004)
8. Hatchuel, A., Weil, B.: C-K design theory: an advanced formulation. Res. Eng. Des. 19, 181–192 (2009)
9. Le Masson, P., Weil, B., Hatchuel, A.: Strategic management of innovation and design. Cambridge University Press, Cambridge (2010)
10. Eberle, B.: Scamper: Games for imagination development. Prufrock Press, Waco (1996)
11. Serrat, O.: The SCAMPER technique. Asian Development Bank, Washington, DC (2010)
12. Burgess, S.C.: A Backwards Design Method for Mechanical Conceptual Design. J. Mech. Des. 134, 031002–1 (2012)
13. Kirkpatrick, J.: The hidden power of Kirkpatrick's four levels. T and D 61, 34 (2007)
14. Alliger, G.M., Janak, E.A.: Kirkpatrick's levels of training criteria: Thirty years later. Personnel Psychology 42(2), 331–342 (1989)
15. Praslova, L.: Adaptation of Kirkpatrick's four level model of training criteria to assessment of learning outcomes and program evaluation in Higher Education. Educational Assessment, Evaluation and Accountability 22(3), 215–225 (2010)
16. Shartrand, A.M., Gomez, R.L., Weilerstein, P.: Answering the call for innovation: three faculty development models to enhance innovation and entrepreneurship education in engineering. In: Proceedings of 2012 ASEE Annual Conference, San Antonio, TX (2012)

Studio-Based Learning as a Natural Fit to Teaching Human-Computer Interaction

Paula Alexandra Silva[1, 2], Martha E. Crosby[1], and Blanca J. Polo[3]

[1] University of Hawaii at Manoa, Department of Information and Computer Sciences
1680 East-West Rd., POST 317, Honolulu, HI 96822, USA
[2] Universidade Portucalense Infante D. Henrique, Departamento de Inovação Ciência e
Tecnologia, Rua Dr. António Bernardino de Almeida, 541, 4200-072 Porto, Portugal
[3] University of Hawaii, Leeward Community College 96-045
Ala Ike, Pearl City, Hawaii 96782, USA
{crosby,paulaale,blanca}@hawaii.edu, palexa@gmail.com

Abstract. The creative element of HCI tends to be neglected due to the rapid advancement of hardware platforms as well as software development. HCI books cannot keep up with this rapid growth, nor can they provide students with the necessary tools to succeed. Considering these facts, HCI instructors need to implement techniques that not just complement but also enhance learning while preparing students for the real world. Studio-based learning, being a constructivist pedagogy that includes critiques and reflection can greatly enhance HCI Education.

Keywords: HCI Education, HCI Pedagogy, HCI Methodologies, Studio-Based Learning.

1 Introduction

Technology and reality are changing at an incredibly fast pace. On the one hand, this imposes an urgency to promptly and constantly be ready to address new challenges on the HCI discipline. The answer to how to address these challenges is largely learned from practice and an acute observation of an ever-changing context. On the other hand, education still relies heavily on books. However, books are often not able to capture the complexity of reality, nor can they provide a methodology to deal with it. Quite opposite, books merely provide a perspective, often the author's perspective, on the subject and, due to their form, are likely to be permanently outdated. Moreover, books do not teach critique, a fundamental tool for disciplines and problems that are heavily dependent on a permanently changing context.

So how can HCI Education bridge the gap between conventional instructional materials and the (unstructured) reality of real-world projects? And most importantly, how can HCI Education prepare students to design the user interfaces of tomorrow and to face the reality they will experience in the job market?

In practice, HCI and the design of user interfaces rarely happens outside of the context of a project and without the involvement of a team. Thus, we need to provide students not only with the core knowledge that is found in books but also with the experience of

M. Kurosu (Ed.): Human-Computer Interaction, Part I, HCII 2014, LNCS 8510, pp. 251–258, 2014.
© Springer International Publishing Switzerland 2014

working in a problem-based environment, in which, collaboration and design critiques play fundamental roles. The authors believe Studio-Based Learning (SBL) is a natural fit for this reality. It is then important to discuss how this methodology can be applied in HCI and HCI-related courses and how it can help HCI educators bridge the gap between HCI instruction and the real-world HCI design process.

2   Studio-Based Learning: Origins and Concepts

The studio-based instructional model originates in the master-apprentice educational system used in the guilds of the Middle Ages [9]. Later, architectural schools of Europe and North America adopted this instructional model in the form of the 'design studio': a place where students set up their own workspaces—drafting tables, books, drawing and modeling materials—and spend much of their lives working individually on common design tasks" [15]. Since then, it has served as an effective pedagogical model in architecture and fine arts Education [8]. More recently, others have been adopting the studio-based instructional model and this methodology is becoming increasingly popular in computer science (CS) Education (see [3] for a review). Examples include SBL being applied to: i) the restructuring of a CS degree [4]; ii) programming [6]; iii) game design [5]; and iv) Human-Computer Interaction courses (e.g. [13] [8]).

To further understand the SBL instructional model, Reimer and Douglas [13] performed an observation of a studio course in architecture. Their observations allowed them to understand that studio classes focus on real-world problems to which the students, often working collaboratively in a team, have to produce a solution through an iterative design process. Also, studio classes are limited to 10-12 students and take place three times a week, four hours a day, in a specially designed room, in which each student has her or his 'own space' for the term (during class and outside class time). Every week the instructor highlights a particular aspect contributing to the overall project (e.g. form or site location). In a highly interactive environment, not only between the instructor and the student but also among students, a studio session will start by having students work on their assigned large-drafting style desks until it is time for them to meet with their instructor for a design critique session (usually referred to as crit session).

The original description of Reimer and Douglas [13] does not include rubrics. However, the authors' experience in using SBL has shown that rubrics should be provided to the students in order to better guide the design critique section. For this reason and also for a sense of completeness, rubrics are introduced from now on and detailed in the next section.

Design crits are a form of teamwork, that will greatly benefit student by providing formal guided feedback. Design crit sessions take-place in a common meeting area and typically involves the instructor plus two to four students guided by the rubric. Students start by presenting their design representations, often low-fidelity sketches, while explaining how the particular design challenge of the week was addressed. The instructor discusses the work of one student at a time for 20 to 30 minutes. The remaining students can contribute to the discussion or concentrate only on the comments made by the instructor and the other students participating in the session. Reviewers highlight the positive aspects of the student's design, before starting to ask strategic questions intended to reveal the weaknesses of the design. Later, the reviewers bring up examples of solutions others proposed to similar design problems and ask the student if she or he has any problems and/or questions. The critique session is guided by the rubric and ends with the instructor providing feedback about the presentation and guidance for future ones (that may happen in or outside class). Crit sessions are key to convey design knowledge.

Besides the day-to-day crit sessions there are also the mid-term and final crit sessions, which are equivalent to midterm and final exams and are therefore more formal. In mid-term sessions, two faculty members and a peer review the student's work for 30 minutes, while others students are welcome to listen and benefit from the knowledge being shared. The final crit session is performed by invited professional architects. The student either Passes or Fails the studio class.

In short the SBL approach involves the concepts of a design studio, a shared physical space in which students work on their assigned problems, and of rubrics and design crit sessions, where students present their evolving design ideas in order to get feedback.

The SBL pedagogy can be implemented in a variety of ways. As long as the basic elements of SBL are present, regardless of the modality it can be considered SBL. The basic SBL elements are: i) The selection of a project that can be correctly executed in a variety ways, ii) Students execute the project either individually or in teams, iii) Students share their project with their peers, either individually or in teams. An instructor is present to answer any questions, iv) The instructor and peers give feedback in the form of a design crit, either individually or in teams, face-to-face or online, v) Students revise the project and resubmit it, individually or in teams. The abovementioned steps represent one iteration, however SBL does not restrict the number of iterations. SBL may be implemented several times during the semester with diverse projects that may vary in complexity. Figure 1 roughly abstracts the Studio-Based Learning process.

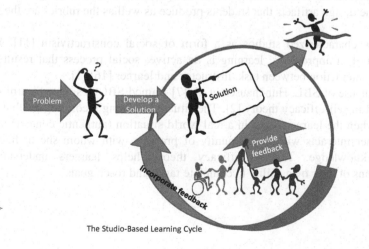

The Studio-Based Learning Cycle

Fig. 1. The Studio- Based Learning Cycle

2.1   Rubrics

In order to guide the SBL process, a rubric should be set into place. A rubric corresponds to a standard of performance for a given population. It specifies the required deliverables of the project and the different levels of achievement, according to specific characteristics. This way, a rubric identifies the important aspects of the design project to be rated as well as what to consider while rating them, and are a useful tool, that provides guidance for design crits session.

Design crits should make sure that the design being presented adheres to the project requirements as well as the rubric. Rubrics have been used for a number of purposes, such as to formalize feedback [21], to guide student game designs evaluations [22], and to develop skills in written communication [24] and ethics [25]. Appendix 1 shows an example of a rubric specifically designed by one of the authors to be used in a SBL class that aimed to support students writing papers and performing peer reviews as part of the studio process.

Design disciplines such as architecture and HCI aim at solving wicked problems [23], where there is not a clear end to the creative process. Rubrics, will suggest a stopping point to SBL iterations.

2.2   Situating Studios in Pedagogical Approaches

As the descriptions above denote, the studio-based learning pedagogy allows for a rich learning environment. Student learning takes place: i) through the execution of projects, which are solved by using real-world processes; ii) by integrating the knowledge obtained from previous lectures; and iii) by taking full advantage of the interactions and collaborations with other students, with the instructors, and sometimes professionals. Moreover, design crits sessions are crucial for learning as it is during those sessions that participants share their knowledge and experience and that the discussion and reflection on the design artifact and the design process takes place. The design artifacts that students produce as well as the rubrics are the basis for grading.

Lebow characterized studios as a form of social constructivism [11]. In social constructivism approaches, learning is an active, social process that results from a dynamic interaction between task, instructor and learner [16] [1].

In their use of SBL, Hundhausen et al. [7] framed SBL in situated learning theory [10], and in self-efficacy theory [2]. The situated learning theory argues that learning occurs when the learner is put in a real world situation (authentic context) and when the learner interacts with a community of practice, with whom she or he then co-creates knowledge. The self-efficacy theory helps learners understand their perceptions of their own ability to complete tasks and reach goals.

3   Studio-Based Learning: A Natural Methodology for HCI Teaching

The challenge of HCI Education is to teach and improve the students' capability to design user interfaces. Due to the complexity of the current shifting reality and the nature of the discipline itself this is not an easy task. In fact, many key skills are only gained in the midst of action, through the active participation and involvement in the development of a given HCI product or project.

Projects are of extreme importance in HCI and that is why students taking an HCI or an HCI-related course often undertake a capstone design project that takes them through all phases of the user-centered design process [12], including the initial phase of user research, the user interface prototyping, and the evaluation of the technology with the users. Having this kind of design projects provides more experience in HCI design, however it still "falls short of teaching the student good design of a real-world artifact while engaging in a real-world design process. In these courses we leave it to faith that students will be able to make the transition from theory to practice." [13].

In 1990 Terry Winograd urged the audience of a plenary session he conducted at CHI to embrace and explore the studio as a teaching concept for HCI Education [17]. Because of its design orientation, HCI Education is an excellent candidate for the application of studio-based instruction.

The literature reports two particularly interesting cases of the application of SBL to HCI, with which HCI educators can gain valuable insight on how SBL can be used in HCI Education. The first example consists of the implementation of an undergraduate HCI course based on the studio model [13]. The second explored the use of the SBL concepts on what the authors called a Prototype Walkthrough [7].

Overall, the authors of those studies [13] [7] confirmed the pedagogical value and the effectiveness of the application of the SBL instructional method and observed that:

- Students willingly helped and offered opinions to their classmates and benefited from the instructor's design experience
- Students critique of the peers' work fostered a highly interactive and constructive atmosphere and promoted the generation and analysis of design ideas
- Students engaged in a critical design dialogue and made valuable and to the point contributions which are relevant not only to the course but also to the design at hand
- Students used these learning opportunities to apply their emerging HCI design knowledge by grounding their design statements in empirical evidence and established theories and principles
- Students presented their work and took ownership and pride and late work was never an issue
- Students gained experience with public speaking and developing writing skills
- Students evaluate the courses positively and stated that they valued witnessing how peers approached the same design problems
- Students had the opportunity to engage in authentic practices that they are likely to encounter in their profession

4   Discussion and Future Work

The SBL approach has proven its potential in HCI Education and in bridging the gap between the reality inside and outside the university boundaries. Also, despite the experienced increased workload, students responded favorably when exposed to this instructional model. So it is up to HCI Educators to adjust and perfect this methodology and bring them into HCI teaching. Building upon the work of Reimer and Douglas [13], Hundhausen et al. [7] and other related ones, in the future, we would like to further understand how to better define the use of SBL theory in HCI and HCI-related courses.

Hundhausen et al. [7] found that the amount of comments on the design was influenced by the students familiarity of the design domain, the clarity of the design domain, tasks, and interface; and the extent to which test users actually encountered user interface problems. These aspects should be taken into consideration when defining the design projects for studio-based courses and activities.

Hundhausen et al. [7] observed that the fidelity of the user interface prototypes influenced design discussions, in that, higher fidelity prototypes tended to discourage them. This impact of high-fidelity prototypes is well-known among the community (see for e.g. [14]). However, Hundhausen et al. [7] also observed that superficial tasks did not allow for much discussion and led to superficial design suggestions. The artifacts to be used in a crit session and the level of fidelity they should entail is an area that requires further investigation. Hundhausen et al. [7] also reported that situations where the test user struggled were the best catalysts for discussion leading to reflections on why the test user struggled and how to redesign the interface to resolve the user interface problem. This aspect deserves further reflection in order to assess if those should also be an important part of crit sessions.

5   Conclusions

The world present-day is changing at an extremely fast pace. HCI design needs to accompany these changes and so does HCI Education.

SBL emerges as an excellent methodology to bridge the gat between HCI and the demands of the real world today. Through the use of the SBL methodology in HCI Education, students reflection and critique skills can be trained, while at the same time, they experience the need to be team players, to carefully observe external needs, and to permanently iterate and be creative. These are some important and necessary tools to approach the complexity of the reality of today.

References

1. Ausubel, D.: Educational Psychology: A Cognitive View. Holt, Rinehart, and Winston, New York (1968)
2. Bandura, A.: Self-efficacy: the exercise of control. Worth Publishers (1997)
3. Carter, A., Hundhausen, C.: A review of studio-based learning in computer science. Journal of Computing Sciences in Colleges 27(1), 105–111 (2011)

4. Docherty, M., Sutton, P., Brereton, M., Kaplan, S.: An innovative design and studio-based CS degree. ACM SIGCSE Bulletin 33(1), 233–237 (2001)
5. Estey, A., Long, J., Gooch, B., Gooch, A.: Investigating studio-based learning in a course on game design. In: Proceedings of the Fifth International Conference on the Foundations of Digital Games (2010)
6. Hundhausen, C., Brown, J.: Designing, visualizing, and discussing algorithms within a CS 1 studio experience: An empirical study. Computers & Education 50(1), 301–326 (2008)
7. Hundhausen, C., Fairbrother, D., Petre, M.: An Empirical Study of the "Prototype Walkthrough": A Studio-Based Activity for HCI Education. ACM Transaction of Computer-Human Interaction 19(4), 1–36 (2012)
8. Hundhausen, C., Fairbrother, D., Petre, M.: The prototype walkthrough": a studio-based learning activity for the next generation of HCI education" (2010)
9. Lackney, J.: A history of the studio-based learning model. Mississippi State University: Education Design Institute (1999), http://www.edi.msstate.edu/work/pdf/history_studio_based_learning.pdf
10. Lave, J.: The practice of learning. In: Understanding Practice: Perspectives on Activity and Context, pp. 3–32. Cambridge University Press, Cambridge (1993)
11. Lebow, D.: Constructivist Values for Instructional Systems Design: Five Principles toward a New Mindset. Educational Technology Research and Development 41(3), 4–16 (1993)
12. Preece, J., Rogers, J., Sharp, H.: Interaction Design: Beyond Human-Computer Interaction. John Wiley and Son, NY (2002)
13. Reimer, Y., Douglas, S.: Teaching HCI design with the studio approach. Computer Science Education 13(3), 191–205 (2003)
14. Rettig, M.: Prototyping for tiny fingers. Communications of the ACM 37(4), 21–27 (1994)
15. Schon, D.: The reflective practitioner: How professionals think in action, vol. 5126. Basic books (1983)
16. Vygotsky, L.: Mind in society: The development of higher mental processes. Harvard University Press, Cambridge (1978)
17. Winograd, T.: What can we teach about Human-computer interaction? In: Proceedings of the CHI 1990 Conference on Human Factors in Computing Systems, pp. 443–449 (1990)
18. Hamer, J., Cutts, Q., Jackova, J., Luxton-Reilly, A., McCartney, R., Purchase, H., Riedesel, C., Saeli, M., Sanders, K., Sheard, J.: Contributing student pedagogy. SIGCSE Bull. 40(4), 194–212 (2008)
19. Emphasizing soft skills and team development in an educational digital game design course. In: Proceedings of the 4th International Conference on Foundations of Digital Games (FDG 2009), pp. 240–247. ACM, New York (2009)
20. Rittel, H.W.J., Webber, M.M.: Planning Problems are Wicked Problems. In: Cross, N.: Developments in Design Methodology, Written Communication Value Rubric. John Wiley & Sons Ltd., Chichester (1984)
21. Written Communication Value Rubric (2009), http://manoa.hawaii.edu/mwp.htm (December 2010) (retrieved)
22. Contemporary Ethical Issues Rubric (2009), http://www.hawaii.edu/gened/cei/cei.htm (December 2010) (retrieved)

Appendix: Example of SBL Rubric

ICS 390 Paper 1 Peer Review Rubric

Reviewer's Name: _____

Reviewee's Name: _____

	Capstone 4	Milestone 3	Milestone 2	Benchmark 1	Not Addressed 0
Context of and purpose for writing	Demonstrates a thorough understanding of context, audience, and purpose that is responsive to the assigned task(s) and focuses all elements of the work.	Demonstrates adequate consideration of context, audience, and purpose and a clear focus on the assigned task(s) (e.g., the task aligns with audience, purpose, and context).	Demonstrates awareness of context, audience, purpose, and to the assigned tasks(s) (e.g., begins to show awareness of audience's perceptions and assumptions).	Demonstrates minimal attention to context, audience, purpose, and to the assigned tasks(s) (e.g., expectation of instructor or self as audience).	Not addressed
Recommendations: (Give specific suggestions to improve this paper to ensure it meets or exceeds the Capstone level)					
Content Development	Uses appropriate, relevant, and compelling content to illustrate master of the subject, conveying the writer's understanding, and shaping the whole work.	Uses appropriate, relevant, and compelling content to explore ideas within the context of the discipline and shape the whole work	Uses appropriate and relevant content to develop and explore ideas through most of the work.	Uses appropriate and relevant content to develop simple ideas in some parts of the work.	Not addressed
Recommendations: (Give specific suggestions to improve this paper to ensure it meets or exceeds the Capstone level)					
Genre and disciplinary conventions	Demonstrates detailed attention to and successful execution of a wide range of conventions particular to a specific discipline and/or writing task (s) including organization, content, presentation, formatting, and stylistic choices	Demonstrates consistent use of important conventions particular to a specific discipline and/or writing task(s), including organization, content, presentation, and stylistic choices	Follows expectations appropriate to a specific discipline and/or writing task(s) for basic organization, content, and presentation	Attempts to use a consistent system for basic organization and presentation	Not addressed
Recommendations: (Give specific suggestions to improve this paper to ensure it meets or exceeds the Capstone level)					
Sources and evidence	Demonstrates skillful use of high quality, credible, relevant sources to develop ideas that are appropriate for the discipline and genre of the writing	Demonstrates consistent use of credible, relevant sources to support ideas that are situated within the discipline and genre of the writing.	Demonstrates an attempt to use credible and/or relevant sources to support ideas appropriate for the discipline and genre of the writing.	Demonstrates an attempt to use sources to support ideas in the writing.	Not addressed
Recommendations: (Give specific suggestions to improve this paper to ensure it meets or exceeds the Capstone level)					
Control of syntax and mechanics	Uses graceful language that skillfully communicates meaning to readers with clarity and fluency, and is virtually error free.	Uses straightforward language that generally conveys meaning to readers. The language has few errors.	Uses language that generally conveys meaning to readers with clarity, although writing may include some errors.	Uses language that sometimes impedes meaning because of errors in usage	Not addressed
Recommendations: (Give specific suggestions to improve this paper to ensure it meets or exceeds the Capstone level, may include in-text recommendations)					

Teaching Design for All Through Empathic Modeling: A Case Study in Tallinn University

Vladimir Tomberg and Mart Laanpere

Institute of Informatics, Tallinn University, Estonia
{vtomberg,martl}@tlu.ee

Abstract. The goal of the paper is to illustrate best practices that can be used in Design for All courses. We implemented the empathic modeling approach in HCI study programme by letting the students simulate users with disabilities in the physical settings in order to increase their understanding of Design for All in their work as HCI designers. The data was collected from students with online questionnaire and open reflections after the course.

Keywords: Accessibility, Design for All, Empathy, Empathic Modeling, Teaching DfA.

1   Introduction

The Pillar VI in European Union's strategy 'Digital Agenda for Europe' sets ambitious goals towards enhancing digital literacy, skills and inclusion [1]. In the context of HCI, the latter of these goals is being targeted by the widening movement called Design for All (DfA). Similar initiatives emerge in other parts of the world, sometimes under other labels like Universal or Inclusive Design. The most notable achievements of DfA community are projects like DfA@eInclusion1 and guidelines for DfA curricula on bachelor and master level in EU and US [2–4].

Considering actions 64 "Ensure the accessibility of public sector websites" and 65 "Helping disabled people to access content" of Pillar VI, the dissemination of knowledge about DfA among software developers seems as especially important. However, no clear guidelines are given to software designers as to how to design for all in practice [5]. There is still no consensus on which phases of software manufacturing cycle should DfA principles to be applied and who should be responsible for the application. As a consequence, there is another threat. Many accessibility principles can be implemented and validated on the level of code. While such low-level implementation is formally valid, it cannot guarantee universal accessibility if DfA principles were not used in the initial phases of design. By focusing mainly on the code, the developers often have no chance to reveal empathy towards potential end-users with different abilities, which is an important prerequisite for inclusive software design.

---

1 http://www.dfaei.org/

M. Kurosu (Ed.): Human-Computer Interaction, Part I, HCII 2014, LNCS 8510, pp. 259–269, 2014.

Our case study demonstrates how these issues can be addressed by applying empathic modeling as a pedagogical approach in teaching DfA as part of a software engineering curriculum.

We validated our assumptions in context of DfA course for HCI master students that took a place in Tallinn University during the first semester of 2013.

2   Reasons for Design for All

Since the 1960s the world population achieved 7 billion, as fertility has exceeded mortality by 200 percent [6]. One noticeable indicator of population ageing is Potential Support Ratio (PSR) — the number of persons aged 15 to 64 per every person aged 65 or older. According to Haux et al [7] only 2 persons will be aged under 64 for each one older person in 2050 in Europe (Table 1).

Table 1.

Year	PSR worldwide	PSR for Europe
1950	12	8
2000	9	5
2050	4	2

These values prompt us that it will be hard for the old people in future to expect the same level of support that they have today. Also it is clear that the number of older people in the population and the length of time these people remain dependent on social security and healthcare systems after retirement will be significantly increased [8]. By considering these circumstances a focus of research nowadays shifts from the life expectancy to the quality of life and to ways of living in the old age. Biologists and health researchers try to reveal the ways for improving personal health of the old people to support their active personal and professional life.

However it is clear that improvement of the personal health only is not enough for supporting active lifestyles. Such personal abilities as vision, hearing, thinking, communication, reach and stretch, dexterity, and locomotion have tendency to degrade with age. This demands from people to leave their habitual jobs and reduce their activities. In addition to improvement of personal health, there is a clear demand for supporting active living by environmental conditions. For example, Ambient Assisted Living (AAL) [9] addresses the needs of the ageing population, and aims to reduce innovation barriers of forthcoming promising markets, and lower future social security costs. In the context of aging societies, ambient intelligence has focused on providing assistive solutions for elders at risk of losing their independence [10]. The understanding of AAL is that it aims:

- to extend the time people can live in their preferred environment by increasing their autonomy, self-confidence and mobility;
- to support maintaining health and functional capability of the elderly individuals, to promote a better and healthier lifestyle for individuals at risk;

- to enhance the security, to prevent social isolation and to support maintaining the multifunctional network around the individual;
- to support careers, families and care organizations;
- to increase the efficiency and productivity of used resources in the ageing societies [11].

Only the second of the aims mentioned above directly addresses personal health, while other four more related to design and development of near and global environments. For achieving such aims Design for All principles should be widely adopted in practice. These principles are intended to ensure accessibility at design time and to meet the individual needs, abilities and preferences of the user population at large, including disabled and elderly people [12]. A core methodology of design for All is User Centered Design, which enables developers to focus on the users as the heart of the design process, and also involves disabled people as an integral part of such design [13].

By following these ideas we presume that software developers should to be involved in co-design process together with the interaction designers and potential end-users. The software designers and engineers should at first be aware about the needs of society for inclusion and different abilities of potential end-users. By being aware of users with different needs the designers should avoid common practice of designing products for 'average' users [14]. They should know how to learn about their potential audience and they should practice empathy to the end-users during the process of development. Finally, developers should have an ability to transfer gathered knowledge about users to the digital realm. Kouprie and Visser ask: how to design a communication product for elderly people, with a design team consisting of marketers, engineers, product designers, usability professionals, etc., if none of them belongs to the user group himself? [15]

To help developers reveal some hidden and not obvious needs of users that can be used in design decisions the *emphatic modeling* method is used.

3   Emphatic Modeling

According to Decety & Jackson an experience of *empathy* is a "natural ability to understand the emotions and feelings of others, whether one actually witnessed his or her situation, perceived it from a photograph, read about it in fiction book, or merely imagined it" [16]. By citing Reik [17], Decety & Jackson described the following four processes that are involved in empathy:

- *Identification*: focusing one's own attention to another and allowing oneself to become absorbed in contemplation of that person;
- *Incorporation*: making the other's experience one's own via internalizing the other;
- *Reverberation*: experiencing the other's experience while attending to one's own cognitive and affective associations to that experience;

- *Detachment*: moving back from the merged inner relationship to a position of separate identity, which permits a response to be made that reflects both understanding of others as well as separateness from them [16].

A similar model that consists of the same amount of properties but stresses them in a slightly different way was proposed by Wiseman:

- See the world as others see it;
- Be nonjudgmental;
- Understand another's feelings;
- Communicate the understanding.

These properties can be considered as useful for designers, who use the user-centered design approach with the aim of identifying user's points of view, abilities and constrains that they may have in interaction with a specific artifact.

Apparently, the goodwill to have empathy without the real experience is not enough to learn about being aged, pregnant or blind. Special activities are required to place the designer "in the shoes" of a person with different abilities. For such kind of activities, a special method of empathic modeling is used.

Torrens defined empathic modeling as "a well-used method through which designers can gain some experience of the constraints of a defined medical condition that manifests itself in a form of impairment" [18]. Nicolle and Maguire describe empathic modeling as the method whereby an individual, using various props and scenarios, is able to simulate the deterioration of physical and perceptual abilities in everyday scenarios [19]. Different empathic tools like wearable and software simulators can be used to restrict the users' capabilities, so that they find it more difficult to see and to move, or to show the effects of vision and hearing impairments on image and audio computer files [20].

Through empathic modeling, the designer aligns with user's emotional aspirations and values, which is critical for effectively providing the basis for product desirability or acceptance [18].

4   Course Design

The experimental DfA course was taught at October - November 2013 within the scope of HCI master curricula in Tallinn University. This blended-learning course included 4 biweekly meetings, each lasting for five hours and several homework assignments that had to be reflected in the Personal Learning Environments (blogs) of the students.

In the class lectures, the students learned about historical roots of Inclusive Design, Universal Design and Design for All. They learned why DfA is an important trend today, and how inclusive design approaches are different from traditional design methods. Information about DfA movement and corresponding legislation acts on worldwide and European scales was presented. Related ICT specifications such as W3C Recommendation, WCAG 2.0 and Accessible Rich Internet Applications Suite WAI-ARIA were described.

The students familiarized themselves with the concept of disability and different types of personal human characteristics such as vision, hearing, thinking, communication, reach and stretch, dexterity, and locomotion. The students learned about differences in the personal abilities between different age groups. After meeting with basic principles of Universal Design [21] such as *ergonomically sound, perceptible, cognitively sound, flexible, error-managed (proofed), efficient, stable and predictable, equitable* [22], the specific design guidances that address limitations for different abilities were presented and examined with the students with corresponding DfA examples.

The course assignments followed the approach of empathic modeling [19], as students were repeatedly invited to put themselves in the shoes of people with disabilities, both as users of a physical environment (university building) and digital environments. During the course students had to complete three home assignments using their personal learning blog: *Observation, Finding the good examples around, and Finding the good HCI examples*.

4.1   Observation

This assignment was the main empathic task for the students. They had to find a way to a specific room in a building by simulating some form of deterioration. This exercise aimed an empathy experience which should be produced by new uncomfortable conditions for the student in the habitual environment (well known building). The students were able to choose a disability on their own. Examples of chosen disabilities were persons in a wheelchair, with a pushchair, with limited vision, with limited dexterity, with osteoporosis, with broken leg, without arms, and a foreigner, to check navigation facilities. All student documented their ways using photo and video cameras and reported stories about their new experience in their personal learning blogs (Fig. 1).

Fig. 1. A student with a handicap in a backpack simulating osteoporosis (left) and a student with tied arms simulating a person without arms (right)

Besides personal reflection the students also had a group work, where they collected all obstacles and design issues they met in the building during implementing task. The obstacles were sorted and prioritized according to level of treat and an amount of people that are affected by each obstacle. On the base of this analysis students proposed several design solutions that may help to avoid problems for people with limited abilities.

4.2   Finding the Good Examples Around

The students had to find, make pictures and describe five examples of physical artifacts around (on a street, in a bus, or in a leaving place).This exercise was implemented after the observation exercise, so students already had an imagination, what kind of design can be hardly accessible by specific people. The aim of this exercise was to train an skill for recognizing real world design issues on the base of experience received during the empathic modeling exercise. The student provided pictures and descriptions of the examples in their personal blogs.

4.3   Finding the Good HCI Examples

After two exercises conducted in the outside environment and getting a base knowledge about different types of abilities the students were assigned with a task related to the digital world. In this homework the students had to find and document five examples of DfA principles implemented in the Web sites, software application, or any other type of electronic services. The aim of this exercise was to transfer knowledge about DfA values and principles to the digital realm.

5   Research Design

After finishing the course the students were asked to reflect upon their learning experience in their blogs and fill in an empathy assessment questionnaire that contained 10 questions with Likert scale. The questionnaire was designed in Limesurvey tool and was provided online on anonymous base. The questionnaire included several general demographic data about participants, one group of questions that measure empathy and one group of questions intended for assessment of results of the course.

There are several studies available on topic of measuring empathy and evaluation of empathy scales [23–25]. The part of questions for the questionnaire was borrowed from Empathy Quotient (EQ) tool that was validated by Lawrence et al and showed High test–retest reliability [23].

Table 2. A subset of items from Empathy Quotient tool to measure general empathy level

To what extent do you agree with the following statements -
I really enjoy caring for other people
I often find it difficult to judge if something is rude or polite
I find it easy to put myself in somebody else's shoes
I am good at predicting how someone will feel
I am quick to spot when someone in a group is feeling awkward or uncomfortable

This comprehensive tool was designed for measuring user empathy in clinical context and was validated in series of four studies examined the reliability and validity of the EQ. While EQ questionnaire is quite big and contains of 60 questions, authors recommend that the different subscales may have clinical applications.

For assessing effect of empathy modeled in real world to understanding needs of people with limited abilities in digital realm we added into questionnaire five specific items relevant for our research focus, these are listed in Table 3.

Table 3. Original Likert-type items added to the survey questionnaire

To what extent do you agree with the following statements -
Understanding the general principles of design for all in physical settings helps a designer to apply them in HCI context
I learned from our exercise with simulation of deterioration something that can be transferred to the context of HCI design
I did not like to play the role of a disabled person during the course assignment
It is important to include such simulation exercises in physical context in the course of universal design for HCI students
Prior to this course I had less empathy towards users with disabilities

We also collected qualitative data by asking students to reflect in their study blogs upon the following open-ended questions:

1. Was the exercise of finding the way in the University building useful for following understanding DfA issues in this HCI examples exercise? How?
2. Was the previous exercise "Good examples of real life DfA artifacts" useful for following understanding DfA issues in this HCI examples exercise? How?
3. From the point of view of DfA, what commons and differences between the physical objects in environmental context and HCI artifacts you can define?

6   Results

The responses to survey questionnaire were submitted by 16 students, half of them were female. The age distribution of respondents matched the typical one for MA study groups in the Institute: two students belonged to the age group 21-22 years, six students to 23-25, four students to 26-30 and four were older than 30. Only two respondents did not have any work experience in IT industry, the others have been working as software developers (3 persons), usability engineers (3), designers (5), QA specialists (2), marketing (3) or HR (1) specialists and managers (4). The prior knowledge about DfA issues was reported as "very low" by 2 students, "low" by 3, "moderate" by 8, "high" by 3 respondents and "excellent" by none.

Figure 2 below illustrates the distribution of responses to five Likert-style items from EQ tool, demonstrating the relatively high level of general empathy among respondents. As we did not assess the level of empathy before the course with the same instrument, we cannot attribute such high values of the EQ items to the course design. All five items (No. 4 is mirrored) show similar distribution of values, which indicates high reliability of EQ tool even on the level of a subset of its items.

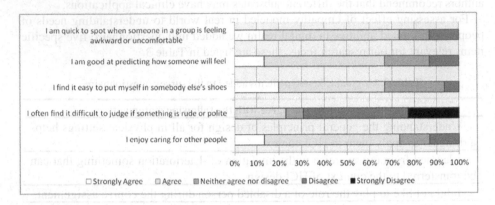

Fig. 2. Distribution of responses to generic EQ items

Figure 3 illustrates the distribution of responses to five Likert-style items that addressed the attitudes towards empathic modeling as the foundation of our course design. Almost half of the students agreed that the course increased their empathy towards users with disabilities, majority (13 out of 16) thinks the empathic modeling in physical settings helps HCI designers to understand better the DfA also in the digital context and considers it important to include such exercises in HCI study programme. There were no respondents who did not like to play the role of disabled person during the exercise, although three students remained hesitated. The general inference that can be drawn from these responses confirms that students were highly satisfied with the pedagogic design of the DfA course based on empathic modeling.

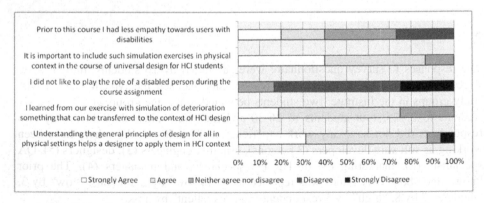

Fig. 3. Feedback from students to the course design based on empathic modeling

When analyzing the open-ended reflections made by students after the course, there are clear indications of students' understanding of DfA issues in line with empathic modeling approach. Several students expressed highly positive attitudes towards empathic modeling exercise:

"For me this exercise was very useful and engaging. I could never imagine how really hard it can be for a person that is limited in motion to get from point A to B in our university. After walking around the university I really understood how necessary it is to communicate to people, while designing for them and to test the creations with them in order to make the design actually usable. Apparently, this principle is fair for every design field, including HCI".

"This exercise was a new experience for me, because I have never put myself in the position of an old or disabled person before and have not thought of all the possible constraints and obstacles that they may meet on their way".

Students who had already previous experience with empathic approaches to design showed more restrained reaction. However, being less enthused about empathic modeling as such, they were able to recognize the professional advantages of such exercise:

" This exercise was a not new experience for me, because I am working in youth centre about 10 years and often we have children and youth with different disabilities. But from another side, it was a new task for me think from the design part about it. I have never put attention on it in my centre or at university. After the task, I started to recognize difficulties for disabled people and what we are able to change".

And almost all students acknowledged that the exercise was a good way for understanding DfA concepts: *"Definitely useful in terms of better understanding what exactly is DfA".*

By answering to the second question related to finding artifacts in outside world the students showed good understanding of DfA issues:

"For me the main and most precious (meaning I will definitely use this in future work, so it's a passive contribution to my qualification) was the realization of a simple fact that "good design" is not design well serving special needs of special people, but serving equally to everybody, without making distinction or exceptions".

By discovering outside world from the new point of view some students concluded:

" Media are every day full of information about new project for people with disabilities. But when I look around in city, especially in city center, I did not see any super or obvious stuff for those people"

Several students mentioned that they didn't pay attention to lack of accessibility artifacts before.

Some students showed good understanding of interrelation between DfA and user-centered design:

"When analyzing HCI examples I can't stop thinking of user-centered design as the primary criteria of assessment. Essentially it is about the same things in the real life defined by Don Norman: the affordances must be clear, there must be clear indication of the state of the system, the error messages must be understandable and the feedback must be relevant, etc".

By answering the last question students demonstrated good understanding of commons and differences between the physical objects in environmental context and HCI artifacts:

"...in digital environments, I think, the focus is shifted towards improving visual and logical representations, rather than appealing to physical capabilities. However, when designing for any of those fields, it is always nice to remember that very various types of people are going to use it, so no matter if we design a pen or a digital payment systems, it should be adopted for different physical and mental capabilities".

"Although physical and virtual objects obviously have different aspects, one thing in common is that both of them must be accessible for all users, but very often they lack this inclusivity. The main distinction between those two types is in different demands of user capabilities. While physical objects rely more on Ergonomic factors and in most cases require Reach & Stretch, Dexterity and Locomotion, virtual objects do not depend on them and are mostly concentrated on Cognition, demanding more Thinking and Communication. However, Perception is important for both, as Vision and Hearing are essential, and both physical and virtual objects should be designed with vision and/or hearing impaired users in mind".

These open-ended responses demonstrate that students have mastered the core vocabulary and value basis of DfA, they are able to apply them in building their argumentation and assessment. Based on our experience from this experimental course, we believe that the students' capability of transferring the knowledge, vocabulary, skills and values of the DfA domain from physical settings to digital realm increases the likelihood of transferring academic knowledge to the world of work.

Based on the quantitative and qualitative analysis of the feedback from students, we can conclude that implementation of empathic modeling as the pedagogical approach for designing a DfA course demonstrated good results and can be recommended for teaching DfA course in HCI curriculum as a starting point for understanding principles of Design for All.

References

1. European Commission: Digital Agenda for Europe - European Commission, http://ec.europa.eu/digital-agenda/en/our-goals/pillar-vi-enhancing-digital-literacy-skills-and-inclusion
2. Aegean, J.D., Rsehf, N.L.U., Romero, R., Engelen, J., Kulrd, S., Carlos, A., Verelst, T., Verbrugge, N., Miesenberger, K.: Teaching DfA Core Knowledge and Skill Sets: Experiences in including inclusive design (2004)
3. Campus, T.P., Road, B., Whitney, G., Keith, S.: Utilising Best Practice in ICT Design for All Teaching, pp. 1–18 (2008)

4. Bohman, P.R.: Teaching Accessibility and Design-For-All in the Information and Communication Technology Curriculum: Three Case Studies of Universities in the United States, England, and Austria (2012)
5. Burzagli, L., Emiliani, P.L., Gabbanini, F.: Design for All in action: An example of analysis and implementation. Expert Syst. Appl. 36, 985–994 (2009)
6. Livi-Bacci, M.: A concise history of world population. John Wiley & Sons, Ltd. (2012)
7. Haux, R., Howe, J., Marschollek, M., Plischke, M., Wolf, K.-H.: Health-enabling technologies for pervasive health care: on services and ICT architecture paradigms. Informatics Heal. Soc. Care 33, 77–89 (2008)
8. Zhavoronkov, A., Litovchenko, M.: Biomedical progress rates as new parameters for models of economic growth in developed countries. Int. J. Environ. Res. Public Health 10, 5936–5952 (2013)
9. Costa, R., Carneiro, D., Novais, P., Lima, L., Machado, J., Marques, A., Neves, J.: Ambient Assisted Living. In: 3rd Symposium of Ubiquitous Computing and Ambient Intelligence, pp. 86–94. Springer (2008)
10. De Ruyter, B., Zwartkruis-Pelgrim, E., Aarts, E.: Ambient Assisted Living Research in the CareLab. GeroPsych J. Gerontopsychology Geriatr. Psychiatry 23, 115–119 (2010)
11. Ambient Assisted Living, http://www.fraunhofer.pt/en/fraunhofer_aicos/research_areas/activity_areas/aal.html
12. Emiliani, P.L., Stephanidis, C.: From Adaptations to User Interfaces for All. In: 6th ERCIM Workshop CNR-IROE, Florence, Italy (2000)
13. Newell, A.F., Gregor, P.: "User Sensitive Inclusive Design" - in search of a new paradigm. In: Proceedings on the 2000 Conference on Universal Usability, pp. 39–44. ACM (2000)
14. Edwards, A.D.N.: Extra-ordinary human-computer interaction: interfaces for users with disabilities. CUP Archive (1995)
15. Kouprie, M., Visser, F.: A framework for empathy in design: stepping into and out of the user's life. J. Eng. Des. (2009)
16. Decety, J., Jackson, P.: The functional architecture of human empathy. Behav. Cogn. Neurosci. (2004)
17. Reik, T.: Character analysis. Farrar, Strauss, Giroux, New York (1949)
18. Torrens, G.E.: Universal Design: Empathy and Affinity. In: Waldemar, K., Marcelo, M.S., Neville, A.S. (eds.) Human Factors and Ergonomics in Consumer Product Design. Methods and Techniques, pp. 233–248. Taylor & Francis Group, Boca Raton (2011)
19. Nicolle, C., Maguire, M.: Empathic Modelling in Teaching Design for All Empathic Modelling. Univers. Access HCI Incl. Des. Inf. Soc. 4, 143–147 (2003)
20. Joy, G.-D., Waller, S.D., John, C.P.: Simulating impairment. In: Proceedings of (re) Actor3, the Third International Conference on Digital Live Art, Liverpool, pp. 3–4 (2008)
21. Center for Universal Design: Universal Design Principles, http://www.ncsu.edu/ncsu/design/cud/about_ud/udprinciples.htm
22. Erlandson, R.F.: Universal and accessible design for products, services, and processes. CRC Press (2010)
23. Lawrence, E.J., Shaw, P., Baker, D., Baron-Cohen, S., David, A.S.: Measuring empathy: reliability and validity of the Empathy Quotient. Psychol. Med. 34, 911–924 (2004)
24. Lietz, C., Gerdes, K., Sun, F., Mullins Geiger, J., Wagaman, M.A., Segal, E.: The Empathy Assessment Index (EAI): A Confirmatory Factor Analysis of a Multidimensional Model of Empathy. J. Soc. Social Work Res. 2, 104–124 (2011)
25. Jolliffe, D., Farrington, D.P.: Development and validation of the Basic Empathy Scale. J. Adolesc. 29, 589–611 (2006)

Models, Patterns and Tools
for UI Development

HCI Prototyping and Modeling of Future Psychotherapy Technologies in Second Life

Sheryl Brahnam

Department of Computer Information Systems,
Missouri State University,
901 S. National, Springfield, MO 65804, USA
sbrahnam@missouristate.edu

Abstract. This paper describes the virtual *MSU SL Prototyping Center for Psychotherapy Technologies* in development at Missouri State University and explores the value of using Second Life (SL) as a prototyping tool for HCI research. The power of SL is illustrated in our use of it to envision applications and usage scenarios for an integrative system for psychotherapy technologies called *MyPsySpace*, a highly flexible and customizable system that can be used by independent therapists trained in a wide range of theoretical orientations.

Keywords: futures studies, second life prototyping, psychotherapy, virtual reality, drama therapy, expressive arts therapy, scenarios.

1 Introduction

Around the turn of the century, many researchers attempted to predict the future of psychotherapy in the 21st century [1-3], discussing such topics as the impact of technological advances [4], ethical and legal issues in the coming age of distance psychotherapy [5], increasing pluralism [6], the future of the mental hospital [7], and the relevance of psychoanalysis [8]. Rarely mentioned in these forecasts were the cutting edge technologies already in development at that time. In the late 1990s, for instance, virtual reality exposure therapy (VRET) was demonstrating its effectiveness in treating people suffering from posttraumatic stress (PTS) and phobias [9, 10]. Serious computer games, alternative realities, and virtual environments (VE) were also beginning to show promise in treating people with body image disorders [11] and in providing people with special needs new expressive therapies, such as sound therapy [12] and audio-visual interactive spaces [13]. Today growth in these areas is exploding, with virtual reality (VR) successfully treating a wide range of psychological disorders [9] and with related technologies supporting the psychological health and well-being of people from all walks of life [14, 15].

A decade into the 21st century, Anthony et al. [16] asked clinical psychologists at the cutting edge to describe their use of technology. The technologies covered in their book included the telephone, SMS, VR, immersive reality, videoconferencing, and such internet tools as websites, wikis, blogging, email, message boards, and Skype.

M. Kurosu (Ed.): Human-Computer Interaction, Part I, HCII 2014, LNCS 8510, pp. 273–284, 2014.

One concern expressed by Anthony et al. is their worry that technology in psychotherapy will remain a niche field. Many therapists are reluctant to accept the new technologies. One reason is that those who use technology as the primary means of conducting psychotherapy typically offer focused, short-term interventions outside the traditional office setting, whether via telephone or some internet service, such as Skype [16] (with distance psychoanalysis being a notable, yet controversial, exception [17]), or through specialized VR systems associated with hospitals and large clinics that have their own IT departments. Most practicing therapists work independently and still believe in the value of seeing clients in private offices, one-on-one and face-to-face. Moreover, most therapists lack training and have insufficient resources for employing technology in the clinical setting. Yet another reason therapists are reluctant to adopt the new technologies is that a majority of them, especially those involving VR, are lopsidedly linked to one theoretical perspective: cognitive behavioral therapy (CBT) [9, 18], with few applications stemming from equally valuable evidence-based humanistic approaches [18], making technology less relevant to a large number of psychotherapists.

In the conclusion to their book, Anthony et al. [16] challenge the reader to imagine future technological innovations in psychotherapy. The project described in this paper envisions how cutting-edge mental health technologies can be integrated and used by independent therapists trained in a wide range of theoretical orientations: humanistic psychology, CBT, depth (Jungian) psychology, drama therapy, and expressive arts therapy (EAT). How best to imagine this integration and expansion into other theoretic modalities is a challenge. As Mankoff et al. [19] recently observed, the literature in HCI offers little guidance in envisioning the future. They suggest that methodologies developed in the field of Futures Studies be tried when attempting to map out future research agendas in HCI, acknowledging that some of these methods mesh well with established practices in HCI, such as prototyping and modeling interactions using gaming engines [20], film [21], science fiction, and scenarios [22]. Mankoff et al. also point out that because prototyping and exploring how future technologies can be used by people is such an important yet difficult task, creating innovative modeling and prototyping approaches has long been a focus in HCI research [19].

The goal of this paper is to explore Second Life (SL) as a fairly rapid and inexpensive prototyping tool for HCI. The power of SL is illustrated in our use of it at the virtual *MSU SL Prototyping Center for Psychotherapy Technologies* developed by the author at Missouri State University. In section 2, I briefly discuss some SL research related to psychotherapy and collaborative design. In section 3, I provide a quick overview of our use of SL for prototyping a system we envision, called *MyPsySpace*, which can be customized to serve both the individual needs of clients and the different theoretical orientations of therapists. In section 4, we summarize some of the advantages SL offers HCI research as a prototyping approach for envisioning future uses of technology and present some ideas for future research.

2 SL for Mental Health Services and Collaborative Design

Developed by Linden Labs and launched in 2003, SL is a free massively multiplayer online environment where residents construct identities, engage in role play, and design, build, and buy their own virtual content (buildings, furniture, clothing, vehicles, etc.). Identities and appearance are easily replaced and modified, with the Second Life Marketplace offering a wide variety of embodiments (free and for sale[1]) that range from hyper-feminine/hyper-masculine physiques to fat suits and a host of child and animal avatars. Communication between SL avatars can take multiple forms: instant messaging, notecard delivery, and voice (via VoIP), the sound of which can be altered to match the chosen identity. SL provides a sophisticated graphics engine for creating custom-made environments and objects, along with the Linden Scripting Language (LSL) to provide avatars and objects with behaviors and animations. Methods for bringing in-world outside content (such as YouTube videos and other media) and for taking snapshots and for filming SL events are also available.

Aside from the creative satisfaction people derive from making things in SL, most people go there primarily to socialize. Popular activities include dancing at nightclubs, attending parties, shopping, and playing sports and games. Many residents of SL form groups to find others who share their interests. Many of these groups involve role playing, with some SL residents living out virtual lives in themed cities and environments (such as Kingdom of Sand) while others take on family roles in SL households. A number of real-life (RL) organizations (such as IEEE) and universities (such as Texas A&M) have also formed SL groups and have built centers on SL to disseminate informational materials to potential recruits and to host distance education and specialized training programs (e.g., mental health nursing [23]). SL is thought to offer many educational benefits, including experiential learning, role playing, theater production, simulations, real-life skills development, and collaborative learning [24].

Other SL groups are formed to provide social support groups (such as Alcoholics Anonymous) and communities (such as the virtual veteran center Coming Home [25]) for people coping with long-term disabilities, chronic diseases, addictions, and mental health issues [26]. Mental health groups are very popular and are said to account for the largest number of participants, approximately 32% of all SL residents [27]. According to the SL community directory (http://secondlife.com/community), over 30 groups offer professional mental health services. [2] The Counseling Center on Wellness Island[3] is one example. A number of independent licensed therapists and counselors also have offices in SL, with some building their offices on land they rent (paying \$20-\$30 per month for 512 m^2) while others negotiate rentals in SL commercial buildings.

---

[1] Purchased with Linden dollars (L\$): 250 L\$ is approximately equal to 1USD.
[2] According to SL community directory searches conducted in February 2014.
[3] See www.slwellness.com

In addition, more than 500 research groups are represented on SL, with over 75 groups devoted to psychological research. One relevant SL project recently reported in the literature assessed the feasibility, acceptability, and effectiveness of treating adults with generalized social anxiety disorder (SAD) with VRET administered in SL [28]. Results of this study showed that the majority of SAD patients found their SL exposure treatments both acceptable and feasible.

Since 2007 SL has been used by many RL companies, universities, and research groups as a rich resource for collaborative design as well as for collaborative learning. The value of building architectural models in SL, for instance, is illustrated in [29], which provides four case studies, with one demonstrating a two way link between a physical dollhouse model and its SL counterpart. In [30] the authors describe how businesses are using SL to try out new ways of delivering business services in order to improve real-world implementations; Starwood Hotels, for example, developed a SL version of its concept hotels, which they improved by eliciting feedback from SL visitors. In [31] the authors describe their SL simulation of a positioning system composed of virtual sensors and emitters (in the form of virtual PDAs worn by avatars), and in [32], the authors report prototyping an automobile heads up display (A-HUD) that projects navigation and traffic information on the windshield of a SL vehicle.

Within the last couple of years, Koutsabasis and Vosinakis [33, 34] not only have explored the benefits of collaborative design in SL for HCI education but have also recently developed a virtual world HCI studio course that takes advantage of problem-based learning in a virtual design studio equipped with tools (such as media players, projectors, bulletin boards, chat recorders, post-it boards, and floating text) that facilitate collaborative design, presentation, critique, and reflection [33]. Unlike traditional design studios, where the typical tools for practicing design are pen and pencil or CAD (Computer-Aided Design) programs, virtual design studios offer a realistic virtual world that can be set up to represent any number of design problems [34]. Moreover, multiple avatar scenarios can be created to explore interaction problems and possibilities. Artifacts, large and small, can be created in-world that exhibit complex behaviors when scripted, and interaction scenarios can be recorded cinematically using machinima techniques [35]. Solutions can also be scaled for better examination and evaluation.

3   MSU SL Prototyping Center for Psychotherapy Technologies

The MSU SL Prototyping Center for Psychotherapy Technologies was recently set up to envision the integration and the further development of state-of-the-art psychotherapy technologies, especially VR, in the typical clinical setting, where clients and therapists meet face-to-face to discuss issues. The first system in development at the center is called *MyPsySpace*, which is intended to be a highly customizable and flexible system enabling activities that accommodate the needs of therapists trained in a range of theoretical orientations. In this section I briefly describe the use of SL as a prototyping tool for the MyPsySpace project. The discussion that follows focuses on three aspects of the project: 1) the physical and conceptual design of the SL prototyping center, 2) the MyPsySpace interface, and 3) the methods used to model VR and distance integration. Figures 1-3 show photographs taken in SL that illustrate these three aspects.

3.1 Conceptual and Physical Design of the MSU SL Prototyping Center

The MSU SL Prototyping Center is currently a one story building that lies on a parcel of land in SL that is $1634m^2$. The center is both a design studio and an exhibition/information center that allows visitors to explore interface designs for MyPsySpace and replay usage scenarios when the center is not being employed by the design teams. At present, the design teams are being formed from CIS faculty and graduate psychology and undergraduate drama students at Missouri State University, as well as professional SL builders. Future teams will include licensed psychotherapists.

People teleporting to the center arrive on a brick landing porch in front of the prototyping center. Two doors lead inside to the main reception area, which contains a bot greeter behind a desk. The reception area and all hallways are always open to the public and provide links to research papers and YouTube videos describing projects and telling users more about the center.[4] The rest of the building is available to the public as well when not in private use by the design teams.

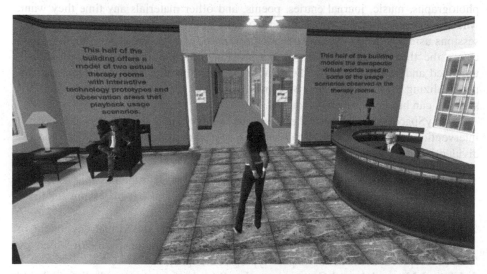

Fig. 1. View of the center's interior as seen from the reception room. The left hand side of the center provides models of two therapy rooms, associated observation areas, and a conference room; the right hand side provides two spaces to model the virtual worlds created and used in therapy session scenarios.

---

[4] The current SLurl for the center's SL location will be available at www.mypsyspace.com

The interior of the building behind the main reception area is conceptually divided into two parts, with one half representing the real world (RW) and the other half representing the virtual world and distance connections (see figure 1). In effect, SL (a virtual world) is being used to model both the real world and other virtual worlds. The RW half of the building is composed of two therapy rooms containing the MyPsySpace interface and two corresponding observations areas. In the back is a conference room, equipped with presentation boards and media players, that can be used for public lectures, team meetings, presentations, displays, critiques, and brainstorming activities. The VR half of the building is composed of two large rooms encased in glass that provide actual models of the therapeutic virtual worlds and VR applications that were created for some of the MyPsySpace usage scenarios explored in the therapy rooms. The center's facilities are discussed in more detail below.

3.2   MyPsySpace Interface

As illustrated in Figure 2, the primary MyPsySpace interface is a large screen that is viewable either on a flat-panel TV or wall projection. MyPsySpace can be controlled using laptop computers, iPads, and smart phones, and requires therapists to create secure user accounts for each client. What appears on the screen varies depending on the client, the applications in use, and the materials in review that have been uploaded to the system by either the therapist or the client. Clients are able to upload photographs, music, journal entries, poems, and other materials any time they want, whether in session or not. Clients also have the ability to access the Internet during sessions using the MyPsySpace screen to project content for discussion. When a client enters the therapy room for his or her session, pictures and materials previously uploaded and produced by the client can appear on the MyPsySpace screen, thereby personalizing the therapy room. Moreover, new and old materials and recorded VR sessions can be accessed when required.

MyPsySpace also allows therapists to select and create any number of interventions for their clients. Interventions accessible on MyPsySpace are loosely divided into seven categories:

1. **Virtual Safe Spaces and Objects**: created in session with the possible assistance of a distance virtual world builder and accessible in and out of session for those suffering from trauma;
2. **Virtual Play Spaces**: painting and music applications, the virtual equivalent of sandplay boxes, virtual dollhouses, and other EAT applications, some of which are in development at the MSU SL prototyping center [18];
3. **Virtual Memorials and Commemoration Spaces:** for trauma and grief work and accessible by clients both in and out of session (figure 3 shows an example of such a space);
4. **Virtual Enactments**: the virtual equivalent of role rehearsal, role expansion, role reversal, narradrama, fixed-role therapy, and the empty chair dialogue intervention [36] (figure 2 shows an example of the virtual empty chair dialogue);
5. **VRET**: VRET applications and virtual worlds for exposure therapy interventions;

6. **Distance Connections**: with specialists, virtual world builders, and playback theatre troupes [36] (discussed below);
7. **Tracking and Assessment**: providing charts and graphs that track depression levels, anxiety attacks, alcohol and drug consumption, etc., over the long and short term. Using smart phone apps, clients can report events to the system as they occur between sessions. Episodes can then be discussed in the next session. These assessments can also be reviewed periodically to evaluate progress.

Fig. 2. View of a therapy room with observation area

The SL therapy and observation rooms are used by the design teams to investigate client and therapist interactions using MyPsySpace as well as to develop novel applications and virtual translations of some of the more traditional techniques listed in the seven intervention categories above. The current focus is on creating multiple usage scenarios in each category for both private and public discussion and evaluation. Students in the MSU drama department and other actors are enlisted to improvise a particular intervention between therapist and client within the parameters of a scene defined by graduate psychology students, CIS faculty, and therapist advisors. The actors are watched and directed in realtime by team members and advisors in the observations areas. The improvisations can be filmed using machinima techniques for later evaluation and iterative development of the scenarios. Movies of scenarios are available for playback in the conference room and as YouTube videos. An advantage using SL for prototyping purposes is the ability to record actor dialogues and avatar movements as they happen in SL and then play them back within the same virtual space at a later time, much like actors repeatedly performing a play on a stage. In this way, interactions can be viewed any number of times from multiple perspectives, unlike film, which can only present the perspective of the camera. Menus in the observation rooms allow team members and visitors to playback and observe the scenarios that are captured live in the therapist rooms.

Figure 2 shows an example of a virtual translation of the empty chair dialogue. Here a man who is grieving the loss of his wife has the opportunity of expressing his feelings and regrets to a projected photograph of his wife who is sitting in a chair in their home. In the iteration of the empty chair scenario portrayed in figure 2, it was observed that the image of the wife was very large and might be overwhelming for the client. It was then realized that tools and gestures for easily resizing images must be readily available in the MyPsySpace interface.

Images for the empty chair dialogue can come from photographs in the possession of the client, or they can be created in SL by builders who construct environments in consultation with client and therapist (as discussed below). In the latter case, an image of someone's face can be mapped to the face of an avatar, which can then be positioned in the environment. A photograph of this SL scene can then be taken. Thus it is possible for any number of empty chair interventions to be created and called up when necessary. These same methods can be extended to create other VR interventions, such as drama therapy and role rehearsing.

Fig. 3. A commemoration space for grief work rendered in one of the VR spaces at the center

3.3   Methods for Modeling VR and Distance Integration

Some of the interventions listed in categories 1-6 may involve VR and necessitate the building of customized virtual spaces. The VR half of the center provides a space to render virtual worlds that are constructed by SL builders for and under the direction of clients and their therapists. As is the case with the therapy rooms, scenarios involving client-therapist interactions and client solo actions in the virtual worlds can be worked out and recorded. The walls in the center containing the VR models, as mentioned above, are constructed of glass thereby enabling people to observe these worlds and what goes on in them from the vantage point of the hallway. When the VR rooms are not in use by a design team, menus are available on the hallway walls that activate what is called a *multi-scene rezzer*, a container that stores virtual environments and renders them within an associated VR space when an environment is selected. Once a virtual environment is rendered, observers can walk inside the space to experience the virtual environment for themselves. Visitors also have the option of playing back scenarios within the virtual environments, much like visitors in the observation rooms can playback and observe prerecorded sessions in the therapy rooms.

Figure 3 shows an example of a virtual commemoration space that was developed as a second intervention for the client depicted in Figure 2 who lost his wife. Explored in a separate therapy session scenario is how a SL builder might come into the therapy room via a remote connection to construct a commemoration space for a client.[5] Once such a space is created, it might be possible to give a client access to it between sessions. It is envisioned that the client sitting on the bench depicted in Figure 3 would have unlimited access to his commemoration space and would be able to write poems, letters, and journal entries on notecards while in the space that he could deposit on one of the grave stones before leaving. These notecards would automatically be uploaded to MyPsySpace where they could be discussed later with the therapist, if so desired. In one rendition of this scenario, it was thought that the client might want to mark some notecards private for personal use; these private thoughts could be emailed to the client instead.

VR spaces can also model distance connections with other specialists while in session. An example would be an encounter with a Playback theatre (PT) troupe, who might be invited into a session, remotely via the MyPsySpace interface, for the purpose of re-enacting traumatic events. PT is a form of improvisational theater where a person called "the teller" tells his or her story to a troupe of actors who then go about dramatizing it [36]. A special member of the troupe called "the conductor" then asks the teller to pick out actors to represent the characters in his or her story. The actors, along with a group of musicians, then improvise the story, with the conductor checking in with the teller to make sure that the actors have depicted the story accurately. If not, the actors are asked to replay these scenes. For more information about the possibilities of virtual drama therapy, see [18].

4   Conclusion

Prototyping and exploring how future technologies can be used by people is an important yet difficult task. For this reason, developing new modeling and prototyping techniques has long been a focus of HCI research. In this paper I describe the virtual MSU SL Prototyping Center for Psychotherapy Technologies at Missouri State University. This center is exploring the value of using SL as both a prototyping tool and exhibition space for HCI research. Reported in this paper are some unique

---

[5] Collaboration would be done in session for ethical reasons and because thinking about memorials for traumatic events could be disturbing for some clients. It should also be noted that we are imagining virtual world builders who would be specialist at building virtual worlds for therapeutic purposes. This certainly will be a profession seen in the future.

benefits offered by SL, which are illustrate by our use of it to envision applications and usage scenarios for an integrative system for psychotherapy technologies called MyPsySpace, a highly flexible and customizable system designed for independent therapists who work in private offices and whose theoretical orientation may or may not be CBT.

My description of the center focused on three aspects of the project: the physical and conceptual design of the prototyping center, the MyPsySpace interface, and the methods used to model VR and distance integration. Described in this paper are some of the techniques used to develop scenarios of therapeutic interventions (some of which are original to the project) within SL models of RW therapy offices and virtual environments.

It is expected that when design teams work out scenarios for MyPsySpace, many ideas for future HCI research will arise. These will be recorded by design team members and collected in a virtual idea box located in the center's conference room. Possible ideas worthy of future investigation include evaluating the acceptance, feasibility, and effectiveness of virtual safe spaces for people suffering from PTS and exploring whether therapists reluctant to accept psychotherapy technologies, but who nonetheless are persuaded to become consultants for a design team at the center, become more accepting of the idea of technology in the clinic when they are given the opportunity of exploring technological implementations based on their own practices of therapy. Another possible area of exploration would be the development of a framework for creating customizable VR applications for psychotherapy. Not discussed in this paper are the practicalities of implementing MyPsySpace. Future studies would also need to address this concern.

Acknowledgments. Special thanks to SL builders Dan Fenwick and Odette Armour for their assistance in building and photographing the MSU SL Prototyping Center for Psychotherapy Technologies.

References

1. Gutkin, T.B.: School psychology and health care: Moving service delivery into the twenty-first century. School Psychology Quarterly 10(3), 236–246 (1995)
2. Worell, J., Robinson, D.: Feminist counseling/therapy for the 21st century. Counseling Psychologist 21(1), 92–96 (1993)
3. Snyder, C.R., Ingram, R.E. (eds.): Handbook of psychological change: Psychotherapy processes & practices for the 21st century. John Wiley & Sons Inc., Hoboken (2000)
4. DeLeon, P.H., Brown, K.S., Kupchella, D.L.: Editorial: What will the 21st century bring? An emphasis on quality care. International Journal of Stress Management 10(1), 5–15 (2003)
5. Koocher, G.P.: Twenty-first century ethical challenges for psychology. American Psychologist 62(5), 375–384 (2007)
6. Norcross, J.C., Freedheim, D.K.: Into the future: Retrospect and prospect in psychotherapy. In: Freedheim, D.K., et al. (eds.) History of Psychotherapy: A Century of Change, pp. 881–900. American Psychological Association, Washington, DC (1992)

7. Persad, E., Kazarian, S.S., Joseph, L.W. (eds.): Mental Hospital in the 21st Century. Wall & Emerson (1992)
8. Wallerstein, R.S.: The relevance of freud's psychoanalysis in the 21st century: Its science and its research. Psychoanalytic Psychology 23(2), 302–326 (2006)
9. Scozzari, S., Gamberini, L.: Virtual reality as a tool for cognitive behavioral therapy: A review. In: Brahnam, S., Jain, L.C. (eds.) Advanced Computational Intelligence Paradigms in Healthcare 6. SCI, vol. 337, pp. 63–108. Springer, Heidelberg (2011)
10. Safir, M.P., Wallach, H.S.: Current trends and future directions for virtual reality enhanced psychotherapy. In: Brahnam, S., Jain, L.C. (eds.) Advanced Computational Intelligence Paradigms in Healthcare 6. SCI, vol. 337, pp. 31–45. Springer, Heidelberg (2011)
11. Riva, G.: Virtual reality in psychological assessment: The Body Image Virtual Reality Scale. CyberPsychology and Behavior 1(1), 37–44 (1998)
12. Swingler, T.: The invisible keyboard in the air: An overview of the educational, therapeutic and creative applications of the EMS Soundbeam. In: 2nd European Conference on Disability, Virtual Reality and Associated Technologies, pp. 253–259 (1998)
13. Brooks, A.: Virtual interactive space. In: World Confederation for Physical Therapy, Yokohama, Japan (1999)
14. Argenton, L., Triberti, S., Serino, S., Muzio, M., Riva, G.: Serious games as positive technologies for individual and group flourishing. In: Brooks, A.L., Brahnam, S., Jain, L.C. (eds.) Technologies of Inclusive Well-Being. SCI, vol. 536, pp. 221–244. Springer, Heidelberg (2014)
15. Stetz, M.M.C., Ries, R.I., Folen, R.A.: Virtual reality supporting psychological health. In: Brahnam, S., Jain, L.C. (eds.) Advanced Computational Intelligence Paradigms in Healthcare 6. SCI, vol. 337, pp. 13–29. Springer, Heidelberg (2011)
16. Anthony, K., Nagel, D.M., Goss, S. (eds.): The use of technology in mental health: Applications, ethics, and practice. Charles C Thomas Publisher, Ltd., Springfield (2010)
17. Scharff, J.S. (ed.): Psychoanalysis Online: Mental Health, Teletherapy, and Training. Karnac Books Ltd., London (2013)
18. Brahnam, S.: Theory-guided virtual reality psychotherapies: Going beyond CBT-based approaches. In: Shumaker, R. (ed.) VAMR 2013, Part II. LNCS, vol. 8022, pp. 12–21. Springer, Heidelberg (2013)
19. Mankoff, J., Rode, J.A., Faste, H.: Looking past yesterday's tomorrow: using futures studies methods to extend the research horizon. In: CHI 2013, pp. 1629–1638. ACM, New York (2013)
20. O'Neill, E., Lewis, D., Conlan, O.: A simulation-based approach to highly iterative prototyping of ubiquitous computing systems. In: Simutools 2009 Article No. 56 (2009)
21. Bardram, J., et al.: Virtual video prototyping of pervasive healthcare systems. In: DIS 2002, London, pp. 167–177 (2002)
22. Blythe, M., Wright, P.: Pastiche scenarios: Fiction as a resource for user centred design. Interacting with Computers 18(5), 1139–1164 (2006)
23. Kidd, L.I., Knisley, S.J., Morgan, K.I.: Effectiveness of a Second Life® simulation as a teaching strategy for undergraduate mental health nursing students. Journal of Psychosocial Nursing and Mental Health Services 50(7), 28–37 (2012)
24. Sidorko, P.E.: Virtually there, almost: Educational and informational possibilities in virtual worlds. Library Management 30(6/7), 404–418 (2009)
25. Morie, J.F.: The healing potential of online virtual worlds. In: Brahnam, S., Jain, L.C. (eds.) Advanced Computational Intelligence Paradigms in Healthcare 6. SCI, vol. 337, pp. 149–166. Springer, Heidelberg (2011)

26. Gorini, A., et al.: A second life for ehealth: Prospects for the use of 3-d virtual worlds in clinial psychology. Journal of Medical Internet Research 10(3), e21 (2008)
27. Norris, J.: The growth and direction of healthcare support groups in virtual worlds. Journal of Virtual Worlds Research 2(2), 4–20 (2009)
28. Yuen, E.K., et al.: Treatment of social anxiety disorder using online virtual environments in Second Life. Behavior Therapy 44(1), 51–61 (2013)
29. Ehsani, E., Chase, S.C.: Using virtual worlds as collaborative environments for innovation and design: Lessons learned and observations from case studies in architectural projects. In: 27th Conference on Education in Computer Aided Architectural Design in Europe, Istanbul, pp. 523–531 (2009)
30. Kim, H.M., Kelly, L., Cunningham, M.A.: Towards a framework for evaluating immersive business models: Evaluating service innovations in second life. In: 41st Annual Hawaii International Conference on System Sciences, Hawaii, p. 110 (2008)
31. Prendinger, H., Brandherm, B., Ullrich, S.: A simulation framework for sensor-based systems in second life. Presence 18(6), 468–477 (2009)
32. Chu, K.-H., Joseph, S.: Using second life to demonstrate a concept automobile heads up display (a-hud). In: MobileHCI, Amsterdam, The Netherlands, pp. 2–5 (2008)
33. Koutsabasis, P., Vosinakis, S.: Rethinking HCI education for design: problem-based learning and virtual worlds at an HCI design studio. International Journal of Human Computer Interaction 28(8), 485–499 (2012)
34. Koutsabasis, P., et al.: On the value of virtual worlds for collaborative design. Design Studies 33(4), 357–390 (2012)
35. Bardzell, J., Bardzell, S., Briggs, C., Makice, K., Ryan, W., Weldon, M.: Machinima prototyping: an approach to evaluation. In: 4th Nordic Conference on Human-computer Interaction: Changing Roles, pp. 433–436 (2006)
36. Landy, R.J.: The couch and the stage: Integrating words and action in psychotherapy. Jason Aronson, New York (2008)

Combining Design of Models for Smart Environments with Pattern-Based Extraction

Gregor Buchholz and Peter Forbrig

University of Rostock, Department of Computer Science,
Albert Einstein Str. 21,
18055 Rostock, Germany
{gregor.buchholz,peter.forbrig}@uni-rostock.de

Abstract. There are two different types of approaches for smart environments. The first group provides an infrastructure that contains mechanisms from artificial intelligence that allow to adapt to certain behavior of users and to support them by performing their tasks. These approaches work fine if the conditions in the environment are not experiencing too many changes. However, when different types of activities have to be supported and participants change a lot there is the problem of getting enough training data to recognize the users' activities with sufficient reliability. In such cases, designing support by providing models for activities of participating users seems to be a solution. Thus, mechanisms from artificial intelligence can be supported by reducing the search space for possible actions.

Designing of activity models can be performed by employing the top-down approach through predefined generic patterns or alternatively the bottom-up mechanism by looking at traces of performed activities (scenarios). Again patterns play an important role as they allow the identification of important parts of traces that lead to parts of models. The identification of such trace sections can be done almost automatically. The mapping to parts of models however, has to be done in an interactive way. Human decisions are necessary to provide good models. Different strategies can be supported by tools in order to make decisions within the models ranging from abstract levels down to the most detailed level.

This paper will provide a discussion of the outlined approach.

Keywords: task models, smart environment, model generation.

1 Introduction

The application of models is a well-established principle of numerous engineering techniques for designing interactive systems. Task model based development approaches highlight on the tasks users want to accomplish while using the system. Thus, not only the requirements analysis and development process are having a strong focus on the users' tasks but also the running system can extensively profit from these models. This is particularly true for Ambient Intelligence Systems like Smart Environments since the utility value and thus the acceptance

M. Kurosu (Ed.): Human-Computer Interaction, Part I, HCII 2014, LNCS 8510, pp. 285–294, 2014.
© Springer International Publishing Switzerland 2014

level among users are dependent to a decisive extent on the usefulness and appropriateness of the system's support. For this purpose, the Smart Environment needs to be aware of single users' movements, positions, etc. among a lot of data describing the current situation, and also has to consider the connections and mutual dependencies between different users fulfilling different (and dynamically changing) roles in order to achieve a common objective. As the variability in human behavior is very high, and potentially unlimited, a real *understanding* of such a complex situation is beyond the possibilities of any computer system. Thus, it might be helpful to provide the system with certain information about what activities to be supported. Applying this concept means to select ("load") a use case description before using the room assistance. Instantiating a use case may involve some customization, for instance the amount of talks in a conference session or the number of groups working temporarily separated in a workshop. Beyond this, an instantiation can include the combination of predefined parts of scenarios, tailored to the current needs of the user(s). Obviously, such adaption operations must be simple to use since the user should not have to delve that deep into the technical details of the room's *intelligence*. Once started, the Smart Environment continuously tries to recognize the given situation and, as soon as the recognition reaches a reasonable degree of certainty, it should give (or propose) assistance as modeled in the previously designed model. Bringing together the room's hardware and high-level models requires some additional effort: The lack of any semantics in the sensor data suggests the introduction of an intermediate language by mapping patterns of sensor signals to basic actions like *sit, walk, talk* etc. which can be seen as triggers and preconditions for specific tasks in the models. Basic actions are supplemented with attributes like timestamp, position information, confidence, and others.

Essentially, the elaboration of task models in the context of Smart Environments comprises:

1. the identification of entities for which tasks have to be modeled
2. the elaboration of these models from the top element (the abstract main goal) down to the tree's leaves describing all single actions necessary for each sub goal (refinements/alternatives)
3. describing the interdependencies between these entities (see [15])

These steps entail a lot of work. For the first step, a thorough understanding of the domain and the users is essential as the defined roles should reflect the users' perspective of the modeled processes. However, the set of roles cannot be determined automatically. As far as the identification of devices involved is concerned, we can derive them from observations of user performances (scenarios) conducted in the Smart Environment. For the second step, domain knowledge and user knowledge are also required. Nevertheless, with increasing level of detail and decreasing level of abstraction (which is the most laborious part of the model as the task tree progressively broadens downwards) some useful time and labour saving assistance can be given to partially automate the construction of the models.

In Section 3, the above-mentioned support type is described in more detail.

2   Related Work

Several approaches adress the scenario-based formalization of human behavior, many of which fall into the field of process mining. A comprehensive collection of such algorithms is implemented in the *ProM* framework [3]. Some of the numerous applications beyond the "basic" mining of processes are the identification of bottle-necks, verification of business rules, and creation of social network graphs. Import from a number of different sources is possible and many plugins for import formats and functionality are available. In common with the majority of process mining approaches, the focus lies in the extraction, visualization and optimization (in terms of resource usage) of processes. Here, it is taken less concern for requirements like human readability and understandability, support for a strong orientation towards a hierarchy reflecting different levels of abstractions from the viewpoint of a user and the suitability of the resulting models for discussions between modeling experts and untrained persons.

An example of a system generating task models is *ActionStream* [10] that records user activities for a long period while all interactions are interpreted as terminals of a grammar. By continuously adapting the grammar's production rules, *ActionStream* learns a formal model of the user's behavior. Such approaches are likely to produce quite precise models successfully covering the learned scenarios, lacking however a semantic meaning of the non-terminals. The resulting models, as "correct" as they may be, are of limited use in the attempt to establish a means of communication between different skilled individuals that is as decisive as easy-to-understand.

Some further references that are very much related to specific parts of our approach will be discussed together with the following presentation of our ideas.

3   Design and Extraction

After the definition of roles and devices (introduced as step 1 in the introduction) the elaboration of task models for all identified entities is our next step. The procedure of constructing role-based task models as proposed in this paper consists of two complementary parts: Taking the role's main goal as starting point, the modeler refines the top goal into sub goals, declares alternatives, temporal dependencies and so on as far as it is known and reasonable from the user's point of view. Part two makes use of recorded scenarios as additional input and synthesizes the task tree following a bottom-up technique, thus completing the manually designed parts. Both parts are highlighted below.

3.1   Top-down Construction of Models

The development process for Smart Environments as proposed here has to start with a careful requirement analysis resulting in, among other things, a set of use cases each comprising a set of roles and devices involved as well as an informal description of what the use case is about and how the roles and devices contribute to the overall objective.

For each role within a use case, the main purpose of a user fulfilling that role has to be identified and is modeled as the root node of the task model. That node is the most abstract description of why a user assumes a certain role for a specific time. Based on the results of the requirements analysis this main task is further decomposed into sub-tasks (i.e. nodes representing tasks with a lower degree of abstraction and vital to achieve the goal related to the parent task) or choice tasks (i.e. the goal related to the parent node can be achieved in more than one way). Between tasks at the same level of abstraction temporal operators, as far as known, can be used to specify the order of task execution. This procedure is continued until all identified activities and their discovered relations are formalized. What emerges from this procedure is a hierarchical model of what constitutes the respective role from the perspective of the user in domain specific terms. It can be supported by patterns that reflect already analysed and specified behavior and characteristics of roles, devices or spaces. Such a pattern-based approach is discussed in [16]. In [17] it is presented how this approach can be used to develop supportive user interfaces for Smart Environments.

However, patterns are available only if the domain is already known and analysed by experts. Knowledge of the domain is a precondition for the top-down approach. Sometimes such kind of knowledge does not exist. In this case the opposite buttom-up approach is worth to be studied. Based on observed scenarios hierarchical models can be constructed. Also combining both approaches seems to be promising. In that way some knowledge of the domain can be combined with information of observed scenarios.

This idea will be explained in more detail in the rest of this paper.

3.2   Bottom-up Synthesis of Models

For the bottom-up synthesis of task models previously recorded traces are essential. These sequences list all events emitted by sensors and devices (e.g. projectors, lamps) during the scenario executions. Thus, the user activities as detected by the system as well as the user interaction with the devices can be analyzed. By applying appropriately configured and trained complex pattern detection algorithms on the sensor traces the event stream is filtered and transformed into new events (in the following referred to as "basic actions") that reach a semantic level suitable for further processing. This transformation itself is a challenging task and requires considerable investment of technical knowledge, experience and work. It has to be set up for each environment separately and has to be extended with the addition of new sensor types, considering the possibilities of new forms of sensor fusion.

Detecting Basic Actions from Sensor Stream. Figure 1 illustrates the detection of complex events and the generation of a basic action stream.

Given a potentially unlimited stream of sensor data from different sources as input, a stream-to-stream transformation is achieved by concurrently running queries in order to find occurences of predefined event patterns. Reducing the

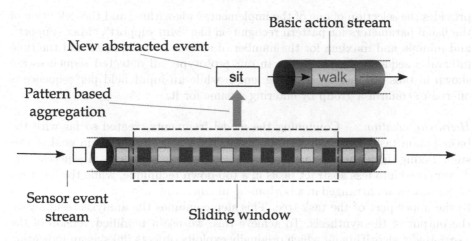

Fig. 1. Complex event detection from sensor stream

scope of queries via *sliding windows* helps restricting resource usage. Krämer et al. [9] suggest a stream processing infrastructure based on an operator and a physical algebra that carries over a wide range of theoretical aspects of stream processing (e.g. windowed aggregation, adaptive resource mangement, and query optimization) into a consistent implementation concept. Furthermore, Hoßbach et al. describe a Java middleware for event processing (JEPC: Java Event Processing Connectivity) in [8].

In the following, we assume that such a transformation with sufficient performance (real time is required for event detection during usage) is available and continue with the basic action stream as the starting point.

Linking Basic Actions to Task Models. After transforming the sensor event stream into a stream of semantically meaningful basic actions, the bottom-up task model construction comprises the following three steps:

1. Pattern recognition
2. Hierarchy creation
3. Identification of temporal relations

Pattern recognition. – Frequently occurring action sequences in the recorded scenarios might indicate a correlation between these actions that can be interpreted as a more abstract task in some cases. Using algorithms like the *Apriori algorithm* [1], *PrefixSpan* [12], and *BIDE+* [14] a set of such sequences can be detected, providing the modeler with groups of potentially combinable actions. Because of the fact that these groups are of algorithmic origin and initially nameless, the reviewing of these groups comprises the check of their reasonableness as well as the specification of a proper label. Once a suggested group is confirmed and labeled, its name is treated as the name of a new task that references the actions of that group as child nodes. Our implementation of the pattern recognition provides the selection of one of the implemented algorithms and the definition of the usual parameters for pattern recognition like "Min support", "Max support", and minima and maxima for the number of actions in a sequence and the time interval a sequence has to fit in. In our prototype, all detected sequences are shown in tabs ordered by sequence length while an input field per sequence is offered to confirm a group by entering a name for it.

Hierarchy creation. – Combining the model fragments created so far with the basic action tasks from the scenario traces (protocols) is the main goal of this step. Taking the identified main goal as the root node, the tasks are successively decomposed into less abstract tasks in a top-down technique, while the recorded action traces are arranged in a bottom-up manner, initially quite loosely coupled to the upper part of the task tree. This step combines the analysis results with the output of the synthesis. To achieve this, we use a modified version of the *LearnModel* algorithm [6] which originally exploits objects links as an indication for probably connected activities. Since we cannot assume the presence of object-related information we decided not to integrate the propagator concept from *LearnModel*. The second modification concerns the set of temporal operators: As the models in our approach should be usable with other tools, our notation and operators have been adapted to the operators of CTT.

During the creation of a hierarchy the *Choice* relation has a special role to play as it crucially influences the emerging structure.

Among the approved action groups detected by the pattern recognition there may be more than one group assigned to a task (called *group set*). In each group set the minimal group (i.e. the group with the lowest number of sub tasks) is determined. The smaller number of basic actions is used as the secondary criterion, in case of equality one group is randomly selected.

Each occurrence of the minimal group within the action sequences of other groups is replaced by this group's assigned task. Then, the group is removed from the group set. This process is repeated until either only one group is left or no more substitutions are possible.

Tasks that were used as replacements for action sequences in other groups as well as the remaining action sequences are considered as alternative realizations of the common super-task.

Finally, the *Align* and *InduceOrdering* algorithms are applied. In short, *Align* generates "recipes" for every group of sequences assigned to the same non-basic task while *InduceOrdering* adjusts the ordering of the sequences. This procedure is repeatedly executed until all protocol actions are assigned directly or indirectly (one or more nodes between the nodes were created during the pattern recognition) to a task node modeled in the top-down modeling process described in section 3.1. Note that only those actions occurring in any of the trace protocols selected for this step are considered.

Identification of temporal relations. – Each task and action can be flagged as optional. Within the establishing of the temporal relations the default value ("mandatory") is considered to be correct until a conflict with the analyzed action traces occurs. Initially, all child nodes of a given node are considered to be in an *enabling* relation with respect to their first occurrence. This assumption may be proved to be incorrect:

- Two actions or tasks a_1 and a_2 with a_1 being assigned to a_i and a_2 to a_j are found to occur in the order $a_2, ..., a_1$. Now, an *order independent* relation between a_i and a_j is suggested because a_1 and a_2 were previously detected in a reversed order and an *enabling* relation to be revoked has been suggested.
- Iterations are suggested for each task or sequence that occurs more than once. Two parameters can be set to control the detection: The minimum number of occurrences of a sequence and the maximum length of sequences that are examined during this step. Thus, the modeler can reduce the computational effort of analyzing large protocols. The number of repetitions is attached as annotation to the iteration.
- End timestamps are synthesized for tasks from the timestamps of the connected basic actions. Based on that, the concurrency of tasks is detected and denoted in the model.

During the derivation of temporal operators each time an already found operator is modified, all operators up to the root are checked and modified, if violated. The process of temporal operator derivation can be repeated any number of times, selecting different sets of task traces recorded before and with varying settings for operator detection. Thus, different rival model versions can be created, discussed and evaluated.

3.3   Example

This section will exemplify the task model synthesis. Space restriction does not enable the example to cover all aspects like pattern recognition but allows us to demonstrate the principle of the proposed approach. Figure 2 depicts the analysis model of a *lecture event* use case: One model (a) describes the whole process and another model (b) defines the tasks of a role *presenter*.

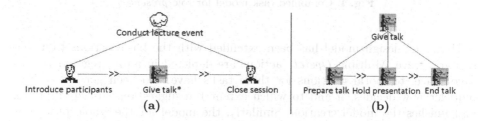

Fig. 2. Analysis models: **(a)** whole process, **(b)** model for role *presenter*

In Figure 3, some excerpts from an example scenario trace (basic action stream) are shown, illustrating how users behave to accomplish the task *Conduct lecture event*.

Timestamp	PID	Basic action	Attr1	Attr2
00:00:24	1	sit	seat3	
00:00:26	2	walk		
00:00:32	2	sit	seat1	
00:00:33	2	talk		
00:01:05	1	walk	pres_zone1	
00:01:17	1	operate	beam4	sw_on
00:01:28	1	operate	beam4	connect
00:01:28	1	operate	lap1	connect
00:01:43	1	operate	screen3	lower
00:01:49	1	walk		
00:01:54	1	talk		
00:02:40	1	talk		
00:03:12	1	operate	lap1	nxt_slide

Timestamp	PID	Basic action	Attr1	Attr2
00:09:02	1	operate	lap1	disconnect
00:09:02	1	operate	beam4	disconnect
00:09:40	1	walk		
00:09:42	2	walk		
00:09:59	1	sit	seat3	
00:10:01	2	walk	pres_zone2	
00:10:36	2	operate	beam2	sw_on
00:10:50	2	operate	lap3	connect
00:10:50	2	operate	beam2	connect

Timestamp	PID	Basic action	Attr1	Attr2
00:23:44	2	operate	lap3	disconnect
00:24:19	2	operate	beam2	disconnect
00:24:30	2	operate	screen2	raise

Fig. 3. Snippets from example scenario trace

Now the modeler has to mark sequences of actions as belonging to tasks or to task trees, be they leaf nodes or inner nodes. Depending on the algorithm selected, a synthesized structure with temporal relations and modifications of existing relations is presented to the modeler (Figure 4).

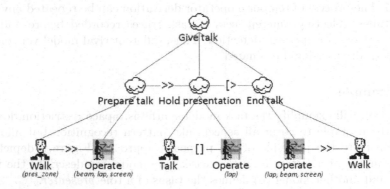

Fig. 4. Combined task model for role *presenter*

Here, the design model has been extended with the basic actions from the scenario trace. Multiple *Operate* actions are depicted in an aggregated way to save space; temporal relations for those tasks have also been generated. The modeler now decides, if and to which extent the suggestions are appropriate, and finishes the model creation. Similarly, the model for the whole process is enriched with generated model fragments.

This partly automated elaboration process results in models bridging the gap between basic action streams as detected from sensor data and the more abstract analysis task models.

3.4   Discussion

The combination of manual creation and semi-automatic generation of models can substantially contribute to a user-centered design of assistance in smart environments. Nonetheless, some effort is needed to prepare and control the generation. The main purpose of this effort is to provide reasonable assurance that the resulting models do not only describe the scenarios in a formally correct way (which could be achieved by fully automated generation) but also in a way that properly reflects the use case from the users' domain specific perspective. The usage of such models is not limited to the derivation of proactive assistance, but also includes the interaction between users and the environment in specific situations: Models can be used as understandable visualizations of the system's state (" *Why* has something just happened?", "What will happen *next?*") as well as for giving specific instructions ("The talk is not over yet.") that may include (or prevent) a number of device actions.

The approach presented here enables modelers to create task models in a more effective and proportionate manner.

4   Summary and Outlook

Using models as primary artifacts in software development to specify user behavior and user tasks is valuable, but requires a lot of work. This is escpecially true for Smart Environments, since the establishing of a link between the rather abstract models and the sensor data as the main input of the system is a very time-consuming task. The combination of manual top-down creation and semi-automatic bottom-up generation of task models based on scenario traces can lead to a considerable reduction in cost and effort. Particular priority is attached to the retaining of the models' character as an easily understandable formalization of tasks and activities from the users' point of view.

Further investigation of possibilities for improving the support of model creation for Smart Environments may include the more effective gathering of scenario data: Thus far, traces are recorded from real users in the environment. It may be useful to allow the recording of traces in a simulated environment. Such an approach would benefit from and rely on the introduction of an intermediate language as outlined in this paper (basic action stream).

Acknowledgements. The work of the first author is supported by DFG graduate school 1424 (MuSAMA) at the University of Rostock, Germany.

References

1. Agrawal, R., Srikant, R.: Fast Algorithms for Mining Association Rules. In: Proc. VLDB 1994, pp. 487–499. Morgan Kaufmann (1994)
2. Chikhaoui, B., Wang, S., Pigot, H.: A Frequent Pattern Mining Approach for ADLs Recognition in Smart Environments. In: IEEE International Conference on Advanced Information Networking and Applications (AINA), pp. 248–255 (2011)

3. van Dongen, B.F., de Medeiros, A.K.A., Verbeek, H.M.W., Weijters, A.J.M.M., van der Aalst, W.M.P.: The ProM Framework: A New Era in Process Mining Tool Support. In: Ciardo, G., Darondeau, P. (eds.) ICATPN 2005. LNCS, vol. 3536, pp. 444–454. Springer, Heidelberg (2005)
4. El-Ramly, M., Stroulia, E., Sorenson, P.: Recovering Software Requirements from System-user Interaction Traces. In: Proc. SEKE 2002, pp. 447–454. ACM Press (2002)
5. Ferilli, S., De Carolis, B., Redavid, D.: Logic-Based Incremental Process Mining in Smart Environments. In: Ali, M., Bosse, T., Hindriks, K.V., Hoogendoorn, M., Jonker, C.M., Treur, J. (eds.) IEA/AIE 2013. LNCS, vol. 7906, pp. 392–401. Springer, Heidelberg (2013)
6. Garland, A., Lesh, N.: Learning Hierarchical Task Models By Demonstration. Technical Report, Mitsubishi Electric Research Laboratories (2003)
7. Hamou-Lhadj, A., Braun, E., Amyot, D., Lethbridge, T.: Recovering Behavioral Design Models from Execution Traces. In: 9th European Conference on Software Maintenance and Reengineering, pp. 112–123. IEEE Computer Society (2005)
8. Hoßbach, B., Glombiewski, N., Morgen, A., Ritter, F., Seeger, B.: JEPC: The Java Event Processing Connectivity. Datenbank-Spektrum 13(3), 167–178 (2013)
9. Krämer, J., Seeger, B.: Semantics and Implementation of Continuous Sliding Window Queries over Data Streams. ACM Trans. Database Syst., 4:1–4:49 (2009)
10. Maulsby, D.: Inductive Task Modeling for User Interface Customization. In: Proc. IUI 1997, pp. 233–236. ACM (1997)
11. Paris, C., Lu, S., Linden, K.V.: Environments for the Construction and Use of Task Models. In: The Handbook of Task Analysis for Human-Computer Interaction, pp. 467–482. Lawrence Erlbaum Associates (2004)
12. Pei, J., Han, J., Mortazavi-Asl, B., Wang, J., Pinto, H., Chen, Q., Dayal, U., Hsu, M.-C.: Mining Sequential Patterns by Pattern-Growth: The PrefixSpan Approach. IEEE Transactions on Knowledge and Data Engineering 16(11), 1424–1440 (2004)
13. Seyff, N.: Exploring how to use scenarios to discover requirements. Requirements Engineering, 91–111 (2009)
14. Wang, J., Han, J.: BIDE: Efficient Mining of Frequent Closed Sequences. In: Proc. ICDE 2007, pp. 79–90. IEEE Computer Society (2007)
15. Wurdel, M., Sinnig, D., Forbrig, P.: CTML: Domain and Task Modeling for Collaborative Environments. Journal of Universal Computer Science 14(19), 3188–3201 (2008) (Special Issue on Human-Computer Interaction)
16. Zaki, M., Wurdel, M., Forbrig, P.: Pattern Driven Task Model Refinement. In: Abraham, A., Corchado, J.M., González, S.R., De Paz Santana, J.F. (eds.) International Symposium on DCAI. AISC, vol. 91, pp. 249–256. Springer, Heidelberg (2011)
17. Zaki, M., Forbrig, P.: A methodology for generating an assistive system for smart environments based on contextual activity patterns. In: EICS 2013, London, pp. 75–80 (2013)

Evaluation of Model-Based User Interface Development Approaches

Jürgen Engel, Christian Herdin, and Christian Märtin

Augsburg University of Applied Sciences, Faculty of Computer Science,
An der Hochschule 1, 86161 Augsburg, Germany
{Juergen.Engel,Christian.Herdin,
Christian.Maertin}@hs-augsburg.de

Abstract. The PaMGIS framework was developed at Augsburg University of Applied Sciences and is aimed at supporting user interface designers without profound software development skills to specify the diverse models which allow for at least semi-automated generation of user interface source code. Currently these are task, dialog, interaction, and layout models as well as user, device, and environment models. The complexity of the model definitions is reduced by the application of patterns of various types and different abstraction levels. These patterns are specified by means of the PaMGIS Pattern Specification Language (PPSL) that is a further refinement of the Pattern Language Markup Language (PLML). Amongst other descriptive information PPSL specifications incorporate sophisticated pattern relationships and model fragments, which are deployed as soon as an individual pattern is applied. In this context we have evaluated existing model-based user interface development frameworks in order to elicit new ideas to improve the applicability of PaMGIS.

Keywords: Model-based user interface development, pattern-based development, user interface modeling, user interface generation, HCI patterns.

1 Introduction

In the scope of our research within the Automation in Usability Engineering group (AUE) at Augsburg University of Applied Sciences we develop an integrated approach for the design and semi-automated generation of user interfaces (UI) of interactive software applications named Pattern-based Modeling and Generation of Interactive Systems (PaMGIS) [9], [10]. It combines both, model-based and pattern-based development techniques and methods. We have identified room for improvement regarding the modeling of dynamic UI behavior and the modeling of UI layout aspects. In addition, we are interested in possibilities to influence the UI appearance at runtime.

In this context we have conducted a literature review of existing model-based UI development environments (MB-UIDE) in terms of their functionality, suitability, adequacy, conformance to the abstraction layers defined by the CAMELEON Reference Framework (CRF), i.e. Model, Abstract UI (AUI), Concrete UI (CUI), and

M. Kurosu (Ed.): Human-Computer Interaction, Part I, HCII 2014, LNCS 8510, pp. 295–307, 2014.

Final UI (FUI) [1], and their general availability. The results will be used to extend the potential of our PaMGIS framework and to overcome the mentioned deficiencies.

The rest of this paper is organized as follows: the review approach is described in Section 2, brief descriptions of the considered MB-UIDEs are provided in Section 3, the review results are summarized in tabular format in Section 4, and our lessons learned and decisions regarding PaMGIS are depicted in Section 5. Finally, Section 0 provides the list of literature being consulted during the review process.

2   Review Approach

Several MBUID reviews have already been carried out and the results are available through the Internet, e.g. [7], [29], [42]. However, two of the documents date from the 1990's [29], [42] and the most current from the year 2001 [7] and therefore they do not cover novel approaches. Nevertheless, these documents delivered valuable input for our updated evaluation, notably for defining the MB-UIDE characteristics to be investigated.

Subject of the literature review has been an assortment of existing MD-UIDEs. Within the current paper we focus on the environments listed in Table 1.

Table 1. MB-UIDEs considered in this paper

MB-UIDE	Originator	Literature reviewed
AME	Augsburg University of Applied Sciences, DE	[24],[25],[26]
ITS	IBM T.J. Watson Research Center, US	[1],[45],[46]
MARIAE	Istituto di Scienza e Tecnologie dell' Inform., IT	[20],[32],[33],[34],[35],[36]
MECANO	Stanford University, US	[38],[41]
MOBI-D	Stanford University, US	[37],[39],[40]
SUPPLE	University of Washington, US	[12],[13],[14],[15][16],[17],[18]
TERESA	Istituto di Scienza e Tecnologie dell' Inform., IT	[3],[4],[27],[28],[31]

Our literature review actually compassed several more MB-UIDEs, including ADEPT [23], FUSE [22], GENIUS [21], HUMANOID [43], JANUS [1], MASTER-MIND [44], TADEUS [8], TEALLACH [19], TRIDENT [5], and UIDE [11]. On the one hand, we could not retrieve any more recent documentation for these fairly old approaches and on the other hand, they have been already covered within the former evaluations [7], [29], [42]. Therefore, and due to space restrictions we picked the most current MB-UIDEs and such systems for that we assumed they would deliver the most promising results for our purposes.

For each of the MD-UIDEs we captured (1) the short name, (2) the full name, if any, (3) its originator, (4) date of first publication, (5) actuality in terms of current version or most current publication, (6) provided functionality in terms of supporting UI modeling, UI generation, UI runtime environment, (7) provided support of CRF abstraction levels, i.e. model, AUI, CUI, and FUI, (8) models actually supported, (9) utilized model notations resp. User Interface Description Languages (UIDL), (10) whether the MB-UIDE was mainly intended to support multi-device, multi- platform, multi-user, or multi-environment developments, (11) tool-support offered with the MB-UIDE, (12) supported target programming languages, (13) supported target devices respectively target platforms, (14) its availability in terms of whether there is a real implementation of the MB-UIDE, meaningful application examples are available and whether the framework can be freely downloaded from the Internet, and finally (15) type of available documentation.

Due to space limits it was not possible to present all details of the evaluated characteristics within this paper. Therefore, we decided to provide as much information as possible within the textual MB-UIDE descriptions (see Section 3) and in summarized tabular form (see Section 4).

3   Description of Considered MB-UIDE

3.1   AME

The *Application Modeling Environment* (AME) was developed at Augsburg University of Applied Sciences between 1992 and 1996 [24], [25], [26]. AME's goal was to tightly integrate the object-oriented software development process with user interface modeling and design starting already in the early phases of the software engineering life cycle and to accompany the software developer until the final implementation of the interactive system. AME used structural information, object-oriented relationships, and semantic knowledge about the application context to automatically generate prototypical MS Windows GUIs for business applications including the dynamic behavior of the UI and the binding to the business objects.

AME uses an object-oriented analysis (OOA) model as starting point. An OOA model defines the domain classes with their attributes and typically contains only abstract specifications of the domain class methods (i.e. method name, calling parameters, calling parameter types, return type) as well as the relationships between classes. OOA models define the domain space of an application. They are created by model editor tools and are transformed into AME's internal model representation. The resulting class models unify the modeling functionality both from Rumbaugh's OMT and Coad and Yourdon's OOA. Attribute names and data types, as well as relationships and their types (generalization/specialization, aggregation, association with semantic information) are parsed by the structure refinement tools to automatically create the window and dialog box structure of the application and for defining abstract interaction objects (AIOs). Domain classes may also include message links (i.e. dynamic relationships to other classes) that can be exploited by AME's behavior tools to automatically create dynamic user interface behavior. No task model is therefore needed. Thus, an OOD model that defines the basis for the solution space, including the user interface structure, can be generated automatically. However, it is also possible for developers to introduce their own OOD classes with AIOs added to the domain objects or to modify the OOD model.

A series of additional knowledge-based automated tools can then be applied to create a prototype of the user interface with concrete interaction objects (CIOs) in the UI builder of Intellicorp's KAPPA-PC development platform including dynamic behavior (i.e. interaction dynamics, navigation, function calls). At this stage, developers and designers can again interfere with the prototype to add their own styles or change the types of the generated CIOs. The UI CIOs are still directly linked to the internal OOD representation. In a final step, the detailed OOD representation is again parsed to finally generate C++ UI code for MS Windows.

3.2   ITS

The *Interactive Transaction System* (ITS) has been developed in the context of a scientific project at the *T.J. Watson Research Center* of the *International Business Machines Corporation* (IBM) in Yorktown Heights. The first publication dates from 1989. ITS provides a rule-based approach for the definition and generation of application and user interface models and incorporates a runtime environment for execution of these models [2]. Amongst others, the visitor information system of the world exposition EXPO 1992 in Sevilla (Spain) has been implemented using ITS [46], [45].

A major principle is the strict separation of the actual content of a software application respectively a user interface from its presentation [2]. The ITS architecture is subdivided into four layers: (1) The *Action Layer* implements the necessary functions of the application's business logic independent of any dialog control matters. (2) The *Dialog Layer* defines the content of the user interface without considering its presentation. Dialogs are specified by means of logical frames and the control flow among them. (3) The *Style Rule Layer* defines the presentation and behavior of the user interface. Based on modifiable rules the system decides automatically by which concrete interaction object every single abstract interaction object will be replaced. Style rules are executed at compile time. (4) Finally the *Style Program Layer* takes care for the mapping of toolkit primitives according to the settings defined within the Style Rule Layer. These decisions are made during runtime, i.e., the final layout is determined not until a frame is displayed on the screen [45].

In the initial step of the ITS development process an expert of the problem domain specifies the data types being exchanged between the UI and the application as well as the dialogs. An application programmer implements the functions of the business logic [45]. From the data type and dialog definitions the *Dialog Compiler* generates a parse tree. This tree is subsequently passed to the *Style Compiler* that assigns the appropriate interaction objects to the tree's nodes by exploiting the *Style Rules*. The resulting full-featured parse tree is processed by the runtime environment that is responsible for calling the application functions and displaying the user interface [2].

3.3   TERESA

The *Transformation Environment for Interactive Systems Representations* (TERESA) has been developed by the Human-Computer Interaction (HCI) group of the *Istituto di Scienza e Tecnologie dell' Informazione* which is an Institute of the National Research Council of Italy (CNR) [4]. This approach supports the design and development of multi-device user interfaces. The work on TERESA started in 2003 [20].

The first step of the TERESA development methodology envisages the creation of a high-level task model which includes not only the actual relevant tasks and sub-tasks, but also information related to contexts of use and involved roles. Additionally, it uses a domain model which describes all interaction objects that have to be manipulated during the task execution as well as the relationships between these objects. From this task model so-called platform-specific system task models are derived by carrying out filtering and optional refinement actions. This forms the basis for generating abstract user interfaces (AUI) consisting of a set of abstract presentations which arise from the analysis of the interrelations of the sub-tasks. The presentations can be understood as compositions of abstract interaction objects resulting from the application of various composition operators, including grouping, ordering, hierarchy, and relation. From the AUI source a platform-dependent UI description is generated considering any specifics of the target device and target operating system. In this stage each abstract interaction object is replaced by a concrete one [28]. From this concrete description (CUI), in turn, the final user interface (FUI), is generated, e.g. in terms of XHTML or Java code [27]. TERESA supports the UI designer by applying different strategies with regard to the fact that it is not necessarily reasonable to implement all the tasks and sub-tasks in a similar way on each intended target platform [4], [27]. Furthermore the construction of multi-modal user interfaces is supported [31].

3.4   MARIAE

The *Model-based Language for Interactive Applications* (MARIA) *Authoring Environment* (MARIAE) is also developed by the HCI group of ISTI-CNR [32]. The initial version has been designed on the basis of the expertise and experiences collected with the predecessor environment TERESA. The first publications date from 2009 [34], [35], [36]. MARIAE is still under development; the current version 1.5.6 can be downloaded from the Internet[1].

MARIAE supports the design and development of Web Service-based interactive applications for multiple target platforms. Usually, Web Services are not constructed in the course of the development of the interactive application, but in fact already existing ones are being accessed. This matter of fact is factored within the MARIAE development process that combines both top-down and bottom-up approaches [36]. Additionally, on the one hand, MARIAE is fully compliant to the CRF degrees of abstraction and hence implements the model level as well as AUI, CUI, and FUI [32]. This implies a top-down development procedure. On the other hand, the analysis and planning regarding the utilization of Web Services demands a bottom-up approach [36].

In a first step the task model of the interactive application is elaborated using the ConcurTaskTrees (CTT) notation [30]. Subsequently, the relations between the task model and the chosen Web Services are established. They are described by means of

---

[1] See http://giove.isti.cnr.it/tools/MARIAE/download

the Web Service Description Language (WDSL)[2] and optionally possess *Annotations* which contain information regarding their later appearance in the user interface. On the basis of the so-called enriched task model the AUI can be generated [32]. The transformation process mainly exploits the hierarchic structure of the task model, the task types, the temporal relationships between the tasks, and the mentioned Web service Annotations. In this stage Presentation Task Sets are identified which consist of tasks being active at the same period of time [33]. In the next step, the AUI is transformed into the platform-specific CUI. This process can be regarded as refinement of the abstract model where essentially the abstract interaction objects are replaced by selected concrete ones. These conversions are specified via *Extensible Stylesheet Language Transformation* (XSLT)[3] [33]. AUI and CUI are described my means of MARIA XML [34]. Finally, the CUI is transformed by means of XSLT into a target language [33], e.g., *Extensible Hypertext Markup Language* (XHTML)[4].

3.5   MECANO and MOBI-D

MECANO was developed at the Department of Medicine and Computer Science at the Stanford University in the context of the Mecano project [41]. The development started in 1995 [38] and the latest publication has been published at the CADUI-Conference in 1996 [41]. MECANO is a model-based interface development environment that enhances the concept of generating interface specifications from data models. It utilizes domain and interface models. The domain model is employed to generate the layout and the relationships inside the model to determine the dynamic behavior of user interfaces [41].

The MECANO Interface Model (MIM) is described by means of the purpose-built MECANO interface modeling language named MIMIC. MIMIC is an object-oriented language that supports modeling at a meta-level and assigns specific roles to each interface element. The grammar of MIMIC is written in Backus-Naur-Form (BNF) [38]. The development environment that supports the MECANO framework in terms of MIMIC and its associated MIMs is called MOBI-D [37].

The Model-based Interface Designer (MOBI-D) is the successor of MECANO [37]. The development started in January 1997 [37] and the last publication dates from 1999 [40]. Like MECANO, MOBI-D supports model-based design of user interfaces. It uses five models to reach this goal: user, task and domain model as abstract models, dialog and presentation model as concrete models [39]. MOBI-D has no support for automatic transformation between the models, but the user can do this conversion manually. All models and mappings are specified with the Mecano Interface Model (MIM) textual notation. The Mecano interface modeling languages (MIMIC) are used to define the components, structure, the elements and relations within interface models [37].

---

[2] See http://www.w3.org/TR/wsdl
[3] See http://www.w3c.org/TR/xslt
[4] See http://www.w3.org/TR/xhtml1/

MOBI-D uses a textual task description of an end user as starting point. The MOBI-D tool U-TEL translates this description into a structured user-task description. The UI developer uses this description to build the user-task and domain models with the help of MOBI-D's model editing tools. MOBI-D uses the user-task and domain models to display suggestions for the presentation and interaction techniques. The developer can select one of these suggestions for the programming of concrete end user interfaces. Finally, the end user conducts a test of the new user interface [39].

3.6   SUPPLE

The SUPPLE system has been developed at the University of Washington in Seattle. The first publication dates from 2004 [14], the most current document we discovered in the Internet is from 2010 [15]. This approach utilizes functional interface specifications as well as device and user models. User interface generation and adaptation are treated as decision-theoretic optimization problems. SUPPLE searches for optimal renditions considering any relevant device constraints and minimizing the user's effort required to carry out the necessary UI actions [14]. In addition, SUPPLE is capable to adapt the user interface to the user's individual work style [13] as well as to personal preferences [16]. UI generation and adaptation is executed during runtime [13]. SUPPLE++ is a variant of the SUPPLE system and supports automatic creation and modification of user interfaces for users with motor and/or visual impairments. The initial publication regarding SUPPLE++ is from 2007 [15].

Within SUPPLE a functional interface specification is defined as a set of abstract interface elements and a set of interface constraints. The elements are specified in terms of their data types that can be either primitive or complex. The constraints are expressed as functions mapping renderings to a Boolean value and allow, for instance, map certain elements to the selfsame widget. The device model comprises of the available widgets, device-related constraints, and two device-specific functions for evaluating the adequacy of the widgets to be used. One function measures the appropriateness of the widgets for interacting with the variables of the given types while the other calculates the user's effort required for navigating through the UI. The user model is defined by means of user traces, which are a type of logs of user actions, recorded at runtime. Supple is aimed at finding the most appropriate rendering for each individual abstract interface element. This is achieved by means of a branch-and-bound algorithm for minimizing a cost function, which is composed of the previously mentioned functions and information from the device and user models [14]. The cost function consists of more than 40 concerted parameters and cannot easily be determined manually. Therefore, a tool named ARNAULD has been developed in order to facilitate this process [16]. SUPPLE++ primarily utilizes even more complex cost functions in order to consider the motor and visual impairments of handicapped users. In analogy to ARNAULD SUPPLE++ is supported by another tool named *Activity Modeler* [12].

4   Summary of Review Results

General MB-UIDE characteristics are depicted in Table 2 in a condensed format.

Table 2. General MB-UIDE characteristics

MB-UIDE	First Publ.	Current Vers. / Latest Publ.	Functionality	CRF Abstraction Levels	Target (Multi~)
AME	1993 [26]	1998 [24]	Model, Generat., Runtime [24][26]	Model, AUI, CUI, FUI [26]	n/a
ITS	1989 [2]	1990 [45],[46]	Model, Runtime [46]	Model, AUI, CUI [2]	Platform, User [46]
TERESA	2003 [28]	Version 3.4 2008 [31]	Model, Generation [27]	Model, AUI, CUI, FUI [27],[28],[31]	Platform [28],[31] Modal [31]
MARIAE	2009 [34],[35]	Version 1.5.6	Model, Generation [34], [35]	Model, AUI, CUI, FUI [34]	Platform [34]
MECANO	1995 [38]	1996 [38]	Model, Generat., Runtime [41]	Model, AUI, CUI [38][41]	n/a
MOBI-D	1997 [37]	1999 [40]	Model, Generat., Runtime [39]	Model, AUI, CUI [39]	n/a
SUPPLE	2004 [14]	2010 [15]	Model, Generation [14],[12], Runtime [15][13]	Model, AUI, CUI [14]	Device [14] User [14],[17]

Details on utilized models and supported target platforms and program languages are provided in Table 3.

Table 3. MB-UIDE models and supported platforms and languages

MB-UIDE	Models	Model notations	Target Platforms	Target Languages
AME	Application, Domain, Kappa PC UI Prototype [26]	OOA, OOD [26]	desktop [26]	C++, KAL [26]
ITS	Domain [46], Dialog [2]	Proprietary [2],[45]	desktop [2],[45],[46]	ITS runtime environment [45]
TERESA	Task, Domain, System Task [28], Interaction [31]	Task: CTT [28], AUI, CUI: TERESA XML [31]	graphical desktop, vocal, cellphone, graphical & vocal, graphical & gestural, digital TV [31]	XForms [27,] XHTML MP, VoiceXML, X+V, SVG, Xlet, Gesture Library for MS [31]

Table 3. (*continued*)

MARIAE	Data, Event, Dialog, Task [34],[35] Transformation [36]	Data: XSD, Task: CTT [35], Transformation: XSLT [34], AUI, CUI: MARIA XML [33]	graphical form-based, graphical mobile form-based, vocal, digital TV, graphical direct manipulation, multimodal desktop / mobile, advanced mobile [34]	XHTML, Java [36]
MECANO	Domain, Interface [38][41]	MIM, MIMIC [38][41]	desktop [38][41]	MECANO runtime environment [41]
MOBI-D	User, User-task, Domain, Presentation, Dialog [40]	MIM, MIMIC [37]	desktop [37][40]	MOBI-D runtime environment [37]
SUPPLE	Interface, Device, User, Data [14], Cost [12], Preference, Ability [18]	Proprietary [14],[12]	mobile phone, touch screen devices [14], desktop computer [12]	SUPPLE runtime environment [14],[12]

Information on comprised tools, availability of the MB-UIDEs, and application examples are summarized in Table 4.

Table 4. MB-UIDE tools, availability, and application examples

MB-UIDE	Tools	Availability	Application Examples
AME	TRANTOOL, OODevelopTool, ODE Editor [26]	Prototype [24]	Small office applications for evaluation purposes
ITS	Dialog Compiler, Style Compiler [2]	Existing framework [45],[46]	Visitor Information System EXPO 1992 [45],[46]
TERESA	CTTE, Editors and Generators [31]	Version 3.4 available at http://giove.isti.cnr.it/tools/TERESA/download	Museum Application [27]
MARIAE	Transformation Editor, Tasks-Services Binding Editor, UI Editor (AUI, CUI), FUI Preview [36]	Version 1.5.6 available at http://giove.ist.cnr.it/tools/MARIAE/download	Pac-Man game [34], Home control application [35], Sales order management [33], DVD management application [32]
MECANO	MOBI-D [37]	Exist. framework [41]	Ship protection system [38]
MOBI-D	TIMM [40], U-TEL [39]	Exist. framework [40]	Logistic example [40]
SUPPLE	ARNAULD [16][18] [13], Activity Modeler [16][18]	Exist. framework [14]	FTP client, Classroom equipment controller [14], Email client, Amazon Web Service interface [12]

5   Conclusion

All the MB-UIDEs considered in our detailed literature review can be regarded as valuable contributions to model-based user interface design and development. However, none of the approaches makes use of a combination of model-based and pattern-based development methods comparable to PaMGIS.

AME integrates an object-oriented software development process with user interface modeling and design and employs OOA and OOD models without requiring an explicit task model. AME aims at desktop computers as target platform.

Compared to PaMGIS, MECANO and MOBI-D use a similar set of models as basis for UI generation. Like AME, the target platform is desktop computer.

SUPPLE and SUPPLE++ start with a data model and treat UI generation as decision-theoretic optimization problem. On the whole we regard this as a very interesting approach, but too different to the current PaMGIS proceeding.

With regard to the further development of our PaMGIS framework, we intend to inspect ITS and MARIAE in more detail. On one hand this decision is based on the fact that these two MB-UIDEs provide solutions for the features we are looking for. On the other hand the pattern-based part of PaMGIS strongly resembles MARIAE in terms of its accordance with the CRF abstraction levels, types of utilized models, and model exploitation. In addition, MARIAE development is still ongoing and the current version is even available on the Internet and allows for practical exertion.

References

1. Balzert, H., et al.: The JANUS Application Development Environment - Generating More than the User Interface. In: Computer-Aided Design of User Interfaces, pp. 183–206. Namur University Press (1996)
2. Bennett, W.E., et al.: Transformations on a Dialog Tree: Rule-Based Mapping of Content to Style. In: Proceedings of the ACM SIGGRAPH Symposium on User Interface Software and Technology, Williamsburg, Virginia, USA (1989)
3. Berti, S., et al.: TERESA: A Transformation-based Environment for Designing and Developing Multi-Device Interfaces. In:Proceedings of ACM CHI 2004 (Vienna, April 2004), vol. II, pp. 793–794. ACM Press (2004)
4. Berti, S., Mori, G., Paternò, F., Santoro, C.: TERESA: An Environment for Designing Multi-Device Interactive Services (2005), http://giove.isti.cnr.it/attachments/publications/2005-A2-80.pdf (last Website call on January 25, 2014)
5. Bodart, F., et al.: Towards a Systematic Building of Software Architectures: the TRIDENT Methodological Guide. In: Design, Specification and Verification of Interactive Systems, pp. 262–278. Springer (1995)
6. Calvary, G., et al.: The CAMELEON Reference Framework. Document D1.1 of the CAMELEON R&D Project IST-2000-30104 (2002)
7. da Silva, P.P.: User interface declarative models and development environments: A survey. In: Palanque, P., Paternó, F. (eds.) DSV-IS 2000. LNCS, vol. 1946, pp. 207–226. Springer, Heidelberg (2001)

8. Elwert, T., Schlungbaum, E.: Modelling and Generation of Graphical User Interfaces in the TADEUS Approach. In: Designing, Specification and Verification of Interactive Systems, pp. 193–208. Springer (1995)

9. Engel, J., Märtin, C.: PaMGIS: A Framework for Pattern-Based Modeling and Generation of Interactive Systems. In: Jacko, J.A. (ed.) Human-Computer Interaction, Part I, HCII 2013. LNCS, vol. 5610, pp. 826–835. Springer, Heidelberg (2009)

10. Engel, J., Märtin, C., Herdin, C., Forbrig, P.: Formal Pattern Specifications to Facilitate Semi-automated User Interface Generation. In: Kurosu, M. (ed.) HCII/HCI 2013, Part I. LNCS, vol. 8004, pp. 300–309. Springer, Heidelberg (2013)

11. Foley, J., et al.: The User Interface Design Environment - A Computer Aided Software Engineering Tool for the User Computer Interface. IEEE Software 6, 25–32 (1989)

12. Gajos, K., Christianson, D., Hoffmann, R., Shaked, T., Henning, K., Long, J.J., Weld, D.S.: Fast and Robust Interface Generation for Ubiquitous Applications. In: Beigl, M., Intille, S.S., Rekimoto, J., Tokuda, H. (eds.) UbiComp 2005. LNCS, vol. 3660, pp. 37–55. Springer, Heidelberg (2005)

13. Gajos, K., Weld, D.: Preference Elicitation for Interface Optimization. In: UIST 2005: Proceedings of the 18th Annual ACM Symposium on User Interface Software and Technology, New York, USA (2005)

14. Gajos, K., Weld, D.S.: SUPPLE: Automatically Generating User Interfaces. In: Proceedings of the 9th International Conference on Intelligent User Interfaces, pp. 93–100 (2004)

15. Gajos, K., Weld, D., Wobbrock, J.: Automatically Generating Personalized User Interfaces with SUPPLE. Artificial Intelligence 174, 910–950 (2010)

16. Gajos, K., Weld, S., Wobbrock, J.: Decision-Theoretic User Interface Generation. In: AAAI 2008, pp. 1532–1536. AAAI Press (2008)

17. Gajos, K., Wobbrock, J., Weld, D.: Automatically Generating User Interfaces Adapted to Users' Motor and Vision Capabilities. In: UIST 2007: Proceedings of the 20th Annual ACM Symposium on User Interface Software and Technology, New Port, Rhode Island, USA (2007)

18. Gajos, K., Wobbrock, J., Weld, D.: Improving the Performance of Motor-Impaired Users with Automaticalls-generated, Ability-Based Interfaces. In: CHI 2008: Proceeding of the 26th Annual SIGCHI Conference on Human Factors in Computing Systems, New York, USA (2008)

19. Griffiths, T., et al.: Teallach: A Model-Based User Interface Development Environment for Object Databases. In: Proceedings of UIDIS 1999, pp. 86–96. IEEE Press (1999)

20. ISTI: MARIA Fact Sheet (2011), http://giove.isti.cnr.it/tools/MARIA/MARIA%20Fact%20Sheet.pdf (last Website call on January 25, 2014]

21. Janssen, C., Weisbecker, A., Ziegler, J.: Generating User Interfaces from Data Models and Dialogue Net Specifications. In: Proceedings of Inter CHI 1993, pp. 418–423. ACM Press (1993)

22. Lonczewski, F., Schreiber, S.: The FUSE-System: an Integrated User Interface Desgin Environment. In: Computer-Aided Design of User Interfaces, pp. 37–56. Namur University Press (1996)

23. Markopoulos, P., Pycock, J., Wilson, S., Johnson, P.: Adept - A Task Based Design Environment. In: Proceedings of the 25th Hawaii International Conference on System Sciences, pp. 587–596. IEEE Computer Society Press (1992)

24. Märtin, C.: Model-Based Software Engineering for Interactive Systems. In: Systems: Theory and Practice. Advances in Computing Science Series, pp. 187–211. Springer, Heidelberg (1998)

25. Märtin, C.: Software Life Cycle Automation for Interactive Applications: The AME Design Environment. In: Computer-Aided Design of User Interfaces, pp. 57–74. Namur University Press (1996)
26. Märtin, C., Winterhalder, C.: Integrating CASE and UIMS for Automatic Software Construction. In: Proceedings of the 5th Int. Conference on Human-Computer Interaction - HCI International 1993, pp. 291–296. Elsevier (1993)
27. Mori, G., Paternò, F., Santoro, C.: Design and Development of Multidevice User Interfaces through Multiple Logical Descriptions. Journal IEEE Transactions on Software Engineering 30(8), 507–520 (2004)
28. Mori, G., Paternò, F., Santoro, C.: Tool Support for Designing Nomadic Applications. In: IUI 2003 Proceedings of the 8th International Conference on Intelligent User Interfaces, pp. 141–148. ACM (2003)
29. Myers, B.A.: State of the Art in User Interface Software Tools. In: Advances in Human-Computer Interaction, vol. 4. Ablex Publishing (1992)
30. Paternò, F.: The ConcurTaskTrees Notation. In: Model-Based Design and Evaluation of Interactive Applications, pp. 39–66. Springer, Heidelberg (2000)
31. Paternò, F., et al.: Authoring Pervasive Multimodal user Interfaces. International Jounal of Web Engineering and Technology 4(2), 235–261 (2008)
32. Paternò, F., Santoro, C., Spano, L.D.: Engineering the Authoring of Usable Service Front Ends. The Journal of Systems and Software 84, 1806–1822 (2011)
33. Paternò, F., Santoro, C., Spano, L.D.: Exploiting Web Service Annotations in Model-based User Interface Development. In: Proceedings of EICS 2010 - 2nd ACM SIGCHI Symposium on Engineering Interactive Computing Systems, pp. 219–224. ACM (2010)
34. Paternò, F., Santoro, C., Spano, L.D.: MARIA: A Universal, Declarative, Multiple Abstraction-Level Language for Service-Oriented Applications in Ubiquitous Environments. ACM Transactions on Human-Computer Interaction (2009)
35. Paternò, F., Santoro, C., Spano, L.D.: Model-Based Design of Multi-device Interactive Applications Based on Web Services. In: Gross, T., Gulliksen, J., Kotzé, P., Oestreicher, L., Palanque, P., Prates, R.O., Winckler, M. (eds.) INTERACT 2009 Part I. LNCS, vol. 5726, pp. 892–905. Springer, Heidelberg (2009)
36. Paternò, F., Santoro, C., Spano, L.D.: Support for Authoring Service Front-Ends. In: Proceedings of EICS 2009 - 1st ACM SIGCHI Symposium on Engineering Interactive Computing Systems, Pittsburgh, PA, USA (2009)
37. Puerta, A., Maulsby, D.: Management of Interface Design Knowledge with MODI-D. In: Proceedings of IUI 1997, Orlando, FL, pp. 249–252 (1997)
38. Puerta, A.: The Mecano Project: Comprehensive and Integrated Support for Model-Based Interface Development. In: Computer-Aided Design of User Interfaces, pp. 19–36. Namur University Press (1996)
39. Puerta, A., Eisenstein, J.: Interactively Mapping Task Models to Interfaces in MOBI-D. In: Proc. Eurographics Workshop on Design, Specification and Validation of Interactive Systems (DSV-IS 1998), pp. 261–273 (1998)
40. Puerta, A., Eisenstein, J.: Towards a general computational framework for model-based interface development systems. In: IUI 1999 Proceedings of the 4th International Conference on Intelligent User Interfaces, pp. 171–178. ACM, New York (1999)
41. Puerta, A., Eriksson, H., Gennari, J., Musen, M.: Beyond Data Models for Automated User Interface Generation. In: Proc. British HCI 1994, pp. 353–366. University Press (1994)
42. Schlungbaum, E.: Model-based User Interface Software Tools - Current State of Declarative Models. Graphics, Visualization and Usability Centre, Georgia Institute of Technology, GVU Tech Report (1996)

43. Szekely, P., Luo, P., Neches, R.: Facilitating the Exploration of Interface Design Alternatives: The HUMANOID Model of Interface Design. In: Proceedings of SIGCHI 1992, vol. 1992, pp. 507–515 (1992)
44. Szekely, P., et al.: Declarative Interface Models for User Interface Construction Tools: the MASTERMIND Approach. In: Engineering for Human-Computer Interaction, pp. 120–150. Chapman & Hall (1996)
45. Wiecha, C., et al.: ITS: A Tool for Rapidly Developing Interactive Applications. ACM Transactions on Information Systems 8(3), 204–236 (1990)
46. Wiecha, C., Boies, S.: Generating User Interfaces: Principles and Use of ITS Style Rules. In: Proceedings of UIST 1990 (1990)

Engineering Variance: Software Techniques for Scalable, Customizable, and Reusable Multimodal Processing

Marc Erich Latoschik and Martin Fischbach

HCI group, University of Würzburg, Germany
{marc.latoschik,martin.fischbach}@uni-wuerzburg.de
http://hci.uni-wuerzburg.de

Abstract. This article describes four software techniques to enhance the overall quality of multimodal processing software and to include concurrency and variance due to individual characteristics and cultural context. First, the processing steps are decentralized and distributed using the actor model. Second, functor objects decouple domain- and application-specific operations from universal processing methods. Third, domain specific languages are provided inside of specialized feature processing units to define necessary algorithms in a human-readable and comprehensible format. Fourth, constituents of the DSLs (including the functors) are semantically grounded into a common ontology supporting syntactic and semantic correctness checks as well as code-generation capabilities. These techniques provide scalable, customizable, and reusable technical solutions for reoccurring multimodal processing tasks.

Keywords: Multimodal processing, interactive systems, software architecture, actor system, DSL, reactive manifesto, software patterns.

1 Introduction

Variance is a central aspect of multimodal utterances. For example, the temporal correlation between the occurrence of deictic markers in gesture and speech has been studied for decades [10]. Such surface patterns identify intervals, not singular points in time, in which a co-occurrence is likely and a semantic relation implied. This variance pervades various aspects of the phenomenology of multimodal utterances. Individual characteristics as given by users' personalities and physiology as well as cultural context have a notable impact on such variances.

As a result, variance has to be a central characteristic at various stages of multimodal processing models. These models must be capable of expressing variance on the surface structures as well as on deeper layers like, e.g., the semantic extend of referential expressions, or the semantic grounding of surface utterances. In addition, multimodal utterances often combine parallel signals from various channels. Sequential processing architectures and strategies often fail to capture this inherent concurrency and have to include technical complexities due to interleaved processing and buffering.

M. Kurosu (Ed.): Human-Computer Interaction, Part I, HCII 2014, LNCS 8510, pp. 308–319, 2014.
© Springer International Publishing Switzerland 2014

Technical systems for processing of multimodal utterances have to cope with the functional aspects implied by variance and concurrency. In addition, a lack of common technical solutions [16] has a negative impact on the overall progress in the field. This article illustrates four software techniques targeted at scalable, customizable and reusable technical solutions for reoccurring multimodal processing tasks.

2   Related Work

Multimodal processing has to deal with variance from low-level sub-tasks like signal processing to high level multimodal fusion and analysis tasks. For example, gesture analysis and detection based on machine learning approaches, e.g., neural networks [17,1] incorporates variance implicitly as predetermined by the variance encoded in the training samples. Template-based approaches like in [14] have to deal with variance explicitly, e.g., by inserting fuzzy constraints.

As a second example, procedural methods (e.g., transition networks [8,13]), alternative parsing strategies [4], and frame-based approaches [11,2] gained a lot of interest as fusion methods in the field of interactive systems due to a potential performance advantage compared to unification [9,7]. They all have to explicitly deal with variance during the central matching operation of two fusion candidates. The advantage of unification is its generalizing aspect due to the abandonment of domain-specific adaptations. Correlations are expressed via the so-called *agreement* between uniform features but agreement is usually mapped to equality which does not consider variance. Similar observations hold true for almost all sub-tasks of multimodal processing.

In addition, software quality requirements have been identified to be a necessity for multimodal processing [16,12]. Tight coupling of the multimodal processing to a predefined execution scheme as well as hard-coded variance-handling code scattered over the various processing sub-tasks greatly weakens scalability, customizability, and reusability. This includes the overall architecture and execution scheme of the processing, i.e., the data and control flow. For example, initial work was characterized by a tight coupling of the gesture processing and fusion with the execution scheme of the simulation middleware used [14]. The Mudra framework–as a recent approach–is coupled to CLIPS as the central rule-based production system and semantic model [6]. Similar approaches often use staged pipeline models. Such models condense and aggregate data from a sensor layer to a final fusion layer, loosely following an hierarchical *from signal to symbol* approach like in [18].

The follow-up sections will introduce the core ideas of the multimodal interaction processing toolkit miPRO. miPRO contains several design and implementation choices which improve scalability, customizability, and reusability and hence provides a sophisticated middleware for engineering variance during multimodal processing tasks.

3   Decomposition of Tasks: Processors and Meshes

The processing of multimodal input is decomposed into a loosely coupled mesh of modular processing units communicating via events (see figures 1 and 2). These processors transform input into output features, e.g., they may map the raw position of the user's left hand or the spoken words to ontology concepts like LEFT_HAND_UP or SPELL_COMMAND respectively. Input and output of processors range from raw sensor signals to intermediate or even end results, all uniformly accessed using concepts from the ontology. Processors define their input requirements and resulting products in terms of these concepts. Input is always buffered: A time series management facility provides simple temporal look-back, interpolation, as well as advanced aggregation facilities potentially necessary. The processor mesh is rearrangeable and provides individual execution schemes, hence fostering customizability, and reusability.

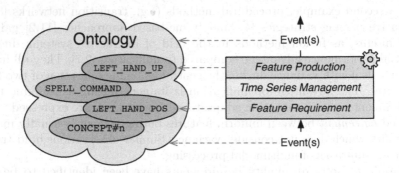

Fig. 1. A single processor (r) and its link into the ontology (l). Processors are executed by individual actors (depicted by the gearwheel) and uniformly communicate with each other by events.

The architecture of the multimodal processing framework is based on Hewitt's actor model [5] to provide scalability based on distribution and concurrency features. It is implemented on top of Simulator X [15], a flexible open-source simulation middleware for realtime interactive systems. This middleware features an entity model to provide an object-centered access to the global simulation state and hence the target domain. In addition, an event system facilitates message passing using a provide/require pattern. Entities and events are grounded into an ontology [19] in order to decouple components, to foster uniform and human readable access patterns, as well as to provide an inherent interface to the domain's semantic description. The latter is highly beneficial for symbolic artificial intelligence (AI) methods, necessary during the semantic and pragmatic interpretation of the multimodal utterances.

Each processor and hence production is concurrently executed by a dedicated actor. Flow of control follows the reactive manifesto. Execution inside of the productions is event-triggered using the underlying actor message system. After receiving new input, the processor executes its local production(s) and sends the result(s) to registered receiving processors in the mesh via events. Currently, the following production methods are supported:

1. **Native:** User-defined tasks (calculus, linear algebra, etc.).
2. **State Wrappers:** State change monitoring.
3. **Native DSL:** User-defined with domain-specific syntax.
4. **Augmented Transition Networks:** Parsing, classification, and fusion.
5. **Unification:** Parsing and fusion.
6. **Supervised learning:** Enhanced classification tasks.

The listed production methods are sorted in increasing levels of abstraction and accompanied decreasing freedom of expressiveness. For example, interaction engineers have to follow a rather predefined syntax inside of the productions of 5 and 6. Here, they don't have to cope with concrete algorithms but have to define parameters for the underlying production method. On the other extreme, the productions inside of native processors (1.) contain code written in the native host language (Scala). Hence, they allow the full scope of potential algorithms and, unfortunately, styles of programming. This expressiveness comes at a price. Missing guidance and standards usually results in highly individual code including self-defined identifiers and idiosyncratic solutions. This typically leads to decreased software quality, i.e., poor comprehensibility, maintainability and reusability.

The production methods 2. to 4. provide an alternative solution to the software quality problem. They restrict the expressiveness to constructs necessary for the domain and hence foster a high comprehensibility. The productions here are based on Domain Specific Languages (DSLs) (see section 5). The DSLs themselves benefit from the semantic grounding of all major constituents involved. Because the building blocks of the DSLs are generated from the ontology in prior, the syntax check–to some extent–simultaneously checks for semantical correctness at compile time. In addition all Scala-capable IDEs provide proper highlighting and auto-completion while editing.

Figure 2 illustrates an excerpt from the processing mesh of a demo application. In SiXton's Curse [3], the user plays a wizard capable of multimodal (speech/gesture) spells. One of the spells in the wizard's arsenal is a protective shield summoned by "*[Move Both hands up] create shield guard*". Movements are tracked by a 6-DOFs (degrees of freedom) sensor and sent to the application via VRPN (Virtual-Reality Peripheral Network). Speech input is captured using the Sphinx speech recognition software. Two components decouple the sensing equipment from the multimodal processing. The input layer of the processing mesh monitors hand and torso movements as well as speech tokens. The intermediate layer consists of two alternative classification methods detecting the occurrence of both hands being above the head. While the neural network processor has learned the variance of the input during training, the fuzzy pattern matcher deals with variance explicitly. Speech tokens are fead into and parsed

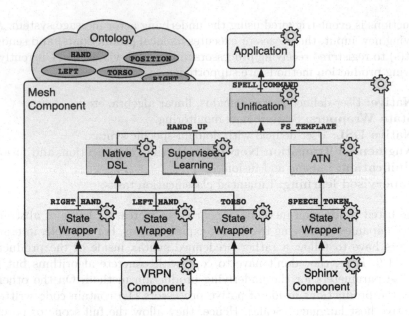

Fig. 2. An excerpt from the processor mesh of a demo application. Input is concurrently processed on two paths with dedicated processors for gesture and speech and finally integrated to form an interaction command provided to the application. Details see text.

by an augmented transition network (ATN). The intermediate layers produce feature structures as input for the multimodal fusion performed by a generalized unification approach. Finally, an application actor registers for changes of the fusion's output, allowing reactions to processed commands.

4   Customizable Operators and Functors

Processing of multimodal utterances has to account for variance even on the level of atomic operations. For example, unification parsers are based on the combination of compatible grammar descriptions called *feature structures*. These structures consist of feature-value pairs or they reference other feature structures recursively. Feature-value pairs represent grammatically relevant aspects like *gender*, *number*, *case*, or–often used in multimodal grammars–*time*. At the lowest level, unification applies a pairwise comparison of features to check if they match, e.g, to check if two parsed words like an article and following noun agree on the *gender* or if the article and the gesture agree on the *time*. Such an agreement is used to define a semantic relation or even an association important for the semantic analysis.

Agreement between matching features is achieved if either only one of the compared features has a value, or if the two compared features have the same value. The *agreement* is the central operator for unification parsers. It relies on equality checks for the atomic feature-value pairs. However, this strict equality does not account for variance: For instance, while a strict syntax check for *gender* or *number* is conceptually sound, real-world utterances often disobey the strict rules of grammar. A similar problem arises for equality checks of *time* features. Technically, strict equality of temporal occurrences is as good as impossible to achieve given a) the independent sample cycles of the underlying hardware, from tracking systems to speech recognition, and b) the internal variances caused by float point representations. In addition, temporal correlations between multimodal streams are observed not to be absolutely precise. If anything, these correlations are better be modeled based on imprecisely delimited time ranges or by some probability distribution.

In summary, comparisons play an important role during multimodal processing. Different types of comparisons are necessary due to inherent or explicit variance. These types could, of course, be programmed individually using tailored code fragments at the appropriate steps, again leading to code hard to maintain with domain-specific parameters scattered around. As a solution to this problem we exploit *functor objects*. Functors are highly customizable. They encapsulate user-defined operations and they make these operations available as first class objects inside of the source code. Functors inherit the type checking feature of the programming language in use, thereby safeguarding against misusage during compile time. In addition, definition and use of functors is now decoupled. This allows developers to build clean and hence maintainable code which, e.g., locates functor definitions at one central place.

A specific processing algorithm like unification now uses functor objects defined like `equals(type_a a, type_b b)` instead of the built-in comparisons of the programming language. These functors are provided for all necessary parameter types and their specific comparison semantic. The choice of the correct functor is automatically performed by the type system, the underlying processing algorithm remains plain and universal. Finally, certain programming languages provide options for an alternative syntax which allows functors to be used as operators. For example, a required fuzzy match functor can be written in Scale like this: `<exp> approximates <exp>`. This feature is highly convenient for the definition of human-readable and comprehensible code, i.e., for the design of domain specific languages as described in the next sections.

5   DSL-supported Feature Processing

The production methods 2. to 6. (see section 3) provide domain specific languages to specify user-defined operations. The constituents of the DSLs are semantically grounded into a common ontology. DSLs are checked for syntactic and (partly) for semantic correctness at compile time. At runtime, terms and expressions are substituted by corresponding implementations of the functors and operators and the resolution result of grounded symbols. Listing 1 defines a set of variables (the left-hand side) used throughout the following examples. The variables further shorten reoccurring access to prominent concepts from the underlying semantic layer.

```
1  val LEFT_HAND   = Position of (left, hand)
2  val LH_REL      = LEFT_HAND relativeTo (Transformation of torso)
3  val LA_LEN      = Length of (left, arm)
4  val HANDS_UP    = Occurrence of (hands, up)
```

Listing 1. Definition of semantically grounded feature descriptions required for the examples. Definitions for torso, elbow, and shoulder as well as for the right side are implemented analogously.

Concepts from the ontology are generated into corresponding static classes (e.g. Position or Length) or variables (e.g. left or hand) and are combined to describe features [19]. In addition, relations between concepts are used to generate corresponding functions that are used to describe processing instructions (e.g. relativeTo). The implementation of these generated functions is application dependent and can be used to cope with the variance of multimodal utterances similar to the functor objects in section 4.

5.1 Unrestricted Native Processing

Listing 2 illustrates a DSL-free code snippet for a native approach to detect HANDS_UP as motivated in the initial example.

```
1   val handsUpEventDescription = EventDescription( hands :+ up,
2     hasToContain = Time :: HANDS_UP :: Nil )
3   val localCps = Map[SVarDescription, Vec3]()
4   EntityDescription(VRPNTarget(trackerUrl, id="8")).realize(e: Entity => {
5     val positionStateVariable = e.get(Position)
6     positionStateVariable.observe(newValue => {
7       localCps += (LEFT_HAND, newValue); produceFeature()})
8   }// ... RIGHT_HAND is processed analogous.
9   def produceFeature() {
10    if (localCps.contains(LEFT_HAND) && localCps.contains(RIGHT_HAND))
11      handsUpEventDescription.emit(
12        Time(System.currentTimeMillis()),
13        HANDS_UP(localCps(LEFT_HAND).y > 2. && localCps(RIGHT_HAND).y > 2.)
14  }
```

Listing 2. Native processing of multimodal input (no DSL). Relative coordinates (e.g. to the torso), or user-specific variance (e.g., the arm length), temporal variances or time series management are missing. Details see text.

Processing starts with the declaration of the resulting event's description (lines 1-2). Then, a data structure for an actor-local copy of the most recent hand positions (localCps) is set up. Next, an entity which wraps access to tracking data is created (realize) and equipped with an individual initializer (lines 5-7). This handler sets-up monitoring for the entity's representation of the hand positions. It registers the executing actor as an observer (observe, line 6) which buffers new positions in localCps (line 7). If new position data for the right and the left hand is available (line 10), a resulting event is emitted. The event contains the current timestamp (line 12) and the result of a pre-defined, hard-coded template match using absolute coordinate axis and values (line 13).

Note that neither individual variances, e.g. hand positions relative to torso and the user's actual arm length, nor temporal variances based on time series management are considered for the sake of simplicity. Still, this example illustrates typical deficiencies arising from missing decoupling. It widely uses concepts from the underlying software framework which makes it hard to understand for non-experts and which complicates portability and hence maintenance. In addition, it hard-codes aspects sensitive to variance which makes it hard to customize and reuse the developed products.

5.2   DSL-supported Processors

The first step to revise the example decomposes the overall task into (1) a layer wrapping the raw sensor data (listing 3, lines 1-4), (2) a layer which transforms absolute coordinates into relative measures (listing 3, lines 5-10), and (3) a layer performing the actual detection (listings 4 to 6). Listing 3 first describes the state wrapper which provides the position data for the user's left hand. These processors use a dedicated syntax to wrap sensor access (line 2) but already use a uniform syntax for the specification of the provided feature(s) (line 3). Wrapping of the user's torso, left and right hand, elbow, and shoulder etc. is performed likewise.

```
1  new StateWrapper {
2    Obtained from Id("8") of VRPNSource(trackerUrl)
3    Produces feature LEFT_HAND
4  }//... RIGHT_HAND, TORSO, LEFT_ELBOW, and LEFT_SHOULDER analogous.
5  new NativeDSL {
6    Requires features (LEFT_HAND, LEFT_ELBOW, LEFT_SHOULDER)
7    Produces feature LA_LEN as
8      (Length of (LEFT_ELBOW - LEFT_SHOULDER)) +
9      (Length of (LEFT_HAND - LEFT_ELBOW))
10 }
```

Listing 3. Implementation of a state wrapper for tracking data and a native DSL processor calculating the length of the user's left arm.

A specific subset of the wrapped input data is then processed and transformed into relative measures. Lines 5-10 illustrate the production of the new feature LA_LEN, the length of the user's left arm. The DSL inside of the productions consists of identifiers which map to concepts and relations from the ontology, or, to be more specific, to auto-generated classes and static variables establishing references to the ontology. The Scala programming language supports the DSL syntax by allowing the definition of operators and thus ease the common handling with vectors in this domain (lines 8 and 9). As can be seen, this code already increases comprehensibility significantly.

The first example to build a HANDS_UP-processor at the detection layer is illustrated in listing 4. It uses a fuzzy template match. The processor requires the hands' positions, the torso, and the length of the left arm (assuming both arms to be approximately equal in length). The required features LEFT_HAND

and RIGHT_HAND are accessed at lines 4 and 5 as LH_REL and RH_REL via functors performing relative transformations.

```
1  new NativeDSL {
2    Requires features (LEFT_HAND, RIGHT_HAND, TORSO, LA_LEN)
3    Produces feature HANDS_UP as
4      ((Height of LH_REL since Time(500)) approximates LA_LEN) and
5      ((Height of RH_REL since Time(500)) approximates LA_LEN)
6  }}
```

Listing 4. A native DSL processor uses a fuzzy match to detect the hands up gesture.

The production defines a conjunction of two fuzzy matches for the left and right hand. The fuzzy matches account for temporal variance using the since operator provided by the implicit time series management available for all features. In addition, they account for individual variance using the predefined functor approximates. This functor is application dependent and auto-generated from the ontology. Finally, the DSL contains additional identifiers providing access to the the ontology, e.g. to resolve the upward direction necessary to determine the Height of a position.

The second example to build a HANDS_UP-processor is illustrated in listing 5. It uses an ATN. In addition to the already described DSL-concepts, it includes ATN-specific identifiers to set-up individual networks consisting of named states, named and directed transitions (arcs), and conditions guarding these transitions. Supplementary, some ATN-specific properties can be set, like an automatic reset of the ATN after 500 ms of receiving no new input.

```
1   new ATN {
2     Requires features (LEFT_HAND, RIGHT_HAND, TORSO, LA_LEN)
3     Create StartState 'start withArc 'lhRaised  toTargetState 'lhUp
4                                 andArc 'rhRaised  toTargetState 'rhUp
5     Create State      'lhUp withArc 'rhRaised  toTargetState 'end
6     Create State      'rhUp withArc 'lhRaised  toTargetState 'end
7     Create EndState   'end
8     Create Arc 'rhRaised withCondition
9       {Height of RH_REL approximates LA_LEN}
10    Create Arc 'lhRaised withCondition
11      {Height of LH_REL approximates LA_LEN}
12    Set autoReset to Time(500)
13    Produces feature HANDS_UP(true) onEntryOf 'end and
14                    HANDS_UP(false) onEntryOf ('start, 'lhUp, 'rhUp)
15  }
```

Listing 5. A DSL-supported ATN processor detecting the hands up gesture.

The ATN-DSL extends the syntax of the productions by explicitly mapping features to be processed to potential transitions (lines 12 and 13) and hence connects the flows of control of the ATN and the processor. Like in the previous example, the concrete implementations of auto-generated ontology relations, e.g. approximates, or the definition of time-related ATN properties, like the auto reset, allow to cope with variance explicitly.

The third example to build a HANDS_UP-processor is illustrated in listing 6. It uses a supervised learning approach, i.e., a neural network. In contrast to the ATN-example, the topology of the neural network is not defined explicitly using the DSL since the variability of useful topologies do not vary as much compared to potential ATNs.

```
1  new SupervisedLearning {
2    Requires features (LEFT_HAND, RIGHT_HAND, TORSO, LA_LEN)
3    Uses NeuralNetwork "./hands-up.nn"
4    Produces feature HANDS_UP
5  }
```

Listing 6. A DSL-supported supervised learning processor detecting the hands up gesture.

The number of input neurons is defined by the number of required features. Converters automatically map the data types of the required features to an array of floating-point numbers. The number of required features determines the number of neurons in the input layer. A default architecture with one hidden layer and a heuristic to determine the optimal number of hidden layer neurons is applied. The number of output layer neurons is implicitly defined by the number of produced features, again using converters to map an array of floating-point numbers to feature types. For many cases this specification already provides a reasonable number of suitable neural network architectures.

The necessary training and supportive tools are not discussed here, since they do not effect the actual description of the SupervisedLearning processor. In contrast to the latter examples, the neural network approach deals with variances implicitly, as they are an intrinsic property of the utilized training set or–later on–a part of the trained neural network parameters.

6 Conclusion

This article presented four software techniques which enhance the overall quality of multimodal processing software as motivated by [16,12] and own preceding work. The techniques target reoccurring multimodal processing tasks, specifically taking into account variance, e.g., due to individual characteristics and cultural context.

The first technique decomposes the overall task into smaller units dedicated to well-arranged and well-defined sub-problems. While this approach is similar to common functional decomposition, the implementation of these units as actors provides concurrent execution schemes and distribution facilities adequately matching the inherent concurrency of multimodal utterances.

The second technique uses functors as a means to weaken the negative impact of often hard-coded constraints dealing with variance. Using functor-objects, the core algorithms stay plain and universal and fundamental features of the underlying programming language like type and syntax check are exploited, which raises the overall code quality.

The third technique uses domain-specific languages to reduce the diversity of user-generated algorithms, idiosyncratic identifiers, and highly individual programming styles. In combination with programming languages which support syntactic variants for method calls, e.g., like Scala, DSLs can conveniently be be expressed and tailored for the application domain.

The fourth technique uses a semantic grounding of the identifiers used for the functors and the DSL tokens in a common ontology. Auto-generated from the ontology, these identifiers match classes, constants, and variables inside of the native programming language. This supports automatic syntax checks, including proper code highlighting in the development environments. In addition, it partly ensures semantic correctness due to the reproduction constancy between the ontology and the corresponding constructs of the programming language. Finally, the ontology binding is highly beneficial during the final semantic and pragmatic interpretation of the multimodal utterances.

All four techniques together provide scalable, customizable, and reusable solutions for reoccurring multimodal processing tasks. They have been implemented inside of miPRO, a realtime-capable processing architecture for multimodal interactions used in Virtual, Augmented and Mixed Reality applications.

References

1. Böhm, K., Broll, W., Sokolewicz, M.: Dynamic gesture recognition using neural networks; a fundament for advanced interaction construction. In: Fisher, S., Merrit, J., Bolan, M. (eds.) Stereoscopic Displays and Virtual Reality Systems, SPIE Conference Electronic Imaging Science & Technology, San Jose, USA, vol. 2177 (1994)
2. Bouchet, J., Nigay, L., Ganille, T.: ICARE software components for rapidly developing multimodal interfaces. In: ICMI 2004: Proceedings of the 6th International Conference on Multimodal Interfaces, pp. 251–258. ACM, New York (2004)
3. Fischbach, M., Wiebusch, D., Giebler-Schubert, A., Latoschik, M.E., Rehfeld, S., Tramberend, H.: SiXton's curse - Simulator X demonstration. In: 2011 IEEE Virtual Reality Conference, VR, pp. 255–256 (2011)
4. Fitzgerald, W., Firby, R.J., Hannemann, M.: Multimodal event parsing for intelligent user interfaces. In: Proceedings of the 2003 International Conference on Intelligent User Interfaces, pp. 53–60. ACM Press (2003)
5. Hewitt, C., Bishop, P., Steiger, R.: A universal modular ACTOR formalism for artificial intelligence. In: IJCAI 1973: Proceedings of the 3rd International Joint Conference on Artificial Intelligence, pp. 235–245. Morgan Kaufmann Publishers Inc., San Francisco (1973)
6. Hoste, L., Dumas, B., Signer, B.: Mudra: A unified multimodal interaction framework. In: Proceedings of the 13th International Conference on Multimodal Interfaces, ICMI 2011, pp. 97–104. ACM, New York (2011)
7. Johnston, M.: Unification-based multimodal parsing. In: Proceedings of the 17th International Conference on Computational Linguistics and the 36th Annual Meeting of the Association for Computational Linguistics, COLING-ACL, pp. 624–630 (1998)
8. Johnston, M., Bangalore, S.: Finite-state methods for multimodal parsing and integration. In: Finite-state Methods Workshop, ESSLLI Summer School on Logic Language and Information, Helsinki, Finland, pp. 74–80 (August 2001)

9. Johnston, M., Cohen, P.R., McGee, D., Oviatt, S.L., Pittman, J.A., Smith, I.: Unification-based multimodal integration. In: 35th Annual Meeting of the Association for Computational Linguistics, Madrid, pp. 281–288 (1997)
10. Kendon, A.: Gesticulation and speech: Two aspects of the process of utterance. In: Key, M.R. (ed.) The Relation between Verbal and Non-verbal Communication (1980)
11. Koons, D.B., Sparrel, C.J., Thorisson, K.R.: Intergrating simultaneous input from speech, gaze and hand gestures. In: Intelligent Multimedia Interfaces. American Association for Artificial Intelligence (1993)
12. Lalanne, D., Nigay, L., Palanque, P., Robinson, P., Vanderdonckt, J., Ladry, J.F.: Fusion engines for multimodal input: A survey. In: ICMI-MLMI 2009: Proceedings of the 2009 International Conference on Multimodal Interfaces, pp. 153–160. ACM, New York (2009)
13. Latoschik, M.E.: Designing Transition Networks for Multimodal VR-Interactions Using a Markup Language. In: Proceedings of the Fourth IEEE International Conference on Multimodal Interfaces, ICMI 2002, Pittsburgh, Pennsylvania, pp. 411–416. IEEE (2002)
14. Latoschik, M.E.: A user interface framework for multimodal VR interactions. In: Proceedings of the IEEE Seventh International Conference on Multimodal Interfaces, ICMI 2005, Trento, Italy, pp. 76–83 (October 2005)
15. Latoschik, M., Tramberend, H.: Simulator X: A scalable and concurrent architecture for intelligent realtime interactive systems. In: 2011 IEEE Virtual Reality Conference (VR), pp. 171–174 (March 2011)
16. Nigay, L., Bouchet, J., Juras, D., Mansoux, B., Ortega, M., Serrano, M., Lawson, J.-Y.L.: Software engineering for multimodal interactive systems. In: Tzovaras, D. (ed.) Multimodal User Interfaces. Signals and Commmunication Technologies, pp. 201–218. Springer (2008)
17. Väänänen, K., Böhm, K.: Gesture-driven interaction as a human factor in virtual environments – an approach with neural networks. In: Gigante, M.A., Jones, H. (eds.) Virtual Reality Systems. Academic Press (1993)
18. Wagner, J., Lingenfelser, F., Baur, T., Damian, I., Kistler, F., André, E.: The social signal interpretation (SSI) framework: Multimodal signal processing and recognition in real-time. In: Proceedings of the 21st ACM International Conference on Multimedia, MM 2013, pp. 831–834. ACM, New York (2013)
19. Wiebusch, D., Latoschik, M.E.: Enhanced decoupling of components in intelligent realtime interactive systems using ontologies. In: Proceedings of the IEEE Virtual Reality 2012 Workshop on Software Engineering and Architectures for Realtime Interactive Systems, SEARIS (2012)

HCI-Patterns for Developing Mobile Apps and Digital Video-Assist-Technology for the Film Set

Christian Märtin[1], Anthony Stein[2,3], Bernhard Prell[2], and Andreas Kesper[2]

[1] Augsburg University of Applied Sciences, Faculty of Computer Science,
An der Hochschule 1, 86161 Augsburg, Germany
Christian.Maertin@hs-augsburg.de
[2] Vantage Film GmbH, Digital Division,
Fuggerstraße 7, 86150 Augsburg, Germany
{AnthonyStein,BernhardPrell,AndreasKesper}@vantagefilm.com
[3] University of Augsburg
Department of Computer Science
86135 Augsburg, Germany

Abstract. Digital cinema technology is now widely accepted by directors, directors of photography, producers, film crews, and during the post-production process. On the film set high-resolution digital motion picture cameras have entered the field. In order to exploit the full creative and organizational potential of the advanced digital production technology and to support the whole shooting process, digital video-assist systems are connected to the cameras, monitors, and auxiliary components on the set to form a computer-supported film set (CSFS). The CSFS around Vantage Film's PSU® family of advanced video-assist systems offers intelligent support for all the roles and tasks on the film set. This paper focuses on the design of the PSU® product generations. Contextual design, agility, and patterns, both for designing control and user interface functionality, have been used extensively in the development process. This is demonstrated for the iPad-based mobile PSU® Satellite and some GUI patterns that were used for different features of the touch-screen based user interface.

Keywords: Digital video-assist, design patterns, HCI-patterns, digital motion picture cameras, iPad, iOS, touch-screen user interface, computer-supported film set.

1 Introduction

For more than a decade digital video-assist systems have been used to support and optimize the production process of feature films and commercials directly on the film set. Such highly interactive systems are responsible for take recording and replay, rendering and pre-screen simulation of special effects, rehearsal purposes, and for improving the user experience of the entire film crew [9], [3].

M. Kurosu (Ed.): Human-Computer Interaction, Part I, HCII 2014, LNCS 8510, pp. 320–330, 2014.
© Springer International Publishing Switzerland 2014

A system that can integrate most of the digital hardware, software functionality, and user-assist technology for all the roles on the set within a common distributed architecture, is called a computer-supported film set (CSFS). When we developed our first CSFS, the PSU®-1 video assist system, using a contextual design process [4], [1], we came up with some solutions for the resulting high-end video-assist-system, like touchscreen-based user interface or content-based retrieval of film takes that even today still define the state-of-the-art in video-assist technology.

Our imagination and the feedback from early contextual inquiry showed us the direction for our future work and provided us with ideas, which roles were needed in the shooting process and which film and IT components should be integrated into a CSFS. At that time we already envisioned and prototyped the *Director's Pad*, a tablet based video-assist client. Only today, however, embedded and wireless technology provides the necessary performance, energy efficiency, reliability and software flexibility for building high-performance mobile video-assist clients for professional use in all imaginable contexts.

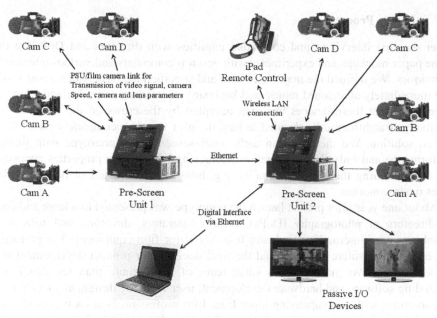

Fig. 1. Computer-supported film set based on the PSU®-3X HD digital video-assist system

The current PSU®3-X HD based CSFS, as shown in figure 1, combines client-supported video recording features with simultaneous multiple camera support, intelligent software functionality for on-the-set effects simulation and rendering (slow-motion, time-lapse, ramping, filtering, mix-and-overlay of takes, blue-, green-screen effects, editing, 3D-support, etc.), shooting day organization, rehearsal mode, and hard- and software-support for active camera control and communication [2].

In the following it will be shown that our development process for advanced video-assist software, could profit enormously from the use of different pattern categories.

We will outline, how contextual design, object-oriented modeling and agile development practices helped us to attain the high quality standards, necessary for a whole class of successful real world products.

2   Mixing Contextual Design and Agile Development

When we started to develop software and digital technology for supporting the movie production process in 1999, we first had to get acquainted with the environmental, contextual and functional requirements of the people working on the film set, their roles, their tasks, their goals, their wishes, and their communication behavior. We formed a joint team of computer scientists and film professionals and started the project that should lead to a widely accepted and reliable CSFS solution. Already in the early planning phase, we de decided to set up a contextual design process [1] – at the time a relatively novel development method for user-centered systems.

2.1   Design Process

After the first interviews and contextual inquiries with directors and DoPs we did some paper mockups and experiments with desktop computers and various interaction techniques. We defined the major use-cases and specified the basic video-assist-tasks. We immediately abandoned mouse and keyboard interaction, as we learned from our interviews, that these devices were not accepted by the crews on the film set. We relatively straightforwardly decided to base the user interface completely on a touch-screen solution. We then built an early touch-screen based prototype with limited performance and only the visualization features and interactive properties necessary for demonstrating the key functionality, e.g. how to record takes, or how to replay takes in slow motion.

About one year after project launch the prototype was presented to a large audience of directors of photography (DoPs), camera operators, directors, and film crew members, at an international industry trade-show for film equipment. The prototype got enormous positive feedback and the final decision for product development was made. Within two more years a small team of never more than ten developers (including software and hardware development, user-interface design, and mechanical construction) with accompanying input from film professionals at each critical stage created a pre-product prototype of the final system that was tested under real-world production conditions by directors and DoPs around the world [4].

Most usability problems resulting from a lack of communication between software engineers and the final users, i.e. our film experts, could be avoided by having the film people evaluate each new interactive feature on the pre-product prototype immediately after the feature was available. This method worked for the first product version of the system, the PSU®-1, and was used in all of the following video-assist products since then. Software features that will be integrated in future product versions today are first integrated into software updates for the current product version and tested and evaluated on real sets. The other way round, ideas for innovative features often come from the people on the set. As we listen to them, our agile process allows us to implement new features rapidly and introduce them in one of the next software updates that are distributed by a remote maintenance process.

It soon became clear that with a rapidly growing interactive functionality a layered design approach was necessary for the user interface in order to maintain the overall look-and-feel of the system. Although the visual design undergoes evolutionary changes from product generation to product generation, each new product will still present its basic take recording and replay functionality on the main screen after power-up. More complex features are hidden below the surface. The more specific or sophisticated the functionality becomes, the more effort is needed by the operator to arrive at the desired level of functional detail. However, several design and HCI patterns guide our layered structuring of the software and the design of the end-user navigation. Examples of such patterns are given in sections 3 and 4.

2.2   Technology Context

In the 15 years since we started to develop systems and components for the computer-supported film set the greatest technology revolution was the migration of the film industry from celluloid film to digital film recording. Today, most advanced video-assist systems are used in combination with highly sophisticated digital motion picture cameras, like the ARRI Alexa [12], the RED Epic [13], or the Sony F65 [14] to name only a few. In contrast to earlier professional electronic cameras, these digital film cameras already are equipped with integrated support for HD video-out signals that can be sent to the video-assist system over the HD-SDI interface. Earlier cameras only provided analog SD video-signals for video-assist purposes. The high-definition 2K or 4K high contrast and high luminosity raw signals of today's most advanced film cameras are used in post-production for preparing the final movie and are not directly used on the set. They have to be stored in separate high-capacity film storage servers.

However, the video signals that arrive over the HD-SDI interface are of remarkably high quality, i.e. available as HD video signals. They can directly be exploited by the digital video-assist technology on the set. The current product generation, the PSU®3-X HD, is able to record up to four takes simultaneously and at the same time replay up to two recorded takes (on different external HD screens). The high computing performance that is needed by the CSFS is made possible by an embedded Intel Core-i7 quad core processor, Nvidia GPUs, several custom-designed FPGA-boards for frame grabbing and visualizing takes, the Linux OS and by highly optimized software using C++, Qt, and OpenGL. The power envelope of the system is nevertheless relatively low (100W). Therefore, the system can be battery-powered for several hours.

To further improve the flexibility on the film set and allow directors, DoPs and crew members the direct interaction with the PSU® systems while moving around at the location, a mobile extension to the CSFS, the iPad-operated PSU® Satellite was recently announced. Its software design is discussed in the following chapter.

3   The Usage of Design Patterns within the iOS Domain

The application discussed in this chapter was developed using a model-based approach, where design patterns serve as the models. On the basis of the so-called *PSU® Take Manager,* which is one of two currently developed iOS applications with the aim to increase the mobility of the CSFS, some well-known design patterns are going to be described for the context of iOS programming. On the one hand the *model view controller (MVC) pattern* – also sometimes denoted as an architecture pattern – gets illustrated. On the other hand some other useful design patterns become the subject matter. To reach the goal of increased mobility on the CSFS, the iOS Device (here the PSU® Satellite, based on the iPad) interacts with the Digital Video-Assist System PSU®-3X HD. To provide an understanding of how this challenge is faced, a short overview of the rudimentary feature set is given [7], [8].

As mentioned above, two independent applications are under development. The *PSU® Take Manager* (fig. 2, left) helps directors to replay already shot takes stored on the PSU® main device. Such takes can also be stored and organized in the iPad's internal storage. To find the right scene to replay, a filter mechanism for a more comfortable browsing through all available takes was integrated. During replay takes can also be viewed frame-by-frame.

Another application, called *PSU Streaming* (fig. 1, right), offers the ability to look at up to four independent live-streams from cameras connected to the PSU® or disc playback. Furthermore some bi-directional conversation functionality was implemented, so that the director can view the scenery from different viewpoints and give instructions to the (human) video-assist operator "over-the-air".

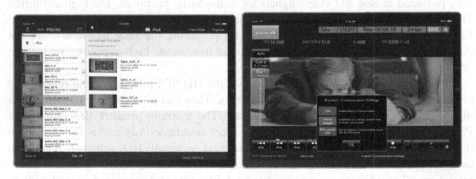

Fig. 2. PSU Take Manager screenshot (left) and PSU Streaming screenshot (right)

For the purpose of iOS-App programming a framework provided by Apple called *Cocoa Touch* comes into operation. This framework makes great use of software design patterns from object-oriented design (OOD) and was an ideal platform for implementing CSFS-mobility. Some of the patterns are described in the following. Figure 3 illustrates the basic concept of the MVC pattern within the iOS domain.

The MVC pattern resembles a three-tier architecture with a database-, a business logic-, as well as a presentation-layer. The model corresponds to the database layer whereas it is not restricted to database connections at all. It could provide data from the web via HTTP or, e.g., from a persistent file. In the case of the *PSU® Take Manager* the model is represented by a WebDAV client, which also handles the connection to the PSU®-3X HD. Over an established WebDAV connection meta-information about the takes stored on PSU can be requested. Files can be accessed via a GET-request. The returned meta-information is stored in the iPad's memory and prepared for further usage within the application.

The middle layer – the controller object – handles the delivery of requested data to the view layer on top. It collects the requested data from the model (pulling), transforms it into an adequate representation and returns the well-formatted data via the return parameter of the callback method invoked by the view.

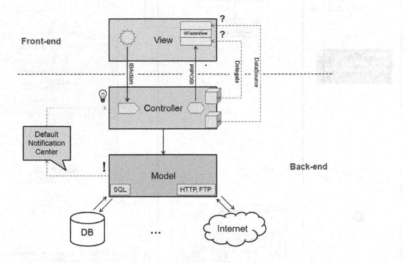

Fig. 3. An MVC illustration for the Cocoa Touch Framework [8]

Figure 4 shows a concrete model-based implementation of the MVC pattern on top of the task of an initial WebDAV request when the PSU® Take Manager App gets launched. The semantics of the red dyed actions is that these actions are invoked or provided by the iOS Framework. The UML signal element was used to illustrate notifications (described below) as well as events on which callback methods will react.

Using callback methods, invoked when needed by the system, is one approach for updating data presented to the user. Another method is pushing new information to the view directly. Therefore Apple provides a macro called *IBOutlet* that allows the graphical interface builder to bind an interaction object, e.g. a label, to a corresponding instance in the source code.

Let's consider the case of a progress view. While downloading a take, the PSU® delivers small data packages that are collected and stored by the model. The view is presenting a so-called *UIProgressView* to let the user know about the status of the download progress. Each time a new data package arrives, the progress has to be

326   C. Märtin et al.

calculated again and passed to the controller that manipulates the view in a direct manner by accessing the bound IBOutlet member.

Pushing the information from the model to the controller is possible through a mechanism called *notification posting*. The sender (here the model) posts an *NSNotification* object with appropriate information to a central message receiving station object (*NSNotificationCenter*). This central instance routes the notification to all objects that have been registered as observers for such a kind of notification. This is an adapted implementation of the well-known *Observer Pattern* [10], [11].

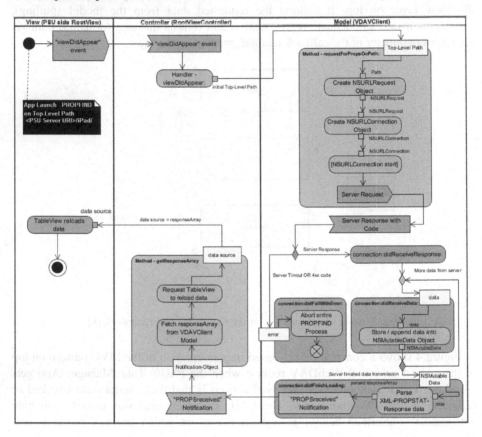

Fig. 4. Activity Diagram – MVC Implementation of WebDAV Request Mechanism [8]

The Cocoa Touch framework makes use of the *Delegation Pattern*, too. The controller responds on requests sent by the view or reacts on notifications about changing data from the model. The implementation of the already mentioned callback methods invoked by the view is mandatory, because these methods are defined in a *protocol*. A protocol equals the concepts of interfaces or pure virtual methods and is a language-level feature of Objective-C. Protocols make it possible to let two objects with different public interfaces communicate with each other. Thus, protocols can be interpreted as an instance of the *Adapter Pattern* [10], [11]. A delegation, e.g., happens when a UI control element is asked how to appear. A delegate object could be set up conforming to a special purpose delegate protocol. An example is the *UITableView* object. A table view needs to know how many rows and sections it will have, how the cells should appear (height, color, etc.), whether there should be a section header or footer describing the individual sections or not, and so on.

The Cocoa (Touch) framework also considers a core problem of graphical user interfaces. A developer of a GUI puts so called interaction control elements on the screen so that a user can interact with the software in the background. The programmer in fact doesn't know at which time or how often a user decides to use the element just as a developer of a GUI library can't know how, e.g., the usage of a button is intended by the developer of a GUI. The flexibility to face this issue is one of the purposes the *Command Pattern* was introduced. When using this pattern a method invocation gets encapsulated by an object. This object usually holds the receiver (also denoted as *target*) of the message, as well as the identifier (*selector*) of the method which should be invoked. The GUI developer defines, which message to which receiver shall be executed and every time a user interacts with a control element, an invocation object is generated dynamically. That, in turn, makes it possible to trigger a method invocation at runtime. Apple conforms to this pattern with the *Target-Action-Mechanism* as well as through *NSInvocation* objects [11].

Another design pattern introduced by Erich Gamma et al. (aka The Gang of Four, see also [10]) is the *Composite Pattern*. This approach allows the programmer to use and implement whole/part-hierarchies of objects. That means that an abstract composite class specifies behavior of individual objects and compositions (container) of such individual objects at the same time. Thus the individuals and compositions of individuals could be used uniformly. With this technique it is possible to build tree-structured hierarchies of objects, whereby the developer doesn't have to handle of which type an instance of a tree-branch (composition) or tree-leave (individual) is.

A more specific example is the view-hierarchy of a graphical user interface. The *UIView* class is a composite class, because it is the base class of most interaction elements like sliders, buttons, etc. If a superview containing some subviews, which are in turn superviews of further subviews (tree-structure), is asked to redraw itself, the redraw message is propagated to all subviews until the leaves are reached. Thus the internal treatment of branches (container) and leaves (individual subviews) is the same [11].

To keep the limited scope of this paper, the focus was set on such design patterns that are related to the User Interface most closely and thus meet the topic of human computer interaction. Of course, some more instances or adaptions of well-known design patterns exist within the Cocoa (Touch) framework. For more details on the mentioned patterns and the usage of them within the iOS-Framework we refer to [10] as well as [11].

4   User Interface Patterns for the Digital Video-Assist

Another area for the successful application of patterns in the CSFS development process is the touch-screen user interface of the PSU® main device. During the evolutionary development process of the PSU® family of video-assist-systems the user interface had often to be adapted to new functionality and new interaction styles. Figure 5 shows an example of the slider user interface pattern.

The slider pattern is always used when a parameter has to be intuitively set, without the necessity for entering an exact value. Implemented as a take slider, it is used to navigate to a specific position within a take. With the slow-buttons, each frame can be directly located. Another implementation would be the use of the slider pattern for the intuitive setting of the overlay intensity, when two image-layers are superimposed as, e.g., for 3D cinema simulation). Finally, the slider pattern can be used for the intuitive setting of brightness, contrast and gamma parameters.

Fig. 5. Implementation of the slider pattern as a take-navigation-slider

Another HCI pattern example that is reused for different functions ist the +/- *display element*. It serves to enter a new value that is not too far away from the current value. If pressing the buttons longer, the rate of the value changes is accelerated. The graphical representation of the pattern can also be seen in figure 5, where it can be used to set the frame rate (original camera speed, or some other value for simulating slow motion or time lapse).

The same pattern is used for setting the length of short takes, that are ignored by the system and will be deleted automatically, or for the fine-tuning of the cooling fan in order to avoid too much noise when shooting takes, or the setting of the microphone volume. If the user presses on the display, a numeric keypad automatically appears for entering an exact value.

Many other user interface patterns were applied for getting a consistent look-and-feel and for reducing the user-interface complexity for the end user [6].

5   Conclusion

Design patterns and HCI patterns can contribute heavily to the successful construction of complex interactive systems. This was shown for the development of an iPad-based mobile video-assist client. The applied structured patterns available in Apple's Cocoa Touch library served as design models and we assume they facilitated the development of several communication tasks between the PSU® main system and the client. At the same time, the use of patterns could accelerate the development process and ensure good coding quality. It was also demonstrated by examples that HCI patterns can be used for keeping navigation and interaction consistent from product generation to product generation and lead to high acceptance by end-users. Our experience with the systems has shown that users in productive environments appreciate, if they quickly recognize functions and can use new functionality intuitively, because interactive behavior is controlled by usage patterns, they already know. Patterns therefore also serve as a means for reducing complexity in rich interactive environments.

References

1. Beyer, H., Holtzblatt, K.: Contextual Design. Interactions, 32–42 (January + February, 1999)
2. Fauer, J.: Vantage PSU-3X HD Digital Video Assist. Film and Digital Times (55-56), 76–77 (2013)
3. QTake (2013), http://qtakehd.com (retrieved on September 13, 2013.)
4. Märtin, C., Prell, B.: Contextual Design of a Computer-Supported Film Set: A Case Study. In: Jorge, J.A., Jardim Nunes, N., Falcão e Cunha, J. (eds.) DSV-IS 2003. LNCS, vol. 2844, pp. 392–405. Springer, Heidelberg (2003)
5. Märtin, C., Prell, B., Kesper, A.: A New Generation Digital Video Assist System with Intelligent Multi-Camera Control and Support for Creative Work on the Film Set. In: Tavangarian, D., Kirste, T., Timmermann, D., Lucke, U., Versick, D. (eds.) IMC 2009. CCIS, vol. 53, pp. 331–332. Springer, Heidelberg (2009)
6. Märtin, C., Prell, B., Schwarz, A.: Managing User Interface Complexity and Usability in Computer-Supported Film Sets. In: Proc. of HCI International, Las Vegas, Nevada, USA, July 22-27, vol. 3. Lawrence Erlbaum Associates (2005) Human-Computer Interfaces: Concepts, New Ideas, Better Usability, and Applications Series
7. Märtin, C., Stein, A., Prell, B., Kesper, A.: Mobile App-Support for Advanced Digital Video-Assist Systems in Computer-Supported Film Sets. In: Proc. 6. Forum Medientechnik, Fachhochschule, St. Pölten, Austria (2013)

8. Stein, A.: Evolutionäre Entwicklung einer proprietären iPad-Applikation für die mobilitätssteigernde Interaktion mit dem digitalen Video-Assist-System PSU®-3, Bachelor Thesis, Augsburg University of Applied Sciences (2012)
9. Vantage Film GmbH (2013), http://www.vantagefilm.com (last access February 4, 2014)
10. Gamma, E., et al.: Design Patterns. Elements of Reusable Object-Oriented Software. Addison-Wesley (1995)
11. Apple Inc.: Cocoa Fundamentals Guide, pp. 165–208 (September 2013)
12. http://www.arri.com/camera/digital_cameras/ (last access: February 4, 2014)
13. http://www.red.com/products/epic (last access: February 4, 2014)
14. http://pro.sony.com (last access: February 4, 2014)

IntNovate a Toolkit to Ease the Implementation of Every Interaction Paradigm on Every Device

Bruno Merlin

Universidade Federal do Pará, FACE, Cametá, Brazil
brunomerlin@ufpa.br

Abstract. With the evolution and diversification of devices and platforms, we observed an evolution of the interaction paradigm usage, but also the emergence of several specific SDKs and toolkits. We present a toolkit, IntNovate, aiming at facilitating every interaction techniques and every interface paradigms in a large set of devices. The toolkit enables to create traditional widget applications, but also incorporates gaming techniques to turn easy animation integration, see-through interactions and direct manipulations. It is compatible with J2SE, J2EE, J2ME and android environments. A first evaluation compared an HMI development using both J2SE and IntNovate none form based application development and illustrated the IntNovate advantages in this context.

Keywords: Toolkit, graphic, direct interaction, multiple devices, multiple platforms.

1 Introduction

During the last decade, the graphic design became a major factor to improve software usability so as to increase software commercial impact. Consequently, the HMI design of commercial software turned to a multidisciplinary task involving HMI developers, ergonomists and graphic designers. In the same time, the number and kind of new devices grew significantly thanks to the evolution of mobile devices and to the integration of computation skills into the traditional appliances (household devices, car dashboard, electronic cash, etc.). At last, the device diversification increased the user's number and amplified their heterogeneity.

The diversity of devices and the evolution of operating systems, the intervention of new actors into the design process, the requirement to turn the software graphically attractive, and the needs to lead with heterogeneous users, changed the way to design graphic interfaces. We observed two mains evolution axes: a convergence between mobile and desktop interaction paradigms and operating systems [14, 15]; and the use of gaming interaction techniques into standard applications. It increased the use of direct interaction [13, 4], animations, gestural interaction [5], marking menu [8], see-through interfaces [3], etc. Graphic interfaces tend to leave their standard rectangular layout and interactive components are frequently integrated into a scene.

M. Kurosu (Ed.): Human-Computer Interaction, Part I, HCII 2014, LNCS 8510, pp. 331–339, 2014.

In spite of these convergences, the HCI development toolkits remain specific for desktop, web or mobile environment, and do not ease the incorporation of gaming techniques into standard applications.

In this article, we present a HCI toolkit, IntNovate (www.intnovate.org), responding to these problems. The Toolkit is developed in Java and offered an implementation for J2SE, J2EE, J2ME and Android enabling to attend the majority of web, desktop and mobile platforms. The toolkit proposes several predefined behaviors, animation motor and skinable widgets that enable to create a compact and high expressive code such as actionscript, whereas beneficing of the java inter-operability. IntNovate also aims at easing the cooperation between developers and graphic designers by loading the graphic scene from vector graphic files generated by drawing and design tools.

In the next chapters, we detail the characteristics of the toolkit, the design process using IntNovate and present a first evaluation of the toolkit aiming at demonstrating its usability.

2   The Toolkit

2.1   Graphical Properties

Such as the majority of drawing toolkits, IntNovate is based on a 2D canvas managing RGB colors, opacity, textures and clipping. The graphical objects composing the application are organized into a single tree. The leafs represented the rendered primitive graphical objects (such as path with one or several contours, ellipses, texts, etc.). The branch nodes manage default properties values for the sub-tree nodes (such as fill and stroke brush, etc.). A local transformation matrix, an opacity coefficient, and a clip may be applied to every node. The tree is rendered by a depth-first traversal from the interface root node. Local node transformation, clip and color opacity are composed with the transformation, clip and opacity of parent nodes.

In fact, displaying a graphical component of the interface consists implicitly in grafting a sub-tree to a main tree branch. Thus, branches are dynamically grafted, cut or just temporarily inactivated to represent the different graphical states of the interface.

Like with scalar graphic drawing tools, the different layers of the interface depend on the graphical position into the tree toward the depth-first traversal order (cf. Fig. 1). The first graphical objects, in depth-first traversal order are painted first, designing the "background" of the application. The last ones are painted in front of every other. This order can be altered.

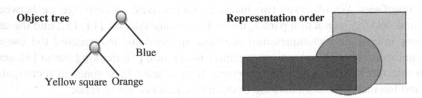

Fig. 1. Layers organization

Simple or complex clips are specified by additional trees. Thus, clips may contain a simple primitive shape so as to a shape composition base (cf. fig. 2). In the same way, texture pattern can be generated from a tree representing the texture pattern (they also can be loaded from an image file).

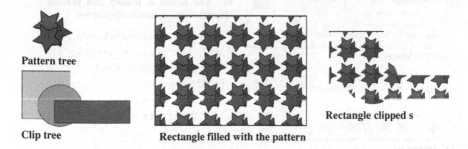

Pattern tree

Clip tree

Rectangle filled with the pattern

Rectangle clipped s

Fig. 2. Using graphic sub-tree as pattern or clip

2.2   Basic Interactions

Tree nodes can handle single and multiple pointer interactions. When e pointer interaction occurred, the toolkit checks if the interaction was performed into the shapes represented by the sub-tree of the handling node (the process consider the specific – and sometime complex – geometry of the shape). Naturally, the evaluation of handled nodes is performed in the inverse depth-first traversal order, corresponding to the order of graphical objects visualized by the user. The events intercepted by a node are propagated to the node ancestors.

Tree node can also handle key events. As standard toolkits, IntNovate manages a focused node, implicitly auto-determined by the last performed click and eventually altered by an explicit request.

At last, tree nodes can handle java and node drag and drop events.

2.3   Graphic Integration

The global structure of IntNovate application, such as the other graphical characteristics (like strokes properties or gradients), is very closed to the SVG and other scalar graphic format definitions.

Because graphic is easier elaborated and altered using drawing tools (graphic designer tools) than described by geometric path or painting directives, IntNovate enables to load graphical sub-trees from scalar graphic files. SVG tree or sub-trees (identified by a node path or node name) are parsed and mapped into IntNovate nodes.

The use of external scalar graphic files enables to ease the interaction between graphic designers and developers. Alterations done by graphic designers are automatically incorporated into the application. Moreover, at the differences with simple images, the loaded graphic objects may be dynamically altered (for instance: colors, transformation and position, or text values, cf. Fig.3).

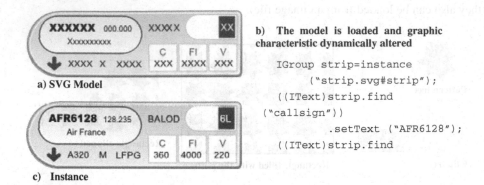

a) SVG Model

b) The model is loaded and graphic characteristic dynamically altered

```
IGroup strip=instance
    ("strip.svg#strip");
((IText)strip.find
("callsign"))
        .setText ("AFR6128");
((IText)strip.find
```

c) Instance

Fig. 3. Dynamic alteration of "images"

In order to increase the loading performances, for every loaded SVG tree or sub-tree IntNovate generates a java object. The object constructor instances the sub-tree nodes. The java class is dynamically compiled and loaded. If the object has ever been created and the graphical files is unchanged, IntNovate reuse the compiled object.

The process enables to speed-up the graphical component loading by skipping the parsing step when the graphical file is unchanged (what is the normal software exploitation situation). But, it also enables to protect the graphic designer work. Thus, at the end the development, the graphic source files may be removed from the project. The graphic design is delivered as java compiled classes.

2.4   Cache

Some branches of the tree may contain several and complex graphical objects. The sub-tree rendering time may be long, prejudicing the number of frames rendered per second. To improve the rendering of these sub-trees, IntNovate enables to create image cache for them. When the application tree is redrawn, if a node of a cached sub-tree has been changes, the cache image is rebuilt; else, the cached image is only rendered.

The cached nodes can be specified by the developers. But, IntNovate can also auto-determines the candidate branches. To evaluate the candidate branches, the toolkit measure the sub-trees drawing time, but also use heuristic such as interaction handled by the nodes, animated nodes, user class of components and sub-trees loaded from scalar graphic files. The aim of this evaluation is to detect the sub-trees that are complex to draw, but also the group of graphical object that make part of the same semantic group of object and which shape and mutual position remain unchanged the most part of the time (for instance background, items of a list, animated object, etc. cf. Fig. 4).

Example: application for air traffic control

a) The background contains several graphical objects that may be configured by the user in function of the context. The most part of the time they remain unchanged. The background may be cached.

b) The flight comets seam to be integrated to the background (at the front), whereas their position change all the time. So they won't be

a) no frequent changes between objects (lines, levels, etc.) at the background ➔ group

c) Frequent changes in the right branch ➔ group not cached

b) Flight comets: frequent changes between object position ➔ group not

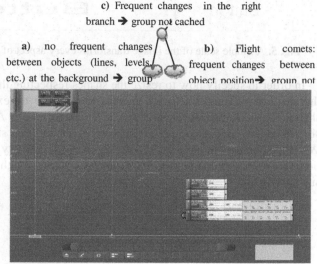

Fig. 4. Principal of cache images

2.5   Widgets

Even if the toolkit is not specifically designed to create form based applications, it proposes a set of skinable widgets containing the principal widgets such as simple, multiline and masked edits, toggle and buttons, radio-buttons, checkboxes, combo-boxes, spinner, list, tables, trees, scrollbar, scroll-panes and split-panes. The widgets have a default skin, whereas the skin can also be specified in SVG.

2.6   Control of Object Transformation: Resizing Specified by Example

Designing widgets with a graphical object tree instead of painting directives introduces a problem in widget resizing. Widgets are normally designed to be represented at different sizes. But, for instance, increasing the size of 25% for a button does not necessarily mean that we are going to increase the size of the border of 25%, neither the size of the font.

In IntNovate, the shapes and their properties are specified with an initial size. A simple way to transform the shapes to make them fit with the other sizes would be to scale them. However, a simple scaling transforms whole graphic without discriminating the semantic aspects of each shape property. Then, it resizes proportionally every graphical property of every shape (the shape but also the borders, text fonts, relative position between shapes, etc.). Consequently, using a simple scale to increase a button size of 25% would also increase of 25% the border, the font size, the text padding, etc (cf. fig. 5).

Fig. 5. A simple scale of the image transforms every aspect of the image proportionally

In order to specify how to resize the shapes respecting the semantic information of the shape properties, IntNovate enables to describe by example how to resize the shapes. The technique is inspired by Flash animations and Artistic Resizing []. It consists in specifying the component appearance at different sizes (key representations). When the component is resized, the value of every property is calculated by interpolation between the property value of key representations with an inferior and a superior size (cf. fig. 6).

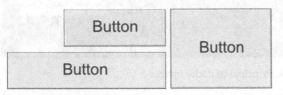

The key representations illustrate how every characteristic of the objects are transformed toward width and height changes

Every characteristics of an instance of the object are calculated by interpolation between the key representation

Fig. 6. Transformation by example

2.7   Animation

The toolkit enables to control animations performed on sub-trees. It proposed predefined animations such as scale, translate, opacity animations, and proposes an animation motor enabling the user to specify his proper animations. Pacers (such as fade-in, fade-out, oscillations, etc.) enable to control the animation rhythmic.

Animations may be sequenced and combined through animation scenario models describing: when the different animations should start and end (relatively to the others animations of the scenario). The transformations performed during scale animations may also be specified by example (cf. 2.6).

2.8   Predefined Behaviors

Out of the animation, several predefined behaviors may be applied to sub-trees. Some behaviors, such, as hover-feedbacks, selection feedbacks, or blinking, enable to control active sub-trees toward interactions.

Motion and inertia enable to move an object into a spaced with or without magnetic anchor and space constraints.

Other behaviors enable to control gesture inputs. The toolkit mainly provides a recognition gesture system based on a neuronal network and electronic ink turning objects scriptable.

At last, some behaviors (such as lasso selection, anti-covering) enable to manage interaction between object groups.

2.9 Synthesis

The toolkit is inspired by the Zinc [12] canvas, IntuiKit [1, 2] graphic cooperation design process between designers and programmers, MTools [10] and Flash [17] behaviors, and power-point [16] and Flash animation design. It regroups those different characteristics into a Java environment. J2SE/J2EE, J2ME and Android wrappers enable to reach the different platforms and devices (web, desktop, mobile platforms and windows, linux and Mac OS operational systems).

3   Evaluation

3.1 Design

To evaluate the toolkit usability, 4 J2SE developers compared the development of the same simple application using both IntNovate and only the J2SE JDK.

The subjects were preliminary trained during 4 hours to use IntNovate. The training consists in reproducing short examples illustrating the main skills of the toolkit: graphic integration, layers organizations, animations, and predefined behaviors integration.

The application to develop consisted in (i) dispatching randomly instances of 3 kinds of shapes into the canvas; (ii) provide an interaction to select the same shapes; (iii) create an animation to group the selected shapes; (iv) provide an interaction to input textual information to the group; (v) provide an interaction to organize the groups into a grid. A demonstration of the required application where presented to the subjects.

Graphic design was not the purpose of the evaluation so graphics were provided both as SVG files and as shape paths and text span descriptions. Thus, the resources were prepared to be directly integrated into IntNovate or J2SE. Algorithms required to implement the different behaviors was also provided.

The evaluation was performed during one day. The morning, 2 developers started the development using only the J2SE JDK and the 2 others started using IntNovate. Then, the afternoon, they switched technology.

3.2 Results

The subjects concluded the application development in less than 2 hours and a half the morning and less than 2 hours the afternoon using the IntNovate, and about 4 hours and a half the morning and 3 hour and a half the afternoon using only J2SE paradigms. So, whatever the order of the technology used, the developers reduced significantly the development time using IntNovate.

The written code was about 2 times shorter using the toolkit due to externalization of graphics and to the use of pre-defined behaviors. The 2D scene resulting of the code developed with IntNovate was drawn 15% faster (in frame/s).

The code developed using IntNovate was compatible with a large set of mobile devices, the code develop with J2SE was not because it was depending on J2SE Graphics2D functions different with J2ME Graphic ones and Android ones.

The user developers expressed that the toolkit was easy to use and powerful.

4   Conclusion

We proposed a toolkit, IntNovate, enabling to create rich graphic and interactive applications. The toolkit developed in Java ensure the compatibility with a large set of devices and platforms (mobile, web and desktop). The graphic integration eases the cooperation between graphic designer and developers. The toolkit also aggregates several predefined algorithm for HMI and behaviors turning the development rapid and simple.

A first evaluation illustrates the toolkit efficiency. It is the same for its usage in research projects.

References

1. Chatty, S., Sire, S., Vinot, J.L., Lecoanet, P., Lemort, A., Mertz, C.: Revisiting visual interface programming: creating GUI tools for designers and programmers. In: Proceedings of the 17th Annual ACM Symposium on User Interface Software and Technology, UIST 2004, Santa Fe, NM, USA, October 24-27 (2004)
2. Chatty, S., Sire, S., Lemort, A.: Vers des outils pour les équipes de conception d'interfaces post-WIMP. In: Proceedings of IHM 2004, Namur, Belgium, pp. 45–52. ACM Press (2004)
3. Bier, E.A., Stone, M.C., Pier, K., Buxton, W., Derose, T.D.: Toolglass and magic lenses: the see through interface. In: Proc. ACM SIGGRAPH 1993, pp. 73–80. ACM Press (1993)
4. Raisamo, R., Räihä, K.: A new direct manipulation technique for aligning objects in drawing programs. In: Proc. ACM Symposium on User interface Software and Technology, UIST 1996, pp. 157–164. ACM Press (1996)
5. Rubine, D.: Specifying gestures by example. In: Proc. ACM Conference on Computer Graphics and Interactive Techniques, SIGGRAPH 1991, pp. 329–337. ACM Press (1991)
6. Dragicevic, P.: Combining Crossing-Based and Paper-Based Interaction Paradigms for Dragging and Dropping Between Overlapping Windows. In: Proceedings of the 17th Annual ACM Symposium on User Interface Software and Technology (UIST 2004), pp. 193–196. ACM Press (2004)
7. Dragicevic, P., Chatty, S., Thevenin, D., Vinot, J.L.: Artistic resizing: a technique for rich scale-sensitive vector graphics. In: Proceedings of the 18th Annual ACM Symposium on User Interface Software and Technology, Seattle, WA, USA (2005)
8. Kurtenbach, G., Buxton, W.: Issues in combining marking and direct manipulation techniques. In: Proceedings of the 4th Annual ACM Symposium on User Interface Software and Technology, UIST 1991, Hilton Head, South Carolina, United States, November 11-13, pp. 137–144. ACM, New York (1991)

9. Merlin, B., Hurter, C., Benhacène, R.: A solution to interface evolution issues: the multi-layer interface. In: Proceeding of CHI 2008, Florence, Italie (2008)
10. Merlin, B., Hurter, C., Raynal, M.: Bridging software evolution's gap: The multilayer concept. In: Kurosu, M. (ed.) HCD 2009. LNCS, vol. 5619, pp. 266–275. Springer, Heidelberg (2009)
11. Merlin, B.: Conception et évaluation des claviers logiciels, Méthodologie et instrumentalisation, Éditions Universitaires Européennes, Berlin (2012)
12. Mertz, C., Chatty, S., Vinot, J.L.: The influence of design techniques on user interfaces: the DigiStrips experiment for air traffic control. In: HCI Aero (September 2000)
13. Shneiderman, B.: The future of interactive systems and the emergence of direct manipulation. In: Proceedings of the NYU Symposium on User Interfaces on Human Factors and Interactive Computer Systems, Norwood, NJ, USA, pp. 1–28. Ablex Publishing Corp. (1984)
14. http://www.itproportal.com/2012/07/10/one-size-fits-all-convergence-desktop-and-mobile-operating-systems/
15. http://www.pcworld.com/article/2047067/how-windows-os-x-and-ubuntu-are-slowly-turning-your-pc-into-a-smartphone.html
16. http://office.microsoft.com/pt-br/powerpoint/
17. http://www.adobe.com/devnet/actionscript.html

One Interface, Many Views: A Case
for Repeatable Patterns

Weston Moran

SugarCRM, 10050 N Wolfe Rd, Cupertino, CA 95014
westonnh@gmail.com

Abstract. Our project looks at modern approaches to template and pattern design in web applications. We designed and implemented a single UI and UX across multiple devices and use cases. We holistically looked at front-end design and the cross over to backend template structure. The UX paradigm was tested to validate the performance gains and efficacy of the concept. The approach was designed to improve the experience, efficiency and understanding for the user as they utilize our application in multiple environments and across all facets of the navigation.

Keywords: User Interface, Repeatable Patterns, Pattern Library, User Experience, Style Guides.

1 Introduction

Speed is born from experience. Consistency promotes intuition. Clarity emboldens an efficient experience. Speed, consistency and clarity together create a pattern that determines the level of success and enjoyment a user experiences to accomplish their tasks.

These concepts of speed, clarity, and consistency are the guiding principles for respecting our users. In the spring of 2012 we began the task of building a team and tools that would strengthen the user experience of our product. We crafted a style guide consisting of a pattern library, visual style guidance, and code guidance to become a toolkit for our product, developers and prototype development.

We built labs for research and enacted test cycles to study our user base. We opened our doors to critique from all internal stakeholders from those who craft the experience to those who use the experience. We consolidated our interfaces into one UI across devices and screen types to simplify and exemplify the user path. We constructed reusable patterns in our own processes as well to strengthen our experience and understanding.

We set out to bring optimum clarity, consistency and speed to the tasks our users perform using SugarCRM application known as Sugar. The path and pattern is a blend of user experience and user interaction skills and practices that strengthen our vision, our team interactions, our product, and ultimately the user satisfaction with our efforts. Having the term "user" in our respective titles reminds every member in this effort of their true mission and job responsibility.

M. Kurosu (Ed.): Human-Computer Interaction, Part I, HCII 2014, LNCS 8510, pp. 340–349, 2014.
© Springer International Publishing Switzerland 2014

2   The User Experience Team

Our team consisted of 8 user experience and user interaction professionals. We supported the front-end efforts in conjunction with engineering, quality assurance, support and product management via an Agile methodology process [1]. We also interacted with a variety of internal stakeholders that ranged from marketing and sales to legal, operations and professional services. Each member of the team had a given focus area but all were free to rotate into whatever roles they preferred.

We all shared tasks at the introduction to the team to develop a path to a given role or focus. Growing or fitting into the correct position was an effort to promote harmony and focus to the individual while also ultimately striving for balancing and harmonizing a team.

When we started, we were a team of two. Lam Hyunh, maintained the current code base from a UI perspective and worked on prototype tasks. I worked with design, research and coding tasks. We quickly saw the need for a bigger team given the task before us. We brought a second designer, Omair Ali, onto the team from the product organization to work with UX related responsibilities. We moved away from being under product management at this point to form a parallel and succinct group within the product organization. We wanted level decision-making and focused priority and understanding in order to remain true to the user, who is our ultimate stakeholder. We also recognized the need for additional research and front-end coders to build prototypes and support engineering with our style guide and over all pattern application. Our engineering group also split into a number of feature-based teams during this time frame and they needed the user experience and user interaction skillset from our team.

Our team grew both in size and in talent areas. Vlad Kulchitski joined to help rapidly generate prototypes and carry designs and patterns into working code. He also led our responsive design efforts for other platform adoption. Henry Rogers was brought on board to foster our data visualization, code performance and consistency. He maintained the growth of our pattern library and tool kit, which we refer to as our Style Guide, and crafted a path for inclusion of it into our product. Ing-Marie Jonsson joined the team in an analytical and research role. She conducted the user testing, competitive research and further developed the UXLabs project. She also handled the coordination of tasks around our efforts. Florence Acevedo joined as an intern to support all efforts and learn the unique blend of user experience and user interaction we were crafting. She was then brought in as a formal team member to conduct research and user interaction tasks. Charles Godewyn was the most recent addition, bringing to the team both design and implementation of mockups.

All team members were encouraged to blend the two disciplines of UX and UI so that a truly holistic discipline is maintained around a singular pattern and design library. Understanding of the engineering complexity of template design and performance issues in the backend, as well as design and research fundamentals has proven to be very effective for a professional to efficiently and effectively apply the craft of user experience and interaction. The design of this creative engineer will lead to a better experience and a better product [2]. One without the other typically leads to longer design cycles, creative dissonance and a lack of confidence in conviction for the interests of the user. Each member has a role with the other functional teams to respect and reserve the user path. They are encouraged to actively share insight and skills with each other, with engineers, quality assurance and with product managers. They moved to different teams when skills were needed, and as a team we adapted to many challenges seamlessly. Now that our team was in place, our next step was to communicate the experience effectively.

3   Communication of Concepts

We learned to adapt our process to those of other groups within SugarCRM to maintain flexibility as the organization matured. We had many new employees and changes in roles that we needed to absorb and adapt to once we began to build our team. We ended up with a centralized warehouse on Google Drive of mockups and presentations to support those mockups. Our team also used this warehouse to store our concepts and explorations per release cycle. We placed all research there as well, creating one collaborative resource, leveraged as needed. The ability for engineers, quality assurance, support, product, sales, marketing, legal, ops and other stake-holders to provide real-time commentary at the appropriate moment has been excellent for efficiency, transparency and reduction of wasted time in procedural or clarifying meetings. We also saved the company considerable cost by streamlining a few processes that used to be scattered on different systems. People commented as inspired and more time was spent designing, researching and implementing. As releases passed we could turn off the older folders and save space on our machines. We could recall older documents as needed from the cloud service.

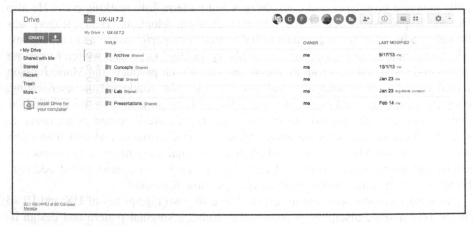

Fig. 1. Google Drive – Release folder assets screen depicted

We combined this established mockup and presentation 3rd generation process of the design and discovery stage with functioning prototypes more in tune with a 5th generation approach [3] in our style guide. The prototyping environment used the same code and CSS as our production environment. SugarCRM utilized GitHub for code revision and this allowed us to build quickly on specialized branch versions of up to date production code for prototypes as well. Having the whole UX and UI team know how to work in this process was critical to the success of this method. The combination reduced time and cost when moving to implementation. It also gave a much more realistic outcome for research and testing.

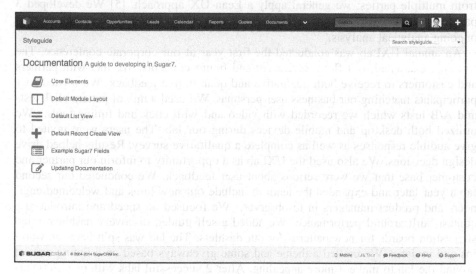

Fig. 2. Style Guide – Introduction and pattern screen depicted

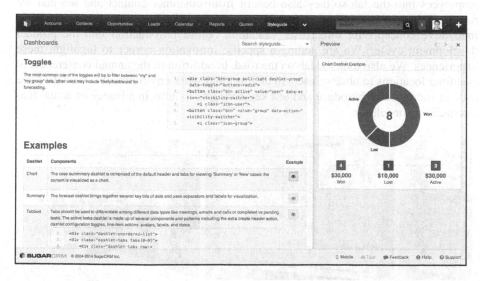

Fig. 3. Style Guide – Dashlets and Dashboards screen depicted

4   Research and Testing

"Indifference towards people and the reality in which they live is actually the one and only cardinal sin in design" – Dieter Rams [4]

The need for repetitive and consistent testing was critical to creating a successful design. We took an iterative usage testing approach to validate concepts with input from multiple parties; we general apply a Lean UX approach. [5] We developed 3 paths for consistent feedback: Conduct annual specific UXLabs, weekly tests, and ongoing analytical analysis.

An annual UXLab was conducted the first year at our corporate conference. The first lab, examined user flows of current and future concepts. We met with partners and customers to receive both qualitative and quantitative feedback. We invited fifty participants matching our business user personas. We used a mix of pattern click tests and A/B tests which we recorded with video and with click and timing tools.   We utilized both desktop and mobile devices during our lab. The users were invited to give audible responses as well as complete a qualitative survey. Results helped drive design decisions. We also used the UXLab as a opportunity to inform our partner and customer base that we were serious about user feedback. We conducted our second lab a year later and expanded the team to include our new hires and welcomed engineers and product managers in to observer.   We focused on speed and introduced a contest built around performance. We added a self-guided discovery dashboard and suggestion boards for new patterns for our dashlets. The lab was split between walk-ins and invitees. We crafted a theme and some giveaways based on a timing contest around the lab to make it more appealing. After 2 successful labs with over 200 participants, we expect continued growth in participation and expansion of tests. The success of this program has led us to expand to include more engineers and product employees into the lab so they also benefit from customer contact and see that we represent the user and are not acting for our own benefit. Lastly we want to build in innovative concepts for direct user validation before introduction into the product development cycle.   We are adding a specific innovation corner to highlight these experiences. We also took the lab on the road, in addition to the annual conference, to customer locations to observe users in their normal work environments. The labs were used to successfully introduce and test key concepts months in advance of actual feature building or release.

Fig. 4. UXLab – Branding and contest performance board

Weekly testing feedback cycles were also conducted with our "Monday Matters" email tests and surveys. We used tools from Zurb [6] such as VerifyApp, to conduct click, A/B and multivariate testing, Solidify, Notable and Insight to mockup feedback. We conducted weekly tests of key concepts with a mix of partner, customer and internal feedback where every employee had a chance to provide input in an unbiased manner. Discovery of new ideas can come from any corner at any time and we embrace that at Sugar. The transparency and opportunity for everyone that was part of a product experience to see and communicate their feedback was valuable for insight and for inclusiveness. Management of that process through the weekly testing proved to be successful, concrete and unbiased when compared to group review sessions. We also conducted timing tests for major releases and sent quarterly assessment surveys in conjunction with regular reviews of support feedback.

Lastly, we have created a program to receive analytical understanding from product based analytical tools. The tool was applied across the suite of products and views of those products to measure user flows, time on functional areas and goals based outcomes. The product team for planning and adjustments to the product leveraged the data.

Data as a stakeholder in the design and implementation process should always be considered. It is one more component of the overall user experience landscape and blends together with consistency, application performance and of course the fit and finish.

5   Fit and Finish

Sugar is very configurable and that strength has lead to some challenges in the final fit and finish around the product. Different components developed by a variety of teams needed a bit of marshaling. We simplified and converged the primary layout, navigational and data elements across devices. The consistency of patterns, accessibility, colors, notifications, status indicators and content modules was crucial to achieving a singular user interface.

Sugar has many partner companies that resell and reconfigure Sugar to meet the needs of their customers. Crafting an interface that can be communicated, adapt and grow to support innovation and our partner's goals involved reducing complexity and enabling consistent repeatable patterns in the interface. When the UX is combined with the implementation of the UI, this provided the product with efficiency in code, templates, quality assurance and ultimately a reduction in support cases.

A predictable interface lead to transparency, intuitive understanding and ultimately for our efforts, speed increases in user flows. Our create flow decreased by 40% by maintaining a consistent pattern in the primary save button position and by making a consistent and clearly identifiable record title. We also made the ability of the pattern to be user configurable and sticky to their workflow.

The interface prior to the recent redesigns was a table or spreadsheet experience. Each module had a slightly different experience or set of labels and buttons. We found anchors in the UI that we could leverage and enhance with UX principals. We standardized the title placement and style as a signal for consistent identification across different views. We created a business card view to only show top line data that would quickly bring the user understanding of the record. In accordance with a mobile first design philosophy [7] we wanted to drive the user to the primary path of information to increase speed and clarity in this data view.

We placed the fields in consistent spots and reduced visual complexity for quick identification. We created a visual pattern consisting of letters and colors to replace icons.

We wanted to reduce confusion in symbol recognition and improve performance, scalability and maintenance by using a purely CSS driven element. These identifiers along with a consistent alert set are the main emphasis items throughout the UI. The goal was to use color only when needed and in order to draw attention of the user. Branding colors and stylistic elements were minimized to reduce contamination of the focus but still enable the user to have a branded app. They could change the color of the navigation bar, which has universal visual prominence, and they could alter the link, highlight and primary button colors. When we studied the usage patterns we actually found that most users were staying with the released theme but found value in the color aspect as a configurable element. Reducing greater stylistic changes in the core of the UI had benefits to engineering, support, and quality assurance by reduction of separate templates and predictability in the UI. It also increased the branding opportunity on the mobile platform, which previously did not exist. Having a solid fit and finish also benefited the consistency of the product line, but the real strength of consistency remained in the 360-degree view content areas.

6   360-Degree Repeatable Pattern

Our previous versions of Sugar were challenged by the user having to click many times to get to views and respective sub views within a record view. We wanted to reduce scrolling and keep the secondary information and flows proximal to the primary content. The 360-degree view involves a main content panel, a grouping of sub panels, activity stream, and a side "intelligence" panel.

Fig. 5. 360 Degree Record View

The business card or primary data on a record view previously consisted of many fields in a tabular or spreadsheet format. Clients typically had many fields in view and the majority remained unfilled forcing the user to have to hunt for their data. The eye movement around the form, the inconsistent placement from record to record and the visual treatment offered little differentiation or consistency. We used a combination of different font sizes, simplification of only showing the required or relevant fields, and increased the white space so the rate of recognition would increase. These patterns were repeated in the mobile views for consistency.

We focused on form inputs as an area to reduce user clicks and application load. We identified that we had some candidates in add/remove flows, drop-down, multisect and actions that applied well across all records. As a result, we removed 3 different add/remove patterns into one, enhanced the select object, and started focusing visibility on next step or primary actions. We used key consistent icons for simple tasks to conserve space and speed recognition but we tried to limit overuse. All icons had tooltips and identifiers.

We looked at the data focus and how search was consumed and performed. Extra clicks were removed by making every user interaction dynamic on the related data set. We removed a long advanced search form that was different from view to view, where the user would have to hunt for specific fields. We replaced it with a chainable, simplified, "add only what you need" dynamic filter. This filter pattern is reused in any data element situation from dashlets to list views. Dynamic search is also applied to all drop-down fields and global search in a consistent manner. All of the patterns were designed from a mobile first perspective as we wanted the user to recognize the patterns in all possible devices or input formats. The universal searches used to be static, where a user would have to type a query and click the search icon to a dynamic set of results in context. Those results were also changed from an experience where the user had to shift their eyes back and forth horizontally for understanding on a variety of elements that changed from search to search. We shifted to a vertical approach allowing for the eye to jump from the line result to a simple vertically balanced line result without this eye shift.

We crafted a side panel "intelligence" dashboard with a set of dashlets that could bring information into a simple, focused, above the fold experience for the user. Information was previously stacked vertically and hidden behind a series of panels and tabs. The information had little visual separation or focus. The side panel was essentially a new ecosystem for integrations and views that is modular. We focused more on a pattern that enables people to create the right set of views rather than dictate them to the user. We also used this space for contextual view help and record previews as well. These elements are designed to keep the user in context to the primary content without the need to click out of the path and then have to return to rediscover. The user could reduce this space or heavily customize if they desire.

One final pattern we wanted to establish was onboarding. We designed a tour into every view that can be programmatically generated off of elements in the UI. We believe this is much more beneficial to the user than a series of slides at the beginning of the product which the user quickly escapes to get to their product. The tour was always available in the respective view in the footer. Next to that we placed a contextual help link, which triggers a help dashboard on the right side of the UI. Always knowing where to go for help, guidance and support is key for new users.

Fig. 6. Contextual Tour on Record

Fig. 7. Inline Help on Record View

By reducing the primary layout flows to this main content and secondary dashboard, which are highly customizable to the user need, we reduced or eliminated the time to navigate and discover on average by 23%. There may be a bit of up-front time for configuring the data filters and dashboards, but it is to the ultimate improvement of the task flow of the user. There is no more time wasted searching for buttons, labels fields or workflows that shift to new positions across multiple views. The UI is not in the way of the user path. It becomes transparent to the task [8] and the user gets things accomplished.

7   Final Thoughts

The path over the past 18 months has been rewarding and educational. We progressed and improved the user experience while discovering improvements in speed, consistency and clarity in our application. We matured a specialized, respected, flexible team and instilled a strong, knowledgeable vibrant user focus to the organization as a whole. Having tools and transparency for the crafters has saved time, energy and spurred innovation. Our testing outcomes showed that we improved the experience in the majority of our key flows and we established goals and patterns to continue testing and communicating those results to internal stakeholders in the future. It has been a fun team experience, efficient to evolve, and ultimately repeatable.

References

1. Beck, K., et al.: Manifesto for Agile Software Development. Agile Alliance (2001)
2. Rams, D.: Design by Vitsœ. New York. Speech (1976)
3. Macefield, R.: Are You Still Using Earlier-Generation Prototyping Tools?: UXmatters (2012), http://www.uxmatters.com/mt/archives/2012/10/are-you-still-using-earlier-generation-prototyping-tools.php
4. Lovell, S.: Dieter Rams: As Little Design as Possible. Phaidon, London (2011)
5. Gothelf, J., Seiden, J.: Lean UX: Applying Lean Principles to Improve User Experience. O'Reilly Media, N.P. (2013)
6. Zurb, Zurb applications (2014), http://zurb.com/apps (retrieved)
7. Wroblewski, L.: Mobile First. Book Apart, New York (2011)
8. Wendt, T.: Designing for Transparency and the Myth of the Modern Interface. UX Magazine (2012), http://uxmag.com/articles/designing-for-transparency-and-the-myth-of-the-modern-interface

Picture-Driven User Interface Development
for Applications on Multi-platforms

Vinh-Tiep Nguyen[1], Minh-Triet Tran[1], and Anh-Duc Duong[2]

[1] Faculty of Information Technology, University of Science, VNU-HCM, Vietnam
[2] Faculty of Software Engineering, University of Information Technology,
VNU-HCM, Vietnam
{nvtiep,tmtriet}@fit.hcmus.edu.vn, ducda@uit.edu.vn

Abstract. Graphical user interfaces are usually first sketched out manually as hand drawing pictures and then must be realized by software developers to become prototypes or usable user interfaces. This motivates our proposal of a smart CASE tool that can understand hand drawing sketches of graphical user interfaces, including forms and their navigations, then automatically transform such draft designs into real user interfaces of a prototype or an application. By using the ideas of modeling and model-transformation in model driven engineering, the authors also propose a mechanism to generate graphical user interfaces as forms targeting different platforms. Experimental results show that our sketch recognition to understand hand drawing graphical user interfaces can achieve the accuracy of 97.86% and 95% in recognizing 7 common UI controls and arrows for navigation respectively. Our model transformation engine can generate user interfaces as forms for applications on 3 different platforms of mobile devices, including Windows Phone, Android, and iOS. This approach follows the trend to develop a new generation of smart CASE tools that can understand and interpret conceptual software design models into concrete software elements and components to assist the software development process in a natural way.

Keywords: picture-driven, graphical user interface, code generation, mobile device, multi-platform.

1 Introduction

Graphical User Interface changed the way people interact with computers and computing systems more intuitively and attractively. By using GUI, a user can easily understand and follow the workflow of a business process in an application. In software development process, early phases are very important, especially in the phase of gathering software requirements. To understand and collect correct and enough information of requirements, developers usually sketch out key ideas, including main user interfaces and their navigations (c.f. Figure 1a), to discuss with customers.

Although there are different tools to assist developers design user interfaces, such utilities still do not have the capability to understand hand drawing user interfaces and

M. Kurosu (Ed.): Human-Computer Interaction, Part I, HCII 2014, LNCS 8510, pp. 350–360, 2014.
© Springer International Publishing Switzerland 2014

the semantic for the navigations between forms and controls. To bridge the gap between user interface designs as sketches and concrete user interfaces, there is a practical need to transform instantly sketch ideas of user interfaces into concrete GUIs for software to avoid misunderstanding and to help developers capture exactly workflows of the system. This opens a new generation of computing, picture-driven computing[1]. Figure 1 demonstrates the idea of turning sketch user interfaces to software prototypes.

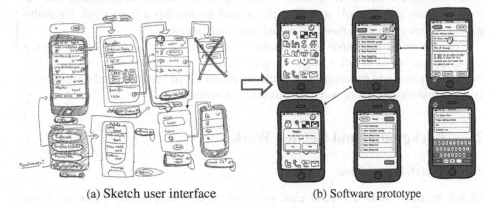

(a) Sketch user interface   (b) Software prototype

Fig. 1. Idea of sketch user interface to software prototype

Moreover, software is often developed with various distributions for multi-platforms with the same user interfaces and functions. It would be time consuming to redesign the user interface of the same software when a developer wants to port that application to another platform. Thus it would be more convenient for developers to automatically transform an abstract UI design that is independent from any specific platform to a concrete realization of the design for a particular platform, such as Windows Phone, Android, or iOS.

In this paper, we propose our idea that to develop a model-driven method to realize user interfaces targeting multi platforms from hand drawing sketches of graphical user interfaces. By understanding the semantic of an image, in this case, a sketch of a user interface design, our system can automatically generate a concrete user interface with required source code for an application on a specific platform. Our idea can be used not only in software prototyping but also in assisting developers to migrate an application to another platform just by model transformations. The two main components to solve two problems in our proposed system are as follows:

- Sketch recognition: this component is responsible for recognizing symbols of UI controls used in the quick sketch design of software user interface. The component also determines the spatial structure of these symbols to capture the topology order and relationship between UI controls, i.e. which object is a control, which object is a container, and what event will be generated when a user interacts with a certain UI object.

- Model-driven code generator: from the spatial structure of symbols, an Abstract User Interface (AUI), a platform-independent UI model of an application, is generated. This AUI model plays the role of the common model to generate different Concrete User Interfaces (CUIs), platform-dependent user interfaces of the same application.

The main contributions of our proposal are to propose a histogram-of-gradient based feature for sketch recognition; to decompose the whole sketch image into separable forms and controls with navigation; and to develop a framework for multi-platform code generation based on model-driven architecture.

The content of the paper is as follows. In Section 2, the authors briefly review some approaches of sketch recognition problem and UI control code generation. Our proposed system and experimental results are presented in Section 3 and 4 respectively. Conclusions and future work are discussed in Section 5.

2   Background and Related Work

2.1   Sketch Recognition

Sketch recognition is a special case of visual object recognition. There are some common approaches for sketch recognition, such as template matching or local feature based matching. Template matching approaches [2] [3] use color information of a template as the main factor to determine the similarity between the template and an extracted pattern from a source image. Edge-based template matching[4] can work well with a low-texture object such as a sketch but it is not robust with some small changes of the sketch.

Local feature based approaches such as SIFT[5], SURF[6] are robust with scale and rotation transformations but these methods are only effective when working with high-texture objects. For the special case of objection recognition problem, a sketch object often has extra useful information such as its shape and directions of movement in the drawing of the sketch. This information can be extracted based on edge features. HoG[7] is a typical feature descriptor that counts the occurrences of gradient orientations in localized portions of an image. This feature is well known in pedestrian detection problem in static image. To work with various types and shapes of sketches, machine learning is a very common approach to think about. There are many learning algorithms and learning models such as: SVM[8], Neural Network[9], Bag of Features[10]. These algorithms often require a large dataset with high computational cost. So in this project, we try to make the implementation process as simple as possible.

2.2   Model Driven Code Generation for Multi Platform Applications

With the rapid development of different mobile platforms, an application can be developed with multiple distributions targeting multiple platforms. It would be waste of time and effort to redesign user interfaces of an application when it is migrated to a new mobile platform. Model-driven approach is one of the promising solutions to help developers in porting applications for multi platforms[11].

In Model-Driven Development (MDD[12]), a software is first designed with high level models that do not depend on any specific technical background. These models are then transformed into low level models that are dependent on a specific platform and linked to a particular technology[13]. By this way, it would be convenient to develop the same application on different platforms simply by transforming the abstract, high level models of the software into different concrete, low level models, even to the source code in a specific development environment.

To solve the problem of generating the same UI design (from sketch drawing) to various mobile platforms, we inherit the concept of Platform Independent Model and Platform Specific Model[13]. A Platform Independent Model (PIM) user interface is independent from any specific mobile platforms while a Platform Specific Model (PSM) is bound to a specific technology, such as Android, Windows Phone, or iOS.

3   Proposed Method

3.1   System Overview

The proposed process consists of three main phases: training phase using sketch image dataset, recognizing phase to identify drawn sketch, and code generating phase. The overview of our system is illustrated in Figure 2.

Training Phase: The input of this phase is a sketch dataset with multiple sketch images of common UI controls, e.g. forms, buttons, textboxes, combo boxes... Each sketch image is labeled corresponding to its UI control type. This module transforms a sketch image into a feature map. These maps are archived in the feature set to be used in next phase. Two feature maps are compared using a distance measure. In this work, Euclidean distance is chosen for simple implementation. Besides sketches of common UI controls, an arrow is proposed as a special sketch with many different characteristics to link a button to a form. Recognizing arrow must be invariant with shape and rotation transformation. We will discuss two algorithms to recognize these types of sketches in section 3.2.

Recognizing Phase: In this phase, new sketches drawn by user when designing graphic user interface are classified into corresponding UI control types. Each feature extracted from a new sketch is compared to trained feature set. Labels of UI new sketches are determined based on best matched sample in the training dataset.

Code Generating Phase: After recognizing a sketched UI, it is necessary to localize its position to determine its corresponding form. Based on its position, our system constructs the spatial structure of all controls that can be used to understand which object is a control, which object is a container, and what event will be generated. Finally, the code generator engine generates software prototype corresponding to the input sketched design targeting a specific platform, e.g. Windows Phones, Android, or iOS.

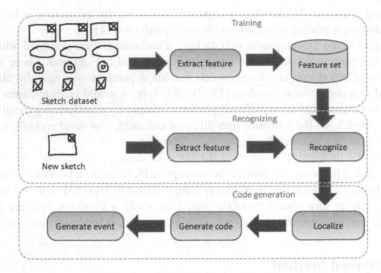

Fig. 2. Overview of the proposed system

3.2   Sketch Recognition Method

Training Phase

In this paper, we focus on recognizing some common UI control in graphic user interface design. There are seven types of controls: main form, tab control, text box, button, combo box, check box and radio button (Figure 3). Among these types, text box and button are very easy to be mistaken if user does not pay attention to some important differences. Button is drawn by smooth curves whereas text box is drawn by straight lines and sharp corners. To connect forms or tab controls together, we use arrow as a special type sketch. An arrow can have many directions, lengths and shapes as illustrated in Figure 4. It is very difficult to use the same method to recognize both graphic controls and arrow sketch. Therefore we propose two distinct algorithms to recognize these types of sketches to take advantages of specific constraints of each problem.

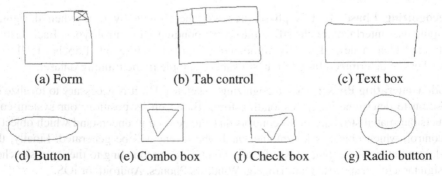

(a) Form   (b) Tab control   (c) Text box

(d) Button   (e) Combo box   (f) Check box   (g) Radio button

Fig. 3. Seven types of UI controls

Fig. 4. Example of various directions, lengths, and shapes or navigation arrows

The main advantage of UI control sketch recognition problem is that it does not need to be invariant with rotation transformation. Inspired by the idea of HoG (Histogram of Gradients)[7], we propose our new simple feature map of sketch. Each sketch is represented as four 16x16 feature maps corresponding to four main directions {0, π /4, π/2, 3π/4}. This feature is used to compare with those of trained sketch samples in the dataset using Euclidean distance for simplicity and ease of implementation. The UI control recognition includes 3 steps:

- **Step 1-Compute Gradients:** To take advantage of order information of points in sketch, angle of gradient vector is computed for each point. Formula of tangent vector at the ith point:

$$\alpha_i = \tan^{-1}\left(\frac{y_{i+w} - y_{i-w}}{x_{i+w} - x_{i-w}}\right)$$

where W is the width of tangle window. After this step, we have a set of (x_i, y_i, α_i) corresponding to each point of sketch and its angle. Spatial information and direction are combined to create feature maps in next steps.

- **Step 2- Normalize Coordinate:** Since UI controls have many different sizes, we normalized original coordinate into feature space to make the algorithm robust with various sizes of control. We use the following formula to transform coordinate:

$$x_{i\_norm} = \left(\frac{x_i - \mu_x}{\sigma_x}\right)\frac{h}{5} + \frac{h}{2}, \ y_{i\_norm} = \left(\frac{y_i - \mu_y}{\sigma_y}\right)\frac{h}{5} + \frac{h}{2}$$

where

$$\mu_x = \frac{1}{n}\sum_{i=1}^{n} x_i, \mu_y = \frac{1}{n}\sum_{i=1}^{n} y_i, \ \sigma_x = \sqrt{\frac{1}{n}\sum_{i=1}^{n}(x_i - \mu_x)^2}, \sigma_y = \sqrt{\frac{1}{n}\sum_{i=1}^{n}(y_i - \mu_y)^2}$$

$h=16$ is size of the feature map.

- **Step 3- Compute Feature Maps:** Since this problem does not need to satisfy invariance with rotation and direction of sketch movement when drawing, only the value of orientation in range of [0, π) is used. In this paper, we divide this range into 4 bin of orientation including {0, π/4, π/2, 3π/4}. Each orientation corresponds to a feature maps. Feature map bases voting principle of intension. After normalization, we accumulate intension of the angle into corresponding map.

For each point in line from (x_{i_norm}, y_{i_norm}) to $(x_{i+1\_norm}, y_{i+1\_norm})$, we accumulate intension of α_i corresponding to four maps of each orientation. Figure 5 illustrates an example of feature maps for a check box sketch.

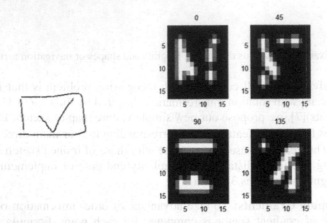

(a) Check box sketch   (b) Feature map for a check box sketch

Fig. 5. An example of feature extraction to feature map

As mentioned before, an arrow that links controls and forms is a special type of sketch in our system. It is very difficult to solve both two types of sketches at the same time. The system is then required to recognize sketches with unpredictable directions and shapes. However, an arrow also has some special characteristics so that we can use to recognize them easier. We inherit the idea of T. A. Hammond [14] to describe an arrow in a specification language to simplify sketch recognition user interface:

- An arrow is formed by three distinct segments. A distinct segment contains all point which has local angle approximate to π. In case a segment has a point that its local angle differs with straight angle, it is separated into two segments. Figure 6 shows an example of segment was separated into two parts.
- Three end points of segments intersect in the same position.
- The longest segment stays at the middle of other ones. All of arrows in Figure 4 satisfy these properties.

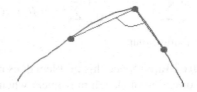

Fig. 6. A segment was separated into two segments

Recognizing Phase

To assist a developer in real-time manner to illustrate how the real user interface looks like as soon as the developer sketches out the draft design of a graphical user interface, we

When the developer designs a form or a set of forms with navigations (denoted by arrows), he or she usually draws on the drawing pad or a sheet of paper only one UI control or a navigation arrow at a time. There is usually a short pause, or idle state, between the drawing of two consecutive UI controls or arrows. Therefore, our system continuously monitors the on-going drawing to detect idle states between the sketches of two UI controls or arrows. By this way, our system can extract a new sketch corresponding to a single UI control or an arrow as soon as the developer finishes drawing it.

When a new sketch is extracted from the current UI design drawing, the system first verifies if it is an arrow, a navigation link between UI controls. If not, the system then continues to pass that new sketch into its UI control recognition module. The sketch is then transformed to its corresponding feature map to be compared with the feature maps of trained samples. For simplicity of implementation, we use Euclidean metric to compute distance between feature maps.

3.3   Code Generating Phase

To generate source code of user interfaces for an application targeting different platforms, we propose a framework following Model Driven Architecture (MDA) to easily transform source code from a platform to another one.

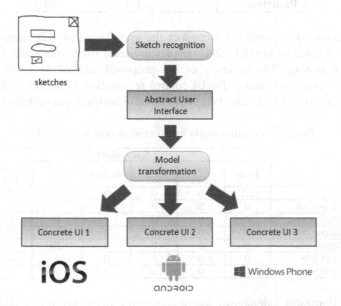

Fig. 7. The overview of code generating phase for multiple platforms

In a model-driven approach, a high level model is required because it is the common model that plays the role of a bridge between different low level models targeting various platforms and technologies. Figure 7 illustrates the overview of our proposed code generating phase for user interfaces on different platforms from a single hand drawing sketch.

We reuse the platform-independent model of user interfaces for application on mobile devices proposed by C. K. Diep et.al[15]. The output of the sketch recognition process is not a concrete user interface that is dependent on a specific mobile platform but an Abstract User Interface (AUI[15]). This model is then transformed into different Concrete User Interfaces (CUIs [15])

4   Experimental Results

For the sketch recognition phase, we conduct two experiments to testing the accuracy of arrow recognition and UI control recognition algorithms. For the proposed arrow recognition algorithm, we create a test set of 100 samples (50 positive and 50 negative tests). The confusion matrix is illustrated in Table 1. We have false positive rate is 4/50 = 8% and false positive is 1/50 = 2%. The total accuracy is (46+49)/100=95%.

Table 1. Confusion matrix for arrow sketch recognition

	Negative	Positive
Negative	46	4
Positive	1	49

For UI control recognition, we conduct the experiment on 420 samples divided equally into 7 types of controls. 280 samples are used for training and 140 samples are used for testing. The accuracy of the proposed method is 137/140 samples (97.86%).The confusion matrix for UI control recognition is shown in Table 2. We can see that, a text box or a radio button can be misclassified as a button (3/40 cases).

Table 2. Confusion matrix for UI control sketch recognition

		Recognized control						
		Form	Tab control	Text box	Button	Combo box	Check box	Radio button
Actual control	Form	20	0	0	0	0	0	0
	Tab control	0	20	0	0	0	0	0
	Text box	0	0	18	2	0	0	0
	Button	0	0	0	20	0	0	0
	Combo box	0	0	0	0	20	0	0
	Check box	0	0	0	0	0	20	0
	Radio button	0	0	0	1	0	0	19

Figure 8 illustrates a demonstration of converting from sketch to a GUI. A sketch is captured by a special device such as stylus pen, tablet (c.f. Figure 8a). The current system can only detect and align which region is label with hand written character.

However, at the meantime, the system does not recognize of a label. A label control is added to the interface but its content must by edited manually by developer. It should be noticed that developer is required to assign text content of the label in an abstract user interface only. Then, this model will be transformed into different CUIs without any modification of the developer.

The source code of graphic user interface is generated automatically for an application targeting iOS, Windows Phone, Android (c.f. Figure 8b,c,d). We also propose an algorithm to align controls of the same type in a specific group to have a better layout. Our system currently supports UI source code generation for 3 main mobile platforms: iOS, Windows Phone and Android.

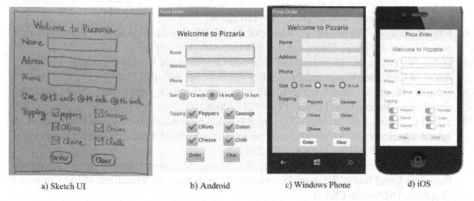

a) Sketch UI   b) Android   c) Windows Phone   d) iOS

Fig. 8. An example of converting a hand drawing UI sketch into three concrete GUIs for an application

5   Conclusion and Future Work

In this paper, we propose a smart tool that can understand a typical hand drawing sketch of a GUI draft design and realize it into concrete user interfaces for a real application on different mobile platforms, including Windows Phone, Android, and iOS. In our system, we propose an algorithm for sketch recognition, an algorithm for separating a sketch image into independent components, and a model-based framework to generate code of user interfaces for applications on multiple mobile platforms.

Currently our solution supports 7 common UI controls, including forms, tab controls, textboxes, buttons, combo boxes, check boxes, and radio buttons. Our sketch recognition module can also identify arrows liking between forms to generate appropriate UI navigations. More UI controls can be trained and added into the sketch recognition module to enrich the usability of our proposed method. With the application of model-driven approach, we utilize the Abstract User Interface and Concrete User Interface to enable our system targeting various mobile platforms. Furthermore, more sets of transformation rules can be added so that our system can support more mobile platforms. For more convenience, we also integrate hand written recognition module to recognize label automatically instead of manually editing by user.

References

1. Hardesty, L.: Picture-driven computing (January 2010), http://web.mit.edu/newsoffice/2010/screen-shots-0120.html
2. Lewis, J.P.: Fast Template Matching. In: Vision Interface 1995, pp. 120–123. Candian Image Processing and Pattern Recognition Society, Quebec City (1995)
3. Ouyang, W., Cham, W.K.: Fast algorithm for Walsh Hadamard transform on sliding windows. IEEE Transaction on Pattern Analysis and Machine Intelligence, 165–171 (2010)
4. Hofhauser, A., Steger, C., Navab, N.: Edge-Based Template Matching and Tracking for Perspectively Distorted Planar Objects. In: Bebis, G., et al. (eds.) ISVC 2008, Part I. LNCS, vol. 5358, pp. 35–44. Springer, Heidelberg (2008)
5. Lowe, D.G.: Distinctive Image Features from Scale-Invariant Keypoints. International Journal of Computer Vision (IJCV), 91–110 (2004)
6. Bay, H., Ess, A., Tuytelaars, T., Van Gool, L.: SURF: Speeded Up Robust Features. Computer Vision and Image Understanding (CVIU), 346–359 (2008)
7. Dalal, N., Triggs, B.: Histograms of Oriented Gradients for Human Detection. In: Conference on Computer Vision and Pattern Recognition, pp. 886–893 (2005)
8. Sun, Z., Liang, S.: Sketch retrieval and relevance feedback with biased SVM classification. Pattern Recognition Letters, 1733–1741 (2008)
9. Su, M.C., Hsio, T.H., Hsieh, Y.Z., Lin, S.C.: A neural-network-based sketch recognition system. In: International Symposium on Intelligent Signal Processing and Communications Systems (ISPACS), pp. 420–423 (2012)
10. Eitz, M., Hildebrand, K., Boubekeur, T., Alexa, M.: Sketch-Based Image Retrieval: Benchmark and Bag-of-Features Descriptors. Transactions on Visualization and Computer Graphics, 1624–1636 (2011)
11. Mourouzis, A., Leonidis, A., Foukarakis, M., Antona, M., Maglaveras, N.: A Novel Design Approach for Multi-device Adaptable User Interfaces: Concepts, Methods and Examples. In: Stephanidis, C. (ed.) Universal Access in HCI, Part I, HCII 2011. LNCS, vol. 6765, pp. 400–409. Springer, Heidelberg (2011)
12. Balagtas-Fernandez, F.T., Hussmann, H.: Model-Driven Development of Mobile Applications. In: International Conference on Automated Software Engineering (ASE 2008), pp. 509–512 (2008)
13. Kherraf, S., Lefebvre, E., Suryn, W.: Transformation From CIM to PIM Using Patterns and Archetypes. In: 19th Australian Conference on Software Engineering (ASWEC 2008), pp. 338–346 (2008)
14. Hammond, T.A.: LADDER: A Perceptually-based Language to Simplify Sketch Recognition User Interface Development, Massachusetts Institute of Technology, Doctor of Philosophy thesis (2007)
15. Diep, C.-K., Tran, Q.-N., Tran, M.-T.: Online model-driven IDE to design GUIs for cross-platform mobile applications. In: The 4th Symposium on Information and Communication Technology, pp. 294–300 (2013)

PeNTa: Formal Modeling for Multi-touch Systems Using Petri Net

Francisco R. Ortega, Su Liu, Frank Hernandez, Armando Barreto,
Naphtali Rishe, and Malek Adjouadi

Florida International University, Miami FL 33199, USA
fort007@fiu.edu
http://www.franciscoraulortega/

Abstract. Multi-touch technology has become pervasive in our daily lives, with iPhones, iPads, touch displays, and other devices. It is important to find a user input model that can work for multi-touch gesture recognition and can serve as a building block for modeling other modern input devices (e.g., Leap Motion, gyroscope). We present a novel approach to model multi-touch input using Petri Nets. We formally define our method, explain how it works, and the possibility to extend it for other devices.

Keywords: Multi-touch, Petri Nets, Modern Input Devices.

1 Introduction

The importance in Human-Computer Interaction (HCI) of descriptive models (e.g., "Three-state model for graphical input"[1]) and predictive models (e.g., Fitts' law) can be seen in the seminal work by[2,3]. A descriptive model is a "loose verbal analogy and methaphore"[4], which describes a phenomenon[5]. A predictive model is expressed by "closed-form mathematical equations"[4], which predict a phenomenon[5]. We present a sound mathematical model using PetriNets for Multi-Touch systems, with the possibility of expanding it to other modern input devices (e.g., Leap Motion). Our motivation is to use a model for simulation of Multi-Touch systems and as a real-time execution system for different 3D applications, such as 3D Navigation[6]. We present **Petri Net Touch** (**PeNTa**), a modeling tool for multi-touch systems.

Input systems formalism is not recent. The pioneer work by Newman (1968) used a state diagram to represent a graphical system[7]. The seminal work by Bill Buxton in a "A Three-State Model of Graphical Input"[1] used finite-state machines (FSM). Around the same time as Buxton's work, a well-rounded model for input interactions was published by Myers[8].

Multi-touch gesture detection, or detection of touch events, have been explored. In 2013, Proton and Proton++ showed the use of Regular Expressions (RegEx) to accomplish gesture detection[9]. Lao et al[10] used state-diagrams for the detection multi-touch events. Context-free grammar was used by Kammer et al. to describe multi-touch gestures without taking implementation into consideration[11]. Gesture Coder[12] creates FSMs by demonstration to later use them to detect gestures. Gesture Works and

M. Kurosu (Ed.): Human-Computer Interaction, Part I, HCII 2014, LNCS 8510, pp. 361–372, 2014.

Open Exhibits by Ideum have a high-level language description, using XML, called GestureML (GML)[1]. A rule-based language (e.g., CLIPS) was used to define the Midas framework[13].

Petri Nets have also been used to detect gestures. Nam et al. showed how to use Coloured Petri Nets (CPN) to achieve hand (data glove) gesture modeling and recognition [14], using Hidden Markov Models (HMM) to recognize gesture features that are then fed to a Petri Net. Petri Nets have been shown to be applicable in event-driven system[15], which is another reason we are interested in them to model input devices. While our approach is based on high-level Petri Nets, Spano et al.[16,17] showed how to use Non-Autonomous Petri Nets[18], low-level Petri Nets, for multi-touch interaction. Also, Hamon et al.[15] expanded on Spano's work, providing more detail to the implementation of Petri Nets for multi-touch interactions.

In our initial approach[19] in 2013, we proposed the use of high-level Petri Nets for multi-touch interaction. In this paper, we defined a formal High-Level Petri Net for the use of Multi-Touch called Petri Net Touch (PeNTa), which is the basis for the Input Modeling Recognition Language (IRML) for input devices.

1.1 Motivation and Differences

Our target audiences for PenTA and IRML are three: (1)Software developers that would like to graphically model multi-touch interactions. (2) Framework developers[2] developers that wish to incorporate modern input to their capabilities. (3) Domain-Specific Language (DSL) developers that create solutions for domain-experts or for other developers.

There are several reasons why we preferred to use high-level Petri Nets versus other approaches. First we must consider the difference between low-level Petri Nets vs high-level Petri Nets. The major difference is that high-level Petri Nets have "complex data structures as data tokens, and [use] algebraic expressions to annotate net elements"[20]. This is similar to the difference between Assembly language versus a high-level language (e.g., Python). For the complete standard defining high-level Petri Nets see [20]. A high-level Petri Net it is still mathematically defined as the low-level petri-net but it can provide "unambiguous specifications and descriptions of applications"[20].

There are further reasons why we decided to use high-level Petri Nets for our approach. These reasons might be better understood when we place the PeNTa in the context of other existing approaches for input modeling: Proton and Proton++[9], Gesture Coder[12], and GestIT[3]. While we find that our approach offers more expressiveness and distributed capabilities, simultaneously providing a solid mathematical framework, the work offered by Proton++, Gesture Coder, and GestIT offers great insight in modeling multi-touch interaction, with different benefits that must be evaluated by the developer. We also like to note that our work is inspired by the contribution of the proponents of Proton and Proton++.

Why Petri Nets to define a multi-touch interaction? Petri Nets provide graphical and mathematical representations, that allows for verification and analysis. Thus providing

---

[1] www.GestureML.org
[2] Library and/or language developers also fit in this category.
[3] Which also refers to Hamon et al.[15].

a formal specification that can be executed. Petri Nets also allow distributed systems to be represented. Finally, a finite state machine can be represented in a Petri-Net but a Petri-Net may not be represented as a FSM. In other words, Petri Nets have more expressive representational power.

Proton and Proton++ offer a novel approach to multi-touch interaction using RegEx. Such approach offers an advantage to those who understand regular expressions. However, there may be some disadvantages in using RegEx for our goals. Expressions of some gestures can be lengthy, such as the scale gesture[9]: $D_1^s M_1^s * D_2^a (M_1^s | M_2^a) * (U_1^s M_2^a * U_2^a | U_2^a M_1^s * U_1^s)^4$. Spano et al.[17] present additional differences between Petri Nets and the use of regular expressions in Proton++. Another potential disadvantage of using regular expressions, is that some custom gestures may become harder to represent.

Gesture Coder offers a great approach to create gestures by demonstration. While we don't follow this approach, PeNTa could also created the Petri Nets by machine learning training. The representation of the training for Gesture Coder results in a FSM. FSMs can become large and do not provide the expressive power and distributed representation of Petri Nets.

We have also looked at GestIT. This is the closest approach to ours. GestIT uses low-level petri nets. While this work represents a valuable contribution, it may lack the expressiveness of using data structures in tokens which are part of high-level Petri Net. We find, nonetheless, that GestIT can provide some great ideas to further improve our approach in PeNTa and IRML.

The approach of GestIT is similar to Proton++ given that the set of points (trace) is broken down into points and the gesture becomes a pattern of those points. While the expressiveness of our HLPN allows to use this approach, we have preferred to define the each token as an individual trace.

Our work includes the novel approach to use high-level Petri Nets for multi-touch recognition including the definition of our HLPN. The fact that we are using Petri Net allows for formal specifications to be applied to multi-touch, and perhaps other modern input devices (e.g., Leap Motion), and enables a distributed framework while keeping the approach simple (in comparison to low-level Petri Nets). This means that by encapsulating complex data structures in tokens and allowing for algebraic notation and function calling in the transitions of a Petri Net, the modeling is not restricted to one individual approach. Furthermore, the data structure kept in each token, can maintain history information that may be relevant to some processes. This will be explained in detail in the following two sections.

2   HLPN: High-Level Petri Nets and IRML

For our model, we define our High-Level Petri Net[21,22], as $HLPN = (N, \Sigma, \lambda)$. This contains the Net **N**, the specifications Σ and the inscription λ.

The Net **N** is formed with places **P**, transitions **T**, and connecting arc expressions (as functions **F**). In other words, a Petri-Net is given by a three-tuple $N = (P, T, F)$, where $F \subset (P \times T) \cup (T \times P)$. Petri Nets' arcs can only go from **P** to **T** or **T** to **P**. This

---

[4] D=Down, M=Move, U=Up; s=shape, b=background, a=any (a—b).

can be formally expressed stating that the sets of places and transitions are disjoint, $P \cap T = \emptyset$. Another important characteristics of Petri Nets is that they use multi-sets[5] (elements that can be repeated) for the input functions, $(I : T \to P^\infty)$ and output functions, $(O : P \to T^\infty)$[23].

The specification Σ represents the underlying representation of tokens. This is defined as $\Sigma = (S, \Omega, \Psi)$. The set S contains all the possible token[6] data types allowed in the system. For our particular case, our data type is always the same, which is a multi-touch token **K**, as shown in Table 1. The set Ω contains the token operands (e.g., plus, minus). The set Ψ defines the meaning and operations in Ω. In other words, the set Ψ defines how a given operation (e.g., plus) is implemented. For our case, we use regular math and boolean algebra rules, without the need to redefine. This is the default for **PeNTa** tokens. It is important that all the tokens in our HLPN are the signature of (S, Ω).

The inscription λ defines the arc operation. This is defined as $\lambda = (\phi, L, \rho, M_0)$. The data definition represented by ϕ is the association of each place $p \in P$ with tokens. This means that **places** should accept only variables of a matching data type. In our case, we have token **K**, which represents the multi-touch structure. The inscription also has labeling **L** for the arc expressions, such as $L(x, y) \iff (x, y) \in F$. For example, a transition that goes from place B to transition 4 will be represented as $L(B, 4)$. The operation of a given arc (function) is given by $\rho = (Pre, Post)$. This are well-defined constraint mappings associated with each arc expression, such as $f \in F$. The **Pre** condition allows our HLPN to enable the function, if the boolean constraint evaluates to true. Then, the **Post** condition will execute the code if the function is enabled (ready to fire). Finally, the initial marking is given by M_0, which states the initial state of our HLPN.

2.1 Dynamic Semantics

In order to finalize the formal definition of our HLPN, we include some basic notes about the dynamic aspects of our Petri Net. First, markings of a HLPN are mappings $M : P \to Tokens$. In other words, places map to tokens. Second, given a marking M, a transition $t \in T$ is enabled at marking M iff $Pre(t) \leq M$. Third, given a marking M, α_t is an assignment for variables of t that satisfy its transition condition, and A_t denotes the set of all assignments. Define the set of all transition modes to be $TM = \{(t, \alpha_t) | t \in T, \alpha_t \in A_t\} \iff Pre(TM) \leq M$. An example of this definition is a transition spanning multiple places, as shown in Figures 1 and 2 (concurrent enabling). Fourth, given a marking M, if $t \in T$ is enabled in mode α_t, firing t by a step may occur in a new marking $M' = M - Pre(t_{\alpha_t}) + Post(t_{\alpha_t})$; a step is denoted by $M[t > M'$. In other words, this is the transition rule. Finally, an execution sequence $M_0[t_0 > M_1[t_1 > ...$ is either finite when the last marking is terminal (no more transitions are enabled) or infinite. The behavior of a HLPN model is the set of all execution sequences, starting from M_0.

---

[5] Also known as Bag Theory.
[6] Some Petri Nets' publications may refer to tokens as "sorts".

2.2 Multi-touch

A multi-touch display (capacitive or vision-based) can detect multiple finger strokes at the same time. This can be seen as a finger trace. A **trace** is generated when a finger touches down onto the surface, moves (or stays static), and it is eventually lifted from it. Therefore, a trace is a set of touches of a continuous stroke. While it is possible to create an anomalous trace with the palm, for example, we are only taking into consideration normal multi-finger interaction. However, our data structure (explained in detail later) could be modified to fit different needs, including multiple users and other sensors that may enhance the touch interaction. Given a set of traces, one can define a **gesture**. For example, a simple gesture may be two fingers moving on the same path, creating a **swipe**. If they are moving in opposite ways (at least one of the fingers), this can be called a **zoom out** gesture. If the fingers are moving towards each other, then this is a **zoom in** gesture. A final assumption we make for the multi-touch system is the following: if a touch interaction is not moving, it will not create additional samples but increment the holding time of the finger. Note that this is not inherently true in all multi-touch systems. For example, in native WINAPI (Windows 7) development, samples are generated, even if the finger is not moving, but holding. We filter those samples out by creating a small threshold that defines that the finger is not moving (even if it may be moving slightly).

2.3 Arc Expressions

Each arc is defined as a function **F**, which is divided into two subsets of inputs **I** and outputs **O**, such that $F = I \cup O$. In the inscription ρ of this HLPN, the arc expression is defined as **Pre** and **Post** conditions. Simply put, the **Pre** condition either enables or disables the function, and the **Post** condition updates and executes call-back events, in our HLPN.

Each function **F** is defined as $F = Pre \cup Post$, forming a four-tuple $F = (B,U,C,R)$, where **B** and **U** are part of the **Pre** conditions, and **C** and **R** are the **Post** conditions. **B** is the boolean condition that evaluates to true or false, **R** is the *priority function*, **C** is the call-back event, **U** is the update function.

The boolean condition **B** allows the function to be evaluated using standard boolean operators with the tokens, in C++ style (e.g., $T_1.state == STATE.UP$). If no condition is assigned, the default is *true*. The priority function **R** instantiates a code block, with the purpose of assigning a priority value to the arc expression. The call-back event **C** allows the Petri Net to have a function callback with conditional *if* statements, local variable assignments, and external function calling. This can help to determine which function should be called. If no callback event is provided, then a default *genericCallBack(Place p, Token t)* is called. The update function **U** is designed to bring the next touch sample using $update(T_1)$, or setting a value to the current sample of a given token using $set(T_1, TYPE.STATE, STATE.UP)$.

Places and transitions in our HLPN have special properties. This is true for **P**, which has three types: *initial*, *regular*, and *final*. This allows the system to know where tokens will be placed when they are created (*initial*) and where the tokens will be located when they will be removed (*final*).

Table 1. Multi-Touch Data Structure

Name	Description
id	Unique Multi-Touch Identification
tid	Touch Entry Number
x	X display coordinate
y	Y display coordinate
state	Touch states (DOWN, MOVE, UP)
prev	Previous sample
get(Time t)	Get previous sample at time t
tSize	Size of sample buffer
holdTime	How many milliseconds have spawn since last rest
msg	String variable for messages

Picking the next transition or place for the case when there is one input and one output is trivial (the next **T** or **P** is the only available). However, when there are multiple inputs or outputs, picking the next one to check becomes important in Petri Net implementation[24]. Our "picking" algorithm is a modified version of the one by Mortensen [24]. Our algorithm combines the random nature found in other CPN[25] selection and the use of *priority functions*. Our algorithm sorts the neighboring **P** or **T** by ascending value, given by the priority function **R**, and groups them by equivalent values, (e.g., $G_1 = 10, 10, 10$, $G_2 = 1, 1$). The last **P** or **T** fired may be given a higher value if found within the highest group. Within each group, the next **P** or **T** is selected randomly.

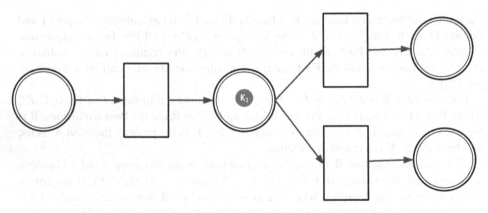

Fig. 1. Parallel PN: State 1

2.4 Tokens and the Structure

A powerful feature of Petri Nets is their discrete markings, called **Tokens**. This feature allows the marking of different states and the execution of the Petri Net. When tokens go through an input function **I** or output functions **O**, they are consumed. For our particular modeling, we use the token as the representation of a data structure, as shown in Table 1. Each token translates to a **trace**. Furthermore, this data structure contains the current sample and a buffer of previous samples(**touches**).

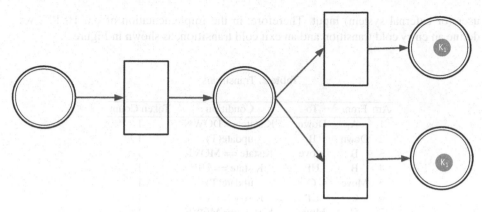

Fig. 2. Parallel PN: State 2

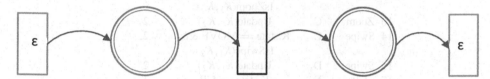

Fig. 3. Cold transitions (Entry and Exit)

When tokens are consumed into a transition, the **Post** condition creates a new token. If the desired effect is of a parallel system, as shown in Figure 1 , then a transition can create n number of tokens based on the original token. In Figure 2, token K_1 is cloned into two identical tokens, both called K_1. To represent the new tokens, different colors were choosen in Figures 1 and 2.

The only token data type for PeNTa in our HLPN is a multi-touch structure, type **K**, as shown in Table 1. The identification given by a system is denoted as **id**. Depending on the system, this may be a unique number while the process is running (integer long) or as a consecutive integer starting from $1 \dots m$, lasting the through the duration of the gesture performed by the user. The latter definition is also contained in the variable **tid**. Display coordinates are given by **x** and **y**. The **state** variable represents the current mode given by "DOWN", "MOVE", "UP". The **holdTime** helps to determine how many milliseconds have lapsed since the user has not moved from the current position. Our data structure assumes that a new sample only happens when the user has moved beyond a threshold. Finally, this data structure acts as a pointer to previous history touches in a buffer of size η. Therefore, the buffer (if it exists,) can be accessed with the function $get\,(Time\,\iota)$ or the previous sample with the variable **prev**.

In Petri Nets or HLPN, at least one initial Marking M_0 needs to be known, especially for analysis. In the case of simulations (which is discussed later), this is not a problem. However, for the case of real-time execution, which is our primary purpose, the initial marking is empty. Remember that the initial marking is the place of tokens in any of the given available places. This is solved by the concept of hot and cold transitions[26], represented by ε. A hot transition does not require user input. A cold transition requires user (or external system) input. Therefore, in the implementation of our HLPN, we define an entry cold transition and an exit cold transition, as shown in Figure 3.

Table 2. Transitions

Arc	From	To	Condition	Token Count
1	A	Down	K.state == DOWN	1
2	Down	B	update(T)	1
3	B	Move	K.state == MOVE	1
4	B	UP	K.state == UP	1
5	Move	C	update(T)	1
6	C	UP	K.state == UP	1
7	C	Move	K.state == MOVE	1
8	C	Move	update(T)	1
9	C	Zoom	K.state == MOVE && IsZoom(K_1, K_2)	2
10	Zoom	C	Update(K_1, K_2)	2
14	Swipe	C	K.state == MOVE && IsSwipe(K_1, K_2)	2
15	Swipe	D	Update(K_1, K_2)	2
17	UP	E	K.state == UP	1
18	UP	E	K.state == UP	1
19	E	Terminate	true	1

3 PeNTa: Modeling with Petri Nets

3.1 User Interface

It is important that our model is mathematically sound. However, it is also very important that it is easy to work with **PeNTa** and our HLPN. While there are great tools for Petri Nets (e.g., CPN Tools) and great frameworks for Domain-Specific Languages (DSL) (e.g., Microsoft Visual Studio DSL), we found that **PeNTa** required its own Graphical User Interface (GUI) to allow for design of input interaction, the ability for HLPN simulation and code-generation for execution. This is the reason that we decided to start developing with the Qt Framework, as well as using well-established Petri Net algorithms, such as [24]. The user interface will serve as a GUI for developers to test their input. While at this point, the model has being designed for multi-touch input, it is foreseeable that this can be expanded to other modern input types.

3.2 Language Choice

CPN uses ML general-purpose language, and it is a very popular HLPN. However, we decided to use a subset of the C++ language to define part of our PeNTa. In a recent information survey in the 3DUI mailing list, C++, C# and Java were the languages of choice in the field of 3D User Interfaces. In a formal survey, Takala et al.[27] said

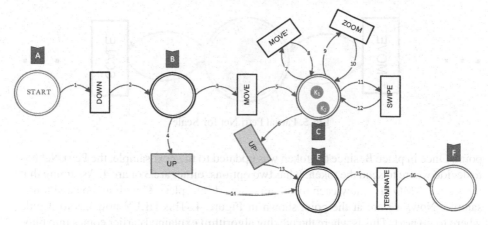

Fig. 4. Multiple Gestures in PeNTa

that the most common programming language was C++. Nevertheless, PeNTa could be implemented in any programming language. The user interface is under development at the time of this writing, and once ready, it will be uploaded into our modeling Web site[7].

3.3   A Tour of PeNTa

A tour of our model is needed to better explain how **PeNTa** works. We start with an example that deals with two gestures using a two-finger interaction: swipe and zoom. A swipe implies that the user moves two fingers in any direction. Therefore, the callback required is always the same, which is a function that reports the direction of the swipe. In the case of the zoom, zoom-in and zoom-out could be modeled separately or together. We chose the latter for our example, shown in Figure 4. This allows us to show how our model can handle gestures that require different call backs. For example, if the user is zooming-in, then it will call a zoom-in only function, otherwise, it will call a zoom-out function.

The example shown in Figure 4 is created for two-finger gestures. The figure has places, arcs, transitions and and two tokens (K_1, K_2), representing two active traces in place **C**. For this particular example, we have added letter labels to places, numbers to the arcs and names to the transitions; however, those are not part of a Petri Net. In addition, Table 2 shows each arc expression with their boolean condition and the tokens that are required to fired (e.g, two tokens). The system starts with a empty initial marking (no tokens), while it waits for the user input. Once the user touches down onto the surface, tokens are created (using the cold transitions) and placed in the START place. Given that the tokens will start with a "DOWN" state, they will move from place **A** into place **C**, using transitions 1 and 2. The first arc just consumes the token, and arc 2 updates the token with the next sample into place **B**. This is done one token a time, by design. The reason for this is that if it required two tokens, the system may starve at this

---

[7] openrml.com

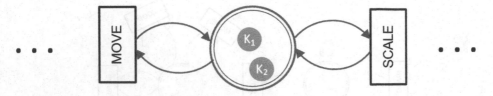

Fig. 5. Partial Petri Net for Scale

point. Once in place **B**, since the token was updated to the next sample, the Petri Net has to decide where to send the token. It has two options, either arc 3 or arc 4. Assuming that the state is "MOVE", now each token gets moved into place **C** with an updated touch sample. Now, we are at the point shown in Figure 4. This HLPN now has to decide where to go next. This is where the picking algorithm explained earlier comes into play. For this example, **MOVE´**, **ZOOM**, **SWIPE**, and **UP** have priority function values 1, 10, 10, and 2, respectively. This means the group with **ZOOM** and **SWIPE**, will be the first to be checked for constraints, since they have the highest values. The HLPN will randomly pick either one and check if it can be enabled (fired) based on the boolean condition. Assume, for example, that it picks **SWIPE** and the boolean condition is *true*. It will be *true* if two tokens are in place **C**, both tokens are in state "MOVE", and the function **isSwipe**, which is an external C++ method, are true. If this is true, then it will call back a swipe function, passing a copy of the token data, and then update to the next sample via arc 12. This finally brings back both tokens into place **C**. At some point, the tokens will have state "UP", and they will move to place **E** and place **F**. The reason for having two places for termination is to allow the designer to choose when to make the final termination. The final state will send two no-longer usable tokens into an **exit** cold transition (not shown in the figure), to be destroyed by the execution system.

While we presented in Figure 4 a single Petri Net that models various gestures, it is possible to create individual Petri Nets as shown in Figure 5, and combine them in a set of Petri Nets. For example, individual Petri Nets PN_i can form a model P = $(PN_1, PN_2, PN_3, ...PN_n)$, where once constructed, the model can be executed. Each PN_i can run in parallel and disabled itself when the condition is not met.

3.4 Simulation and Execution

Petri Nets could be used for analysis (e.g., Linear Temporal Logic), simulations and execution. We have concentrated **PeNTa** for simulation and execution, as we find it the most critical aspect needed for input devices. Nevertheless, analysis could be implemented into PeNTa.

There are different ways to simulate **PeNTa**. Non-user-generated data could be used for the simulation, providing an initial marking with a history of the possible samples. Another option it is to record the user interaction creating tokens and a buffer to feed those tokens. There are multiple ways to go about this, but we used MySQL to store the data. This is a very useful way to test new gestures, create custom gestures, and troubleshoot problems with an existing system.

Execution is the primary purpose of PeNTa. Given a well-defined model, this can run in real-time, using the definitions of our HLPN. As stated before, our HLPN would need additional **cold** transitions (entry and exit), since this is user-generated input.

4 Conclusion

We presented a novel modeling approach to multi-touch interaction, named **PeNTa**. This is given by our High-Level Petri Net, defined with input systems in mind. We also showed an example of a model. In the near future, we will complete the GUI tool to design, execute and simulate **PeNTa**. We will also look into the use of other input devices, as well as combining our HLPN model with multiple devices in one design.

Acknowledgements. This work was sponsored by NSF grants NSF-III-Large-MOD 800001483,HRD-0833093, CNS-0959985, CNS-0821345, and CNS-1126619. Francisco Ortega is a GAANN fellow (US Department of Education) and McKnight Dissertation Fellow (Florida Education Fund).

References

1. Buxton, W.: A three-state model of graphical input. In: Human-computer Interaction-INTERACT 1990, pp. 449–456 (1990)
2. English, W.K., Engelbart, D.C., Berman, M.L.: Display-Selection Techniques for Text Manipulation. IEEE Transactions on Human Factors in Electronics (1), 5–15 (1967)
3. Gray, W.D., John, B.E., Atwood, M.E.: Project Ernestine: Validating a GOMS analysis for predicting and explaining real-world task performance. Human–Computer Interaction 8(3), 237–309 (1993)
4. Pew, R.W., Baron, S.: Perspectives on human performance modelling. Automatica 19(6), 663–676 (1983)
5. Mackenzie, I.S.: Human-Computer Interaction. An Empirical Research Perspective. Newnes (December 2012)
6. Bowman, D.A., Kruijff, E., LaViola Jr., J.J., Poupyrev, I.: 3D user interfaces: theory and practice. Addison-Wesley Professional (2004)
7. Newman, W.M.: A system for interactive graphical programming, pp. 47–54 (1968)
8. Myers, B.A.: A new model for handling input. ACM Transactions on Information Systems (TOIS) 8(3), 289–320 (1990)
9. Kin, K., Hartmann, B., DeRose, T., Agrawala, M.: Proton++: a customizable declarative multitouch framework. In: UIST 2012: Proceedings of the 25th Annual ACM Symposium on User Interface Software and Technology, ACM Request Permissions (October 2012)
10. Lao, S., Heng, X., Zhang, G., Ling, Y., Wang, P.: A gestural interaction design model for multi-touch displays, pp. 440–446 (2009)
11. Kammer, D., Wojdziak, J., Keck, M., Groh, R., Taranko, S.: Towards a formalization of multi-touch gestures. In: ITS 2010: International Conference on Interactive Tabletops and Surfaces, ACM Request Permissions (November 2010)
12. Lü, H., Li, Y.: Gesture coder: a tool for programming multi-touch gestures by demonstration, pp. 2875–2884 (2012)
13. Scholliers, C., Hoste, L., Signer, B., De Meuter, W.: Midas: a declarative multi-touch interaction framework, pp. 49–56 (2011)

14. Nam, Y., Wohn, N., Lee-Kwang, H.: Modeling and recognition of hand gesture using colored Petri nets. IEEE Transactions on Systems, Man and Cybernetics, Part A: Systems and Humans 29(5), 514–521 (1999)
15. Hamon, A., Palanque, P., Silva, J.L., Deleris, Y., Barboni, E.: Formal description of multitouch interactions. In: EICS 2013: Proceedings of the 5th ACM SIGCHI Symposium on Engineering Interactive Computing Systems, ACM Request Permissions, New York, USA, pp. 207–216 (June 2013)
16. Spano, L.D., Cisternino, A., Paternò, F.: A compositional model for gesture definition. In: Winckler, M., Forbrig, P., Bernhaupt, R. (eds.) HCSE 2012. LNCS, vol. 7623, pp. 34–52. Springer, Heidelberg (2012)
17. Spano, L.D., Cisternino, A., Paternò, F., Fenu, G.: GestIT: a declarative and compositional framework for multiplatform gesture definition. In: EICS 2013: Proceedings of the 5th ACM SIGCHI Symposium on Engineering Interactive Computing Systems, ACM Request Permissions, New York, USA, pp. 187–196 (June 2013)
18. David, R., Alla, H.: Discrete, Continuous, and Hybrid Petri Nets. Springer (November 2010)
19. Ortega, F.R., Hernandez, F., Barreto, A., Rishe, N.D., Adjouadi, M., Liu, S.: Exploring modeling language for multi-touch systems using petri nets. In: ITS 2013: Proceedings of the 2013 ACM International Conference on Interactive Tabletops and Surfaces. ACM (October 2013)
20. High-level Petri Nets-Concepts: Definitions and graphical notation. Final Draft International Standard ISO/IEC 15909 (2000)
21. Genrich, H.J., Lautenbach, K.: System modelling with high-level Petri nets. Theoretical Computer Science 13(1), 109–135 (1981)
22. Liu, S., Zeng, R., He, X.: PIPE-A Modeling Tool for High Level Petri Nets (2011)
23. Peterson, J.L.: Petri net theory and the modeling of systems. Prentice Hall (1981)
24. Mortensen, K.H.: Efficient data-structures and algorithms for a coloured petri nets simulator, pp. 57–74 (2001)
25. Jensen, K., Kristensen, L.: Coloured Petri Nets. Basic Concepts, Analysis Methods and Practical Use. Springer (1996)
26. Reisig, W.: Petri Nets. An Introduction. Springer (July 2012)
27. Takala, T.M., Rauhamaa, P., Takala, T.: Survey of 3DUI applications and development challenges, pp. 89–96 (2012)

An Iterative and Incremental Process
for Interaction Design
through Automated GUI Generation

David Raneburger, Roman Popp, Hermann Kaindl,
Alexander Armbruster, and Vedran Šajatović

Institute of Computer Technology, Vienna University of Technology
Gusshausstrasse 27-29, 1040 Vienna, Austria
{raneburger,popp,kaindl,armbruster,sajatovic}@ict.tuwien.ac.at

Abstract. Model-driven generation of graphical user interfaces (GUIs) for multiple devices requires a model representing an interaction design. High-quality interaction models are a prerequisite for achieving a good level of usability for the corresponding applications. Our tool-supported process facilitates the exploration and evaluation of interaction design alternatives in an iterative and incremental manner, using automated GUI generation to achieve a running application more quickly and with reduced effort in comparison to manual (prototype) development. This allows the designer to quickly find a suitable alternative and to build more complex applications incrementally.

Keywords: Interaction design, automated GUI generation, iterative and incremental process.

1 Introduction

According to Preece et al. [1], creating an interaction design typically involves designing alternatives, prototyping and evaluating, and these activities are to be repeated for informing each other. We recently presented an iterative process for facilitating interaction design through automated GUI generation in [2]. While Preece et al. have strong emphasis on iterations, they do not even mention incremental development, which is widely used in software development, however (see, e.g., [3]).

Our objective in the current paper is to facilitate interaction design in a defined iterative and incremental process, utilizing automated GUI generation tool-support for fast, inexpensive, and still high-fidelity prototyping. So, we present a defined process for this kind of development based on automated GUI generation, and experience from its application during the interaction design of a larger trial application. This process is iterative and incremental and, in principle, facilitates both improvements and extensions to the interaction design in each iteration. It starts with the creation of an initial design using certain heuristics. This initial interaction design is *not* supposed to be complete in our proposed

M. Kurosu (Ed.): Human-Computer Interaction, Part I, HCII 2014, LNCS 8510, pp. 373–384, 2014.
© Springer International Publishing Switzerland 2014

process in the sense of covering all the interaction possibilities yet. Especially for relatively large applications, providing an already complete initial model of the interaction design is too difficult. So, like in usual approaches to software development in general, it is preferable to start with an essential part first, to get cyclic feed-back to the current version, to adapt accordingly, and to add an increment in a defined iteration.

The remainder of this paper is organized in the following manner. First, we relate this new process to existing work and provide some background material in order to make our paper self-contained. Then we present this tool-supported process for iterative and incremental interaction design in detail. After that, we describe an informal evaluation in the course of developing a trial application. Finally, we discuss our approach more generally and conclude.

2   Related Work and Background

A thorough discussion of related work on academic and industrial state-of-the-art design-time GUI generation approaches can already be found in [2]. So, we restrict our discussion on major work on life-cycle models for iterative and incremental development. Subsequently, we provide background information on the design-time GUI generation approach that we used to evaluate our new process, the Unified Communication Platform.[1]

2.1   Related Work

Software development has generally changed from a 'waterfall' approach to an iterative and incremental development (IID) approach. The basic approach is much older than usually acknowledged, see, e.g., [4]. However, IID became much more wide-spread in use with the Rational Unified Process (RUP) [5], or 'agile' approaches such as Extreme Programming, see, e.g., [6], where the most popular one today is *Scrum* [7].

Recently, more and more literature suggests to use some kind of iterative and incremental process also for the development of general systems. In particular, RUP has been extended for the engineering of general "large-scale systems composed of software, hardware, workers and information components" [8], and is supported in a process management platform as a plug-in. One of the authors of the current paper proposed a life-cycle model for iterative and incremental systems engineering in [9].

2.2   Background on the Unified Communication Platform

The Unified Communication Platform (UCP) uses a Discourse-based Communication Model [10] to model the communicative interaction between two parties, which can be assigned to the Tasks & Concepts Level of the CRF [11]. In the

---

[1] http://ucp.ict.tuwien.ac.at/

context of UI Generation, one communication party is the human user interacting with the application via a UI. A Discourse-based Communication Model specifies interaction based on discourses in the sense of dialogues. It consists of a Discourse Model, which models all the possible dialogues, a so-called Domain-of-Discourse (DoD) Model, which models the concepts that can be exchanged between the user and the application, and an Action-Notification Model (ANM), which models Actions and Notifications that can be performed by one of the communicating parties (either the user or the application). UCP already provides a so-called 'basic ANM' that specifies basic Actions like get, set, or selecting, and basic Notifications like presenting.

The basic interaction units in such Discourse Models are so-called Adjacency Pairs, like question–answer or offer–accept/reject. Each such Adjacency Pair consists of one or two Communicative Acts (e.g., a question and an answer). These units are connected via so-called Discourse Relations, such as *Alternative*, *Title*, *Switch* or *IfUntil*, in a hierarchical way. An *Alternative* relation specifies that the connected sub-branches can, in principle, be executed concurrently, but that only one sub-branch can be finished, in contrast to a *Switch* relation, where each sub-branch specifies a condition and only one sub-branch can be executed (which sub-branch is executed is determined through evaluating the corresponding condition). A more complex relation is *IfUntil*, which is a combination of a loop with a condition. A specified sub-branch is repeated until a condition is fulfilled. After the condition is fulfilled, another sub-branch is executed. All three relations are assigned to one of the interacting parties, which evaluates the corresponding conditions. A *Title* relation, in contrast, specifies that its Nucleus and its Satellite branch can be executed concurrently without any conditions, and does not depend on a specific interaction party. For more details see [10].

UCP supports modeling such Discourse-based Communication Models with a dedicated editor [12]. Most importantly, UCP can fully-automatically generate GUIs from such models [13]. UCP also provides a message-based run-time environment [13], which allows deploying the generated GUIs and application back-ends. This run-time environment uses the Communicative Acts as messages and provides a generic function-based interface for the back-end integration. The functions are implicitly defined in the Discourse-based Communication Model through the *propositional content* of the Communicative Acts and the interface can be generated automatically. UCP uses a run-time architecture that is based on the Model-View-Controller pattern [14], but does not impose any constraints on the technology to be used to implement the functionality.

3   Our Tool-supported Process for Iterative and Incremental Interaction Design

Larger and more complex applications typically involve more complex interaction. Such applications are typically developed in an iterative and incremental manner. Therefore, we extended our process for iterative interaction design presented in [2] to support incremental development as well. Figure 1 shows

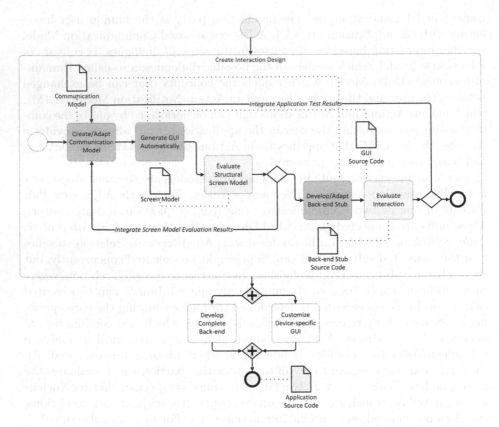

Fig. 1. Our Tool-supported Process for Iterative and Incremental Interaction Design Embedded in our Communication Model-based Application Development Process

our extended Communication Model-based application development process in BPMN.[2] Analogously to our iterative development process, it includes and starts with the tool-supported process named *Create Interaction Design*. Once a stable interaction design is available, the activities *Develop Complete Back-end* and *Customize Device-specific GUI* can again be performed concurrently. These activities focus on GUI customization and manual back-end development and are out of the scope for this paper.

In Figure 1, all activities shown in orange (dark) result in new or customized artifacts, while all activities shown in yellow (light) are evaluation activities. Our iterative and incremental process *Create Interaction Design* starts with the *Create/Adapt Communication Model* activity. This activity creates the initial **Communication Model** and adapts it in subsequent iterations. Such adaptations can either be modifications due to the results of an evaluation activity, or incremental extensions, or both. Incremental extensions of the interaction design

---

[2] http://www.omg.org/spec/BPMN/2.0

may concern any of the three models that constitute the Communication Model (i.e., the Domain-of-Discourse, the Action-Notification or the Discourse Model).

Once a `Communication Model` is available, it can be transformed in the activity *Generate GUI Automatically* to a `Screen Model` and the `GUI Source Code` fully automatically using UCP. The Structural Screen Model can be used for a first evaluation in the *Evaluate Structural Screen Model* activity. These evaluation results can be immediately used to customize the `Communication Model` by following the path labeled *Integrate Screen Model Evaluation Results* in Figure 1. This allows iterating on design alternatives in micro-iterations, much as in our previous purely iterative process [2].

Once the results from the evaluation of the screen model are satisfactory, our process continues with the *Develop/Adapt Back-end Stub* activity. Developing a back-end stub is the same activity as in our purely iterative process and means its initial creation. Adapting the back-end stub can be modifications due to the results of an evaluation activity, or incremental extensions, or both. Incremental extensions implement the new functionality introduced through an extension of the Communication Model. This activity results in a prototypical application back-end stub, as required to achieve a running application prototype. It can be used in the *Evaluate Interaction* activity, where the focus is on its external behavior in the course of interacting with a user. The results of this evaluation can be used to customize the `Communication Model`. In effect, this allows iterating on design alternatives in macro-iterations.

Overall, this process is similar to the iterative design process presented in [2], but additionally includes incremental extensions of various artifacts. To make this paper self-contained, we include as short description of the *Generate GUI Automatically*, the *Evaluate Structural Screen Model* and the *Evaluate Interaction* activities here, based on [2].

The *Generate GUI Automatically* activity is essentially a machine task performed fully-automatically by UCP as presented in [13]. It generates the `Screen Model` (as an intermediate result) and the `GUI Source Code`. The Screen Model specifies the GUI's behavior through a Behavioral Screen Model and the GUI's structure through the Structural Screen Model. The Structural Screen Model is a screen-based graphical representation on Concrete UI Level [11] comparable to GUI mock-ups.

The *Evaluate Structural Screen Model* activity evaluates the screens of the Structural Screen Model. It allows identifying missing interaction elements and thus shortcomings of the interaction model through comparing the generated GUI model to the functional requirements (e.g., given through use cases) that the resulting application needs to satisfy. Importantly, this is feasible even without the availability of an application back-end (prototype or final). Therefore, it allows for micro-iterations in our process. UCP provides a dedicated graphical editor for the Structural Screen Model, which supports this evaluation activity through visualization of the generated screens.

The *Evaluate Interaction* activity uses the running application prototype to evaluate the interaction. This may be done informally by the developer, again through comparing the interaction to the functional requirements for the application, but is typically achieved through *heuristic evaluation* performed by usability experts, or possibly even through *usability tests*, but always with a focus on the interaction rather than the GUI screens per se. Only problems or violations of heuristics concerning the external behavior are relevant, because layout and style are not reflected in the interaction design.

4   Evaluation Using Vacation Planning

We built a vacation planning application according to our process, in effect evaluating it. In particular, we use this trial application in this paper to illustrate all activities of our process and present how we developed the corresponding interaction design incrementally in several micro- and macro-iteration, using UCP tool support.

Our vacation planning application is based on a commercial accommodation booking Web-site of an Austrian province and implements a subset of this Website's functionality. In particular, our application supports searching for an accommodation either through text search or through more specific search masks. In addition, it provides information on events, articles that report on different topics, and information on how to get to this Austrian province. Finally, it allows a user to send a booking request to a specific accommodation or to book an accommodation directly. Below we use excerpts of the corresponding Communication Model to illustrate the enactment of our new process.

4.1   Initial Iteration

The basis for our interaction development was a set of tasks that should be supported through the vacation planning application to build, and an existing commercial Web-site that supported them. Such tasks were, for example, get information on events, book a specific accommodation or find out how to get there. These tasks were already supported by the commercial Web-site, and we basically re-engineered its interaction. Our aim was to allow for a comparative usability evaluation of our application through a user study in the end. This user study is, however, out of scope for this paper.

The interaction required to support the tasks could be triggered on the commercial Web-site through links labeled *Home*, *Search Accomodation*, *Plan Vacation*, *Get There* and *Events*. The Web-site allowed for switching between these categories at any time, which decouples the interaction attached to each category and facilitates incremental development of the interaction model.

The *Home* link, for example, led to the start-page that displayed a welcome message and presented a list of events and a list of articles. Selecting a specific event or article led to a Web-page with more detailed information on the selected event/article.

When developing our interaction design, we started with modeling these alternative selections and the interaction provided by the start-page. Figure 2

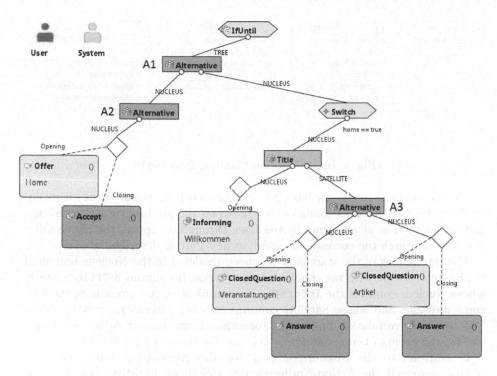

Fig. 2. Excerpt of Initial Vacation Planning Discourse Model

shows an excerpt of the corresponding Discourse Model. This model has German content descriptions for the Communicative Acts, because the language of the application was German and these descriptions are used as default labels by our GUI generation framework. We will use English translations in this paper, providing the original German words in italics next to the translation.

The interacting parties in our Communication Model are a User (green/dark fill-color) and the System (yellow/light fill-color), depicted in the upper left corner of Figure 2. The top-level `IfUntil` relation is assigned to the System (indicated through its yellow/light fill-color) and specifies a so-called `Tree` branch without a condition only and no `Then` or `Else` branch. This models an endless loop used for restarting the application (i.e., to display the home screen again) after the interaction has been finished.

The Alternative relation labeled A1 has been assigned to the User, which means that the User can alternatively perform any interaction specified in its `Nucleus` branches. Its left Nucleus contains another Alternative relation (A2), which we used to model the selection between the five links that should be available at any time for the user during the run-time of the application. We built our interaction model incrementally starting with the Home link, which is modeled through the `Offer-Accept` Adjacency Pair. The corresponding interaction is modeled in the second Nucleus branch of Alternative A1. This nucleus contains a `Switch` relation that has been assigned to the System. This means that the

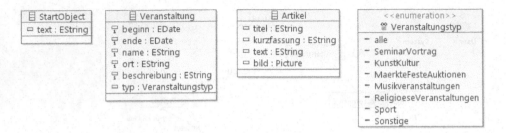

Fig. 3. Initial Vacation Planning DoD Model

condition assigned to the Switch's Nucleus branch (i.e., `home==true`) is evaluated by the System. This condition is true when the application is started and can be set to true at any time by the User through accepting the Home Offer (modeled through the corresponding Adjacency Pair as described above).

The interaction of the start-page has been modeled in the Nucleus branch of the Switch relation with the condition `home==true`. It contains a `Title` relation, whose Nucleus contains the `Informing` Communicative Act presenting the welcome message, and whose Satellite contains another Alternative relation (A3). This Alternative relation links two `ClosedQuestion-Answer` Adjacency Pairs, one for the events (*Veranstaltungen*) and one for the articles (*Artikel*).

In addition to the Discourse Model, we also created the initial Domain-of-Discourse and the Action-Notification Model in an iterative way. The initial Domain-of-Discourse Model is shown in Figure 3. It defines the classes `StartObject`, `Event` (*Veranstaltung*) and `Article` (*Artikel*) with their respective Attributes. Moreover, it defines `EventType` (*Veranstaltungstyp*) enumeration, which is used by the `type` (*typ*) attribute of the event class.

The initial ANM model contained a `home` Action only, as the remaining actions used in our initial Communication Model were already specified in the basic ANM model. Both, the concepts specified in the DoD Model and in the ANM were referenced through the propositional content of the Communicative Acts in our Communication Model.

After having created these three models, we generated the corresponding GUI, evaluated the Screen Model and implemented the back-end stub. Then we iteratively refined the interaction.

4.2   Generated GUIs and Incremental Extensions

The generated GUI of the start-page of our application is shown in Figure 4 on a smartphone device. Our generation framework split the Alternative relation A1, rendering it as a tabbed pane, to avoid horizontal scrolling, and to keep the vertical scroll-limit of five times the screen length (as defined through the smartphone platform model). Figure 4(a) shows the GUI for the Home branch of the Switch relation (as sketched in Figure 2).

We modeled the interaction following the selection of a specific event or article on the start-page in our first incremental iteration. This interaction intuitively

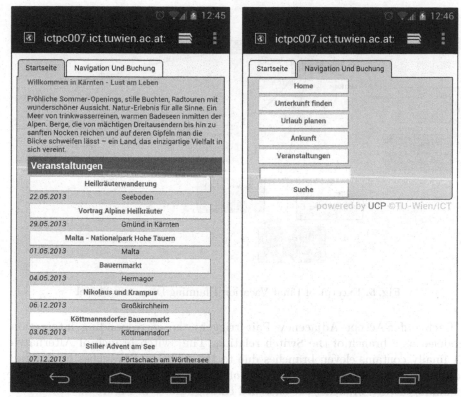

(a) Vacation Planning Smartphone Home (b) Vacation Planning Smartphone Menu
Screen.   Screen.

Fig. 4. Vacation Planning GUI Displayed on a Samsung Galaxy Nexus Device

belongs to the home Sub-Discourse presented above, but we modeled it in a new branch of the Switch relation instead, as it should be reachable from different points of the final interaction model, and subsequently again evaluated and refined this new branch iteratively. Another example for interaction that should be reachable from different points is the payment interaction that finalizes the booking process for a specific accommodation, which we added in another incremental iteration. In general, we modeled all interactions that should be reachable from different points in the interaction model as sub-branches of the Switch relation, extending the existing interaction model and developing the final interaction model in increments.

Figure 5 illustrates the structure of the final Discourse Model. This model offers six options in the navigation (i.e., Alternative) branch of Alternative relation A1. Five of these options were Offer-Accept Adjacency Pairs, which are sketched in Figure 5 through the Home and the Events (*Veranstaltungen*) Adjacency Pairs with dots in between. The sixth branch contains the text search (*VeranstaltungenSuche*), modeled as OpenQuestion-Answer Adjacency Pair.

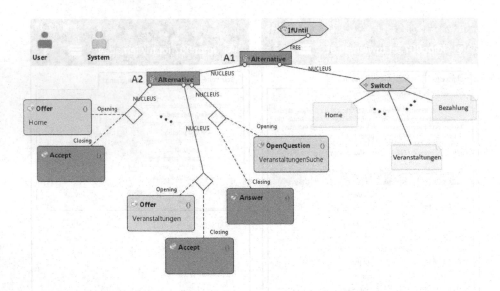

Fig. 5. Excerpt of Final Vacation Planning Discourse Model

Each Offer-Accept Adjacency Pair triggers the corresponding interaction, modeled as a branch of the Switch relation. The Switch branch of Alternative A1 finally contains eleven branches due to the additional branches for interaction that was reachable from different points of the final interaction model. The remaining Switch branches are sketched through notes in Figure 5.

The five branches corresponding to the Offer-Accept Adjacency Pairs are sketched through the Home and the Events (*Veranstaltungen*) notes with dots in between. The remaining six branches, that model interaction that is reachable from different points in the final interaction model, are sketched through the dots between the Events (*Veranstaltungen*) and the Payment (*Bezahlung*) notes. Such interaction is the display of text search results, which typically contains a list of accommodations, events and articles. All items in these three lists can be selected to provide further details, which triggers the interaction in the corresponding branch of the Switch relation. We provided three branches for this interaction, one for Accommodation details, which also allowed for booking a specific accommodation, one for Event and one for Article details. The remaining two branches model the interaction for getting information on how to get there by a specific means of transport (i.e., plane, train or car) and the interaction required for completing the booking process for a specific accommodation through payment.

Overall, we performed 11 incremental iterations while developing the Communication Model. After each increment, we evaluated and refined the Communication Model iteratively. Extending and refining the Discourse Model also included extensions and modifications of the DoD Model and the ANM. The final DoD Model specifies 18 classes and 8 enumerations, and the final ANM specifies 11 Actions and 2 Notifications.

Figure 4(b) shows the GUI for the final Alternative branch A2, as sketched in Figure 5. The complete GUIs of our vacation planning application are accessible in the Web for Smartphone[3] and Desktop[4].

5   Discussion

As an empirical evaluation, we presented the application of our iterative and incremental interaction development process during the development of a more complex vacation planning application. We found, however, that even a high-quality interaction model requires further GUI customization to achieve a good level of usability and the desired "look & feel". We will, therefore, extend our iterative and incremental process to support GUI customization as well, concurrently to interaction design. This will facilitate the evaluation of the interaction design through heuristic evaluations and user studies, and become a synthesis of the approach in the current paper and our previous approach to perfect-fidelity prototyping [15].

6   Conclusion

In this paper, we present a new iterative and incremental process for creating a (high-level) interaction design in the context of model-driven generation of GUIs, and its enactment in the course of a trial application. For such an automated generation, a (good) interaction design (represented as a corresponding model) is a prerequisite. We show, that such generation can actually be utilized for the creation of an improved interaction design. This defined and concrete process is consistent with the usual approach to interaction design in general. It involves designing alternatives, prototyping and evaluating, and how these activities are to be repeated for informing each other. In terms of process execution, it adopts from software development, where the artifact (here an interaction design) grows incrementally, iteration by iteration.

The significance of this work is that GUIs for multiple devices are typically derived from the same interaction model, which in case of UCP also specifies the interface between GUI and application back-end. Achieving a stable interaction model allows developing the GUIs and the back-end concurrently, which (potentially) shortens the development time of the overall application.

Acknowledgment. Part of this research has been carried out in the GENUINE project (No. 830831) funded by the Austrian FFG.

---

[3] http://ucp.ict.tuwien.ac.at/UI/accomodationBookingSmartphone
[4] http://ucp.ict.tuwien.ac.at/UI/accomodationBookingDesktop

References

1. Preece, J., Rogers, Y., Sharp, H.: Interaction design: beyond human-computer interaction, 3rd edn. John Wiley & Sons (2011)
2. Raneburger, D., Kaindl, H., Popp, R., Šajatović, V., Armbruster, A.: A process for facilitating interaction design through automated GUI generation. In: Proceedings of the 29th Annual ACM Symposium on Applied Computing (2014)
3. Larman, C.: Applying UML and Patterns, 3rd edn. Prentice Hall (2005)
4. Larman, C., Basili, V.: Iterative and incremental development: a brief history. Computer 36(6), 47–56 (2003)
5. Jacobson, I., Booch, G., Rumbaugh, J.: The unified software development process. Addison-Wesley Longman Publishing Co., Inc., Boston (1999)
6. Beck, K., Andres, C.: Extreme Programming Explained: Embrace Change, 2nd edn. Addison-Wesley (2004)
7. Deemer, P., Benefield, G., Larman, C., Vodde, B.: The Scrum primer, Version 1.2 (2010)
8. Cantor, M.: Rational unified process for systems engineering. Rational Edge, IBM (August 2003)
9. Kaindl, H., Falb, J., Arnautovic, E., Ertl, D.: Increments in an Iterative Systems Engineering Life Cycle. In: Proceedings of the 7th European Systems Engineering Conference (EuSEC 2010), Stockholm, Sweden (April 2010)
10. Popp, R., Raneburger, D.: A High-Level Agent Interaction Protocol Based on a Communication Ontology. In: Huemer, C., Setzer, T., Aalst, W., Mylopoulos, J., Sadeh, N.M., Shaw, M.J., Szyperski, C. (eds.) E-Commerce and Web Technologies. LNBIP, vol. 85, pp. 233–245. Springer, Heidelberg (2011)
11. Calvary, G., Coutaz, J., Thevenin, D., Limbourg, Q., Bouillon, L., Vanderdonckt, J.: A unifying reference framework for multi-target user interfaces. Interacting with Computers 15(3), 289–308 (2003)
12. Falb, J., Kavaldjian, S., Popp, R., Raneburger, D., Arnautovic, E., Kaindl, H.: Fully automatic user interface generation from discourse models. In: Proceedings of the 13th International Conference on Intelligent User Interfaces (IUI 2009), pp. 475–476. ACM Press, New York (2009)
13. Popp, R., Raneburger, D., Kaindl, H.: Tool support for automated multi-device GUI generation from discourse-based communication models. In: Proceedings of the 5th ACM SIGCHI Symposium on Engineering Interactive Computing Systems, EICS 2013. ACM, New York (2013)
14. Popp, R., Kaindl, H., Raneburger, D.: Connecting interaction models and application logic for model-driven generation of Web-based graphical user interfaces. In: Proceedings of the 20th Asia-Pacific Software Engineering Conference, APSEC 2013 (2013)
15. Falb, J., Popp, R., Röck, T., Jelinek, H., Arnautovic, E., Kaindl, H.: UI prototyping for multiple devices through specifying interaction design. In: Baranauskas, C., Abascal, J., Barbosa, S.D.J. (eds.) INTERACT 2007. LNCS, vol. 4662, pp. 136–149. Springer, Heidelberg (2007)

Adaptive and Personalized Interfaces

A Model and Guidelines for the Interface Design Process for Adaptive Web Applications (IDPAWA)

Claudia Regina Batista[1], Vania Ribas Ulbricht[1], and Adhemar Maria do Valle Filho[2]

[1] Federal University of Santa Catarina, Department of Graphic Expression, Trindade,
88040-900 Florianópolis – Santa Catarina, Brazil
claudia.batista@ufsc.br, vulbricht@gmail.com
[2] University of Vale do Itajaí, Computer Science, Itajaí – Santa Catarina, Brazil
adhe.valle@gmail.com

Abstract. This paper shows a model and guidelines for the Interface Design Process for Adaptive Web Applications (IDPAWA) proposed to guide and aid the designer on taking decisions during the interfaces development. The model schematically describes five steps of an interactive process: analysis, concept, development, prototype and test. In order to support the model, eight guidelines were developed to deal with the requirements and configuration of adaptive techniques.

Keywords: Design Process, User Interface, Visual Design, Adaptive Web Applications.

1 Introduction

The World Wide Web, or simply Web, became a powerful electronic vehicle of global proportions. The interaction, the non-linearity, the freedom of navigating thru a wide informational space and the media plurality made Web attractive and engaging. However, there is still a long way to be pursued regarding usability.

Problems related to users disorientation and cognitive overload resulted on the growth of interest on researches that present solutions for a better working when it comes to users' variety. One alternative that promotes a better assistance to the heterogeneity of profiles and users is the Adaptive Hypermedia. According to Brusilovsky (2007): "Adaptive hypermedia systems (AHS) offer an alternative to the traditional 'one-size-fits-all' hypermedia and Web systems by adapting to the goals, interests, and knowledge of individual users as they are represented in the individual user models" [3]. These environments potentiate an approach focused on the user, since the system adapts the visible aspects according to the 'user model' (build based on the user's information) creating an interface that offers appropriated information, with the right layout for each user [10].

On the other hand, it is noticeable that the design and development of Web applications and services that meet the needs and requirements of as many diverse users as possible is still a difficult and demanding task [10].

M. Kurosu (Ed.): Human-Computer Interaction, Part I, HCII 2014, LNCS 8510, pp. 387–398, 2014.
© Springer International Publishing Switzerland 2014

2   A Contribution to Interface Design Process for Adaptive Web Applications (IDPAWA)

2.1   Research Problem

The design and implementation of adaptive hypermedia systems or Adaptive Web Applications represents a time-consuming and difficult job, which make them complex and expensive systems [10].

There are support tools to interface design such as ISO standards [7] [8] [9] and others described on the literature [1] [5] [11] [13] [14] [15] that establishes rules, principles, guidelines, criteria, recommendations, methods and are useful to assist the designers by contemplating from the conception to the evaluation of interfaces along with the user. However, these support tools to interface design were not conceived under the perspective of Adaptive Hypermedia, therefore they don't present guidance on the specificities of these systems (as example, the requirements for application of content, navigation and presentation adaptation techniques) [2].

According to the presented context, it is observed the lack of support to Interface Design Process for Adaptive Web Applications. The incipient orientations to interface design induce the designers to adjust the generic orientations to their needs and adopt inappropriate developing processes, which might result in interfaces without usability, with communication failures, compromised interaction, inappropriate layout and others. "If" poorly projected, the interface impairs the functionality and endangers the quality of web adaptive applications [2].

The lack and/or incipience of orientations to the interface design to Adaptive Web Applications constitute a lacuna of knowledge in this area. Therefore, it is proposed a research which objectives are presented on the following lines.

2.2   Objective and Methods

The main objective of research was the development of a model and guidelines to Interface Design Process for Adaptive Web Applications (IDPAWA) in order to guide and support the web interface designer on taking decisions during design process.

This applied research approached the problem in a qualitative way and adopted the technic procedures of bibliographic research and study of case. The research was accomplished in four phases: survey, analysis, proposition and validation.

- In the survey phase, it was performed a bibliographic research and with the collected data it was possible to consolidate the theoretical foundation and establish the "state of art" in Adaptive Web Applications.

- In the analysis phase, the collected data on the bibliographic research was analysed and by that way it was possible to define the interfaces' properties to Adaptive Web Applications, as well as identify the designer's specific tasks during the development of an adaptive website.

- In the proposition phase, the qualitative research was accomplished by crossing the information that was collected on the bibliographic research and by an inductive analysis of data related to the properties and requirements of Adaptive Web

Applications where it was possible to outline a task flow to be accomplished by the designer during the IDPAWA. Initially it was proposed a model that schematically describes a structure of concepts and steps, in order to guide the designer during the IDPAWA. The guidelines were established as a set of instructions with the objective of supporting the proposed model and guide the designers thru the configuration of adaptive techniques and interface requirements.

* In the validation phase, the Model and Guidelines to IDPAWA were available to designers that composed the sample to be validated during the interface development to the adaptive website. The population research was composed of web interface designers. The sample was determined by the inclusion and exclusion criteria. As inclusion criteria, were defined: act professionally as a web interface designer; and agree with being a volunteer on the project. Analogously, the exclusion criteria were: having experience for less than two years on developing web interfaces.

2.3   Results

The interface characteristics, the task flow of the interface designer, the proposal for a model of design process and guidelines constitute the research results and are presented below.

The Identification of Interface Characteristics for Adaptive Web Applications.
The essential characteristics that define an interface to Adaptive Web Applications are presented on the concept board[1] (figure 1).

The elements presented on the concept board are described next:

* TRANSFORMABLE: the Interface for Adaptive Web Applications transforms itself. In other words, it changes itself in order to fit preferences, needs and users' characteristics. The adaption methods and techniques allow the necessary transformations.
* ASSEMBLE and DISASSEMBLE: the Interface for Adaptive Web Applications must be a dynamic interface. It is possible to make an analogy with the LEGO™ toy: "with the same pieces" it is possible to assemble different solutions; and with the same content (stored in the database) it is possible to assemble dynamically different ways for interaction and presentation of information. The fact that the content is separated from presentation/formatting is also significant, which provides better accessibility.
* FLEXIBLE: the Interface for Adaptive Web Applications must reflect the system's flexibility, providing ways of action for the user in order to take command (he can skip the system's recommendations and redefine his own way of information visualization if he so desires). There also must be flexibility to resize it in different screens and resolutions.

---

[1] On a *concept board* it is visually and/or verbally presented an idea for a product or service; usually described its' attributes or benefits.

- SPEEDY: the Interface for Adaptive Web Applications must load instantly. The interfaces with valid code, accessible code, semantically correct code (Web Standards) are going be rapidly interpreted by browsers.
- LIGHT: the Interface for Adaptive Web Applications must be composed by light image, videos and audio files, in order to provide speed when loading it.

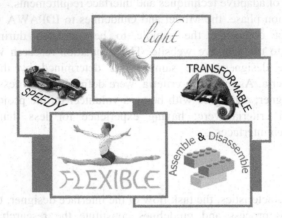

Fig. 1. Interface Concept Board for Web Applications (Source: Batista, 2008, p. 64)

Interface Designer's Task Flow to Adaptive Web Applications. During the development of an Adaptive Web Application, the interface designer works along with the multidisciplinary developing team. The interface designer must analyse the software artefacts (domain, navigation and adaption models) produced by other team members, in order to extract the requirements to the interface project.

From the investigation and data analysis concerning the developing process of Adaptive Web Hypermedia Systems and Adaptive Applications, from the developed activities by the multidisciplinary team and the characteristics of Interface for Web Applications, it was possible to outline a task flow to be accomplished by the designer during the IDPAWA.

The task flow presented on Figure 2 was the fist step to develop the Model for IDPAWA, since it was necessary to understand which activities are involved with the interface design for Adaptive Web Applications, in order to visualize the complete developing process.

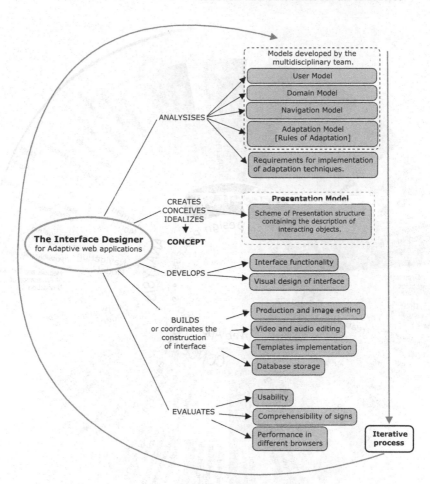

Fig. 2. Interface designer's task flow during the IDPAWA (Source: Batista, 2008, p. 66)

Process Model of Interface Design for Adaptive Web Applications. Considering that the interface developing process is not a top-down activity, a model that describes an iterative sequence of steps was proposed, in order to guide the designer during the process of Interface Design for Adaptive Web Applications (IDPAWA). The model presented on Figure 3 allows the designer to obtain a global vision of the design process and accomplished a structured, systematic and organized job. The analysis initiates the sequence; when coursing the clockwise direction, the transition for the following steps is made: concept, development, prototype and test.

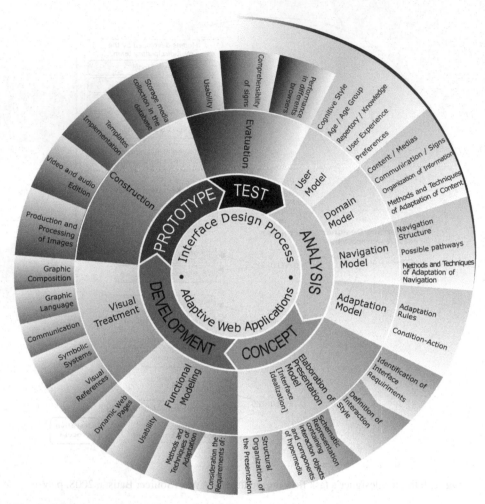

Fig. 3. Model of Interface Design Process for Adaptive Web Applications (Source: Batista, 2008, p. 67)

Next it is made a description of steps from the Interface Design Process for Adaptive Web Applications:

- ANALYSIS step: While on the development of non-adaptive systems the designer starts the process by the data collection step, on IDPAWA he will begin his activity analysing the models made by the multidisciplinary team involved on the Adaptive Web Application project. It means that the multidisciplinary team has already accomplished the data collection step to build the user's models, of domain, navigation and adaption. They have also already defined the methods and adaption techniques that will be utilized.

Then, the designer's task is to understand how the system will operate, the context of use and the adaption techniques requirements, in order to establish goals and objectives of interface to the Adaptive Web Application.

- CONCEPT step: After understanding how the Adaptive Web Application will be, the designer is going to list the interface requirements, define the interaction style; in other words, will idealize the interface. After it is done, the designer will schematically represent it by describing the location of interaction objects, hypermedia elements and the structural organization of presentation. This schematic representation is the Presentation Model.

- DEVELOPMENT step: After building the Presentation Model, the design will develop the interface. He will make the functional modeling, where is necessary to generate interface elements in order to attend the requirements of methods and adaption techniques, of usability and dynamic web pages. To accomplish the visual treatment (create interface layout) the designer must search visual references in agreement with the user model, generate symbolic and communicational systems, identify the graphic language pertinent to the user model and define the graphic composition of the interface.

- PROTOTYPE step: If the designer has skills and ability to implement the prototype, then within the multidisciplinary team he can assume the programmer function. Otherwise he can coordinate the prototype construction. In this step, it is accomplished the production and treatment of images, video and audio edition, templates implementation and storage media collection in the database.

- TEST step: The same interface evaluation processes of non-adaptive systems can be applied on Adaptive Web Applications. In this step it should be accomplished usability tests (before and after the implementation), of comprehensibility of signs (icons and others) and the application performance in different browsers.

After accomplishing a cycle, which means accomplishing the test step, the process is not yet finished, because based on the evaluation feedback the cycle can be repeated as many times as necessary.

The proposed model reflects the logic of the Interface Design Process for Adaptive Web Applications, but does not guarantee the project's success. It is relevant to mention that the final quality of the interface is also related to some of the designer attributes, such as knowledge, abilities, experience and sensibility to create visual communication and accomplish the visual treatment.

Guidelines for Interface Design for Adaptive Web Applications. According to the IDPAWA model, the designer must identify the methods and adaption techniques that will be used on adaptive systems and establish ways to enable them on the interface.

The designer will work directly with adaption techniques, since they implement the adaption methods [4] [2]. Therefore, the designer needs to know the characteristics and particularities of adaption techniques. To help the designer task and support the proposed model, guidelines for IDPAWA were developed. The Guidelines[2] for Interface Design for Adaptive Web Applications are a set of interactions that deal with requirements and the adaption techniques configuration. It was made one guideline for each one of the adaption techniques related below:

- Strechtext - Content Adaption Technique
- Conditional Fragment - Content Adaption Technique
- Page Variants - Content Adaption Technique
- Direct Orientation - Navigation Adaption Technique
- Links Note - Navigation Adaption Technique
- Hiding/Removal of Links - Navigation Adaption Technique
- Page Variants - Presentation Adaption Technique

The guidelines present descriptions of adaption techniques concerning function, objective, properties, operation description with examples, strategy and requirements for the interface design. However, some guidelines are longer than others, since some adaption techniques require specific interface elements. It brings more orientations and examples to support the interface designer. The adaption techniques that require more interface elements development are the Stretchtext (Content Adaption Techniques), the Direct Orientation and the Links Note (both are Navigation Adaption Techniques). They demand the development of specific areas on the interface, of interaction objects and visual treatment in order to call the user's attention. However, the content adaption techniques Conditional Fragment and Page Variants; and the navigation adaption techniques Hiding/Removal of Links and Links Ordination do not require the interface elements development, which means that they do not infer on the interface configuration.

Validation. Seven designers (whose profile were compatible with the sample criteria) participated in the research to validate the model and guidelines. The Model and the Guidelines for IDPAWA were provided to the seven designers during the interface design for an adaptive website entitled *"Diferente todo mundo é!"* / "Everyone is different!"[3].

According to designers, the model shows clearly the design process. It was easy to understand all steps. In respect guidelines, it was perceived that the interface designers needed more data. At the initial stage of the work, it was difficult for designers to understand the characteristics of adaptation techniques, because the guidelines had only a description about them. They have suggested the inclusion of examples with graphic elements that should appear on the interface.

---

[2] The Guidelines were commented briefly, in order to fit the size of this article. In Batista (2008) the guidelines are fully presented.

[3] "Everyone is different!" is an Adaptive Web Application that offers information about Down Syndrome. The content, navigation and presentation are adapted according to the "user model".

The designers' feedback led to revision, restructuring and improvement of the guidelines. It is important to emphasize that this phase of research was crucial to make guidelines more complete. After the application, it was noticeable that the model and guidelines for IDPAWA accomplished its' purpose (provide the necessary support during the project), since the designers who were unaware of this particular area were able to develop the interface for Adaptive Web Application.

The Personalised Interfaces Created for the Website about Down Syndrome. Besides the Model and Guidelines for IDPAWA, the designers received information about the project "Everyone is different!" and software artefacts produced by the development team, such as: user model, domain model, navigation model and adaptation rules. They analysed these documents to understand the logic of the system. This website provides the adaptation of content, navigation and presentation to three user profiles: child, teenager and adult. In this project was used the adaptation techniques presented next:

- The Presentation Adaption Technique - Page Variants: it provides a mode of presentation and interaction consistent with the cognitive characteristics of each user class. Thus, to meet the attributes of each user class, the designers created three distinct modes of presentation, i.e., the child template, the teenager template and adult template, presented below.

Fig. 4. Content, Navigation and Presentation personalized for child (Source: Reginaldo, 2012)

Fig. 5. Content, Navigation and Presentation personalized for adolescent (Source: Reginaldo, 2012)

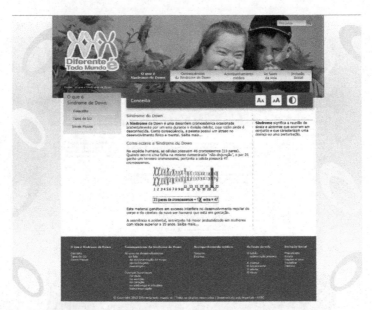

Fig. 6. Content, Navigation and Presentation personalized for adult (Source: Reginaldo, 2012)

- The Content Adaption Technique - Strechtext: it includes additional / complementary explanations, definitions, concepts, examples, by expandable paragraphs and/or marginal notes. The Figure 7 shows an example of use of Strechtext.

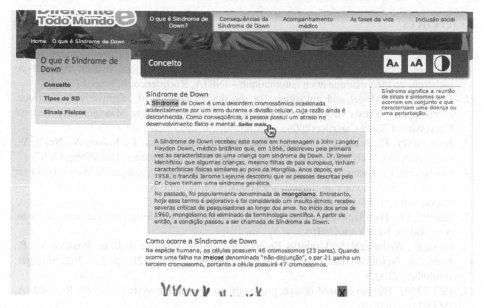

Fig. 7. Complementary information is added in expandable paragraphs (Source: Reginaldo, 2012)

3   Final Considerations

The scope of this study consisted on the proposition of a solution to guide de designer during the interface design process for Adaptive Web Applications, contemplating aspects regarding the dynamic structure of web document, graphic presentation quality, implementation technology, the interface elements performance that provide navigation and adaptive presentation.

The model and guidelines for IDPAWA bring contributions in order to facilitate the tasks of professionals from the Design and Communication and Information Technology areas.

However, it was noticeable that the authors of content/specialists on domain (professionals who were not graduated on computation) also need orientations concerning the use of content adaption techniques. Therefore, the possibility of developing guidelines dedicated to authors of content is foreseen.

It is also necessary to investigate if the utilized solutions by the adaptive techniques provide accessibility to the web document.

There is space for new researches in the usability sphere of adaptive websites. The adaptive hypermedia development represents a promising area of investigations. However, in Brazil, the researches in this area are still in an early stage. Therefore, it is the interested people's mission to participate of this new model of information, acquire knowledge, discuss and propose solutions that might contribute to the consolidation of this new media.

References

1. Bastien, J.M.C., Scapin, D.L.: Human factors criteria, principles, and recommendations for HCI: methodological and standardization issues, Internal Report, Institut national de recherche en informatique et en automatique – INRIA, Rocquencourt, France (1993)
2. Batista, C.R.: Model and guidelines for the design process of adaptive web interface. Florianópolis. Thesis (Doctorate in Engineering and Knowledge Management). Federal University of Santa Catarina (2008)
3. Brusilovsky, P.: Adaptive Navigation Support. In: Brusilovsky, P., Kobsa, A., Nejdl, W. (eds.) Adaptive Web 2007. LNCS, vol. 4321, pp. 263–290. Springer, Heidelberg (2007)
4. Doulgeraki, C., Partarakis, N., Mourouzis, A., Stephanidis, C.: Adaptable Web-based user interfaces: methodology and practice. eMinds: International Journal on Human-Computer Interaction I(5), 79–110 (2009)
5. Garrett, J.J.: The elements of user experience: user centered design for the web, 2nd edn. New Riders, New York (2010)
6. Gena, C., Weibelzahl, S.: Usability Engineering for the Adaptive Web. In: Brusilovsky, P., Kobsa, A., Nejdl, W. (eds.) Adaptive Web 2007. LNCS, vol. 4321, pp. 720–762. Springer, Heidelberg (2007)
7. ISO 13407. Human-centred design processes for interactive systems (1999) Revised by: ISO 9241-210 (2010)
8. ISO 9241-11. Ergonomic requirements for office work with visual display terminals (VDTs) – Part 11: Guidance on usability (1998)
9. ISO 9241-12. Ergonomic requirements for office work with visual display terminals (VDTs) – Part 12: Presentation of information (1998)
10. Koch, N.P.: Software Engineering for Adaptive Hypermedia Systems: Reference Model, Modeling Techniques and Development Process. Munich, Thesis (Doctor of the Natural Sciences at the Faculty for Mathematics and Computer Science), Ludwig Maximilians University Munich (2000), http://www.pst.informatik.uni-muenchen.de/~kochn/PhDThesisNoraKoch.pdf
11. Nielsen, J., Loranger, H.: Prioritizing Web Usability. New Riders Press, Berkeley (2006)
12. Reginaldo, T.: Personalised interfaces design for adaptive website "Everyone is different!". Florianópolis. Monograph (Bachelor's degree in Design) Federal University of Santa Catarina (2012)
13. Rosenfeld, L., Morville, P.: Information Architecture for the World Wide Web, 2nd edn. O'Reilly, Sebastopol (2002)
14. Sharp, H., Rogers, Y., Preece, J.: Interaction Design: Beyond Human-Computer Interaction, 3rd edn. John Wiley & Sons, Inc., Chichester (2011)
15. Shneiderman, B., Plaisant, C.: Designing the user interface: Strategies for effective Human-Computer Interaction, 5th edn. Addison Wesley Longman, Inc., Berkeley (2009)

A Model to Promote Interaction between Humans and Data Fusion Intelligence to Enhance Situational Awareness

Leonardo Botega, Cláudia Berti, Regina Araújo,
and Vânia Paula de Almeida Neris

Federal University of São Carlos
Computer Science Department
Wireless Networks and Distributed Interactive Simulations Lab (WINDIS)
235, Washington Luís Road, São Carlos, São Paulo State, Brazil
leonardo_botega@dc.ufscar.br

Abstract. The operator of a Command & Control (C2) system has a crucial role on the improvement of information that is processed through data fusion engines to provide Situational Awareness (SAW). Through direct access to data transformations, operators can improve information quality, by reducing uncertainty, according to their skills and expertise. Uncertainty, in this work, is considered an adverse condition, which can make the real information less accessible. Although relevant solutions have been reported in the literature on innovative user interfaces and approaches for quality-aware knowledge representation, these are concerned mostly on transforming the way information is graphically represented and on quantitatively mapping the quality-aware knowledge acquired from systems, respectively. There are few studies that deal more specifically with accessibility for decision-makers in safety-critical situations, such as C2, considering the aspect of data uncertainty. This paper presents a model to help researchers to build uncertainty-aware interfaces for C2 systems, produced by both data fusion and human reasoning over the information. Combined to environmental and personal factors, a tailored and enriched knowledge can be built, interchangeable with systems intelligence. A case study on the monitoring of a conflict among rival soccer fans is being implemented for the validation of the proposed solution.

1 Introduction

Major Events require effective and efficient operational responses. Frequently, unexpected incidents arise and demand time-critical decisions from a commander of the state police, security managers or governmental members. Such decisions might involve the deployment of new tactics and the allocation of human resources and equipment. Automatic and semi-automatic monitoring systems for the security and safety of major events can be highly complex; they provide the operators awareness about what is going on at the event location. For that, Data Fusion processes fed by multiple, heterogeneous sources (physical sensors, social networks,

M. Kurosu (Ed.): Human-Computer Interaction, Part I, HCII 2014, LNCS 8510, pp. 399–410, 2014.
© Springer International Publishing Switzerland 2014

databases, etc.), and computational intelligence are used to help providing the operators not only with the perception and understanding of what is going on at the environment, at a certain time and space dimension, but also anticipation of events to come. This is known as situational awareness (SAW) [1].

Devices and innovative interfaces are being devised for better supporting the situational awareness visualization process, what can be a great challenge for two main reasons: such devices might have to be used in harsh conditions, for instance, command and control interactive devices might be used in moving vehicles, poor lighting conditions and noise; and operators might be subject to long hours of work, under emotional stress. Also, considering that commanders are expected to make decisions based on his/her understanding of what is going on, and his expertise, skills, and past experience can be a valuable asset in the comprehension of current and even anticipation of future issues, it is crucial that SAW systems interfaces provide for that expertise/experience to be used as another source of information.

The physical and emotional stress to which SAW systems users/operators can be subject to, besides potential harsh conditions of the environment, the always emerging new technologies [2], and even pervasive multiculturalism, in which commanders from different regions of the world with distinct cultural backgrounds might have to work and make decisions collaboratively, add to the challenge of devising accessible interfaces. Relevant interface solutions to accessibility for users with different abilities, capabilities, needs and preferences in a variety of contexts are reported in the literature. However, as far as the authors investigated, there are few studies that deal more specifically with accessibility for professionals acting under uncertainty and harsh conditions, such as decision-makers in safety-critical situations, as the monitoring emergency situations (incidents) in major events.

This paper introduces a model to promote interaction between humans and the data fusion intelligence to enhance situational awareness. With our model, the data fusion process can be fed the experience of operators/skilled professionals, and imperfections of data and situations can be reduced. The model supports the management of uncertainty-aware information flow, led by the propagation of evidences along the flow, and the operators' belief driven by data transformations across the process. The paper is organized as follows: Section 2 presents Approaches for Improving Information Quality to Enhance SAW; the Model for Promoting interactions between Humans and the Data Fusion Process is introduced in Section 3, followed by Conclusions.

2   Approaches for Improving Information Quality to Enhance SAW

Situation awareness systems, specially applications of command and control relies on information quality to provide operators a better view of the analyzed scenario for making improved decisions. If imperfect information is provided to SAW systems, the operator may be uncertain on what he perceives and understands and the quality of decision will be compromised. For such, this paper presents a model comprising of a user interface and an extended Dempster-Shafer approach for reasoning from uncertain information and storing knowledge about assets and situations obtained with or without transformations. Hence, this combination will provide a model for building accessible interfaces for operators in adverse conditions through the interaction with fusion systems under uncertainty. The State-of-the-Art reveals advances in two main related fields: the development of innovative user interfaces and techniques for the enhancement of operator's understanding of information and the approaches for the management of the knowledge generated by systems and humans.

2.1 Interactive Interfaces and Visualization Techniques

Regarding interactive interfaces and techniques for quality-aware data information exploration and transformation, Xie *et al.* [3] created an interactive interface to enable users to explicitly explore that data quality information. They also created a framework for the coupling data space and quality space for producing multivariate visualizations. Authors also introduced two novel techniques, quality brushing and quality-series animation, to help users with the exploration of this connection between spaces. Their case study they conclude that the solution on quality information is more effective than traditional multivariate visualizations. To improve their framework, they point the creation of a tighter link between data and data quality, whereas brushing data can conduct to quality inferences, that is, to perform tasks related to the quality of the data abstraction. Friedemann *et al.* [4] created an uncertainty interaction model to reduce the probability and consequences of poor decisions on the detection of tsunamis. Such model implies on representing all quality measurements in unique graphs allowing pre-defined combinations. All classification and quantification of imperfect information are done by the system, with no human involved. Summers *et al.* [5] developed a user interface for C2 environments with the capability of visualization customization based on the situation, user role, individual preferences and the size of the display. Clustering and de-clustering were implemented to make information filtering and the integration of new information as the situation evolve. This work generalizes all types of data quality issues and uses the same approach to mitigate them (requesting more and more data).

2.2 Models for Improving and Quantifying Information Quality

Regarding the advances on models for improving and quantifying information quality, Wen and Zhou [6] presented an approach with two comparative experiments on examining how data transformation impacts user task performance in various visualization situations. They proved that data and information transformation significantly improves user performance in both single-step and multistep difficult analytic tasks. They also identified three types of data transformation techniques that help to produce a quality visualization and developed a set of guidelines that suggests when and what types of data transformation are most useful. The effects of data transformation is evaluated only in the end of the process. Angelini *et al.* [7] presented a visualization model to support analytical interactive exploration of information retrieval results with the focus on supporting the failure analysis and the understanding of a system behavior, conducting a *what-if* questions to have estimations of the impact of modifications into the system. The authors overall goal of the paper is to provide users with tools and methods to infer the effectiveness of a system and explore alternatives for improving it. The methods used by authors allow users to dynamically quantify quality improvements and rank gains/losses as the system under examination, instead of the method of the previous approach. The effects of quality assessment are given back to the visualization part, allowing users a smooth interaction of the user with the results. Only real-time evaluations are possible with no temporal analysis allowed. In their work Correa *et al.* [8] proved that when users is about to make decisions under an uncertain environment, it is important to quantify data and present to them both the aggregated uncertainty of the results and the impact of that uncertainty. In such paper, it was presented a new framework to support uncertainty-aware in a visual analytics process, using statistic methods. They show that data transformations, such as regression, principal component analysis and k-means clustering, can be used to take account for uncertainty identification and quantification. This framework leads to better visualizations that improve the decision-making processes and help analysts to perform new inferences. There is no qualitative assessment by this framework.

Authors agree with contributions of their approaches e.g. the interaction techniques to brush data, assess information from new inferences and access associated data quality inferred by a system. Overall limitations are the need for data evaluation on every interaction step for a better data quality quantification, the development of new interaction techniques to assess high level information and a more tight coupling between human judgments and data representation.

2.3   Human's Knowledge Management

Regarding approaches for the management of the knowledge generated by systems and humans, McKeever [9] and Zhang *et al.* [10] both presented approaches based on the Dempster-Shafer theory for the recognition of situations under uncertainty environments. The formed included the knowledge about the sensors and their attributes, and the temporal aspect of the evidences as part of the belief functions. The latter created an approach to allow context reasoning from incomplete pieces of information aiming to infer situations. Blasch *et al.* [11] built a complementary model of the well known JDL model involving humans in the process. Such model supports the modeling, method, management and the design of fusion systems that demand high level information fusion and the evaluation of information driven by the humans. Laskey *et al.* [12] built a model that describes the role flow of information since the description of the data quality as it is acquired, the storing quality into metadata, the propagation of uncertainty by fusion process, the exploration with decision support tools until the communication to users as the final product. This model considers the whole process but does not takes into account the information judgment by experts.

Although several attempts succeeded on infer and reason on contexts that aim to include data quality with known evidences and beliefs, authors agree on suggesting that the human judgment is essential to infer data quality from an expert point of view. All quality attributes must be know as new evidence arise and be applied by human input. We envision that our work innovate in the human-information discourse propagating and refining uncertainty information previously identified by systems. From user interfaces, operators iteratively interact and transform information and its representation requesting functions of the fusion process, and then re-evaluate the information based on their own conceptions. A new knowledge involving interactive visualizations and the transformed information will be conceived and can be used to enrich system's intelligence .

3 A Model for Promoting Interactions between Humans and Data Fusion Intelligence

The main goal of our work is to devise interfaces to critical security systems that takes in consideration operators' skills and experiences to enhance the decision making process even in harsh conditions. For that, a model is being created to support human's knowledge as input to the data fusion process via novel and accessible interfaces to be used also in challenging environmental, physical and emotional conditions. Figure 1 depicts an overview of the model, which comprises two main modules: SAW-oriented user interface and a DSET (Dempster-Shafer Evidence Theory)-based knowledge manager, which are described below:

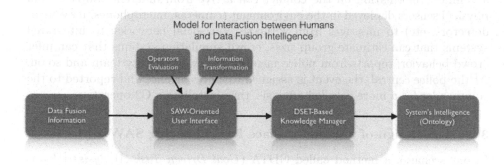

Fig. 1. Model for Promoting Interactions Between Humans and Data Fusion Intelligence

- SAW-oriented user interface: A user interface that supports information acquisition from the Data Fusion systems (fused or not) about one or more assets. The way this information is acquired and processed can present imperfections on its structure, composition and meaning - thus, uncertainties can arise on the operators' SAW. Operators must re-evaluate information to update the previous evaluation made by the systems intelligence. To obtain more evidences on the quality of information and provide more reliable evaluation, operators must be able to perform transformations with new combinations and corrections of data.

- DSET-Based knowledge manager: An approach for acquiring, processing and storing the knowledge generated from operators via the proposed interface, considering the used sources, discovered assets, applied transformations and the revealed situations. The product of this module is an uncertainty-aware information flow, driven by the users interactions to apply information transformations on-demand to reduce such uncertainty. The combination of these two modules aim to enhance SAW by providing means for humans to iteratively improve the quality of the information that operators rely on to make critical decisions, reducing her/his uncertainty on what s/he perceives and understands by her/his own choices on how information is obtained and presented.

3.1   The Problem

The application domain considered in this work focus on C2 for the monitoring of large events. A case study is being developed considering incidents of social disorder (e.g., hooliganism) inside a subway station that can occur after a major event (e.g., soccer game). The goal is to monitor assets for the maintenance of public order and safety, given high population density and constraints of the contingency plans. Rival soccer fans meet inside the subway station, starting a conflict. Information on the conflict can arrive from different sources: from physical sensors deployed in the environment (cameras, microphones, movement detectors, etc) to messages from witnesses via social networks, to integrated systems that can estimate group sizes, crowd simulation systems that can infer crowd behavior, reports from police members, subway security team and so on. At the police central, the event is assigned to an occurrence and reported to the commander for a more detailed analysis, thus installing a C2 operation.

3.2   The Design of a User Interface for Enhancing SAW

In our scenario, a method called GDTA (*Goal Driven Task Analysis*) [1] was adopted in order to elucidate the information required for each decision commanders must make. All decisions are stablished in order to accomplish tasks to reach minor and major goals. Such goals were determined following guidelines from literature and validated with a São Paulo State Police commander.

One of the major goals is "*Monitoring*", which can be specified into the goal of "*Evaluating activities at the subway station*", or even more specified, "*Evaluating the event status at the subway station*". Based on these goals, at least one decision must be made, such as "*Should commander take any additional action besides the stablished contingency plans?*" This question leads to a set of information required to make such decision, divided by SAW levels. With this set of required information to make the decision, a user interface and visualizations can be designed. For the accomplishment of this design, the guidelines for user-centric user interface design by [1] were adopted. In their work, eleven principles are depicted. Also, new interactive visualizations were conceived to overcome the uncertain information that may cause mental confusion on operators. Such visualizations were based on the work of [13] and [14].

Quality-Aware Interactive Visualizations

The user interface (Figure 2) accommodates quality-aware interactive visualizations to perform the information transformations. If the information looks uncertain to operators, new inferences must be revealed for building new knowledge and contributing to a better SAW [13,14].

The first action the operator must take is to tell the system about his first impression on information. If the operator indicates that the information is imprecise, incomplete or even vague, the system will be able to provide a transformation toolbox, aiming to empower operator toward the experience of building his own awareness. The main objective of using information transformation is to provide better suitable contexts to reach the required goals by means of his will in an iterative fashion. Hence, operators are able to refine, correct or compose new information that may be uncertain to him or just represent it again in a better way to reach SAW.

Our approach envision to apply transformations in a way to promote what authors call high-level information fusion (HLIF) [15]. Such concept emerged once information is already produced but it wasn't enough for human purposes, being needed new information to be brushed, inferred or just aggregated once data fusion systems already provided initial results. Hence, users can acquire new data by choosing new sources in the side panel, to populate the interface with new perception items; aggregate the new data into the current data/information, promoting HLIF; split already fused data/information, useful to reveal SAW hierarchy of information and start a whole new HLIF; filter relevant information, for reducing cognitive workload; and correct data/information that system and/or humans can acquired or process. Transformations can trigger operations that a data fusion system performs through its phases in a high level manner, such as data acquiring and pre-processing (e.g., image/signal processing), information processing (e.g., mining, correlation, fusion), visual representation (e.g., filtering, presenting) and user refinement (e.g., insertion, evaluation and correction).

By the end of the user interface development we will be able to provide guidelines for the design of user interfaces for uncertainty mitigation by interacting with visualizations.

The Human in the Information Evaluation Process

System's intelligence may be capable of inferring quality-aware data, allowing user to reason over pre-evaluated information. Such a priori evaluation may be derived from past experiences from other users or by automated process

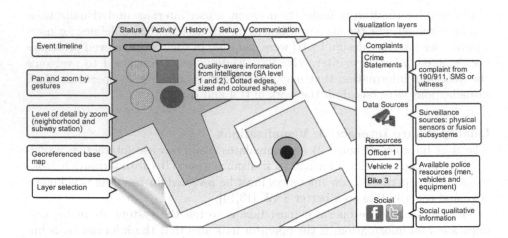

Fig. 2. User Interface to accommodate quality-aware interactive visualizations

of identifying quality issues on data or information, such as incompleteness or imprecision, which both can lead to uncertainty.

Such users evaluation on C2 information can confirm, contradict or even improve systems evaluation and is based on observational evidences of the warfare environment or on his personal experiences on similar situations. Stress, experience and workload are factors that can be weighted and accounted as evidences for determining certainty on information. Such factors directly influences how commanders see and process information, improving or decreasing their trust on the information and its source.

Consider the following example of our scenario: surveillance sensors and system's intelligence determine that in a specific region of the subway station there is a set of tracked persons denoted by {team1_fans, team2_fans, passengers, officers, offenders}. The tracking system determine (in a range of 0.0 (imperfect) - 1.0 (perfect) possibilities in a Likert scale) that in a certain group there is a possibility of 0.7 that they are team1_fans; 0.8 they are offenders and also they represent a 0.9 possibility of threat to a group of team2_fans, considering their attitude and position at the station. The system also detected a 0.7 chance that team1_fans is carrying sticks and stones. Furthermore, experience is crucial to trust or contradict the situation that has been presented. Analyzing the images from the surveillance system, the operators experience can lead his assessment to reason over the information that has been presented, e.g., the operator can conclude that the persons must be offenders by only 0.3 possibility and then represent a 0.1 chance of threat, given the isolated area and the 0.8 chance of presence of officers near the analyzed area. Also, by requesting another source of data (witnesses for instance) or a new fusion event, the operator can discover, for instance, that there is a chance of 0.1 of presence of sticks at the scene. Such inferences by the operator also obey the scale used by the system and the evaluation possibilities will be suggested through the interface.

Making the interface accessible for human participation in the information evaluation process is in progress, as much as the evaluation of the impact of physical and emotional stress of operators on the decision-making and how this can affect SAW. SPAM (Situation Present Assessment Method) will be adopted to measure such impact.

3.3 The Operator's Knowledge Management

The knowledge obtained from the interaction with information over the interface may enrich modules of intelligence services (or inference engines) of Data Fusion systems. Such services can "learn" from operators past experiences and help other operators to improve comprehension under C2 critical domain in cases of similar contexts and situations. The knowledge manager module shown in Figure 1 deals with the management and display of the knowledge obtained from evidences. Dempster-Shafer Evidence Theory (DSET) [16] is used, with changes on how evidences are propagated as masses change. Inspired by [10] we model knowledge as a set of sensors, assets, transformations and situations. In the example shown in Figure 3 the asset A2(a gun) is inferred from the transformation T1(image processing) applied to A1(a man carrying an object captured by image); the asset A4(a group of fans of team 1 at the left side of the station) is inferred from the transformation T2 (aggregation of new information) applied to A3 (incomplete information about the presence of team 1 fans); both A2 and A4 combined provide the situation U1(armed group of team 1 fans); A7 is comprising from A5(passengers) and A6(persons in green shirts) just by observations; A8 (possible group of team 2 fans) is inferred from the transformation T3 (disaggregation) applied to A7(unarmed people) and result on the situation U2 (presence of team 2 fans); both U1 and U2 can be used to infer a new situation U3 (imminent threat and risk to life).

Such mapped contexts and situations can be used to establish the basis of a knowledge about to be formalized by the DSET-based theory. Besides managing the transformation-driven knowledge until it reaches a situation, our approach registers a quality index (measured by system) before transformations and a quality index (measured by operator) after information transformation. Such indexes reflect directly on the masses that represent beliefs on hypothesis of what assets A are or what situations U represent. Figure 3 also shows the stored knowledge with the quality index update.

3.4 Accessibility and Uncertainty as an Accessibility Dimension

The goal of Command and Control systems is to support operators in complex tasks for safety-critical decision-making in a highly restrictive environment [17]. Most of the restrictions arise from the usage of user interfaces that need to be "aware" of the amount of data, operator's physical and cognitive factors and the inherent aspects of the information, such as quality attributes. Besides, multi-sensors for C2 systems typically produce big data and the assessment of current situations can be severely compromised if relevant information is not

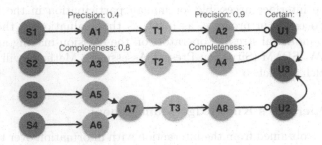

Fig. 3. An example of the working model for the management of the operator's knowledge. The organization of the information flow and the quality index updating after transformations.

properly presented to operators in a timely fashion [18]. Operators may not be prepared to deal with such burden and may not know how to handle it. User Interfaces must provide means for users on qualifying information. Moreover, environment impairments situationally induced [19], i.e., adverse conditions regarding the operation environment of the interface may influence how operators perceive and understand information, e.g., noisy surroundings, poor lighting conditions and devices used on moving vehicles. Also, physical limitations such as motor disabilities, stress, fatigue and emotions must be known and captured by such interface [20]. To overcome such conditions, adaptive interfaces become inevitable to support access to information regardless the context of use, providing timely information on demand and formatted to specific information, operator and environment [21].

Furthermore, during the processes of information acquiring, computation, representation and refinement in a multi sensor scenario, imperfect information may be propagated until it reaches the user interface. Added to other human constraints, the result may not be promising. Uncertainty about information is also an adverse condition and can make the real information less accessible. The presence of uncertainty can lead to a poor SAW about what the assets are and what is going on with them. Reducing such uncertainty is crucial for decision-making and part of this is humans' responsibility [22]. For such, it must be accounted, besides the other factors, the experience, expertise and the operator's training, which may guide operators in their tasks, help them to infer new information and customize the interface. Hence, interacting with and transforming the uncertain information can become an additional instrument for reaching accessibility due to its potential for adapting the way information is composed or visually represented.

The model presented in Section 3 provides the support for the interaction and transformation required to reduce information uncertainty. Further research is now underway to integrate our model to an interface solution for users operating under the adverse conditions presented in this sub-section. The necessary dimensions (e.g., disability types) were identified and will be mapped against required context processing and adaptation rules.

4   Conclusions

The physical limitations of users, their different capabilities, needs and preferences, besides the situationally induced environment impairments, make accessibility a critical and challenging issue, especially when users access a critical security system. Added to that, uncertainty about information is also an adverse condition and can make the real information less accessible. Human intervention on the information flow can reduce uncertainty. For that, interfaces that support such intervention are necessary. This paper introduced a model that can offer operators of critical security systems, interface for direct access to data transformations to improve information quality according to operators' skills and expertise. The model also provides support for the knowledge management from the uncertainty-aware information flow – the used sources are mapped, the assets are identified, transformations are applied and patterns and situations are revealed. As a result, system's intelligence can be enriched and the operators' situational awareness potentially enhanced. The interface is being implemented and will be validated by Sao Paulo police commanders. As future work, our model will be integrated to an interface solution for users operating under different dimensions of adverse conditions.

References

1. Endsley, M.R., Jones, D.G.: Designing for Situation Awareness: An Approach to User-Centered Design, 2nd edn. Taylor & Francis (2012)
2. Emiliani, P.L., Stephanidis, C.: Universal access to ambient intelligence environments: Opportunities and challenges for people with disabilities. IBM Systems Journal 3(44), 605–619 (2005)
3. Xie, Z., Ward, M.O., Rundensteiner, E.A., Huang, S.: Integrating Data and Quality Space Interactions in Exploratory Visualizations. In: Fifth International Conference on Coordinated and Multiple Views in Exploratory Visualization (CMV 2007), pp. 47–60 (July 2007)
4. Friedemann, M., Raape, U., Tessmann, S., Schoeckel, T., Strobl, C.: Explicit Modeling and Visualization of Imperfect Information in the Context of Decision Support for Tsunami Early Warning in Indonesia. In: Smith, M.J., Salvendy, G. (eds.) Human Interface, Part I, HCII 2011. LNCS, vol. 6771, pp. 201–210. Springer, Heidelberg (2011)
5. Summers, V.A., Jones, R.L., Flo, R.: Increasing Situational Awareness by Visualizing Uncertainty (2005)
6. Wen, Z., Zhou, M.X.: An Optimization-based Approach to Dynamic Data Transformation for Smart Visualization. In: Proceedings of the 13th International Conference on Intelligent User Interfaces, IUI 2008, pp. 70–79. ACM, New York (2008)
7. Angelini, M., Ferro, N., Granato, G., Santucci, G., Silvello, G.: Information retrieval failure analysis: Visual analytics as a support for interactive what-if investigation. In: IEEE Conference on Visual Analytics Science and Technology, pp. 204–206. IEEE (October 2012)
8. Correa, C.D., Chan, Y.H., Ma, K.L.: A framework for uncertainty-aware visual analytics. In: 2009 IEEE Symposium on Visual Analytics Science and Technology, pp. 51–58 (2009)

9. McKeever, S.: Recognising Situations Using Extended Dempster-Shafer Theory (February 2011)

10. Zhang, D., Cao, J., Zhou, J., Guo, M.: Extended Dempster-Shafer Theory in Context Reasoning for Ubiquitous Computing Environments. In: 2009 International Conference on Computational Science and Engineering, pp. 205–212 (2009)

11. Blasch, E., Stampouli, D., Costa, P.C.G., Laskey, K.B., Valin, P., Ng, G.W., Schubert, J., Nagi, R.: Issues of Uncertainty Analysis in High-Level Information Fusion. Technical report (2012)

12. Laskey, K.B., Wright, E.J., da Costa, P.C.: Envisioning uncertainty in geospatial information. International Journal of Approximate Reasoning 51(2), 209–223 (2010)

13. Keim, D.A., Bak, P., Bertini, E., Oelke, D., Spretke, D., Ziegler, H.: Advanced visual analytics interfaces. In: Proceedings of the International Conference on Advanced Visual Interfaces - AVI 2010, p. 3 (2010)

14. Riveiro, M.: Evaluation of uncertainty visualization techniques for information fusion. In: 11th International Conference on Information Fusion, pp. 1–8 (July 2007)

15. Hall, D., Jordan, J.: Human-centered information fusion. Artech House (2010)

16. Mahadevan, S.: Visualization Methods and User Interface Design Guidelines for Rapid Decision Making in Complex Multi-task Time-critical Environments. PhD thesis (2009)

17. Martinie, C., Palanque, P., Ragosta, M.: Some Issues with Interaction Design and Implementation in the Context of Autonomous Interactive Critical Systems. In: Workshop on End-user Interactions with Intelligent and Autonomous Systems. ACM SIGCHI Conference on Human Factors in Computing Systems (2012)

18. Verma, S., Vieweg, S., Corvey, W.J., Palen, L., Martin, J.H., Palmer, M., Schram, A., Anderson, K.M.: Natural Language Processing to the Rescue? Extracting "Situational Awareness" Tweets During Mass Emergency. In: Fifth International AAAI Conference on Weblogs and Social Media (2011)

19. Sears, A., Young, M., Feng, J.: Physical disabilities and computing technologies: An analysis of impairments. In: Sears, A., Jacko, J.A. (eds.) Human-Computer Interaction Handbook, pp. 829–852. Lawrence Erlbaum Associates (2008)

20. Chambers, L.: A hazard analysis of human factors in safety-critical systems engineering. In: 10th Australian Workshop on Safety Critical Systems, vol. 55 (2006)

21. Caminero Gil, F.J., Paternò, F., Motti, V.G.: Context-aware service front-ends. In: Proceedings of the 5th ACM SIGCHI Symposium on Engineering Interactive Computing Systems - EICS 2013, p. 339 (2013)

22. Mirhaji, P., Richesson, R.L., Turley, J.P., Zhang, J., Smith, J.W.: Public Health Situation Awareness, towards a semantic approach. Multisensor, Multisource Information Fusion: Architectures, Algorithms, and Applications 5434, 339–350 (2004)

Visualization Adaptation
Based on Environmental Influencing Factors

Dirk Burkhardt[1], Kawa Nazemi[1], Jose Daniel Encarnacao[1],
Wilhelm Retz[1], and Jörn Kohlhammer[2]

[1] Fraunhofer Institute for Computer Graphics Research (IGD), Darmstadt, Germany
```
{dirk.burkhardt,kawa.nazemi,jose.daniel.encarnacao,
        wilhelm.retz}@igd.fraunhofer.de
```
[2] Technische Universität Darmstadt, Darmstadt, Germany
```
joern.kohlhammer@gris.informatik.tu-darmstadt.de
```

Abstract. Working effectively with computer-based devices is challenging, especially under mobile conditions, due to the various environmental influences. In this paper a visualization adaptation approach is described, to support the user under discriminatory environmental conditions. For this purpose, a context model for environmental influencing factors is being defined. Based on this context model, an approach to adapt visualizations in regards of certain environmental influences is being evolved, such as the light intensity, air quality, or heavy vibrations.

Keywords: Adaptive Visualization, Information Visualization, User-centered Interaction, User Experience, Sensor Fusion.

1 Introduction

The work efficiency and effectiveness with information visualization systems may depend on the user-centered adaptation capability considering various influencing factors. Therewith, human information retrieval systems with strong user-centered approaches provide sufficient support for the diversity of information-related tasks. The user-centered approaches are commonly developed as static systems supporting in particular specific stakeholders in various domains, e.g. analysts. The static approaches have various advantages for the specific and known users and tasks, but in domains with variety of users the "one-system-fits-all" approach does not support the user sufficiently.

Adaptive information and adaptive visualization approaches model users' behavior based on the implicit users' interactions or by identifying users' tasks focus in particular on such user-driven influencing factors. However, the effectiveness of information visualization may be influenced by further factors too. One of these indirect factors is the environmental influence. Today, the environmental influencing factors are commonly investigated in environments with extreme conditions, such as manufactories or computer systems that are used in dusty, noisy, very hot and very cold

M. Kurosu (Ed.): Human-Computer Interaction, Part I, HCII 2014, LNCS 8510, pp. 411–422, 2014.

environments. In perspective of the increasing relevance of mobile computing, the considerations of environmental issues get important for the everyday use too. In mobile environments a couple of factors have influences on users and their interaction behavior. Among others, common aspects are changes of light (bright conditions outside under the sun, dark in some rooms, which makes it hard to watch information on screens), vibrations (as they effect during travels in trains, which limit the precision of pointing interactions) or sticky air conditions (heavy weather in summer or bad air in smaller rooms, which limits the mental conditions of users and restricts the use, e.g. of complex visualizations, too).

There are approaches that adapt systems based on environmental aspects. Some basic approaches are also integrated in notebooks and smartphones, for instance the use of light sensors to change the brightness of the screen. However, these concepts are designed to adapt the general system on the environmental factors, but these concepts lose sight of adapting the visualizations based on the environmental factors. Also the transfers of environmental aspects to concrete adaptations of the visualizations are less regarded. But adapting visualizations in a more appropriate way to the environmental factors, and in a well configurable way, can increase the usability of visualizations and thus increase the efficiency of the user working with it.

Therefore, first of all this paper introduces different influencing factors that might be useful for adapting visualizations. To investigate the variety of possible influencing factors, we introduce a conceptual framework of environmental influencing factors. In this context, the most obvious sensor-types will be investigated and modeled to a "context model". This context model is the baseline of investigating further factors of influence, but refers in its first version on data about light intensity, temperature, humidity, air quality, and vibrations. In a proof of concept we consider these sensor data to adapt the visualization during a common search scenario.

2   Environment Based User-Interface Adaptation

To realize adaptive systems, it is required to consider the relevant information about the user and the context [1]. Meanwhile, many adaptation strategies do regard the user and his behavior as main actor on the technical system, whereas other aspects, such as the process or the environment as influencing factor, is less considered. But, the additional contextual information, such as GPS information from physiological sensors, can be valuable, as far as they can help to identify relevant information for the user in more concise manner [2,1]. To summarize, research on user-adaptive systems focused on variables corresponding to the categories: current state of user, longer-term properties of user, user's behavior with state, and consequences for user [1]. Whereas the main focus in the area of context-aware computing has been on the categories: readings from context sensors, readings from physiological sensors, and features of the situation [1].

The complexity of how many and which factors do influence a user can be very heterogeneous. This depends on a couple of aspects. Therefore Motti [3] defined a 7 dimensional context-aware design space that encompasses, among other, technical, environmental, process and user aspects. Malek et al. [4] defines the context from a generalized point of view and distinguishes between internal and external environmental factors on the highest level. He classified the user model and the current state during interaction as internal environmental factors. As external environmental factors, he classified physical (location, temperature, light etc.), temporal, hardware (bandwidth, processor speed, etc.), software (e.g. the used OS) and social (e.g. connected users) environmental aspects. Especially the adaptation capabilities of external environmental factors, more precisely the physical aspects, are in focus of our work. One representative is the system of Samulowitz et al. [5], which aims to adapt the user-interface and the presented information based on the current user location. Therefore they adapt primary on the data level to filter and highlight certain pieces of data. Most other systems and approaches focus on the adaptation of physical aspects in mobile environments, and more precisely on mobile devices, such as PDAs or smartphones [6,7]. In all of these adaptation approaches - with respect to environmental factors - they aim to adapt the entire user-interface, such as rotating the entire presentation, if the device is rotated, or changing the contrast and brightness, if the environment is very bright (bright sunshine) or dark (in close rooms with dimmed lamps). The used approaches, to adapt the entire user-interface, are currently also standard in notebooks and smartphones, but only on a very basic level with limitation on just one or two sensors.

To the best of our knowledge, there is no application or prototype available that aims to adapt concrete visualizations based on the environmental influence factors.

3   Visualization Adaptation Based on Environmental Influencing Factors

3.1   Overview

The adaptation needs to focus on two major parts. The first part is the most technical, because it concentrates on the sensor data acquisition and processing pipeline. The second part is a more conceptual one, it specifies how the visualization needs to be adapted based on the influencing factors.

Fig. 1. The abstracted sensor data processing pipeline, starting from the sensors, where the data are captured to adapt the visualizations

To adapt visualization based on environmental influencing factors, it is essential to measure environmental constraints. Therefore it is necessary for the first part, to define a pipeline where sensors measure these constraints and transform and prepare them for the adaptation of the visualizations.

For this purpose, we defined a canonical processing pipeline for the processing of environment sensors, which is illustrated in Fig. 1. At the initial point, sensors (as part of a sensor board) are measuring a certain aspect, e.g. light intensity or noise level. Afterwards all the sensor data are collected and summarized at middleware service, which we mentioned as Environment Adaptation Service. Here, the data can be further prepared and will be provided through an API to frontend programs, which use these information to optimize the visualization based on the environmental factors.

3.2   The Environment Context-Model

Currently, a number of environment context-models exist [4,6,15]. For our concrete adaptation purpose, we focus on those models, which focus mainly on the environmental factors in a physical manner. As a baseline, we orient our specification primarily on the work of Malek et al. [4]. They distinguish between internal environmental factors, such user models and current states, and external environmental factors, such as physical, temporal, hardware, software and social environments.

As we aim to adapt on the application level, the applicable environmental influences are limited. Therefore, we reduced the major categories of Malek et al. [4] on physical and hardware factors. We extended their list of factors, because they provided only some examples. Our final environment context model is than specified as follows:

3.3   Architecture and Sensor Processing Pipeline

One major challenge in adapting visualization within programs is the collection of relevant sensor data. On mobile devices, for instance on modern smartphones, it can be easy, because they provide these information directly. On computers and notebooks it is more challenging, because only a very limited number of computers contain integrated sensors that measure the environment. Therefore, it is essential to provide a middleware to consider this issue and provide alternative interfaces for external sensor boards. These boards should not be limited on specific and established sensors, for example because the light intensity can be measured through a light sensor, the distribution in the histogram of a web-cam picture, indirect through the eye size, and user made contrast and brightness changes of the monitor. For each kind of input sensor, the middleware can define a possible environmental influencing factor.

In fact, the adaptation of the visualization has to follow a simple data procession pipeline (see Fig. 2), beginning with the sensors, for instance a temperature or light sensor, or in indirect form, e.g. through a camera or audio sensor as part of a webcam. These sensors are connected to a sensor board, for instance an Arduino that directly connects some sensors, or a webcam that includes a video and audio sensor. These sensor boards are connected to the middleware, we mentioned as Environment Adaptation Service. On this service, the sensor values will be stored and additionally used to generate abstract environment conditions, such as bright, humid or hot environment. This sensor data acquisition can be very easy, if just specific sensors are used, and can become more complex, if environment factors have to be calculated e.g. from a webcam picture. At the end, the server owns a couple of environment conditions and the raw sensor values.

Table 1. The environment influencing factor context (based on Malek et al. [4]). Each category consists of some environmental influencing factors that can be measured and used to adapt the visualization.

Category	Influence factors	Examples
Physical environment	Location and orientation	- Changes of light intensity, e.g. bright sun outside and dark rooms
	Noise	
	Dirt	
	Weather	
	Temperature	- Reduced air quality in rooms without air conditions
	Humidity	
	Pressure	
	Light	
	Air quality/concentration	
	Vibration	
Hardware environment	Device capabilities	- Changes of the resolution needs changes at the application
	Bandwidth	
	Network capacity	
	Connectivity	- Support of special interaction devices, e.g. an 3D-Mouse to navigate to 3D Visualizations
	Processor speed and supported processing features	
	Graphic card speed and supported processing features	
	Caching/Memory capacity	
	Storage capacity	
	Resolution	
	Sound Quality	
	Sound Power	
	Battery	
	Input Devices	
	Output Devices	

To adapt visualizations, there must be an application that allows considering such environment conditions in the visualization generation. Therefore, it needs a connection possibility to connect to the Environment Adaptation Service to request the environment conditions (or the raw data). To have a flexible API with extension ability for further adaptation strategies, we used a simple socket API, but it can also be integrated on a webserver as web-service. To consider the environmental influencing factors in a sufficient way during the visualization generation, sensor data processing should base on a stable processing concept.

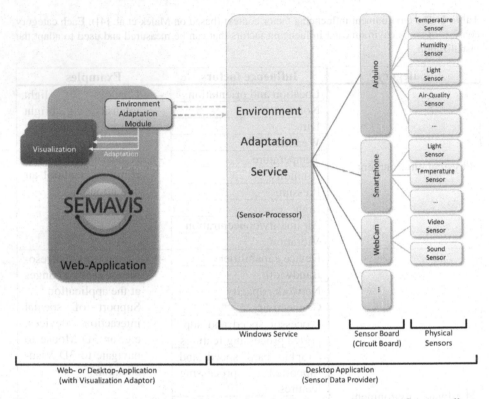

Fig. 2. Overview over the general architecture where the *Environment Adaptation Service* collects the values of different sensors from various sensor boards and processes environmental conditions. These conditions are provided to applications that use the data for adaptation purposes.

3.4   Adaptation Concept

In the previous section, the technical architecture was described, which is responsible to measure environmental and process it for the provision for the final application or program that needs to use this information for the adaptation purposes.

We have the data for the general visualization purpose at the visualization application, e.g. Linked-Open Data for visualizing the semantic information, and we have the environment condition data, which should be used to optimize the visualizations. Because of the fact that the sensor data are not that complex, we generally can confine the further processing strategies to adapt the visualization on two methods. The first methods are machine learning approaches. Machine learning approaches are useful, if the system should learn what conditions are appropriate for which changes/parameterization of the visualizations. The advantage would be that the threshold when and which graphical primitive etc. has to be changed, is set automatically on an optimal value. The second approach is a rule-based approach. Here, the parameterization will be applied based on some (static/fix) defined rules, e.g. if the light sensor value is higher than 300 lumen, then the contrast and brightness should be increased.

In our adaptation concept, we chose a rule-based approach, because training of the system gets very difficult, since we just have novice and advanced users, who use the system not regularly. Another advantage of the rule-based approach is the easier extension with further sensors, where only new rules for these new sensors have to be specified.

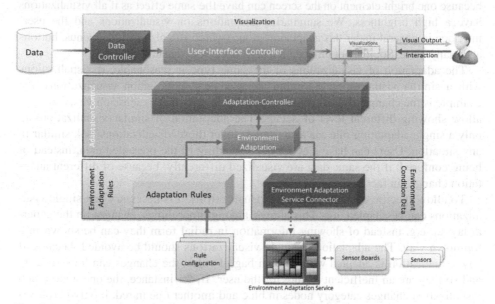

Fig. 3. This illustration shows how the adaptation will be applied on the visualization. Therefore, the adaptation rules from a configuration will be used and compared in the in the *Environment Adaptation* with the condition data from *Environment Adaptation Service*.

In Fig. 3 we show the internal adaptation processing. On the top we have the normal data processing for the visualization generation. On the bottom, we have a configuration with the concrete adaptation rules and the connection module to the Environment Adaptation Service, which provides the environment conditions. Based on both information, the *Environment Adaptation* generates the required changes on the user-interface and – more important – on the visualizations. The *Adaptation-Controller* has just a managing functionality, because our system supports a number of adaptation capabilities [11,12,13,14]. Such a certain *Adaptation-Controller* is not required if visualizations should only be adapted on environmental factors.

The generated changes on the user-interface and the visualizations were considered during the user-interface and visualization generation. Therefore it is essential that both parts provide the required adaptability.

3.5   Definition of Adaptation Rules

As mention above, the adaptations are specified in a static manner through adaptation rules. These rules can (1) address the entire user-interface, (2) visualizations of the same type, and (3) a concrete visualization. What adaptation should be performed in case of which environment factor change, needs to be defined by experts.

The application of adaptation on the entire user-interface can be useful, if the effect is not limited on a specific visualization. For instance, if the contrast and brightness of the general user-interface should be reduced, it is mandatory to change all visual elements, because one bright element on the screen can have the same effect as if all visualizations have a high brightness. We summarize adaptations on visualizations and the user-interface in general under this adaptation group, which can also include menus, buttons and many more. So, it is not limited on real information visualizations.

The adaptation of visualizations of the same type is reasonable, if visualizations with a similar visualization algorithm are used, e.g. node-graph visualizations. An example is the change of the level-of-detail, which only makes sense on visualizations allow showing different level of details. The adaptation of similar visualizations in only a single adaptation rule can also support to let those visualizations look similar in any situation. Users can have a better understanding of the presented data, instead of being confused, if the same data are visualized differently, because of different adaptation changes in fact of different rules.

To allow specific changes on certain visualizations, it is necessary that single visualizations can be adapted, too. This allows, among other things, changes on the general layout, e.g. instead of showing information in radial form they can be shown in a top-down way. The adaptation of single visualizations should be avoided, because if any visualization is adapted with its own bag of rules, the changes can look random and so they are an inefficient feature for the user. If, for instance, the one node-graph visualization changes category nodes in blue and another one in red, it only perplexes the user. Thus, it is recommended to use adaptation approaches, which taking care for the entire user-interface or for a group of visualizations of the same type. Rules for single visualization should only be used to enable or disable very visualization specific aspects.

3.6   Towards a Multi-adaptation Visualization System

Adaptation of visualizations is often a beneficial strategy. Most often the user is in focus and it is aimed to adapt visualization to the user factors. In the past, we have therefore conceptualized and implemented a couple of adaptation approaches [11,12,13,14], which take just a single aspect into account. Each of the presented approaches helps the user to work with the visualizations in a more efficient (solve tasks faster) or a more effective way (solve tasks more comfortable).

A crucial point is to enable more than one of these approaches at the same time, especially, if different adaptation methods affecting a visualization. To avoid unwanted effects in the visualizations, e.g. different node color changes because of user adaptation and environment adaptation, we currently allow only one adaptation technique at the same time. But this idea limits the possibilities, because the visualization can only be optimized by a single influencing factor.

Hence, we conceptualized an adaptation manager (the adaptation manager is equal to the adaptation controller in Fig. 3). The adaptation manager organizes all adaptation actions. So, all changes on graphical primitives, layout aspects etc. are notified to the adaptation manager. The adaptation manager stores all changes (by type and value) for any visualization (the name) and what adaptation technique has done that in a large list. These four properties build a quadruple and are stored as one entry in the list. In case that another adaptation technique wants to make similar changes in a single visualization, e.g. changing the color of a node, the entire change will be blocked, until the other technique revert the adaptation to the previous state. This approach avoids most unwanted curious states of visualization, because of many independent operating adaptation techniques.

4   Implementation

We applied the described concept through the integration of an Arduino (Fig. 4 shows the circuit), which connecting a number of sensors. We focused on physical environmental influencing factors for the prototype. By way of example, we included a temperature and humidity sensor pro to measure the environment temperature and relative humidity. We also integrated a light sensor to detect the ambient light intensity, and an air quality sensor to monitor over indoor air conditions. We tested a tilt switch, to detect vibrations. A small program runs on the Arduino that provides the sensor values over the USB connection to the computer.

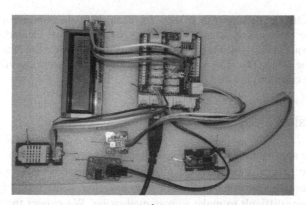

Fig. 4. To test our concept, we use an Arduino[1] with a couple of sensors that shares the sensor values with the Environment Adaptation Service. Instead of the Arduino Board also other kinds of sensor systems can be connected.

A simple Java program acts as our Environment Adaptation Service. It collects the sensor values and generates the environment conditions. Other applications can

---

[1] The Arduino is a programmable microcontroller that allows easily connecting various sensors and other kinds of electronic bricks for different use cases. More information on: http://arduino.cc (last accessed: 21/01/2014).

connect to this service and can request the environment conditions or the raw sensor values through a separate provided socket connection.

The adaptation functionalities are implemented in the web-application SemaVis, which is used in a common search scenario. SemaVis is a web-technology to visualize heterogeneous kinds of data. A separate module requests the current environment conditions and based of pre-defined rules, the visualizations will be adapted. In this very first implementation we only considered adaptations based on the light, which adapts the contrast and brightness of the visualization, on motions, which adapts the size of some nodes/buttons, and the air quality, which adapts the complexity of some visualizations. Fig. 5 shows the adaptation on the visualizations based on the light intensity and the air quality.

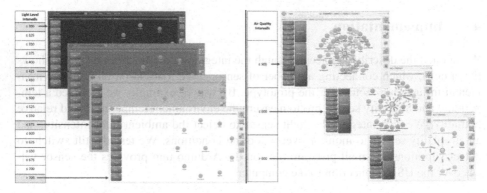

Fig. 5. On the left side, the screenshots show the changes of the contrast and brightness in dependence of the environment lightness. The darker the environment the darker the visualizations will be drawn. On the right side the visualization complexity (level of detail) is changed in dependence of the air quality. The worse the air quality of the environment is detected, the more reduced the complexity of the visualization.

5   Discussion

To validate our approach to adapt the visualization based on environmental influencing factors, we noticed the challenge of evaluating adaptive visualizations. In contrast to implementation of other features, e.g. to visualize some issues in an improved manner, it is more difficult to make a cross-evaluation. We expect the reason for this circumstance is that the provided visualization functionalities have not been changed. Even more, they are just refined slightly through an improved subjective perception. These subjective perceptions are mainly interpreted as User-Experience, and the evaluation of User-Experience is a complex topic [10,8]. In the most evaluation experiments the time is measured to compare (e.g. [9]), if users could solve certain tasks faster [10]. But, for the evaluation of the subjective perceptions such experiments will not be suitable. However, questionnaires can give feedback on personal perception, but whether this is also a practical and beneficial approach cannot be determined.

It is also critical how an evaluation should be realized in practice, because it is not so easy to change the environmental factors in a natural way. Simulated environment changes, e.g. vibrations or changes of the temperature in offices, give a quite surreal impression. To evaluate adaptations based on environment factors is a challenge, since it is mostly not perceived as something normal.

6   Conclusion

In this paper we introduced an adaptive visualization approach based on environmental influencing factors. For this purpose we investigated similar approaches in research and already existing implementations in the market, especially in mobile devices. Furthermore, we investigated the variety of possible influencing factors and defined a context model, which builds the baseline for further influencing factors. Based on this theoretic context model, we described a conceptual framework of an adaptation system that adapts visualizations based on the influencing factors.

In the first prototype we utilized data on light intensity, temperature, humidity, air quality, and vibrations. In a proof of concept, we considered these sensor data to adapt the visualization during a common search scenario.

Acknowledgments. Part of this work has been carried out within the FUPOL project, funded by the European Commission under the grant agreement no. 287119 of the 7th Framework Programme. This work is based on the SemaVis technology developed by Fraunhofer IGD (http://www.semavis.com). SemaVis provides a comprehensive and modular approach for visualizing heterogeneous data for various users.

References

1. Zimmermann, A., Specht, M., Lorenz, A.: Personalization and Context Management. User Modeling and User-Adapted Interaction 15(3-4), 275–302 (2005)
2. Jameson, A.: Modelling both the Context and the User. Personal Ubiquitous Comput. 5(1), 29–33 (2001)
3. Motti, V.G.: A computational framework for multi-dimensional context-aware adaptation. In: Proceedings of the 3rd ACM SIGCHI Symposium on Engineering Interactive Computing Systems (EICS 2011), pp. 315–318. ACM, New York (2011)
4. Malek, J., Laroussi, M., Derycke, A.: A Multi-Layer Ubiquitous Middleware for Bijective Adaptation between Context and Activity in a Mobile and Collaborative learning. In: International Conference on Systems and Networks Communications (ICSNC 2006), p. 39 (2006)
5. Samulowitz, M., Michahelles, F., Linnhoff-Popien, C.: Adaptive interaction for enabling pervasive services. In: Banerjee, S. (ed.) Proceedings of the 2nd ACM International Workshop on Data Engineering for Wireless and Mobile Access (MobiDe 2001), pp. 20–26. ACM, New York (2001)
6. Schmidt, A., Beigl, M., Gellersen, H.-W.: There is more to Context than Location. Journal of Computers and Graphics 23, 893–901 (1998)

422   D. Burkhardt et al.

7. Hinckley, K., Pierce, J., Sinclair, M., Horvitz, E.: Sensing techniques for mobile interaction. In: Proceedings of the 13th Annual ACM Symposium on User Interface Software and Technology (UIST 2000), pp. 91–100. ACM, New York (2000)
8. Arhippainen, L., Tähti, M.: Empirical evaluation of user experience in two adaptive mobile application prototypes. In: Proceedings of the 2nd International Conference on Mobile ldots (2003)
9. Van Velsen, L., Van der Geest, T., Klaassen, R., Steehouder, M.: User-centered evaluation of adaptive and adaptable systems: A literature review. Knowl. Eng. Rev. 23(3), 261–281 (2008)
10. Vermeeren, A.P.O.S., Lai-Chong Law, E., Roto, V., Obrist, M., Hoonhout, J., Väänänen-Vainio-Mattila, K.: User experience evaluation methods: current state and development needs. In: Proceedings of the 6th Nordic Conference on Human-Computer Interaction: Extending Boundaries (NordiCHI 2010), pp. 521–530. ACM, New York (2010)
11. Nazemi, K., Breyer, M., Forster, J., Burkhardt, D., Kuijper, A.: Interacting with Semantics: A User-Centered Visualization Adaptation Based on Semantics Data. In: Smith, M.J., Salvendy, G. (eds.) HCII 2011, Part I. LNCS, vol. 6771, pp. 239–248. Springer, Heidelberg (2011)
12. Nazemi, K., Burkhardt, D., Praetorius, A., Breyer, M., Kuijper, A.: Adapting User Interfaces by Analyzing Data Characteristics for Determining Adequate Visualizations. In: Kurosu, M. (ed.) HCD 2011. LNCS, vol. 6776, pp. 566–575. Springer, Heidelberg (2011)
13. Burkhardt, D., Ruppert, T., Nazemi, K.: Towards Process-Oriented Information Visualization for Supporting Users. In: IEEE Education Society: ICL 2012: 15th International Conference on Interactive Collaborative Learning and 41st International Conference on Engineering Pedagogy. IEEE, Inc., New York (2012)
14. Burkhardt, D., Nazemi, K.: Dynamic Process Support Based on Users' Behavior. In: IEEE Education Society: ICL 2012: 15th International Conference on Interactive Collaborative Learning and 41st International Conference on Engineering Pedagogy. IEEE, Inc., New York (2012)
15. Castillejo, E., Almeida, A., López-de-Ipiña, D.: User, Context and Device Modeling for Adaptive User Interface Systems. In: Urzaiz, G., Ochoa, S.F., Bravo, J., Chen, L.L., Oliveira, J. (eds.) UCAmI 2013. LNCS, vol. 8276, pp. 94–101. Springer, Heidelberg (2013)

Intelligent Document User Interface Design Using MVC and UIML

Lawrence Henschen[1], Ning Li[2], Yunmei Shi[2], Yuhan Zhang[2], and Julia Lee[1]

[1] Northwestern University, Evanston, Illinois, USA
henschen@eecs.northwestern.edu, julialee@agep.northwestern.edu
[2] Beijing Information Science and Technology University, Beijing, China
{lining,sym}@bistu.edu.cn, zhangcong668@163.com

Abstract. We describe a method for generating dynamic user interfaces for document processing systems by using MVC as a guide and UIML as the method to describe the model, view, and controller. Our approach implements the notion of intelligent documents, that is, documents whose processing is richer than processing applied to paper documents. Using our approach, the interface may include new operations not included in the normal document processing system. Moreover, the functions used to implement those operations may be any service available on the web. Finally, because we use UIML, the interface and implementation of services is easily changeable. Thus we achieve the goal of any document originated from anywhere in the world (globalization) being displayed in a usable way (usability) in any environment in a dynamic and platform independent way.

Keywords: intelligent document, user interface, MVC model, UIML , dynamic configuration.

1 Introduction and Background

As globalization continues, the need for document systems that do more than just traditional editing and saving functions has grown. Examples of this need include dynamically selecting spell checking programs for international companies that communicate in many languages or that use special sets of terms, private encryption/decryption for heightened security in both international and domestic transmission of files, the ability to embed special features in documents and process them with proprietary software (for example for specialized engineering enterprises), and many more. Moreover, it is expected that these needs will extend over an increasing variety of computing platforms. No single document processing system is likely to provide such a vast array of services or to be adaptable to the needs of such a variety of individual enterprises, much less run on a variety of platforms. Thus, there is a need to make document processing systems extendible, adaptable, and interoperable. A major aspect of achieving this goal is to design a user interface mechanism that will allow enterprises to augment the capabilities of document processing systems, allow

M. Kurosu (Ed.): Human-Computer Interaction, Part I, HCII 2014, LNCS 8510, pp. 423–432, 2014.

users convenient access to those capabilities with a high degree of learnability, and do so in a platform-independent way.

The notion of "active document" and, later, "intelligent document" [1,2] encompasses many of the features mentioned above. Intelligent documents can interact with other programs besides just the word processing system itself, should be interoperable, and in general should adapt to the users' needs. Even more importantly, intelligent document systems should be able to smoothly integrate new operations that are specific to a particular type of enterprise but not generally available in word processing systems. Intelligent documents require a user interface that can change dynamically to adapt to the user's needs based on the content of the document and the actions of the user, thereby providing a much richer interface than those provided by traditional word processing software. Such a user interface must accommodate a wide variety of computing environments and platforms as well as major differences in document format (e.g., OOXML vs. UOF).

Some attempts have been made to implement intelligent document processing systems, for example, HotDoc [3] and to some extent Microsoft Office 2007 [4]. The approaches that they used to implement intelligent documents vary, for example, through embedding some micro scenario or some plug-ins, using XML extended packages plus a second document that describes the first document's characteristics, and using a dynamic link library (DLL) to achieve dynamic operation. In the first approach, dynamic operation depends on the specific programming language or script language. Such approaches are not platform independent. Similarly, approaches based on DLLs are not platform independent. Finally, the actual user interfaces used in these approaches are relatively static and not so easy to modify to be responsive to users' needs. Many of these attempts use the Model-View-Controller (MVC) [5] approach as a guide. Although a step in the right direction, unless the model, view, and controller are themselves described in a high-level descriptive language as opposed to a specific language, the resulting interface is again static and platform dependent.

We propose combining the MVC approach to system development with the use of User Interface Markup Language (UIML) [6], a high-level description language, to generate document processing systems that satisfy the requirements mentioned above – platform independent, easily maintainable and modifiable, responsive to users' needs, and able to access required services anywhere on the web. Our approach contributes to reaching the goal of any document originated from anywhere in the world (globalization) being displayed in a usable way (usability) in any environment and adapting to the needs of any enterprise. Although the goal of complete platform independence is not reached, our method reduces the dependence to a small portion of an overall system, the renderer, which is discussed in Section 3. We only note here that the renderer connects the platform-independent interface description in a UIML document to the specific widgets (e.g., WPF widgets) used by a particular document processing system. It is written only once, can be used for many different UIML files, and is generally much smaller than application libraries that might be used for special functions being added to a system. Therefore, the benefits of the intelligent document concept can be achieved with a very small one-time software effort.

We note that our work is orthogonal to the work on automatic user interface generation, such as described in [7]. We propose a method by which a system designer (i.e., a human) can specify a user interface that meets the needs of a particular class of applications – intelligent document processing. As such, our work represents a case study in applying HCI tools to meet a particular need.

In the next section we describe the actual interface that we implemented and the rationale for our choices of interface features. In the section Implementation Details we describe how we used MVC as a guide and UIML as the technique to actually implement the interface for a specific set of new document operations. Our goal for this work was to demonstrate that MVC and UIML were adequate tools to isolate platform dependence while still providing a high degree of flexibility in interface design and document processing feature set. Finally, we provide some closing remarks on our work and its contributions to HCI.

2   Our Interface

The interface we implemented is shown in Figure 1. We implemented our system using the add-on feature of common document processing systems. The left side of Figure 1 shows the initial user interface, with the specific additions marked by the red box. The left button changes the menu bar to a list of the new operations that a user can perform, as shown on the right (the actual intelligent operation interface). The right button in the red box opens a dialogue interface (not shown for reasons of space) that allows the user to select which intelligent operations he or she wants to use.

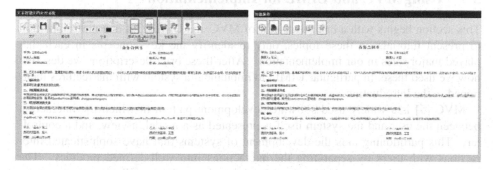

Fig. 1. Normal System View and Intelligent Operation Menu

There are many ways an interface to intelligent document processing could be designed. We chose the above design based on standard HCI principles – learnability, flexibility, and robustness [8]. Regarding learnability, this design maximizes familiarity, consistency, and predictability. The same menu process that is built in to almost every document processing system is used for selecting standard of intelligent operations, selecting a particular intelligent operation, and selecting the configuration. The standard operations are used in exactly the same way as before the addition of intelligent operations. Users who do not need the new operations require no learning at all, and even novice users can easily tell how to access the new operations or access the configuration interface. Flexibility is evidenced in several ways. The user can select which intelligent operations he or she wants to use, thereby customizing the interface for that particular user. The choice to use the operations is completely the user's choice; the dialogue is completely user-driven as opposed to system-driven, at least for the top level selection of operations. Because our system allows essentially any application to become part of the document processing system, it is of course impossible to ensure user-driven dialogue beyond the top level. Similarly, the degree of multi-threading and task migration is determined by the applications being added to the system and are again beyond the scope of the basic interface methodology we have proposed. Thus, our approach provides as much flexibility as possible given that we cannot know further details of the specific intelligent operations being added to a specific system. Finally, similar remarks apply to robustness. For example, the user can easily close the intelligent operation menu if he or she made a mistake in opening it. The internal state regarding standard mode vs intelligent mode is readily apparent. Other issues of robustness, like responsiveness and conformance, are tied to both the implementation and location of the individual intelligent operations. Location now plays an important role because our system allows the intelligent applications to use any software available anywhere on the web. Feedback that an intelligent operation has been selected is instantaneous, but if the implementation is somewhere else on the web the user may not be able to observe the progress. Thus, we claim that our design provides a very high level of learnability, flexibility, and robustness.

3   Using MVC and UIML for Implementation

This section begins with a brief overview of MVC and UIML. It is not our intention to present tutorials on these topics, only to identify the key concepts in each that played major roles in our implementation. After these brief descriptions we describe how we used these, in particular UIML, to implement a system with the features mentioned in the Introduction

MVC [5] is a widely used software development pattern in which the interaction between the user and the system itself is presented as a model, a view, and a controller. This partitioning aids the development of systems that have sophisticated interactions with users by separating the interactions into well-defined modules. The model contains the general rules, logic, and functions of the application and specific data of the system. The view is what the user sees. The controller accepts inputs from the user and passes information along to the model. In the original, simple MVC methodology, the interaction between these three components is straightforward: the model informs the view regarding how to present information to the user, and the controller receives inputs from the user and informs the model. The model changes accordingly and again informs the view what to display to the user and how. Recent applications of this pattern allow the controller to also serve as the translator or interpreter between the user's language and the system's language [8]. There are many other variations of this approach. Our system allows the controller component to interact with both the view component and the model component.

UIML [6], introduced in 1998, is an XML-based (OASIS) standard for designing and specifying user interfaces. Its goal is to allow interface designers to specify in an abstract way what an interface should have and then to connect terms used in the abstract description with real applications. This separation allows interface designers to develop portable and dynamic interfaces without having to become experts in web programming. The abstract description is portable because it uses only abstract terms and does not depend on specific applications or hardware. The application logic, given in a separate part of the UIML file, then implements the abstract description in a specific computing environment.

The two major components of a UIML specification, interface and peers, make UIML highly compatible with the MVC approach. The interface component specifies the view portion of the system in an abstract way that is completely platform independent. The interface elements structure, style, and content are used to specify the corresponding view elements. The behavior element of the interface portion of a UIML file describes the abstract operations that are to be performed in response to conditions, typically user inputs. All of these elements within the interface component, even the behavior elements, are specified in a completely abstract and platform independent way. The connection to platforms and the actual functions that implement the abstract concepts in the interface section are given in the UIML peers section through the use of several types of elements. The d-component element maps abstract concepts in the interface section to specific classes in an actual software system. The d-method elements map specific abstract operations to actual methods, and the d-param sub-elements map specific pieces of the user interaction to the parameters for the corresponding method. Finally, we note that UIML, like other XML-based languages, uses the standard namespace technique to allow the writer of a UIML-based application to access a myriad of existing systems and vocabularies that already define concepts and applications. In particular, the ability to use any namespace to access implementations of intelligent operations anywhere on the web is a key component for achieving our goals.

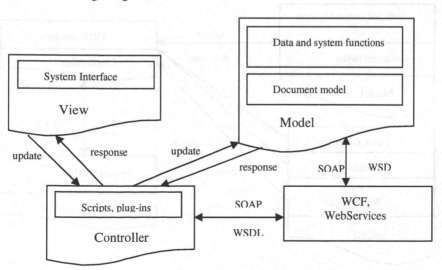

Fig. 2. Overview of the System from the MVC Point of View

Figure 2 outlines the major pieces of our intelligent document processing system from the MVC point of view. The intelligent processing section has its own model, view, and controller. The view portion interfaces with the traditional document processing system, which may have its own MVC model independent of the intelligent portion of the whole system. We describe the intelligent model and controller in more detail in the following paragraphs.

The Model component in our approach includes all aspects (logic, functions, as well as data) of the intelligent portion of the document processing system. The View component includes all the user interface views that allow user to observe all system state changes. The Controller component serves as the translator or interpreter for the Model component and the View component. It translates the user language (inputs) into the system language (commands/function calls/messages, etc.). We utilize Web services and Windows Communication Foundation (WCF) in both the Controller component and the Model component.

Note that the UIML document is used to generate the system user interface. There are two different ways to utilize a UIML specification in a system. One possibility is to write a UIML renderer as a compiler which produces a UI and its interaction operations. Another way is to write a renderer as an interpreter; that is, the UIML specification and the renderer are parts of the run-time system. Our system used the latter approach. Figure 3 shows how the UIML document and renderer fit into our MVC approach for our system.

Note that the UIML renderer takes the role of Controller in our system since it dynamically interacts with other parts of the system and creates the system interface. The UIML document and the vocabulary table, which maps the UIML terminology into specific toolkit terms or commands, are used by the renderer. In our system the toolkits used were WCF and WebServices. The UIML document and the vocabulary

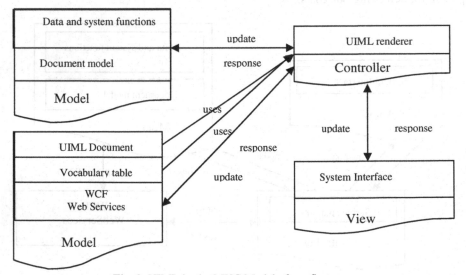

Fig. 3. UIML in the MVC Model of our System

are considered as system data in MVC and, hence, belong to the Model component. The WCF and Web Service functions are not part of the essential intelligent document model, but they are parts of the system functions to dynamically form the system interface.   Our model also includes information required by the Controller to apply intelligent operations to user documents in different standard format systems, such as UOF or OOXML. Any required translation in our implementation is performed by using XSLT. In our MVC approach, the documents in different format and the XSLT document are all system data, and the XSLT Processor is part of the system functions. All the original intelligent document model and operation functions are certainly parts of the Model component in the MVC of our system.

Figures 4, 5, and 6 give examples from the UIML file used in our demonstration implementation to illustrate the concepts described above. So that the reader can better understand the examples, we mention that our demonstration system implemented six different intelligent operations – spell checking, verbal read out of selected text, encryption and decryption of selected text, annotation, and database lookup relevant to selected text. All of these were specific for Chinese text. We provided XSLT translation for documents in the Chinese standard, UOF.

Figure 4 shows portions of the UIML interface section. It specifies that in this model there is an appliance by which the user can invoke the verbal read-out intelligent operation. The appliance consists of a button, which has certain properties and behaviors. For example, the button has an image, width, etc. and causes an intelligent operation (TextToSpeechService.speaker) to be invoked when the button is pressed. Figure 5 shows a portion of the UIML peers section that connects the abstract intelligent operation named in the rule in Figure 4 to an actual implementation for that abstract operation.   In this case, the abstract operation TextToSpeechService is mapped to a function on the same computer, localhost:8081/TextToSpeechService. As can be seen, the location parameter is a general URL, so a document processing system can use services anywhere on the web. This feature could be important for some applications. For example, companies that have international communications and use many different languages may need access to special software not built in to typical document processors but available on different web sites in different countries. Another important use is a company that uses special software for their documents, but whose employees travel and do most of their document processing on their laptops. If the special software is large or frequently updated, it would not be effective to download on every employee's laptop; accessing a single, up-to-date version through the web in a way that is directly accessible in the document processor is the optimal approach. We used many Web service functions that will also utilize the URL notation where they are reference in UIML document. Figure 6 shows a portion of the vocabulary, contained in a separate XML file. In this case, the vocabulary file specifies a standard library, WPF_1.0_ZYH_1.0 as specified in the base attribute, for concrete definitions of abstract concepts used in the UIML file. For the selected library Figure 6 shows how the abstract concept "Button" in the UIML file maps to a concrete implementation in the WPF library. Fortunately, there are many common vocabularies available free on the web; however, system designers can also define their own vocabularies and reference them through base and namespace attributes.

```
<uiml:interface id="WPF">
    <uiml:structure>
        ...
        <uiml:part class="Button" id="btnSpkr">
            <uiml:part class="Image" id="imgSpkr" />
        </uiml:part>
    </uiml:part>
    </uiml:structure>
    <uiml:style id="WPFstyle">
        ...
        <uiml:property part-class="Button" name="Width">40</uiml:property>
    </uiml:style>
    <uiml:behavior>
        <uiml:rule>
            <uiml:condition>
                <uiml:event part-class="ButtonPressed" part-name="btnSpkr" />
            </uiml:condition>
            <uiml:action>
                <uiml:call name="TextToSpeechService.speaker">
                    <uiml:param name="text">
                        <uiml:property part-name="r" name="Selection.Text" />
                    </uiml:param>
                </uiml:call>
            </uiml:action>
        </uiml:rule>
        ...
    </uiml:interface>
```

Fig. 4. Portion of the Structure Section of the UIML File

```
<uiml:peers>
    <uiml:presentation base="WPF_1.0_ZYH_1.0" />
    ...
    <uiml:d-component id="TextToSpeechService"
    location ="http://localhost:8081/TextToSpeechService/Speaker.svc">
        <uiml:d-method id="speaker" maps-to="speak">
            <uiml:d-param id="speakertext" type="string" />
        </uiml:d-method>
    </uiml:d-component>
    ...
</uiml:peers>
```

Fig. 5. Portion of the Peers Section of the UIML File

```
<template id="WPF">
  <presentation base="WPF_1.0_ZYH_1.0">
    <d-class id="Button" maps-type="tag" used-in-tag="part" maps-to="Button">
      <d-property id="VerticalAlignment" maps-type="attribute"
                  maps-to="VerticalAlignment">
        <d-param type="System.Windows.VerticalAlignment"/>
      </d-property>
      ...
    </d-class>
  </presentation>
  ...
</template>
```

Fig. 6. Portion of the Vocabulary XML File

As already noted, the goal of complete platform independence is not achieved. There are two reasons for this. First, the target applications, document processing systems, typically do not have built-in interfaces to UIML. Each product has presentation and interface software that is specific to that product. Therefore, in our approach a small software interface is needed to connect the UIML elements into the document processing system. We call this software the renderer. The renderer transforms the platform independent user interface description contained in the UIML file into the widgets in the specific visual library being used to display and interact with the user. In particular, a major responsibility for the render is to check rules in the UIML to see which, if any, need to be invoked when the user has provided some input. The second reason that complete independence is not possible is that different implementations of the interface widgets (e.g., WPF, JavaSwing, etc.) use different representations of the actual documents. Our approach allows the system designer to select arbitrary implementations for the actual interface functions, and therefore for each such choice we may need to translate an individual document being processed from its source format (e.g., UOF or OOXML) into the format required by the chosen implementation (WPF, JavaSwing, etc.). In our demonstration system this was accomplished by an XSLT file. The renderer was implemented with 550 lines of C# code, the UIML file was 560 lines, the vocabulary file 223 lines, and the XSLT file 340 lines.

4   Conclusion and Future Work

The major contribution of our work described in this paper is that by combining the MVC model and the UIML language we were able to implement a rich user interface for intelligent documents that includes dynamic reconfiguration of the interface, access to services appropriate for individual documents regardless of where they were originally written or where they are currently being viewed, the ability to specify and dynamically change the application logic to be any service anywhere on the internet, interface design reusability, and other significant features. We believe this approach can be the foundation for other efforts at implementing interfaces for intelligent documents.

A long-term goal of our project at Beijing Information Science and Technology University is to use our approach, in particular the UIML approach for describing interfaces, to describe the entire office software and thereby provide even the basic operations, like insert/delete, as web services. In this way we would be able to dynamically generate a complete word process like MS-WORD and customize it in literally any way a client wants.

Acknowledgements. This work was supported in part by the Opening Project of the State Key Laboratory of Digital Publishing Technology, China.

References

1. Spinard, R.: Dynamic Documents. Harvard University Information Technology Quarterly 7, 15–18 (1988)
2. Willet, E.: Microsoft 2003 Bible. Wiley Publishing Company, Indianapolis (2004)
3. Buchner, J.: A Framework for Compound Documents. Journal of the Association for Computing Machinery 32, 33–36 (2000)
4. Janus, P.: Pro InfoPath 2007. Springer, New York (2007)
5. Krasner, G., Pope, S.: A cookbook for using the model-view-controller user interface paradigm in Smalltalk-80. Journal of Object-Oriented Programming 1, 26–49 (1988)
6. Abrams, M., Phanouriou, C., Batongbacal, A., Williams, S., Shuster, J.: UIML: An Appliance-Independent XML User Interface Language. Computer Networks: The International Journal of Computer and Telecommunications Networking 31, 1695–1708 (1999)
7. Calvary, G., Graham, T., Gray, P.: Proceedings of the 1st ACM SIGCHI Symposium on Engineering Interactive Computing Systems (EICS 2009). ACM Press, New York (2009)
8. Dix, A., Finlay, J., Abowd, G., Beale, R.: Human Computer Interaction, 3rd edn. Pearson/Prentice Hall, New York (2004)

Log-Based Personalization Tool
as an Assistive Technology

Vagner Figueredo de Santana and Maria Cecília Calani Baranauskas

Institute of Computing, University of Campinas (UNICAMP) Albert Einstein Av.,
1251, Campinas, São Paulo, Brazil
{vsantana,cecilia}@ic.unicamp.br

Abstract. Solutions for personalizing websites by automatically changing user interfaces (UI) to fit users' needs have been proposed by the industry and the academy in order to provide individualized user experience. However, the users' perception of changes in the tailored UI is still a topic to be studied. This work presents a tool developed to capture logs, generate, and apply individual adjustments, personalizing websites as people use it. In addition, the tool is proposed as a log-based personalization assistive technology and it is published to the community. The tool was evaluated in depth, qualitatively, counting with the participation of 4 blind users fluent in using the Web, knowing personalization existing features, and fluent on using computers. They were invited so that the understanding of outcomes and limitations of the personalization features offered could be better understood. Based on the results, we highlight possible scenarios where similar approaches could be used to assist people with disabilities and reinforce the importance of considering the users' perception of changes automatically performed in UIs.

Keywords: Self-tailoring website, adaptive website, website evaluation, user interface evaluation, remote evaluation, accessibility, usability, event logs.

1 Introduction

Accessibility is already recognized as a fundamental requirement of user interfaces (UIs). Moreover, the task of removing accessibility barriers to guarantee accessibility is motivated by legislation and guidelines from organizations and governments.

Although there are worldwide organizations and legislation supporting Web accessibility, more than 95% of the websites fail when confronted to minimum accessibility requirements, such as to provide adequate descriptions of visual elements [24].

Web Accessibility means that people with different types of limitation can perceive, understand, navigate, interact, and contribute with the Web. Accessibility barrier is anything that makes difficult or impossible for people with disability to use the Web [25]. The traditional concept of Usability – as the capacity of a product to be used by specific users to achieve certain goals with efficiency and satisfaction, in a certain context of use – already brings to focus the context of use, which involves

M. Kurosu (Ed.): Human-Computer Interaction, Part I, HCII 2014, LNCS 8510, pp. 433–444, 2014.

users, tasks, equipments (hardware, software, and other materials), physical and social environment in which the product is used [11].

The evaluation of websites is a way of identifying issues and supporting the removal of accessibility barriers. When an evaluation aims at improving accessibility, characteristics related to the context of use need to be considered. However, as software configuration and environment variables are difficult to replicate in labs, remote evaluation is an interesting approach for analyzing the real context of use.

After the analysis of data resulting from UI evaluations, tools can provide reports on features, suggest improvement, or they can change the UI in order to remove any identified issue. This last action is referred in literature as UIs that are personalized, adaptive, individualized, or self-tailored. However, such approach on changing the UI is only part of the solution, since it is also important to analyze the users' perception and the users' satisfaction with the changes. Thus, the objective of this work is two-fold: to present a self-tailoring evaluation tool and to analyze how blind users perceive, interact, and deal with a website tailored according to a previous usage.

This paper is organized as follows: section 2 gathers definitions and the background of the work; section 3 presents the developed tool; section 4 details method and experiment design; section 5 shows the results; section 6 draws the conclusions.

2 Background

The automation of evaluation tools may involve the following steps: **capture** (i.e., logging the usage data), **analysis** (i.e., identification of problems), **critic** (i.e., suggestions on how to improve the evaluated UI) [12]. In addition, it may also involve **adjustments** (i.e., the elimination of identified problems by changing UI elements).

UI events are a natural result of the usage of UI based on windows and their components (e.g., mouse clicks, key strokes). Moreover, from the possibility of recording these events and the fact that they indicate users' behavior during UI usage, they represent an important data source regarding UI evaluation; they allow to analyze performed paths, repeatedly triggered events, time spent to perform certain actions, etc. [9]. In this context, event logs can be seen as a temporized set of UI events.

Evaluation of UI can be **local**, when the participant and evaluator are in the same place (e.g., a UI evaluation lab), or **remote**, when participant and evaluator are in different places. Moreover, evaluation can be considered **synchronous** (evaluator and participant are working on the evaluation at the same time) or **asynchronous** (there is no need for evaluator and participant to work on the evaluation at the same time).

Asynchronous remote evaluation is interesting for the context of website evaluation because it avoids biases (e.g., related to environmental, software, and hardware variables) in the use of UI and, consequently, in the data logged. It is also a way of enabling the number of sessions to scale up. In the context of accessibility, it is an interesting approach because it is hard to replicate configurations of hardware and software when users are using assistive technology (AT) support [5]. Another point in favor of this combination is that, according to Rubin [22], tests in controlled environments are artificial and may influence the results. In addition, the variety of needs and the wide diversity of physical, sensorial, and cognitive characteristics of users make the UI design very complex [1]. However, this approach has also limitations, e.g., capturing users' verbalizations, expressions, and actions performed before the event logging takes place. Literature presents different tools for evaluating UIs; in what follows we present a brief history of related tools.

WebVIP is a logger for formal tests; i.e. when the participants are required to execute specific and predefined tasks. The vocabulary of events, which stands for the number of different event types, is restricted to a few events (i.e., press/hold keys, press/hold/move the mouse pointer, enter/leave a widget, and enter/exit the window). The environment configuration requires a local copy of the entire website being evaluated [18]. **WET** is another example of a logger for formal tests. It uses cookies to store logged data, which leads to the reduction on the vocabulary of events due to storage issues [7]. These tools represent the first efforts to capture client-side events.

WebRemUSINE is a tool that performs the automatic capture and analysis of website interaction logs in order to detect usability problems through remote evaluation. The analysis of logs is based on the comparison between the paths used by users and the optimum task model previously defined. The user must select the tasks she or he is performing to allow comparison of the captured events with the task selected by the user [19]. **MultimodalWebRemUSINE** is the latest version of the tool that aims at exploiting the possibilities opened up by recent technologies to gather a richer set of information regarding user behavior. The tool allows traditional graphical logs to be analyzed together with the logs from webcams and portable eye trackers [20].

Google Analytics is an example of automatic capture and analysis tool. The default data source used by the tool represents page-views. The tool requires the evaluator to register him/herself and to insert a JavaScript code into the Web pages to be evaluated. It provides different report formats, allows actions to be registered as virtual page-views, and has a feature to register customized events at the client-side. These customized events in Google Analytics are events that can be named by the evaluator and triggered in any Web page component configured to communicate with the JavaScript data-logger (e.g., a Flash video or HTML event handler). However, the tool has a limit of logging 500 customized events per visit [8].

WebQuilt is an automatic capture and analysis tool that uses page-view level logs as data source. It uses a proxy-logger that mediates between users and Web servers and stores the communication between them [10]. **MouseTrack** is a proxy-based usability evaluation system that performs automatic client-side capture and analysis. It provides an online configuration and visualization tool that shows the mouse path followed by website visitors [2]. **UsaProxy** is a proxy-based usability evaluation system that performs automatic capture and analysis of client-side events. It uses JavaScript and focuses on usability tests [3]. **WebinSitu** is an enhanced version of UsaProxy that focuses on behavior comparisons between blind and sighted users [5]. **WAUTER** is a proxy-based Web usability evaluation tool, which employs a functional set of tools that automate the capture and analysis by considering client-side logs and task models [4]. **Web Usability Probe** (WUP) is a proxy-based remote usability evaluation tool that considers formal use situations. The data source considered is client-side data on user interactions and JavaScript events. In addition, it allows the definition of customized events, giving evaluators the flexibility to add specific events to be detected and considered in the evaluation. The tool supports evaluation of any Web site by exploiting a proxy-based architecture and enables the evaluator to perform a comparison between actual user behavior and an optimal sequence of actions [6]. In some cases, proxy-based tools require reconfiguration of the user's browser or a proxy setup. Moreover, they may result in Web server processing overhead, due to additional requests/responses, or compatibility problems, which may occur when inserting JavaScript code into the evaluated Web pages.

The presented tools have drawbacks, e.g., limited vocabulary, dependency of task model development, limit of events captured, among others. Thus, the proposed tool (detailed in the next section) addresses the presented shortcomings. Next we present the background on personalization and how it is considered in the proposed tool.

According to Pierrakos et al. [21], personalization improves the experience of a visitor by presenting the information she or he wants, in an appropriate way, and at the appropriate time. Mobasher et al. [15] define personalization as any action that adjusts Web experience to a particular user or group of users. Nielsen [17] defines personalization as when the computer changes its behavior to adequate itself to the users' interests. Mikroyannidis and Theodoulidis [14] define self-adaptive UIs as those that improve their structure and design by learning how the UI is used. Model-Based User Interfaces Incubator Group (MBUI-XG) [13] defines adaptive UI as a UI that is capable of considering the usage context and (automatically) reacts to context changes in a continuous way, changing presentation, content, navigation, or even behavior. Mørch [16] uses the term tailoring as the adaptation of information systems to specific practices of developers, end users, or group of users. The author presents a classification of 3 levels for tailoring, as follows: Customization – Modification of the objects presentation or edition of attributes by the selection of predefined values; Integration – Creation or recording of a sequence of actions that result in a new functionality, stored within the application as a component or a command; Extension – Improvement of the functionality of an application by the insertion of new code.

Considering the related works, the tool proposed in this work advances the state of the art by presenting an approach that generates adjustments code based on client-side events captured continuously. The proposed tool identifies usage patterns, generates adjustment codes, and applies the adjustments, evaluating whether the change was well succeeded or not. Thus, considering the presented terms, the tool continuously applies Mørch's tailoring of level 3 (i.e., extension); next section details the functioning of the proposed tool.

3   The Proposed Tool

The proposed evaluation tool, called WELFIT (Web Event Logger and Flow Evaluation Tool), supports remote/non-remote, synchronous/asynchronous, and formal/informal tests. The data source considered is client-side events log. Regarding the effort level to configure an evaluation, the evaluator is required to register and to insert the logger into Web pages; on the part of the participant, it requires the acceptance of the invitation to participate in the evaluation. The automation performed by the tool involves logging client-side events, generating graphical/statistical reports, and generating UI adjustments automatically.

The basic requirement of the developed system is to capture and log user interface events, which is available in interactive systems, reducing the need for specific evaluation devices (e.g., eye tracking) that take for granted certain characteristics of the user population (e.g., sight). The system is composed by two main modules:

- Client module, which is responsible for: capturing events at the client-side; iteratively compacting log lines using the Run Length Encoding algorithm; transmitting the packages of logged data asynchronously to the server; controlling that logged data is only discarded when the server confirms the proper storage, and; inserting adjustment code to the evaluated website.
- Server module, which is responsible for: receiving the data sent by the client module; unpacking the lines; storing received data; generating reports using JGraph[1] library, and; generating the adjustment codes.

For the evaluator, the environment configuration requires the following steps:

- The website administrator must register him/herself at the tool's Web administrative interface.
- Once logged, the administrator must register the websites s/he wants to evaluate.
- Once the website is registered, s/he includes the call to the JavaScript client-module in all website's pages that are to be evaluated.

At the client module, as soon as a package containing the logged data reaches the configurable size limit, it is sent to the server. Thus, as soon as some interaction data is stored at the server, the evaluator can login and view the resulting usage graph, which is the digraph representing the UI usage in which each node represents an event triggered in a certain Web page element. The report format used follows the structure presented by Santana and Baranauskas [23].

The usage graph can also be seen as the combination of walks (non-empty alternating sequence of nodes and edges) representing what, where, and when users performed actions. In the usage graph, a node is identified by its label, which is the concatenation of the event name and an identifier of the UI element where the event occurred. Each node counts on information regarding the total of sessions in which they occurred, mean distance from the root node, mean timestamp, among others.

The generated adjustments aim at reducing the identified usage incidents, available at the usage graph structure built from the client-side events log. Thus, after each visit, the rules matching previously identified patterns with adjustments are verified and, if it is the case, one or more adjustments are generated to next sessions. Then, in the next visit the tool applies the adjustment and the new observation is compared to previous ones in order to verify whether the number of usage incidents was reduced. Finally, if it is the case, the adjustment is applied in the future visits, else, the applied rule is marked as not well-succeeded for the specific participant.

---

[1] http://www.jgraph.com/

Regarding the insertion of adjustment code, at each new visit, the client-side module requests any generated adjustment for the current participant. Thus, if there is any adjustment code to be applied, then the client-module receives it and applies it to the current Web page.

The developed tool avoids the limit of client-side events captured, captures all types of events triggered at the client device, provides simple environment configuration, summarizes usage patterns, and points out usage incidents. This work contributes to the field by detailing an approach and providing a tool to evaluate how UIs are used by people with/without disabilities under the Universal Design philosophy. Moreover, a case study was carried out to increase the understanding of how the participants perceive adjustments performed by such tool.

4 Method and Experiment Design

This section presents characteristics of participants, materials, and the experiment design considered in the case study. The objective of the experiment was to investigate how IT experienced blind users perceive, interact, and deal with a website tailored according to a previous usage.

Participants: The participants invited to be part in the evaluation are blind people that are researchers, workers, or students at the university where the project was conducted. They had already had previous contact with the evaluated website, as this condition is essential for getting their perception to adjustments in the website. The point in inviting users with experience on IT is that they might present a more critical point of view, enriching the results of the study, since they have contact with different initiatives on evaluation of UI and insights involving the proposed approach may emerge. To invite participants, we counted one people that mediated the interaction with the team and the participants. The invitation was sent by email to 13 persons; 4 accepted to participate in the evaluation. Regarding gender, 2 are men and 2 are women. Regarding screen reader, 2 participants use NVDA and 2 use JAWS.

Materials: The website that was object of the evaluation is the portal of a research group from the university where the study took place. The research group develops research on topics related to accessibility and the support needed for the access and the permanence of people with disabilities in higher education. The target audience of the research group and its website is composed by students, researchers, and teachers. The website was chosen because it was developed and it is maintained considering accessibility requirements. Thus, the probability of users to face accessibility barriers is reduced and then interaction techniques can be analyzed with minor impacts of coding problems. Other important characteristic of the evaluated website is that part of its audience is composed by people with disabilities. The website uses the Plone® Content Management System (CMS), which is one of the most popular CMSs.

The tool developed in this research supports remote informal and formal tests. For a formal test, which is the case reported in this study, it requires the evaluator to send specific URLs to each of participants. These URLs help evaluators to track sessions and to identify tasks performed as well. The tool also allows evaluators to insert specific adjustment code into the URL in order to evaluate adjustments generated by the evaluator instead of adjustments generated automatically by the tool. Moreover, the adjustments can be plain JavaScript or jQuery code. In this study the adjustments were sent via URL to participants.

Design: The experiment design considered two evaluation stages. The first one to capture detailed data on how participants performed the tasks. The second one to apply adjustments and to analyze how participants interacted with the adjusted UI. All the tasks initiated from predefined links sent to the participants. For each participant, these links provide information allowing us to identify details of the evaluation (e.g., tasks performed) and to apply changes in the UI being evaluated (e.g., adjustments).

The tasks were proposed to identify usage patterns and ways that the evaluation tool could adjust the UI to allow detailed analysis of a posterior adjustment. The tasks were defined to observe how users access certain linked images, available resources, and the contact page. The tasks involved in the study were the following: Search and access the link to an audio book available at the research group portal; Search and access the link to the website used as a reference to develop accessible websites, available at the research group portal; Access the contact page and send a message informing what AT is being used and what is your opinion about the website, including any difficulty faced. The last task was proposed to evaluate the contact page channel, to gather information regarding the user software context (i.e., AT), and, considering the profile of the participants, to ask about difficulties or missing features.

In the second stage the link sent to participants already had the adjustments designed to shorten the tasks considering the interactions strategies used by the participants in the first stage. The adjustments were generated after detailed analysis of each usage graph resulting from each of the sessions. The adjustments are presented in details in the results section. In addition, a questionnaire was sent to the participants in order to gather further opinions on the adjustments applied and on the proposed approach. The questionnaire was composed by the following questions: A) Have you noticed any change in the website? If this is the case, which one? B) In your opinion what are the negative and positive aspects of this kind of evaluation in which the participants use their own computer, but have not explicit contact with evaluators? C) If a website under evaluation informs that it changed to fit the strategies you use to interact with it, what would be your opinion regarding this feature? D) What features do you think a self-tailoring system should have?

5   Results

In the evaluation, from the 13 invitations sent by email to blind users of the website who are also experienced IT users, 4 accepted to take part in the evaluation. Thus, the acceptance rate was 30.77%.

First Stage: the tasks performed by the participants were analyzed and the path performed by them was considered in the generated adjustments. The tool provides reporting features that summarize the actions performed by the participants. These reports were analyzed, the incidents indicated by the tool were mapped back to the studied UI, and the adjustments were created in order to reduce the incidents identified.

The participant 1 mentioned that the evaluated website is very concerned about accessibility and that she did not face any difficulty when performing the tasks. In addition, she said that she uses the shortcut 'H', available at NVDA, to navigate through all Web page's headers. She reported that this feature allows users to navigate through the content quicker than, for example, using the TAB key. During the first task, the participant also identified that one Web page had a missing link to the appropriate file; this fact was also pointed out by participant 3.

The participant 2 informed that he did not find any difficulty to use the evaluated website. However, the participant reported that the calendar feature, available at the right side of the homepage, has links that are not read by the screen reader. According to the participant, it is hard to understand what is available in the calendar, which is a standard feature offered by the Plone® CMS and it is located at the right hand side of the website (Figure 1).

Fig. 1. Plone®'s calendar feature

The participant 3 commented that the shortcuts (using the ALT key) available at the web page did not work. Moreover, she identified that a flash movie available at the homepage (showing different pictures) affected negatively the navigation.

The participant 4 mentioned he performed the tasks without problems. He also reported that the level of accessibility of the evaluated website is "very good [...] excellent for what is found in our country." The participant also informed that the submit button, at the contact page, was not accessible and that he had to ask for help to someone else that could see the link.

As a result of the interactions of these participants, it was possible to observe the following issues that led to the adjustments applied during the second stage (Table 1).

Table 1. Features and respective adjustments generated for all participants of the second stage

Feature/issue	Adjustment
The flash animation, located at the homepage, interfering negatively in the navigation.	Remove the flash animation, which has only decorative information.
Contact links available at the accessibility toolbar.	The structure of the accessibility tool bar was changed in order to show the contact link as the first item of the list.

Besides the issues regarding the animation available at the homepage and the submit button, participants reported that UI elements were easy to reach.

Second stage: The adjustment codes generated to address the incidents pointed out by the tool are presented in Table 2. Following we present participants' comments and questionnaire answers regarding the second stage:

- **Question A):** one answer pointed out that "[...] it looks like some accelerators were created and content was inserted [...]"; however, two participants commented that they did not noticed any change. These comments suggest that the adjustments applied were rated by one participant as an accelerator, suggesting improvement in the usage. Additionally, for other participants the adjustments were not noticed, meaning that at least they did not disturb the interaction.

- **Question B):** one participant mentioned that a positive point for developer is that "he can reach more participants." Another fact reported was that "for the developer it may not be evident whether the portal is working with the most used screen readers, because, in the course of time, users end up using features offered by these systems and beginners may find it difficult to navigate." As a positive point, a participant also highlighted that "[...] the remote evaluation without the presence of the researcher makes the user feel more comfortable [...]" These comments bring interesting facts related to the skill level of participants on using screen readers and about the comfort level of users participating remotely.

- **Question C):** one participant informed that he "would be very happy and satisfied because [...] [he] uses the internet a lot [...]"; another comment pointed out that "it is a big frustration to try to access something and fail to do it due to lack of accessibility." Moreover, one participant opined that "when we talk about changes to be applied to a website, they should be thought as a whole, and not only for the most accessed items." Another participant mentioned that she "would be satisfied for the [application of adjustments] and would focus on verifying the changes in order to report my opinion." These opinions suggest that participants would receive positively the information that a website applies adjustments considering the user´s strategies to navigate through some website. It is also worth noting the wish of participants on expressing opinions and giving feedbacks on tailoring features.

- **Question D):** the participants indicated the following features: "adjust the web page so that all the content can be accessed by the keyboard, insertion of accelerators in the most accessed items"; "at websites that require users interaction as drag and drop an item, that should be adjusted into something accessible and to be manipulated in other ways instead of by clicking and dragging"; "adjustment of improving contrast for people with difficulty on seeing", and; "reduction of the complexity for typing CAPTCHAS".

The features pointed out are strongly related to barriers faced by people with disabilities and, with exception of the CAPTCHA issue, all of them can be addressed as adjustments in an analogous way as presented in this study. One participant informed the following: "I do not know to what extent it is possible to adjust functionalities of an information system according to the strategies used by the users either because of the plurality of the strategies used or because of the generality of foreseen and unforeseen situations." In this comment the participant seems somewhat skeptical. The participant is right when pointing out the plurality of strategies used, however, all strategies are sequences of actions that, in turn, underneath the UI, are translated to UI events. Thus, the challenge resides on identifying who is using assistive technology and then analyzing patterns in these UI events streams. Moreover, the emphasis on foreseen and unforeseen situations corroborates the approach of the continuous evaluation supported by the WELFIT.

Table 2. Adjustment codes applied in the second stage related to the results of the Table 1

Adjustment code	Effect of applying the adjustment
document.getElementById('region-content'). getElmentsByTagName('p')[1]. setAttribute('style', 'display:none');	Plain JavaScript code used to change the layout of the web page, hiding the flash movie for the participants of the second stage of this evaluation.
$('#portal-siteactions').prepend($('#siteaction-contact').html()); $('#siteaction-contact'). style('display', 'none');	jQuery style of code used to change the structure of the accessibility toolbar, placing the contact link as the first element of the toolbar.

6   Conclusion

The evaluation of websites is essential for identifying issues and supporting the removal of accessibility barriers. Evaluation tools provide reports on problems, suggest improvements, or they can change the user interface in order to remove an identified issue. While solutions for adapting websites to fit users' needs are being proposed by the industry and academy, the users' perception of the changes in the tailored UI has not received the same attention.

The evaluation of adjustments is a key step for personalization systems, since an adjustment may solve an issue for a certain context of use, but the same adjustment might cause a usability problem or hamper access for others. This case study presented the perception of blind users to adjustments made in a website they use, based on their previous experience with it.

The first stage supported the identification of issues related to content (missing link) and to markup (calendar coding). In addition, the data generated in the first stage was analyzed with the support of the reporting features provided by the evaluation tool used and then used as input for generating adjustments. It is worth noting that the type of analysis performed in this study, in which UI events were analyzed one by one, was only possible because of the limited number of participants. Such detailed analysis does not scale if the number of participants grows. In cases where there is a large number of participants, it is required to consider summarization features highlighting the most relevant patterns, the most critical sequences, the usage incidents that have greater impact, to name a few.

The second stage findings suggest that the adjustments were not harmful for the evaluated UI in the presented case study and that they were perceived as accelerators or bypassed by participants. In addition, participants reveal that adjustment features are welcome and that one interesting application of such feature is to fix known accessibility problems, providing such a tool as an assistive technology.

Despite involving the participation of only 4 users, the data set obtained is rich in details and the presented results may help people working with personalization in the context of Web Accessibility. The gathered data is rich in the sense that the participants are real users, they were willing to be part in the evaluation, and they provided detailed information regarding how they perceive a self-tailoring website, using their own configurations of software and hardware. It was possible to verify that, when noticed, adjustments were perceived as improvements.

The presented approach supported the test of UI and UI adjustments remotely, in the real environment of the users. This work presented a promising direction regarding UI evaluation tool in the context of accessibility, supporting the fix of common accessibility barriers.

Acknowledgements. We would like to thank the participants, Deise Pupo for the support in contacting participants, and FAPESP for supporting this research (grant #2009/10186-9).

References

1. Abascal, J., Nicolle, C.: Moving towards inclusive design guidelines for socially and ethically aware HCI. Interacting with Computers 17(5), 484–505 (2005)
2. Arroyo, E., Selker, T., Wei, W.: Usability tool for analysis of web designs using mouse tracks. In: Proceedings of ACM CHI 2006 Conference on Human Factors in Computing Systems, Work-in-Progress, vol. 2, pp. 484–489 (2006)
3. Atterer, R., Schmidt, A.: Tracking the interaction of users with ajax applications for usability testing. In: Rosson, M.B., Gilmore, D.J. (eds.) CHI, pp. 1347–1350. ACM (2007), http://doi.acm.org/10.1145/1240624.1240828
4. Balbo, S., Goschnick, S., Tong, D., Paris, C.: Leading web usability evaluations to wauter. In: AusWeb 2005 - Australian World Wide Web Conference 2005 (2005)
5. Bigham, J.P., Cavender, A., Brudvik, J.T., Wobbrock, J.O., Ladner, R.E.: Webinsitu: a comparative analysis of blind and sighted browsing behavior. In: Pontelli, E., Trewin, S. (eds.) ASSETS, pp. 51–58. ACM (2007), http://doi.acm.org/10.1145/1296843.1296854
6. Carta, T., Paternò, F., de Santana, V.F.: Web Usability Probe: A Tool for Supporting Remote Usability Evaluation of Web Sites. In: Campos, P., Graham, N., Jorge, J., Nunes, N., Palanque, P., Winckler, M. (eds.) INTERACT 2011, Part IV. LNCS, vol. 6949, pp. 349–357. Springer, Heidelberg (2011)
7. Etgen, M., Cantor, J.: What does getting WET (web event-logging tool) mean for web usability? In: Proceedings of 5th Conference on Human Factors & the Web (1999)
8. Google analytics (2009), http://www.google.com/analytics
9. Hilbert, D.M., Redmiles, D.F.: Extracting usability information from user interface events. ACM Comput. Surv. 32(4), 384–421 (2000)
10. Hong, J.I., Heer, J., Waterson, S., Landay, J.A.: Webquilt: A proxy-based approach to remote web usability testing. ACM Transactions on Information Systems (2001)

11. International Standardization Organization: ISO-9241 - Ergonomic requirements for office work with display terminals (VDTs), Part 11: Guidance on usability (1998)
12. Ivory, M.Y., Hearst, M.A.: The state of the art in automating usability evaluation of user interfaces. ACM Comput. Surv. 33(4), 470–516 (2001)
13. MBUI-XG – Model-Based UI XG. Model-Based UI XG Final Report (2010), http://www.w3.org/2007/uwa/editors-drafts/mbui/Model-Based-UI-XG-FinalReport.html
14. Mikroyannidis, A., Theodoulidis, B.: A Theoretical Framework and an Implementation Architecture for Self Adaptive Web Sites. In: Proceedings of the International Conference on Web Intelligence (WI 2004), pp. 558–561 (2004)
15. Mobasher, B., Cooley, R., Srivastava, J.: Automatic Personalization Based on Web Usage Mining. Communications of the ACM 43(8) (2000)
16. Mørch, A.: Three Levels of End-User Tailoring: Customization, Integration, and Extension. In: 3rd Decennial Aarhus Conference, Aarhus, Denmark (1995)
17. Nielsen, J.: Customization of IUs and Products. Jabob Nielsen's Alertbox (2009), http://www.useit.com/alertbox/customization.html
18. NIST – WebVIP (2002), http://zing.ncsl.nist.gov/WebTools/WebVIP/overview.html
19. Paganelli, L., Paternò, F.: Intelligent analysis of user interactions with web applications. In: IUI 2002: Proc. of the 7th Int. Conf. on Intelligent User Interfaces, pp. 111–118 (2002)
20. Paternò, F., Santoro, C.: Remote usability evaluation: Discussion of a general framework and experiences from research with a specific tool. In: Maturing Usability (2008)
21. Pierrakos, D., Paliouras, G., Paratheodorou, C., Spyropoulos, C.D.: Web Usage Mining as a Tool for Personalization: A Survey. User Modeling and User-Adapted Interaction 13, 311–372 (2003)
22. Rubin, J.: Handbook of Usability Testing: How to plan, design, and conduct effective tests, 1st edn. John Wiley & Sons Inc. (1994)
23. Santana, V.F., Baranauskas, M.C.C.: Summarizing observational client-side data to reveal web usage patterns. In: Proc. of the 2010 ACM Symposium on Applied Computing, SAC 2010 (2010), http://doi.acm.org/10.1145/1774088.1774344
24. Santana, V.F., Paula, R.A.: Web Accessibility Snapshot: An Effort to Reveal Coding Guidelines Compliance. In: 10th Int. Cross-Disciplinary Conf. on Web Accessibility (2013)
25. Web Accessibility Initiative – Introduction do web accessibility (2005), http://www.w3.org/WAI/intro/accessibility.php

A Practical Solution for the Automatic Generation of User Interfaces – What Are the Benefits of a Practical Solution for the Automatic Generation of User Interfaces?

Miroslav Sili[1], Christopher Mayer[1,*], Martin Morandell[1], Matthias Gira[1], and Martin Petzold[2]

[1] AIT Austrian Institute of Technology GmbH, Health & Environment Department, Biomedical Systems, Donau-City-Str. 1, 1220 Vienna, Austria
[2] ProSyst Software GmbH, Dürener Str. 405, 50858 Köln, Germany
{miroslav.sili,christopher.mayer,martin.morandell, matthias.gira}@ait.ac.at, m.petzold@prosyst.com

Abstract. Older adults benefit from information and communication technology solutions in the Ambient Assisted Living (AAL) domain. The offered user interfaces for these ICT solutions often do not take the special needs, preferences and the physical and mental capabilities of older adults into account. The project AALuis focuses on solutions to increase accessibility, adaptability and usability of user interfaces in the AAL domain. The paper describes the functionality of the AALuis layer and the different steps involved stakeholders have to cover to benefit from the user interface generation framework. A detailed comparison between the traditional user interface design and the AALuis approach lists similarities and identifies differences in the user interface generation process.

Keywords: Ambient Assisted Living, Human-Computer Interaction, User Interface, Framework, Task Model, Automatic Adaptation.

1   Introduction

Needs and wishes regarding the interaction with ICT solutions change over time and vary between older adults. They depend on the user's physical and cognitive capabilities and his/her preferences. Thus, the user interface (UI), which can be critical to the success or failure of an ICT service, needs to be flexible and adaptable to support the user's abilities. AALuis[1] focuses on solutions within the Ambient Assisted Living (AAL) domain and provides an open middleware layer to guarantee accessible and usable UIs for different services [1].

---

[1] www.AALuis.eu

M. Kurosu (Ed.): Human-Computer Interaction, Part I, HCII 2014, LNCS 8510, pp. 445–456, 2014.
© Springer International Publishing Switzerland 2014

2   Objectives

The main objective of AALuis is to provide the possibility to connect different types of ICT services to various user interfaces and offers thereby an interaction in the user's preferred way. The basic concept is to detach the functionality of the service and its representation to the user, and to provide a standardized way to use the framework embedded into or connected to existing platforms in use, such as HOMER [2] or UMO [3]. This concept supports service developers (SD), user interface designers (UID) and service providers (SP) in providing the services in a usable and accessible way. The end-user (EU) is not directly affected by the separation of concerns, but can benefit from the consistent look and feel of user interfaces for various applications.

The developed solution closes the gap between the functionality of the service and the automatically generated UI (figure 1). Automatic UI generation and runtime adaptation enable reaction to changing needs and preferences regarding the interaction with ICT solutions over time and variations between older adults. As the group of older adults is very heterogeneous the personalization and customization possibilities offered to each single user by AALuis are of high importance.

AALuis uses an interaction model in Concur Task Trees (CTT) notation [4][5] describing the interaction flow of the service. The UI generation process takes into

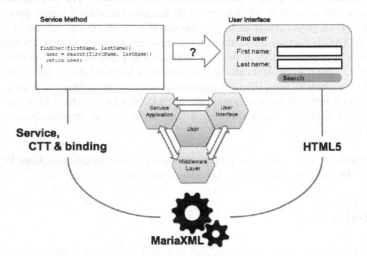

Fig. 1. The UI generation process in AALuis. Service methods and the interaction model in CTT notation are used to generate intermediate steps in MariaXML. The final transformation leads to the concrete UI in HTML5.

account the user's preferences and capabilities as well as the context of interaction (e.g., properties of available devices, etc.) [6]. The intermediate steps from the service description to the concrete UI in HTML5 are represented in Model based lAnguage foR Interactive Applications (MariaXML) [7].

Who are the main stakeholders to benefit from the UI generation framework and what do they need to do to benefit? The solution mainly helps service developers, service providers and finally older adults using the provided services and their functionality. To finally reach the beneficial solution, of customized service interaction, each stakeholder group has to conduct certain tasks, which are described in the methodology section.

3   Brief State of the Art

In recent years, an increasing amount of research focused on the user interface and thus on the representation of services in general and in particular for older adults. In the following some selected and relevant research projects and their approaches are described. GUIDE has focused on a novel adaptive accessibility framework and a characterization of individual users for creating accessible TV applications [8]. MyUI has addressed the provision of individualized UIs which are accessible to a broad range of users by the collection of information about the user during the interaction and updating the user profile accordingly [9]. EGOKI uses a similar approach as presented in the paper. It is based on the UCH [10], which acts as a middleware for ubiquitous interaction, and UIML for the abstract representation of the UIs [11]. The Universal Remote Console (URC) framework facilitates pluggable and handcraft user interfaces, which are designed for a specific target group, context of use and application based on the so-called (user interface) socket [12]. The project universAAL follows an automatic UI generation approach [13] and is based on the usage of XForms for the definition of an abstract data model combined with a set of abstract user interface components [14]. The Cameleon Reference Framework (CRF) distinguishes four layers of user interfaces, namely tasks and concepts, the abstract user interface, the concrete user interface, and the final user interface [15]. A similar concept is applied in the AALuis approach.

4   Methodology

In order to achieve the above mentioned objectives the layer is developed in a flexible way. The different involved stakeholder groups (figure 2) have to cover the following steps to benefit from the user interface generation framework.

Service developers (SD) need to develop the service functionality in a first step. The service can be either included as a web service or as a separate Open Service Gateway initiative (OSGi) [16] component. Besides the implemented service, the interaction model, which represents the logical activities to be conducted to reach the user's goal, has to be provided using the CTT notation, a W3C working draft [17]. Alongside, a binding file in XML format connects concrete service methods to its corresponding CTT tasks. An optional content file can be used by the service developer to provide necessary additional resources for the UI generation (e.g., sign language videos, pictures). If there is a need, user interface designers (UID) can optionally update and change the used transformation rules for optimizing (e.g., corporate identity) the UI and add additional I/O modalities.

The service providers (SP) need to deploy the AALuis middleware layer and to provide access to the connected services. Additionally, they have to enable the I/O devices to be used by the end-user. These devices run a dedicated application responsible for communication with the AALuis layer and presenting the final UI. A user model can be selected and adapted to meet the user's preferences and to map his/her physical and cognitive capabilities, as used in the transformation process. These user preferences can be modified at any time (real-time) by either the end-user or his/her (in-) formal caregiver.

The end-user (EU) can directly use the AALuis service on all enabled I/O devices and benefit from the dynamically adaptable UIs.

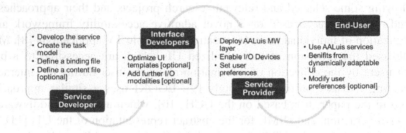

Fig. 2. Tasks to be fulfilled by the different stakeholder groups to benefit from AALuis

4.1   The User Interface Development Process

During the development process, service developers and UI designers have to consider several steps from the service on the one side, towards the final user interface on the other side. Table 1 depicts required and optional steps in a traditional, handcrafted UI design process and in the AALuis UI design process. The aim of the table is to uncover benefits, but also potential weaknesses, of the AALuis layer in comparison to a traditional, handcrafted UI design process.

The comparison illustrates that both approaches have some steps in common (steps A, D, E and F), but also that one step on the traditional approach (step H) and three steps on the AALuis approach (steps B, C and G) are not necessary in the other approach. The different colors in the table refer to the different stakeholders to be involved in each step. The blue color indicates the service developers, and in contrast the green colors stand for the user interface designer. The service provider is represented by the yellow colors in step I. The final step J is performed by the end-user interacting with the user interface and thus the service.

The table illustrates also mandatory steps (A, B, C, D, E for handcrafted approach and A, D, E for the AALuis approach) and optional steps (F and G for handcrafted approach and F and H for the AALuis approach).

Table 1. Comparison of required and optional steps that different stakeholder groups have to consider during the user interfaces generation process

Step	Traditional UI generation process	AALuis UI generation process
A	(SD) Define the service (business logic)	
B	(UID) Select the target device (tablet, PC, TV, other)	-
C	(UID) Select the application type (web, native, hybrid)	-
D	(UID) Implement UIs for the target device	(SD) Create the interaction model
E	(UID) Implement connectors, handlers, listeners etc. to connect the service and the UIs	(SD) Create the binding file which defines connections between the service and the interaction model
F	(UID) Optional: Implement or adopt UIs for different target devices	(UID) Optional: Crate new transformations for new target devices which are not provided so far
G	(UID) Optional: Adopt UIs to special user needs	-
H	-	(UID) Optional: Adopt the transformation if the generated UIs do not fulfil the expected results
I	(SP) Publish the service and the UIs	
J	(EU) Use the service and the UIs	

Step A. The separation of the service from the final user interface is an important issue in the UI development process. Both approaches have this step in common. Regardless of the approach – the business logic defined in a remote web service or in the same application – a back-end side is necessary, to which an UI can act as a front-end. A clear separation between this back-end and the UI allows service developers to focus on the service functionality, rather than on the user interface. They need not be concerned with requirements for specific users or specific target groups regarding service data representation. Responsibility for a suitable, user-specific representation of data and interaction of a service is at the UI designer or in the case of AALuis mainly in the layer itself.

As mentioned before, the AALuis layer is able to generate user interfaces for any kind of service. Generally a service can be described as a piece of software program that is able to exchange data with a user or another service. By using this description it becomes clear, that AALuis can be used for remote located web services but also for the interaction with a local application or device. The following two examples illustrate the usage of the AALuis layer with two complementary types of services:

- AALuis in the context of interaction with a local heating control device in a smart home environment.
- AALuis in the context of an external mobile caregiver and its "meals on wheels ordering" web service.

To facilitate the service inclusion process for already existing services, but also to reduce frame conditions for new, upcoming services two different approaches for the service integration in the AALuis have been developed. Services can be integrated via the Simple Object Access Protocol (SOAP) [18] but also via the OSGi specification. The former offers a great opportunity for service developers because it allows the service implementation on any machine, any platform or in any programming language. The only two constrains for this approach are: a) the service is reachable via LAN or WAN and b) the service is accessible via SOAP. The latter approach, the service definition via the OSGi specification, is especially useful for local devices or for local services provided by an OSGI based AAL middleware platforms like HOMER and universAAL [19].

Step B. In the traditional UI generation process the UI designer has to select a specific target device or at least to be aware of its technical constraints. In contrast, the AALuis approach comes already with a default set of supported target devices, like the tablet/smartphone, PC or TV. Thus, using the AALuis layer neither service developers nor user interface designers have to select a specific target device for the new service.

Step C. Step C is closely related to Step B. In many cases application types are determined by the device constrains. However, in the traditional approach UI designers have to decide the best suited application type for the service and for the selected target device(s). Service developers using the AALuis approach do not need to decide this for a new service. The built in set of default target devices are already implemented as hybrid applications. They benefit from the native hard- und software advantages of the specific target device but use also web based methods for the communication with the AALuis layer.

Step D. Traditional, handcrafted UIs can be built in many different ways. UI designers may use their preferred programming langue to generate a graphical user interface (GUI), use HTML for web based UIs or proprietary implementations for specific devices. One of the advantages of this approach is the possibility to tailor a specific UI for a specific use case. At the same time, this can be considered a disadvantage of tailored UIs, since every new service requires a newly tailored user interface.

Regarding the interaction model, handcrafted UIs have an implicit user-service interaction model. The front-end knows how to handle user actions and how to send them to the service in the back-end. The services in the back-end know how to update the UI in the front-end. In contrast, AALuis needs, an explicit interaction model. The interaction model describes possible interaction steps between the user on the one side and the service on the other side in a formal way. This formal description becomes necessary when both sides have the potential to alternate. AALuis provides automatic generated user interfaces (alternation on the one side) for different services (alternation on the other side).

For the interaction model in AALuis the Concur Task Trees (CTT) notation is used. The CTT notation distinguishes between interaction, system, user and abstract tasks. Interaction tasks are performed by user interactions with the system. User tasks represent internal cognitive or physical activities performed by the user and abstract tasks are used for complex actions which need sub-tasks of different categories [20]. Service developers may use a graphical user interface tool, namely the Concur Task Trees Environment (CTTE), to design and test interaction models for their services [21].

Step E. Step E focuses on the connection between the service, and the user interface and the interaction model, respectively. Handcrafted UIs have usually a concrete connection to the service via a specific controller, some handlers or listeners. The UI is aware of the service in the back-end and vice versa. This awareness is not directly present in the AALuis approach, because the layer is designed to generate multiple user interfaces for multiple services. In this case, each service needs to be connected to the interaction model and not to a concrete user interface. Figure 3 illustrates two common and very often used design patterns (figure 3a and figure 3b) for software development and their connection between the front-end (viewer or user interface) and the back-end (model or service). Moreover, figure 3 clarifies the correlation related to the front-end-back-end communication between the design pattern in figure 3b and the AALuis approach in figure 3c.

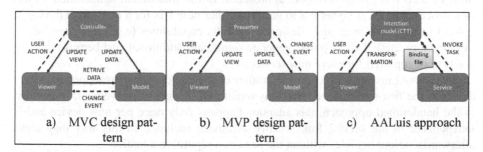

a) MVC design pattern   b) MVP design pattern   c) AALuis approach

Fig. 3. Visualization of data and event flow in the a) Model Viewer Controller (MVC) design pattern, the b) Model Viewer Presenter (MVP) design pattern and in the c) AALuis approach

The MVC design pattern was developed at Xerox PARC in the late 1970's [22]. As illustrated in figure 3a, the pattern is based on three components the viewer, the controller and the model. The model contains the data which should be represented by the viewer. In most cases this component also contains the business logic and the backend service, respectively. The model is loosely coupled with the viewer and separated from the controller. It may send notifications towards the viewer about change events in the related data. The viewer is responsible for rendering the retrieved model data. It also relays user actions towards the controller. The controller determinates how to act on user actions and updates the model data accordingly. In most cases the controller has a reference to the view and may cause the viewer to update the current shown view.

The MVP design pattern, as illustrated in figure 3b, was developed at Taligent in the 1990's [23][24]. The viewer and the model have the same functionality as in the MVC design pattern. In contrast to the MVC design pattern, the MVP completely separates the view from the model. In this case, the communication is carried out by the presenter. Seen from the viewer side, the presenter is responsible to receive user actions and to cause the viewer to update the current shown view. Considered from the model side, the presenter is responsible to receive change events from the model and to cause an update on the models data.

The AALuis approach, as illustrated in figure 3c, follows roughly a MVP design pattern. The interaction model acts as the presenter in the MVP design pattern and it is aware of the viewer but also of the service and model, respectively, or the business logic. The viewer in the AALuis approach achieves the same goal as in the MVP pattern. The main difference is that AALuis automatically generates the viewer on-the-fly and the interaction model is used as the basis for this transformation process. The service contains the data that the viewer should present but also the business logic. A simple binding file in XML format connects the interaction model with the service. Moreover the binding file defines the mapping between interaction tasks (CTT tasks) and input/output parameters of the service functionality.

Step F. Step F is optional in both approaches. In the traditional, handcrafted UI design process, the UI designer has to generate either new UIs for a new target device or at least to adapt the previously designed UI to its capabilities (e.g. screen resolution, I/O modality, etc.). This step may generate significant additional cost because the step needs to be repeated for every new service.

In the AALuis approach, the integration of a new, currently unsupported, target device is the first optional step that may require UI designer involvement. In contrast to the handcrafted approach, this adaption happens only once per new device and is independent of the service functionality. A device included in this way may serve afterwards various services without the need of a repetitive adaption.

The transformation is composed of three separate phases. The output of the first transformation is the Abstract User Interface (AUI), which is modality and device independent. Based on the AUI the Concrete User Interface (CUI) is generated. The CUI is more specific and modality and device dependent. The final phase uses the CUI to create the Renderable User Interface (RUI). This represents the final user interface and is already enriched with preferred user settings. The AUI and the CUI are represented in MariaXML whereas the RUI may vary from used device and output modalities. The current implementation returns HTML5 as output but also other output formats like VoiceXML [25] are possible and already under development.

Step G. Step G, the adoption of user interfaces to special user needs, is optional for traditional UI creation, and obsolete for the AALuis approach. Traditionally, to achieve accessibility and making a service, or interaction, available to as many people as possible, demands a high level of expertise in the domain of assistive technologies and underlying impairments. A thorough understanding of the target group of the service at hand, and additionally multiple international standards, guidelines, like the Web Content Accessibility Guidelines (WCAG) [26] or legal obligations, may also apply.

This knowledge and practices have to be applied to every single user interface to achieve accessibility. Appliers of AALuis on the other hand, can forget the above mentioned methods and strategies. Accessibility is provided "out-of-the-box". The user generation process of AALuis utilizes a user context model, which is currently based on the MyUI approach. Through the description of the user, his/her preferences, capabilities and limitations, AALuis automatically selects suitable input/output devices and creates suitably adopted user interfaces for them. In contrast the traditional UI designer may have to target larger categories (e.g. visually impaired, hearing impaired, etc.) of users to limit resource spending. He also has to ensure that each user employs the "correct" UI, suited best for him.

Thus Step G, adopting the UI to a certain user is managed by the AALuis layer automatically and does not demand additional human interference, to achieve accessibility or usability.

Due to the nature of AALuis, it is also possible to react to future requirements of accessibility that go beyond the current state. Adopting the user profile, the transformation process, or adding device technology is possible. This would immediately benefit all other services and users as well.

Step I. Step I is mandatory for both approaches. The service providers have to distribute services and UIs accessible to the end-users. Unfortunately it is not possible to generalize the distribution possibilities for traditional UIs because this can be realized in different ways. Concerning AALuis, service providers have to fulfil the following distribution tasks:

- Deploy the AALuis middleware layer and make it available to the target devices via LAN or WAN.
- Initialize a default user preference set for each AALuis user.
- Enable and configure I/O devices so that they are able to connect to the deployed AALuis middleware layer.

Step J. The final Step J represents the end-user who interacts with the provided UIs and the underlying services. This step is also common for both approaches.

5   Results and Conclusion

This paper has given an overview of the functionality of the AALuis layer and its practical deployment of automatic user interface generation. The presented comparison between the traditional, handcrafted approach and the AALuis approach listed similarities, and identified differences in the UI generation process. Although both procedures are able to produce user interfaces that satisfy the needs and preferences of the end-user, the comparison has shown that the two approaches differ regarding the effort each stakeholder has to fulfil to achieve this goal. One of the most significant findings to emerge from this comparison is that the AALuis layer is able to generate UIs for different services without any involvement of the user interface designer. In general, the overall goal of AALuis project is to provide a common tool which is able to reduce the development costs for new and innovative user interfaces and services especially for the target group of older adults. AALuis is currently still in the development stage. The upcoming user trials will help to identify weaknesses in the UI generation process as well as in the interaction with the implemented services. AALuis will be released as open source in autumn 2014.

Acknowledgement. The project AALuis is co-funded by the AAL Joint Programme (REF. AAL-2010-3-070) and the following National Authorities and R&D programs in Austria, Germany and The Netherlands: bmvit, program benefit, FFG (AT), BMBF (DE) and ZonMw (NL).

References

1. Mayer, C., Morandell, M., Hanke, S., Bobeth, J., Bosch, T., Fagel, S., et al.: Ambient Assisted Living User Interfaces. In: Gelderblom, G.J., et al. (eds.) Everyday Technology for Independence and Care, AAATE 2011. Assistive Technology Research Series, vol. 39, pp. 456–463. IOS Press (2011)
2. Fuxreiter, T., Mayer, C., Hanke, S., Gira, M., Sili, M., Kropf, J.: A modular platform for event recognition in smart homes. In: 2010 12th IEEE International Conference on e-Health Networking Applications and Services (Healthcom), pp. 1–6. IEEE (2010)
3. Verklizan: Intelligent software for monitoring centres, http://verklizan.info/content/umo-platform/system-overview/ (accessed: January 2014)
4. Paternó, F., Mancini, C., Meniconi, S.: ConcurTaskTrees: A Diagrammatic Notation for Specifying Task Models. In: Proceedings of the IFIP TC13 International Conference on Human-Computer Interaction, INTERACT 1997, pp. 362–369. Chapman & Hall (1997)
5. Paternó, F.: Concur Task Trees: An Engineered Notation for Task Models. In: The Handbook of Task Analysis for Human-Computer Interaction, pp. 483–503. Lawrence Erlbaum Associates (2003)
6. Mayer, C., et al.: User interfaces for older adults. In: Stephanidis, C., Antona, M. (eds.) UAHCI/HCII 2013, Part II. LNCS, vol. 8010, pp. 142–150. Springer, Heidelberg (2013)

7. Paternó, F., Santoro, C., Spano, L.C.: MARIA: A universal, declarative, multiple abstraction-level language for service-oriented applications in ubiquitous environments. ACM Trans. Comput.-Hum. Interact. 16, 19:1–19:30 (2009)
8. Duarte, C., Langdon, P., Jung, C., Coelho, J., Biswas, P., Hamisu, P.: GUIDE: Creating Accessible TV Applications. In: Gelderblom, G.J., et al. (eds.) Everyday Technology for Independence and Care, AAATE 2011. Assistive Technology Research Series, vol. 29, pp. 905–912. IOS Press (2011)
9. Peissner, M., Häbe, D., Janssen, D., Sellner, T.: MyUI: generating accessible user interfaces from multimodal design patterns. In: Proceedings of the 4th ACM SIGCHI Symposium on Engineering Interactive Computing Systems, EICS 2012, pp. 81–90. ACM, New York (2012)
10. Zimmermann, G., Vanderheiden, G.: The Universal Control Hub: An Open Platform for Remote User Interfaces in the Digital Home. In: Jacko, J.A. (ed.) HCI 2007. LNCS, vol. 4551, pp. 1040–1049. Springer, Heidelberg (2007)
11. Miñón, R., Abascal, J.: Supportive adaptive user interfaces inside and outside the home. In: Ardissono, L., Kuflik, T. (eds.) UMAP Workshops 2011. LNCS, vol. 7138, pp. 320–334. Springer, Heidelberg (2012)
12. ISO/IEC. ISO/IEC 24752. Information Technology - User Interfaces - Universal Remote Console. Part 1: Framework. 1st edn. ISO/IEC (2008)
13. Stocklöw, C., Grguric, A., Dutz, T., Vandommele, T., Kuijper, A.: Resource Management for Multimodal and Multilingual Adaptation of User Interfaces in Ambient Assisted Living Environments. In: Stephanidis, C., Antona, M. (eds.) UAHCI/HCII 2013, Part III. LNCS, vol. 8011, pp. 97–106. Springer, Heidelberg (2013)
14. Boyer, J.M.: XForms 1.1. W3C Recommendation (October 20, 2009), http://www.w3.org/TR/xforms/
15. Calvary, G., Coutaz, J., Thevenin, D., Limbourg, Q., Bouillon, L., Vanderdonckt, J.: A Unifying Reference Framework for Multi-Target User Interfaces. Interacting with Computer 15(3), 289–308 (2003)
16. OSGi Service Platform Core Specification (2011), http://www.osgi.org/download/r4v43/osgi.core-4.3.0.pdf (accessed: February 2014)
17. W3C MBUI - Task Models, http://www.w3.org/TR/2012/WD-task-models-20120802/ (accessed: October 2013)
18. W3C SOAP Version 1.2 Part 1: Messaging Framework (2nd edn.), http://www.w3.org/TR/soap12-part1/ (accessed: February 2014)
19. Hanke, S., Mayer, C., Hoeftberger, O., Boos, H., Wichert, R., Tazari, M.-R., Wolf, P., Furfari, F.: universAAL – an open and consolidated AAL platform. In: Ambient Assisted Living, pp. 127–140. Springer (2011)
20. Miroslav, S., Matthias, G., Christopher, M., Martin, M., Martin, P.: A Framework for the Automatic Adaptation of User Interfaces. In: Assistive Technology: From Research to Practice: AAATE 2013, pp. 1298–1304 (2013)
21. Mori, G., Paternó, F., Santoro, C.: CTTE: Support for Developing and Analyzing Task Models for Interactive System Design. IEEE Transactions on Software Engineering 28(8), 797–813
22. Burbeck, S.: Applications Programming in Smalltalk-80(TM): How to use Model-View-Controller, MVC (1992), http://st-www.cs.illinois.edu/users/smarch/st-docs/mvc.html (accessed: February 2014)

23. Potel, M., MVP: Model-View-Presenter; The Taligent Programming Model for C++ and Java (1996), http://www.wildcrest.com/Potel/Portfolio/mvp.pdf (accessed: January 2014)
24. Zhang, Y., Luo, Y.: An architecture and implement model for Model-View-Presenter pattern. In: 2010 3rd IEEE International Conference on Computer Science and Information Technology (ICCSIT) (2010) doi: 10.1109/ICCSIT.2010.5565090
25. W3C Voice Extensible Markup Language (VoiceXML) 3.0, http://www.w3.org/TR/voicexml30/ (accessed: January 2014)
26. W3C Web Content Accessibility Guidelines (WCAG) 2.0, http://www.w3.org/TR/2008/REC-WCAG20-20081211/ (accessed: February 2014)

Proposal of Collaborative Learning Support Method in Risk Communications

Hiroshi Yajima, Naohisa Tanabe, and Ryoich Sasaki

Tokyo Denki University 2-2 Kanda-Nishiki Cho, Chiyoda-Ku, Tokyo, Japan
yajima,sasaki@im.dendai.ac.jp

Abstract. In this paper, we propose the supporting method of the risk communications that use the collaborative learning. Using collaborative learning, participant of risk communication can acquire not only knowledge that participant is interested in, but also the intention and knowledge of other party who do not concern the participant's concern. In the process of collaborative learning, participants of risk communication get the mutual understanding about risks. The feature of this method is to use the "Externalization" form that use concept map and the construction drawing of the opinion understanding made from Fishbone

Keywords : Risk Communication, Collaborative Learning, Participant.

1 Introduction

A social risk is diversified as the information society develops, and a complex social trouble like the youth information restriction problem occurs. And. the enterprise and the society are holding various risks respectively. Recently, the phenomenon in which one risk measures generates a new risk is caused. For instance, security countermeasures such as the encryption and introduction of the public key certificate for the digitalized signature cause the personal information leak such as the address and date of birth, and the risk concerning privacy is generated as a result.

Thus, requesting the combination of preferable measures ideas (optimum solution), while considering two or more risks and costs becomes very important in the situation in which correspondence to a certain risk, increases other risks.

It is finally essential to find the most suitable solution which can form an agreement among people of decision making participation. It is need in consideration of interests between people of participation to solve these problems. At the same time, not only knowledge and judgment of the expert but also opinions of participants are necessary.

Therefore, the risk communications (RC) that are the processes to do the consensus building among those with different standpoint and aspect (the stake holder and the decision-maker are included) and specialists are needed.

As the risk communications supporting tool to solve the social risk problem and the social mutual agreement problem in the information society, the multiple risk communicator (MRC) is developed [1].

M. Kurosu (Ed.): Human-Computer Interaction, Part I, HCII 2014, LNCS 8510, pp. 457–465, 2014.

It has been understood that in the process applying MRC to the large-scale, social mutual agreement problem, the participation person's prior study is important for participation person's decision making, and also the consensus building among those who take part is moreover difficult if participation person's decision making is not enough.

In this paper, to do the mutual understanding between participants smoothly, the risk study supporting method that uses cooperative study [4] is proposed. In the proposal technique, participant studies risks concerning the interested field, and this is put into writing. Participant clarifies own intention while requesting the opinion of other participants by showing the study result, and decides the optimum solution that he consents. Communications are done among participants for each participant's optimum solution, and the final mutual agreement solution is obtained. Those of the feature of the proposed method is first participant can know intentions and the finding of other participants during the risk study period, so multipronged study can be done, and secondly each participant knows other party's intention at early stages, so mutual understanding can be achieved smoothly. The utility of the proposed method is shown by the verification experiment.

2   Risk Communications Support Problem

2.1   Outline of MRC for RC

In MRC, participant support part consists of three stages of the following (a)(b)(c). [2][3]. The RC support process is shown in Fig. 1.

(a) 1stRC : Information acquisition phase for each participant to attempt clarification of self-opinion

(b) 2ndRC : Phase in which the mutual understanding between participants is attempted.

(c) 3rdRC : Phase to plan the agreement formation between participants.

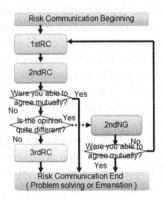

Fig. 1. RC support process

In this paper, we propose an RC support method for 1stRC and 2ndRC

2.2   A Risk Learning Problem for the Participants

We performed an experiment. As a result of experiment, the argument between participants took much time in 2ndRC and did not advance smoothly. In 2ndRC, An argument between participants is performed so that participants find respected measures considering each other's intention. As the result, it has understood that the support of this phase is necessary for agreeing. The following issues are made clear.

Difference of the Intention between Participants and Participant's Risk Understanding Shortage. When participant adopts risk measures, participant emphatically take care about own risk. In that case, the participant's intention to the risk is different according to the difference of each participant's standpoint. Evaluation figure of measures was different according to this difference in each participant (Fig.2).This phenomenon caused the discussion in 2ndRC not to go well. Because only the risk study along own intention of participant was done. Therefore these two points were made clear, that is (1)in the sturdy of participant, the important study range that is valued originally for RC was lacked. (2)Time has hung in the understanding of participant about the proof that is behind another participant's opinion.

Moreover, as for the content that became proof of the testimony of another participant, the participant's concern was left in low level.

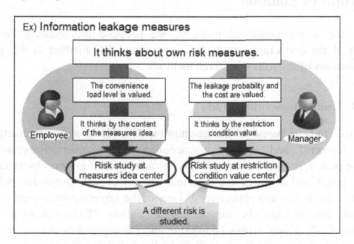

Fig. 2. Evaluation figure and risk study

Timing of Information Exchange and Information Log. In the RC support method that uses above-mentioned MRC, it is necessary to execute a lot of study processes in 1stRC. For instance, when those who take part study the information of the measures idea, participant should study "Leakage probability", "Measures cost", "Convenience load level", and "Privacy load level", etc. for the individual information leakage problem. In that case, participant study each item with the measures idea unit. Participant should study at the same time again while combining these items.

In this case, when the risk measures ideas are 15 pieces, participant should think about the combination of these measures ideas. In a word, various study cases exist for participant. Therefore, it becomes difficult for participant to integrate and understand study content that be studied in the first stage, while becoming the latter half of study.

Moreover, as the result, the chance of the information exchange in this phase was few though 2ndRC was being offered in the RC support method described in 2·1 as a place for the information exchange. This issue cause by difference of the content type that participants study and by the difference of the amount of study. In 2ndRC, participants discuss and negotiate solution based on the knowledge that they obtained in their risk study. In that case, the amount of unknown content or hearing only in the word for certain participant has increased when there is a study difference among participants. As a result, the following inconvenient cases were generated as the discussion was done repeatedly.

(1) Case where important points for participant became indefinite in the discussion
(2) Case where participant missed relativity with own risks in the discussion. Therefore, the discussion for the consensus building was not settled well.

3   Proposed Solution

To solve the above-mentioned problem, we propose the solution that adds the viewpoint of the cooperative study to conventional RC method in this paper. This solution consists of the following three methods.

3.1   RC Using Cooperative Study

Cooperative study is based on the assumption of a close, active interaction activity between learners, and enables metacognition formation (Expression power, persuasive power, problem discovery way, problem solving way, observation method of others speech and behavior and look into oneself of self-speech and behavior) and deepen the knowledge, and gives overall view of the target to participant of RC.

One of the features is the technique called "Externalization". In the "Externalization", people writes knowledge and the reproof as documents or figures, and these documents or figures are left as the log for study. Participant can review the study finding and the self-intention at any time by looking at "Externalization". Therefore, an active discussion becomes possible by executing "Externalization".

3.2   Cooperation Type Risk Study Method

In considering collaboration type risk study, we propose two types of methods, that is "Allotment type study" and "Development type study".

Allotment Type Study. The risk is studied to the event based on own necessities of each participant. Next, the content that participants studied mutually is given each other. It aims that all participants cover about the range of study necessary for RC by this procedure.

Participant independently decides the individual participant's range of study. However, the facilitator intervenes the participant's study according to the study theme, and in this case, participants study separately mutually. In that case, the difference of the recognition between participants becomes clear by comparing the study results between participants. Moreover, the study range that all participants did not study at all is covered by what the specialist explains based on "Externalization" information. (Fig.3)

Moreover, the following effects arise so that the learner may teach the content of study to another learner in Allotment type study.

(a) Participant has a sense of responsibility for his study.

(b) Participant does an independent study action.

(c) The interpersonal relationship between Participants is formed

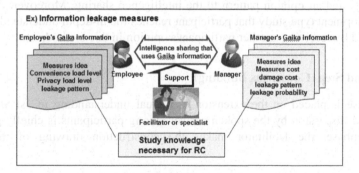

Fig. 3. Range of knowledge necessary for RC

Allotment type study can be used as a personal cure for Epistemic Egocentrism Epistemic. Egocentrism is a bias through that the other person also knows what I know. In allotment type study, participant examines whereabouts and the bigness and smallness of an actual risk closely. Allotment type study makes participant's acknowledged risk visible, makes participant conscious of the risk, and, in addition, corrects the risk acknowledgment of participant.

Development Type Study. The development type study uses participant's "Opinion" and "Actual experience", etc. in "Externalization" that is the feature of the cooperative study. The chance to think about the problem, the finding, and the opinion which is not studied for myself alone, by knowing another participant's intention and finding through "Externalization" arises. In a word, deep risk understanding arises by facing the problem, the finding, and the opinion that are not studied for himself alone.

4   RC Process Using Cooperative Study

This chapter describes a concrete process procedure of the proposal method described in Chapter 3 (Fig.2).

4.1   1stStep   Risk Study and Mutual Understanding

In this phase, the information gain (risk study) done with 1stRC and discussion done with 2ndRC is united in the technique. There is a feature of this phase in the point for participant to study the risk while sharing information with other participant. However, there is no place of the spoken answer discussion among participants, and mutual understanding among participants is achieved by sharing information by "Externalization" form that is based on concept map.

In this paper, the cooperation type risk study is done in the form of decentralized study., In the process, participants advance self-study (individual study) and the intelligence sharing and these studies are advanced concurrently. Two kinds of "Externalization" patterns are set. In a word, these are "Externalization" pattern by self-study, and an opinion pattern to the intelligence sharing. Moreover, the form of the development type study that participant reaches the in-depth understanding further is adopted by receiving another participant's opinion in this method.

4.2   2nd Step (Consensus Building)

This phase is placed on the extension of mutual understanding in 1st Step. In this phase, the discussion by the spoken answer among participants is chiefly performed. In this phase, the facilitator makes the construction drawing of the opinion

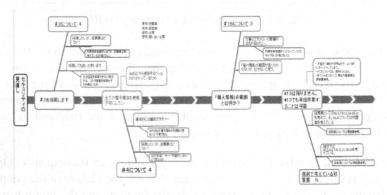

Fig. 4. Construction drawing of opinion understanding (usage example by Manager)

understanding (Fig.4) based on the hope solution on each participant by putting out first of all with 1st Step and "Externalization" information. Participants discuss about final solution by using this construction drawing. The construction drawing of the opinion understanding is an improvement of Fishbone figure to understand the situation of the development type study of other participant and the intention by present quickly.

In the construction drawing for the opinion understanding, a horizontal axis is a time axis, and content of "Externalization" of participant and "Externalization" content of other participants who see the content of each participant's "Externalization" is described. In this figure, the RC name is described in the screen left end, and the first "Externalization" of the event on an upper and lower edge is described, and, in addition, final "Externalization" is described on a fat line at the center. The first "Externalization" and final "Externalization" are tied in the line, and other "Externalization"'s are on the way of the line Final "Externalization" is decided from "Externalization" from other participants to the first "Externalization", and Final "Externalization" is put out by receiving these "Externalization". When the discussion emanates without the mutual agreement solution's to which all participant's opinions correspond or when mutual agreement solution among participant is obtained, this phase is assumed to be an end. (The above-mentioned mutual agreement solution contains the proposal of concerning alternatives about the measures idea that MRC offers and proposal and the adoption of compromise solution about the change of the measures idea setting etc.)

5   Verification Experiment

5.1   Experiment Purpose

The proposal technique is applied to the individual information leakage problem, and whether the problem described in 2·2 is solved is verified.

5.2   Precondition

In this experiment, RC intended for the security review is performed, for the enterprise that has urged by the necessity to solve the individual information leakage problem. A student in one's twenties performed the manager post and the employee as a testee. Eight students participated, and experiments on four cases are performed each by two students. The facilitator advised the testee on each phase at any time while experimenting. The following three points were required for participants.

(a)The manager and the employee take cooperated each other, standpoint for the company.
(b)Participant doesn't keep a secret to another.
(c)Participants agree on the final search of each other for the solution to satisfy.

5.3   Outcome of an Experiment

All groups reached the consensus building as a result of applying the RC support method described in Chapter 4. (Fig.4 shows the construction drawing of understanding of the opinion between participants made as a result of the experiment.

5.4   Consideration and Finding

The proposed method to use the cooperation type study was found to be effective for smooth RC, that is, smooth selection of optimal solution and the consensus building from the outcome of an experiment. An insufficient points were observed about the risk understanding by participant and the understanding of the risk structure   by participant. The information exchange at the timing that the risk was studied and the consensus building support by the construction drawing of the opinion understanding were effective for RC. For the "Externalization" form, the evaluation value was obtained from the testee with the high appraisal of four or more, including the following comment.

(a)Participation person's "Externalization" is easy.
(b)The understanding of other participant's "Externalization" was easy.

It was clarified that the intelligence sharing at an early stage was effective from the free description type questionnaire that had been done at the same time after experiment, including the following opinions.

1. Participant worked on RC valuing other participant's opinions.
2. The utility of measures was able to be discussed among participants.
3. It became easy to compromise because it was able to confirm other participant's intentions before own opinion hardened.

As a whole, the process to which the discussion for the consensus building was done from the risk study was observed, and the problem described in 2.2 was solved.

6   Conclusion

In this paper, we proposed information acquisition methods that consists of the development type study for the cooperative study, and allotment study method, as a support method of the risk communications in the cooperation type study. In this sturdy, mutual understanding and the consensus building supporting tools such as Externalizationform and Fishbone were introduced. As a result of the RC experiment, the effectiveness of the proposed method became clear.

We will develop with a more effective method by systematizing the proposal method in the future.

Reference

1. Sasaki, R., Hidaka, Y., Moriya, T., Taniyama, M., Yajima, H., Yaegasi, K., Yoshiura, Y.: Development and application of the multiple risk communicator's. Journal of Information Processing of Japan 49(9), 3180–3190 (2008)
2. Watanabe, T., Yamamoto, H., Yajima, H., Sasaki, R.: Evaluation of participant information acquisition support method in multiple risk communicator. IEEJ Trans. EIS 128(2), 310–317 (2008)
3. Matsumoto, S., Hiroshi, Y., Sasaki, R.: Proposal of smooth risk communications support method in multiple risk communicator. In: Symposium on Cryptography and Information Security, SCIS 2006 (2006)
4. Miyake, N.: Cooperated study and AI. Journal of the Japan Society of Artificial Intelligence 23(2), 174–183 (2008)

Evaluation Methods, Techniques
and Case Studies

Towards Qualitative and Quantitative Data Integration Approach for Enhancing HCI Quality Evaluation

Ahlem Assila, Káthia Marçal de Oliveira, and Houcine Ezzedine

L.A.M.I.H. – UMR CNRS 8201
UVHC, Le Mont Houy, 59313 Valenciennes Cedex 9, France
assila.ahlem@gmail.com,
{Kathia.Oliveira,Houcine.Ezzedine}@univ-valenciennes.fr

Abstract. Over the two past decades, various HCI quality evaluation methods have been proposed. Each one has its own strengths and its own shortcomings. Different methods are combined to enhance the evaluation results. To obtain better coverage of design problems and to increase the system performance, subjective and objective methods can complement each other. However, the variability of these methods features poses a challenge to effectively integrate between them. The purpose of this paper is to enhance the evaluation of HCI quality by suggesting new approach intended for improving evaluation results. This method supports a mapping model between evaluation data. It aims to specify new quality indicators that effectively integrate qualitative and quantitative data based on a set of pre-defined quality criteria. Qualitative (items) and quantitative data are respectively extracted from highly cited HCI quality questionnaires and from existing tools.

Keywords: Human-Computer Interface, HCI evaluation, subjective, objective, qualitative, quantitative, integration, mapping; data, indicator.

1   Introduction

The evaluation of Human Computer Interaction (HCI) quality is an important issue increasingly attracting researchers in the field of the software engineering1]. Quality[1] evaluation is a process assessing the extent of the system's functionality; the impact of the interface on the user; and identifying the specific system problems [2].

Over the past decades, several quality evaluation methods and tools have been proposed. Some of them provide a quantitative (objective) evaluation based on analytic and quantitative data retrieved from various tools such as electronic informers [3]. Other methods perform a qualitative (subjective) evaluation exploiting for instance questionnaire and/or interview methods [4] [5]. They focus on the direct interaction with users to ask them about their opinions and their preferences about the evaluated interface. However, all the methods do not perform the same measuring procedures.

---

[1] In this paper, we address by the quality evaluation to the quality of the user interface evaluation.

M. Kurosu (Ed.): Human-Computer Interaction, Part I, HCII 2014, LNCS 8510, pp. 469–480, 2014.
© Springer International Publishing Switzerland 2014

Some of them use only questionnaires and others include additional tools to perform more accurate evaluation [6]. Many authors have argued for employing various methods for quality evaluation so that these methods supplement each other rather than compete [7] [8]. However, strengths and limitations of each evaluation method can guide researchers and practitioners. It can help them to determine how these methods complement each other. Nevertheless, the variability of these methods features and drawbacks poses a challenge to effectively integrate between them. This integration is an important issue in order to obtain better coverage of design problems and to increase the system performance.

In this paper, we are interested to enhance the evaluation of quality by proposing a new evaluation approach. This approach is intended for improving evaluation results issued from both various tools. It supports a mapping model between evaluation data. It specifies new quality indicators integrating qualitative and quantitative data.

The reminder of the paper is organized as follows. Section 2 reviews the works related to existing approaches that combined multiple HCI quality evaluation methods. Section 3 explains on one hand, an accurate description of our approach of the defined mapping models and indicators. On the other hand, it explains our approach using a case study between some items from CSUQ questionnaire and the tools based on quantitative data. Section 4 draws conclusions and future work.

2   Related Works

Several research efforts about quality evaluation have been established. They concern various methods and approaches for evaluating HCI quality (e.g. the questionnaires or the interviews as subjective tools [19] and the electronic informer as an objective tool [3]). Recent researches have investigated the possibility of employing different methods to improve evaluation results [10] [11].

The need for supporting evaluation using different methods has been emphasized by Grammenos et al. [12] in their framework for defining an integrated environment supporting guidelines: the Sherlock guideline management system. It is structured following a client/ server architecture and aims to facilitate the detection of usability problems. The evaluation has been preceded by two methods independently employed. The first is a static method for assessing interface presentation quality. The second present a dynamic method that uses two IBM usability satisfaction questionnaires (i.e. After Scenario Questionnaire (ASQ) [23] and Computer System Usability Questionnaire (CSUQ) [21]) for measuring the user's subjective opinion in a scenario-based situation.

Some approaches have suggested combinations of various evaluation methods for improving evaluation [11] [13]. In [13], authors are interested to use three evaluation tools separately: (1) the eye tracker for capturing information about the user eye movements and view localization during tasks execution, (2) the electronic informer for capturing user action, and (3) the questionnaire for measuring users' satisfaction. However, this approach has used a paper questionnaire. It's will be better if it is used an automatic questionnaire to facilitate the evaluators task.

In [11], authors are suggested an evaluation framework named RITA (useR Inerface evaluaTion frAmework). It combines between three different evaluation tools, respectively: a questionnaire, EISEval electronic informer and the ergonomic guidelines inspector. Despite this approach leads to inspect a broad outfit of utility and usability problems in user interfaces, it has two main limits. On one hand, the questionnaire was developed based on a set of predefined questions without taken into consideration the existing predefined questions that can be extracted from standardized questionnaires which have a good score in terms of validity and reliability measures. In the other hand, the evaluation results are presented with a separate manner, which implies the lack of the integration aspect.

Al-Wabil and Al Khalifa [8] have developed a framework for integrating usability evaluations methods by matching the methods' capabilities and limitations through a classification of usability problems. The adopted evaluation approach is based on the usability problem profile of Chattratichart and Lindgaard [20]. It is initially based on the classification of the usability issues according to usability problem profile and secondly on the classification of these problem profiles according to the usability evaluation methods. This approach considers three usability evaluation methods: (1) the eye tracking method which deals with the problems related to visibility of user interface elements, (2) the card sorting usability evaluation method for detecting the problems related to disorientation, and (3) the focus group discussions for assessing subjective satisfaction. Although this framework is interesting, it remains very critical. On the one hand it is related only to evaluate web user interfaces. On the other hand, this approach is focused mainly in determining how the combination between usability evaluation methods can complement each other rather than how combining usability evaluation methods with integrated and complementary forms.

In a study, Nikov et al. have proposed an approach that combines between subjective and objective usability parameters for inspecting usability problems [14]. This approach exploits a neuro-fuzzy model to aggregate between data. Furthermore, it was implemented in a MS EXCEL software tool. Nevertheless, there are some limits to consider; this approach is only dedicated to evaluate web user interfaces. Moreover, the selection of the gathered measurements is still ambiguous mainly when these data are not extracted using universal usability evaluation methods.

A recent research method proposed by Kerzazi and Lavalée has been designed for combining both objective and subjective usability evaluations [15]. It aims to provide more complete view of usability. However, gathering qualitative and quantitative metrics and analyzing it in a separate manner presents a weakness that can only be solved through the combination of qualitative and quantitative data.

This section describes a panorama of existing approaches based on combining different evaluation methods to enhance evaluation results. Indeed, these approaches attempt generally to combine methods in a separate manner. However, they do not consider the specificities of evaluation data and the possibility to combine them with in integrated form. There is still a lack to determine how effectively integrate qualitative with quantitative data for improving evaluation results. In consequence, a new approach for integrating qualitative and quantitative evaluation data will be presented in the next section.

3   Proposition of an Evaluation Approach for Integrating Qualitative and Quantitative Data

We are interested in proposing an evaluation method including a mapping model aiming to define new quality indicators integrating qualitative and quantitative data based on a set of quality criteria. These data are relatively related to both ergonomic and functional aspects of interactive systems. That is why our aim is: (1) to identify the tools used to extract the qualitative and quantitative evaluation data, and (2) to determine how to integrate these data.

3.1   Specification of the Tools Used for Extracting Qualitative and Quantitative Data

As the proposed method integrates and synthesizes the data issued from different evaluation tools, it exploits different tools that have been developed to facilitate and to automate a variety of quality evaluation aspects.

The tools related to the quantitative data are:

- The ergonomic guidelines inspector [11]: aids for ergonomic quality evaluation of interactive systems. It evaluates the ergonomic consistency of a HCI according to ergonomic guidelines in order to detect the ergonomic inconsistencies. It consists on comparing a referential model entitled the evaluation model to an object model [11]. This parses the interface graphical components attributes. The evaluation model is defined as the configuration specified by the evaluator before starting the usability test [11]. It provides the evaluator by a set of ergonomic recommendations. Comparison results are generated as textual files.
- EISEval electronic informer (Environment for Interactive System Evaluation) [3]: is a generic and configurable electronic informer used for agent-based interactive systems [3]. It is based on Petri Nets for modeling the interaction sequences between the user and the system to evaluate to detect eventual usability problems in the evaluated user interface [9]. Moreover, it automatically captures Human-Computer Interaction information as user actions and their consequences on the interactive system. Thus, it analyzes these various captured interaction information using its confrontation module [3].

To perform a qualitative evaluation, we use questionnaires as tools for inspecting users' satisfaction degree to the evaluated interface. Over the past twenty years, several questionnaires have been putted forward by researchers for HCI quality evaluation. For our study, we performed a large state of the art of the most known and the most validated questionnaire tools. In the first stage, 23 questionnaires with good scores in validity and reliability measures are selected. In the second stage, we only selected five questionnaires considering various constraints such as the higher reliability degree and the type of application for which they are defined. These questionnaires are: QUIS[2], PSSUQ[3], SUMI[4], SUS[5] and CSUQ[6].

---

[2] QUIS: Questionnaire for User Interface Satisfaction (http://lap.umd.edu/QUIS/about.html).

3.2 The Defined Mapping Model and the Quality Indicators: How to Integrate Qualitative with Quantitative Data?

The proposed mapping model and the quality indicators. Qualitative and quantitative data are related to a set of quality criteria such as the ISO 9241-11 standard criteria (i.e. satisfaction, efficiency, and effectiveness). These criteria can be evaluated first through questionnaires qualitative data and second through quantitative data extracted from the existing tools. Nevertheless, as explained in the last section, the combination or the integration of qualitative and quantitative data leads to use the evaluation data with a separate manner. The lack in determining how to integrate qualitative with quantitative data leads to an intensified need to define a full structural mapping model to specify new quality indicators based on the existing quality criteria.

As defined by the ISO/IEC 15939 [16], an indicator is a measure that provides estimation or evaluation of specified attributes. These attributes are quantified based on the type of measurement method which can be subjective or objective. To propose quality indicators based on the existing quality criteria, we first performed a deep study to define a mapping model between quality criteria used by the tools quantitative data and the questions (items) extracted from the selected questionnaires. This mapping model allows specifying the required attributes for the construction of indicators. It links each questionnaire item with the appropriate quantitative data with a complementary manner. Further, the proposed mapping model is based on both ISO 9241-11 quality criteria [17] and Bastien and Scapin ergonomic criteria [18] to evaluate both functional and ergonomic aspects of the interface. Figure 1 illustrates our proposed mapping model. As depicted in this figure, each item can be related in the same time to more than one quantitative data.

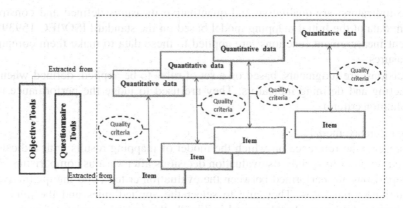

Fig. 1. Proposed mapping model

---

3 PSSUQ: Post-Study System Usability Questionnaire [22].
4 SUMI: Software Usability Measurement Inventory (http://sumi.ucc.ie/en/).
5 ASQ: After Scenario Questionnaire [23].
6 CSUQ: Computer System Usability Questionnaire [21].

Defining a mapping model is the first step to integrate qualitative with quantitative data. To ensure effectively this integration, defining and constructing new indicators (measures) based on this specified mapping model that combines qualitative with quantitative data is a crucial task. For our study, we adapted the ISO/IEC 15939 Measurement Information Model to define new quality evaluation indicators for HCI quality evaluation of interactive system. These measures are able to cross implicitly qualitative with quantitative data. As defined by ISO/IEC 15939, the Measurement Information Model is a structure linking the needs to the relevant entities to the attributes of concern. It describes how the relevant attributes are quantified and converted to indicators that provide a basis for decision making [16].

These indicators aim to directly measure the performance of quality criteria and enhance evaluation results.

Our approach is based on three models: (1) the initial mapping model, (2) the results mapping model with indicators, and (3) the reference model.

— The initial mapping model:
  It consists of three components: the evaluation criteria, the qualitative data, and the quantitative data. This model specifies the evaluation criteria with their corresponding data. This model links and associates each qualitative data with appropriate quantitative data.
— The results mapping model with indicators:
  This model presents the evaluation results. It is based on the specified initial mapping model. As illustrated in Fig. 2, it consists of six components: evaluation criteria, users list, the qualitative and quantitative measures values obtained after evaluation, the applied rules for each criterion, and the final decision of evaluation. This model can be divided into two main parts:

• The indicators: are qualitative and quantitative measures defined and constructed from data of the initial mapping model based on the standard ISO/IEC 15939. Different measurement functions[7] are applied to these data to make them computable measures.
• Decisions: are judgments, based on a set of rules to be applied, defined when constructing and defining indicators. They are used to judge the performance of the evaluation criteria.

— The reference model:
  It presents the reference on which the model of mapping results with indicators is based, in order to specify its evaluation decisions after various comparisons. These comparisons are performed between the evaluation criteria and the qualitative and quantitative measures. They aim to select the applied rules and the appropriate evaluation decisions. As illustrated in Fig. 1, this model consists of four components: the evaluation criteria, the qualitative and quantitative measures, the applied rules and their evaluation decisions.

---

[7] Measurement function: is an algorithm or calculation performed to combine two or more base measures [16].

Fig. 2 synthesizes our approach for the integration of qualitative with quantitative data and illustrates the mapping phase and indicators.

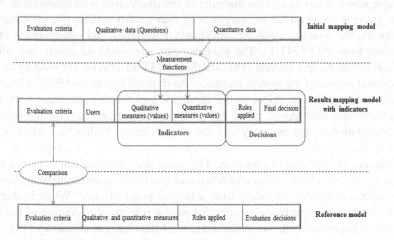

Fig. 2. The proposed approach (mapping model and indicators)

In the next section, we explain our approach through a case study between a set of items from CSUQ questionnaire and quantitative data issued from the specified tools. Thus, we introduce an example of an indicator of HCI quality evaluation. It is constructed for evaluating the effectiveness criterion defined by the standard ISO 9241-11 based on the defined mapping model data.

A case study of a mapping between CSUQ items with quantitative data. To demonstrate how our approach can be applied to evaluate the quality of interactive systems interfaces, we present a case study of the mapping between some items from CSUQ[8] questionnaire with the quantitative data of the specified tools based on a set of quality criteria. The mapping results are presented into the initial mapping model to illustrate how this mapping is specified for defining new quality indicators. This mapping involves three steps, starting with the identification of the specified tools' data and the evaluated quality criteria to the presentation of results.

Since our intention is to evaluate any WIMP interface of interactive systems, we opt as qualitative data some items of CSUQ. We choose CSUQ for our mapping study due to the fact that it is: (1) a successful record of practical and academic applications in its original; (2) a continuing relevance to current researchers; and (3) supporting an applicability in usability evaluation of computer systems in various areas as well as in research into the measurement of the construct of usability [19].

For the quantitative data, we opt for data extracted from the ergonomic guidelines inspector (e.g. writing size, writing color, informational density) and the EISEval elec-

---

[8]   CSUQ (Computer System Usability Questionnaire) is an IBM questionnaire tool designed for the purpose of assessing users' perceived satisfaction with their computer systems in the field, modeled directly on the Post-Study System Usability Questionnaire (PSSUQ) for conducting this type of assessment at the end of a lab-based usability study. In its current form, the CSUQ is a 16-item instrument [21].

tronic informer (e.g. the rate of completion of correct tasks, time of tasks execution) to evaluate respectively the ergonomic and the functional aspects of the system interface.

The extraction, analysis and the mapping of the qualitative with quantitative data in this case study is based on the measurement of four quality criteria (the efficiency, the effectiveness, the guidance, and the workload). Efficiency and effectiveness criteria are selected from ISO 9241-11. The guidance and the workload criteria are selected from Bastien and Scapin criteria [18]. The ISO 9241-11 criteria are used to evaluate the functional aspect of the system interface. As defined by the ISO 9241-11standard, the effectiveness criterion refers to the accuracy and the completeness with which users achieve specified goals, while the efficiency criterion refers to resources expended in relation to the accuracy and the completeness with which users achieve goals [17]. Nevertheless, Bastien and Scapin criteria are used to evaluate the ergonomic aspects of the system interface. The guidance criterion refers to the means available to: advise, orient, inform, instruct, and guide the users throughout their interactions with a computer, including from a lexical point of view. Whereas workload criterion concerns all interface elements that play a role in the reduction of the users' perceptual or cognitive load, and in the increase of the dialogue efficiency [18].

The used data and mapping results for this example are specified in Table 1 which presents the initial mapping model.

Table 1. The initial mapping model

Evaluation criteria	Mapped data		Relative quantitative data
	Qualitative data		
	Items	Items keywords	
Effectiveness: ISO 9241-11	It is simple to use this system Strongly agree 1 2 3 4 5 6 7 Strongly disagree	simple	The rate of completion of correct tasks
	CSUQ questionnaire		EISEval
Efficiency: ISO 9241-11	I am able to complete my work quickly using this system Strongly agree 1 2 3 4 5 6 7 Strongly disagree	complete quickly	The rate of completion of correct tasks Time of tasks
	CSUQ questionnaire		EISEval
Guidance (readability): Bastien and Scapin criteria	The information provided with this system is clear Strongly agree 1 2 3 4 5 6 7 Strongly disagree	clear	Writing font Writing size Writing color
	CSUQ questionnaire		The ergonomic guidelines inspector
Workload (Informational density): Bastien and Scapin criteria	It is easy to find the information I needed Strongly agree 1 2 3 4 5 6 7 Strongly disagree	find, easy, information	Workload density Components dimension
	CSUQ questionnaire		The ergonomic guidelines inspector

As illustrated in the table above, the results of the mapping data from the initial mapping model provide evaluators with a combination of qualitative and quantitative data. It shows how the quantitative data can complement the qualitative data to increase the performance of the measurement of evaluation criteria and subsequently help evaluators to inspect accurately the quality problems. A quantitative data can complement different questionnaire items that cover diverse quality evaluation criteria. These mapped data will be as parameters used to define and to produce new quality indicators based on the ISO/IEC 15939 Measurement Information Model [16]. These indicators allow crossing items with quantitative data to inspect quality criteria. They aim to measure directly the performance of quality criteria and to enhance evaluation results. They are presented into the reference model. An example of a defined indicator, their related measures with their applied rules and evaluation decisions suggested by the indicator specification are presented in Table 2.

Table 2. An indicator example from the reference model

Evaluation criteria	Indicator and decisions		
	Qualitative and quantitative measures	**Rules applied**	**Evaluation decisions**
Effectiveness of correct performance of tasks in a HCI	- Rate of correct completion of each Task in a session (RT) - Number of tasks performed - Number of users involved in the evaluation (users: novice, medium (students) and experts in the field of HCI) - Response to question for each user (Rep) - Rate of Correct performance of Tasks for a user session (RCT) - Rate of user Responses to a question (RRep)	- Rule 1: More than the RCT measure is large (tends to 100%), more than the Rep measure is small (tends to the value 1: strongly agree) - Rule 2: More than the RCT measure is low (tends to 0), more than the Rep measure is large (tends to the value 7: strongly disagree)	• Case 1: compliance with rules - The interface is effective: If the majority of subjects (participants) respect the rule 1. - The interface is less effective: If subjects follow the two rules with an average way. The interface has some problems in term of execution of tasks - The interface is ineffective: If the majority of subjects respect the rule 2. The interface has a lot of problems in term of execution of tasks
			• Case 2: No respect for rules A problem of imbalance between the two measurements is detected. It requires a revision of the evaluated interface with taken into account the users' profiles.

Table 2 explains new quality indicator able to judge the performance of the effectiveness criterion in term of execution of tasks. This indicator is constructed based on a set of mapped evaluation data extracted from the initial mapping model. It performs the crossing between qualitative with quantitative measures which are the bases of the defined applied rules and the evaluation decisions.

This case study illustrates different examples of the mapped data specified into the initial mapping model and an example of a new indicator specified into the reference model. These two models will be the basis to provide evaluation and to obtain results based on the principle of the integration between qualitative and quantitative data. These results after evaluation will be presented into the model of the results mapping model with indicators.

4   Conclusion and Perspectives

A new proposition for the evaluation of HCI was presented in this paper. This proposition allows supporting quality evaluation. It aims to demonstrate how integrating qualitative with quantitative evaluation in order to enhance HCI quality evaluation results. For this purpose, this paper introduces a method that defines and constructs new quality indicators based on a mapping model that combine qualitative with quantitative evaluation data. These indicators integrate effectively data by crossing qualitative with quantitative measures.

As a part of our future work, different experimental tests will be done for ensuring the validation of our approach. This method will be implemented into a new quality evaluation tool.

Acknowledgments. The present research work has been supported by International Campus on Safety and Intermodality in Transportation the Nord Pas-de-Calais Region, the European Community, the Regional Delegation for Research and Technology, the Ministry of Higher Education and Research, nd the National Center for Scientific Research.

The authors gratefully acknowledge the support of these institutions.

References

1. Fernandez, A., Abrahão, S., Insfrán, E.: A systematic review on the effectiveness of web usability evaluation methods. In: Proceedings of the 16th International Conference on Evaluation & Assessment in Software Engineering (EASE 2012), Ciudad Real, Spain, pp. 52–56 (2012)
2. Khan, M., Sulaiman, S., Tahir, M., Said, A.M.: Research approach to develop usability evaluation framework for haptic systems. In: Proc. of NPC, Tronoh, Malaysia, pp. 1–4. IEEE (2011)

3. Tran, C., Ezzedine, H., Kolski, C.: EISEval, a Generic Reconfigurable Environment for Evaluating Agent-based Interactive Systems. International Journal of Human-Computer Studies 71(6), 725–761 (2013)
4. Yang, T., Linder, J., Bolchini, D.: DEEP: Design-Oriented Evaluation of Perceived Usability. International Journal of Human Computer Interaction, 308–346 (2012)
5. Assila, A., Ezzedine, H., Bouhlel, M.S.: A Web questionnaire generating tool to aid for interactive systems quality subjective assessment. In: IEEE International Conference on Control, Decision and Information Technologies, CoDIT 2013, Tunisia, pp. 1–7 (2013)
6. Alva O., M.E., Martínez P., A.B., Cueva L., J.M., Sagástegui Ch., T.H., López P., B.: Comparison of Methods and existing tools for the Measurement of usability in the web. In: Cueva Lovelle, J.M., Rodríguez, B.M.G., Gayo, J.E.L., del Pueto Paule Ruiz, M., Aguilar, L.J. (eds.) ICWE 2003. LNCS, vol. 2722, pp. 386–389. Springer, Heidelberg (2003)
7. Lindgaard, G.: Notions of Thoroughness, Efficiency, and Validity: Are they Valid in HCI practice? Proceedings of the 4th International Cyberspace Conference on Ergonomics 36(12), 1069–1074 (2005)
8. Al-Wabil, A., Al-Khalifa, H.: A Framework for Integrating Usability Evaluations Methods: The Mawhiba Web Portal Case Study. In: The International Conference on the Current Trends in Information Technology (CTIT 2009), Dubai, UAE, pp. 1–6 (2009)
9. Charfi, S., Trabelsi, A., Ezzedine, H., Kolski, C.: A User-Oriented Test environment based on User-Interface evaluation graphical controls. In: 12th Symposium on Analysis, Design, and Evaluation of Human-Machine Systems, IFAC, Las Vegas, USA, pp. 494–504 (2013)
10. Koutsabasis, P., Spyrou, T., Darzentas, J.: Evaluating Usability Evaluation Methods: Criteria, Method and a Case Study. In: Jacko, J.A. (ed.) Human-Computer Interaction, Part I, HCII 2007. LNCS, vol. 4550, pp. 569–578. Springer, Heidelberg (2007)
11. Charfi, S., Ezzedine, H., Kolski, C.: RITA: a Framework based on multi-evaluation techniques for user interface evaluation, Application to a transport network supervision system. In: ICALT, May 29-31, pp. 263–268. IEEE, Tunisia, ISBN 978-1-4799-0312-2
12. Grammenos, D., Akoumianakis, D., Stephanidis, C.: Integrated support for working with guidelines: the Sherlock guideline management system. Interacting with Computers 12(3), 281–311 (2000) ISSN 0953-5438
13. Ezzedine, H.: Méthodes et Modèles de Spécification et d'Evaluation des Interfaces Homme-Machine dans les systèmes industriels complexes. HDR memory, University of Valenciennes and Hainaut-Cambrai (December 2002)
14. Nikov, A., Vassileva, S., Angelova, S., Tzvetanova, S., Stoeva, S.: WebUse: An approach for web usability evaluation. In: Proc. 3rd Symposium on Production Research, Istanbul, April 19-20, pp. 511–518 (2003) ISBN 975695731X
15. Kerzazi, N., Lavallée, M.: Inquiry on usability of two software process modeling systems using ISO/IEC 9241. In: CCECE, pp. 773–776 (2011)
16. ISO/IEC 15939 Systems and software engineering — Measurement process (2007)
17. ISO/IEC. ISO 9241-11 Ergonomic requirements for office work with visual display terminals (VDT) s- Part 11 Guidance on usability. ISO/IEC 9241-11: 1998(E) (1998)
18. Bastien, J.M.C., Scapin, D.: Ergonomic Criteria for the Evaluation of Human Computer interfaces. Technical Report n° 156, Institut Nationale de Recherche en Informatique et en Automatique, France (1993)
19. Erdinç, O., Lewis, J.R.: Psychometric Evaluation of the T-CSUQ: The Turkish Version of the Computer System Usability Questionnaire. International Journal of Human and Computer Interaction 29(5), 319–326 (2013)

20. Chattratichart, J., Lindgaard, G.: A Comparative Evaluation of Heuristic-Based Usability Inspection Methods. In: The Conference on Human Factors in Computing Systems, CHI 2008, pp. 2213–2220. ACM (2008)
21. Lewis, J.R.: IBM computer usability satisfaction questionnaires: Psychometric evaluation and instructions for use. International Journal of Human Computer Interaction (7), 57–78 (1995)
22. Lewis, J.R.: Psychometric evaluation of the PSSUQ using data from five years of usability studies. International Journal of Human Computer Interaction (14), 463–488 (2002)
23. Lewis, J.R.: Psychometric evaluation of an after-scenario questionnaire for computer usability studies: The ASQ. ACM SIGCHI Bulletin 23(1), 78–81 (1991)

Efficiency in Performing Basic Tasks Using Word Processing Programs by the Elderly as a Measure of the Ergonomic Quality of Software

Krzysztof Hankiewicz[1] and Marcin Butlewski[2]

[1] Poznan University of Technology, Chair of Management and Computing Systems
krzysztof.hankiewicz@put.poznan.pl
[2] Poznan University of Technology, Chair of Ergonomics and Quality Management
marcin.butlewski@put.poznan.pl

Abstract. Computers and the opportunities they offer are no longer the domain of the young, and the ability to use a multitude of computer software has become a basic skill both in private and professional life. Therefore, it is no wonder that increasing attention is paid to the design of interfaces adapted well to groups of users with specific needs, like the elderly. Such measures are broadly reflected in scientific works, however, commonly available software is rarely marked by an adequate concern for the needs of seniors. Additionally, the elderly usually gain access and opportunity to work on a computer during old age, being outpaced by their younger, and somewhat more predisposed to computer technology, colleagues. The prevalence of computer needs and growing number of elderly people means that seniors are condemned to using computers. How effectively and enthusiastically they will use them will be largely dependent on the ergonomic quality of the offered software.

Keywords: elderly design, ergonomic evolution, software usability.

1 Introduction

Working with programs such as word processing is the most common operation performed during typical office work and private activity. The software that is used for this purpose is largely a different variety of Microsoft products [14]. However, the need to sell next editions of the program requires continuous changes that do not always meet with enthusiasm of users. Especially older users are resistant to such alternations as they became accustomed to certain solutions and such a situation may create a considerable consternation. The problem has become even more serious because the population of the elderly is increasing year by year. For example, in Poland in 2011 nearly 35% of the population has exceeded the age of 50 years (34.89%)[19]. It is expected that in view of the ageing population this percentage will grow, which will also affect the labour market. In addition, the extension of working time will cause that more and more elderly people will have to perform work that has been previously carried out by much younger people. This results in a much higher demand

M. Kurosu (Ed.): Human-Computer Interaction, Part I, HCII 2014, LNCS 8510, pp. 481–488, 2014.
© Springer International Publishing Switzerland 2014

for solutions with the right level of ergonomic quality [5]. Solutions of this type will be needed at each stage of production [10]. Aging of workforce will also affect office workers who use a variety of software, including most often text editors. The purpose of this article is to present the studies that have been undertaken in order to verify differences regarding particular solutions concerning text editors for the elderly in the context of work efficiency.

2   Literature Review

The use of a computer is caused by a need, but also contributes to the improved well-being of older people who got familiar with the computer technique, which has been shown on 222 older adults in south Florida. It indicates that players awaiting a tournament start are more computer savvy and more self-satisfied with life [11]. As elderly persons increased their experience with computers, they achieved more positive attitudes toward a computer technology [6]. Lack of interest in the computer techniques does not result from the inability of older people to use the computer techniques, but it is due to the fact that they lack the habit and do not see the need for it-elderly people are just as technologically savvy as the rest of the population [17]. Therefore, there is a demand for adapting the software to their needs.

Designing ergonomic interface of any program that is friendly to the elderly people requires, like all kinds of different items, the principles of universal design. Among a number of publications on the subject [3], [4], [15] ones that should be mentioned are those relating to the problem of transferring the principles of universal design for usability [7]. Among the features that must be met are: effectiveness, affordability, reliability, portability, durability, securability, physicalsecurity/safety, learnability, physical comfort, acceptance, ease of maintenance/repairability and operability.

Among reported trials to examine how older people work with typical office software it is worthwhile to cite a study conducted on patients of a nursing home [12]. The experiment that was carried out with office software exposed dialectal difficulties in understanding instructions and texts. The subjects had particular problems with the word "cursor", with many other terms (e.g. "backspace", "page up = down", "enter", "ctrl key", "alt key" "ESC" and function keys) were confusing, and players awaiting tournament start could not remember their relative functions [12]. For those who did not have any previous experience with computer technology the biggest problem was double-clicking the mouse which was probably the most difficult manoeuvring task to learn in a menu-driven environment. In the case of writing texts, the problem was a size of the cursor, which exceeded the size of the text in too little extent to be recognized. This problem is present in a wider problemacy range of control accuracy and abilities to recognize small objects by the elderly [9]. An additional factor which limits the efficiency of the implementing these steps is stress resulting from contact with new technical equipment [1], which may additionally curb the efficiency of the performed activities.

3   Research Method

Numerous authors have isolated three areas of IT product quality - internal quality, external quality and quality in use. Internal quality is the "core" of product quality, which determines the quality of other areas. It's a static design quality dependent on code, programming style, etc. External quality refers to performance and behaviour of the product regardless of the user. This quality is expressed by dynamic characteristics of the operating product. Both internal and external qualities are potential – they characterize quality before application and evaluation by the actual user. However, quality in use (QIU) is defined as the ability of software to enable users to achieve specified goals with effectiveness, efficiency, security and user satisfaction in a specified context of use. QIU is observed by the user and measured by the result of software application, rather than by its inherent qualities. QIU is therefore a resulting quality and characterizes an IT product in the broad context of use in order to perform real tasks in a real work environment.

As a direct result of the design process, the internal and external qualities influence QIU, but are not themselves indicators of the overall quality of the product.

To evaluate usability, methods based on observation and measurement are used, with the most popular including heuristic evaluation, usability inspection and usability testing.

A previously developed model of testing QIU [16] is used during research, in which group criteria are expanded to precisely defined elementary criteria. The developed criteria are supplemented by rules from principles of universal design and persuasive design. Thus, for each of the criteria groups a set of detailed sub-criteria is created. A set of group criteria included:

— Easiness of use
— Error tolerance
— Comprehension
— Using fastness
— Usefulness
— Adequateness
— Ease learning of use
— Accessibility
— Self-descriptiveness
— Integrity
— Aesthetics

Typical word processors are analyzed, accounting for changes in ergonomic quality in consecutive versions of software. For this purpose, the program versions are tested in variable order. The study selected the most commonly used word processing programs, which are an example of a computer tool independent of interest or age. The execution time of basic tasks, saved as user instructions with no technical hints, is used as a measure of efficiency. Tasks are designed with three levels of difficulty.

1. The first level – entering a simple text and its formatting which was limited to paragraph alignment, modifications of the font type and size along with its bold,

italic, underline and line spacing. Other features of the document remained unchanged, according to their initial settings.

2. The second level – additionally took into account paragraph formatting, page settings, zooming and inserting the table.

3. The third level – additionally took into account an application of styles, inserting graphics, page numbering, inserting a table of contents and other features. The use of advanced features could be preceded by searching the help system.

At each of these levels a number of elderly people aged over 70 years were examined. These people had varied levels of experience, starting from the smallest, and so those who had no previous contact with the computer or their contact was limited to occasional and random activities, in comparison with the people who previously used the editorial programs for writing documents. For research the method of ethnographic research, which includes participant and nonparticipant observation, focus on natural settings, use of participant constructs to structure the research, and investigator avoidance of purposive manipulation of study variables [18]. The implementation of ethnographic design was used to see discrepancies between verbal assessment of the user and the real way of task implementation [2]. In the highest level of difficulty, a comparison is made with a control group comprised of persons under the age of 40 years.

4   Results

The first level of task difficulty was designed for people who have never created documents in a text editor. As might have been surmised, these subjects were focused on the introduction of characters and any unpredictable software reactions aroused concern. In the case of this group, the differences between the older and newer Microsoft Word software interface did not have greater importance.

For this group of users the criterion for Easiness of use would be best met if it was possible to hide most of the options. Their number scares inexperienced older users. A typical element of the intuitive operation is a ruler, however, the required precision makes it difficult and sometimes even prevents the use of it by the elderly.

Another criterion, Error tolerance should involve, for example, blocking the function of replacing the selected text, and moving a text by means of the mouse. The criterion called Comprehension and Adequateness was more acceptable when all the settings were similar to what the users associated with the final version of the paper document.

Therefore, despite the need to reduce the size of the font display, users wanted to work in print layout view with visible edges of the page. It should be noted that this system is also preferred by young users.

The criterion of Self-descriptiveness could be evaluated by novice users on the level of the subtitles displayed after moving the mouse cursor on the selected item. In this case, the new interface of Microsoft Word 2007 version and higher was better assessed due to more elaborate descriptions.

Because of the simplified interface resulting from limited functionality, the most appropriate for this beginner group of users is considered WordPad program which is a component of Windows accessories. This choice applies to the modified version available in Windows 7. Versions that were previously available in Windows XP and

Windows Vista – were not accepted by older users due to the lack of possibility to work in the system of visible edges of the page.

The second level of task difficulty was designed for people who previously dealt with writing text documents on a computer. These people could already better evaluate the meaning of different interface versions. The preferred version was traditional interface with toolbars, where the selected stripes are constantly displayed and execution of other commands requires checking the menu or short-term display of additional bar, for example, the Tables and borders toolbar. Some users claim that a banner with hidden buttons proved to be such a big problem that when they do not see a certain group of buttons, they simply do not use it. An example of such unused function in the new interface is the zoom view, previously easily available in the standard bar.

Most of the ratings given by the users of the first group were confirmed by the people from the second group. In addition, due to the use of a greater number of features, this group could refer to a bigger amount of features. The Accessibility criterion has been assessed in terms of the assistance available in particular dialog boxes. The function that was highly rated was the help assistance available in the windows dialog box for MS Word 2003. Analogous help of the newer versions was assessed by the users as not fully linked with the instructions to which it was attached.

Variability in the size and position of the command on ribbons at different screen resolutions, and even the change of the window size was considered a characteristic worsening the assessment of a criterion called Ease learning of use. For this reason, many users must again seek the position of well known commands.

The third level of tasks difficulty was intended for people who use text editors more often. Most of the earlier assessment was confirmed, although simplifications that were given for first group do not apply to them and a help system in each version is treated as useless.

This group of older users was compared with a group of people under the age of 40. Table 1. presents a summary of the assessment results in the percentage (0-100%) of the satisfaction level of elderly users whether their expectations were met in each group category. Table 2. contains an analogous correlation for younger people.

Table 1. Satisfaction level of the elderly users regarding their expectations in particular group categories

Group criterion	MS WORD 2000-2003	MS WORD 2007-2013
Easiness of use	83%	78%
Error tolerance	80%	79%
Comprehension	93%	86%
Using fastness	95%	81%
Usefulness	94%	84%
Adequateness	89%	78%
Ease learning of use	87%	75%
Accessibility	81%	74%
Self-descriptiveness	82%	82%
Integrity	91%	73%
Aesthetics	89%	95%

Table 2. Satisfaction level of the younger users regarding their expectations in particular group categories

Group criterion	MS WORD 2000-2003	MS WORD 2007-2013
Easiness of use	85%	82%
Error tolerance	88%	85%
Comprehension	92%	87%
Using fastness	94%	83%
Usefulness	91%	86%
Adequateness	87%	82%
Ease learning of use	92%	81%
Accessibility	84%	81%
Self-descriptiveness	83%	87%
Integrity	88%	81%
Aesthetics	86%	96%

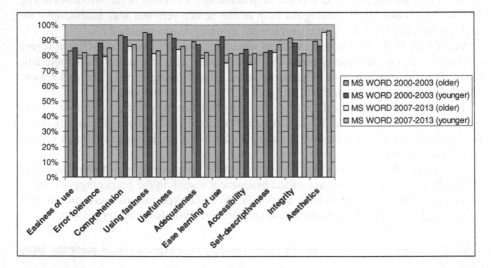

Fig. 1. Satisfaction level of the older and younger users regarding their expectations in particular group categories

Summary of the results from table 1. and table 2. is described in Figure 1.

5   Conclusion

Many elementary conclusions were mentioned in the description of the achieved results and made observations. For users who in the past did not use text editors, all interfaces regardless of the WORD program version and WinWORD proved to be too complex. Their expectations were aimed at searching for much simpler program that involves little precision in operating the mouse. It turns out that the assessment of a given criterion also depends on the users level of expertise and experience to use a particular software. In order for the impact of this experience on the differences between the elderly and the control group was the smallest, the control group of younger users were people with similar experience. This problem is typical for the cross-sectional studies and is associated with a cohort effect.

By comparing the results of evaluations between versions with an older and a newer interface, it can be concluded that, in general, the old interface had better evaluations. The exception is the criteria of *Aesthetics*, which was assessed similarly both by younger and older people as more efficient. It ought to be noted, that the assessment of younger people only slightly differentiate evaluations for both interfaces.

For the elderly those differences are larger and can mean that it is more difficult for them to adapt to new solutions. Younger people with a lot of experience better cope with new trends, often treating them as a challenge for their intelligence, and thus are not critical of the software creators new ideas. Older people require, however, a much stronger stimulus to overcome fear of new technology. The solution can be manuals written specifically for seniors to learn WORD [13], [8].

Materials from these books take older adults step by step through the basic features and the entire new tab format of the program. Such an approach will definitely help many senior to overcome their fear and will enable them to acquire new skills and develop their independence.

Most seniors and beginner computer users will use Word for typing a letter to a family member or friend, typing up a recipe or creating a fun card or flyer.

Research found that most office software insignificantly reflects the needs of the elderly. Among the most significant problems are small intuitiveness of operation and small tolerance for error. Elderly people have navigation problems and take an increased amount of time to discover unknown functions than in the case of younger people. An important factor is the tendency of software producers to modernize and move away from previously developed schemes. For elderly people who utilize earlier versions of software the "modern design" of the following versions becomes a major obstacle to effective work. A particular obstacle is a program's drop-down menu, which requires considerably precise motion of the computer operator. The efficiency of performing work is proportional to the perceived ergonomic quality of programs. The biggest impact on the results has the intuitive operation of the program – its ease of use.

In summary, with the increasing proportion of elderly people in Polish society and the dissemination among them of computer technology, there will be an increase in the demand for senior-friendly computer programs. Even when taking into account technologically-advanced future seniors, this group due to declining organ reserves and cognitive abilities will experience deficits in the ergonomic quality of programs, costing them a reduced efficiency or even an inability to work with a computer in its current form. Moreover, even seniors experienced with computers are exposed to exclusion due to rule changes of program interfaces, which also indicates the need to develop methods of design with a focus on elderly people.

References

1. Bajda, A., Wrażeń, M., Laskowski, D.: Diagnostics the quality of data transfer in the management of crisis situation. Electrical Review 87(9A), 72–78 (2011)
2. Bichard, J.-A., Greene, C., Ramster, G., Staples, T.: Designing ethnographic encounters for enriched HCI. In: Stephanidis, C., Antona, M. (eds.) UAHCI/HCII 2013, Part I. LNCS, vol. 8009, pp. 3–12. Springer, Heidelberg (2013)
3. Branowski, B., Zabłocki, M.: Creation and contamination of design principles and construction principles in the design for people with disabilities. In: Ergonomics of the Product. Ergonomic Principles of Products Design (2006) (in Polish)
4. Butlewski, M., Tytyk, E.: The assessment criteria of the ergonomic quality of anthropotechnical mega-systems. In: Vink, P. (ed.) Advances in Social and Organizational Factors, pp. 298–306. CRC Press, Taylor and Francis Group, Boca Raton, London (2012)
5. Butlewski, M.: Extension of working time in Poland as a challenge for ergonomic design. Machines, Technologies, Materials, International Virtual Journal VII(11) (2013)
6. Czaja, S.J., Sharit, J.: Age differences in attitudes toward computers. Journal of Gerontology 53(5), 329–340 (1998)
7. Follette, M.S.: Maximizing Usability: The Principles of Universal Design. Assistive Technology: The Official Journal of RESNA 10(1), 4–12 (1998)
8. Free Computer Tutorials, http://www.free-computer-tutorials.net/word-2010.html
9. Hertzum, M., Hornbæk, K.: How Age Affects Pointing With Mouse and Touchpad: A Comparison of Young, Adult, and Elderly Users. International Journal of Human-Computer Interaction 26(7) (2010)
10. Jasiulewicz-Kaczmarek, M.: The role of ergonomics in implementation of the social aspect of sustainability, illustrated with the example of maintenance. In: Arezes, P., Baptista, J.S., Barroso, M., Carneiro, P., Lamb, P., Costa, N., Melo, R., Miguel, A.S., Perestrelo, G. (eds.) Occupational Safety and Hygiene, pp. 47–52. CRC Press, Taylor & Francis, London (2013)
11. Karavidas, M., Lim, N., Katsikas, S.: The effects of computers on older adult users. Computers in Human Behavior 21(5), 697–711 (2005)
12. Namazi, K.H., McClintic, M.: Computer use among Elderly persons in long-term care facilities. Educational Gerontology 29(6) (2003)
13. Microsoft Office 2010 and 2007 for Seniors, http://www.visualsteps.com/officeseniors/
14. Microsoft Office wciąż niekwestionowanym liderem, http://www.chip.pl/news/wydarzenia/statystyka/2013/10/microsoft-office-wciaz-niekwestionowanym-liderem
15. Newell, A.F., Gregor, P.: Design for older and disabled people – where do we go from here? Universal Access in the Information Society 2(1), 3–7 (2002)
16. Prussak, W., Hankiewicz, K.: Usability estimation of quality management system software. In: 11th International Conference on Human - Computer Interaction, July 22-27. Caesars Palace - Las Vegas, Nevada, USA (2005)
17. Rousseau, G.K., Rogers, W.A.: Computer usage patterns of university faculty members across the life span. Computers in Human Behavior 14, 417–428 (1998)
18. Smith, L.M.: An evolving logic of participant observation, educational ethnography, and other case studies. Review of Research in Education 6, 316–377 (1979)
19. The results of the National Census of Population (2011), http://www.stat.gov.pl/bdl/app/strona.html?p_name=indeks

Guidelines for Usability Field Tests in the Dynamic Contexts of Public Transport

Stephan Hörold, Cindy Mayas, and Heidi Krömker

Ilmenau University of Technology, Ilmenau, Germany
{stephan.hoerold,cindy.mayas,heidi.kroemker}@tu-ilmenau.de

Abstract. Public transport is one of many fields of application where a system is not used in only one context of use, but in different and varying contexts. Evaluating these systems in lab-based tests can only cover a small part of the real context. This paper describes a usability field test of a mobile passenger information application in public transport, the challenges of testing in a highly dynamic context, and also solutions to overcome these challenges. As a result, a classification of the variety of dynamic factors in public transport and guidelines for typical test contexts in public transport are derived from the gained experiences and empirical findings.

Keywords: usability, field test, public transport, tasks, context.

1 Introduction

In recent years, many public transport companies have extended their passenger information offerings with mobile applications and real-time information, in order to fulfill the information needs of the passengers [1] [2]. The integration of mobile applications into the existing passenger information system requires user and task analysis, as well as usability tests in different contexts. These mobile applications often serve as personal assistant for different kinds of passengers [3]. Along the journey, these passengers pass through varying environmental contexts with many different tasks and subtasks, such as: travel planning, getting on and off a vehicle at the right stop point changing between vehicles, etc. [4]. The aim of this paper is to classify this dynamic context in public transport, in order to derive guidelines to improve the manageability of these factors in field tests.

In current discussions on testing mobile applications with lab-based or field-based usability tests, typical advantages and disadvantages of both testing methods are widely identified and discussed controversially [5] [6]. Lab-based tests, e.g. often lack a realistic setting, while field-based tests, for instance are time consuming and hard to control. Nevertheless, the real complexity of public transport cannot be simulated in a lab, e.g. because a real journey has a high amount of physical tasks and provides a highly dynamic context of use.

M. Kurosu (Ed.): Human-Computer Interaction, Part I, HCII 2014, LNCS 8510, pp. 489–499, 2014.
© Springer International Publishing Switzerland 2014

2   Testing in Dynamic Contexts of Public Transport

The ISO/IEC 25062 Common Industry Format (CIF) for usability test reports defines usability as "the extent to which a product can be used by specified users to achieve specified goals with effectiveness, efficiency and satisfaction in a specified context of use" [9]. The context of use is shaped by the users and tasks as well as the technical parameters and social and physical environment, in which the systems will be used [7]. Bevan points out that for usability testing, the context of use should be as close as possible to the real context, in order to provide valid results [10].

Thus, for usability testing, it is essential to have a clear understanding of users, tasks and the environment. In order to reach this clear understanding of the context of use, an analysis of the dynamic factors of the mobile context of use is needed initially. Krannich defines two dimensions of the mobile context of use, the situative and the cognitive dimension, in which different dynamic factors are identified [8].

The cognitive dimension deals with the individual characteristics and problem solving strategies of the users [8]. The situative dimension deals with the social and physical environment [8]. Before conducting a usability test, these dynamic factors have to be mapped to the context of use and the impacts on usability tests have to be identified.

2.1   Dynamic Context Factors

Users. The users of public transport can differ widely, depending on their capabilities and activities in public transport [3]. Krannich points out, that within the dynamic mobile context of use, especially the following user dependent characteristics shape the context of use [8]:

- Prior knowledge
- Individual perception
- Level of attention
- Individual goals and motivation

Task. More than ninety public transport special tasks are done along a journey, depending on the kind of passenger [2]. These tasks differ in complexity and difficulty. Some of these tasks are accomplished to obtain information, while others are performed to physically travel from one point to another. Task specific dynamic context factors include:

- Complexity of tasks
- Difficulty of tasks
- Time for task completion
- Dependences between tasks

Environment. Depending on the kind of public transport system and region, as well as time, day and season, the environmental context in public transport can differ as well [4]. Krannich identifies several dynamic factors, which result from the dynamically changing environment [8]:

- Local environment
  - Weather conditions
  - Noises
  - Traffic density
- Social situation
- Local objects and equipment

Additional Influencing Factors. In addition to the context of use, the development and test of a product or system can be influenced by organizational, legal and social conditions. A key part of a usability test is the system or product, which will be tested. The state of the system, whether it is a prototype or a final system, might influence the test concept and the test itself, as well. Interdependencies between the state of the system and the context of use should be considered early in the preparation of a test.

2.2 Impacts of Dynamic Context Factors

To measure effectiveness, efficiency and satisfaction within the context of use, a usability test can be conducted as a lab-based or a field-based test. As mentioned before, advantages and downsides are widely discussed within the HCI community [5][6]. A decision should be made, based on the area of application and the phase of the development. The context of use in public transport is shaped through different users, tasks and environments. A natural behavior of test users can only be reached if the users actually have to perform all the tasks along the journey and the information needs arise from a concrete situation, which can only be completed when the information is acquired. In lab-based tests, a journey often has to be divided into different phases, as a physical journey is not performed. The user has to imagine a complex journey while essential physical tasks are left out and consequences e.g. a missed vehicle, are hard to simulate. In contrast, field-based tests are hard to control and difficult to analyze [11] because the running public transport system cannot be adjusted to the needs of a usability test.

In the following two examples, the influences of the context of use on field-based tests are described.

Example 1: Level of attention. Within a usability field test, the level of attention can differ from lab-based tests, because in addition to the concrete task, the surroundings have to be observed, e.g. to prevent collisions with other people or objects. This may result in an increase of the task's complexity.

Table 1. Example for Factor: Level of Attention

Task to perform during journey	Task Complexity in lab-based test	Reason for lack of attention	Task Complexity in field based test
Checking arrival times	Low	Standing within a crowded vehicle	middle
Finding the way to the stop point	Middle (e.g. with a map)	Walking, objects and people	High

Example 2: Time for task completion. Along a journey, several tasks have to be completed under defined time constraints. If an interchange is not performed within a specified interchange time, a vehicle may be missed and the passenger has to wait for the next vehicle. A lab-based test can simulate such constraints, but the consequences for the test users, are minimal. Within a field test, these consequences become quite real and may extend the test significantly.

Table 2. Example for Factor: Time for task completion

Task to perform during journey	Task Complexity in lab-based test	Reason time constraint	Task Complexity in field based test
Finding alternative routes in case of disturbances	Middle	Time pressure resulting form planned arrival	High
Identifying the needed track	Low	Small time slot for interchange	middle

In general, a task is not only influenced by one dynamic context factor, but by a combination of different factors, resulting, e.g. in stress, time pressure and low level of attention. Within a complex field-based test, these can effect several parts of the test and may result in unforeseen reactions of the test persons. Wrong decisions may result in the test person not reaching the destination, or the test time frame is enormously extended. Therefore, the results of the test may not be comparable anymore and too many individual differences make an analysis of the results difficult.

3   Field-Based Usability Tests in Public Transport

The following test concept describes a public transport field-based test for a mobile application, which serves as the basis for the identified solutions and derived guidelines.

3.1   Field Test Concept

Test object. The test object is a new standardized IP-based interface, which was implemented in a prototype of a smart phone application for public transportation. The application includes the functions of travel planning, itinerary, departure timetables and event management with push services.

Test Objectives. The primary objective of the study is to evaluate the flow of information in relation to the locations of use and phases during the travel chain. Other points of focus are: which functions satisfy the information needs of users and which additional information resources are required.

Test Area. The test is conducted in Stuttgart, a state`s capital city in Germany, with about 600 000 inhabitants. The test track is located on the outskirts of the city and has an overall length of 11 km (6.84 miles). The test starts at a metro station and includes a metro ride, a footpath necessary to change between two stops and a bus ride. Each context of the test track, which is identical for each test person, provides specific characteristics of crowding, environmental influences, and information needs for different times and dates.

Test Participants. In total 36 test persons, which are local inhabitants of the town, are acquired with the kind assistance of the local transportation company. The main screening characteristics of the test persons are: their age, their knowledge of the place, their frequency of use, and their experiences with smart phones. Only test persons, who are experienced users of smart phones, are invited to the test, in order to prevent influences of the learnability of the hardware in the test.

Evaluation Methods. Prior to and after the test, a standardized questionnaire is used to confirm the screening characteristics, to allow further insight into knowledge and usage of public transport and to retrieve feedback to the test object. In addition, a retrospective thinking aloud [14] is performed by commentating the audio and video material recorded with the test equipment, during the test trip, afterwards. For later evaluation the thinking aloud is recorded as well.

Test Equipment. The interaction of the test person with the smart phone is recorded by a focused spy camera, which is integrated in a backpack worn by the test person. In addition, each request of the application is logged and the screen is captured, including the visualized interaction points. The use of video glasses also enables the evaluation of available further public information in the field of view. At least, the position of the test person is observed, by tracking the smart phone.

Test Tasks. The main test task is to reach a predefined point of interest from a predefined starting point. This task includes several subtasks: trip planning, getting on and off, riding along, changing, managing disturbances and sending stop requests. The test persons were introduced to the application before, and had to solve the tasks independently, by using the test application and public information. Each of the 36 test persons had to fulfill the same tasks along the journey, in dynamic contexts.

3.2   Dynamic Field Test Challenges

Resulting from the different dynamic factors, as mentioned before, the field-based test provides several challenges. The basic test concept had to be extended by methods to overcome these challenges, respectively and to ease the effects on the test or enable the test team to react to unforeseen circumstances. Based on the dynamic context factors and a conducted pre-test, the following challenges were identified.

User Dependent Challenges. The context factors resulting from the users, especially prior knowledge, individual perception, level of attention and individual goals and motivation [8], highly influence the usability test. Mainly, these influences are desired, to receive results from different user groups and to be able to test the system for all potential users. Nevertheless, in a field environment like public transport, these factors provide different challenges:

• Keeping track of the passenger in the field
• Providing secure and trustworthy conditions, even for less experienced users

In addition, the context factors resulting from users directly influence tasks through different knowledge and task completion strategies.

Task Dependent Challenges. The main influencing factors in a field test are different durations for task completion as well as the changing difficulty and complexity levels. Task completion in public transport often depends on performing a series of task, physical as well as cognitive, which influence each other. The environment, the tasks themselves, the time and how the user reacts, all influence each other. The following challenges where identified, in relation to task complexity and time constraints:

• Simple tasks may become very complex, when influenced by time constraints, missing information and the environment
• Time for task completion can differ, depending on timetables and events

Environment Dependent Challenges. Local circumstances, social situation and equipment differ widely in public transport [4]. A field test should integrate these factors , as they are vital for a realistic setting. In contrast, especially the changing social situations, disturbances and traffic density, provide the greatest challenges:

• Disturbances of different scope occur spontaneously and are hard to plan
• Daytime and weather conditions may provide additional challenges for the user

3.3   Artifacts through Test Equipment

In addition to the influences of the context of use, the test equipment may affect the test as well. Visible test equipment, e.g. video recording equipment, may create conflicts with other passengers or make the test user feel uncomfortable. Thinking aloud in public may feel strange to the test users and a retrospective thinking aloud may not provide real insight into the users thoughts. These effects were analyzed prior to the field test, to identify a test setting with minimal artifacts [12].

3.4   Field Test Results

The test results show that the inclusion of different and varying contexts into the test concept provides profound and highly differentiated feedback on the user specific task completion strategies, the use of the application, and the parallel use of other information systems [13]. Each test context imposes special characteristics in regard to the criteria time, place and environmental context.

4   Guidelines

Before conducting the field test, solutions for the context challenges were identified and integrated into the test concept. In the following, these challenges and solutions, as well as the assessment after the usability field test in public transport, are described.

4.1   Context Factor User

Challenge: Keeping Track of the Test Person. Test participants in a field test in public transport have to change their positions quickly during the test. The chance of getting lost or leaving the route is high, especially when stations and stop points are complex and prior knowledge, as well as the level of attention, is low.

Solution: Tracking and Contact Information. The test team developed three ways, which were used altogether, to keep track of the test person along the journey.

- The first solution is the tracking of the geo-positions of the smartphone. It enables the test team to monitor the test person and to decide if an intervention is needed.
- In addition, an undercover observer can follow the journey of the test person. The decision, however, of having someone follow the test person's journey is quite controversial, from an ethical point of view. So this solution should be carefully discussed, before it is used.
- We also provided a rescue card providing the route and contact information of the test team.

Assessment: Vital in Combination for a Fluent Field Test. The solution worked very well in combination. Due to patchy connections, the tracking might be unreliable, especially when inside a vehicle. Having an observer provides a backup for such situations. During peak times, it is hard for the observer to keep track of the test person. In such cases, the smartphone tracking can provide necessary information to locate the test person. The rescue card was never used within our tests, but provided security for the test persons and the test team and should be a given standard for field test within such dynamic contexts.

Challenge: Providing Secure and Trustworthy Conditions. Test participants in a field test in public life are exposed to several social factors. Uncertainty, resulting from missing knowledge and individual perception of the actual context, combined with the situation of a usability test, may result in unusual behavior and have negative reflection on the test system or product. In addition, due to the technical recording equipment they may feel observed by other passengers or even uncomfortable and threatened.

Solution: Professional Document and Information. We provided a professional document to verify their activity as test participants and additional information, in case of uncertainty. A standardized questionnaire was used after the test to evaluate how the test person felt during the test regarding the equipment itself and the behaviour of others.

Assessment: Essential for Natural Behavior. Only few of our test participants were addressed by other passengers regarding the test equipment. In average, these test interruptions took less than 60 seconds. None of them felt disturbed or unpleasantly observed [12]. The document provided security and information, making it easier for the test users to behave naturally.

4.2   Context Factor Tasks

Challenge: Simple Tasks Might become Very Complex in the Field. Some tasks might seem very simple in a lab test or when designing a field test. For example, an interchange between two vehicles in public transport is very simple, if the participant has all needed information. Tasks like this can become very complex when they depend on other tasks which have to be done correctly, and have to be conducted in a short time frame, or else it is uncertain whether the information is available or not, due to dynamic information systems. As a result, a vehicle could be missed or the participant could lose the right track.

Challenge: Time Frame for Task Completion Can Differ. Throughout the day, time to check departure times, interchange times and other time frames, can differ through the different time tables and occurring events. As time is a key factor for task completion in public transport, smaller or longer time frames may influence the user's individual task completion, resulting in different behaviors for different users.

Solution: Controlling Dependencies and Effects. For both challenges, it is essential to know the dependencies between different tasks and the available time frame for task completion. In addition to the described solutions to track the passenger, we prepared an easy-to-use timetable for the metro and the bus ride, which enabled the test team to calculate possible effects of different interchange times, missed vehicles and alternative routes. The available dynamic information systems were carefully analyzed and observed during the test. Due to this, the test team was able to monitor the actual situation, especially regarding unforeseen events and could document the influences for later integration into the field test evaluation.

Assessment: Dynamic Contexts Need Dynamic Reactions of the Test Team. The task completion not only depends on the task and the user but on the influences of the context as well. The field test showed that even if all tasks were performed on time, a connection can be missed and a delay within the test procedure is inevitable. Having information about the actual situation and possible alternatives is essential to judge the effect. The tested solution, enabled the test team to observe the situation and calculate the effect, and decide whether the test was still within in the defined test framework or not.

4.3   Context Factor Environment

Challenge: Disturbances Occur Spontaneously and Are Hard to Plan. Disturbances are part of public transport. They range from longer delays to complete breakdown of parts of the transportation systems, e.g. in hard winters. While a public transport field test should incorporate disturbances to evaluate, e.g., how the information needs are fulfilled, unforeseen disturbances may interrupt the test.

Solution: Planned Disturbances and Direct Influence on Communication. The test included a simulated disturbance, which for the test users, could not be distinguished from real disturbance information. Due to this, a comparable disturbance could be introduced in every test. In case of real disturbances, this system allowed the possibility to provide additional information in order to reduce the effect on the test.

Assessment: Disturbances Need Careful Planning and Reactions. The use of simulated disturbances worked quite well. A realistic situation and information has to be produced, to be able to convince even high experienced users. With this system, other unusual disturbances could be alleviated. In case of one greater disturbance, effecting major parts of the test track, a normal test could not be conducted. This demonstrates the limiting boundaries of being able to control a dynamic environment.

Challenge: Daytime and Weather Conditions Provide Additional Challenges.
During peak times, public transport vehicles are often crowded and task complexity
rises. Additionally, new challenges arise, e.g. getting on and off the vehicle or
performing an interchange in time. In the evening or early morning, the dark
environment may reduce the feeling of security and makes it hard, e.g. to identify the
right way or read signs. Rain or intensive sunlight may reduce the visibility of
information and in addition to normal travel tasks, the user has to find shelter or use
an umbrella.

Solution: Provide Security and Adjustable Equipment. In case of the changing
weather conditions, the equipment could be adjusted by, e.g. changing from video
sunglasses to normal video glasses. The test track was evaluated and carefully chosen
to minimize the security risk and the rescue card, as well as the observer, provided
additional security. As one of the objectives was the evaluation of realistic behavior in
different contexts, the test track provided stop points with and without public
transport shelters. These effects where recorded and later evaluated.

Assessment: Users Deal Quite Easily with Such Challenges. For commuters, as well
as less frequent users, adjusting to weather conditions was quite easy. Test users cared
more for the test equipment than for themselves, making it important to assure them of
the needed weather resistance. Only very few of the participants felt insecure on the test
track. Especially in the evening, they feared someone could take away the test
smartphone. The observer feedback shows, that no threatening situations occurred, but
the subjective feeling shows, the importance of the described measures taken.

5   Conclusion

Conducting field tests is challenging and requires thorough planning and preparation.
Nevertheless, not all situations can be predicted prior to the start of the test.
Especially in public transport, disturbances of different size and scope can occur any
minute. Tests in dynamic contexts, imply a high risk, that tests fail, due to unforeseen
circumstances, or due to the fact that the test situations of the different users are not
comparable. As a solution, additional measures, e.g. tracking of the test person and
monitoring of occurring disturbances, are used, in order to enable the test team to
react appropriately. Other challenges result from the complexity of tasks and
providing secure and trustworthy conditions for the test persons.

The described solutions show how field tests can be conducted to deal with the
influences of the dynamic context. More studies are needed to develop a framework
with dynamic factors, challenges and solutions, which make field-based testing more
controllable.

Acknowledgements. Part of this work was funded by the German Federal Ministry of
Economy and Technology (BMWi) grant number 19P10003L within the IP-KOM-
ÖV project. The project develops an interface standard for passenger information in
German public transport.

References

1. EN 13816:2002: Transportation - Logistics and service - Public passenger transport - Service quality definition, targeting and measurement. German version. Beuth Verlag GmbH, Berlin (2002)
2. Hörold, S., Mayas, C., Krömker, H.: Identifying the information needs of users in public transport. In: Stanton, N. (ed.) Advances in Human Aspects of Road and Rail Transportation, pp. 331–340. CRC Press, Boca Raton (2012)
3. Mayas, C., Hörold, S., Krömker, H.: Meeting the Challenges of Individual Passenger Information with Personas. In: Stanton, N. (ed.) Advances in Human Aspects of Road and Rail Transportation, pp. 822–831. CRC Press, Boca Raton (2012)
4. Hörold, S., Mayas, C., Krömker, H.: Analyzing varying environmental contexts in public transport. In: Kurosu, M. (ed.) Human Computer Interaction, Part I, HCII 2013. LNCS, vol. 8004, pp. 85–94. Springer, Heidelberg (2013)
5. Nielsen, C.M., Overgaard, M., Pedersen, M.B., Stage, J., Stenild, S.: It's worth the hassle!: the added value of evaluating the usability of mobile systems in the field. In: Proceedings of the 4th Nordic Conference on Human-Computer Interaction: Changing Roles, NordiCHI 2006 (2006)
6. Sun, X., May, A.: A Comparison of Field-Based and Lab-Based Experiments to Evaluate User Experience of Personalised Mobile Devices. Advances in Human-Computer Interaction 2013, Article ID 619767 (2013), doi:10.1155/2013/619767
7. ISO 9241-210:2010: Ergonomics of human-system interaction – Part 210: Human-centred design for interactive systems, German version. Beuth Verlag GmbH, Berlin (2010)
8. Krannich, D.: Mobile System Design – Herausforderungen, Anforderungen und Lösungsansätze für Design, Implementierung und Usability-Testing Mobiler Systeme. Books on Demand GmbH, Norderstedt (2010)
9. ISO/IEC 25062:2006: Software engineering - Software product Quality Requirements and Evaluation (SQuaRE) - Common Industry Format (CIF) for usability test reports. ISO, Switzerland (2006)
10. Bevan, N.: Using the Common Industry Format to Document the Context of Use. In: Kurosu, M. (ed.) Human-Computer Interaction, Part I, HCII 2013. LNCS, vol. 8004, pp. 281–289. Springer, Heidelberg (2013)
11. Kjeldskov, J., Skov, M., Als, B., Høegh, R.: Is It Worth the Hassle? Exploring the Added Value of Evaluating the Usability of Context-Aware Mobile Systems in the Field. In: Brewster, S., Dunlop, M.D. (eds.) Mobile HCI 2004. LNCS, vol. 3160, pp. 61–73. Springer, Heidelberg (2004)
12. Mayas, C., Hörold, S., Rosenmöller, C., Krömker, H.: Evaluating Methods and Equipment for Usability Field Tests in Public Transport. In: Kurosu, M. (ed.) Human-Computer Interaction, Part I, HCII 2014. LNCS, vol. 8510, pp. 545–553. Springer, Heidelberg (2014)
13. Hörold, S., Mayas, C., Krömker, H.: Passenger Needs on mobile Information Systems – Field Evaluation in Public Transport. In: 5th International Conference on Applied Human Factors and Ergonomics, AHFE 2014, Krakow (accepted 2014)
14. Dumas, J.S., Fox, J.E.: Usability Testing. In: Jacko, J.A. (ed.) The Human-Computer Interaction Handbook: Fundamentals, Evolving Technologies and Emerging Applications, 3rd edn., pp. 1221–1241. CRC Press, Boca Raton (2012)

Integrating Usability Evaluations into Scrum: A Case Study Based on Remote Synchronous User Testing

Fulvio Lizano[1], Maria Marta Sandoval[2], and Jan Stage[1]

[1] Aalborg University, Department of Computer Science, Aalborg, Denmark
{fulvio,jans}@cs.aau.dk
[2] National University, Informatics School, Heredia, Costa Rica
msandova@una.cr

Abstract. The tendency to empower users in the software development process encourages the continuing search for ways to reconcile the interests of agile methodologies and Human-Computer Interaction (HCI) activities. The practice of agile methods, e.g. Scrum, is normally focused on high productivity, sometimes leaving aside other important aspects of software development such as usability. On the other hand, HCI methods usually attempt to reach solid conclusions through extensive and formal studies, which can consume significant resources and time. In this paper we present an instrumental single case study which offers an example of how usability evaluations can be integrated into a Scrum project by using Remote Synchronous User Testing (RS). Our approach suggests that the RS process should be conducted by the same developers who integrate the developing team. Our results indicate that RS can be used as a strategy to efficiently and easily integrate usability evaluations into Scrum projects. The most valuable benefit obtained in this integration is related to the opportune feedback offered by usability testing, which can be incorporated to the developing process immediately as is provided through agile principles. Other elements of our approach could help solve other problems normally present in other efforts made in order to integrate usability evaluations into agile methods. The major problem in our case study was related to the difficulty presented by software developers in terms of changing their usual focus when they have to conduct usability evaluations.

Keywords: Software development, usability evaluation, Remote Synchronous User Testing (RS), SCRUM, integrating RS into SCRUM.

1 Introduction

Scrum, as well another Agile methodologies, emphasizes simplicity and speed in the software development process [4]. This explains why these methodologies have become popular in numerous organizations [12].

However, simplicity and speed could make any integration of these development methods with formal usability techniques (e.g. usability evaluations) difficult. Considering the valuable feedback obtained in usability evaluations [9], there is an in-creasing interest in the integration of these kinds of tests into Scrum and other agile methods.

M. Kurosu (Ed.): Human-Computer Interaction, Part I, HCII 2014, LNCS 8510, pp. 500–509, 2014.
© Springer International Publishing Switzerland 2014

In this paper we present an instrumental single case study [15], [24] which offers an example of how to integrate usability evaluations into a Scrum project.

The case study has two aims. Firstly, considering the Scrum iterative approach, we are interested in exploring which usability evaluation activities/artifacts should be used throughout the process. Secondly, considering that we propose extensive participation from software developers, we want to explore the implications that such participation has in the integration, mainly in terms of how the developers' focus changes during the integration.

In the second section of this paper we present the related works. Next, we present the method used in this case study. After that, we describe the methodological approach for integrating usability evaluations into Scrum. The paper subsequently describes and analyzes the main results of our case study. The remaining sections cover discussion and conclusions, which includes future works proposals.

2   Related Works

Notwithstanding the interest in integrating usability into agile methods, literature is prolific in terms of references to obstacles to achieving this purpose [2, 3]. In the particular case of Scrum, there are deeper differences originating from the foundations of both approaches. Usability is focused on how users will work with the software, whereas agile development is centered on how software should be developed [23].

It is possible to identify different viewpoints regarding the integration between usability evaluation and Scrum. Sohaib and Khan [23] identified several tensions between usability and agile methods: the agile approach is characterized by a focus on the client more than the user, it develops functional software that is not necessarily useful, there is an emphasis on acceptation and unit testing more than usability testing, and finally User-Centered Design (UCD) is not normally a priority in agile projects. Lee and McCrickard [18] identified the origin of these tensions in the differing aims and motivations of Software Engineering (SE) and HCI practitioners, combined with a significant quantity and variety of techniques and methodologies existing in both fields.

It is a fact that the differences of aims between SE and HCI practitioners negatively affect the aforementioned integration. There are different perspectives about what is important in software development [17]. SE practitioners focus on designing, implementing and maintaining software, minimizing the relevance of human-computer interfaces. On the contrary, HCI practitioners focus on developing software with high orientation to users in order to allow them to work with the soft-ware effectively.

This dissimilarity of goals could lead to a lack of collaboration between software developers and HCI practitioners. Jerome and Kazman [11] found that SE and HCI practitioners do not closely collaborate with other professionals outside their knowledge areas. The limited collaboration tends to occur too late in the software development process, which reduces its effectiveness.

Finally, the lack of formal application of HCI and SE methods is another factor that could complicate integration. For example, Jia [12] found that only the 38% of participants in her study reported using Scrum "by the book". This issue could explain why the UCD community complains about the limited application of some agile principles (e.g. individuals and interactions over processes and tools, and customer collaboration over contract negotiations) [21].

Several solutions have been suggested in order to integrate usability in software development process. Sohaib and Khan [23] proposed increasing the iterative approach and testing throughout the lifecycle, adopting usability activities by integrating user scenarios and including usability practitioners in agile teams.

Alternatively, Fischer [8] proposes an integration approach based on international standards, which are the result of the consensus of experts, by providing consistency, repeatability of processes, independence of organizations, quality and facilities for communication.

Coincidentally, Ferré, Juristo and Moreno [7] proposed the integration of HCI activities into software projects by using SE terminology for HCI activities in order to allow developers to understand HCI concepts. The Ripple framework could be used as an example of such an approach [19]. This framework proposes an event-driven design representation that offers developers and HCI practitioners a common framework to represent artifacts generated at each stage of SE and HCI lifecycles.

Other practical considerations were recommended by Hussain et al. [10], e.g. smaller tests with iterations to test only certain parts of the software and using smaller groups of 1-2 users into each usability evaluation.

3   Method

The case study was developed considering a small core system designed to manage the data resulting from the supervision process of undergraduate system engineering students' projects. The supervision process is carried out by regular professors of the system engineering courses.

We decided to define a case protocol based on the widely accepted Yin theory [24] for case studies. Our case protocol included specifications such as period of time for the case study, location, hypothesis, research questions, unit of analysis, data analysis plan and also a proposed outline for the future paper.

Data collection is based on several theoretical approaches. Our case protocol primarily considers the documents resulting from the tests (e.g. usability plan, user tasks, usability final report and guidelines) [13], [20]. We also used some Scrum documents [14] and other secondary sources of data collection (e.g. emails, personal interviews, a focus group meeting and videos of sessions).

The analysis used the general analytic strategy of relying on theoretical propositions [24]. We mainly focused on the data resulting from usability evaluations in order to contrast the results of the case study against other findings reported in the literature.

Data evaluation was focused on assessing usability reports delivered during the integration process. We used a checklist based on Capra approach [6]. Additionally, the data collected was triangulated with results obtained in personal interviews and a focus group meeting [16].

4   Integrating Usability Evaluations into SCRUM: A Proposal for a Methodological Approach

Our proposal of integration is based on usability evaluations created by Remote Synchronous User Testing (RS) [1]. We organized the tests in an iterative scheme of smaller usability evaluations [10]. In each sprint, we made a small usability evaluation by using only two users. Each user participated in a single test and we recruited different users in each test. We also used a few tasks related to specific parts of the software (normally 4-5 tasks per test). The software developers were in charge of conducting the usability evaluation [5], [22].

This approach allowed a simple and practical integration. By using RS in an iterative scheme, we achieved enough test coverage. More importantly, conduction of the evaluations by developers allowed them to easily realize and understand the main usability problems present in their software.

5   Case Description and Analysis

This section covers the description and analysis of the case study. The first sub-section covers the first actions that took place at the beginning of the case. The remaining two sub-sections present the project and the main usability evaluation issues. Although the aim of the study is to explore how integrate usability evaluations into a Scrum project, the description of the case study will focus on usability evaluations.

5.1   Prologue: First Actions in the Case

It is possible to consider a simple spreadsheet with crude data related to students' projects as the foundations of the project. The professors had used this spreadsheet as a master record of projects, students, contacts, etc. The evident limitations related to security and the lack of control over this data management provides adequate reasons for developing a software system that could make the management process of the data related to the students' projects more secure and practical. Because of the urgency of the project, there was a consensus to develop the software using an agile methodology, specifically Scrum. In addition, among other factors, the usability of the final software product was cited as a highly desirable feature.

In early August 2012, a web-conference was made between the authors of this study, the professors' coordinator and members of the Scrum team. In this web-conference, we took several decisions. Firstly, bearing in mind resource limitations regarding staff, the project's roles were defined considering the product owner (the professors' coordinator), three developers and one usability adviser (co-author of this paper). Secondly, we decided on the software tools that should be used in the project. The final accord was related to the definition of the project's schedule.

5.2   The Project

An initial definition of the project considered three sprints with several main activities. The sprints were coded as '0', '1' and '2'. Sprint '0' was focused on definition-planning matters. After finished sprint '2', together with the product owner we decided to add an additional sprint coded as '3'. Our intention was explore an improvement of some usability artifacts.

5.3   Usability Evaluations

Sprint '0' was used in definition-planning issues. The main activities were related to defining the team and roles during the different sprints, defining the preliminary software architecture facts, defining the business value project, and finally other activities more connected to the usability evaluations that will be conducted by RS (i.e. the settings of RS software tools and training).

Starting from sprint '1', the developers conducted several usability evaluations. The tests included sessions with two users and a final analysis session conducted by a facilitator. In Figure 1 a session with users (section A) and the final analysis session (section B) can be observed.

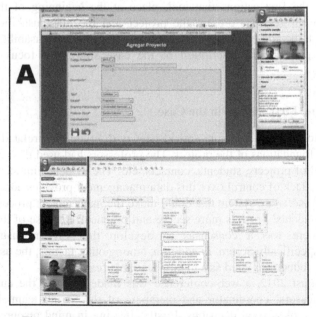

Fig. 1. A: User test session. B: the final analysis session.

In Table 1 is possible to see the main results of the case study. In the table it is also possible see the main artifacts designed for the tests, which were based on Rubin and Chisnell [20]. In sprint '0' a usability plan was defined along with several usability tasks and guidelines. Only in the case of the usability plan and the guidelines for the remote analysis final session was a second release of such documents necessary, specifically during sprint '2'. In sprint '0', no usability evaluation was conducted. Some of the usability tasks also required a second release. The main data from the usability evaluations and the assessment of the usability problem reports is also presented in the table.

Table 1. The case study main facts

Activity	Deliverable / results	Sprint 0	Sprint 1	Sprint 2	Sprint 3
Usability evaluation artifacts	Usability Plan	1-R1		1-R2	
	User Tasks	T1-R1 T2-R1 T3-R1 T4-R1 T5-R1 T6-R1 T7-R1	T1-R1 T2-R1 T3-R1 T4-R1	T1-R1 T4-R1 T5-R1 T6-R1 T7-R1	T1-R2 T4-R2 T8-R1 T9-R1
	Usability Problems Report	0	1	1	1
	Test-Monitor guideline	1			
	Logger guideline	1			
	Remote Analysis Final Session guideline	1-R1		1-R2	
Test facts	Average per user/task		220,75	300,7	210,25
	Critical usability problems			3	2
	Serious usability problems		1	3	2
	Cosmetic usability problems		6	1	1
Assessment of Usability Problem Report	Final result		6,5	9	9

6   Discussion

This case study presents an example of how to integrate usability evaluations into a Scrum project. One of the aims of the study was related to exploring which usability evaluation activities/artifacts should be used during the process. The other aim is connected to the effects of developers' participation in such integration. Considering that we proposed extensive participation from developers, we were interested in exploring the implications that such participation has in the integration, mainly in terms of how the developers' focus changes during the integration. In the following sub-sections, we will discuss these research questions in more detail.

6.1   Usability Evaluation Activities/artifacts Considered in the Integration

The results of our study confirmed that Scrum emphasizes simplicity and speed [4] and can be compatible with usability evaluations by using RS. The iterative schema of Scrum allows for the implementation of several usability evaluations on a software system, something that was also proposed by Sohaib and Khan [23]. Practical usability evaluations can be conducted by using smaller tests on certain elements of the software with smaller groups of users as was suggested by Hussain et al. [10]. In the case study we conducted short evaluations in one day where smaller groups of only two users performed a small number of tasks (i.e. 4-5). Several test iterations with different users carrying out different tasks allowed us to achieve adequate testing coverage.

This iterative approach allows a set of usability activities/artifacts that could change from one sprint to another to be used. Thus, it is possible to use only the strictly necessary activities or artifacts in every sprint, e.g. designing a single usability plan which could be upgradeable if necessary, defining several usability tasks for the entire project, etc.

The fact that practical tests can be conducted in Scrum by using the strictly necessary forms, guidelines, etc. makes integration feasible, practical and easy. The usability feedback which is obtained as a direct result of the usability evaluations fits perfectly into the agile principles [21]. Indeed, the limited application of Scrum [12] could be improved through the aforementioned integration.

6.2   Changing the Focus in the Usability Evaluation Iterations

Our study found that the main challenge of the integration between usability evaluation and Scrum was to change the focus of software developers in the usability evaluations conducted in the iterations. During the first evaluation, the developers who participated in usability evaluation had forgotten or simply ignored the specific rules documented in the guidelines. This attitude, although apparently unintentional, could be another manifestation of the software developers' mindset [2, 3]. During the second evaluation, the re-training efforts produced good results; audio video recording, notes and the results of closing meetings confirmed that the problem had decreased.

The problem can be handled by using guidelines and giving developers training that emphasizes not only the techniques required to conduct the tests but also those specific rules related to how they should conduct themselves during such tests. These guidelines, which are based on Rubin and Chisnell approach [20], implement the

Fischer approach [8] regarding international standards in the integration. The use of guidelines and the iterative schema of usability evaluations were easily understood by developers as these elements are well-known to them. This is another example of the integration proposed by Ferré, Juristo and Moreno [7] through using SE terminology for HCI activities in order to facilitate developers' understanding of HCI concepts.

Changing the focus of developers is a complex issue due to the developers' mindset [2, 3] and the difference of perspectives between developers and HCI practitioners [18], [23]. However, even considering the limitations of this case study, it is possible to identify certain improvements in developers' focus regarding usability matters when they are interacting with usability activities, especially in an iterative scheme of usability evaluations. This improvement process will definitely reduce the lack of collaboration between SE and HCI practitioners [11].

7 Conclussion

Usability evaluations conducted using RS can be integrated into Scrum projects, regardless of the formal assumptions presented in this evaluation method. RS does not create major obstacles for the Scrum principles of simplicity and speed. In this single instrumental case study, we proposed a methodological approach that considers using RS conducted by software developers in Scrum projects as a way to integrate usability evaluations into this agile method. Throughout the case we identified the specific RS activities or instruments involved in the Scrum's sprints. We also studied changes in software developers' focus when they conducted usability evaluations and the major implications of the interchanging roles system used by developers in the Scrum's sprints.

Our approach to integrating RS into Scrum presents several interesting advantages. Firstly, the iterative strategy required by the Scrum dynamic makes it unnecessary to use all the activities and artifacts normally used in a usability evaluation process. Secondly, it is relatively easy for developers to conduct usability evaluations by using RS; the use of guidelines and basic training has confirmed the feasibility of such an aim. Finally, because this integration has shown to be practical, it is possible to use a similar approach in order to increase the chances of applying usability evaluations in other agile methods. This case study has shown how it is possible to handle some problems presented in the efforts to integrate usability evaluations into agile methods, e.g. the inherent tensions found between these approaches, the difference in aims and the lack of collaboration between the SE and the HCI practitioners, the lack of a formal Scrum application and usability evaluation approaches, etc.

The main problems present in this integration are related to the changes of focus of developers when they have to conduct usability evaluation. Despite the fact that we implemented some correcting actions relatively successfully, it seems that this issue could affect the quality of the evaluation results, at least in the first ones. Fortunately, the approach used in this case of study and the iterative dynamic which is presented in the Scrum method allow the problem to be detected in a relatively short period of time in order to adjust the guidelines, training, etc.

Future works include developing a more extensive longitudinal study in order to explore, over longer periods of time, the effectiveness and sustainability of the corrective actions used in this case study. This study should use a more extensive number of cases that could include different sizes and compositions of software development teams.

Acknowledgments. The research behind this paper was partly financed by National University (Costa Rica), Ministery of Science and Technology – MICIT (Costa Rica), National Council for Scientific and Technological Research - CONICIT (Costa Rica), and the Danish Research Councils (grant number 09-065143).

References

1. Andreasen, M.S., Nielsen, H.V., Schrøder, S.O., Stage, J.: What happened to remote usability testing?: an empirical study of three methods. In: Proceedings of the SIGCHI Conference on Human Factors in Computing Systems, pp. 1405–1414. ACM (2007)
2. Ardito, C., Buono, P., Caivano, D., Costabile, M.F., Lanzilotti, R., Bruun, A., Stage, J.: Usability Evaluation: a survey of software development organizations. In: Proceedings of 33rd International Conference on Software Engineering & Knowledge Engineering, Miami, FL, USA (2011)
3. Bak, J.O., Nguten, K., Risgaard, P., Stage, J.: Obstacles to Usability Evaluation in Practice: A Survey of Software Development Organizations. In: Proceedings of the 5th Nordic Conference on Human-Computer Interaction: Building Bridges, pp. 23–32. ACM, New York (2008)
4. Beck, K., Beedle, M., Van Bennekum, A., Cockburn, A., Cunnimgham, W., Fowler, M., ...Thomas, D.: Principles behind the agile manifesto (2001) (retrieved 11, 2008)
5. Bruun, A., Stage, J.: Training software development practitioners in usability testing: an assessment acceptance and prioritization. In: Proc. OzCHI, pp. 52–60. ACM Press (2012)
6. Capra, M.G.: Usability problem description and the evaluator effect in usability testing (Doctoral dissertation, Virginia Polytechnic Institute and State University) (2006)
7. Ferré, X., Juristo, N., Moreno, A.: Which, When and How Usability Techniques and Activities Should be Integrated. In: Seffah, A., Gulliksen, J., Desmarais, M.C. (eds.) Human-Centered Software Engineering - Integrating Usability in the Software Development Lifecycle. Human-Computer Interaction Series, vol. 8. Kluwer, Dordrecht (2005)
8. Fischer, H.: Integrating usability engineering in the software development lifecycle based on international standards. In: Proceedings of the 4th ACM SIGCHI Symposium on Engineering Interactive Computing Systems, pp. 321–324. ACM (June 2012)
9. Hoegh, R.T., Nielsen, C.M., Overgaard, M., Pedersen, M.B., Stage, J.: The impact of usability reports and user test observations on developers' understanding of usability data: An exploratory study. International Journal of Human-Computer Interaction 21(2), 173–196 (2006)
10. Hussain, Z., Lechner, M., Milchrahm, H., Shahzad, S., Slany, W., Umgeher, M., ...Wolkerstorfer, P.: Practical Usability in XP Software Development Processes. In: The Fifth International Conference on Advances in Computer-Human Interactions, ACHI 2012, pp. 208–217 (January 2012)

11. Jerome, B., Kazman, R.: Surveying the solitudes: An investigation into the relationships between human computer interaction and software engineering in practice. In: Human-Centered Software Engineering—Integrating Usability in the Software Development Lifecycle, pp. 59–70 (2005)

12. Jia, Y.: Examining Usability Activities in Scrum Projects–A Survey Study, Doctoral dissertation, Uppsala University (2012)

13. Kjeldskov, J., Skov, M.B., Stage, J.: Instant data analysis: conducting usability evaluations in a day. In: Proceedings of the Third Nordic Conference on Human-Computer Interaction, pp. 233–240. ACM (October 2004)

14. Kniberg, H.: Scrum and XP from the Trenches. InfoQ Enterprise Software Development Series (2007)

15. Lazar, J., Feng, J.H., Hochheiser, H.: Research methods in human-computer interaction. Wiley (2010)

16. Lazar, J., Feng, J.H., Hochheiser, H.: Research methods in human-computer interaction. Wiley (2010)

17. Lee, J.C.: Embracing agile development of usable software systems. In: CHI 2006 Extended Abstracts on Human Factors in Computing Systems, pp. 1767–1770. ACM (April 2006)

18. Lee, J.C., McCrickard, D.S.: Towards extreme (ly) usable software: Exploring tensions between usability and agile software development. In: Agile Conference (AGILE), pp. 59–71. IEEE (August 2007)

19. Pyla, P., Pérez-Quiñones, M., Arthur, J., Hartson, H.: Ripple: An event driven design representation framework for integrating usability and software engineering life cycles. In: Human-Centered Software Engineering—Integrating Usability in the Software Development Lifecycle, pp. 245–265 (2005)

20. Rubin, J., Chisnell, D.: Handbook of usability testing: how to plan, design and conduct effective tests. John Wiley & Sons (2008)

21. Seffah, A., Desmarais, M.C., Metzker, E.: HCI, Usability and Software Engineering Integration: Present and Future. In: Seffah, A., et al. (eds.) Human-Centered Software Engineering. Springer, Berlin (2005)

22. Seffah, A., Metzker, E.: The obstacles and myths of usability and software engineering. Commun. ACM 47, 71–76 (2004)

23. Skov, M.B., Stage, J.: Training software developers and designers to conduct usability evaluations. Behaviour & Information Technology 31(4), 425–435 (2012)

24. Sohaib, O., Khan, K.: Integrating usability engineering and agile software development: A literature review. In: 2010 International Conference on Computer Design and Applications (ICCDA), vol. 2, p. V2-32. IEEE (2010)

25. Yin, R.K.: Case Study Research: Design and Methods. Sage, Thousand Oaks (2003)

Evaluating an Automatic Adaptive Delivery Method of English Words Learning Contents for University Students in Science and Technology

Shimpei Matsumoto[1], Taiki Kurisu[2], Tomoko Kashima[3],
and Masanori Akiyoshi[4]

[1] Faculty of Applied Information Science, Hiroshima Institute of Technology, Japan
[2] Graduate School of Science and Technology, Hiroshima Institute of Technology,
2-1-1 Miyake, Saeki-ku, Hiroshima 731-5193, Japan
[3] Faculty of Engineering, Kinki University,
1 Takaya Umenobe, Higashi-Hiroshima City, Hiroshima, 739-2116, Japan
[4] Faculty of Engineering, Kanagawa University,
3-27-1 Rokkakubashi, Kanagawa-ku, Yokohama, Kanagawa 221-8686, Japan

Abstract. Today's e-Learning, blending portable digital devices and common PC devices under well-maintained Internet infrastructure, provides convenient learning environment where everyone can learn when they need. In particular, self-study with simple multiple-choice questions with LMS (Learning Management System) is available with no need to score by lecturer because usual LMS implements automatic scoring capability. Since LMS is useful for both lecturers and students, in Japan it has been already accepted as being indispensable in educational institutions around universities. However, this type of learning can only support just gathering of knowledge, but not assist the improvement of the skill to leverage knowledge. Currently it has not been enough to provide e-Learning with capabilities of both knowledge acquisition and utilization, so to realize it the authors started the development of user adaptive learning service which deals with English learning. This paper focuses on the automatic delivery of learning contents for each user's mobile device, and verifies practical effectiveness of item response theory for user adaptive learning contents provision. This paper develops a server program to automatically deliver learning materials consisted of some multiple choice questions. Based on the result of preliminary experiment, for realizing e-Learning service with learner adaptation functionality, the conceptions to evaluate each user's learning effort and to realize the learning of knowledge acquisition are discussed.

Keywords: push-based e-Learning, mobile learning, English words learning, user adaptive, item response theory.

1 Introduction

Today LMS (Learning Management System) based e-Learning is widely-accepted mainly by higher education institutions including universities. Previously the

M. Kurosu (Ed.): Human-Computer Interaction, Part I, HCII 2014, LNCS 8510, pp. 510–520, 2014.
© Springer International Publishing Switzerland 2014

objective of using LMS had been to widely publish and to smoothly distribute educational materials, but recently various types of e-Learning, multifunctional LMS, have been developed for a variety of purposes. A recent hot topic of e-Learning is supporting learners' interactions with the feature of SNS (Social Networking Service) and utilizing its log data stored by the database; for instance, systems cooperating major SNS services such as Twitter or combining ICT software such as Skype have been actively reported by a lot of educational journals. Similarly another hot topic has been introducing mobile communication devices including smart phones. By using high-performance mobile devices recently cheaply available, not only interactive lectures but also supporting school life are being realized.

In the aspect of knowledge acquisition, general LMS still has been the mainstream, and Moodle is well-known as the most common open source LMS package. With Moodle, a lecturer can easily publish learning materials, and can practice an education on social constructionist pedagogy [1][2] with Moodle's various functions called Wiki, chat, and forum. Other than that, recently there are various approaches for supporting knowledge acquisition by focusing on a certain category of learners and by applying a business model of information and communication fields. As an example of supporting learners who has more difficulty in learning categorized as "Negative Learners", Ooki, Kashima, and Matsumoto have developed a push-based e-Learning using mobile phone's e-mail transfer feature toward the support of self-study [3]-[5]DThis system aims to make learners aware of daily constant learning by giving convenient exercises routinely, and holistic educational support, which is not enough with only usual LMS functions, was archived by combining common LMS environment. As an example of not only assisting education but also achieving business, Akiyoshi et al. proposed an educational service[6]. The Akiyoshi's educational service generates each learning content from the learning source scattering in the "cloud", and judges the scoring result by crowdsourcing to improve the establishment of learning in response to the scoring result of each learner's simple tests mainly given by multiple-choice. They provided an important conception to prepare learning contents for knowledge acquisition, and to automatically generate learning contents from the "cloud " space for practical skill learning. Both of them gives interesting suggestion about utilizing mobile devices for automatic delivery of learning contents and estimating each learner's understandings from the result of the mobile learning.

From among the previous reports, this paper focuses on the user adaptive learning and the automatic delivery of learning contents. This paper considers the automatic delivery of learning contents for mobile devices is effective to provide opportunity of knowledge utilization according to user's learning level. This paper deals with English learning strongly requiring both knowledge acquisition and utilization. Automatic learning contents delivery system is constructed by the efforts of push-based e-Learning previously developed by the authors, and then multiple-choice English words exercises are continuously provided by using this system. Since the learning of knowledge acquisition tends to monotonous task, maintaining learner's motivation is important for user adaptive learning. Therefore this paper verifies practical effectiveness of item response theory for establishing user adaptive exercise delivery algorithm. Preliminary experiment applying item response theory showed the tendency in response to learner's characteristic. Finally based on the present effort, conceptions about user evaluation method based on his/her efforts, contents generation method to improve knowledge acquisition, and presentation method of exercises to be effective on digital devices, are discussed respectively.

2   Push Based e-Learning as Learning Contents Delivery System

Push-based e-mail transfer system adopted by mobile phones is applied as automatic learning content delivery system. The proposed system automatically creates exercise mails, and each student can continually receive the questions based on his/her system configurations such as the delivery time and the number of questions. All user do not have to access learning contents by oneself, and the scoring and evaluation about each user's answer is automatically operated. This system follows three procedures: (1) One or more questions are continuously delivered by an e-mail to a user automatically. (2) A user adds his/her answer to a received e-mail. (3) By replying the e-mail to the system, a user can obtain scoring result immediately.

The learning protocol is shown in Fig. 1. All questions are given in the form of multiple-choice. After receiving an exercise e-mail as shown in Fig. 1 (a), a user has to select the function "reply with received text as citation" on e-mail software and replies the e-mail with his/her best option at designated section as shown in Fig. 1 (b). After replying to the e-mail, the user's scoring result as shown in Fig. 1 (c) is instantaneously available. The system can support each individual user by giving opportunities to study through a convenient and easily accessible system, which targets students whose effective study habits are not yet established.

The learning contents delivery system consists of two principal functions: LMS service and e-mail exchange service. The service of LMS works LAMP environment, which is constructed by Linux kernel 2.6.38, Apache 2.2.22, PHP 5.3.5, MySQL 5.1.54, and CakePHP 2.2.5 for user interface. With the service of LMS, various functions are available via Web browser. The types of service are different between learners and lecturers. On the learner side, there are following services: score inquiry, learning history inquiry, and some user settings such as exercise delivery time, the number of questions, and user information. On the lecturer side, there are following services: user management, exercise management, history management of e-mail exchange, dialogue function with a user, and analysis function of user's learning history data. Various kinds of data, such as the number of delivery of each English word and its accuracy rate, user's reply rate, user's accuracy rate, and user's experience point, are stored in database uniquely developed by this study, and they are always available.

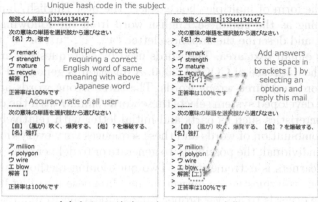

(a) Automatic learning contents delivery

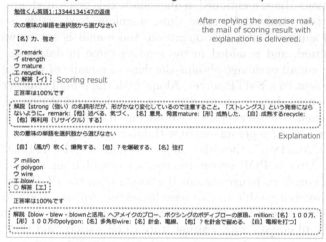

(b) Automatic delivery of scoring result

Fig. 1. Learning Protocol

This paper uses COCET 3300 as database of exercises. COCET3300 is an educational material to support English words for students of science and technology in higher education, and it has achieved satisfactory results at some educational institutions mainly national college of technology. As each English word in the corpus has Japanese meaning, related term, related phrase, and explanation, the proposed system uses these attributes to create each exercise e-mail. Each word is divided into 7 levels according to its difficulty. In the learning contents delivery system, there are 3 server applications which work on java 1.6.31, and the one server application of them provides e-mail exchange (sending and receiving). An e-mail with questions is routinely delivered on a time that is set by a student registered to the developed system. The server application monitors e-mail exchange at 10 seconds interval. When it is time to deliver an exercise e-mail, the other server application to generate exercise statement is called. All questions are given in the form of multiple-choice: select the best English/Japanese word of same meaning as the Japanese/English word from the following options to each question, and describe the Japanese letter "a", "i", "u", or "e" to the place in brackets at e-mail text area. The words used by each question are randomly chosen from the database of COCET 3300. A question is generated by selecting one correct word and three wrong words. The three wrong words are randomly given, but the developed system selects these words similar with the correct word in some characteristics such as parts and initial letter with relatively high rate.

Since the combination of words and these sequences vary every time and from individual to individual, the possibility to generate or to deliver same question for two or more learners is extremely low. Two questioning methods are randomly decided; the one is a question to answer proper Japanese meaning from English words, and the other is to answer proper English meaning from Japanese words. By the operations above mentioned, a question text is generated, and it is added to an e-mail text, and at the same time, a unique hash value is also added to the e-mail subject. After this operation, the e-mail is set to waiting state to be transmitted, and is added to the sending table in database. The server application of e-mail exchange obtains the data of e-mails of waiting state, and then they are sent to a SMTP server. Along with the e-mail transfer operation, the state of e-mail data is changed to transmission completion. After a user received the e-mail, the user replies the e-mail with his/her answer at designated point. All users should reply an e-mail with hash value at the subject, i.e., if the subject is "12126221801", then the subject should be "Re: 12126221801" or a similar form. After a POP server receives an e-mail from a user, the server application of e-mail exchange obtains the e-mail from the POP server, and it is added to the receiving table in database by setting waiting state to be scored. The other server application of automatic scoring which is working as other thread obtains all e-mails with waiting state to be scored, and they are scored. At the same time with scoring, some statistic information is updated. A scored e-mail is set to waiting state to be transmitted, and then it is added to the sending table. By the above processes, a user can receive scoring result with explanation immediately. Each word in COCET3300 is given the value of difficulty, so every time a user has the correct answer, the user obtains experience point depending on the value of difficulty.

3   Learning Contents Delivery Method for User Adaptive Learning

3.1   Previous Works Aiming User Adaptive Learning

To realize user adaptive education through automatic learning contents delivery, recommendation techniques [7] is considered to be effective. Application examples of recommendation techniques for educational support, Matsuzawa et al. developed bidirectional recommendation system that extracts the relationship among learning texts with historical logs and recommends effective texts for learners[8]. Kai et al. proposed a learning contents recommendation method of e-Learning for Japanese language education to improve the ability of self-study [9]. The authors previously focused on collaborative filtering, the most typical recommendation method, to archive user adaptive education with push-based e-Learning based on mobile e-mail technology, but from the result of preliminary experiments, some critical problems were clarified [10]DTherefore to judge whether the contents of questions are proper or not for learners, this paper focuses on item response theory [11] which can estimate each subject's understanding and each question's difficulty from examination result.

3.2 Application of Item Response Theory

A study on assessment using item response theory was addressed by Nobehara et al. [12]. They showed a method to present a next question by estimating the parameter of learner's understanding generally called " ability level" θ successively. Each θ is calculated by Bayesian estimation method every time the system receives user's answer. By providing questions with the difficulty around the value of θ, each learner's ability is continued to be estimated. This method has accomplished certain results including practical efforts.

To prepare user adaptive learning environment with item response theory, a framework to utilize estimated parameters for the presentation of learning contents was given by Sasaki et al. [13] and they provided the basic guideline as follows.

1. For learners in the upper level group who have less weak subjects than a certain rate, their learning is concentrated on overcoming weak subjects. In this case, one learning policy of the following two is adopted depending on the rate of weak subjects.
2. (a) If the rate of weak subjects is less than a certain value, the ability to think is developed by giving the qustions of the most difficult level.
   (b) If the rate of weak subjects is greater than a certain value, the questions of the easiest level are given which can be solved with minimum effort.
3. For learners in the lower level group who have more weak subjects than a certain rate, questions are given by choosing questions with no difference between learner's ability and question's difficulty (questions with high accuracy rate), so they can be solved with minimum effort. As the results for learners whose weak subjects becomes less than a certain rate, learning contents are delivered by changing the learning policy to 1.

Since the response pattern obtained by the user adaptive learning contents delivery is incomplete defect matrix, parameters are not obtained directly. Therefore a method to cover a loss of response pattern by using item response theory was proposed by Kuwabata et al. [14]. The adaptive test was archived by calculating ability level every time a user answers questions, and by presenting questions of the closest difficulty with user's ability level.

4 Experiment and Result

This paper uses 2 parameters logistic model of item response theory given as follow.

$$p_j(\theta) = \frac{1}{1 + \exp\left(-Da_j(\theta - b_j)\right)},$$ (1)

where θ is subject's ability level, a is the discrimination power of question j, b is the difficulty of question j. When the difficulty and the ability level are same value, i. e. $\theta = b$, the percentage of questions is 0.5 [15].

This paper examines the application possibility of item response theory from the experiments with 10 senior university students as subjects. 20 questions requiring proper Japanese mean of English word are prepared, and parameters are estimated from the response pattern obtained by subjects' answers. Next, the parameter of learner's characteristic, ability level θ and SE corresponding to standard deviation are calculated. In Table 1, "Score" denotes raw score of test and "Person-Fit" is an index to represent the degree of adequacy of the test for subject. The ability level is considered to be high when the value of θ is large. When a subject mistakes an easy question and correctly answers a difficult question, SE becomes large.

Table 1. Parameters estimated by item response theory

Subject ID	Score	θ	SE	Person-Fit
1	18	1.4744	0.5482	0.5947
2	12	-0.0681	0.3588	-0.5629
3	17	1.0981	0.4711	0.7986
4	10	-0.4373	0.3521	-0.3717
5	10	-0.4373	0.3521	0.5504
6	18	1.4744	0.5482	0.3946
7	11	-0.2544	0.3538	0.1992
8	10	-0.4373	0.3521	-1.1703
9	13	0.1254	0.3674	0.2439
10	13	0.1254	0.3674	0.3526

The parameter of difficulty b and the ability level θ are compared when a question is selected to realize adaptive learning. These parameters are same scale, so they are directly comparable. As the subject's ability is not always constant but has surely a margin for error, the error is assumed to be same as SE. Based on the value of SE, learner's ability level is assumed to be within the range $\theta \pm SE$. A question is provided as the standard of adaptive learning under the assumption that the range $\theta \pm SE$ is appropriate difficulty for a subject. The relation between θ and SE is shown in Fig. 2, and from here we can see that SE becomes large with increasing θ.

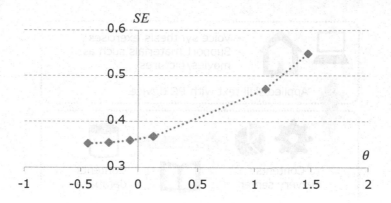

Fig. 2. Relation between θ and SE

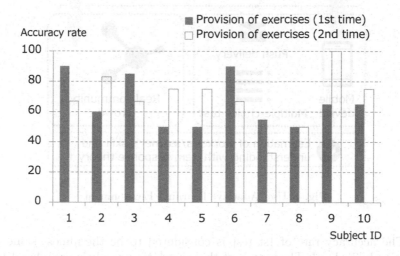

Fig. 3. Influence of the adaptive learning for the accuracy rate

By using parameters SE and θ, the simulation of adaptive learning is performed. Other 20 questions different from the earlier test are given by the subjects different with the earlier test, and parameters of item response theory mainly difficulty level b are estimated. After 2nd test, only questions of 2nd test with $\theta - SE \leq b \leq \theta + SE$ are presented for subjects of the 1st test, then this result is assumed to be the adaptive learning. English words in the 1st and 2nd test are randomly selected among the 548 noun words of COCET 3300 classified into the easiest level.

The experimental result is shown in Fig. 3. Fig. 3 shows each subject's accuracy rate of 1st and 2nd test, and 2nd test is assumed to be the adaptive learning. From the result, we can see the tendency that the accuracy rate of subjects with high accuracy rate of 1st test decreased in 2nd test, and on the contrary, the accuracy rate of subjects with low accuracy rate of 1st test increased in the 2nd

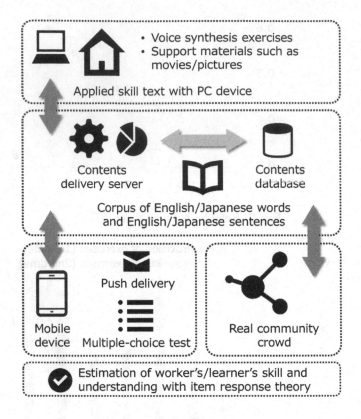

Fig. 4. User Adaptive Learning Environment

test. The accuracy rate of 1st test is considered to be the almost same with subject's ability level. The reason of this simulation result is considered to be affected by the operation that relatively high level questions were presented for subjects with high ability level depending on the volume of SE.

5   Conclusion

This paper proposed a user adaptive learning method for automatic learning contents delivery and scoring system previously developed by the authors. The learning service of mobile device cannot provide high capability because of mobile device's limitation such as screen size and input device, so based on the mobile learning's advantage, multiple-choice based contents are considered to be appropriate to realize simple and convenient learning. On the other hand, maintaining motivation is important because multiple-choice based English words learning is monotonous rote exercise. Therefore the adaptive learning with item response theory was examined, and the effectiveness was confirmed from the preliminary experiment. From the experiment, subjects with high accuracy rate decreased comparing with the test without adaptive method, and the accuracy rate came close to $\theta = b$.

In the near future, the proposed algorithm will be implemented for the automatic learning contents delivery system, and the effectiveness will be examined from the result of long term massive real operation based on the user's subjective evaluation and the objective data from ability test conducting before and after the system operation. By evaluating questions presented by the algorithm based on the user's subjective aspect like precision, recall, and f-value, the effectiveness will be verified.

In addition, the constructing result of learning environment for knowledge utilization will be continually reported. In the whole conception of user adaptive learning environment blending mobile and PC devices as shown in Fig. 4, an exercise presentation method with PC devices according to each user's understanding will be examined, which provides knowledge utilization test and fully uses the feature of PC device: large screen, multimedia function, and high performance PC resources. Regarding "real community crowd" providing learning environment for PC device, it is realized by the people who participating in indicated by Akiyoshi et al. indicated the craowd community is realized by the people who are not learner but participates in the learrning environment [6]. Therefore along with the construction of user adaptive learning environment, we will examine the application method of item response theory for matching learning contents and workers in the crowd community. In this case, matching an efficient combination between a worker and a task is attempted by item response theory, and then the user adaptive learning on PC device, mainly scoring and evaluation of English writing, will be realized.

References

1. Richardson, V.: Constructivist Pedagogy. Teachers College Record 105(9), 1623–1640 (2003)
2. Doise, W., Mugny, G.: The social development of the intellect. Pergamon Press, Oxford (1984)
3. Ooki, M., Matsumoto, S.: How to Nurture Students' Study Habits Using a Handy E-Learning System with Cell Phones. J. of The Society for Teaching English through Media 12(1), 231–255 (2011)
4. Kashima, T., Matsumoto, S., Ihara, T.: Proposal of an e-Learning System with Skill-based Homework Assignments. In: Proc. of the International MultiConference of Engineers and Computer Scientists, pp. 1405–1410 (2011)
5. Matsumoto, S., Akiyoshi, M., Kashima, T.: Development of Push-Based English Words Learning System by Using E-Mail Service. In: Kurosu, M. (ed.) Human-Computer Interaction, Part II, HCII 2013. LNCS, vol. 8005, pp. 444–453. Springer, Heidelberg (2013)
6. Akiyoshi, M., Matsumoto, S., Araki, N.: E-learning cloud service for promoting consolidation of the learning content. In: Proc. of the 27th Annual Conference of the Japanese Society for Artificial Intelligence, 3M3-OS-07d-5 (2013) (in Japanese)
7. Jannach, D., Zanker, M., Felfernig, A., Friedrich, G.: Recommender Systems. Cambridge University Press (2013)

8. Matsuzawa, S., Yamaguchi, M., Wada, Y., Dohi, S.: Implementation of recommend system for learning texts. Technical Report of Information Processing Society of Japan 13, 127–132 (2008) (in Japanese)
9. Kai, A., Nemoto, J., Matsuba, R., Suzuki, K.: Designing a Recommendation System of e-Learning Materials for Non-native Speakers of Japanese to Develop Learner's Autonomy. In: Proc. of the 26th Annual Conference of Japan Society for Educational Technology, pp. 615–616 (2010) (in Japanese)
10. Ishizaki, T., Matsumoto, S., Kashima, T.: Automatic Exercise Delivery to Portable Digital Terminal for Supporting Self-Study. In: Proc. of IEEE SMC Hiroshima Chapter Young Researcher Workshop, pp. 97–98 (2011) (in Japanese)
11. Ayala, R.: The Theory and Practice of Item Response Theory. Guilford Pr. (2008)
12. Nobuhara, T., Koyama, Y., Miyake, S., Shoji, N., Liu, B., Yokota, K.: Adaptive e-Learning System Corresponding to Learners' Performance. The Institute of Electronics, Information and Communication Engineers Technical Report, Data Engineering 104(178), 7–12 (2004) (in Japanese)
13. Sasaki, D., Matsuzaka, T., Kurihara, N.: Adaptive distribution of e-learning contents using item response theory. The Bulletin of Hachinohe Institute of Technology 27, 53–60 (2008) (in Japanese)
14. Kuwabata, T., Sakumura, T., Hirose, H.: Adaptive Online IRT System. Information Processing Society of Japan SIG Technical Report A-1-4 (2012) (in Japanese)
15. Sugiura, M., Shoji, Y., Ooiwa, G.: An Analysis of Qualification Tests for IT Education at University: Through Classical Test Analysis and Applicability of Item Response Theory. In: Proc. of Information Processing Society of Japan Symposium, vol. 2008(6), pp. 87–93 (2008) (in Japanese)

Can Users Speak for Themselves? Investigating Users Ability to Identify Their Own Interactive Breakdowns

Bernardo A.M. Mattos, Raquel L.S. Pereira, and Raquel Oliveira Prates

Department of Computer Science, UFMG
Belo Horizonte, Brazil
{bemattos,raqlara,rprates}@dcc.ufmg.br

Abstract. The Communicability Evaluation Method (CEM) is based on Semiotic Engineering HCI theory and involves observing users in a controlled environment and capturing with software the user-system interaction. The analysis involves 3 steps: (1) tagging: watching the user-system interaction video, identifying the communicative breakdowns, associating one of CEM's utterance (from a predefined set of 13) to the breakdown; (2) interpretation: interpreting the problems that are being indicated by the tagging performed in the first step; (3) semiotic profiling: reconstructing the intended communication being conveyed by the system and the problems identified. Originally CEM requires the evaluator to perform all 3 steps. In this paper we investigate the possibility of users themselves performing the tagging step of the analysis and the costs and benefits of such a procedure. If users are able to identify and tag breakdowns they can directly communicate the problems they have experienced. Our results have shown that user tagging is possible and pointed to various directions in which it could be very useful. We present the case study performed, the results found and discuss costs and benefits of such procedure.

Keywords: Evaluation, user participation, communicability, semiotic engineering, communicability evaluation method (CEM).

1 Introduction

Empirical studies have played a major role in creating the knowledge in HCI available today [11],[1]. Researchers in the field have pointed out the need for more theoretical approaches and a theory of HCI [1] and called attention to the fact that usability is not the only important aspect to be evaluated in user interfaces [5]. They have also criticized the excessive emphasis the HCI community has given to quantitative evaluation and identified the need for more theoretically based methods [5]. This paper investigates the possibilities a theoretical based evaluation method – Communicability Evaluation Method – offers to involve users in part of the analysis of their own interaction with the system.

Semiotic Engineering theory [2] has been proposed as a theory of HCI that aims at explaining (not predicting) the phenomena involved in the designing and using of interactive systems. It is based on Semiotics and takes a communicative approach to

M. Kurosu (Ed.): Human-Computer Interaction, Part I, HCII 2014, LNCS 8510, pp. 521–532, 2014.
© Springer International Publishing Switzerland 2014

HCI. Semiotic Engineering theory perceives an interactive system as a communicative act from designers to users. In the message being sent (i.e. the system) designers convey to users who the system is meant to, what problems it can solve and how to interact with it to solve them. This message is an indirect message that users understand as they interact with the system. In this theoretical framework a good interface is one that conveys to users, efficiently and effectively, their underlying design intent and interactive principles, in other words one that has a high **communicability** [9].

The Communicability Evaluation Method (CEM) [9]. [2], [3] has been proposed within the Semiotic Engineering framework and aims at evaluating the system's communicability. To do so, the method identifies communicability breakdowns – that is, problems that have taken place in the user-system interaction. Each breakdown is associated to an utterance that represents what users potentially may have said to the designers of the system when facing the breakdown. It is as if evaluators *"put words into the users' mouth"*. Based on the breakdowns identified and their tagging, the evaluator proceeds to describing the communicability problems of the system, and contrasting them to designers' original intent.

Communicability Evaluation Method has been applied to a number of different contexts [12] [3] [8]. Other works have shown how the interactive breakdowns changed as users interacted with the system over time [10] and how it compares to other evaluation methods [14]. The participation of users in helping evaluators understand their actions has been the focus of all verbal protocol methods [4], [11]. Other researches have investigated in which moment of the evaluation users can best support evaluators' interpretation [13], [7], [6].   Although user participation in supporting evaluation analysis has been explored for other methods, and in spite of CEM authors having raised the hypothesis of the possibility of users performing the tagging step [9], to the best of our knowledge this investigation has not yet been performed. Therefore, in this paper we investigate the possibility of having not evaluators put words in users' mouth, but rather users themselves apply the tagging step of the method. Performing this step requires users to identify the communicative breakdowns they have experienced and to associate it to the tag that describes it. A communicative breakdown occurs when the user does not understand the communication intended by the designer through the system, which can hamper or even preclude the use of the system. If users are able to identify and tag breakdowns they can communicate directly the problems they have experienced.

The first step in investigating the possibility for users to identify breakdowns and associate to them an utterance from the CEM set was to perform regular communicability tests using CEM. As soon as the test was completed the procedure continued and the evaluators guided the participant through the tagging step. The user tagging was conducted in the following steps: (1) brief explanation of what a breakdown is; (2) watching the interaction movie of the test and annotating it with breakdowns identified by the user; (3) brief explanation of CEM's predefined set of utterances used to describe breakdowns; (4) reviewing the breakdowns identified and associating to each one an utterance from CEM's set; (5) a post-tagging interview about their experience.

Eight people participated in the user-tagging investigation. All of them were undergrad or master students and were experienced in the use of technology, but had never taken any courses in or worked with HCI or interface evaluation. Our main findings were that users were able to identify breakdowns and tag them. They felt comfortable with the procedure and with the set of utterances and felt that they could perform it by themselves.

In the next section we briefly present the Communicability Evaluation Method. Then, we describe the user-tagging experiment performed. In the following section we present and discuss the results from the user-tagging experiment. Finally we conclude with our final remarks and possible future directions in this research.

2   The Communicability Evaluation Method

As described, the Communicability Evaluation Method (CEM) is based on Semiotic Engineering and aims at evaluating qualitatively the communicability property of an interactive system. The CEM involves evaluators observing users interacting with a system in a controlled environment. The preparation and application steps of the CEM are very similar to other user tests in controlled environments [12], [2]. A few aspects that are important to highlight are (1) user interaction with system must be recorded by use of an interaction recording software; (2) two evaluators are recommended: one to conduct the test and another one to take notes during the test; (3) an interview with the user after the test is strongly recommended. Once the test has been applied, the evaluator proceeds to the analysis of the data collected.

The analysis of the data requires three steps: tagging, interpretation and semiotic profiling [9], [2], [3]. In the **tagging** step the evaluator watches the movies of user-system interaction and identifies communicative breakdowns that have taken place. To each communicative breakdown the evaluator associates one utterance from a predefined set of 13 utterances (see Table 1) that best describes it. Utterances are stereotypical expressions users could potentially express (to the designer) when having difficulties interacting with the system, such as *Where is...*<specific function>? In this step the evaluator "*puts*" words in the participant's mouth [9].

Once breakdowns have been identified and tagged, the next step in the analysis is interpretation step, in which the evaluator assigns meaning to the tagging done in the previous step and evaluates whether there are or not communicability problems with the system. Finally, in the last step, the semiotic profiling step, the evaluator reconstructs the global message being sent from designer to users, and then contrasts this global intended message with the problems identified.

The interpretation and semiotic profiling steps require expertise in CEM and Semiotic Engineering theory, which is not necessarily the case for the tagging step. Thus, authors of the method have raised the hypothesis that users may be able to do the tagging themselves and that this could provide a more precise tagging, since users would utter the expressions themselves [9]. Although the utterances are based on natural expressions, their use is directed by a specific set of symptoms which limit their natural use. The goal in this paper is to investigate whether users could identify their own communicative breakdowns and associate the expected utterance from the CEM's predefined set of tags, in other words, if tagging could be used to provide a direct communication between users and designers (or evaluators). In the next section we explain the method adopted and the case study performed.

Table 1. Brief description of CEM set of utterances

Utterance	Description
What's this?	Occurs when the user does not know the meaning of an interface element.
Where is it?	The user knows what he would like to do, but demonstrates difficulty in locating it.
What now?	It applies when a user does not know what to do next and thus searches for the next step.
What happened?	The user does not perceive or is unable to assign meaning to the function's outcome, or the system does not present any feedback.
Oops!	The user performs some action to achieve a specific state of affairs, but the outcome is not the expected one. The user then immediately undoes the action.
I can't do this way	The user goes into a path of interaction composed of many steps and decides to abandon the path.
Why doesn't it?	The user insists on an action path that does not produce the expected outcome.
Where am I?	User does not realize the context he is in and tries to perform actions that only make sense in another context of the system.
Looks fine to me...	The user is convinced he has achieved his goal, but in fact he has not.
I give up.	The user runs out of resources (time, patience or motivation) and interrupts a task performance.
I can do otherwise.	The user is unaware of some preferential intended affordance present in the interface and manages to achieve his goal some other way.
Thanks, but, no, thanks	The user understands some preferential intended affordance present in the application's interface but decides to do it in another way.
Help!	The user explicitly asks for help.

3   User Tagging Experiment

The first step in the experiment was to perform a system evaluation using CEM. The user tagging experiment immediately followed this system evaluation in the same controlled environment. The reason for this was to allow users to perform the tagging while they still had their interaction with the system fresh in their memory, not adding an issue regarding the time spent between the test and their analysis of it. The interaction was recorded and the test videotaped. Two evaluators were required: one to guide the user through the experiment, and another one to observe and take notes (behind a one-way mirror). The experiment was organized in 5 steps:

1. **Brief presentation:** Once participants completed a regular CEM test, the evaluators explained to them what the next steps in the process were. At this moment the evaluator explained briefly to them Semiotic Engineering perspective of an interface as a communicative act, the communicability property and the definition of a communicative breakdown.
2. **Identifying communicative breakdowns:** In this step, participants watched the movie of their own interaction, and identified communicative breakdowns they had experienced. The description of each breakdown given by the participant was annotated in the movie by the evaluator. If the participant became too quiet the evaluator encouraged his/her participation by asking questions about what was going on at a point of the movie.
3. **Presentation of CEM utterances:** After the breakdowns had been identified, the evaluator explained to participants the tagging process and the utterances. To do so, a slide show was used in which each utterance was briefly explained, its symptoms presented and an example made available. Two short movies illustrating an example of a breakdown associated to an utterance were shown to participants, and they were asked whether they would like to see other ones. Participants at this point were given a list of the utterances they could refer to during the following step (similar to the one shown on Table 1).
4. **Associating utterances to breakdowns:** In this step, evaluators guided users through the breakdowns annotated in the movie and then users associated an utterance to each breakdown.
5. **Post-tagging interview:** In this step the evaluator conducted a semi-structured interview with the participant about the tagging.

In the case study conducted the software chosen was a personal organizer (Student Life – http://www.tesorosoft.com/studentlife.htm) for college students. The software handles everything related to the life of a typical student, such as classes, homework and tests, contacts, calendar, reminders and a degree tracker. The software was chosen because it did not require any specific domain knowledge, college students were available as volunteers and the in a previous HCI class students had evaluated it and reported having found many communicative breakdowns in interacting with it.

The requirements to select volunteers were: (1) be a college student (undergrad or master level); (2) understand English well (the system's interface was in English); (3) not have any experience with HCI and interface evaluation; (4) not have used the system before; (5) be experienced in the use of technology. One pilot test was done to adjust the material and how the test would be conducted. The study was conducted with eight volunteers (5 men and 3 women), ages ranging from 20 to 28 years old. Students were distributed into different courses: 4 in computer science, 2 in information science and 2 in engineering. Each test lasted about 1:40 hours. The test of the personal organizer was comprised by 3 different tasks: editing an instructor's information, entering a new class in an existing semester, entering a new semester. All users were able to complete all three tasks. After they completed the tasks they were interviewed about the system (as they would in a regular application of CEM).

The system test lasted around 15 minutes. Once it was over, the tagging step of the analysis was performed as described in the beginning of this section. The explanation required to apply the method was brief – step 1 (brief explanation) took about 3 minutes and step 3 (presentation of utterances) lasted around 10 minutes. At this step none of the participants asked to see any other examples besides the two that were shown. At the utterance association step (step 4) some users (5 of them) added a few (varying from 1 to 3) new breakdowns to their interaction they had not identified in step 2. Finally the post-tagging interview script included asking the participants what they thought about tagging their own interaction; if it had changed their view of the system; whether they felt the explanation on the utterances had been enough for them to perform the tagging; if they felt they had done a good job tagging their interaction; whether they had felt the need for utterances that were not available; what were the difficulties they had had during the tagging and whether they felt they could perform the tagging by themselves.

At the end of the experiment the participants' tagging were analyzed by the evaluators. The analysis was mainly qualitative and aimed at identifying whether users were able or not to identify breakdowns and associate utterances to them and what were the main challenges involved in these tasks.

4   Results and Discussion

The experiment intended to provide indicators to two main questions: (1) Can users identify their own breakdowns?; (2) Can users associate utterances from CEM's predefined set to breakdowns? Our analysis has shown that most of the time users are able to perform the tagging step, but they faced some challenges in doing so.

4.1   Identifying Breakdowns

To verify whether users would be able to identify their own breakdowns, evaluators analyzed the breakdowns they had identified and contrasted them with their own identification of user-system breakdowns. Five out of eight participants were able to identify most (over 55%) of the breakdowns they experienced. One participant correctly identified 85% of her breakdowns. An analysis was done to understand if there were specific situations or breakdowns that users missed. First of all, we checked whether users who experienced more breakdowns missed more in the identification, but there was no correlation between the number of breakdowns found and the number of breakdowns experienced.

The next step in the analysis was to verify what breakdowns had been missed. Note that two of the breakdowns considered in CEM users were not expected to identify (*Looks fine to me.* and *I can do otherwise.*), since they represent some aspect the user did not perceive at the interface. Thus, in order to identify them, at the tagging step users would have to perceive something about the system they had missed minutes before. Thirteen (13)% of the breakdowns that were not identified corresponded to these two types of breakdown. Nonetheless, some users were able to identify a few of these breakdowns. It usually was possible when during the interaction users learned more about the system and understood something they had missed before.

There were 4 instances of *Looks fine to me* type breakdown that were correctly identified (i.e. 31% of the total number of breakdowns). One of them was due to filling in a numeric field with the wrong information. The participant realized the mistake in the analysis of his own interaction movie. One other participant did not understand what a Set button in the interface was for, so she clicked on it after each action unnecessarily, introducing a spurious action in her sequence of actions. Later on in a following task she realized what it was meant for, and during the analysis was able to identify the spurious action in two different moments. The last one was not sure which field she was meant to fill in, so she chose the wrong one.

Out of the two *I can do otherwise* breakdowns that took place, one of the participants was able to identify one of them. The user did not find a piece of information (available in the system) referred to in the task scenario and created a new one. Later on, during another task he found the information and realized he did not have to create it, identifying the breakdown. Although this situation might have been caused by the test situation (in a real context he would have created the information the task referred to at some previous time), it still indicated that the difficulty the user had in finding the information led him to an alternative action.

It was interesting to notice that a great number of *Where is it? What is this?* and *Oops!* types of breakdowns were not identified (together corresponded to 67% of the total of breakdowns not identified). These are usually considered easy to identify by evaluators who are beginners because their symptoms are easily identified (as shown in Table 1). The reason for this came up during the step in which they identified the breakdowns. When the evaluator noticed the symptom and the participant did not identify it as a breakdown, he asked whether they had had any problems at that point. They usually responded that *"No, I was just looking for <something>"* or *"No, I was just checking what that was."*. This means that even though users had to change their attention focus from the task to the interface they did not consider it a problem. This could be either because this was the first time they were using the system, and thus expected to look for functions and ask what interface elements meant as a way to learn the system, or because once they found what they were looking for, then later on they minimized the problem (effect noticed in Post Think Aloud experiments [13]). The former situation was verified in an experiment over time. A study of how breakdowns change over time has shown that these types of breakdowns decrease as users become more familiar with the system [10]. Thus, a future study could verify if once they learned the system, they would still consider these situations natural or would perceive them as breakdowns.

Another situation that happened that is worth noticing was when a participant experienced a breakdown and in trying to solve it went through other breakdown situations. For instance the participant was looking for a specific action, so he waited for tool tips on interface elements (*What's this?*) and opened options and closed immediately as they realized it was not what they were looking for (*Oops!*). A couple of times the participant identified the higher level breakdown (typically *Where is it?* or *What now?*) but did not identify the smaller ones as breakdowns, probably because they were efforts to solve the higher level one.

The other types of breakdowns that were not identified represented a smaller percentage of the situations, but two cases are interesting to comment. In the first one a participant did not identify a "*I give up*" breakdown, which may seem odd. The participant tried to set the initial and end date of the semester being created, but was unable to do so. She then abandoned the task to do something else. At that moment, it configures a breakdown since she gives up on the action of setting the date. However, in her analysis she did not define it as a breakdown because she said she had not given up yet, she had decided to do another action and go back later to try again. She actually did so, and then when she was still unable to set the dates she identified the breakdown. In this case, what was taken into account by the user were not her actions (she did give up at that point) but rather her global intention to try it again later.

The other situation was that 3 participants when finished a task were not able to tell whether they had succeeded or not. They then went on to try and verify whether what they had intended to do had actually been done. Although, these actions indicate a breakdown – system did not communicate back to them in a way they understood what had been done (symptoms of a *What happened?* breakdown) – even when they commented what their intention was at that point, they did not consider it a breakdown. We believe that one possible reason for it was that they all realized they had achieved their goal, so nothing had gone wrong in the task, so they did not consider that a breakdown.

None of the users experienced breakdowns related to the utterances *I can't do it this way.* , *Thanks, but no thanks!* or *Help!*.

4.2   Associating Utterances to Breakdowns

Another goal was to verify whether users, having identified breakdowns, could associate the expected utterance to it. The analysis on this step of the experiment yields indicators on how natural the expressions are to users. One potential difficulty is that even though the utterances are natural the situations they apply to are limited or determined by the symptoms. In tagging the breakdowns five out of eight users chose the utterance correctly over 70% of the times. The other three chose correctly over 49% of the times. Two out of these three also had more difficulties in identifying breakdowns. An analysis of the mistaken tags was done to investigate whether there was a pattern in changing one for the other, and also if mistakes took place in a specific context. However, this analysis showed that there were no patterns in making a wrong choice or in the context in which it was made.

Nonetheless, the analysis indicated that most of the choices of wrong tags can be explained by two different situations. The first one, as we had foreseen, was when in a natural context (but not if symptoms described were considered) both utterances would apply. The second situation that led users to choose the wrong tag was when users identified the breakdown as part of a higher level goal or context and associated the tag to this higher level, as opposed to the symptoms of the breakdown. For instance, one participant opened a dialog realized it is not what she was looking for and immediately closed it – the symptoms characterize the breakdown as an *Oops!*. However, she commented that at that point she could not find what she wanted and was lost in the system, so she chose the tag *Where am I?*

It is important to notice that explanation on utterances given to participants was very brief (around 10 minutes). The reason for this short explanation was to investigate the execution cost with a minimal learning cost on the users' side. However, it seems that with a more detailed explanation or even a short training (users would tag some examples first) users could perform even better at the tagging step.

4.3   Evaluator's Accuracy

This study has also provided some indicators about how accurately evaluators can identify problems experienced by users, and correctly tag it – that is, "put the *correct* words in the users mouth". It was interesting to notice that most of the time evaluators correctly identified breakdowns (99%) and tagged it (95%).

There were only two breakdowns that evaluators had not considered as a breakdown and participants identified as such. In the first case, the participant interacted with a dropdown list to select the year of interest. He chose one year, changed to another and went back to the first. Evaluators considered he had understood the interface element and was just exploring the different years. However, the participant identified it as a breakdown and later tagged it with *Oops!* because he had thought the choice of year would change the options in the semester list. When he made the choice and the expected change did not take place, he undid his action by returning the year to its previous value. The other breakdown was when another participant put her mouse over an interface element expecting a tool tip. However, she did it quickly and no tool tip was available and she went on to do something else. The evaluators did not perceive that the cursor had been intentionally moved to the interface element in search of a tool tip (symptoms of a *What's this?*, which the user correctly tagged) and did not identify the action as a breakdown. Although these two breakdowns are not very serious ones, it shows that sometimes evaluators may miss symptoms when the users' intention is not clear from their interaction with the system. In these situations the participation of the user in the tagging step can be crucial.

One other aspect the case study indicated was that although symptoms limit the application range of the tags minimizing some ambiguities, some still take place. In some situations evaluators perceive the ambiguity and if that is done during the test they have the chance at the post-test interview to understand what happened. However, in other situations the evaluator does not even perceive it and the user is actually the only who could tag it correctly. In this case study both situations were observed.

In this case study instances of the first situation were not solved during the test because participants were expected to continue with the tagging step so these kinds of issues were not raised at the post-test interview. For instance, one participant had filled out some pieces of information and clicked on the button labeled Set. He then stopped for a moment and continued his interaction. The Set button was not associated to the pieces of information he had filled in. Since he then continued evaluators took that he believed he had to click on that button, and tagged that as

Looks fine to me. However, since it was not clear what had led him to click on the button, during the interview evaluators could ask him why he had done so to eliminate any misunderstanding on their part. In fact at the tagging step the user identified the breakdown and tagged it as an *Oops!*. He explained that as soon as he clicked on the button, he realized he did not have to do so. However, since the Set button had not generated any valid action there was nothing to undo, so he just continued the interaction.

There was one situation that the evaluators had no idea the tagging was incorrect until the point the user explained it and tagged it himself. This happened when one participant wandered with the cursor on the screen without actually doing anything, which led evaluators to tag it with a *What now?*. However, the participant explained that he knew what to do next and was actually trying to identify which element in that dialog represented the function he wanted, so he correctly tagged it as a *Where is?*.

The case study shows that the evaluators tagging was very accurate (95%), and although evaluators had experience with CEM, but were not experts yet. Of the few mistakes that did happen, some could have been solved at the post-test interview. However, the system evaluated was a very simple general purpose one and the tasks were simple as well. Further studies considering more complex or domain specific systems that require more complex tasks should be pursued to investigate how it would affect evaluators' accuracy.

4.4   Participant's Comments about Tagging

In the experiment users were interviewed twice, once about the system after the CEM regular test, and another about the tagging after the user-tagging experiment. None of the users changed their opinion about the system after the tagging, however, they were much more critical about the interface and also volunteered many suggestions or comments for alternative designs.

Some of the users clearly were enthusiastic about the tagging, and even when evaluator was explaining the utterances they would make comments about them. For instance, when the evaluator explained the *Where is?* tag a participant said[1] *"Oh! I had a couple of Where is?"* and then when he explained the *What's this?* tag the participant said *"Oh when I checked out that button it was a What's this? then"*. When asked about the tagging, four participants said they had difficulties in making a distinction between a few of the utterances, and one of them said that he thought that the time they had do learn them was too short. In spite of the difficulties, seven out of eight participants believed they could perform the tagging by themselves. Only one participant said that she felt that some utterances were very simple such as *Where is it?*, but others (she mentioned *Oops!, I can't do it this way.*, and *Why doesn't it?*) she believed she would have difficulties in using. One participant said: *"I thought it was interesting because you can identify exactly where the problem is, you can distinguish among the many problems in the system."*. Another one commented that: *"This*

---

[1] All participants' comments were translated from users' first language to English by the authors.

tagging part I thought was really cool because the expressions are the same as the doubts we have. We really identify ourselves!"

They all felt that their participation in the interpretation process was very useful to the evaluation. Some commented that otherwise how could the evaluator have known what was going on. Most users felt that the utterance set was comprehensive. Only one user suggested the inclusion of an utterance, but when he explained what it meant evaluators identified it as being the same description as the *Oops!* tag. One other user commented that it would be nice to have some positive utterances as well to be able to tell when the system had been clear or a goal easy to achieve.

5   Final Remarks and Next Steps

In this paper we have presented a case study that investigates the possibility of users performing the first step in the CEM analysis of their interaction with the system – the tagging step. Although investigation on user participation in supporting evaluators has been done in other contexts [13], [7], [6], it had not yet been done for the CEM. The relevance of investigating this for the CEM is that this research increases the knowledge regarding CEM and its applicability. This is useful not only for Semiotic Engineering Theory research but also for HCI since this community has pointed out the need for more theoretical based methods for HCI [1], [5]. Furthermore, the breakdown identification and tagging is based on natural users' expressions, and could be an appropriate language for user to designer communication about the system.

This study has shown that the user participation during tagging step could provide for a more precise identification of problems experienced. Although in cases like the one investigated (simple general purpose system with simple tasks) more precision may not be necessary since evaluators tagging was also accurate, in others, in which tagging requires a domain specific knowledge (e.g. educational systems) it could have a relevant contribution in eliminating ambiguities.

One other result noticed after having performed the tagging step was that users discussed more aspects of the system's interface and alternative design options. Thus, an interesting future investigation would be to use CEM (or the user tagging step) as a method to involve users in the design process. In this situation positive utterances, as suggested by one of the participants, could be useful to allow users to express the aspects of the system they thought had high communicability.

Participants' interviews about the tagging have shown that users have identified themselves with the tags and felt comfortable using them to indicate the problems they had experienced. In spite of the brief explanation on tagging they received, most of them were able to tag over 70% of breakdowns correctly. Thus, further studies are needed to evaluate if users would be able to tag breakdowns by themselves.

As for the breakdowns users missed, they could probably be solved with a longer explanation or training. In that case benefits of user investment must be weighed, since the time invested and thus cost of the method would increase. At any rate, some of the breakdown misses per se may be an interesting information for evaluators. The fact that users do not consider a breakdown as such could provide indicators on the higher level task they were focusing on, as well as the breakdown's severity and priorities for redesign. In the case study presented the focus was on the tagging step, so the impact of users tagging on the other analysis step (interpretation and semiotic profiling) was not investigated. Nonetheless, such a case study could provide more indicators on the potential benefits of user tagging.

Finally, this paper was a first step in the investigation of the cost and benefit of user tagging in CEM. It has shown that user tagging is possible and pointed to various directions in which it could be very useful. Furthermore, the challenges faced by users are potentially challenges for evaluators who are applying the method for the first time. Thus, pointing out the challenges and potential reasons for them is useful for evaluators who want to apply the method, as well as for educators who teach them.

Acknowledgements. We thank all the participants of the tests and also Fapemig and INWeb (MCT/CNPq/ grant 57.3871/2008-6) for partially supporting this work.

References

1. Carroll, J.M.: HCI models, theories, and frameworks: toward a multidisciplinary science. Morgan Kaufmann, Menlo Park (2003)
2. de Souza, C.S.: The semiotic engineering of human-computer interaction. MIT Press, Cambridge (2005)
3. de Souza, C.S., Leitão, C.F.: Semiotic engineering methods for scientific research in HCI. Morgan & Claypool, Princeton (2009)
4. Ericsson, K.A., Simon, H.A.: Protocol analysis: Verbal Reports as Data. MIT Press, Cambridge (1993)
5. Greenberg, S., Buxton, B.: Usability evaluation considered harmful (some of the time). In: Proceedings of ACM CHI 2008, Italy, pp. 111–120 (2008)
6. Frøkjær, E., Hornbæk, K.: Cooperative usability testing: complementing usability tests with user-supported interpretation sessions. In: Proc. of CHI 2005, pp. 1383–1386. ACM (2005)
7. Guan, Z., Lee, S., Cuddihy, E., Ramey, J.: The validity of the stimulated retrospective think-aloud method as measured by eye tracking. In: CHI 2006, pp. 1253–1262. ACM (2006)
8. Mattos, B., Prates, R.: An overview of the communicability evaluation method for collaborative systems. In: IADIS International Conference WWW/Internet, pp. 129–136 (2011)
9. Prates, R.O., de Souza, C.S., Barbosa, S.D.J.: A method for evaluating the communicability of user interfaces. ACM Interactions 7(1), 31–38 (2000)
10. Prates, R.O., Barbosa, S., de Souza, C.S.: A case study for evaluating interface design through communicability. In: Proceedings of DIS 2000, pp. 308–317. ACM (2000)
11. Preece, J., Rogers, Y., Sharp, H., Benyon, D., Holland, S., Carey, T.: Human-computer interaction. Addison-Wesley, Reading (1994)
12. Sharp, H., Rogers, Y., Preece, J.: Interaction Design: Beyond Human Computer Interaction. Wiley (2011), Case Study 14.3 Communicability Evaluation, http://www.id-book.com/casestudy_14-3.php (last visit Januaury 2014)
13. Teague, R., et al.: Concurrent vs. Post-Task Usability Test Ratings. In: Proc. CHI 2001, pp. 289–290. ACM Press (2001)
14. Salgado, L.C.C., Bim, S.A., de Souza, C.S.: Comparação entre os métodos de avaliação de base cognitiva e semiótica. In: Proceedings of IHC 2006. SBC, pp. 158–167 (2006)

Reflections on the Cross-Platform Semiotic Inspection Method

Rodrigo de A. Maués and Simone Diniz Junqueira Barbosa

Informatics Department, PUC-Rio
Rua Marques de Sao Vicente, 225/410 RDC
Gavea, Rio de Janeiro, RJ, 22451-900, Brazil
{rmaues,simone}@inf.puc-rio.br

Abstract. Evaluating cross-platform systems can be quite challenging. Unfortunately, despite the increasing number of such systems and therefore growing need for evaluation methods, little work has been done on the matter. We have extended the Semiotic Inspection Method (SIM), a Semiotic Engineering evaluation method, to evaluate cross-platform systems, producing the CP-SIM variant. However, despite its support in identifying and classifying several potential issues particular to cross-platform systems, the cross-platform aspects of the method (called 'horizontal analysis') were only briefly illustrated by an analytical study in the original work. This paper provides deeper reflection and a more detailed account of the horizontal analysis in order to support evaluators in using the method. It also situates CP-SIM among related work on cross-platform system evaluation.

Keywords: Cross-platform, user interface design, communicability, semiotic inspection method, semiotic engineering.

1   Introduction

Users increasingly expect to have access to the same applications and services with a multitude of computing devices (e.g., PCs, smartphones, tablets, digital TVs), which differ greatly in their capabilities and constraints (e.g., screen size and resolution, input mechanisms, etc.) [1, 2, 3, 4, 5]. Traditional evaluation methods are not entirely adequate to assess the quality of these cross-platform systems, since the evaluated quality of separate parts (i.e., system versions on each platform) does not necessarily correspond to the quality of the whole cross-platform system [2]. However, despite the increasing number of such systems and therefore growing need for specific evaluation methods [1], little work has been done on the matter.

This paper advances a line of research that evaluates cross-platform systems based on Semiotics rather than cognitive theories [2, 5, 6]. In a previous work [7], we extended the Semiotic Inspection Method (SIM) [8] in order to provide a systematic way to evaluate cross-platform systems, resulting in the Cross-Platform Semiotic Inspection Method (CP-SIM). However, we only briefly illustrated the cross-platform aspects of CP-SIM (called 'horizontal analysis') by an analytical study. This paper

M. Kurosu (Ed.): Human-Computer Interaction, Part I, HCII 2014, LNCS 8510, pp. 533–544, 2014.
© Springer International Publishing Switzerland 2014

provides deeper reflection on and a more detailed account of the horizontal analysis in order to support evaluators using the method. It also situates CP-SIM among related work on cross-platform system evaluation.

This paper is organized as follows. We begin by presenting the theoretical background and related work. We then take a deeper look at the horizontal analysis of CP-SIM, discussing further about each sign manipulation type and about other key concepts for CP-SIM, relating them with concepts found on cognitive theories literature. Finally, we present our conclusions and future work.

2   Theoretical Background

This section presents some basic semiotic engineering concepts, necessary to understand the Semiotic Inspection Method, also described here.

2.1   Semiotic Engineering Basics

Semiotic Engineering [9] is a reflective and explanatory (as opposed to predictive) theory of human-computer interaction (HCI) that focuses on communicative rather than cognitive aspects of HCI analysis and design. It views the user interfaces of interactive systems as meta-communication artifacts, i.e., through the user interface, designers1 convey to the users their understanding of who the users are, what they know the users want or need to do, in which preferred ways, and why. Users then unfold and interpret this message as they interact with the system. This meta-communication message can be paraphrased as [9]:

"Here is my understanding of who you are, what I have learned you want or need to do, in which preferred ways, and why. This is the system I have therefore designed for you, and this is the way you can or should use it in order to fulfill a range of purposes that fall within this vision." (p.25)

The designer-to-user message is comprised of signs [9, 10]. A sign is anything that stands for something else, to somebody in some respect or capacity [11]. Signs compose one or more signification systems that arise from culturally (and, in the case of HCI, also artificially) encoded associations between content and expressions [9, 10, 12]. For example, words and images typically come from signification systems that exist in a culture outside the specific context of HCI, whereas mouse pointers belong to signification systems that are native to computer applications.

Semiotic Engineering classifies the signs in three different types [9]: static, dynamic and meta-linguistic. Static signs express and mean the system's state (*e.g.*, icons, text areas, buttons at a given moment, menus). Dynamic signs express and mean the system behaviour and emerge during interaction (*e.g.*, a save button becomes enabled after entering the name of a client in a registration form). Meta-linguistic signs refer to other interface signs and are used by the designer to explicitly

---

[1] In this paper, designers should be interpreted as whoever speaks for the design team of a given application.

communicate to users the meanings encoded in the user interface and how they can be used (*e.g.*, instructions and explanations, error and warning messages, hints and tooltips).

Based on this theoretical framework, the quality of a user interface is given by its *communicability*, which is "the system's property to convey effectively and efficiently to users its underlying design and interactive principles" [9]. On the one hand, when a user can comprehend how the system works because the designer expressed himself properly through the user interface (communicability), it becomes easier to learn how to use it (usability) [9, 10]. On the other hand, when the user fails to understand the communication intended by the designer, a communication breakdown takes place that may hinder or even preclude the use of the system [10].

2.2   The Semiotic Inspection Method

The Semiotic Inspection Method (SIM) [8] is a qualitative inspection method grounded in Semiotic Engineering that allows the evaluation of the communicability of a computer system through the analysis of its signs. The goal is to identify communication breakdowns that may take place during the user-system interaction and to reconstruct the designers' meta-message conveyed by the user interface.

SIM requires a preparation phase, in which the evaluator defines the purpose of the inspection, performs an informal inspection by navigating through the system to define the focus of the evaluation, and finally elaborates the inspection scenarios. Next, the evaluator proceeds to the execution of the inspection. To execute the method properly, the evaluator must assume a "user advocate" position. The execution of the method is carried out in five distinct steps: (1) a meta-linguistic signs inspection; (2) a static signs inspection; (3) a dynamic signs inspection; (4) a contrastive comparison of designer-to-user meta-communications identified in steps (1), (2), (3); and, finally, (5) a conclusive appreciation of the overall system communicability. In the first three steps, the evaluator inspects the signs within the scope of the evaluation and reconstructs the meta-messages conveyed by them at each level, filling out the template of the designer-to-user meta-communication and identifying potential communicability problems at each level. In step (4) the evaluator contrasts the meta-messages generated in the previous steps and checks for potential ambiguities among them. Finally, in step (5), the evaluator qualitatively assesses the system communicability by unifying the meta-communication messages and then generates a report.

3   Related Work

Despite the proliferation of cross-platform systems, when it comes to evaluating such systems, it is not yet very clear which evaluation techniques should be used [1]. A great body of work has been done over the last years regarding the design and development of such systems [3, 4, 13, 14, 15, 16]. However, a rare few have focused on their evaluation, which is one of the main needs of practitioners [1].

Öquist and coauthors discuss a method to assess usability of different interfaces by taking into account the different environments or contexts where different devices and interfaces are used, and by identifying some environmental variables that affect the usability of different devices and interfaces in those contexts of use [17]. However, this evaluation is not sufficient to guarantee the quality of cross-platform systems, since, as argued by Denis and Karsenty, the evaluated quality of each separate platform does not necessarily correspond to the quality of the whole cross-platform system [2]. People alternately use the "same" application in different platforms, frequently switching from one to the other. When traversing between system versions of a cross-platform system, a person should be able to reuse his or her knowledge of the available functions and of how to perform tasks. Based on that, Denis and Karsenty introduced the concept of inter-usability to designate "the ease with which users can reuse their knowledge and skills for a given functionality when switching to other devices" [2]. They also introduced a conceptual framework for achieving inter-usability, which proposes design principles addressing inter-device consistency[2], transparency and adaptability. They focus on knowledge and task continuity, and on how these can be better supported through design.

Huang and Strawderman [6] also acknowledge that the knowledge gained from the previous platform may greatly affect users' performance in the following platforms, but they believe that a lack of theoretical support weakened the generalization of the approaches proposed in [2]. Hence, they proposed the Usability Paradigm for Multiple Device System (UPMDS), a conceptual framework that relies on the area of transfer of learning [18], which embraces many theoretical and empirical studies rooted in behavioral and cognitive psychology. In their framework, usability is composed of two attributes: transferability and user perception, with transferability further divided into effectiveness, efficiency and user perception further divided into satisfaction and attractiveness. They define transferability as "the ease with which users switch between using different interfaces". Their work is still in its initial stages, and more studies are needed to empirically validate the framework.

Instead of focusing on the usability as the aforementioned studies, Wäljas et al. investigated the key elements that characterize the user experience when users exploit web-based applications through different computing platforms [5]. They conducted their analysis focusing on three key themes: composition, continuity and consistency. Based on their findings, they proposed an initial conceptual framework of cross-platform user experience, in which the central elements include: fit for cross-contextual activities; flow of interactions and content; and perceived service coherence.

Maués and Barbosa [7] have shifted the focus from cognitive theories to semiotic engineering [9] and provided a systematic way to evaluate cross-platform systems: the cross-platform semiotic inspection method (CP-SIM). Having a method specific for evaluating cross-platform system, instead of only conceptual frameworks, meets the practical needs of practitioners. We discuss CP-SIM in detail next.

---

[2] In this paper we follow a definition of consistency similar to the one adopted in [2]: striving for uniformity regarding the system's appearance, presentation and offered functionalities.

4   CP-SIM

When evaluating each platform of a cross-platform system separately, each one may have high communicability. However, when traversing between platforms, the user brings his or her understanding of one version that may not be applicable to another, creating or enhancing conflicts and communication breakdowns. Hence, the designer-to-user messages within a cross-platform system should not be conflicting; instead, they should complement each other.

With that in mind, we introduced the quality attribute named *cross-communicability* [7]: the cross-platform system property of each of its platforms being able to convey effectively and efficiently to users not only its individual underlying design and interactive principles, but those of the cross-platform system as a whole. Just like high communicability consequently leads to a better usability [9], it is expected that high cross-communicability will result in a better inter-usability.

To assess the cross-communicability of a cross-platform system, we proposed CP-SIM [7], an extension of SIM [8]. After the SIM's traditional preparation, the execution of the method is involves two phases: vertical (within-platform) analysis and horizontal (between-platform) analysis.

We designed the vertical analysis to evaluate the communicability of the system in each platform individually. Hence, it consists of conducting the same five steps of the traditional SIM, with one difference: the evaluator should also highlight the signs that denote any compositional aspects of the cross-platform system (e.g., a sign that acknowledges the existence of another version of the system).

After completing the vertical analysis, the horizontal analysis consists of contrasting the meta-communication messages of each system version in order to assess the system's cross-communicability. This analysis is based on a semiotic framing of design changes initially proposed for End-User Development (EUD) [12], where the differences between the system versions are related to possible manipulations made to signs on each interface. The horizontal analysis is composed of three steps: (1) to identify the sign manipulations in each pairwise combination of the evaluated platforms; (2) to examine the manipulations collated and categorized in the previous step to assess how they could negatively affect the horizontal meta-communication messages by intensifying already identified vertical communication breakdowns (e.g., causing ambiguities) or even by creating new ones; and (3) to qualitatively assess the system cross-communicability by unifying the meta-communication message obtained in each previous step, judging the costs and benefits of the identified manipulations made between platforms. After going through the three analysis steps, the evaluator generates an evaluation report.

5   Reflections on the Horizontal Analysis

There already is a good body of work explaining and exemplifying how to properly apply the traditional SIM [9, 10], and therefore it is safe to assume that it would not be difficult to conduct the vertical analysis. However, the same cannot be said about the horizontal analysis, which is a significant part of the proposed method. As mentioned before, the horizontal analysis relies on concepts taken from [12], namely, impermeability, semiotic dimensions and computer manipulation of signs. However, in [7], we could barely mention the concept of semiotic dimensions and we could only briefly discuss about the manipulation types that were found in their analytical study. In order to support evaluators to better identify and analyze the manipulations of signs, in this paper we discuss the aforementioned concepts in more details later in this section, and we contrast them with concepts found on related work to provide a better understanding and to avoid ambiguity.

From the nature of the manipulation, we can identify potential cross-communication breakdowns [7]. Regardless whether the signs were manipulated or conserved across platforms, the evaluator should intentionally explore the possibility of assigning plausible contradictory or ambiguous meanings to the signs that constitute the messages in the evaluated platforms. We derived some questions from our previous analytical study [7] that can serve as scaffolds for the evaluators' analysis:

1. Would the user plausibly be able to interpret this sign differently in other platform? How? Why?
2. Would the misinterpretation of this sign propagate and affect the interpretation of the same or other signs in other platforms? How? Why?
3. Would the user plausibly be able to interpret this sign consistently in this particular platform regardless of the amount and order of platforms that he previously interacted with? Why?

These questions are not the only ones that the evaluator can or should ask, but they provide useful guidance and input for conducting a productive horizontal analysis, which is especially useful for less experienced evaluators. Next we discuss in detail and in the context of cross-platform systems the aforementioned concepts of impermeability, semiotic dimensions and computer manipulation of signs.

5.1 Impermeability of Signs

The concept of impermeability [12] is related to the encapsulation of signs, i.e., when the sign meaning is in an atomic capsule and therefore it cannot be altered. Thus, the originally encoded meaning of impermeable signs is always preserved. Impermeable signs can be essential or accidental. Essential impermeable signs can only be used in monotonic manipulations, i.e., those that do not destroy the basic meanings (identity) of the application. For instance, essential impermeable signs cannot be removed from the application. Accidental impermeable signs may not be changed either, but they may be subtracted from the application by means of a manipulation called *pruning* (a type III manipulation, as seen in the next section). For instance, let us consider a "skip to the next track in the playlist" button in a music player. It is an impermeable sign and thus its meaning of skipping to the next track on a playlist should not be changed, otherwise it may confuse the user (e.g., if the next track button is used to skip to the next playlist instead). If this sign is essential (i.e., part of the system identity), it should also be present in any other platform. However, if it is not part of the system identity (i.e., it is an accidental sign), it may be pruned in any platform.

5.2   Semiotic Dimensions and Manipulation of Signs

According to [12], the underlying signification system (i.e., the computer languages to which users and programmers have access) has three semiotic dimensions: lexical, syntactic and semantic. Manipulations of these three dimensions effect different symbolic transformations (numbered from I to VII; see Fig. 1). The designer of a cross-platform system did not necessarily consider making these modifications, but based on the differences between supposedly equivalent signs we can assume which manipulations are capable of transforming a system version into another [7].

The lexical and the syntactic dimensions of computer languages are related to the surface features of the user interface, i.e., the look or appearance of a user interface. These dimensions are addressed in the perceptual or terminology and visual appearance inter-device consistency level in [2]. However, these two are different from the perceptual (look and feel) consistency dimension mentioned in [5] because they are not related to the feel (the behavior associated to interface elements).

The lexical dimension encompasses the color, shape and typefaces of labels and icons signs in the user interface, which corresponds to the lexical consistency level in [2] and to the semantic consistency level in [5]. The syntactic semiotic dimension relates to the layout or spatial organization of graphical signs. It encompasses the navigation and the arrangement of steps in a procedure or the ordering of operations in order to accomplish a task. In [2] this latter aspect is addressed in an inter-device consistency level called syntactical consistency, and in [5] it is called syntactic or interaction logic consistency.

The semantic dimension relates to the feel of the user interface, which corresponds to the semantic or partition of data and functions inter-device consistency level in [2]. This dimension is related to the meanings expressed by signs in the system and it allow us to identify two different subsets of manipulations to signs (Fig. 1): meaning-preserving manipulations (types I, II, and III) and meaning-changing ones (types IV through VII). Meaning-preserving manipulations affect only impermeable signs and preserve the application identity. Every application requires that users learn a new and unique signification system used in HCI [12]. Therefore, the application's identity and the notion of impermeability are important to keep the user's semiosis sufficiently tied to the designer's vision, so that productive interpretations can be motivated, and unproductive ones discouraged. This is especially important when it comes to cross-platform systems, since you have many versions of the same system and they cannot or should not be entirely consistent in every case [2]. A coherent user experience is the ultimate target of cross-platform service design [5]. Meaning-changing manipulations, however, can threaten the application's identity (and consequently the system's perceived coherence), and therefore should be avoided whenever possible in order to minimize more serious conflicts between system versions.

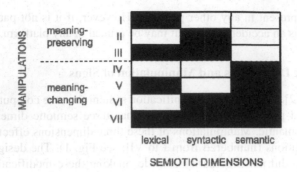

Fig. 1. Semiotic manipulation possibilities of symbols and signs from a computer symbol-processing perspective

Type I Manipulations. Type I changes correspond to *renaming* and *aliasing* operations that affect only the lexical component. This manipulation is partially related to the simplification and magnification content adaptation strategies mentioned in [19] and to the transducing adaption approach in [20], because it modifies the appearance of some piece of information (signs) present in the user interface. Changing the label of a button and changing an icon appearance are both examples of renaming. Renaming should be limited to lexical items that are not part of the application identity [12]. Besides, it should be used only when imposed by the device's constraints (e.g., summarizing a description or using synonyms for a label in order to fit in the screen) or the platform patterns (e.g., changing the appearance of a component or icon from the Android platform to accommodate the patterns in the iOS platform and vice-versa) to avoid unnecessary inconsistencies.

Whenever a sign is renamed between platforms (i.e., receives different names in each one), the user must follow a reasoning process to establish whether the object has the same function (meaning) as its instance in another version of the application [2]. Depending on the degree of the lexical inconsistency, the user might fail to associate an object (sign) with its function (expected meaning), causing a communication breakdown and a continuity problem. Resizing a user interface element is usually not a problem since users still have enough visual clues to judge whether the different sized objects are similar [2, 19]. Changing the color of an element, however, can lead to some issues since a color is by itself a sign and therefore express its own meanings (e.g., the red color is commonly associated to cancel or removing operations).

Type II Manipulations. Type II manipulations involve making changes only to syntactic components, i.e. *reordering* items: changing the layout placement of user interface elements (the adaptation strategy called rearrangement in [19]); or changing the navigation or the order in which operations are performed.

Type II manipulations are most common and inevitable when it comes to cross-platform systems. Resizing elements is often not enough to adapt the application interface when the display sizes and resolutions are different, which forces the designer to reorganize the layout to fit all the interface elements (or even to separate elements into two or more screens) to avoid pruning essential impermeable signs.

However, is worth noticing that any reordering in the layout, when not imposed by the device's space or resolution constraints, is unnecessary and counterproductive, negatively affecting the continuity or inter-usability of the system [2]. Keep in mind that, whenever this sort of manipulation occurs, users will have to make an effort to locate the object. At best, this will increase their workload (e.g., a person who is already used to the order of some labels in a platform will have to learn the order of the such elements again in the other platforms); at worst, if they can't locate the object quickly, they could conclude that the related function is unavailable on the new device [20]. Also, if the reordered interface elements were buttons, a distracted person might press the wrong button and perform some undesired action because the order with which this person was already familiar has changed. Moreover, from a semiotic perspective, the order of elements may also convey a relation of importance between them, and therefore such inconsistencies may cause an ambiguity when communicating to the user what the designer thought was more important. Finally, as shown in the analytical study in [7], a misplacement of even a simple element as a label may mislead the user and hinder the use of the system.

Type III Manipulations. Rearranging (type II) or changing the appearance (type I) of some components is often not enough. Type III manipulation (also known as *pruning*) corresponds to the possibility of selecting non-essential (accidental) components to be included in or excluded from the application (which corresponds respectively to the increase and reduction adaptation strategies mentioned in [19]). Not only must pruning preserve the identity of the application, but also the impermeability of the pruned components. Thus, an important design decision is to select which of the impermeable signs are essential and thus cannot be pruned i.e., which signs constitute the application identity [12].

As in type II manipulations, one of the reasons why type III manipulations are likely to occur arises from differences between platform capabilities. However, even when technologically feasible, some functionalities and signs should still be distributed across platforms according to their utility (i.e., if they will be useful considering the platform or device context and purpose of use) in order to reduce the complexity on each application version [5]. However, if the composition of applications and devices and the way they are combined is not in line with the user's activity or needs, it may essentially hinder the resulting user experience [5]. From an inter-usability perspective this happens because the lack of some expected features hinders both knowledge and task continuity [2]. From a semiotic perspective, this mismatch relates with poorly defining the application's identity.

The negative effect of such inconsistencies may be mitigated by an appropriate degree of system transparency [2, 5]. The system should help the user to understand the potential and limitations of distinct technologies, and the different useful ways to combine the system versions altogether. We go even further to say that whenever an appropriate degree of transparency is not reached, the user might end up thinking that some pruned feature is actually present in some other part of the system (type II manipulation) and therefore he will eventually get frustrated after endlessly looking for it. Alternatively, also due to a transparency problem, the user might think that some feature is not present (since it was not present in the other version) while it actually is. Although being unaware of an extra feature may not seem to lead to a problem, it will in case this feature performs some automatic operation without the user being aware of it. For instance, when first launched, most Android users were not aware of Instant Upload, a feature that allows you to upload photos and videos taken from your device automatically to a private album on Google+. These users ended up uploading undesired pictures and videos to their profiles, often consuming their 3G data allowance (when no Wi-Fi was available) without even noticing it.

Type IV Manipulations. A type IV manipulation affects the semantic (meaning), but not the lexical and syntactic dimensions. Hence, it involves using existing signs to mean something different from what they mean in another platform (e.g. the same button triggers different actions on each platform). As a result, when transitioning from one version to another, users may feel frustrated because of this conflict of meanings. This manipulation should be avoided since, to ensure continuity, the effect or result of the operations (i.e. their meanings) should be as similar as possible across devices [20]. Besides, if the user does not notice the functional inconsistency the failures may be even more frustrating and harder to recover from. For instance, the user might expect that, when pressing a button, an e-mail will be sent to the trash can just like when pressing a similar button in another version of the system. However, it might actually delete the e-mail permanently.

Type V Manipulations. A type V manipulation makes changes to meanings and lexical items but not to grammatical structures. In this case, it is important to mention that only because signs in different platforms have the same grammar structure (syntactical base), but different lexical and semantic bases, it does not necessarily mean that they represent the same sign. We can consider, for instance, that instead of a Type V manipulation, two type III manipulations took place: a sign was pruned and another one was added. Therefore, when the lexical bases of two signs are different enough from each other, such Type V inconsistencies may impair the use of a cross-platform system only as much as a type III inconsistency would. However, if the lexical base is somewhat similar, the user may not expect that some sign will have a different meaning across platforms, which will lead him to failures such as the ones that arise from a type IV manipulation.

Type VI Manipulations. Type VI affects both syntactic and semantic dimensions, and therefore it may involve reordering components or even eliminating components that change the conveyed meaning. As in type IV manipulations, since the lexical base does not change, the user may not understand or perceive at first that there are different grammatical structures associated with same sign across platforms, which will lead to different effects. For instance, when closing an application in a platform there might be an intermediate step asking the user whether he wants to save or discard unsaved changes to a document, while in another version this step might be eliminated, leading the user to lose this data, a failure from which he may not be able to recover. Regarding rearranging graphical elements instead of operations, users will hardly assume that the same element (sign) will have a different meaning and purpose only because it is in a different place of the user interface.

Type VII Manipulations. Type VII makes changes to meanings, grammatical structures and lexical items. This manipulation can freely affect the inside of any sign capsule and thus it can potentially override the limits of the application identity. As discussed before, the application cannot be entirely consistent across platforms, but it should at least be coherent, otherwise they user will not be able to reuse any of the knowledge acquired when transitioning between platforms (i.e., knowledge continuity). Moreover, it may even seem to the user that such versions are not part of the same system. The concept of application identity helps to draw the boundary of how inconsistent, in the worst-case scenario, a cross-platform system might be: at least the signs that constitute the application identity should be should never be pruned or changed. Therefore, such manipulations should be avoided at all costs.

6   Conclusion and Future Work

This paper discusses the Cross-Platform Semiotic Inspection Method, CP-SIM, an extension of the Semiotic Inspection Method designed to evaluate cross-platform systems. In order to support evaluators using this method, we presented a more detailed account of the horizontal analysis of the method. In this paper, we contextualized (in the cross-platform scenario) the concepts used in the method better and also related these concepts to the ones found in literature about cross-platform systems evaluation based on cognitive theories. We believe this link is extremely helpful especially for evaluators that are not so familiar with Semiotics or Semiotic Engineering. Finally, we discussed in detail each type of sign manipulation, providing a better perspective on their actual and potential impact on the quality of cross-platform systems.

As future work, we plan to conduct several analytical studies to investigate further and to better characterize each type of sign manipulation in the context of cross-platform systems. We also plan to investigate the learning curve of the method in order to decide how to improve it.

Acknowledgments. Simone Barbosa thanks CNPq (process #308490/2012-6) for the support to her research work.

References

1. Antila, V., Lui, A.: Challenges in designing inter-usable systems. In: Campos, P., Graham, N., Jorge, J., Nunes, N., Palanque, P., Winckler, M. (eds.) INTERACT 2011, Part I. LNCS, vol. 6946, pp. 396–403. Springer, Heidelberg (2011)

2. Denis, C., Karsenty, L.: Inter-usability of multi-device systems - a conceptual framework. In: Seffah, A., Javahery, H. (eds.) Multiple User Interfaces: Cross-Platform Applications and Context-Aware Interfaces. Wiley & Sons (2004)
3. Paternò, F.: Designing multi-device user interfaces: how to adapt to the changing device. In: Baranauskas, C., Abascal, J., Barbosa, S.D.J. (eds.) INTERACT 2007, Part II. LNCS, vol. 4663, pp. 702–703. Springer, Heidelberg (2007)
4. Seffah, A., Forbrig, P., Javahery, H.: Multi-devices "Multiple" user interfaces: development models and research opportunities. Journal of Systems and Software 73(2), 287–300 (2004)
5. Wäljas, M., Segerståhl, K., Väänänen-Vainio-Mattila, K., Oinas-Kukkonen, H.: Cross-platform service user experience: a field study and an initial framework. In: Proc. MobileHCI 2010, pp. 219–228. ACM (2010)
6. Huang, Y., Strawderman, L.: Introducing a New Usability Framework for Analyzing Usability in a Multiple-device System. In: Proc. Human Factors and Ergonomics Society Annual Meeting, vol. 55(1), pp. 1696–1700. SAGE Publications (2011)
7. de A. Maués, R., Barbosa, S.D.J.: Cross-communicability: Evaluating the meta-communication of cross-platform applications. In: Kotzé, P., Marsden, G., Lindgaard, G., Wesson, J., Winckler, M. (eds.) INTERACT 2013, Part III. LNCS, vol. 8119, pp. 241–258. Springer, Heidelberg (2013)
8. de Souza, C.S., Leitão, C.F., Prates, R.O., da Silva, E.J.: The Semiotic Inspection Method. In: Proc. IHC 2006, vol. 1, pp. 148–157. SBC (2006)
9. de Souza, C.S.: The Semiotic Engineering of Human-Computer Interaction. The MIT Press (2005)
10. Barbosa, S.D.J., Silva, B.S.: Interação Humano-Computador. Campus-Elsevier (2010)
11. Peirce, C.S.: The essential Peirce. In: Houser, N., Kloesel, C. (eds.), vols. 1&2. Indiana University Press (1992)
12. de Souza, C.S., Barbosa, S.D.J.: A semiotic framing for end-user development. In: Lieberman, H., Paternò, F., Wulf, V. (org.) End User Development: People to Flexibly Employ Advanced Information and Communication Technology, pp. 401–426. Springer (2006)
13. Florins, M., Vanderdonckt, J.: Graceful degradation of user interfaces as a design method for multiplatform systems. In: Proc. IUI 2004. ACM (2004)
14. Lin, J., Landay, J.A.: Employing patterns and layers for early-stage design and prototyping of cross-device user interfaces. In: Proc. CHI 2008, pp. 1313–1322. ACM (2008)
15. Ghiani, G., Paternò, F., Santoro, C.: On-demand cross-device interface components migration. In: Proc. MobileHCI 2010, pp. 299–308. ACM (2010)
16. Paternò, F., Zichittella, G.: Desktop-to-mobile web adaptation through customizable two-dimensional semantic redesign. In: Forbrig, P. (ed.) HCSE 2010. LNCS, vol. 6409, pp. 79–94. Springer, Heidelberg (2010)
17. Öquist, G., Goldstein, M., Chincholle, D.: Assessing usability across multiple user interfaces. In: Multiple User Interfaces: Cross-Platform Applications and Context-Aware Interfaces, pp. 327–349 (2004)
18. Haskell, R.E.: Transfer of learning: cognition and instruction. Academic Press (2000)
19. Berti, S., Paternó, F., Santoro, C.: A Taxonomy for Migratory User Interfaces. In: Gilroy, S.W., Harrison, M.D. (eds.) DSV-IS 2005. LNCS, vol. 3941, pp. 149–160. Springer, Heidelberg (2006)
20. Paternò, F., Santoro, C.: A logical framework for multi-device user interfaces. In: Proc. EICS 2012, pp. 45–50. ACM (2012)

Evaluating Methods and Equipment for Usability Field Tests in Public Transport

Cindy Mayas, Stephan Hörold, Christina Rosenmöller, and Heidi Krömker

Ilmenau University of Technology, Ilmenau, Germany
{cindy.mayas,stephan.hoerold,christina.rosenmoeller,
heidi.kroemker}@tu-ilmenau.de

Abstract. Usability experts require high quality of evaluation data, in order to achieve detailed and meaningful results. In particular, evaluation in public environment, e.g. in public transport, involves influences of different contexts. In order to observe these context factors, a wide range of technical test equipment, for instance eye-tracking or video glasses, are available. This paper describes the evaluation of different combinations of test methods and equipment for a field test in public transport. The goal of this study is to identify a test setup which enables a natural behavior of the test persons and a high quality of data.

Keywords: usability, field test, methods, test equipment, context.

1   Introduction

Usability field tests analyze the use of systems in their real context of use [1]. In field tests, effectiveness, efficiency, and satisfaction [2] of the task performance depend on where and in which context a task is performed respectively. Bevan points out that for usability testing especially the context of use should be as close as possible to the real context, in order to provide valid results [3]. On the one hand, field tests provide this highly realistic context, but on the other hand the reality setting includes a high number of variable actions and influences [4], which have to be observed. Especially in public transport, field tests pass different contexts along a journey, for instance stations, vehicles and footpaths. Consequently, public transport sets the following challenges for field tests:

- Discontinuity of actions along variable locations
- Variable external influences, for instance waiting times vs. time pressure for changing or rainy footpaths vs. crowded stations
- Higher workload due to high autonomy for reaching the destination

In this context, stationary equipment is not sufficient to observe the actions of the user and the possible influences. The equipment has to be extended with other observation methods and mobile observations techniques. In addition, the objectively observed data has to be interpreted. These interpretations require information about the subjective impressions and feelings of the users [5].

M. Kurosu (Ed.): Human-Computer Interaction, Part I, HCII 2014, LNCS 8510, pp. 545–553, 2014.
© Springer International Publishing Switzerland 2014

The aim of this paper is to design and evaluate a mobile test setup, as combination of test methods and equipment, for field tests with mobile devices in public transport. The challenge is to observe sufficient objective data about the interactions of the users in specific tasks and also data about the variable environmental influences [4]. The designed test setup has to ensure valid and reliable data, which is not influenced by the technical equipment or lacking acceptance of the observation methods by the users.

2   Analytical Pre-study

Usability tests include different qualities of data. First of all, objective data are gathered by quantified data or video and audio recordings. The next step is to interpret the objective data. The interpretation requires more detailed data about the subjective feelings and emotions of the users. The subjective data reveal motivations of the users for specific actions, as well as feelings and perceptions, according to the test incidents [5]. The following analysis is restricted to methods which are realizable in a field test in public transport.

2.1   Methods for Objective Data Collection

Position Tracking. Gathering detailed information about the varying local test position, which is combined with the synchronized test time, enables conclusions on additional usage contexts. Position tracking can be combined with most mobile smart phones or additional tracking devices. The detailed geo coordinates can be displayed on maps, for instance to compare routes and analyze differences in way-finding strategies.

Function Tracking. Server log files of user requests give an overview of the used functions during the test. More detailed technologies even provide log files, which record every single user action with screenshots [6] and the point of time, but require additional software installations on the test platform.

Screen Capturing. In every usability test it is essential to record the user interface of the test object as detailed as possible. But additional cameras, attached to the smartphone, influence the user comfort and the ease of use. The focus of cameras with other perspectives highly depend on the user's handling position and the incidents of light on the screen. In contrast, software solutions, which enable a directly and synchronized capturing of the smartphone screen, is independent from external influences and nearly imperceptible for the test users. Important criteria for the choice of screen capturing software are the sufficient resolution and recording duration.

Performance Measurement. According to the results of time measurement, tracking, or capturing, performance measurement compares the users' times of task completion [5]. This method provides information about the efficiency of a task completion process. But due to the variety of influences, field tests generate widespread results of task completion times, which can be hardly interpreted.

Interaction Camera. Cameras, which can be flexibly attached and adjusted, provide the possibility to focus the test observation on a specific aspect [7]. For example, the interaction with smartphones can be observed by an interaction camera in field tests. Due to its small and unobtrusive construction, interaction cameras can be attached to the user's clothes without causing limitations the mobility and free movements of the user.

Table 1. Comparison of methods for objective data collection

	Advantages	Disadvantages
Position tracking	— highly mobile — cost-effectively integrated in most smartphones	— Inaccuracies of GPS positioning
Function tracking	— Exact action traceability — cost-effectively integrated in data collection	— low context-sensitiveness — high amount of data
Screen Capturing	— detailed synchronized recording of the user interface	— low relation to user actions
Performance measurement	— directly comparable data of efficiency	— low relation to user actions
Interaction camera	— High acceptance of users — High qualitative data about special aspects	— Limited field of observation — Risk of position shifting
Point of view recording	— Audio and video observation of test context and surroundings	— problems with spectacles — no observation of the test user
Eye tracking	— information about point of view and fix points of the user interface	— High effort of equipment — High effort of calibration

Point of View Recording. The challenge to observe the variable context of actions prompts the use of video observations in field tests. However, in public spaces, a continuous static observation by cameras is not allowed and additional camera operators could influence the behavior of the users. In contrast, point of view recordings, for instance with video glasses, are directly worn by the users and observe the field of view of the test person, in reference to their actions. According to the actual weather conditions, the video glasses should be adjusted to sunglasses or transparent glasses.

Eye Tracking. The use of eye tracking technologies provides information about the focused pix points by the users in the field of view. The quality of the revealed data varies, depending on the adjustment of the eye tracker to the user and external influences, e.g. the incidence of light [8]. In order to analyze and compare eye-tracking results, the recognition of fixed markers is recommended, which is hardly realizable in variable public contexts.

Summary. Table 1 summarizes the key advantages and disadvantages of the introduced methods of objective data collection. Analytical pre-study results revealed that the methods of position and function tracking in combination with screen capturing and interaction camera are basic methods for the field test.. In addition, point-of-view-recording and eye tracking are varied in three test setups (see chapter 3).

2.2   Methods for Subjective Data Collection

Thinking Aloud. Thinking Aloud is one of the most frequently applied methods in lab-based usability tests [9]. The user is asked to formulate the feelings and thoughts, which come to his mind during the interaction with the system. This method provides a direct feedback on user interpretations and motivations in reference to the user interface elements and tasks. But thinking aloud of users also prolongs the execution times of tasks und reduces the concentration on task completion, due to the additional verbal effort. In addition to single user tests with thinking aloud, also co-discovery methods are established, which allow a more natural communication behavior of the test users. Finally, active-intervention methods also encourage a verbalization of the user thoughts during the test. For active-intervention, an interviewer moderates the content by requesting.

Retrospective Thinking Aloud. In contrast to thinking aloud, the method of retrospective thinking aloud is conducted after the practical test [10]. During the practical test, the test user only concentrates on the task completion, which is observed by video recording. On the basis of these recordings, the test user comments the conducted actions. In this process, the video recording supports the memorization of the test users and can be stopped or replayed for critical incidents.

Coaching-Method. The coaching method not only involves an interviewer in the test session but also allows the test user to ask questions about the test system and the task solution process. The interviewer explains the system to the user and suggests required functions. In this method, the questions of the user display the user feedback and indicate potential for improvements for the system [5].

Post-test Interview. Interviews provide the possibility of gathering both qualitative and quantitative data. Open, semi-standardized or standardized questions allow a wide range of results, especially regarding a valid and reliable assessment of products' characteristics. From face-to-face- to paper-and-pencil interviews, different methods are established according to the test setups.

Summary. Table 2 summarizes the key advantages and disadvantages of the introduced methods of subjective data collection. In reference to the planned field test with an unknown system, the coaching method was applied in a short introduction trip, in order to ensure a better feeling for the test users. A post-test questionnaire is used to quantify the acceptance of the system and the test equipment. The methods thinking aloud and retrospective thinking aloud are varied in the test setups (chapter 3). In order to reduce the disadvantages of thinking aloud, traditional thinking aloud is modified with parts of active-intervention.

Table 2. Comparison of methods for subjective data collection

	Advantages	Disadvantages
Thinking Aloud	— Direct user feedback in relation to the tasks — No memorizing effects	— Influences on task completion and performance measurement
Retrospective Thinking Aloud	— Detailed user feedback on critical incidents in retrospection	— Missing information due to memorizing effects — video recording as reminder
Coaching Method	— Natural user behavior by questioning	— Interviewer influences
Post-Test Questionnaire	— Possibility of qualitative and standardized quantitative data — Highly structured feedback	— Constrained user feedback on specific aspects

3   Empirical Field Study

In order to evaluate application prototypes for a new communication interface standard in public transport, a three week field test [11] was conducted on in a state's capital city in Germany. The field test with real passengers was preferred due to the more realistic context with more changing circumstances than laboratory test environments, which could only simulate selected external influences.

Test Objective. Each of the test persons was instructed with the same task, to reach a defined destination, and equipped with the evaluation equipment and a mobile passenger information application. Along the test track of 17.5 miles, the traveler experienced different contexts, for instance metro rides, bus rides, interchanges and footpath. In addition, the participants were allowed to use every available public information during the test.

Test Persons. The test was conducted with 12 male test persons between the ages of 18 and 35 years. Every test person had a high knowledge of the public transport system, but limited knowledge of the place. All were very experienced smartphone users.

Test Methods. Three different combinations of the analyzed methods and equipment, shown in table 3, are tested, in order to identify a test setup, which provides valid and reliable data with a minimum of interference. The different combinations are assessed in reference to the recorded interviews or actions and a questionnaire after the test. The test setups were created according to the functional conjunction of the several test components, as well as the synchronicity, accuracy, and completeness of the data. That is why all three test setups include five standardized basic elements: position tracking, function tracking, screen capturing, and interaction camera for objective data collection, coaching method and post-test questionnaire for subjective data collection.

The key task, reaching the prescribed aim, was conducted either with thinking aloud during the test or with retrospective thinking aloud after the test. The retrospective thinking aloud was supported by the videos of the interaction camera, the point of view recording, and the screen capturing. Some test persons with thinking aloud also wore video glasses for the point of view recording and the others used eye tracking.

Table 3. Evaluated field test setups for public transport

Test setup	Objective data	Subjective data
Setup 1	Position tracking Function tracking Screen Capturing Interaction camera (IC) *Point of view recording (PVR)*	Coaching Method *Retrospective Thinking Aloud (RTA)* Post-Test Questionnaire
Setup 2	Position tracking Function tracking Screen Capturing Interaction camera (IC) *Point of view recording (PVR)*	Coaching Method *Thinking Aloud (TA)* Post-Test Questionnaire
Setup 3	Position tracking Function tracking Screen Capturing Interaction camera (IC) *Eye tracking (ET)*	Coaching Method *Thinking Aloud (TA)* Post-Test Questionnaire

4   Results

4.1   Physical and Social Comfort

The post-test questionnaire included a segment of seven questions about the direct limitations and uncomfortableness due to the technical devices, which were worn by the test users. The questions were answered on a scale from 1 to 5: 1 signifies very comfortable feelings during the test, 5 signifies very uncomfortable feelings.

Table 4 displays the mean value and standard deviation data of the three test setups. Overall, every setup was assessed as rather comfortable than uncomfortable. The setup 1, with the point of view recording and retrospective thinking aloud, was most comfortable to the users, especially regarding the indirect influences from people's reactions. The direct influences on free movements and physical stress according to the test equipment were very low for setup 2 und setup 1. The differences between setup 1 and 2 with the same technical equipment might be caused by the accompanying interviewer during the test, who potentially causes more attention to the test user. Particularly setup 3 with the eye tracking equipment, which included a heavier backpack and a more conspicuous eye-glasses construction than setup 1 and 2, is assessed as considerably more uncomfortable for the users.

Table 4. User assessment of physical and social comfort

	Setup 1 (PVR, RTA)	Setup 2 (PVR, TA)	Setup 3 (ET, TA)
Direct uncomfortableness with equipment [a]	$\bar{x} = 1,65$ $\sigma = 0,62$	$\bar{x} = 1,50$ $\sigma = 0,73$	$\bar{x} = 2,75$ $\sigma = 0,71$
Indirect uncomfortableness with people's reactions [a]	$\bar{x} = 1,80$ $\sigma = 1,18$	$\bar{x} = 2,20$ $\sigma = 1,10$	$\bar{x} = 2,67$ $\sigma = 1,41$

a. scale from 1 to 5 points: 1 very comfortable; 5 very uncomfortable

$\bar{x}$ = mean; σ = standard deviation

More physical and social comfort with the test equipment imply more natural behavior of the user. This natural behavior is the key characteristic of the field test, which should not be restricted by the technical equipment.

4.2   Reliability

The subjective feedback of the users is an important indicator for usability problems. In the field test the user should commentate each function usage with their motivation of use, in order to discuss potential deviations of the user interface to the users' expectations and goals. The analysis of the objective data and the subjective data revealed a high difference between the number of real function calls in different situations and the number of commented function calls (see table 5).

Both test setups with thinking aloud and retrospective thinking aloud detect the same mean value of 26 function uses during the test. But in the retrospective thinking aloud interview, the test users commented nearly 20% more function calls than in the thinking aloud interviews. The users explained with averaged 16 comments in retrospective thinking aloud test four functions calls more than in thinking aloud test. Nevertheless, in both test situation the minimum of commented functions is with 35% respectively 40% considerably less than half the function calls in reality.

Table 5. Comparison of used and commented functions

	Function calls	Commented function calls	Share of results
Thinking Aloud	$\bar{x} = 26$ $\sigma = 9$	$\bar{x} = 12$ $\sigma = 4$	$\bar{x} = 45\%$ $\sigma = 7\%$
Retrospective Thinking Aloud	$\bar{x} = 26$ $\sigma = 5$	$\bar{x} = 16$ $\sigma = 5$	$\bar{x} = 64\%$ $\sigma = 20\%$

4.3   Quality of Methods

A key factor of the field test is the natural and independent behavior of the test users. The mere presence of the interviewer in thinking aloud influenced the behavior and way-finding process of the test users. The technical equipment has less influences on the quality of the subjective data.

Furthermore, the content of the user feedback was much more detailed in the test with retrospective thinking aloud. During the thinking aloud test, the users had to manage the high autonomy of the tasks and partly the time pressure activities, simultaneously to the commentating action. Additionally, the interviewer could request for critical incidents detailed in retrospective thinking aloud tests. In contrast, in the thinking aloud test, the interviewers were not able to go into detail of special aspects of the user interface, due to the time restriction and the fact, that the smartphone   was often hidden from the view of the interviewer.

5   Conclusion

The analytical and empirical studies reveal different advantages and disadvantages of the test setups in mobile field tests. According to the described criteria, a combination of methods and equipment is derived, which possesses a low interference to the test persons and the task performance process, as well as a high quality of data of the primary and secondary context. The final setup consists of   the following parts:

(1) Objective data collection with position and function tracking, screen recording, interaction camera, and point of view recording
(2) Subjective data collection with coaching method, retrospective thinking, and questionnaire.

This test setup is applied again in the field test by a larger number of users and provided valid and reliable data with satisfied test users.

The fast-growing technical possibilities of observation technology refines the fields of application of usability tests in the evaluation of different contexts. Field tests especially benefit from this development. But these possibilities also imply the challenges of higher efforts to synchronize and analyze the data. The final combination used in the field test shows that even with some additional equipment, users still feel comfortable and behave naturally. In addition, ethical and social parameters have to be included in the assessment of the equipment, in reference to decreasing size and visibility of video and audio camera systems.

Acknowledgements. Part of this work was funded by the German Federal Ministry of Economy and Technology (BMWi) grant number 19P10003L within the IP-KOM-ÖV und Dynapsys project. The project develops an interface standard for passenger information in German public transport with focus on the connection between personal mobile devices, vehicle systems and public transport background computer systems.

References

1. Kaikkonen, A., Kekäläinen, A., Cankar, M., Kallio, T., Kankainen, A.: Usability testing of mobile applications: a comparison between laboratory and field testing. Journal of Usability Studies 1(1), 4–16 (2005)
2. ISO 9241-210:2010: Ergonomics of human-system interaction – Part 210: Human-centred design for interactive systems, German version. Beuth Verlag GmbH, Berlin (2010)
3. Bevan, N.: Using the Common Industry Format to Document the Context of Use. In: Kurosu, M. (ed.) Human-Computer Interaction, Part I, HCII 2013, Part I. LNCS, vol. 8004, pp. 281–289. Springer, Heidelberg (2013)
4. Krannich, D.: Mobile System Design – Herausforderungen, Anforderungen und Lösungsansätze für Design, Implementierung und Usability-Testing Mobiler Systeme. Books on Demand GmbH, Norderstedt (2010)
5. Nielsen, J.: Usability Engineering. Academic Press, Inc., London (1993)
6. Kawalek, J., Riebeck, M., Stark, A.: A New Approach to Analyze Human-Mobile Computer Interaction. Journal of Usability Studies 3(2), 90–98 (2008)
7. LaRosa, M., Schusteritsch, R., Wie, C.Y.: Towards the Perfect Infratsructure for Usability Testing on Mobile Devices. In: Proceedings of the 8th Conference on Human-Computer Interaction with Mobile Devices and Services (MobileHCI 2006), pp. 187–190. ACM Press, New York (2007)
8. Brau, H., Sarodnick, F.: Methoden der Usability Evaluation: wissenschaftliche Grundlagen und praktische Anwendung. Verlag Hans Huber, Bern (2011)
9. Boren, T., Ramey, J.: Thinking aloud: reconciling theory and practice. IEEE Transactions on Professional Communication 43(3), 261–278 (2000), doi:10.1109/47.867942
10. Plaisant, C., Shneiderman, B.: Designing the user interface: strategies for effective human-computer interaction, 5th edn. Addison-Wesley Publ. Co., Reading (2010)
11. Hörold, S., Mayas, C., Krömker, H.: Guidelines for Usability Field Tests in the Dynamic Contexts of Public Transport. In: Kurosu, M. (ed.) Human-Computer Interaction, Part I, HCII 2014. LNCS, vol. 8510, pp. 489–499. Springer, Springer (2014)

ErgoSV: An Environment to Support Usability Evaluation Using Face and Speech Recognition

Thiago Adriano Coleti, Marcelo Morandini, and Fátima de Lourdes dos Santos Nunes

University of Sao Paulo
{thiagocoleti,m.morandini,fatima.nunes}@usp.br

Abstract. Usability test is a group of activities that should be performed by all designers in order to identify interaction problems. Filming and Verbalization are two techniques widely used due to the reason that they provide real information about the software interaction capacity. Filming is performed using one or several cameras and the verbalization is done encouraging the participant to verbalize what he/she is thinking about the software. Both techniques register the data in video and audio files to be analyzed forward. Although these techniques has been widely used, the analysis process is considered slow, difficult and expensive because the evaluator may need to review all the data registered from the first second until the end of the test to identify possible usability problems and this task could take from 2x to 10x the test time. This paper presents the ErgoSV Software, a tool to support usability evaluation test using speech processing that recognize specific keywords pronounced by the participants and face images processed during the test. These data are used to provide organized and relevant information to support the data analysis and the identification of interfaces with possible usability problems. Experiments performed in three different softwares presented that this tool reduced the time of analysis to 1,5 times the test time considering the keywords as the main data.

This research is supported by FAPESP.

Keywords: Usability Evaluation, Usability Test, Face Recognition, Speech Processing, Automatic analysis information.

1 Introduction

Usability is the main feature of interactive systems and, according to ISO 9241 should allow the users to perform their tasks with effectiveness, efficiency and satisfaction. Evaluating the software usability can guarantee that the users performs all their tasks in the system and do not reject the systems [4, 12,13].

Usability tests can be performed by designers in order to analyze whether the interaction has problems and so decrease the interface quality. Two techniques are widely used to test the usability: (1) filming: in this technique, the evaluator places one or several cameras to register images by the user, computer, environment and more information that they consider relevant; (2) think-aloud: the evaluator encourage the participant (final user) to verbalize what he/she is thinking about the system and

M. Kurosu (Ed.): Human-Computer Interaction, Part I, HCII 2014, LNCS 8510, pp. 554–564, 2014.
© Springer International Publishing Switzerland 2014

register the data in paper or audio files. The verbalization can be done simultaneously or consecutive with the test. In simultaneously approach, the participants perform their task and express in the same moment their opinion. In consecutive, the participant verbalizes after finishing the test and due to this reason, the consecutive approach is considered slower [4].

These techniques of test are considered too effectiveness due to the reason that provide real information about the software interaction capacity and so, allows the evaluator do input improvements in the interface besides to submit the software to real situations that could not be predicted by designers. However, the filming and the verbalization analysis data are slow and expensive and according to [12] can take long two to ten times the evaluation time [4, 15].

This paper presents the ErgoSV Software, an application developed by researchers of the University of Sao Paulo (Brazil) to support the usability test using filming and verbalization techniques. This tool was developed to register two events used as data: user face images collected by a image processing framework; keywords pronounced by participants that were registered by a speech recognition software.

The ErgoSV was developed and tested by real participants that performed real activities in three different systems and provided events that allow the evaluator to analysis the software usability.

The next section presents the bibliographic review used in this research.

2   Bibliographic Review

This section presents a bibliographic review performed in order to identify researches related with verbalization/think aloud method concepts and applications.

2.1   Speech Processing

People have several mechanisms to express their emotions and one of the more important ways is the voice. Due to the importance in human life, the voice became an important area of research in computing [16]. Speech Recognition (SR) is the voice interpretation process performed by a computer. It receives an external signal and through computational algorithms performs the transformation of the input data to obtain an output that can be analyzed as a text [11,17].

There are several methods and techniques to perform the SR. The main difference among the techniques is the number of processes performed to transform the voice signal in text, but the basic activities are the same: (1) collect sounds using a resource such as microphone; (2) processing the signal and generating the text; and (3) display the final result [11, 17, 19].

The use of speech processing in different areas such as software development and biometrics raised the needs of tools to easily support the recognition activities in such way that developers do not need to know specific models. Aiming to solve this gap, the Laboratório de Processamento de Sinais (LAPS) in Federal University of Para – Brazil had developed the Coruja Application [17]. This application allows the use of complex speech processing functions in development environments such as Visual Studio coding few and little instructions, since the Coruja has all the complex algorithms implemented in low level.

2.2   Verbalization/Think Aloud

The Think Aloud Method (Verbalization) is a widely used technique that supports usability evaluation. However the initial studies using it were performed in the psychology area. Ericsson and Simon encouraged this technique and began using it similar way of the usability evaluation technique [1,3].

In an evaluation supported by verbalization, the evaluator encourages the participants (traditional users) to verbalize (speak) what they are thinking about the system allowing the evaluator collect real data about the user satisfaction with the system [4,2,13].

The verbalization can be performed according to two strategies [4]: (1) Simultaneously: the participants verbalize what they are thinking about the software in the same time that execute the task. This approach is considered effective because the participants are using the system and all their ideas can be clear in their minds. However this technique requires mental workload due to the reason that the users need to share attention with the verbalization and the use of the system, converting what they are seeing in an word and pronounce it; (2) Consecutive: the participants verbalize what they are thinking about the software after finishing all the tasks. This approach is considered less intrusive because users only perform their tasks using the system and, after finishing, they verbalize what they were thinking about the system, but it is considered slow due to the reason that the participants need to verbalize after the test and so, retarding the evaluation process. Although the participants do not share attention in using the system and in the verbalization, they need to remember what and why they did the activities, requiring a high mental workload.

Using this strategy, the evaluator should work as a manager in order to guarantee that the participants always verbalize some words. Whether the participant keeps more than sixty seconds without pronouncing a word, the evaluator should notify them with several terms such as 'Keep talking', 'Is there any Doubt ?', or 'Do not stop talking' [1,4].

The participants can pronounce any word or phrase according to their opinion such as 'it is good', ' I did not understand this screen', 'the colors are not good' and any other that they think appropriate [1,4,12,13].

The data collection can be done in papers which the evaluator writes what the participants pronounce. The use of microphones, computers and voice recorders are also considered in order to facilitate de collecting and the processing [4]. The use of simultaneously or consecutive verbalization approach is a choice of the evaluator and the results of each test can vary according to user, software and test environment [1].

The verbalization is considered one of the most effective usability evaluation techniques and is used and encouraged by many researchers and specialists due to the reason that it provides real data about user satisfaction. The results of evaluations performed using this technique can vary according to specific contexts that are defined by the evaluators, tasks, participants and software contexts. The use of simultaneous or consecutive approach is an evaluator decision and must be done according to the evaluations needs as well as the data interpretation can be influenced by this choice [1,2,4].

A research performed by [8] presents that the use of the Think Aloud technique to support usability evaluation is considered as suitable by a great number of HCI designers and evaluators. In this study, ninety percent of the researchers and students used the verbalization in order to perform usability evaluation, as well as, seventy percent of the developers.

The next section presents the ErgoSV environment.

3   ErgoSV Software

The ErgoSV Software was developed in order to support usability test using face and speech recognition as data to providing inputs that should allow the evaluator to identify interface with possible usability problems easily and safe.

Aiming to perform the data collect the system was developed using the Microsoft Visual C# Express Edition and contained two resources supported by frameworks: (1) Coruja [11,17]: this framework was used in ErgoSV to perform the speech recognition and write in the software a text with the word pronounced by user; (2) OpenCV [7]: used to perform the face recognition and the image processing activities. These frameworks were chosen because it can be used into the Visual C# Express easily and provide all the resources to access the image and speech recognition functions using few procedures and functions.

ErgoSV was divided in two modules in order to improve the evaluation/monitoring process. One module is used to performing the data collect and process initial data and; the other provides the information processed and organized with the data registered in the first module besides available screen images and details about the user´s events.

3.1   ErgoSV – Collect and Initial Processing

The data collecting stage is performed by the in order to support speech and face images recognition. The first step of the test is to fill a form with user self data. These data are used in the analysis stage to create cross reference information and identify who performed the tests. The next step is the configuration of the ErgoSV. This activity is necessary to guide the monitoring system in the test, and can be done in the ErgoSV main interface, presented in the Figure 1.

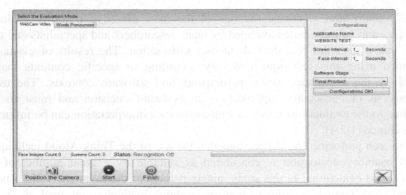

Fig. 1. ErgoSV Initial Screen

The main interface is composed by three sections: tabs; form panel and button panel. The first section has two tabs: the firs tab (WebCam Video) presents the face images during the test in order to position the camera in front of the participant face and verify whether the application is recognizing the face; the other tab (Words Pronounced) presents a list of words recognized by ErgoSV using Coruja application. The tab also shows the register time and the confidence rate.

The form panel has fields to be filled by test self data such as the software tested name, the Screen Interval and the Face Interval. These data should receive inputs to guide the ErgoSV in the images registration activities. The intervals fields receive the time that the software will collect images of the participant face and software snapshots. There are not specific values, however, the ErgoSV suggests the time of three seconds due to reason that according to [12,13] is the middle time of a emotion expression, but the time should by a chosen of the evaluator.

To start the test, the participant should click in the button "Position the Camera" in order to position the webcam in front of their face and after this stage they can select the option "Start". The Start Function starts the ErgoSV monitoring activities and minimizes the application aiming a less interference in the user activities.

The ErgoSV recognizes five keywords pronounced by participants: "Excellent", "Good", "Reasonable", "Bad" and "Terrible" by default but can be replaced by any other group of words as wishes the evaluator.

3.2   ErgoSV Analyzer – Data Analysis and Information Generation

The data analysis is performed using the Analyzer module. The main objective of ErgoSV is the decreasing of the analysis time allowing the evaluator to identify easy and safe interfaces and resource with possible usability problems.

Initially, the software was tested using three different analysis approaches: only words data; only face images data and both words data and face images simultaneously. However, the use of the face image was not considered safe due to the reason that did not allow the easy and safe usability problems identification.

The use of words pronounced was considered appropriate to identify usability problems and provide safe information allowing the identification of possible interface to be reviewed. The analysis data should be performed according to the following steps: (1) select relevant words; (2) Insert interval value; (3) View interfaces or face images; (4) View face images easily; (5) Visualize and analyze interface or face images.

(1) Select relevant words
The evaluator should select a word pronounced by the participant that he/she considered relevant to analyzing. The ErgoSV highlights words considered as bad opinions such as "Regular", "Bad" or "Terrible" due to the reason that these words can present interfaces that must be reviewed by designers.

(2) Insert Interval Value
The interval is the value of time that the ErgoSV should consider to select interfaces and/or face images from the word pronounced time. For example, a word "Bad" was pronounced in the time 10m20s after start the test. If the evaluator input the interval time as 4 seconds, the ErgoSV must select all interfaces image from 10m16s until 10m24s. The same search is performed using face images data.

(3) Select interfaces or face images
After the interval time had been defined, the evaluator can visualize the interfaces used by the participants or their face images from a word pronounced or from a specific interface.

(4) View face images easily;
The evaluator can access the participant face images in the pronounced moment using the image present in the words list right side.

Figure 2 presents the ErgoSV Analyzer interface with highlights to the four resources previously explained named as (1)..(4) in red colour.

Fig. 2. ErgoSV Analyzer Interface

(5) Visualize and analyze interface or face images

This resource presents the interfaces or participant face images in moments near the moment of the word pronunciation. Figure 3 shows the resource to visualize the interfaces images.

Fig. 3. Interface Visualization Resource

The interface visualization presents the snapshots registered in the moment of an event and near to it (considering the interval value). This resource has a main panel to present the image and a panel in the bottom of the interface with some information such as Registration Time, Total of Images loaded, navigation bar, and a image of a ray that highlight the interface used in the exactly moment of the event of pronounced the word.

A hyperlink name "View Face Images" provides a second interface that allows the visualization of an array of face images based on the time of interface registration and the interval input in the resource. Figure 4 presents the interface to visualize and navigate through participant face images.

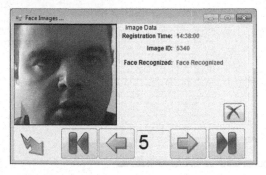

Fig. 4. Face Images Visualization Interface

The use of the keywords as parameters to identify participant's opinions and the use of interfaces and faces images to support the analysis stage allowed the creation of the approached named as "Environment Tree" presented in the Figure 5.

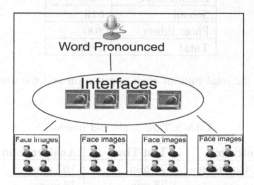

Fig. 5. Environment Tree by ErgoSV

4 Validation and Results

The validation of the ErgoSV tool was performed using three different software: an e-commerce website, a school website and a photo editor desktop software. All of participants performed several activities according to the application type such as searching for a product, buying a product, visualizing professor profile, modified a picture color or create a new pictures based on other images. Two hundred and one words were registered in the tests and distributed according to Table 1.

Table 1. Words Pronounced and Recognized by ErgoSV

	Excellent	Good	Reasonable	Bad	Terrible
E-Commerce	1	59	14	1	2
School	1	16	6	1	0
PhotoEditor	3	27	10	1	0
Total	5	102	30	3	2

Besides the words pronounced, the ErgoSV registered the participants' face images. Table 2 presents the numbers of images registered.

Table 2. Face images registered

Software	Images
E-Commerce	364
School	618
Photo Editor	800
Total	**1778**

Table 3 presents the total time of each application and the time limit of analysis presented in minutes.

Table 3. Time of test and analysis

Software	Test Time	Analyze limit
E-Commerce	71 min.	107 min.
School	25 min.	38 min.
Photo Editor	57 min.	86 min.

The analysis time limit was determinated as 1,5x the time test. There is no scientific parameter to this value, it was choosed due to the reason that it is less than the time presented by [12,13] as minimum time to analyze data and generate relevante information.

The analysis sequence was definied considering the keywords that could be collected in the experiments as tha main parameter to identify possible usability problems interface. Thus, the analysis was done studing:

- Keywords that meant opinions such as "Reasonable", " Bad" or "Terrible";
- Keyword that meant the great user opinion: Excellent;
- Special cases with the keyword "Good".

The data analysis was performed using two different approaches: only words data; and both words data and faces images. Both approaches used the snapshots registered during the test.

The "Only Words" analysis approach was considered satisfactory, easy to use and fast. So, it allowed the evaluator to identify which interfaces were not good according to participants opinions. The time to identify the interfaces was low and the keywords selected to the experiments supported this activities appropriatedly because all the words had clear means, i.e., it was easy to identify whether the participant liked or disliked the interface.

However, this approach presented a problem: the evaluator did not identify which was the user focus in the moment of an event. For example, it was possible to find a bad interface, but this interface had several resources and the evaluators did not identify what resource were used by the participants. This problems was solved using the face imagens since the images provide the eyes position and so, it was possible to identify what was the focus of the participant in the moment of an event reducing the area to be analysed by the evaluator and providing a safe information about the resource classified by participant.

Figure 6 presents the time analysis comparing to time test and analysis time limit.

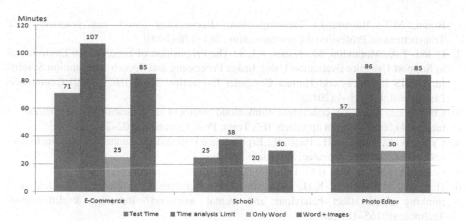

Fig. 6. Times achieved in the tests

5 Conclusions

Usability evaluation is a group of activities that must be performed in order to verify whether the interface has usability problems. The usability test is a technique of usability evaluation that must be realized to test the software interaction capacity, i.e., how the interface/interaction interfere in the participant activities.

Filming and verbalization are two widely used techniques, however are considered slowed due to the reason that the evaluator needs to review a vary amount of data manually and sequentially.

This paper presented the ErgoSV software, a tool that uses speech and face images recognition to support the collection and data analysis in usability tests. The focus of this research was the decrease of the time to identify possible usability problems in the interfaces. The use of keywords with significant means supported the identification of users opinions reducing the time to identify possible problems. The ErgoSV provided a highlight to keywords that could be relevant for analysis and so, the evaluator could easily and safely identify the problems. The interface and face images visualization resource allows the evaluator to accomplish what happen in the moment of an event and few seconds before and after this moment.

Finally, the experiments presented that this tool reduced the time to identify the interfaces with possible usability problems from 2 to 10 times the test time to 1,5 times. The use of face images allowed the identification of the user focus supporting the analysis of the interface and the classification of which resources were used by the user.

Acknowledgments. The authors are grateful to Fundação de Amparo à Pesquisa do Estado de São Paulo (FAPESP).

References

1. Boren, M.T., Ramey, J.: Thinking aloud: Reconciling theory and practice. IEEE Transactions on Professional Communication, 261–278 (2000)
2. Coleti, T.A., Morandini, M., Nunes, F.L.S.: The Proposition of ErgoSV: An Environment to Support Usability Evaluation Using Image Processing and Speech Recognition System. In: IADIS Interfaces and Human Computer Interaction 2012 (IHCI 2012) Conference, Lisbon, vol. 1, pp. 1–4 (2012)
3. Cooke, L.: Assessing concurrent think-aloud protocol as a usability test method: A technical communication approach. IEE Trans. Prof. Commun., 202–215 (2010)
4. Cybis, W.A., Betiol, A.H., Faust, R.: Ergonomia e Usabilidade: conhecimentos, métodos e aplicações, 2nd edn., Novatec, São Paulo (2010)
5. Gonzalez, R.C., Woods, R.E.: Digital image processing. Addison-Wesley, Reading (1992)
6. Hertzum, M., Hansen, K.D., Andersen, H.H.: Scrutinising usability evaluation: does thinking aloud affect behaviour and mental workload? Behavior & Information Technology, 165–181 (2009)
7. Lima, J.P.S.M., et al.: Reconhecimento de padrões em tempo real utilizando a biblioteca OpenCV. Técnicas e Ferramentas de Processamento de Imagens Digitais e Aplicações em Realidade Virtual e Misturada, 47–89 (2008)
8. Mcdonald, S., Edwards, H.M., Zhao, T.: Exploring think-alouds in usability testing: An international survey. IEEE Transactions on Professional Communication (2011)
9. Morandini, M.: Ergo-Monitor: Monitoramento da Usabilidade em Ambiente Web por Meio de Análise de Arquivos de Log. Tese (Doutorado) - Universidade Federal de Santa Catarina (2003)
10. Morandini, M., de Moraes Rodrigues, R.L., Cerrato, M.V., Chaim, M.L.: Project and Development of ErgoCoIn Version 2.0. In: Jacko, J.A. (ed.) Human-Computer Interaction, Part I, HCII 2011. LNCS, vol. 6761, pp. 471–479. Springer, Heidelberg (2011)
11. Neto, N., Patrick, C., Klautau, A., Trancoso, I.: Free tools and resources for Brazilian Portuguese speech recognition. J. Braz. Computing Society, 53–68 (2011), doi:10.1007/s13173-010-0023-1
12. Nielsen, J.: Usability Engineering. Morgan Kaufmann, Moutain View (1993)
13. Nielsen, J.: Designing Web Sites - Designing Web Usability, Campus (2000)
14. Nunes, F.L.S.: Introdução ao processamento de imagens médicas para auxílio a diagnóstico – uma visão prática. In: Livro das Jornadas de Atualizações em Informática, pp. 73–126 (2006)
15. Preece, J., Rogers, Y., Sharp, H.: Design de Interação: Além da interação homem-computador, Bookman, Porto Alegre, Rio Grande do Sul – Brasil (2005)
16. Shariah, M.A., et al.: Human computer interaction using isolated-words speech recognition technology. In: International Conference on Intelligent and Advanced Systems (2007)
17. Silva, P., et al.: An open-source speech recognizer for Brazilian Portuguese with a windows programming interface. In: The International Conference on Computational Processing of Portuguese (PROPOR) (2010)
18. http://www.laps.ufpa.br/falabrasil/ (accessed in December 2011)
19. Agus, T., et al.: Characteristics of human voice processing. In: Proceedings of 2010 IEEE International Symposium on Circuits and Systems (ISCAS), pp. 509–512. [S.l.: s.n.] (2010)
20. ISO9241. Ergonomic requirements for office work with visual display terminals

Identifying Intention and Perception Mismatches in Digitally Augmented Museum Settings

Hanna-Liisa Pender and David Lamas

Tallinn University
Institute of Informatics
Narva mnt. 29, 10120 Tallinn
Estonia
{hanna-liisa.pender,david.lamas}@tlu.ee

Abstract. The key aim of introducing information and communication technology (ICT) in museum settings is to enhance the visitors' experience. However, the concrete strategies or best practices for digitally augmenting the museums remain to be determined. The main role of the ICT solutions in a museum context should be the mediation of the communication between the visitors and the museum artefacts to support the meaning making process. However, a large number of existing solutions fail to fulfil this task. In this paper we evaluate two digital interactive displays in different museums with Semiotic Engineering methods to detect mismatches between designers' intentions and visitors' perceptions in this communication process.

Keywords: Evaluation methods and techniques, semiotic inspection method, communicability evaluation method, museums.

1 Introduction

There is a growing tendency to use information and communication technology (ICT) in museums is to enhance the visitor experience and many museum researchers have agreed that the visitor experience can be adequately described in terms of meaning making. *Meaning making* generally refers to an active interpretation of objects and events, through which an individual or a group develops a personal meaning, deeply integrated with ones own values, beliefs, feelings, and aspirations [3].

With some exceptions, designing ICT solutions for museums is currently a variety of *black art* [3] i.e. there are no clear guidelines or strategies that would support the design processes for this particular context. While there are some extraordinary museum exhibits and settings designed by skilled and creative people, the results of the design processes related to the domain of cultural heritage are far too often discouraging, as...

- ICT solutions fail to actively engage the museum visitors and do not provide sufficient support for the meaning making process [3].

M. Kurosu (Ed.): Human-Computer Interaction, Part I, HCII 2014, LNCS 8510, pp. 565–576, 2014.
© Springer International Publishing Switzerland 2014

- The design solutions are in most cases intuition based, i.e. no methodology or analytical approach has been used in the design process [4].
- Further, the ICT solutions implemented in museums fail to meet even the real needs of the visitors as well as museum staff and are plagued with usability problems [4].

This papers working hypothesis is that one of the reasons for the apparent lack of success of ICT solutions in museum settings is a mismatch between designers' intentions and users' perceptions. And therefore the aim is to identify these mismatches with the help of Semiotic Engineering methods.

2   Semiotic Engineering

Semiotic Engineering methods were chosen to address the challenge of identifying mismatches between designers' intentions and users' perceptions due to their emphasis on communicability.

Communicability is seen as an attribute of software artefacts related to how efficiently and effectively their underlying design intents and interaction principles are conveyed to their users.

The two qualitative methods for evaluating the communicability of software artefacts are:

- The Semiotic Inspection Method (SIM) [7]; and
- The Communicability Evaluation Method (CEM) [5].

The goal of SIM method is to examine the meta-message being sent by the designer. The high level message will be reconstructed using the Semiotic Engineering template [2].

CEM is based on the observation of how a small group of users interacts with a specific system. It focuses on identifying communication breakdowns users may experience while having to interpret the designers message.

Although described as technology and application independent, until now, the semiotic engineering methods have mainly been used in a controlled lab setting and in most cases for evaluating application software [6][1]. This study will apply the methods in a field context where the users have different expectations towards the software artefacts, namely in the context of using ICT in museums.

3   The Study

Considering the above described context, the goals of the work herein reported are:

- To reify the hypothesis that one of the reasons for the apparent lack of success of ICT solutions in museum settings is a mismatch between designers' intentions and users' perceptions; and

- To assess the effectiveness of the combined use of the semiotic inspection and communicability evaluation methods to identify and explain these intention and perception mismatches.

In order to fulfil the above-mentioned goals, a parallel study was deployed in two museums in Tallinn, Estonia. These museums will be referred to as Museum A and Museum B from now on:

- Museum A is a recently renovated museum that has a digitally augmented exposition about the history of the financial system and an overview of how the contemporary financial system functions. The renovated exposition was opened in January 2013 and it was designed with the intention to engage a younger audience.
- Museum B is situated in a 314 meters high communications tower that was opened after an extensive renovation in spring 2012. The entire exhibition consists of digital interactive displays that aim to give an overview of the progress and achievements of the nearby region.

The main rationale behind the choice of the museums was the extensive integration of digital interactive displays in the expositions. Both exhibitions were developed as a whole i.e. the digital interactive solutions were a part of the initial vision, not secondarily added to already existing exhibitions.

3.1 Method

The procedure comprised the application, to the materials of both museums, of the semiotic inspection method (SIM) to identify the designer teams' intentions, and of the communicability evaluation method (CEM) to render the visitors' perceptions.

While applying SIM, the goal was to reconstruct the designers intended message to the system user by identifying answers to following orientation questions [6]:

- What is the designer communicating?
- To whom is the designer's message addressed?
- What effect(s) does the designer expect his communication to cause?
- How is the designer signifying his communication?
- What expectations does the designer have about what users will want to communicate to the system?
- How, where, when, and why does the designer expect users to engage in communication with the system?

The method includes the analysis of the project documentation and the solution deployed in the museum followed by a discussion with the design team. It consists of five core steps [6], including...

- Analysing metalinguistic signs, in this case the documentation from the design and development process.

– Analysing static signs. Static signs are those that do not change when interaction takes place e.g. buttons state, interactive element used, selected options;
– Analysing dynamic signs. The dynamic signs represent the system behaviour, in other words, they can only be perceived through the interaction with the system (e.g., action triggered by a button);
– Comparing the results of first three steps to determine the consistency of designers metacommunication message; and
– Evaluating the inspected system's communicability.

The visitors' perceptions were depicted with CEM using data collected about the visitors' semi-directed activities. The focus questions [6] were:

– How is the user interpreting the designer's communication?
– What does the user want to communicate and how can she do it?
– What effect does the user want her communication to produce?
– How is the user signifying her communication?
– How is the user communication being interpreted by the system?

The method was enacted in three steps:

– Tagging the passages where communication breakdown was noticeable with a set of tags [6];
– Interpreting the meaning of the set of dispersed tags; and
– Characterising the metacommunication message's reception by composing a semiotic profile.

3.2 Participants

Seven museum visitors participated in the CEM study in museum A and six visitors in museum B. The participants in museum A were all female with at least a bachelor's degree. The average age of the group was 29. They evaluated themselves as being rather novice users of large touch screens and only one person identified herself as being knowledgeable about the topic presented by the interactive display. The participants in museum B were five females and one male and the average age of the group was 21. Only one participant had a bachelor's degree, others were still students or had graduated high school. Most of the participants in museum B evaluated their expertise in using large touch screens above average and their knowledge of the topic presented by the display below average. None of the participants of either group had ever participated in the development process of a similar interactive display.

Relevant input for the SIM study was acquired with the help of museum representatives, the museum directors in both cases, who took part of the development process of the exhibitions and the interactive displays under investigation.

3.3   Materials

For both museums, the materials of the study were:

- The documentation from the design and development process (system requirements documents);
- Semi-structured interviews with museum representatives;
- One interactive display in each museum;
- The data collected while monitoring and recording the semi-directed activities of the CEM study participants (video recordings, observation notes);
- Pre- and post-session interviews with CEM study participants.

3.4   Procedure

Although there were several displays with similar design in both museums, the content and structure of these was in general comparable and therefore only one display was chosen for in depth analysis in both museums to avoid unnecessary repetition. Both of the displays chosen were 40" touch screens integrated in custom design frames.

Further more, both of the chosen displays had more than one topic stream that could be explored from the main menu (display in museum A — 3 streams, museum B — 4 streams). State transition diagrams (e.g. Fig. 1.) were drawn for both software artefacts under investigation and the streams with most complex interaction possibilities were chosen for further evaluation:

- The aim of the interactive display in museum A was to explain how different types of electronic payment systems function. Semiotic evaluation methods were applied to one specific stream of the display, concerned with electronic card payments.
- The aim of the interactive display stream in museum B was to explain the historical development of the region that could be seen from the telecommunication tower windows behind the display.

Field Data Collection for the Semiotic Inspection Method. The implementation of SIM started with systematically photographing all possible states of the interactive displays for the analysis of static signs. A systematic video recording was done for the purpose of analysing the dynamic signs. The input for metadata analysis was the system requirements document.

Empirical Data Collection for Communicability Evaluation Method. The application of CEM started with preparing a scenario for the study. The scenario determined the context for the study participant and introduced the purpose of the study. The study was conducted by the two authors of the paper. The task of one of the authors was to recruit the participants, explain them the purpose of the study, get their informed consent to participate in the study, conduct a short interview with the purpose of determining their profile and to

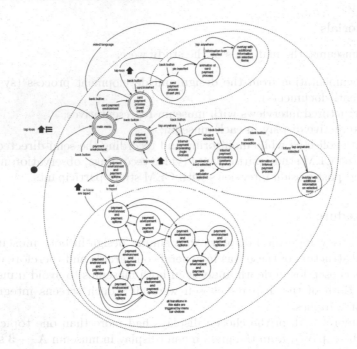

Fig. 1. State transition diagram for the selected interactive display of museum A

explain the tasks to be completed. The other author of the paper was observing the participants from a distance while they were completing the tasks and making notes about the communication breakdowns on the printouts of the state transition diagrams of the software artefact (e.g. Fig. 1).

The participants of the study were asked to complete four tasks:

1. Exploring the display stream without any time constraint while commenting aloud what they were doing.
2. Looking for the answer to a more specific question about the content. The specific question depended on their behaviour in first task i.e. to what extent they explored the artefact content.
3. Explaining their understanding of the structure of the information displayed.
4. Pointing out a surprising or new fact that they discovered while exploring the display.

The participants were video recorded with two cameras while completing the tasks. One camera was recording the face impressions and other the hand movements on the interactive display.

A post-session interview was conducted after the participants had completed all four tasks. The questions were based on the observation notes and aimed to clarify the communication breakdown situations.

3.5   Results

Results are presented grouped by method. First the results of applying the SIM will be presented to describe the designers intentions, then the CEM results will follow to give an overview of visitors perception of the intended messages.

Results of Applying the Semiotic Inspection Method. SIM aims to re-construct the designer's message in its entirety. The results of the SIM study are displayed in Table 1. The High level messages were re-constructed by answering the Semiotic Engineering method template question: Who the user is, what does the user want or need to do and which are the preferred ways for the user to achieve these goals and why?

From the process it became clear that there were mismatches between the supplied documentation and the static and dynamic signs. These differences are apparent, for instance, in the underlying distinct understandings of who the user is. Mismatches, or at least, a very particular interpretation of what the initial documents described also surfaced in the case of the authentication simulation, that ended up being implemented as partially physical authentication simulation comprised of a card, a card reader and a digital simulation of an ATM keyboard.

In case of museum B we see an evident mismatch between the museum representatives expectations and designers intentions that are clearly reflected in the outcome of the design process. The software artefact presents a partial overview of the most important developments (four events per each period in addition to forest and coastline changes) in the region and manages to contextualize these spatially to some extent.

Results of Applying the Communicability Evaluation Method. CEM results were generated from the collected data by tagging the passages where communication breakdown was noticeable, by interpreting the meaning of the set of dispersed tags, and by composing a semiotic profile in order to characterise the metacommunication message's reception.

Regarding museum A, tagging and interpreting the resulting tags uncovered a number of communication breakdowns. Half of the breakdowns lead to complete failures (50%), equally distributed between abandonment (issues tagged with "I give up") and clueless behaviour (issues tagged with "looks fine to me"). Giving up was systematically related with the need to act upon a physical card and card reader set instead of manipulating their digital representations. The clueless behaviour was mostly due to missing the intended and hinted connections between some of the different types of information presented.

The remaining breakdowns mostly lead to temporary sense making failures (issues tagged with "What now?" were predominant but "Where am I?" and "Where is it?" tags were also assigned). "What now?" tags were mostly related with failure to realise that the illustrations and process steps, depicted in the screen, are clickable and can be explored. The remaining temporary sense making failures are also related to the visualization of the electronic payment system but denote disorientation rather than uncertainty. For example, one participant tried

Table 1. SIM results: reconstructing the meta-communication message

	Museum A	Museum B
Documentation	The users are visitors at least 10 years old, seeking an introduction to how a card payment system works and after an initial authentication simulation, they will get interactive, visually appealing and informative information about the electronic card payment process.	The visitor speaks Estonian, English or Russian and needs to get a versatile and exciting overview of the development of city that can be seen from the tower windows by manipulating 3D models of the city that represent different periods of it's development in history. The 3D models are equipped with an additional information layer that explains the most important developments of the period.
Static Signs	Visitors are tall enough to reach the screen with or without the help of a stool and speak Estonian, English or Russian. After a partially physical authentication simulation (the card and card reader are physical but the PIN number is introduced in a simulated keyboard on the screen), these visitors, will get interactive, visually appealing and informative information about the electronic payment process.	The user is a visitor who speaks at least one of the three languages mentioned, can reach the display and needs to know about four historical events or facts from different periods of history about the city as well as the changes that have taken place on the landscape (decline of forest and sea line) that is displayed on a panorama photo of the surrounding area that can be see from the tower windows.
Dynamic Signs	Visitors are tall enough to reach the screen with or without the help of a stool, speak Estonian, English or Russian. After a partially physical authentication simulation (the card and card reader are physical but the PIN number is introduced in a simulated keyboard on the screen), these visitors, will need to be able to follow interactive and visually appealing information simultaneously in different parts of the screen and to make sense of the complex banking terminology used to explain the card payment process.	The user is a visitor who speaks at least one of the three languages, can reach the screen and needs to know about four historical events or facts from different periods of history about the city as well as the changes that have taken place on the landscape (decline of forest and sea line). The extra layer of information is represented by and related to the spatial dimension with the help of small tappable icons situated on a 180 degrees panorama photo that needs to be scrolled from left to right.

to click on the description of the steps of the process before the animation was finished not realizing that the steps were not actionable before the end of the animation.

The fact that half of the issues consisted of complete failures seems to indicate that the interface's semiotic resources failed to scaffold the participant in the process of grasping how the system works. This interpretation is further supported by the fact that 50% of these communication breakdowns resulted in abandonment. Further the interface's semiotic resources lead otherwise to states of clueless behaviour, uncertainty and disorientation. Taking these findings into consideration, it is reasonable to infer that the semiotic resources have systematically failed to enable valid understandings about how the system works, although, in most cases, there were enough clues to enable recovery after mediated interventions. In other words, provided the assistance needed to recover from the complete failures, most participants were eventually able to make sense out of the available resources.

Finally, as for museum B, after tagging and subsequently interpreting the resulting set of tags, it surfaced that most of the temporary errors were recurrent and therefore represented 80% of the total communication breakdowns that occurred, while only 20% of the failures were complete and no partial failures were revealed.

Within the temporary failures, the study participants mainly manifested short-term sense-making issues equally distributed between past events (issues tagged as "What happened?") and future possibilities (issues tagged as "What now?"). The most common communication breakdowns were related with missing affordances e.g. most of the participants of the study had difficulties accessing the additional information layer from the landscape panorama. Relevant icons were interpreted as directions to scroll from left to right instead of as access points to additional information. Another major communication error was related to the navigation principles - half of the study participants did not understand the basic navigation principles, namely scrolling the panorama landscape. The scrolling only functioned with one finger and using more than one finger triggered an unwanted zoom in.

4   Discussion

Although in case of museum A the deviations of the metacommunication message of the static and dynamic signs compared to the initial documentation were only mild, these influenced the perception of the messages considerably. For example:

- The most evident and complete communication errors were caused by the design decision to bring the simulation of a card payment process partially off the digital screen and into the physical realm. Although the requirements document asked the designers to simulate the initiation of a card payment to make it the following process more relatable for the visitor, it was not specified that it should be done off screen;

- The decision to to bring the card payment partially off the screen would have required further instructions indicating towards the physical card and card reader that was hardly noticeable to the visitors standing in front of the digital display;
- Another common communication error was caused by the fact that the design team dismissed the initial definition of the user profile - the content of the interactive display was supposed to be clearly understandable for visitors older than 10 years;
- The animation of the card payment process aimed to explain the structure and logic of the process by depicting the six different parties involved in the process and the transactions between them represented by colour coded and numbered 14 arrows. The numbers were related to the 9 steps of the process that were shown appearing on the right side of the screen, one after another, at the same time that the related transactions took place in the animation. The whole animation lasted for 45 seconds. The CEM study indicated that no participants were able to follow the animation and make the connections between the colour coded and numbered arrows and similarly colour coded and numbered steps of the process. Only two participants out of seven figured out the connection after the animation had ended and one was able to connect the steps with the animation from the start. However she was not able to follow it in real time and needed to use both of her hands to keep track of the steps and transactions indicated in the animation.

The CEM study clearly indicated that study participants without extensive knowledge about the domain were unable to grasp most of the content during the short period such displays are usually explored. When asking from the study participants in the interview after the CEM session if they understood how the explained process works, four persons out of seven indicated that their knowledge level about the process was still below average. They understood that the process contains multiple parties and is much more complicated than they would have expected. One study participant explained that the topic was not engaging for her and since it was not explained in a easily comprehensive way, she did not bother to follow the information. Two of the participants with above average knowledge of the domain to start with were able to follow the process, which might be partially related to confirming their previous knowledge of the system.

In the case of museum B we saw a strong difference between the initial expectations of the museum representatives and the design team that lead to an incomplete solution. For example:

- The initial requirements for the design and development team clearly expected a virtual reality solution with 3D models from four historical periods of the city that could have been manipulated on the screen by the visitors. Instead the solution was a panorama photo that could be scrolled from left to right.
- The 3D models were required to include an extra information layer that would have explained the most important developments of the city during the

four different periods. Instead, the panorama picture contained four spatially situated facts or events about each period that did not give a comprehensive overview of the developments.

As for the perception mismatches, apart from the fact that missing affordances rendered museum visitors incapable of accessing most of the available information, the designers intention of using large touch screens as augmented reality periscopes was totally lost. For example:

- It was difficult for the study participants to understand that there was a panorama photo of the surrounding area on display that needed to be scrolled left and right to access a large part of the additional information layer. For two participants this resulted in a complete communication error - they gave up exploring the screen because they did not find any additional information.
- The *play* icons representing the spatially situated extra information layer on the panorama picture were un-obvious access points in most cases. For three participants the icons signified *scroll right* instead of access point to additional information.

As such, in the case of Museum B, the effects of the mismatches between intentions and perceptions are abundant and mainly related to the fact that the initially intended augmented reality experience was scaled down to an information kiosk solution without adequate reframing of the enabling interaction metaphors. For instance, the interface retained the initial *information layer* layer metaphor but did no longer include the actual landscape to support it. The result was the provision of information bubbles on top of a static but wide panorama, that by being static, failed to evoke the possibility of panning and thus prevented visitors from finding most of the information bubbles.

Finally and when reflecting about the results obtained through applying SIM and CEM in these two settings, a common cause for the identified issues emerged: although the design teams were able to apprehend the requirements outlined by the museum representatives, they failed to understand the wider context of the solutions they worked on. In other words, they failed to understand the implications their design decisions had beyond the interface.

This single but relevant fact suggests the need for common ground between all involved in the design of ICT solutions for museum settings, eventually manifested as a framework that scaffolds such design processes.

5   Conclusion

On one hand, the results of the study indicate why and where the mismatches between intent and perception occur and how it would be possible to avoid these when designing digital installations for the cultural heritage setting. On the other hand, the study fostered the understanding of how can both SIM and CEM be applied in a cultural heritage setting, where, as mentioned before, the role of the digital solutions should be to support the meaning making process.

It can thus be concluded that the combined use of the semiotic evaluation methods enabled us to identify the mismatches between the designers intentions and the users perceptions as well as helped to shed light to the reasons why these mismatches occur.

In fact, using SIM enabled not only the identification of mismatches between users and designers but also between designers and museum representatives. There were clear communication errors during the design process that resulted in failures to understand the design implication that were supposed to support the meaning making for the visitors in both museums.

On the other hand, CEM proved useful highlights about the effects of these mismatches and therefore in large part confirmed the results of the SIM study.

Finally, there is clearly the need to further investigate the causes of expectation and intention mismatches as these might, after all, be influenced by factors not typically stressed by the literature, such as poor articulation within the teams designing, developing and deploying ICT solutions in museum settings.

References

1. De S. Reis, S., Prates, R.O.: Applicability of the semiotic inspection method: A systematic literature review. In: Proceedings of the 10th Brazilian Symposium on on Human Factors in Computing Systems and the 5th Latin American Conference on Human-Computer Interaction, IHC+CLIHC 2011, pp. 177–186. Brazilian Computer Society, Porto Alegre (2011), http://dl.acm.org/citation.cfm?id=2254436.2254468
2. De Souza, C.S., Leitão, C.F.: Semiotic engineering methods for scientific research in HCI. Synthesis Lectures on Human-Centered Informatics 2(1), 1–122 (2009)
3. Kaptelinin, V.: Designing technological support for meaning making in museum learning: an activity-theoretical framework. In: 2011 44th Hawaii International Conference on System Sciences (HICSS), pp. 1–10. IEEE (2011)
4. Pierroux, P., Kaptelinin, V., Hall, T., Walker, K., Bannon, L., Stuedahl, D.: MUSTEL: Framing the design of technology-enhanced learning activities for museum visitors. In: ICHIM (2007)
5. Prates, R.O., de Souza, C.S., Barbosa, S.D.J.: Methods and tools: A method for evaluating the communicability of user interfaces. Interactions 7(1), 31–38 (2000), http://doi.acm.org/10.1145/328595.328608
6. de Souza, C.S.: The semiotic engineering of human–computer interaction. MIT Press, Cambridge (2005)
7. de Souza, C.S., Leitão, C.F., Prates, R.O., da Silva, E.J.: The semiotic inspection method. In: Proceedings of VII Brazilian Symposium on Human Factors in Computing Systems, IHC 2006, pp. 148–157. ACM, New York (2006), http://doi.acm.org/10.1145/1298023.1298044

Heuristics for Assessing Emotional Response of Viewers during the Interaction with TV Programs

Kamila Rios da Hora Rodrigues, Cesar Augusto Camillo Teixeira,
and Vânia Paula de Almeida Neris

Department of Computer Science, Federal University of São Carlos/UFSCar,
São Carlos, Brazil
{kamila_rodrigues,cesar,vania}@dc.ufscar.br

Abstract. The analysis of emotional cues can provide practitioners a more accurate understanding of the user's experience. The literature mentions several techniques for gathering affective data which do not involve questioning users. However, most of them have drawbacks as they can be intrusive, expensive or require additional evaluation. To minimize these problems, methods using inspection based on heuristics have been employed. These methods, on the other hand, do not consider emotional responses. There are gestures and facial expressions which are inherent in the interaction with this kind of media and must be taken into account. We propose the TV Emotion Heuristics (TVEH), a set of 23 heuristics that represent viewer's behavioral patterns when interacting with TV programs or movies. These heuristics allow a comprehensive assessment of the viewers' emotional responses. This paper reports the creation process of the TVEH and describes how to apply the method. Two case studies are reported using the proposed heuristics and we discuss some of the lessons that have been learned.

Keywords: Heuristic Evaluation, Emotional Response, Interactive Media, TV Emotion Heuristics, Assessment Methods.

1 Introduction

Studies of the human emotions are essential to obtain an understanding of users, as these can assist in providing information about their interest in a subject or goal [1]. An analysis of this affective dimension can help designers and developers ensure that the users will be engaged and motivated while using computational systems. Analyzing and evaluating emotional cues can provide practitioners with a more accurate understanding of the user's experience [1].

There is a growing number of HCI researchers that have been investigating the role of emotions in the design and evaluation of a UI [2], [3]. Zhang and Li [4], for instance, suggest that the quality of interactive products in general, consists of three elements: utility (usefulness), ease of use (usability), and enjoyment (affective quality).

According to Chorianopoulos and Spinellis [5] emotional issues, such as viewer satisfaction, are usually measured by eliciting the users' opinions about specific issues and may also include questions about subjective (perceived) usefulness and ease of use.

M. Kurosu (Ed.): Human-Computer Interaction, Part I, HCII 2014, LNCS 8510, pp. 577–588, 2014.
© Springer International Publishing Switzerland 2014

In the literature, it is possible to find techniques for gathering affective data, many of which do not involve questioning users. However, most of the methods have limi- · tations as they can be intrusive for the user, incur high costs and require additional evaluation. Some authors propose the use of Heuristic Evaluations to overcome this problem. This technique can be used to help understand the emotional response of a person during the interaction with systems, and supplements current methods by adding another dimension to the evaluation process [1].

The studies found in the literature about heuristic evaluation for TV programs, in a particular way, describe heuristics related to usability [6], [7], [8] and sociability [9] with regard to interactive applications (iTV). Solano et al. [8] propose 14 usability heuristics based on Nielsen's heuristics. Chorianopoulos [6] and Collazos et al. [7] also use heuristics that are similar to those proposed by Solano et al. [8] to evaluate usability in an iTV application. Geerts and Grooff [9] outline 12 sociability heuristics for evaluating aspects of sociability on TV. The heuristics are based on several studies involving social TV systems and viewers.

With regard to heuristics used to evaluate other interactive media such as games, Desurvire et al. [10] describe Heuristic Evaluation for Playability (HEP), a comprehensive set of heuristics for playability. The authors defined four heuristic categories (game play, game story, game mechanics and game usability). These authors believe that HEP is helpful in early game design and that user studies are best suited to locate specific problems and make it easier to think about the design from the user's standpoint.

The heuristics and assessments cited, do not consider emotional responses. However, during an interactive session there are gestures and facial expressions, for example, which are inherent in the interaction with this kind of media and reveal a lot about what is experienced by the user.

Lera and Domingo [1] formalized a set of heuristics to evaluate the user's affective dimension more easily and in a cost-effective way. These heuristics allow the users' behavior to be observed and determine their emotional state during their interaction with computer systems. However, the writers state that the Ten Emotion Heuristics are appropriate for systems in which designers are looking for a neutral and relaxed interaction with the application. This does not apply to media such as interactive movies and interactive TV programs, which are the focal point of our studies [11], [12] or to games.

Some of the gestures and expressions observed in a TV session are not covered by the Ten Emotion Heuristics [1], nor are they evaluated by the heuristics of usability and sociability proposed in the literature.

In this scenario, we propose a set of twenty-three heuristics that represent viewers' behavior when interacting with TV programs or movies. We call them TV Emotion Heuristics (TVEH). The new heuristics emerged from a period of 3 years´ observation and evaluation of a sample of 43 different viewers, making a total of 1055 minutes of video recorded from several sessions of different TV programs and movies. The new heuristics were formalized by a certain methodology and allowed a comprehensive assessment of the viewers' emotional response in a TV session. The set incorporates Lera and Domingo's heuristics.

This paper is structured as follows: Section 2 outlines reports the creation process of the TVEH. Section 3 describes how to apply the method that contains the new heuristics and how to evaluate the incidence of heuristics to determine the viewers' emotional response. Section 4 examines two case studies; carried out in different scenarios; using the proposed heuristics. Section 5 addresses the problem of some limitations and discusses the lessons learned.

2   The TV Emotion Heuristics Creation Process

As mentioned earlier, media such as interactive movies and interactive TV programs or games, do not provide a neutral and relaxed interaction. These media are usually longer and, probably, arouse a wider range of emotions and types of reaction in users who interact with them. The TV Emotion Heuristics allow a comprehensive assessment of the gestures and expressions revealed during a TV session.

The heuristics formalization process followed the methodology proposed by Rusu et al. [13] where 6 stages are outlined to establish new heuristics for specific applications, which are as follows: STEP 1, an *exploratory* stage, to collect bibliographic material related to the main topics of the research: specific applications, their characteristics, general and/or related heuristics (if they exist); STEP 2, called the *descriptive* stage, to highlight the key features of the previously collected information, to formalize the main concepts associated with the research; STEP 3, a *correlational* stage, to compare similar characteristics between the proposed heuristics and the heuristics outlined in the literature for specific applications. This stage is based on traditional heuristics and an analysis of case studies; STEP 4, was an *explicative* stage, to formally specify the set of the proposed heuristics, using a template; STEP 5, a *validation* stage, to compare the new heuristics with traditional heuristics by conducting experiments involving heuristic evaluations carried out with selected case studies, and supplemented with user tests; STEP 6, a *refinement* stage, based on feedback from the validation stage.

STEP 1: The authors conducted an exploratory study in the literature which entailed looking for studies with heuristic evaluations related to emotion and applied to interactions with TV programs. This requirement arose from the need to assess the emotional responses of viewers during a TV session. On the basis of this exploratory study of the literature, and by drawing on the expertise of research colleagues, the data collected in previous studies with viewers, were evaluated, following the hybrid approach proposed by Xavier and Neris [14]. This approach is adopted for the emotional evaluation of the users while they interact with information systems and considers the observations that were made from different components. One of these components is motor expression and to assess this component, Xavier and Neris [14] recommend the Ten Emotion Heuristics [1]. This has been the method applied in the case studies of this group of researchers.

Moreover, in this exploratory phase, some authors were found in the literature who describe heuristics with regard to assessing aspects of TV. Among these writers are: Collazos et at. [7] and Solano at al. [8] from the standpoint of usability and Geerts and Grooff [9] from the standpoint sociability.

STEP 2: In this descriptive stage, relevant studies were analyzed and the most important characteristics were collected. However, it was clear that the techniques and approach adopted did not consider emotional factors. Furthermore, the Ten Emotion Heuristics [1] do not include all the gestures and expressions that occur in the interaction with TV programs. In the first case studies evaluated by means of the Ten Heuristics it was evident that it left blanks.

STEP 3: This correlational stage is based on traditional heuristics and an analysis of case studies. Thus, the Ten Emotion Heuristics [1] approach was employed in the evaluation of the emotional responses of viewers from videos collected of case studies over 3 years of research. These viewers were observed during interactive TV sessions and their physical and facial images were captured.

After observing a scenario in which other heuristics were applied and examining the previous evaluations of these authors when the Ten Emotion Heuristics [1], we noted that these methods fail to evaluate the viewers' emotions with precision and that, by relying on them alone, it is not possible to infer whether the viewer is satisfied or not with the displayed content.

For this reason, we proposed creating a new set heuristics that represent the viewer's behaviors when interacting with TV programs or movies.

STEP 4: In this stage, the set of proposed heuristics was formally specified, using a template. The template used in STEP 4 is shown in Table 1.

The set of heuristics (14-23) were incorporated from Lera and Domingo [1]. Some of them the name, description and status of experience were adapted to suit the TV domain and other kinds of interactive media.

Table 1. Emotion Heuristics for TV programs

ID/ TVEH	Name	Description	Experience
colspan header	TV Emotion Heuristics – TVEH		
01	Restless feet and/or legs	Signs of irritation, impatience, dislike.	Negative
02	Crossing/ Uncrossing arms	Signs of irritation, impatience or desire to escape from this situation.	Negative
03	Physical Adjustments	Looking for a way to. May be a sign of relaxation. It can also be a sign of annoyance.	Positive Negative
04	Nodding one´s head	Showing agreement with a situation.	Positive
05	Shaking one´s head	Disagreeing with a situation. It may also represent a sign of detachment.	Negative
06	Moving one´s hands	Sign of impatience, frustration or tension.	Negative
07	Crying	Sign of disappointment, sorrow, regret or affliction. It can also be a sign of being moved or an upsurge of sudden, relief and joy.	Negative Positive
08	Shouting/ Scared	Sign of protest, extreme expression of dissatisfaction, annoyance or an expression of being scared. It may also shown someone´s full involvement with the scene.	Negative Positive

Table 1. (*continued*)

09	Breathing Deeply	Sign of irritation or musing. It may be a sign of a desire to escape from a situation. It can also be a sign of involvement with the scene.	Negative Positive
10	Sleeping /Dozing off / Yawning	Sign of boredom, dissatisfaction or desire to get away from a situation.	Negative
11	Turn one´s face away from the scene	Sign of fear, repugnance, disbelief or irritation.	Negative
12	Watching everything in a scene or paying attention	Shows involvement with the scene. The viewer wants to observe more closely what is being displayed.	Positive
13	Getting up and/or Leaving a place	Sign of irritation, distress, fatigue, fear, repugnance or disbelief.	Negative
14	Frowning	Sign of experiencing difficulty in a necessity to concentrating or understanding, showing displeasure or disapproval.	Negative
15	Brow Raising	Sign of uncertainty, disbelief, surprise, exasperation or ironical attitude.	Negative
16	Gazing Away	May be perceived as a sign of disappointment or lack of involvement/concentration or disgust/disapproval/embarrassment.	Negative
17	Smiling/ Raising the corners of one´s mouth/Sneer	Sign of satisfaction and involvement. The viewer may have encountered a degree of amusement during the session. It also may represent a sign of indignation and contempt.	Positive Negative
18	Compressing the Lip	Sign of frustration and confusion. Lip and jaw tension clearly reflect anxiety, nervousness and worry.	Negative
19	Moving the Mouth/ Speaking to himself/herself	Sign of being lost or in doubt. May also represent a sign of reflection and involvement with the scene.	Negative Positive
20	Expressing Vocally	Sighs, gasps, coughs, grunts - the volume of the expression, the tone or quality of the expression may be signs of frustration or disappointment. It may also represent interaction with other viewers and involvement with the scene.	Negative Positive
21	Hand Touching the Face	Sign of confusion and uncertainty, generally a sign that the viewers are lost, tired or indignant. It may also be a sign of contemplation and involvement with the scene	Negative Positive
22	Drawing Back on one´s Seat	This may reflect negative emotions such as refusal. By drawing back on the seat, the viewer may be showing a desire to withdraw from the present situation.	Negative
23	Forward Leaning the Trunk	Leaning forward and showing a sunken chest may be a sign of depression and frustration with the session. The viewer might be lost but instead of showing a lack of interest, leaning forward is often a sign of attentiveness, of "getting closer".	Negative

STEP 5: The set of heuristics defined in STEP 4 was evaluated. The use of TV Emotion Heuristics was checked, and a comparison made with the use of the Ten Emotion Heuristics [1], to evaluate emotional responses during the interaction with TV programs. The same images of viewers, captured from a previous case study, were evaluated by means of the Ten Emotion Heuristics and TV Emotion Heuristics [1]. The validation was carried out by 5 specialists in emotion heuristic evaluation and it was confirmed that only relying on the Ten Emotion Heuristics is not enough to evaluate the interactions with TV programs. In some cases, 67% of the observed heuristics were part of TVEH (see Table 2, Elderly 5) –This means that out of nine heuristics, six were represented by TVEH).

These results corroborate the observation made previously by the authors of this new set of heuristics, which is result of the experiential gains from the application of the Ten Emotion Heuristics [1].

STEP 6: This stage refines the set of heuristics defined in STEP 4. This refinement is based on feedback from the validation stage and was carried out by the specialists. In this step, for example, the name of some heuristics has been improved, as well as the descriptions of heuristics and the experience. Issues concerning the application of the evaluation method were also refined on the basis of the specialists' feedback. The specialists also alerted that when a video is too long, this may have a harmful effect on its evaluation because the evaluator may feel tired and impatient.

The application of the evaluative method of TV Emotion Heuristics is described in the following section.

3   Applying the TVEH Method

In general, a heuristic evaluation is carried out in two stages - an individual stage and a group stage [15]. In the individual stage, the evaluator must observe a given system and investigate whether there has been violation of a set of predefined heuristics. The evaluator fills out a specific form in which he records which heuristic was violated, at what time it occurred and how this violation was evaluated. In the group stage, all the evaluators meet to assess the system again and discuss the violations found in the individual stage. A single document is prepared that contains a summary of these violations.

The evaluation of TVEH is similar. In the individual stage, the evaluator receives the video which has captured the viewers' interactions and fills in a form to describe details of the heuristics observed. For each heuristic observed in the viewer during the interaction, the evaluator must describe the time of the video in which the reaction occurred and what the observed heuristic was. It is also necessary to indicate what kind of experience was associated with that reaction and provide a brief description to clarify the situation. This procedure must be repeated for all the viewers on the video.

TV emotion heuristics may be classified as Positive, Negative or Neutral. However, if the evaluator does not feel the urge to characterize the experience, or has doubts about whether the heuristic that was observed can be directly related to the media on display, he/she should use the 'Nothing Can Be Concluded' (NPC term in Portuguese) text. This means that the user experience and the feelings associated with this experience should be defined on the basis of an interaction scenario and on interventions arising from it.

During the second evaluation stage, which is carried out in-group, all the evaluators meet to review the video collectively, and evaluate the observed heuristics that have been pointed by each evaluator. They prepare the document by recording the final experience of the viewers. In defining this experience, the evaluators have to assess the set of observed heuristics with respect to two metrics: 1) Impact (how often has the heuristic occurred) and, 2) Frequency (how often the same heuristic was observed in the viewer).

The experience will be considered negative if eight heuristics, defined by the evaluators as negative, were incident. However, to consider the degree of incidence of a given heuristic, it is necessary for it to occur at least twice during the same viewer interaction with the media on display. Otherwise, it will be considered to be positive or neutral.

The number of the evaluators should follow the recommendations of Nielsen and Molich [15] who are proponents of the Usability Heuristic Evaluation [15]. These authors recommend that a heuristic evaluation be conducted with the participation of 3-5 evaluators. With regard to the evaluators' experience, the classification should take into account the number of times that the evaluators applied the emotion heuristics evaluation. Hence, the following classification should be considered: above 5 applications: expert evaluator; 2-5 applications: evaluator with little experience; 0-1: inexperienced evaluator.

The videos with viewers' images may be made available to the evaluators in their entirety or just with the movie clips of the scenes in which one wishes to evaluate the interaction with the programs. This decision is made by the person responsible for the evaluation. It should be is noted, however, that longer videos can cause fatigue and impatience in the evaluator, and this can have an adverse effect on the results of the evaluation.

In the following section, are described two case studies are described that were carried out in different scenarios, using the proposed heuristics.

4   Case Studies

The TVEH method was used to evaluate the emotional experience of viewers in two different scenarios. In the first scenario, an elderly group participated in an interactive TV session in which the program on display was enhanced with additional multimedia content [17]. In the second scenario, some families were filmed during their interaction with a fiction movie and the purpose was to determine at what times during the movie, the viewers had difficulty in understanding the content displayed and/or felt dissatisfaction with it. The case studies will be examined in more detail in the sequence.

4.1   Case 1

This case study was carried out with 8 elderly viewers to analyze their degree of satisfaction when watching a movie and observe whether the level of satisfaction increases while they are watching programs that are enhanced with additional multimedia content in the parts that have a complex narrative structure.

The media used in the study was approximately 14 minutes long and the genre was fiction. The sample of the elderly from the treatment group (TG) watched the movie when it was enhanced with three additional content and the control group (CG) watched the movie without any additional content. The video had approximately 2 hours, and the images from the elderly group and their interactions, underwent heuristic evaluative analysis conducted by five evaluators.

One of the evaluators was considered inexperienced, three had little experience and one of them was an expert in the field. The classification of the experience took into account the number of times that the evaluators applied the emotion heuristics evaluation.

Table 2 summarizes the obtained results when the TVEH method was employed. This shows which heuristics were observed during the interaction for each elderly person evaluated, as well as the incidence and frequency in which they occurred (how many heuristics considered to be negative, were observed more than twice) and the final experience attributed to the interaction of that viewer.

Table 2. TVEH results for Case 1

		Observed Heuristics	Incidence/Frequency	Final Experience
TG	E 1	IDs: 1, 2, 3, 5, 6, 9, 10, 14, 15, 16, 18, 22, 20.	10 negative heuristics observed more than twice - IDs: 1, 2, 3, 5, 10, 14, 15, 16, 18, 22.	Negative
	E 2	IDs: 1, 2, 3, 6, 9, 11, 14, 16, 18, 19, 21.	8 negative heuristics observed more than twice - IDs: 18, 21, 3, 16, 19, 9, 2, 1.	Negative
	E 5	IDs: 1, 2, 5, 6, 10, 14, 15, 18, 19, 20, 21.	2 negative heuristics observed more than twice – IDs: 1, 14. The other heuristics were observed only once.	Neutral
	E 6	IDs: 1, 2, 3, 6, 9, 11, 14, 15, 16, 17, 18, 19, 20, 21, 22, 23.	8 negative heuristics observed more than twice - IDs: 1, 2, 3, 6, 14, 16, 19, 21.	Negative
CG	E 3	IDs: 1, 2, 3, 6, 7, 11, 18, 19, 20, 21.	Only 3 negative heuristics observed more than twice – IDs: 1, 7, 19. The other observed heuristics were considered to be positive.	Positive
	E 4	IDs: 2, 3, 6, 9, 10, 14, 16, 19, 21.	Only 4 negative heuristics observed more than twice – IDs: 2, 6, 14. The other observed heuristics were considered to be positive.	Positive
	E 7	IDs: 3, 6, 10, 11, 14, 16, 18, 19, 21.	2 negative heuristics observed more than twice – IDs: 14, 1. The other heuristics were only observed a few times.	Neutral
	E 8	IDs: 2, 5, 18, 19, 22.	Only 2 negative heuristics observed more than twice – IDs: 5, 19. The other observed heuristics were considered to be positive.	Positive
E => Elderly		TG => Treatment Group		CG => Control Group

When the results using the TVEH method were collected, they suggested that the elderly in treatment group (TG) had a more negative experience than the elderly from the control group (CG).

Figure 1 illustrates some of these elderly participants during the session. In the case of the elderly people shown in Figure 1 (a) it is possible to determine the occurrence of heuristics: 2 - Crossing arms, 3 – Physical Adjustments and 17 - Smiling. In Figure 1 (b) we can identify the occurrence of heuristics: 6 - Moving hands, 15 - Brow Raising and 21 - Hand Touching the Face.

Fig. 1. Expressions of the elderly viewers

As shown, some of the heuristics observed during the interaction of the elderly were not foreseen in the Lera and Domingo heuristics [1]; however, they represent important information that should be taken into account when assessing the viewers' experience and how it came to be represented by TVEH.

Approximately 49% of the heuristics observed in the participants in this case study are represented by TVEH. The Elderly 5, for instance, had 67% of heuristics from TVEH (six out of nine observed heuristics – see Table 2).

4.2   Case 2

This case study was carried out with 3 families with three, two and two members. The families were observed during their interaction with a fiction movie. The purpose was to determine at what times during the movie, the viewers expressed emotional responses related to difficulty in understanding and/or dissatisfaction with the media. We wanted to find out if these times were related to the narrative structures incorporated in the movies.

The video had approximately 4 hours, and contained images from the families and their interactions; it underwent a heuristic analysis conducted by 3 evaluators. One of them was an expert, one with little experience and one was considered to be inexperienced.

Table 3 summarizes the results obtained from the application of the TVEH method. This shows which heuristics were observed during the interaction, for each member of the family evaluated, as well as the incidence and frequency in which they occurred (how many heuristics considered to be negative were observed more than twice) and the final experience attributed to the interaction of that viewer.

In general, the data point to a negative outcome for viewers' experience with regard to the movie displayed.

Table 3. TVEH results for Case 2

		Observed Heuristics	Incidence/Frequency	Final Experience
F1	M 1	IDs: 2, 3, 4, 14, 15, 17, 18, 19, 22, 20.	Only 3 negative heuristics observed more than twice - IDs: 14, 15, 18.	Positive
	M 2	IDs: 2, 3, 6, 9, 12, 15, 16, 19, 20, 21, 22.	5 negative heuristics observed more than twice - IDs: 2, 9, 16, 19, 20.	Neutral
	M 3	IDs: 1, 2, 3, 5, 6, 9, 10, 13, 14, 15, 16, 22, 23.	10 negative heuristics observed more than twice -IDs: 1, 2, 5, 6, 9, 14, 15, 16, 22, 23.	Negative
F2	M 1	IDs: 1, 3, 5, 12, 15, 17, 18, 20, 21.	Only 2 negative heuristics observed more than twice - IDs: 20, 21.	Positive
	M 2	IDs: 1, 2, 3, 4, 5, 6, 9, 10, 14, 15, 16, 17, 18, 20, 21, 22, 23.	13 negative heuristics observed more than twice -IDs: 1, 2, 5, 6, 9, 10, 14, 15, 16, 18, 20, 22, 23.	Negative
F3	M 1	IDs: 6, 9, 12, 15, 16, 19, 20, 21, 22.	4 negative heuristics observed more than twice - IDs: 9, 16, 19, 20.	Neutral
	M 2	IDs: 1, 2, 5, 6, 9, 13, 16, 18, 19, 20, 23.	9 negative heuristics observed more than twice -IDs: 1, 2, 6, 9, 10, 16, 18, 20, 23.	Negative
F => Family M => Member				

In the case of the excerpts with a narrative structure, it was observed that this triggered feelings of doubt, dissatisfaction or excerpts that require a prior knowledge on the part of the viewer. In these situations, a higher incidence of heuristics observed such as ID: 1, 2, 5, 6, 9, 13, 14, 15, 16, 18, 19 and 20, most of which can be regarded as negative experiences (a half of these heuristics is represented by TVHE). In most of the cases in which the final experience was considered to be negative, there was an incidence of at least six of these heuristics.

Figure 2 illustrates some of the families that took part in a session.

Fig. 2. The expressions of the families

With regard to the family shown in Figure 2 (a) it is possible to determine the occurrence of heuristics: 10 – Dozing off, 14 – Frowning, and 21 - Hand Touching the Face. In Figure 2 (b) the occurrence of heuristics can be detected: 2 - Crossing arms, 6 - Moving hands, 21 - Hand Touching the Face, and 22 - Drawing Back on one´s Seat.

In this case study, approximately 45% of the heuristics observed in the participants are represented by TVEH. Member 3 of the Family 1, for instance, had 61% of heuristics from TVEH (eight of thirteen observed heuristics – see Table 3).

5   Limitations and Lessons Learned

The analysis of the signals or emotional cues showed that all the viewers expressed feelings related to frustration and/or satisfaction while watching TV programs. In several situations the reactions were similar. Some signals or emotional cues were more difficult to identify because the viewers did not display many facial or physical expressions. Other viewers were more expressive.

In line with the proposals of Xavier and Neris [14] and Chorianopoulos and Spinellis [5], we believe that the heuristic evaluation put forward in this paper should be used in combination with other techniques to provide a more accurate understanding of the viewers' experience and their levels of satisfaction. One problem is that often participants want to please the researcher, and avoid criticism, and thus do not want to provide an overall evaluation that is negative. In view of this, both the viewer's report and the specialist's evaluation should be taken into account.

However, the use of the TVEH method may require extra effort on the part of the evaluators, especially if the videos are too long and the viewers show a wide range of reactions during the session. These issues were noted during the stage of heuristics validation and were also recorded by the evaluators.

In the validation stage, it was also observed that when associating an experience with a viewer, it is necessary to determine whether this interaction can indeed be attributed to the displayed contents or is the result of external issues. Hence it is important to evaluate   the general context of the media and also the social context of the viewer. One heuristic that normally represents a positive experience may, in a given context, represent the exact opposite. The Crying heuristic, for example, may represent a feeling of joy if the viewer is watching a comedy or represent fear and sadness if the genres of the movies are connected with horror or a sentimental novel.

With regard to the time that the evaluator takes to analyze the video interactions, it is observed that this is at least twice as long as for the video itself. Those responsible for carrying out the research can help to ease the burden of the evaluator´s task when they are assessing the viewers' emotional response during a period of interaction, by restricting the media excerpts so that they contain only a limited amount of material. This strategy, however, can mean that there is a loss of general context with regard to viewer's interactions and this can cause an erroneous assessment of the emotional reactions caused by the media.

We expect that the new set of heuristics can help in the evaluation of the viewer's experience and offer assistance for designers and entertainment producers in making their work increasingly interesting and enjoyable.

Acknowledgements. We would like to thank CAPES for its financial support and the colleagues from the LIFeS and Lince labs for agreeing to participate in the TVEH validation stage.

References

1. Lera, E., Domingo, M.G.: Ten Emotion Heuristics: Guidelines for assessing the user's affective dimension easily and cost-effectively. In: Proceedings of the 21st British HCI Group Annual Conference on People and Computers: HCI, pp. 163–166. British Computer Society, Swinton (2007)
2. Norman, D.A.: Emotional Design: why we love (or hate) everyday things. Basic Books (2004)
3. Draper, S.W.: Analysing fun as a candidate software requirement. Personal and Ubiquitous Computing 3(3) (1999)
4. Zhang, P., Li, N.: The importance of affective quality. Communications of the ACM 48(9), 105–108 (2005)
5. Chorianopoulos, K., Spinellis, D.: User interface evaluation of interactive TV: a media studies perspective. Universal Access Inf. Soc. 5(2), 209–218 (2006), http://dx.doi.org/10.1007/s10209-006-0032-1, doi:10.1007/s10209-006-0032-1
6. Chorianopoulos, K.: User interface design principles for interactive television applications. Journal of Human-Computer Interaction 24(6), 556–573 (2004)
7. Collazos, C., Rusu, C., Arciniegas, J., Roncagliolo, S.: Designing and Evaluating Interactive Television from a Usability Perspective. In: Proceedings of 2nd International Conferences on Advances in Computer-Human Interactions (ACHI 2009), pp. 381–385. IEEE Press (2009) ISBN: 978-1-4244-3351-3
8. Solano, A., Rusu, C., Collazos, C., Roncagliolo, S., Arciniegas, J.L., Rusu, V.: Usability Heuristics for Interactive Digital Television. In: Proceedings of the Third International Conference on Advances in Future Internet (AFIN 2011). Nice/Saint Laurent du Var, France (2011)
9. Geerts, D., Grooff, D.: Supporting the social uses of television: sociability heuristics for social TV. In: Proceedings of the CHI 2009, pp. 595–604. ACM, New York (2009)
10. Desurvire, H., Caplan, M., Toth, J.A.: Using heuristics to evaluate the playability of games. In: Proceedings of the CHI 2004. Vienna, Austria (2004)
11. Rodrigues, K.R.H., Melo, E.L., Nakagawa, P.I., Teixeira, C.A.C.: Interaction with Additional Content to Support the Understanding of Television Programs. In: Proceedings of the IX Brazilian Symposium on Human Factors in Computing Systems (IHC 2010), Belo Horizonte-MG, Brazil, vol. 1, pp. 91–100 (2010) (in Portuguese)
12. Rodrigues, K.R.H., Pereira, S.S., Quinelato, L.G.G., Melo, E.L., Neris, V.P.A., Teixeira, C.A.C.: Interaction with Additional Content Using Multiple Devices to Support the Appreciation of Television Programs. In: Proceedings of Brazilian Symposium on Multimedia and the Web (WebMedia 2011). Porto Alegre-SC, Brazil (2011) (in Portuguese)
13. Rusu, C., Roncagliolo, S., Rusu, V., Collazos, C.: A Methodology to establish usability heuristics. In: Proceedings of 4th International Conferences on Advances in Computer-Human Interactions (ACHI 2011), pp. 59–62 (2011) ISBN: 978-1- 61208-003-1
14. Xavier, R.A.C., Neris, V.P.A.: A Hybrid Evaluation Approach for the Emotional State of Information Systems Users. In: International Conference on Enterprise Information Systems (ICEIS 2012), vol. 202, pp. 1–9. SciTePress (2012)
15. Nielsen, J., Molich, R.: Heuristic evaluation of user interfaces. In: Chew, J.C., Whiteside, J. (eds.) Proceedings of the SIGCHI Conference on Human Factors in Computing Systems (CHI 1990), pp. 249–256. ACM, New York (1990)
16. Rodrigues, K.R.H., Teixeira, C.A.C., Neris, V.P.A.: Assessing the elderly's emotional responses while interact with movies enriched with additional multimedia content. In: Stephanidis, C., Antona, M. (eds.) UAHCI/HCII 2014, Part III. LNCS, vol. 8515, pp. 158–169. Springer, Heidelberg (2014)

Evaluation of Industrial Touch Interfaces Using a Modular Software Architecture

Philipp Tiefenbacher, Fabian Bumberger, and Gerhard Rigoll

Institute for Human-Machine Communication,
Technische Universität München, Germany
philipp.tiefenbacher@tum.de
http://www.mmk.ei.tum.de

Abstract. In the highly automated industry process surveillance is crucial for understanding current states and decisions of certain parts of the industrial line. Specific parts of the industrial line, however, may have their own user interfaces right beside of the machine. Thus obtaining a holistic impression of the state of the industrial line might be complicated. So on the one hand, important functionalities should be summarized into one user interface. On the other hand, the user interface must be mobile and easily accessible to have the information on site of the inspected part of the machine. In this work, we propose three different navigation concepts for touch interfaces and evaluate them on a thinkable story board based on tasks of an industrial plant. These concepts can be compared this way, as the single functional components of the interfaces are the same. All three concepts are evaluated on two different mobile devices with a 7" and a 12" screen. We show that the objective metrics of all concepts are invariant to the screen size. The subjective results in regard to the screen size, however, differ for the most flexible user interface (UI). We determine the best concept based on users' preferences and the obtained objective metrics.

1 Introduction

Touch interfaces are wide spread due to the current success of smart phones and tablet PCs [4]. The consumer can choose between a wide range of devices with different form factors. Furthermore, industry foresees advantages in mobile process surveillance and error handling. Thus, the desire for both rugged touch devices and optimized industrial touch interfaces increases [1].

In an average industrial plant the user interface must be a complete desktop replacement, as the working personnel should not be able to change some fundamental settings of the device, as it is the case in the project Hol-I-wood PR. Additionally, persons with different backgrounds have to work with the system. This can be a technician, who inspects the service intervals of maintainable parts or an inspector, who wants an overview of today's yield. So, the user interface must be able to adapt to these authorization changes.

M. Kurosu (Ed.): Human-Computer Interaction, Part I, HCII 2014, LNCS 8510, pp. 589–600, 2014.
© Springer International Publishing Switzerland 2014

1.1 Framework

Figure 1 depicts the devised architecture. The major advantage of this concept is the independence of the single functionalities, here shown as components. Each component may have a variety of different views. The "Interface" module, however, loads the desired views dynamically based on the requirements of the defined user interface. This way, a new user-interface can easily and quickly created and the "Interface" module loads the best fitting view to a new concept. The before mentioned case of loading a specific content based on the authorization level of the user can be achieved, by creating a distinct view for each of these levels. The logic of each component is encapsulated in the "Component" box and does not need to be touched for new designs.

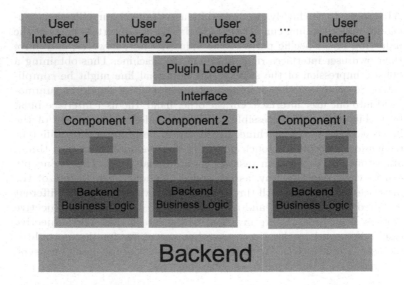

Fig. 1. The developed architecture for the user study. Multiple interfaces can be created, but at start of the application one is selected. The "Plugin Loader" loads the available components into the graphical representation. The "Interface" combines the function components with the chosen textural designs and also determines a general interface between the "Plugin Loader" and arbitrary "Components". The "Components" hold the function of the application, here multiple components are possible and loaded through the "Plugin Loader" at the start of the application. The "Backend" at the bottom mainly works as a simple data storage for XML files.

2   GUI Concepts

The concept of a GUI is basically the structure and interaction technique of the interface. We develop three different interface concepts based on the architecture proposed before. Each concept enables a consistent interaction scheme with the functional components [7]. Each concept is based on a different interaction and navigation behaviour. We named the three concepts the *tile*, *swipe* and *widget* concept. In the following sections each concept is explained in detail.

2.1 Tile Concept

The menu structure of the *tile* concept consists of multiple tiles, which display only the title of the component. After a click or a touch on a menu item, extended information regarding this tile is shown. Hereby, a rotation transition from the normal to the preview state of the tile animates the process. In this way, the user receives the most important information of a menu item without entering the full screen mode of that item. Through another click at "View", the tile opens in full screen mode. The full screen mode includes a button "Minimize" at the top right corner, which allows to close the component at any time. When the component closes, the user ends up in the former menu structure.

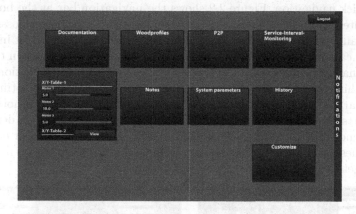

Fig. 2. The standard view for the *tile* concept. Each tile is a single component, with just the title of the component loaded into the tile. When a single tile is selected, the state of the tile changes to the extended view. The right side holds the notification manager in the collapsed state. On the right top, a "logout" button enables to close the view.

The notifications appear on the right hand side. In Figure 2 the notification centre is minimized. By clicking on the collapsed notification manager, the bar extends and shows the full message module. When a new messages arrives, a blinking animation of the notification bar informs the user. As there is a central navigation screen, the tile overview, the UI concept might be easy to use without further instructions or training. This should be achieved according to [3] as the users commonly do not want to study the documentation. Ideally, the preview of the tile shows in some cases enough information to the user, so that the user does not enter the full screen mode. In this case, the UI could increase the efficiency.

2.2 Swipe Concept

The second UI variant is named the *swipe* concept. In this concept, the single components are shown in full screen mode and listed besides each other. Each representation almost fits the full screen. Thus, in this variant only one single component can be displayed at once. The concept is named *swipe*, as through a swipe gesture on the touch screen (dragging the finger on the touch screen in horizontal direction) the direct neighbour of the current component on the right or left side is loaded. The moving direction of the finger determines the direction of the switch. Figure 3 shows this kind of navigation exemplarily. This selection method alone, however, would take too long as no overview of all the components is available. When the user wants to start a component right on the other side of the list, the user has to open all components until reaching the desired one. Therefore, an additional navigation bar at the bottom of the UI shows all the components. The components on this bar can be selected through a touch or mouse click, then the interface jumps directly to this component. This enables quick navigation. Figure 2.2 shows the navigation bar at the bottom of the user interface. So the *swipe* concepts connects two navigation possibilities. The user can navigate through a swipe gesture to the next component in the list or the user can directly select the component in the navigation bar. On the right side of the navigation bar, a button is placed, which opens the notification centre. When touching the button, a pop-menu appears, which lists current notifications. After the arrival of a new notification at the mobile device, the notification button starts blinking until the button is clicked. The blinking changes depending to the urgency of the arrived messages. This way, an experienced user can differ different messages without further interactions. Additionally, more important messages get higher and faster attention from the user.

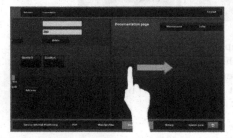

Fig. 3. On the left side, a user swipes the finger to the right. The component of the user interface moves to the right. The new component is shown in the right image after the completion of the gesture.

Fig. 4. Navigation bar in the *swipe* concept. If the list exceeds the available space at the bottom, the user can swipe inside the bar to see the other available components. A click or touch at a component, opens the component. On the right side, a button for opening the notification centre exists.

2.3   Widget Concept

The last concept is the *widget* concept. This variant is based on multiple scalable windows, which is quite similar to the Windows desktop [6]. Each window, the so called widget, displays one component. The user can resize the widget through a pinch gesture. A pinch starts, when two touch points are recognized at one widget. Moving the fingers together or apart minimizes or maximizes the widget. Figure 5 depicts the *widget* method. As it is necessary to detect two touch points at the same time, this concept can only be used on multi touch screens. Also working in this UI with a mouse on a desktop PC is not possible. This method makes use of progressive disclosure. Here, the content of a component adapts to the size of the widget at runtime. Depending on the size of the widget, more or less information is presented in the UI. Each widget can be translated to a different position during the pinch gesture or during a drag gesture (dragging off the element with just one finger). One advantage in comparison to the other methods is the support of multi-tasking. The user can open two or more components and interact with them at the same time. Hereby, the widget can be arranged besides or above each other.

Fig. 5. The two images depict two different sizes of the same component. In the first image, on the left side, the component is rather small and only a title is presented. When the component is emphasized due to a pinch gesture, the preview mode of the component is shown (right image).

In the case of starting a video chat, this option might be important. The video stream can be opened right besides a component, which includes the machine parameters. Thus, the working personnel is able to communicate over the video chat and to survey the machine status in parallel. However, the navigation bases on gestures and the arranging of the components is more complex than in the other variants. That is the reason, why we expect the users to need a phase of training to be able to work with this UI. The notification centre in this variant is a component like the other ones. However, when a message arrives, the whole component starts blinking.

3   Experiment

This section presents and discusses the experiment of the three user interface variants on the two form factors. As the different UI methods shall be evaluated, the storyboard should involve multiple context switches within the UI. That at the end, the different navigation concepts can be compared. Each participant received the storyboard in hard copy. Before the experiment starts, the subjects had the time to read the whole storyboard. The experimental procedure is the following:

1. First, a user logs into the interface.
2. Then the user overviews the most urgent service intervals of the plant.
3. As the subject is not familiar with one serviceable part of the machine, the user opens the related documentation.
4. The worker chooses and edits a profile, which defines important quality levels of the process.
5. Afterwards, the most recent produced items of the plant are shown in a comprehensive history view.
6. Meanwhile, an error appears in the notification centre and the subject has to initiate a video conference with a technician, who recommends to adjust a parameter of the machine.
7. The user checks the current state of the plant.
8. Lastly, the user logs off.

The necessary components to conduct these story board have been implemented.

3.1   Participants

A total of 18 (3 female and 15 male) subjects took part in the final experiment. 12 participants were students of Electrical Engineering and Information Technology at the Technische Universität München, 5 participants were engineers, and one was an architect and one a trainee. The age of the candidates lied in-between 20 and 46 years, with a mean age of 28.06 years. Every subject owns a smart phone with multi-touch screen. Half of the test persons possess a mobile tablet device also. Hence, the test subjects are very familiar with the use of touch screens.

3.2   Devices

All three GUI concepts are evaluated on both, a 7-inch and a 12-inch, mobile device. Besides the difference in size, also the weight differs from 950 grams for the big to 425 grams for the small device. Each participant tests every concept on both devices. Consequently, each subject finishes the storyboard 6 times.

3.3   Design

The order of the different UI variants for the experiment is determined by the Latin square method, which reduces fatigue and learn effects. Furthermore, the order of the devices changes between the candidates with the same order of UI variants. After each turn, the participant completes the SUS [2] form. Hereby, the results can be distinguished between objective and subjective metrics. The objective metrics are directly logged to the hard disk during the test. This includes the number of clicks and the completion time. The subjective metrics are obtained through the completed SUS forms of the subjects. The completion time is the time, the subjects needed to accomplish the tasks of the story board. The "clicks" are the total number of clicks received during the user's progression in the story board. The participants were instructed to work as quickly and accurately as possible. The hypotheses of the study are the following:

H0 The size of the screen has no significant influence on the objective data.

H1 The *swipe* concept needs significant less time and touch clicks than the other concepts.

H2 The subjective results of the *swipe* variant will depend on the screen size.

H3 The concept with the best objective data is preferred by the users.

4 Results

At first, the recorded data was tested for normal distribution. Therefore, the Shapiro-Wilk normality test was applied. Table 1 shows that neither the logged data on the small device nor the data on the big device are all normally distributed based on a significance level of $\alpha = .05$. For that reason, we perform the Friedman's test over the factors of the hypotheses. If the p value of the Friedman's test is near zero, at least one column of data differs significantly from another one. In that case, we test the columns pairwise with Tukey's honest significant test (HSD).

Table 1. Results of the Shapiro-Wilk normality test: On the left side the results of the normality test for the total number of clicks is presented, the table on the right side depicts the corresponding results for the completion time

Device	Concept	W	p-Value	N	Device	Concept	W	p-Value	N
big device	Swipe	0.87	0.0335	0	big device	Swipe	0.92	0.0122	0
	Tile	0.92	0.2161	1		Tile	0.87	0.2390	1
	Widget	0.96	0.7330	1		Widget	0.96	0.4968	1
small device	Swipe	0.87	0.0360	0	small device	Swipe	0.94	0.1636	1
	Tile	0.94	0.6619	1		Tile	0.87	0.0291	0
	Widget	0.94	0.4890	1		Widget	0.94	0.5588	1

4.1 Task Completion Time

Figure 6 shows that the task completion time of the *swipe* concept is the shortest on both devices and therefore performs best with a mean time on the big device of M_{big}: 268.06s and a corresponding standard deviation of SD_{big}: 94.90s. The completion time decreases on the small device even further to M_{small}: 248.95s,

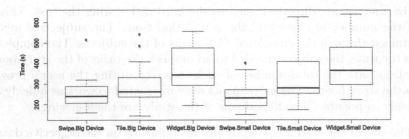

Fig. 6. The mean and standard deviation of the three concepts on both mobile devices for the completion time (s)

SD_{small}: 66.85s. The *swipe* concept is followed by the *tile* concept (M_{big}: 300.61s, SD_{big}: 110.04s and M_{small}: 334.72s, SD_{small}: 136.38s) and *widget* (M_{big}: 374.61s, SD_{big}: 120.34s and M_{small}: 384.94s, SD_{small}: 123.28s) is the slowest variant. This is true for both form factors. The Friedman's test results in a significant difference between the concepts on the big device as well as on the small device ($\mathcal{X}^2_{big}(.95) = 10.11$, $p_{big} = 0.01$ and $\mathcal{X}^2_{small}(.95) = 12.33$, $p_{small} = 0.00$). Table 2 shows the results of the pairwise examination of the mean values with Tukey's HSD test. When the subjects used the *swipe* concept, they have been significantly faster than with the *widget* concept. This coherence is true on both devices. The other combinations are not significantly different. Furthermore, the completion time of a concept is independent of the two screen sizes.

Table 2. Results of Tukey's range test for a pairwise comparison between the completion times of the concepts

Device	Group I	Group J	MD(I-J)	Std. Error	CI(95) Low	CI(95) High
	swipe	tile	-0.44	0.24	-1.23	0.34
big device	swipe	widget	-1.06	0.24	-1.84	-0.27
	tile	widget	-0.61	0.24	-1.39	0.17
	swipe	tile	-0.67	0.24	-1.45	0.11
small device	swipe	widget	-1.17	0.24	-1.95	-0.39
	tile	widget	-0.50	0.24	-1.28	0.28

4.2   Total Clicks

Figure 7 shows that the *swipe* concept needs the least clicks on both devices (M_{big}: 82.67, SD_{big}: 20.03 and M_{small}: 94.11, SD_{small}: 23.41). The *swipe* concept is followed by the *tile* (M_{big}: 112.78, SD_{big}: 30.58 and M_{small}: 127.94, SD_{small}: 31.63) concept and the participants had the highest number of clicks for *widget* (M_{big}: 148.83, SD_{big}: 39.75 and M_{small}: 158.72, SD_{small}: 44.25). This is true

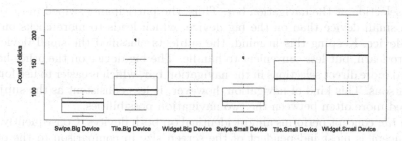

Fig. 7. The mean and standard deviation of the three concepts on both mobile devices for the total number of clicks

on both devices. The Friedman's test results in a significant difference on the big device and also on the small device between the concepts ($\mathcal{X}^2_{big}(.95) = 20.82$, $p_{big} = 0.00$ and $\mathcal{X}^2_{small}(.95) = 26.06$, $p_{small} = 0.00$). Table 3 presents the detailed results of Tukey's HSD test, which shows that the subjects needed significantly less clicks with the concept *swipe* in comparison to both other methods. Again, the screen size of the device does not matter.

Table 3. Results of the Tukey's range test for a pairwise comparison between the total number of clicks of the concepts

Device	Group I	Group J	MD(I-J)	Std. Error	CI(95) Low	CI(95) High
	swipe	*tile*	-1.03	0.23	-1.80	-0.25
big device	*swipe*	*widget*	-1.47	0.23	-2.25	-0.70
	tile	*widget*	-0.44	0.23	-1.22	0.33
	swipe	*tile*	-1.00	0.23	-1.77	-0.23
small device	*swipe*	*widget*	-1.67	0.23	-2.44	-0.90
	tile	*widget*	-0.67	0.23	-1.44	0.10

4.3 Questionnaire

This section presents the results of the SUS questionnaire. At first the SUS scores are compared in regard to the screen size. Followed by a discussion of the results between the concepts. Figure 8 displays the medians of the results of the SUS form. The *swipe* concept at the top left shows that the three factors "small inconsistency", "easy to learn" and "easy to handle" differ the most between the both devices. The first two factors are higher for the small device and the latter one is higher for the big device. The total number of clicks deliver a possible explanation for these differences. The participants clicked more often on the small device than on the big device when comparing the *swipe* concept solely. The *swipe* concept enables two kinds of navigation, the swipe and the direct selection at the navigation bar. Thus, the participants swiped more often on the small device than on the big device, which leads to more clicks on the small device. Keeping this in mind, the subjects classified the small device as easier to learn, but less convenient to handle. The big device on the other hand, received more direct selections in the navigation bar, which is easier to use for the test persons. This kind of navigation, however, is less consistent as the subjects switched more often between the two navigation possibilities.

The *tile* concept performs almost identical on both devices. Consequently, the *tile* concept is most independent of the screen size in comparison to the other concepts. The SUS graph regarding the *widget* concept shows that it is more difficult to use on the small device. This also corresponds to the lower factor "using regular" on the small device. We calculate the overall SUS score based on the work of Tullis *et al.* in [8]. Furthermore, we also separate the factors of the SUS scores into learnability and usability as proposed from Lewis *et al.* in [5]. Table 4 lists all three scores. The *swipe* concept on the small device received the highest ratings, closely followed by the same concept on the big device. When comparing the impact of the form factor within a concept, the scores of the *tile* concept are the closest. Whereas, the *widget* concept is most dependent on the screen size with a SUS score of 44.0 on the small device and 55.0 on the big device. The learnability for the *widget* concept is similar, but the usability greatly differs.

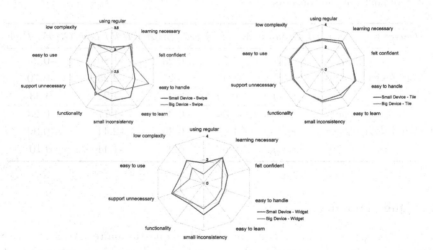

Fig. 8. The SUS results separated into the three UI concepts. The blue line refers to SUS results of the small device, the red line to the big device.

5   Discussion

The hypothesis **H0** can be classified as true as all the statements of the objective data are valid on both devices. The SUS-, learnability- and usability-scores of a

Table 4. Overview of the SUS-Scores of the different variants. The classification of the results is presented as well as the scores for learnability and usability.

Device	Concept	SUS-Score	CL	Learn.	Usabil.
big device	swipe	77.36	B+	77.08	77.43
	tile	71.94	C	72.53	72.05
	widget	55.00	D	68.06	52.95
small device	swipe	**78.19**	B+	**78.47**	**78.13**
	tile	71.39	C	71.92	72.01
	widget	44.00	F	67.36	39.06

concept are almost identically on both devices, except for the *widget* concept. A comparison of the completion time of the *widget* concept between the two devices shows no significant difference (ANOVA: $F(4.45)=0.12$, $p=0.7372$). A test of the number of clicks (ANOVA: $F(4.45)=1.49$, $p=0.2392$) leads also to no significant difference. Hence, the objective performance of the developed UI variants are independent of the screen size. Our hypothesis **H1** is only partly valid. The necessary clicks for completing the story board with the *swipe* variant are fewer than in the other methods. However, this is not true for the completion time. Here the *tile* concept performs equally well. Therefore, *swipe* had the least clicks, but it was not beneficial for the completion time.

We could not determine an effect of the screen size in relation to the objective data. Although, the SUS scores within the *widget* variant differ much. Additionally, the participants had to select their favourite device for each concept. Here, 17 out of 18 participants chose the big device, when working with the *widget* variant. Thus, hypothesis **H2** is true. We further conclude that a 7" mobile device is too small for a satisfactory operation, when multiple windows (nine windows in our case) are presented in parallel. The interaction becomes even more difficult, when all windows can freely resized through touch gestures. Finally, **H3** is true, as the *swipe* concept with the best SUS score has also the best objective outcomes in our study.

6   Conclusion and Outlook

We define a new architecture for quickly creating graphical user interfaces without the necessity of re-implementing the functionality. We deploy this framework to create three different interface variants. Afterwards, we evaluate possible differences between the variants but also between the screen sizes of the mobile devices. The best concept (*swipe*) enables two ways of navigation, through a gesture and through a navigation bar. The *tile* concept shows the least difference in subjective feedback between the two form factors. The tile structure of an interface has the advantage that menu items have an acceptable size on big and on small screens, since the whole display can be used for showing navigation items. Furthermore, when a functional component is maximized to full screen mode it fills the whole screen. This is beneficial when working on small screens. The *swipe* concept always displays an additional navigation bar, which occupies a certain area. Therefore, the maximum size of a component window decreases.

The biggest improvements are possible for the *widget* variant, which also has the lowest overall SUS score. We suggest for this variant to restrict the scaling of the components. Currently, the scaling is completely free. A modification to a more structured grid based scaling could be advantageously. Here, the size of the components should always fit to an underlying grid. Other sizes between the knots of the gird should not be possible. Furthermore, an additional help for overlaying components would improve the usability.

Acknowledgement. The research leading to these inventions has received funding from the European Union Seventh Framework Programm (FP7/2007-2013) under grant agreement n° 284573.

References

1. Bonomi, F.: The future mobile infrastructure: challenges and opportunities. Wireless Communications 17(5), 4–5 (2010)
2. Brooke, J.: Sus-a quick and dirty usability scale. Usability Evaluation in Industry 189, 194 (1996)
3. Krug, S.: Don't make me think: A common sense approach to web usability. Pearson Education (2009)
4. Laugesen, J., Yuan, Y.: What factors contributed to the success of apple's iphone? In: Proc. ICMB-GMR, pp. 91–99 (2010)
5. Lewis, J.R., Sauro, J.: The factor structure of the system usability scale. In: Kurosu, M. (ed.) HCD 2009. LNCS, vol. 5619, pp. 94–103. Springer, Heidelberg (2009)
6. Nielsen, J.: Usability engineering. Elsevier (1994)
7. Shneiderman, B., Plaisant, C.: Designing the user interface, 4th edn. (2005)
8. Tullis, T., Albert, W.: Measuring the user experience: collecting, analyzing, and presenting usability metrics. Morgan Kaufmann (2010)

Visualisation Methods and Techniques

3D Face-Aware Electronics with Low-Resolution Imaging

Yu-Jin Hong[1], Jaewon Kim[1], Junghyun Cho[2], and Ig-Jae Kim[1]

[1] Korea University of Science and Technology
[2] Imaging Media Research Center, Korea Institute of Science and Technology, Korea
{hyj,jaewonk,jhcho,kij}@imrc.kist.re.kr

Abstract. What if your electronics with cheap cameras can reveal 3D faces of captured people? In daily life, we use a lot of consumer electronics employing cameras such as a mobile phone, a tablet PC, a CCTV, a car black box, and so on. If such devices provide 3D facial shapes of 2-dimensionally framed people, it would benefit new applications and services in higher dimensional imaging, security, HCI (Human-Computer Interaction), AR (Augmented Reality), and mobile applications like phone games. This paper introduces a novel method to realize the functionality in computational electronics with low-resolution imaging.

Keywords: 3D face reconstruction, Smart devices, High-resolution imaging, Image processing.

1 Introduction

Today, many people spend every day with camera-equipped consumer electronics such as digital cameras, cellphones, tablets, PCs, CCTVs, and car black boxes. Thanks to them, shooting photos and videos became an easy and routine job. There are many commercial applications associated with them as well. For example, QR code is widely used with potable camera-equipped devices in shopping payment system and AR (Augmented Reality) applications allow users to access to digital contents overlaid with real world view through smart devices. Also, they can be used for virtual trying of various hair wigs and glasses. The smarter camera-equipped devices are with high computation power and camera resolution, the more chances can be provided for advanced AR and computer vision applications, which were available in only PC environment a few years ago.

While techniques and applications have focused on the smart use of captured photos and videos in camera-equipped devices, this paper throws a question that the photos and videos themselves are indeed in a smart shape. At this viewpoint, this paper proposes a smart way to convert facial information in photographs or videos into higher dimensional information. Our method is composed of two steps, super-resolution (SR) and 3D facial reconstruction. The first SR step enhances low-resolution facial regions to higher geometrical dimension, which are commonly captured with camera-equipped electronics, not DSLR cameras. The second 3D facial reconstruction step reconstructs 3D facial shape from a set of 2-dimensional photographs or video frames which are processed by the first step.

M. Kurosu (Ed.): Human-Computer Interaction, Part I, HCII 2014, LNCS 8510, pp. 603–610, 2014.
© Springer International Publishing Switzerland 2014

With our method, we expect a lot of new applications and services can be inspired as shown in Fig. 1. Users can view 3D facial shapes of people in photographs and videos through IT devices (Fig. 1.(A)). At live video chat, the other party's 3D face can be freely viewed according to user interaction (B). Also, in security monitoring suspect's 3D facial information can be revealed from CCTV frames (C).

Fig. 1. Various application scenarios with our method, 3D facial reconstruction from a video. 3D facial visualization (A) for a video clip in a smart device (B) at live video chat (C) at CCTV monitoring.

2   Contributions

This paper presents a novel technique to provide 3D facial shape from a set of photos or video frames at a cheap computational cost. Specific technical contributions are the followings:

- A SR method optimized for captured faces in large scale and rotation variation.
- A novel 3D facial reconstruction method from a set of 2D images, based on iterative 3D model refinement through feature point matching between 2D input images and a 3D reference model.
- Practical applications and services (Fig. 1) associated with a new paradigm of 3D facial visualization.

3   Related Work

3.1   Super-Resolution

Previous SR literatures can be roughly divided into five categories: interpolation-based [1], reconstruction-based [2], classification-based [3], learning-based [4] [5], and probability-based methods [6]. Protter and Elad's method [6] (PME: Probabilistic Motion Estimation) works well with sequenced facial photos when the scale and rotation are invariant. We propose an improved SR method to cover large scale and rotation variation over facial region, which is a general imaging condition in consumer electronics.

3.2   3D Facial Reconstruction

A number of researchers have worked to directly recover 3D facial shapes from images. Pighin et al. [7] reconstructed a parametric 3D model with five viewpoints of faces based on feature points. Blanz and Vetter [8] reconstructed a realistic 3D face with PCA (Principle Analysis) and modified the facial appearance based on 3D human scanned database. Kim and Ko [9] proposed a novel technique to compensate errors between manually generated basis and statistically generated models. Smith et Hancock [10] showed how to capture facial shape via statistically varied models in a shape-from-shading algorithm. K.Shlizerman and Basri [11] presented a method to reconstruct 3D model from a single face image by using only single reference model to overcome limitations in previous reconstruction methods. Conventional model-based approaches took significant time to build a 3D facial model with detailed texture, making them inapplicable for smart devices with low computing power. While, our adaptive basis model approach resolves this matter.

4   Super-Resolution Process

Our SR process uses low-resolution photos or video frames as input data, which are not necessarily consecutive. We assume the input data include a target person's whole face. Our SR algorithm consists of three steps. The first step is detection of facial feature points by STASM [12] as shown in Fig. 2(B). Since the original STASM didn't work for such low-resolution images, we used interpolated images in three or four times larger scale. Next step is warping data frames toward a reference frame using the facial feature points. Through this step, data frames are normalized over scale and rotation with regard to the reference frame (Fig. 2(C)).This is a critical process to achieve a good SR result. Typically, a human face shows huge movements at photograph and video shooting and consequently imaging factors like zoom, translation and rotation of the face significantly varies in the captured data. Although PME method has strength in the usage of pixels uncovered by explicit motion estimation, pixels in significant zoom and rotation variation regarding a reference patch are still in low utilization. Accordingly, same input images can produce a better PME result after compensating scale and rotation variation by warping.

We applied two warping methods for each input frames: TPS (Thin Plate Spline) and PA (Piecewise Affine) warping. First, TPS warping was performed to compensate overall zoom and rotation as shown in (Fig. 2). Then, PA warping compensated local shapes such as eyes, a nose, and a mouth over scale and rotation variation (Fig. 3).
The final super-resolution step was performed by a simplified PME method based on patch-based similarity computation (Fig. 4(B)) over the warped data frames. In the Fig. 4, I_p means central intensity of a patch, P. PME method computes patch similarities S_n between the target I_{p_0} and other frames $I_{p_{1\sim n}}$ as follows. p_0 and $p_{1\sim n}$ are patches in a reference and input frames, respectively.

606   Y.-J. Hong et al.

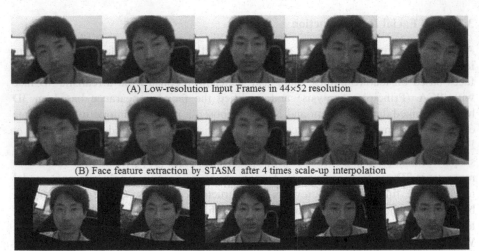

(A) Low-resolution Input Frames in 44×52 resolution

(B) Face feature extraction by STASM after 4 times scale-up interpolation

(C) Compensation of rotation, location, and scaling over the reference frame in the middle by TPS warping

Fig. 2. TPS warping process. The middle column is a reference frame and the others are data frames.

$$S_n = \sum_{k=1}^{m}(I_{P_0}^k - I_{P_n}^k)^2 \qquad (1)$$

Weights for each patch, W_n, is defined in (2) regarding S_n and a super-resolution image is produced by weighted average of patches in (2).

$$I_{Ps} = \frac{\sum_{j=1}^{n} I_{P_0} + I_{P_0}W_j}{\sum_{j=1}^{n} I + W_j}, W_n = e^{-\frac{S_n}{2\sigma^2}} \qquad (2)$$

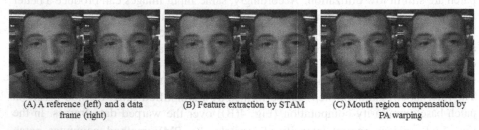

(A) A reference (left) and a data frame (right)

(B) Feature extraction by STAM

(C) Mouth region compensation by PA warping

Fig. 3. PA warping process for compensating local shape variation in a frame of Avatar

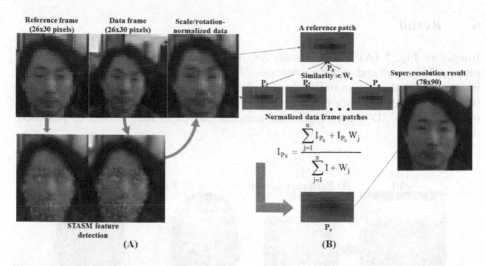

Reference frame (26x30 pixels)   Data frame (26x30 pixels)   Scale/rotation-normalized data   A reference patch

Similarity ∝ W_a

Normalized data frame patches

$$I_{Ps} = \frac{\sum\limits_{j=1}^{n} I_{P_0} + I_{P_0} W_j}{\sum\limits_{j=1}^{n} 1 + W_j}$$

Super-resolution result (78x90)

STASM feature detection

(A)   (B)

Fig. 4. Our super-resolution computation based on PME mothod. (A) Normalization of data frames over scale and rotation variation. (B) Patches in normalized data frames are compared with reference frame patches to compute similarity, which is used as a weight for the patch's contribution on a SR image by the given equation.

5   3D Facial Reconstruction

Our 3D facial reconstruction method has a novelty in fast 3D shape estimation from a set of video frames. The key idea is iteratively refining a 3D reference model by the time when the minimum feature difference reaches between input SR images (SRIs) and the 3D reference model (Fig. 5(B)). Linear blending [10] was used to express a 3D reference model via the weighted combination of 8 basis models with 3,500 vertices. Equation (3) formulates blendshape technique.

$$V = \sum_{i=1}^{n} \alpha_i V_i, \qquad \sum_{i=1}^{n} \alpha_i = 1 \qquad (3)$$

where α_i are the blending weights, V_i is the position of the vertex in the blend basis i, and n is the number of blend shapes. V are the coordinates of a vertex of result 3D shape.

The basis models are adaptively chosen most similarly to the face type   in a SRI among a 3D facial database which includes 100 head data of 15~73 year-old male and female scanned by HDI Advance system [13]. Our method can reconstruct a 3D face with at least a single SRI. In that case, the 3D result means a statistical transformation from 2D to 3D. A more precise 3D result can be acquired with processing more different views. Note that 3D reconstruction results from a low- resolution image show significantly worse quality that the results by a SRI in Fig.6, which demonstrates the importance of the SR step for fair 3D reconstruction quality.

6   Result

Images in Fig. 5 (A) are the results SR images from low-quality images (D) by proposed method and (C) demonstrates 3D reconstruction results of LR and SR images. Since the texture of 3D shape is dependent on input image, final face shape (C,left) has higher quality than the result model (C, right) and it takes 2-3 seconds to generate the 3D shape. Fig.6 also presents our experiment result of proposed method.

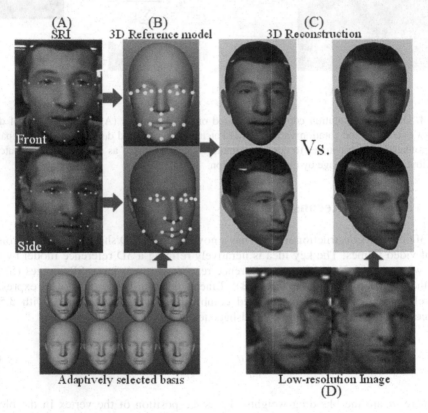

Fig. 5. 3D facial reconstruction pipeline based on SRI (column A) and 3D reference models (column B) generated with 8 adaptive blendshape basis (left bottom). The spots indicate corresponding features between the SRI and the 3D model. Column C compares 3D reconstruction results generated by SRIs and low-resolution images (column D). Both column A and D are frames from Avatar.

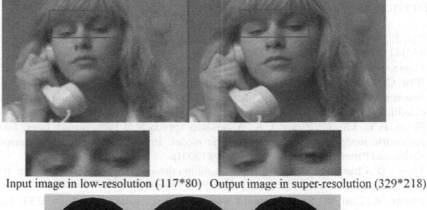

Input image in low-resolution (117*80)   Output image in super-resolution (329*218)

3D reconstruction result

Fig. 6. A low resolution input frame (top-left) and our SRI (top-right) using Protter and Elad's data [6]. The bottom shows 3D reconstruction result generated by the SRIs.

7   Conclusion

This paper describes a novel 3D facial reconstruction method via video or sequenced photos captured by camera-equipped electronics. We propose a patch-based SR method with normalizing scale and rotation in input video frames. Also, a fast cheap 3D facial reconstruction method is proposed based on feature matching between 2D video frames and a 3D model. We hope our method leads new applications and services to various camera-equipped consumer electronics by providing higher dimensional face information.

Acknowledgements. This research was supported by a grant from the R&D program, "Development of 3D Montage Creation and Age-specific Facial Prediction System", funded by the MKE, Republic of Korea and the KIST Institutional Program (Project No. 2E24790).

Photo Credits: Original image in Fig.1: Paramount Pictures. Original image in Fig. 3 : 20th century Fox.

References

1. Xin, L., Orchard, M.T.: New edge-directed interpolation. IEEE Trans. Image Processing, 1521–1527 (2001)
2. Morse, B.S., Schwartzwald, D.: Image magnification using level-set reconstruction. In: IEEE Conference on Computer Vision and Pattern Recognition, pp. 333–340 (2001)
3. Bouman, C.A., Atkins, C.B., Allebach, J.O.: Optimal image scaling using pixel classification. In: IEEE Conference on Image Processing, pp. 864–867 (2001)
4. Shum, H.Y., Liu, C., Zhang, C.S.: A two-step approach to hallucinating faces: Global parametric model and local non-parametric model. In: IEEE Conference on Computer Vision and Pattern Recognition, pp. 192–198 (2004)
5. Yeung, D., Chang, H., Xiong, Y.: Super-resolution through neighbor embedding. In: IEEE Conference on Computer Vision and Pattern Recognition, pp. 275–282 (2004)
6. Protter, M., Elad, M.: Super resolution with probabilistic motion estimation. IEEE Trans. Image Processing 18(8) (2009)
7. Pighin, F., Hecker, J., Lischinski, D., Szeliski, R., Salesion, D.H.: Synthesizing realistic facial expressions from photographs. In: Proceedings of SIGGRAPH, pp. 75–84 (1998)
8. Blanz, V., Vetter, T.: A morphable model for the synthesis of 3d faces. In: Proceedings of SIGGRAPH, pp. 187–194 (1999)
9. Kim, I.J., Ko, H.S.: Intutitive quasi-eigen faces. In: ACM International Conference on Computer Graphcis and Interactive Technique, pp. 33–38 (2007)
10. Smith, W.A.P., Hancock, E.R.: Recovering facial shape and albedo using a statistical model of surface normal direction. In: IEEE Conference on Computer Vision, pp. 588–595 (2005)
11. Shlizerman, I.K., Barsi, R.: 3D facial reconstruction from a single image using a single reference face shape. IEEE Trans. Pattern Analysis and Machine Intelligence 33, 394–405 (2011)
12. Milborrow, S., Nicolls, F.: Locating facial features with an extended active shape model. In: Forsyth, D., Torr, P., Zisserman, A. (eds.) ECCV 2008, Part IV. LNCS, vol. 5305, pp. 504–513. Springer, Heidelberg (2008)
13. http://www.3d3solutions.com

Timeline Localization

Ilona Nawrot[1,2] and Antoine Doucet[1]

[1] Normandy University — Unicaen, GREYC, HULTECH,
Campus Côte de Nacre, F–14032 Caen, France
[2] Poznań University of Economics, WIGE, KEM
al. Niepodległości 10, 61-875 Poznań, Poland
{ilona.nawrot,antoine.doucet}@unicaen.fr

Abstract. The research findings provide evidence that time-oriented data visualizations can contribute to faster information processing, better understanding and improved recall. Thus, they are used in many application domains – medicine, law enforcement, traffic and navigation control to name but a few. Simultaneously, human's time perception varies depending *inter alia* on culture, language, personal experience and situational factors. Although, the differences caused by the aforementioned aspects were acknowledged and addressed in the Human Computer Interaction (HCI) field for decades their impact on time-oriented data visualizations was largely neglected.

To fill this gap, we investigate the influence of time spatializations (organization of time along axes) on the response time and accuracy of inferences based on time-oriented data visualizations. Moreover, we examine users' preferences toward different time arrangements. Our findings show that user-adapted organization of time along axes can speed up the decision-making process and increase the user experience.

Keywords: timeline, localization, time perception, time spatialization, performance, preferences.

1 Introduction

Despite the importance of time in every aspect of people's lives relatively little attention has been paid to it in the HCI field. Typically it is considered an implicit, yet well defined, variable in the system design. Empirical research investigating cognitive performance of different time-oriented data visualizations, particularly accounting for individual or cultural diversity in time perception, is very limited. Moreover, a number of culture and language related differences in time conceptions and representations were not addressed at all.

In this paper the problem of information flow in time-oriented data visualizations is addressed and empirically investigated.

According to comparative linguistics and cognitive psychology studies, in order to conceptualize time, people rely on space. Nevertheless, factors like long-term cultural, linguistic and personal experience, as well as proximal situational context affect the conceptualization process. Consequently, time organization

M. Kurosu (Ed.): Human-Computer Interaction, Part I, HCII 2014, LNCS 8510, pp. 611–622, 2014.
© Springer International Publishing Switzerland 2014

along axes in mental and physical time-oriented data visualizations can differ significantly. In particular, people can represent time along horizontal or vertical axis and in both possible directions (it is from left to right or from right to left and from top to bottom or from bottom to top) [1–3].

Due to globalization interdependencies among the markets are growing. The flow of human capital in between countries is either opened or facilitated. Global corporations are being developed. Multicultural research groups are being formed. Simultaneously, owing to the accelerated pace of life, the need of fast decision-making is growing. Thus, as a consequence of information overload, the upsurge of reliance on data integration systems is observed. However, software in domains depending heavily on fast time-oriented data analysis (e.g. medicine [4–6], law enforcement [7, 8], military [9, 8] or air traffic and navigation control [10]) does not account for the fact that people can perceive, process and interact with temporal information differently. In general, it's design to follow western cultural cues and does not allow for the manipulation of time arrangements along axes.

This phenomenon raises the question of whether differences in time organization observed in between cultures affect the performance in the interaction with the system and user experience. In the empirical study presented in this article we examined the inference time and error rate depending on time arrangements in the scenario of simple information retrieval task, as well as users' preferences toward those arrangements. Moreover, based on the obtained results we formulated the recommendations for software and Web developers and designers.

The rest of the paper is organized as follows. First, we give an overview of the related work in Section 2. In Section 3, we describe the methodology of the experiment conducted to evaluate the possible differences in performance and preferences caused by the interaction with different time arrangements in time visualizations. Section 4 details its results whereas Section 5 provides the discussion and the summary of the paper.

2   Related Work

This work explores the role of time organization along axes in reasoning process based on time-oriented data visualizations. Time organization along axes depends on the culture and language experience. Further, it can be also affected by the situational context in which the reasoning takes place [1–3]. Thus, we firstly review the seminal works on localization and cultural adaptivity whose principal goal is to provide users with personalized experience catering their cultural or individual expectations. Then, we discuss the findings of comparative linguistics and cognitive psychology studies on time spatializations. Finally, we survey research on cognitive performance in time-oriented data visualizations.

2.1   Localization and Cultural Adaptivity

The minimization of restrictions on access to markets brought about increased competition. The amount of products that is aimed at international audience is constantly growing [16, 11]. This gives more choice to consumers. Hence, businesses to be competitive must meet the needs and expectations of customers to the highest extent. Nevertheless, cross-cultural differences can hinder achieving this goal. Such variations can impact user performance in the interaction with a product, his/her satisfaction and finally its acceptance. In the HCI field, these factors were particularly analyzed in the context of applications or Web sites implementation and design [11–16].

A great deal of research has been focused on the identification of cultural markers, it is elements typical of members of a given culture and likely affecting their preferences. It was demonstrated that software and Web designers should be aware of *inter alia* colors and fonts usage; wording of warning, error and help messages; or menus' architecture [12, 11, 13, 16]. Thus far, the following temporal cultural markers have been distinguished and examined: 1) date and time format [16]; 2) style of time management (mono-chronic culture[1] versus poly-chronic culture[2]) [17]; 3) time orientation (importance people attach to the past, present and future) [19]; 4) long-term or short-term orientation (degree to which people in a given culture are willing to defer present gratification for the sake of greater future reward) [18].

The knowledge on cultural differences stemmed from the research on cultural markers and it is used to adapt software and Web sites (on both functional and presentation level). Initially, the adaptation was being achieved through largely manual localization process. Firstly, during internationalization phase, culturally sensitive elements were being identified, isolated and all the preparatory tasks facilitating their subsequent adaptation were being performed (e.g. text containers' dimensions had to account for varying translations lengths). Then, during localization phase, the culture-specific content was being infused into previously isolated elements [20, 16]. Recently, due to expensiveness and high time consumption of manual localization, culturally adaptive systems are being proposed [12]. Such systems using a provided knowledge base and artificial intelligence techniques (usually ML or PGM modeling) automatically create initial user model and adapt culturally sensitive elements accordingly. Then, they analyze users' behavior and refine his/her model. Hereby, they also account for needs of culturally ambiguous individuals [12].

2.2   Time Spatialization

Despite extensive research and widespread interest in cross-cultural differences, including aforementioned temporal cultural markers, still a great deal of findings

---

[1] Mono-chronic cultures (e.g. Germany, Japan, most parts of the United States) are characterized by the tendency to handle tasks sequentially. Their members appreciate time and treat time commitments very seriously, strongly adhering to schedule [17].

[2] Multitasking and flexible plans are indicative of the poly-chronic cultures (e.g. China, Mexico, India). Individuals belonging to such cultures view time commitments as goals that can be easily changed depending on the situation [17].

from related domains were not evaluated in the HCI context. This applies particularly to the studies exploring the concept of time and especially the way people
spatialize time. Comparative linguistics and cognitive psychology research has
revealed an extensive flexibility, as well as cultural and linguistic variability in the
way people perceive and conceptualize time. People differ *inter alia* in whether
they see time as limited or open-ended; as static or dynamic with respect to an
observer (*ego-moving* or *time-moving* metaphor) or moving independently of any
observer (*time reference point* or *time-RP* metaphor). Moreover, some tend to
see time as moving along horizontal axis while others along vertical one [1, 3].
The axis can also be oriented in various directions (e.g. from bottom-to-top in
Zapotec [3] or from east-to-west in Pormpuraaw [1]). In this paper we focus on
cross-cultural differences in the space-time mappings and people's preferences
with respect to those conceptualizations.

Previous work has established that although wide diversity can be observed
between cultures in the way people spatialize time, three main classes of time
arrangements can be distinguished [1][3]: 1) along horizontal axis from left to right
or 2) from right to left and 3) along vertical axis from top to bottom. First, typical
of languages written from left to right (e.g. English), places past on the left side
and future on the right side of the horizontal axis [1, 3, 23, 24, 26, 27]. Second,
common among languages written from right to left (e.g. Arabic), locates time
on the horizontal axis but past on its right side and future on its left side [24–
27]. Third, observed in languages traditionally organizing text in columns (e.g.
Mandarin Chinese), position past on the top and future on the bottom of the
vertical axis [2, 21–23].

Although language and in particular the writing direction are used as an
organizing structure for time-space mappings presentation, those are neither the
only nor the deciding factors affecting the choice of spatialization. Thus far, the
following factors influencing the specific time arrangement along axis activation
have been distinguished and acknowledged by the scientific community [1, 22,
2]: 1) spatiotemporal metaphors (e.g. *Christmas is quickly approaching, The
meeting has been moved forward two days* or *He left sad memories behind* [3,
2]); 2) spatial representations available to co-opt with time; 3) organizational
patterns in cultural artifacts (e.g. writing direction, clocks, calendars, gestures);
4) cultural or personal experience and dispositions; 5) context.

The aforementioned factors were distinguished based on the studies analyzing
free productions, images' arrangements, response time and accuracy in different
conditions. Alternative spatializations were proven to be generally available (yet
sometimes very rarely used) in each culture. Nevertheless, differences in performance (usually measured by response time in various temporal reasoning tasks)
can be observed depending on the salience of the chosen time representation in
the given culture[4].

---

[3] Classification based on the number of people using the given time spatialization
frequently.
[4] It was proven that bilinguals can possess two mental timelines. In their case differences in performance are not statistically significant [2].

Finally, the consensus on the mechanism through which the abstract notion of time is conceptualized still has not been reached and is further researched.

2.3 Cognitive Performance in Time-Oriented Data Visualization

Time, and particularly the timeline metaphor, is an omnipresent organizational structure used in data visualizations [28]. It is established in scientific literature that time-oriented data visualizations can increase information retrieval performance, aid memorization and insight discovery processes. Nevertheless, studies investigating the aforementioned potential benefits of time visualizations are very sparse and limited.

Thus far, it was demonstrated that visuo-spatial timeline (ViST) format[5] outperforms both: traditional alphanumeric timeline (AnT) format[6]; and table-based data visualizations; in terms of reaction and task completion times [29, 30]. It was also shown, that in order to visualize space, time and agents, matrix representation with time as rows or columns, and space and agents as either entries or remaining axis (rows or columns)[7] is the most intuitive and effective model choice [31]. Moreover, the timeline metaphor was proven advantageous in reducing the first impression biases by increasing the accuracy of initial situation judgments [30]. Further, it was determined that it can mitigate the negative impact of large number of objects to monitor on response time and accuracy [9]. Finally, timelines and particularly timelines annotated with public or personal landmark events were found to benefit both the free and cued recall processes [30, 32, 29].

Although pointing out numerous advantages of time-oriented data visualizations, the results of the presented research studies are very constrained. Firstly, they do not account for differences in time perception and conceptualizations. Secondly, the research hypotheses are tested on a very specific, homogeneous sample (usually western undergraduate or graduate students) what makes the generalization of the results to the population questionable. Thirdly, comparative studies analyzing the differences in cognitive performance in between various types of time-oriented data visualizations are very limited. Thus, further research in this direction is indispensable.

3 Methodology

The aim of this paper is to evaluate whether time spatializations in data visualizations can affect the cognitive performance and satisfaction of individuals exposed to different linguistic or cultural norms. Thereby, whether time organization along axes adaptation should be incorporated as a standard feature in visualizations. An experiment was designed in order to investigate the effects

---

[5] Based on parallel, horizontal time lines.
[6] Based on vertical, subsequent lists of events.
[7] Depending on which dimension was ascribed to time.

of time arrangements along axes on user cognition and experience. It involved temporal reasoning over simple schedules visualizations.

The benefit of time organization along axes adaptation was hypothesized to be two-fold. Firstly, it was expected that the interaction with preferred time arrangement along axes, compared with other well known and frequently used by a user arrangement, would elicit faster reaction time. Secondly, it was assumed that such arrangements in juxtaposition with not-adapted ones would increase the overall user experience. In line with previous comparative linguistics and cognitive psychology findings, the accuracy of inferences was predicted not to be affected by time spatialization manipulations.

Participants. Ninety individuals who reported being fluent in two languages with different most salient time spatializations, yet not being bilingual in those, were recruited to participate in the experiment. Fifty-six of them were male, 34 female, ranging in age from 15 to 55 $(median = 28; \sigma = 7)$. The subjects represented 18 nationalities, were currently living in 15 countries and were speaking 21 different languages. Thus, their cultural and linguistic backgrounds varied. Over 84% of the participants already graduated from a university (about 61% receiving bachelor, 17% master and 4% doctoral degree). All but one of them, who reported using the Internet only on weekdays, were using computer and Internet on a daily basis.

Materials. The target stimuli comprised 2 sets of schedules of four individuals depicted on the common matrix-based visualization. Space and agents variables were categorical and both assumed 4 different values: *dorm, library, bookstore, gym* and *Justin, Alex, Sammy, David* respectively. Time in the experiment was mapped on the 4-valued ordinal variable taking the *morning, noon, afternoon* and *evening* values. Locations and times were represented either as columns or as rows, whereas agents were encoded via 4-colored dots[8]. For each set of schedules 28 true-false statements requiring temporal reasoning were being displayed under the matrix (Fig. 1). Within each set, half of the utterances were true. The number of syllables in each query was equated to a high degree. The statements' wording in both sets was similar to a great extent. Both, visualizations and questionnaires, were devised by Kessell [33, 31].

Design. The experiment was a within-subjects design with time arranged along different axes in the matrix-based schedule visualization as the main experimental factor. The effectiveness of inferences (response time and number of correct answers) was measured based on the questionnaires developed by Kessell [33, 31].

---

[8] Lines representation was found to be advantageous in inferences requiring time sequences analysis and in time trends identification tasks. Nevertheless, the participants of the ramp-up phase of the experiment reported to be confused at first once given 2 representations. Since, it could introduce differences in response time due to learning effects, only dots representation was used in the final experiment set up.

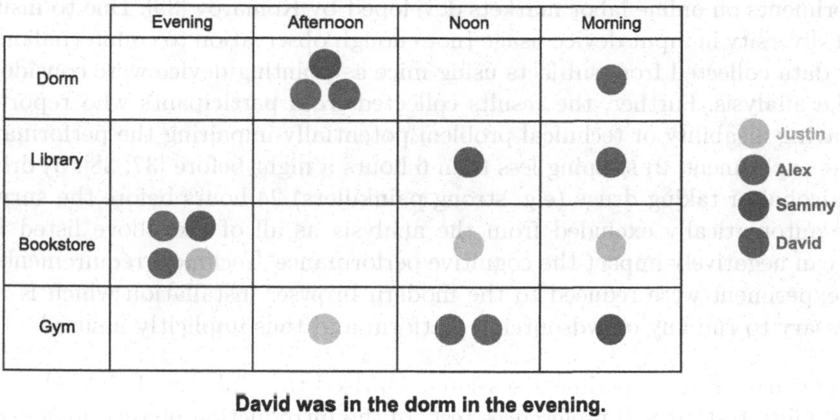

	Evening	Afternoon	Noon	Morning
Dorm				
Library				
Bookstore				
Gym				

Justin
Alex
Sammy
David

David was in the dorm in the evening.

Fig. 1. Example user stimuli

The users' preferences toward different time arrangements were assessed via self-developed 7-point Likert scale, where 7 represented time spatialization typical of the participant's mother tongue whereas 1 was mapped to the one common in the other language respondent reported was fluent in. Additionally, open question allowed the participants to indicate the conscious reasons behind their time spatialization choice. Finally, the information on participants' performance expectancy was collected using *Unified Theory of Acceptance and Use of Technology* (UTAUT) [34] which was previously validated cross-culturally [35, 36]. The overview of used assessment metrics is presented in Tab. 1.

Table 1. Summary of evaluation methods used in the experiment

Attribute	Assessment Method
Usability	Overall task completion time
	Geometric mean of task completion time [41]
	Number of correct answers
Preferences	4-item usability scale on a 7-point Likert scale on performance expectancy [34][a]
	2-item preferences scale on a 7-point Likert scale[b]
	open question[b]

[a] indirect measure
[b] direct measure

The study was run in an online scenario. The participants were recruited via *CrowdFlower* (a crowdsourcing platform) or *Facebook* advertisement. The experiment design accounted for the suggestions on conducting human subjects experiments on online labor markets developed by Komarov [39]. Due to insufficient diversity in input device usage (not enough observation to counterbalance), only data collected from subjects using mice as pointing device were considered in the analysis. Further, the results collected from participants who reported: 1) having disability or technical problem potentially impairing the performance in the experiment; 2) sleeping less than 6 hours a night before [37, 38]; 3) drinking alcohol or taking drugs (e.g. strong painkillers) 24 hours before the survey; were automatically excluded from the analysis as all of the above listed factors can negatively impact the cognitive performance. Technical requirements of the experiment were reduced to the modern browser installation which is also necessary to run any crowdsourcing platform and thus implicitly assured.

Procedure. Each experiment session comprised three phases: 1) introduction; 2) usability test; and 3) preferences test. In the introduction phase, participants were explained the test routine and in order to proceed, they were required to accept the informed consent form. In addition, demographic, cultural and linguistic background, as well as computer literacy information were collected at this stage.

The second phase started with the group assignment questionnaire establishing participant's language and time spatialization preferences and further checking for factors potentially affecting cognitive performance. Each usability test consisted of 2 blocks of 28 trials. In the *congruent scenario (CS)* block, subjects interacted with visualization in which time was organized according to his/her reported preferences. In the *incongruent (IS)* one the other, familiar to him/her time arrangement was used to provide structure to the visualization. In both scenarios, participants were given 1 matrix-based schedule visualization. On each trial, a statement requiring true-false temporal judgment based on the provided visualization was shown under the matrix. Participants were instructed to answer the questions as quickly, yet as accurately, as possible. They were asked to indicate their responses by clicking *True* or *False* button.

The usability test was preceded by 4 trials training block assuring the comprehension of the instructions. Scenarios' order was counterbalanced across participants to minimize the learning effects. To avoid ordering effects, the sequence of questions within each scenario was randomized. Furthermore, the participants were tested entirely in English to reduce the effects of proximal language context [23, 2, 26]. The choice of English was motivated by the fact that still a great deal of popular software and Web pages are available only in English. Moreover, it is used as a *lingua franca* among people working in multicultural environments.

Finally, in the third phase, participants preferences toward different time spatialization survey was carried out.

4   Analysis and Results

Data collected from the crowdsourcing platforms are susceptible to the extreme outliers problem [39]. To reduce the impact of abnormal observations on the final results, a method based on the inter-quartile ranges was applied [39]. It detected no extreme outliers, thus no data were excluded from the further analysis.

Visual inspection of data (histograms, normal Q-Q plots, box plots) indicated that overall completion time and number of errors samples are strongly right skewed which is consistent with other literature findings [40, 41]. The formal inspection of data using Shapiro-Wilk's and Anderson-Darling's tests ($p < 0.001$ for all variables) confirmed this hypotheses. Thus, the assumption of normal distribution of data was rejected. Since the assumption of normality was not met, the nonparametric Wilcoxon Signed-Rank Test for matched pairs were used to test the one-sided hypotheses of the superiority of adapted time visualizations over non-adapted ones. Moreover, the mean completion time metric was replaced with the geometric mean completion time, as the latter was proven to be a much more powerful estimate of the population center in skewed samples. All p-values (including non-significant ones) were adjusted using Benjamini-Hochberg correction to account for multiple hypotheses testing.

The results indicate that even though, as expected, the accuracy of inferences is not affected by time arrangement changes, the response time is (see Tab. 2).

Table 2. Usability results

Measure	Congruent scenario	Incongruent scenario	p-value
Overall task completion time	+	−	0.0002
Geometric mean completion time	+	−	0.0097
Number of correct answers	=	=	0.7076

Cronbach's alpha was used to test the Likert scale items' internal consistency and thus overall scales' reliability. Both scales were found to be valid, with excellent α scores about 90%. Therefore, the average overall ratings were computed for them (see Tab. 3). The results reveal strong preferences toward the adapted time arrangement. Interestingly, the preferences could rarely be correlated with the participant's mother tongues. The primary language of education appears to be a much better heuristic.

Table 3. Scales preferences results

Likert scale	Cronbach's alpha	Average overall rating
Performance expectancy (UTAUT)	0.886	23.71/28[a]
Preferences scale	0.900	11.97/14[a]

[a] preferences toward congruent time arrangement

The qualitative analysis of users' comments revealed: 1) decreased cognitive load and relatively greater ease in data decoding, interpretation and understanding (29 indications); 2) routines or cultural customs (13 indications); 3) habits established as part of education process (5 indications); 4) intuitiveness and naturalness (4 indications); as the main conscious reasons explaining their preferences.

5   Conlusions and Future Work

The evidence provided in this paper extends and partially contradicts the findings of Kessell [31]. It shows that time arrangement along axes can significantly influence performance and user experience in the interaction with time-oriented data visualizations. Consequently, we argue to enrich the time-oriented data visualizations with features allowing time spatialization adaptation and changes. We particularly recommend their inclusion in systems requiring fast information processing (e.g. medical, military systems), as well as in systems underlying on user engagement (e.g. personal storytelling, narrative visualizations). Although, present results demonstrate the impact time spatialization can have on visualizations, they open also many avenues for future research. It includes its influence on information recall and cumulative effects of more complex tasks.

Acknowledgments. This work has been supported by The French Ministry of Foreign Affairs through the Eiffel Excellence Scholarship.

Appendix

The questionnaires and data collected during the experiment are available to the scientific community and can be accessed at: https://nawrot.users.greyc.fr/resources/.

References

1. Boroditsky, L.: How Languages Construct Time. In: Dehaene, S., Brannon, E. (eds.) Space, Time and Number in the Brain: Searching for the Foundations of Mathematical Thought, pp. 333–341. Academic Press (2011)
2. Miles, L.K., Tan, L., Noble, G.D., Lumsden, J., Macrae, C.N.: Can a mind have two time lines? Exploring space-time mapping in Mandarin and English speakers. Psychon. Bull. Rev. 18(3), 598–604 (2011)
3. Santiago, J., Román, A., Ouellet, M.: Flexible foundations of abstract thought: A review and a theory. In: Maass, A., Schubert, T. (eds.) Spatial Dimensions of Social Thought, pp. 39–108. DE GRUYTER (2011)
4. Rind, A., Wang, T.D., Wolfgang, A., Miksch, S., Wongsuphasawat, K., Plaisant, C., Shneiderman, B.: Interactive Information Visualization to Explore and Query Electronic Health Records. Foundations and Trends in Human-Computer Interaction 5(3), 207–298 (2011)
5. Park, H., Choi, J.: V-Model: A New Innovative Model to Chronologically Visualize Narrative Clinical Texts. In: Konstan, J.A., Chi, E.H., Höök, C. (eds.) Proc. of the SIGCHI Conf. on Human Factors in Computing Systems, pp. 453–462. ACM, New York (2012)
6. Wang, T.D., Deshpande, A., Shneiderman, B.: A Temporal Pattern Search Algorithm for Personal History Event Visualization. IEEE Transactions on Knowledge and Data Engineering 24(5), 799–812 (2012)

7. Kwon, B.C., Javed, W., Ghani, S., Elmqvist, N., Yi, J.S., Ebert, D.: Evaluating the Role of Time in Investigative Analysis of Document Collections. IEEE Transactions on Visualization and Computer Graphics 18(11), 1992–2004 (2012)
8. Eppler, M.J., Pfister, R.: Best of Both Worlds: Hybrid Knowledge Visualization in Police Crime Fighting and Military Operations. In: Lindstaedt, S., Granitzer, M. (eds.) Proc. of the 13th Int. Conf. on Knowledge Management and Knowledge Technologies, pp. 17:1–17:8. ACM, New York (2013)
9. Willis, R.A.: Effect of Display Design and Situation Complexity on Operator Performance. In: Proc. of the Human Factors and Ergonomics Society 45th Ann. Meeting, pp. 346–350. Human Factors and Ergonomics Society, Santa Monica (2001)
10. Cordeil, M., Hurter, C., Lesbordes, R., Letondal, C., Vinot, J.-L., Conversy, S.: Tangible Encoding of Temporal Data in Air Traffic Control (2013), http://chi2013time.wordpress.com/accepted-papers/
11. Su, Y., Liu, D., Yuan, X., Ting, J., Jiang, J., Wang, L., Gao, L.: Webpage Designs for Diverse Cultures: An Exploratory Study of User Preferences in China. In: Kotzé, P., Marsden, G., Lindgaard, G., Wesson, J., Winckler, M. (eds.) INTERACT 2013, Part I. LNCS, vol. 8117, pp. 339–346. Springer, Heidelberg (2013)
12. Reinecke, K., Bernstein, A.: Improving Performance, Perceived Usability, and Aesthetics with Culturally Adaptive User Interfaces. ToCHI 18(2), A:1–A:29 (2011)
13. Marcus, A., Baumgartner, V.-J.: A Practical Set of Culture Dimensions for Global User-Interface Development. In: Masoodian, M., Jones, S., Rogers, B. (eds.) APCHI 2004. LNCS, vol. 3101, pp. 252 261. Springer, Heidelberg (2004)
14. Barber, W., Badre, A.: Culturability: The Merging of Culture and Usability. In: Proc. of the 4th Conf. on Human Factors and the Web (1998)
15. Evers, V., Day, D.: The Role of Culture in Interface Acceptance. In: Howard, S., Hammond, J., Lindegaard, G. (eds.) Proc. of the IFIP TC13 Int. Conf. on Human-Computer Interaction, INTERACT, pp. 260–267. Chapman & Hall, London (1997)
16. Russo, P., Boor, S.: How fluent is your interface? Designing for international users. In: Ashlund, S., Mullet, K., Henderson, A., Hollnagel, E., White, T. (eds.) Proc. of the INTERACT 1993 and CHI 1993 Conf. on Human Factors in Computing Systems, pp. 342–347. ACM, New York (1993)
17. Hall, E.T., Hall, M.R.: Understanding Cultural Differences: Germans, French and Americans. Intercultural Press, Boston (1990)
18. Hofstede, G.: Culture's Consequences: Comparing Values, Behaviours, Institutions and Organizations across Nations, 2nd edn. Sage Publications, Thousand Oaks (2001)
19. Adler, N.J., Gundersen, A.: International Dimensions of Organizational Behavior, 5th edn. Thompson South-Western, Mason (2007)
20. De Troyer, O., Casteleyn, S.: Designing Localized Web Sites. In: Zhou, X., Su, S., Papazoglou, M.P., Orlowska, M.E., Jeffery, K. (eds.) WISE 2004. LNCS, vol. 3306, pp. 547–558. Springer, Heidelberg (2004)
21. Boroditsky, L.: Does language shape thought? Mandarin and English speakers' conceptions of time. Cogn. Psychol. 43(1), 1–22 (2001)
22. Boroditsky, L., Fuhrman, O., McCormick, K.: Do English and Mandarin speakers think about time differently? Cognition 118(1), 123–129 (2011)
23. Fuhrman, O., McCormick, K., Chen, E., Jiang, H., Shu, D., Mao, S., Boroditsky, L.: How Linguistic and Cultural Forces Shape Conceptions of Time: English and Mandarin Time in 3D. Cogn. Sci. 35(7), 1305–1328 (2011)
24. Fuhrman, O., Boroditsky, L.: Cross-cultural differences in mental representations of time: evidence from an implicit nonlinguistic task. Cogn. Sci. 34(8), 1430–1451 (2010)

25. Nunez, R.E., Sweetser, E.: With the Future Behind Them: Convergent Evidence from Aymara Language and Gesture in the Crosslinguistic Comparison of Spatial Construals of Time. Cogn. Sci. 30(3), 401–450 (2006)
26. Ouellet, M., Santiago, J., Israeli, Z., Gabay, S.: Is the Future the Right Time? Exp. Psychol. 57(4), 308–314 (2010)
27. Tversky, B., Kugelmass, S., Winter, A.: Cross-Cultural and Developmental Trends in Graphic Productions. Cogn. Psychol. 23(4), 515–557 (1991)
28. Aigner, W., Miksch, S., Schumann, H., Tominski, C.: Visualization of Time-Oriented Data. Springer, London (2011)
29. Bahr, G.S., Walwanis, M.M., Wheeler Atkinson, B.F.: Musically Inspired Computer Interfaces: Reaction Time and Memory Enhancements in Visuo-Spatial Timelines (ViST) for Graphic User Interfaces. In: Stephanidis, C., Antona, M. (eds.) UAHCI/HCII 2013, Part II. LNCS, vol. 8010, pp. 555–564. Springer, Heidelberg (2013)
30. Alonso, D.L., Rose, A., Plaisant, C., Norman, K.L.: Viewing personal history records: A comparison of Tabular format and graphical presentation using Life-Lines. Behaviour & Information Technology 17(5), 249–262 (1998)
31. Kessell, A., Tversky, B.: Visualizing space, time, and agents: production, performance, and preference. Cognitive Processing 12(1), 43–52 (2011)
32. Ringel, M., Cutrell, E., Dumais, S.T., Horvitz, E.: Milestones in Time: The Value of Landmarks in Retrieving Information from Personal Stores. In: Rauterberg, M., Menozzi, M., Wesson, J. (eds.) Human-Computer Interaction, INTERACT, pp. 184–191. IOS Press (2003)
33. Kessell, A.M.: Cognitive Methods for Information Visualization: Linear and Cyclical Events. PhD Dissertation (2008), https://www.stanford.edu/dept/psychology/cgi-bin/drupalm/system/files/Kessell_Dissertation.08.pdf
34. Venkatesh, V., Morris, M.G., Davis, G.B., Davis, F.D.: User acceptance of information technology: toward a unified view. MIS Quarterly 27(3), 425–478 (2003)
35. Venkatesh, V., Zhang, X.: Unified Theory of Acceptance and Use of Technology: U.S. vs. China. J. of Global Information Technology Management 13(1), 5–27 (2010)
36. Oshlyansky, L., Cairns, P., Thimbleby, H.: Validating the unified theory of acceptance and use of technology (UTAUT) tool cross-culturally. In: Ramduny-Ellis, D., Rachovides, D. (eds.) Proc. of the 21st British HCI Group Ann. Conf. on People and Computers: HCI...But Not as We Know It, pp. 83–86. BCS, Swinton (2007)
37. Killgore, W.D.S., Weber, M.: Sleep deprivation and cognitive performance. In: Bianchi, M.T. (ed.) Sleep Deprivation and Disease. Effects on the Body, Brain and Behavior, pp. 209–229. Springer, New York (2014)
38. Alhola, P., Polo-Kantola, P.: Sleep deprivation: Impact on cognitive performance. Neuropsychiatric Dis. Treat. 3(5), 553–567 (2007)
39. Komarov, S., Reinecke, K., Gajos, K.Z.: Crowdsourcing performance evaluations of user interfaces. In: Bødker, S., Brewster, S., Baudisch, P., Beaudouin-Lafon, M., Mackay, W.E. (eds.) Proc. of the SIGCHI Conf. on Human Factors in Computing Systems, pp. 207–216. ACM, New York (2013)
40. Ratcliff, R., McKoon, G.: The diffusion decision model: theory and data for two-choice decision tasks. Neural Computation 20(4), 873–922 (2008)
41. Sauro, J., Lewis, J.R.: Average task times in usability tests: what to report? In: Proc. of the SIGCHI Conf. on Human Factors in Computing Systems, pp. 2347–2350. ACM, Atlanta (2010)

Design Criteria for Public Display User Interfaces

Alessandro Bendinelli and Fabio Paternò

CNR-ISTI, HIIS Laboratory, Via G.Moruzzi 1, 56124 Pisa, Italy
{alessandro.bendinelli,fabio.paterno}@isti.cnr.it

Abstract. Recent technological advances have made large displays available on the mass market at affordable prices. We present a set of design criteria that support those who want to exploit such displays effectively to select the relevant content and present it in such a way to take into account the features of the specific devices and the context in which they are used. The discussion is exemplified with concrete example application of the design criteria.

Keywords: Public Displays, Guidelines and heuristics, Presentation design.

1 Introduction

Recent technological advances have made available on the mass market large displays in the range of 40 – 60 inches at affordable prices. Such displays can vary in terms of orientations and technologies used (LCD, plasma, various types of projectors, …). Given the low cost such devices are being installed in great numbers in a variety of public places (train stations, airports, hospitals, public offices, museums, universities, shop centers, bars and restaurants, …). Thus, their deployment can occur both in outdoor and indoor environments for providing various types of contents (informative, entertainment, advertisements, …).

Unfortunately, often this widespread distribution has occurred without paying sufficient attention to how information is provided through such devices, thus diminishing their potential effectiveness. Indeed, some authors introduced the concept of display blindness [1] to indicate an effect similar to banner blindness on the Web: displays for which users expect uninteresting content (e.g. advertisements) are often ignored; an example taken from the Pisa (Italy) train station is shown in Figure 1.

Thus, it becomes important to think carefully about what information to provide through such screens and how to present it. Indeed, this work was stimulated by a project of a regional public authority in the health domain in which a number of large displays were bought for their deployment in various hospitals, first aid centers, and health offices and they needed to identify guidelines regarding information selection and presentation in such devices.

The purpose of this paper is to introduce a set of design criteria for public displays that can be installed in various contexts of use and indicate some examples of their application. We focus on public displays, which provide dynamic output but do not support the possibility of user interactions, since this is still the most common case of

M. Kurosu (Ed.): Human-Computer Interaction, Part I, HCII 2014, LNCS 8510, pp. 623–630, 2014.
© Springer International Publishing Switzerland 2014

their use and, even if technically possible, for various reasons organizations sometimes do not wish to allow interaction with them. The only interactive element that we have considered is the use of QR codes in public displays user interfaces since it is easy even for non-technologically expert users and content providers. Thus, its use can be recommended even if user interaction is not contemplated because it can be a simple mechanism to provide additional related information on the users' smartphones.

Fig. 1. Example of display blindness in a train station

In the paper, after discussing related work, we introduce the dimensions characterising the proposed set of design criteria, we then discuss how to apply them more in detail, and provide some example applications. Lastly, we draw some conclusions and provide indications for future work.

2   Related Work

Designing user interfaces for large displays has some differences with respect to the case for Web desktop applications, which are the most common applications. In desktop Web applications users usually   access their applications alone, while sitting, and with the possibility of spending   some time for searching and reading information, which can be located on any Web server, public displays are usually accessed in public areas, where people are on the move and have little time to observe them. Moreover, the information that is accessible in such displays is predefined, with limited or no possibility for users to select the content.

While many user interface guidelines exist for desktop and mobile devices, little has been proposed to capture the specific aspects of public displays. Nebelling et al. [2] addressed issues related to the overall use of the screen, the proportions between different content elements and the readability of larger amounts of text but only in the context of news web sites accessed through large screens. They pointed out that Web sites made with older technologies or that are not designed from scratch with a view to adapting show various problems. Some common causes of problems are: the fixed vertical layout, i.e. with default columns width that cannot be modified and do not allow easily readable distribution of content in the space provided; poor layout with large centre or left areas, leaving large unused spaces; the intrinsic characteristics of texts and fonts used (weight, size, etc..) that, when set in absolute rather than relative terms, do not fit the browser window. The authors indicate possible solutions based on automatic font scaling, elements adaptation, use of CSS3 multi-column attributes, and automatic content pagination.

Muller et al. [3] found that the specific requirements for public displays are that they need to grab the attention of passers-by, motivate passers-by to interact with them, and deal with the issues of interaction in the public. Thus, they identified a taxonomy for existing display installations according to four possible ways (posters, window, mirror, and overlay) to use interactive public displays and briefly discuss the most suitable interaction modalities and interaction techniques for each of them without providing a set of concrete design criteria. Huang et al. [4] report on the findings of a field study examining the current use practises of large ambient information displays in public settings. They found that the technology and content being widely used was relatively simple. The set of public displays for ambient information that they found deployed consisted almost entirely of non-interactive vertical displays consisting of announcements for services, events, resources, "fun facts," or products, as well as more abstract artistic content. From their analysis they derived some general recommendations that concern brevity of glances, positioning of displays, content formats and dynamics, catching the eyes, and display size. We have considered also them in elaborating our proposal with the aim to provide more concrete indications for user interface designers and developers. Alt et al. [5] have considered how to evaluate public displays rather than the design of their user interfaces: they identified five evaluation paradigms either used to inform the design of a prototype (ethnography, asking users) or to evaluate a prototype (lab study, field study, deployment-based research), and they ended up with some other general recommendations as well: choose your focus on internal, external, or ecological validity; consider the impact of the content; understand the users; and check for common problems.

Examples of interesting applications in the public displays area are reported in [6, 7]. In particular, [6] reports on the design, development, and deployment of Digifieds (derived from digital classified), digital public notice area, and the findings from its evaluation: the preferred content is events, sales, and community-based information; both the mobile and the display client could be easily used, preferences depend on the user's situation and privacy concerns. The other application [7], Agora2.0, is a system that aims to foster the dialog between citizens and their political representatives and administrators, composed of two equally relevant features: an online system for voting ideas and an interactive public display deployed in a public space that is relevant to the community, a public relations office. However, a set of structured guidelines for designing user interfaces for public displays has not emerged from such works either.

3   The Design Space

Based on our experiences and discussions with target users and domain experts, and the analysis of previous work in the area of public displays, we have identified nine aspects that are relevant when designing user interfaces for public displays.

They can be grouped according to three main dimensions: the context of use in which the public display is deployed and accessed, how to select and organise the content to provide through it, and how to present the content in such a way to allow effective and efficient access to it.

In particular, the most relevant contextual aspects are:

- Position: where the display is located has an impact on the choice of the most suitable type of information and presentation, some locations are suitable for longer information access while others are places of transit and thus users dedicate rapid limited attention;
- Time: different contents can be more relevant depending on the time they are shown, for example if the display is located in places where new events occur frequently, then it is useful to exploit such changing events and immediately indicate those happening in the upcoming relevant time period;

The content-related aspects are:

- Type: it is important to carefully select the type of information, the source channel and media used to communicate, this depends on the environment in which the display is located, the target users, and its purpose;
- Number of information items: refers to the number of information topics presented with a specific style. Usually, the public display user interface is structured in a number of distinct areas, each of them presenting information associated with a specific topic. Overall, the screen should be exploited in its entirety without becoming too cluttered;
- Text: it refers to what various textual styles to adopt, how to structure them, the number of words associated with each of them, and how they should be presented.

The presentation-related aspects are:

- Layout: The visual structure of the user interface should consider the screen dimensions and exploit them in terms of number of internal areas, associated with the various information topic addressed, their positions, and dimensions;
- Colour: the choice of the colours for the user interface elements should facilitate visual interpretation for users viewing from distances greater than desktop users (usually between 1 and three meters instead of less than half meter);
- Font: the most suitable font attributes for the textual content in this type of display;
- Dynamicity: how the content presentations change over time and how their transitions should be represented.

4   How to Consider the Design Space

In this section we detail and discuss how to address the various dimensions of the proposed design space, and which aspects to consider for each of them.

For the context of use we have identified the position and the time as two important factors. Regarding the position, the choice of the place where to locate the display is fundamental: it should be accessible, visible, in a heavily trafficked place, at eye level or above. It can be indoor or outdoor (e.g. streets, train stations, …). Some typical indoor locations are entrances, waiting rooms, hallways, shop windows, counter of an information point, … Depending on the position various aspects can vary: the information displayed, the dynamicity of the information, the structure of the layout, timing, For example, a display at the entrance can show various screens with essential information repeated periodically, while a display in a waiting room can show various, more detailed, pieces of information at the same time, available for longer time. In a street it can be useful to have some multimedia elements with animations in order to draw the attention.

The scheduling is another important aspect as well: the type of content should be well suited to the time of its display in order to highlight useful information for the next hours. Such information can be general or specific to the context in which the public display is located. For example, in the morning it can be useful to show weather forecast for the day or the timing for public opening, while in the afternoon it can be useful to indicate events that occur in the evening nearby, while in the evening it can be useful to show the weather forecast and meetings that are scheduled for the day after.

Regarding the content types, in order to make them more visible and pleasant they should be multimedia, by integrating various types of texts with images, videos, maps, … but they should also simple to ease their interpretation. QR codes can be useful to provide related additional information directly in the users' smartphones. The sources of the contents can be heterogeneous, some of them can be static and others dynamic, provided by external sources, which can be local or remote. The important point is that external content should be filtered and structured in order to be included consistently in the public display user interface. The use of content derived from social networks depends on the application domain considered. For example, in the project about deployment of large displays in the health sector we discussed the use of Twitter as a source of information. However, this possibility was discarded since in some cases the information provided needs to be first carefully checked, and may even have some legal implications. While in the same domain the display of content derived from news channels was considered useful in order to provide up-to-date information on a variety of subjects and does not suffer from such drawbacks.

The number of information items to provide depends on the purpose of the display, the user interface structure and where it is located. For example, if the purpose of the display is informative then greater amount of information is expected, even provided dynamically through multiple presentations. The location is relevant since it determines how long people can look at the screen, and consequently the number of topics that can be considered: waiting rooms or public offices imply the possibility of standing for longer time than entrances and corridors where people have to move and so the texts should be read quickly. Each topic is associated with an area in the public display, usually we have a range from 3 to 6 informative areas.

Regarding the text, usually it should be communicated with short clear expressions, in very few lines, left or centre aligned, sometimes using bulleted lists. In the design of digital signage slides, some authors [8] indicate that, in order to provide clean, simple, attractive, and appropriate content, the main message should be communicated with a few, clear, and simple words (from 2/3 to 5/6 words), and a limited number of rows (from 1/2 to 6/7 rows). Titles should be with at most 22 characters, texts with at most 27-30 words, verbs used in active form, describing actions and stimulating involvement by using key words. In any case, secondary information can be structured in longer and more discursive paragraphs with the goal to provide additional information to the main message and stimulate the viewers' reading and deepening.

For the presentation, various aspects should be considered. The layout should be organised in such a way to capture the users' attention and drive their visual scan. It should be composed of three to five areas associated with the main information topics whose space depends on their importance. The resulting structure should be regular and easy to interpret. In general, there is one main area in the central part, which should attract the user's attention and provide the most important information, and some secondary areas with various spaces. Thus, symmetric layouts where two or more main areas have similar size do not seem to provide a useful hierarchy for driving the user view.

The public displays often should grab attention and communicate a message quickly and effectively. When too many colours are used, our eyes do not know where to look first. Thus, the classical 7± 2 colours can be applied. Indeed, by simplifying the colour number it will be possible to more effectively guide viewers. Contrast is a key element in colour choice in order to make sure that the message is easily readable. The choice of the colour should also consider the type of lighting available in the location where the public display is deployed.

The font should be simple and readable in order to better support the communication. It is better to avoid the use of fanciful or small fonts, which can be difficult to read. The titles should have a font size larger than texts with a ratio that can go from 1 : 1,5 up to 1 : 2 (for example, titles with 40 pts and text body with 24 pts or titles with 72 pts and body text with 36 pts) [8].

There are two types of dynamic behaviours in public displays: one is related to animated content often used to attract user's attention and one is more oriented to provide pleasant effects during the transition between showing two different pieces of information. Usually the interaction between the user and the display is short and casual. The user's full attention is usually limited to 2-3 seconds. Then, before deciding whether reading carefully or moving the gaze somewhere else the content is looked for 10-15 seconds. The overall average observation time depends on the purpose of the display and its location and is usually between 3 and 7 minutes. In an entrance or hallway it can be 2-3 minutes while in a waiting room it can be 7-8 minutes. In the case of various pieces of information that are shown in a cyclic way then the average time for each presentation should be around 3-5 minutes with some variations depending on the location [9].

5   Three Example Applications

We have considered three example applications for our guidelines for public displays: a hospital waiting room, a museum, and a research centre. Such contexts are different and thus determine the communication of different types of information in a different way.

In a museum context using a public display to show static information such as fares and opening time would have limited effectiveness, while exploiting the large screen in order to show dynamic content that supplements the static descriptions accompanying the various artworks could improve the user experience. For example, in a museum showing sculptures, it can be used to show where the quarries from which the material for such sculptures was extracted are located, the techniques used to extract such material, where the artists processed them, other artworks made by the same artists or similar artworks that are located in other museums.

Hospital waiting rooms are destined for use by people who often have to wait for long times, and thus may be willing to read more elaborated content. Health organizations can take this opportunity to provide users with information regarding the current services situation and how to access them (waiting list, expected duration, booking modalities, services currently available) but also for stimulating interest on how to improve personal behaviour and health or for some prevention and awareness campaign. For example, they can use them also for some campaign against smoking or alcoholism or for suggesting better diets and physical exercises. They can also be exploited for advertising events such as donor days. In order to enrich the informative content some information not strictly health related can be provided, such as local and national news, weather forecast, photo galleries of the sights of the area.

In the case of a research centre, an example is shown in Figure 2, public display represents a tool that can be exploited for providing students and visitors with overviews on the most recent research results and activities, also through images and videos showing some engaging demos, in order to stimulate interest in them. Such content can be accompanied by some general information regarding the town and weather forecast, and news related to the relevant research areas (such as forthcoming conferences, recently published papers by other groups, …).

Fig. 2. Example of public display in a research context

6   Conclusions

We have presented a set of design criteria for public display user interfaces in order to support organizations that have to deploy them in their environments. In this work we have focused on how to provide output information through such devices. For this purpose we have identified a set of relevant dimensions and discussed how to consider them through a number of related design aspects. We also discuss their use in three specific application domains.

We plan to further detail such design criteria in order to obtain a set of guidelines that can also be supported by an authoring environment able to implement them when selecting content and designing user interfaces for specific public displays. A further planned extension is to supplement the guidelines with indications on how to interact with such user interfaces, when possible. Such refinements will also be obtained through a number of user tests that will be carried out in order to empirically validate the final guidelines set.

References

1. Müller, J., Wilmsmann, D., Exeler, J., Buzeck, M., Schmidt, A., Jay, T., Krüger, A.: Display Blindness: The Effect of Expectations on Attention towards Digital Signage. Pervasive, 1–8 (2009)
2. Nebeling, M., Matulic, F., Norrie, M.: Metrics for the Evaluation of News Site Content Layout in Large-Screen Contexts. In: Proceedings CHI 2011, pp. 1511–1520. ACM Press (2011)
3. Müller, J., Alt, F., Schmidt, A., Michelis, D.: Requirements and Design Space for Interactive Public Displays. ACM Multimedia, 1285–1294 (2010)
4. Huang, E.M., Koster, A., Borchers, J.: Overcoming Assumptions and Uncovering Practices: When Does the Public Really Look at Public Displays? In: Indulska, J., Patterson, D.J., Rodden, T., Ott, M. (eds.) Pervasive 2008. LNCS, vol. 5013, pp. 228–243. Springer, Heidelberg (2008)
5. Alt, F., Schneegaß, S., Schmidt, A., Müller, J., Memarovic, N.: How to Evaluate Public Displays. In: Proceedings PerDis 2012, p. 17. ACM Press (2012)
6. Alt, F., Kubitza, T., Bial, D., Zaidan, F., Ortel, M., Zurmaar, B., Lewen, T., Sahami Shirazi, A., Schmidt, A.: Digifieds: insights into deploying digital public notice areas in the wild. In: MUM 2011, pp. 165–174 (2011)
7. Schiavo, G., Milano, M., Saldivar, J., Nasir, T., Zancanaro, M., Convertino, G.: Agora2.0: enhancing civic participation through a public display. In: C&T 2013, pp. 46–54 (2013)
8. University of British Columbia, Guidelines for digital signage, http://digitalsignage.ubc.ca/current-clients/content-guidelines/ (last accessed on February 5, 2014)
9. Rafi Elettronica S.p.A., Digital Signage Project – Content Strategy, http://www.rafi.it/pdf/digital_signage.pdf

Recommender System to Support Chart Constructions with Statistical Data

Taissa Abdalla Filgueiras de Sousa[1,2] and Simone Diniz Junqueira Barbosa[1]

[1] Departamento de Informática, PUC-Rio, Rio de Janeiro, RJ, Brazil
[2] IBGE
{tsousa,simone}@inf.puc-rio.br

Abstract. Research on statistical data visualization emphasizes the need for systems that assist in decision-making and visual analysis. Having found problems in chart construction by novice users, we researched the following question: *How can we support novice users to create efficient visualizations with statistical data?* To address this question, we proposed ViSC, a recommender system that supports the interactive construction of charts to visualize statistical data. It explores a visualization ontology to recommend a set of graphs that help to answer information-based questions related to the current graph data. By traversing the recommended graphs through their related questions, the user implicitly acquires knowledge both of the domain and of visualization resources that represent the domain concepts of interest well. We report here a qualitative study conducted to evaluate ViSC using two methods: the Semiotic Inspection Method (SIM) and a Retrospective Communicability Evaluation (RCE). We first analyze how the questions influence the users' traversal through the graph and then address the broader question. We concluded the questions were important to generate efficient visualizations and thus, an efficient solution to help novice users in chart constructions.

Keywords: Statistical data visualization, recommender systems, semiotic engineering, human-computer-interaction.

1   Introduction

The goal of visualization is to aid understanding of data, leveraging the ability of the human visual system to identify patterns, detect trends and discrepancies [15]. Visualizations can be an effective means of communication when it takes advantage of human perception and cognition [22], esp. the human ability to recognize visual patterns [23]. However, chart creators or designers can confuse the reader either by selecting misleading graph types or by distorting representations. Tufte [27] describes methods to create well-designed charts, but also common techniques that obscure the reader's understanding, such as lack or forgetfulness of scale; omission of the initial value, which should be always zero (otherwise it may cause disproportion between the compared values); and comparison between part and the whole (comparisons between the past whole year with the current one). Thus, an efficient visualization can help in comprehension, memory and decision-making. On the other hand, inadequate visualizations can confuse the user, causing misinterpretation of data.

M. Kurosu (Ed.): Human-Computer Interaction, Part I, HCII 2014, LNCS 8510, pp. 631–642, 2014.
© Springer International Publishing Switzerland 2014

To promote an adequate interpretation and to avoid mistakes, students need not only perceptual experience but also mathematical knowledge [12]. Chart interpretation requires specific knowledge of graphic systems, which are not easy to learn [4, 13]. This problem is aggravated in countries with high rates of functional illiteracy and cultures that promote information absorption without questioning.

Computational systems that allow users to interact with charts can also influence to the data interpretation and the graphic system understanding. These systems aim to improve the user experience in data visualization and motivate his interest. Among the visualization tools to present statistical data in the Web, we find:[1] Manyeyes, GapMinder, Worldmapper, Statplanet, Google Public Data, several multimedia atlas, SIDRA, and Statistical Series. There are also several available toolkits that allow chart creation, such as:[2] Flare, Silverlight, JavaScript InfoVis toolkit and ivtk. However, many tools for novice users restrict users to a single visualization, and toolkits usually need additional programming to make the operations to the visualization creation, i.e., they target expert users [10].

Mackinlay et al. state "all analysts have knowledge about their problems domain, but only few have skills to design effective graphic presentations of information", and "people need systems of visual analyses that automatically present data using the best practices of graphic design" [19]. Sousa reached a similar conclusion when she analyzed problems of chart construction and interpretation through a qualitative research evaluation with some Web visualization tools [25].

Sousa also verified that the phrasing of the information-seeking question is a central step for reading and designing charts [1]. To help novice users in creating efficient visualizations, we created ViSC — Visualization with Smart Charts —, a visualization tool for displaying statistical data that helps users to explore the information visualization space by recommending related visualizations based on typical information-seeking questions.

In the next section, we list some internet visualization tools and explain why they do not meet users' requirements for visualizing statistical data. Section 3 describes ViSC, our visualization tool. In section 4, we report a study to evaluate ViSC. Finally, section 5 presents concluding remarks and discusses future work.

2   Related Work

Our work draws on research on graphic systems, visualization techniques for interactive systems, automatic presentation techniques and tools.

---

[1] http://www-958.ibm.com/software/analytics/manyeyes/;
http://www.gapminder.org/; http://www.worldmapper.org/;
http://www.sacmeq.org/interactive-maps/statplanet/StatPlanet.html;
http://www.google.com/publicdata/directory?hl=en_US&dl=en_US#;
http://www.sidra.ibge.gov.br/;
http://seriesestatisticas.ibge.gov.br/
[2] http://flare.prefuse.org/;http: //www.silverlight.net/;
http://thejit.org/; http://ivtk.sourceforge.net

With regard to the rules of reading and constructing charts, we followed Bertin's semiology of graphics [1] and the Few's guidelines [11]. According to Bertin [1], the basic problem of chart construction is the selection of representation, which depends on the evaluation of specific properties and efficiency of each language. Heer and Shneiderman [16] describe three design solutions for data visualization. The first solution uses chart typology, a palette of available visualizations for analysts to show their data. Despite its simplicity and familiarity, especially to spreadsheet users, this approach may become cumbersome when trying out different visualizations with the same data. The second solution consists of using data-flow graphs, in which the visualization process is composed of a set of operators to enable tasks like data import, transformation, layout, coloring, etc. It allows flexible combination of systems and more design variations, but it also requires more effort than chart typologies. The third and last solution involves formal grammars for building visualizations. These grammars are high-level languages that describe how data should map onto visual features. Some examples of this type of solution are toolkits, such as: *ggplot for the R statistical analysis platform*,[3] Protovis [2] for HTML5, and Google Chart Tools.[4] However, as described before, toolkits require some programming skill. As these methods are not mutually exclusive, ViSC uses chart typology and formal grammar. However, our grammar is used only internally by a recommender system, and thus ViSC does not require programming skills from the user.

Tableau[5] and Explorations Views (EV) [10] are recent visualization tools developed for both novice and expert users. Show me [19] is an integrated set of interface commands that add automatic presentation in Tableau, a commercial system designed to be used by novice and expert users to create effective visualizations based on Bertin's semiology of graphics [1] and on the algebra of APT [20]. The Show Me panel consists of a dialog of choices with tooltips that describe conditions for a choice to be available. Exploration Views (EV) is still a prototype but also suggests charts and templates to create dashboards by novice users.

The next section describes ViSC, the proposed tool whose design draws on Bertin's and Few's rules and guidelines, as well as on the methods of automatic presentations used in Tableau and EV.

3   The ViSC Tool

Results of a qualitative user evaluation study of visualization tools [25] also influenced the design of ViSC interface. Similar to both EV and Tableau, ViSC generates visualizations of aggregated multidimensional data from selecting only two variables, while assigning default initial values to the remaining variables. As part of the process of information seeking, ViSC differs from the others because includes a knowledge-based recommender system [3]. Based on ViSC's ontology [24], the interface recommends charts to help meet user needs. From the selected data and visualization, ViSC attempts to infer questions the user might want to answer at each moment.

---

[3] http://had.co.nz/ggplot2/
[4] https://developers.google.com/chart/interactive/docs/index
[5] http://www.tableausoftware.com/

ViSC's ontology [24] was inspired on the ontology of the Visko project [28], the visualization ontology of UK National e-Science Center [21] and the data taxonomy of Tory *et al.* [26]. It has five high-level classes: data, display attribute, visualization, task and transformation.

The ontology associates eight kinds of visualization — clustered columns, multiple columns, stacked columns, time series, multiple time series, stacked series, scatterplot and table —, questions related to these visualizations and characteristics of the selected data such as type of component and nature. The questions were classified according to the taxonomy of Amar *et al.*, which covers a set of ten task related to specific questions of a user may ask while work in a set of data [1]. The covered tasks are: retrieve value, filter, compute derived value, find *extremum*, sort, determine range, characterize distribution, find anomalies, cluster and correlate. In ViSC, the questions are dynamically generated based on templates stored at the database, such as:

- How many <persons> with <10 years of study> are in <Rio de Janeiro>? (task: retrieve value)
- What is the average of <grade average> in <disciplines> of the selected set? (task: compute derived value)

The relation between data characteristics and display attributes defines preconditions to map variables onto display attributes. We have also attributed scores (from 1 to 5) to the relation data-question-visualization. Therefore, besides data characteristics, the ontology presents selection conditions according to the number of selected elements at each dimension.

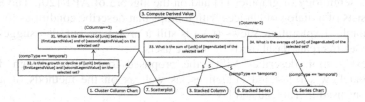

Fig. 1. Ontology fragment related to the task Compute Derive Value

Figure 1 presents a fragment of the ontology relating the task Compute Derived Value, its questions, conditions and effective visualizations. You can see that, regarding question 31, which calculates the difference between two quantitative values, the selection condition is to have 3 columns among the selected data. To answer this question, our visualization shows the scatterplot as the most highly rated (score equal to 5), so it is the most efficient between the options.

Figure 2 presents the ViSC main user interface. Area 1 displays the menu of elements to each dimension. Area 2 provides the visualization menu, whose items are enabled and disabled according semantic characteristics of the selected data (preconditions). Area 3 presents buttons to sort the data into the displayed chart. Area 4 is the main area, where the system displays charts. Finally, area 5 shows the related questions to recommend different visualizations.

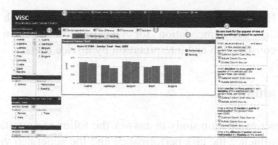

Fig. 2. ViSC Interface

The questions are generated by the user's interaction with the system in the following way: after the user selects the data, ViSC presents questions related to the current displayed visualization and recommends other efficient visualization to a different set of questions related to the selected data.

The questions aim to enable a user-system dialog in close-to-natural language, so that the user traverses through other visualizations related to the answer he seeks. For each interaction, the displayed questions can be changed or highlighted at the user interface, to reflect their relevance to the selected data. Thus, the system guides the user in searching for an effective visualization to answer her question. All visualizations related to the question are displayed at the interface sorted by score in decreasing order. The score is shown at the interface inside the star icon beside the name of the chart.

According to Semiotic Engineering, the user interface is a metacommunication artifact through which the designer sends to users a *metamessage* of why and how the users can and should use the system 9. From previous studies we defined the following ViSC metamessage: *"I think you are a student or a professional from a field related or not to statistics and need to create efficient visualizations. As you may not have total domain about the graphic system, you would like to have an interface that, with little interaction, creates a chart. From this chart you would like to easily change selected values or representation. You also want to be able to compare the displayed chart with other visualizations. Thus, we designed a system that, from the selection of the theme and two more variables, displays a chart with some dimensions selected automatically by default. You need only to include or switch the pre-defined values and select by one of the avialable visualizations. In order to help you to choose the most efficient visualization, the interface recommends visualizations based on questions you may want to answer. You can select the visualization through options of menu or through the questions. By selecting this kind of interaction you only need to find the sought question and to choose one or some among the recommended visualizations. The interface shows how to obtain the answer and highlight it in the chart. Each recommended visualization also has a score related to your selection and to a question you may want to answer. The interface displays these scores to help in your choice. You can also try other options to improve your chart such as switch axis, include difference, change scales, remove zero or sort values."*

The main difference between ViSC and the other tools is exactly the dialog ViSC exchanges with the user through the related questions. Thus, we have aimed to contribute to the Human-Computer-Interaction (HCI) field through this proposal of interaction based on recommendation for visualization tools in order to solve problems of chart construction and interpretation by novice users.

4   ViSC Evaluation

We conducted a user evaluation study to answer the following question: "How do the related questions influence the task performance and the generated visualizations?" In this study, we compared ViSC with Tableau Public,[6] to understand the chart construction process with and without the interface questions. We selected two qualitative methods to triangulate results: the Semiotic Inspection Method (SIM) [6] and a method we named *"Retrospective Communicability Evaluation* (RCE)"*, which involves user observation, Retrospective Think Aloud (RTA) [14] and the tagging step of the Communicability Evaluation Method (CEM) [8].

4.1   Methodology

SIM [6] is the proposed method by Semiotic Engineering [9] to analyze the diversity of signs and sign systems that compose the metamessage. After inspecting the metalinguistic signs (found in the system documentation and in natural language messages), static signs (composed of images, icons, colors, etc.) and dynamic signs (animations and generated behaviors from events), we compare the designer-to-user metamessage generated in each previous inspection and, finally, analyze the quality of the overall metacommunication. The *Retrospective Communicability Evaluation* consists of three main phases: 1) user observation, 2) retrospective think aloud (RTA) and 3) tagging. The observation phase consisted in observing and recording the user interacting with the tools and taking notes about relevant occurrences. The second phase (RTA) consisted in observing, recording and later transcribing each users' speech while he was watching the recording created in the previous phase. Based on CEM [7], in the tagging step we identify breakpoints of communication, and then we map these breakdowns onto HCI problems and rewrite the semiotic profile with the general metamessage emitted by the system. For each breakdown, we assign one of the thirteen tags proposed by Semiotic Engineering, which are common expressions at the human communication and they are: "Where is it?", "What now?", "What's this?", "Oops!", "Where am I?", "What happened?", "Why doesn't it?", "I can't do it this way.", "I can do otherwise.", "Thanks, but no thanks!", "Looks fine to me.", "Help!" e "I give up." Later, at the interpretation stage, with the tagged material, the evaluator aims to identify the main metacommunication problems, analyzing the frequency and context of each type of tagging, the existence of sequence of patterns to each type of tagging, the level of the analyzed problem and the communicability problems that caused the observed breakdowns.

---

[6] http://www.tableausoftware.com/public

We defined a scenario with two tasks with similar difficulty: one performed with ViSC and the other with Tableau Public. In order to reduce the learning effect of the evaluation results, we used the Latin square method [18] to distribute tasks and tools between the two groups of users. The tasks were the following:

1. Show whether the education level of Brazilian students between 7 and 9 years old increased in the period from 2003, 2006 and 2009.
2. Analyze the average of grades in the PISA exam from Brazil, Canada and Australia in 2003 and 2009, and then identify the country with highest increase.

The participants had to have some skill in reading graphs but not be professional statisticians, journalists or data analysts, nor have previous experience in using Tableau. We recruited six students (undergraduate and graduate) in engineering, informatics, and computer science. In order to assess their initial skills and compare the results, we asked them to perform two tasks with pen and paper before the test sessions.

4.2   Findings

SIM and RCE were effective methods to help us find HCI problems in ViSC. Through SIM, we reconstructed the ViSC metamessage and checked that it was consistent with the designer's metamessage (described in section 3). However, this method revealed inconsistencies and ambiguities in some signs, meaning that the users could misunderstand them. RCE allowed us to understand the processes of user's reasoning and formulation of hypotheses, related to both the tools and the generated visualizations; to evaluate how the questions influenced the results; and to understand, through the reconstruction of the received metamessage, the signs actually misunderstood by the user.

Task 1 asked the user to show if there the total number of students between 7 and 9 years of schooling in 2003, 2006 and 2009 has increased. The first one, as a summation could be answered with both the stacked column (Figure 3b) and the stacked series (second chart of Figure 3a) in ViSC and the stacked bars in Tableau. All of the three users of ViSC used questions to perform the task and all generated efficient visualizations. The first one created a composite of two charts including the stacked series and the others created the stacked column chart.

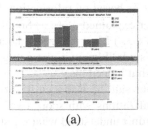
(a)

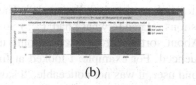
(b)

Fig. 3. (a) Result of the first user, cluttered column chart and stacked series; (b) Result of the second user, stacked columns

One of the HCI problems we analyzed with both methods was the selecting of the field difference (checkbox), because in some conditions it did not return any feedback. The RCE allowed us to find even more breakdowns, because the users sought a functionality not developed to the tool. Two of the three users who performed task 1 with ViSC tried to gather the three colors in a column with only one color. The users also did not understand well the sorting buttons. One of them tried to reorder variables by removing and including elements in the new order. We concluded that the sorting buttons did not emit a clear message to the user. RCE allowed finding other problems and HCI features that fumbled the user, such as: lack of understanding due to lack of metadata; and the need to relate the displayed graphics with the selected item in the graphic menu.

Regarding the features that helped the user, we verified, through explicit comments, that questions had major influence and led the user to efficient results. According to the first user, the questions were crucial for him to find the desired response. His answer about satisfaction with the result is consistent with the given explanation during the RCE and show that he really compared visualizations to achieve the given result: "*I decided to show the two graphs because I thought it would be more complete.*"

Other users employed the questions to check whether the graphic was correct. According to the second user, the questions were neutral to the obtained result. However, we assess that they had a higher importance because when he compared his chart to the recommended chart, he stopped seeking the consolidated sum, which expedited the completion of the task. According to him, his first impulse would always try to draw the graphic. Furthermore, when asked about other recommended alternative, he said: "It was interesting because I don't know if I would have thought to draw stacked series".

Despite having developed the same reasoning, intending to build a graphic that the tool did not allow (with the total sum), the third user chose the recommended solution. For him, as well as speed, this strategy also returned a better result than the one he had thought. These two users' statements show that some learning may have taken place during interaction with the system.

In order to evaluate the users' understanding of the questions, we asked them to explain how they thought the questions were generated and what they understood about the scores. The first user explained: "I honestly do not know how they are made, but it seems to have the information available to you and recommend some related information. (...) Either based on the chart or based on information. It shows what can be cool for you to show." The second user explained : " (...) So, at the first moment, I didn't realize that they were facilitators (...) I just realized it later when I got to click on the chart I've made". The third one said: "I knew it was going to show questions related to what I had. (...) So that was what helped me."

About sorting through scores, only the third user said he had seen it: "It has also influenced. For example: I looked at first at visualizations with score five." For the second user, it was not noticeable. "I saw it but I didn't understand what the star was."

Two users demonstrated awareness they did not create the most efficient chart but considered the task as complete. Although Tableau allowed more interaction than

ViSC and was apparently more attractive to users, the produced charts were considered less satisfactory, and the tool was considered more difficult. Between the two tools, one of the users stated he wanted thumbnails of graphics in ViSC as in Tableau.

Task 2 asked the user to observe the average grade on the PISA exam from Brazil, Canada and Australia in 2003 and 2009, and to identify the country where the increase was higher. The recommended visualizations were scatterplot (with score five) and clustered column chart (with score three).

The first two users used the questions to help in performing the task. However, none of them created the chart with the highest score. Two of them created the clustered column chart (Fig. 4a) and the other one, series chart (Fig. 4b).

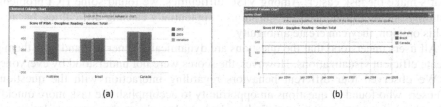

(a)   (b)

Fig. 4. (a) Clustered column chart with the column difference; (b) series chart

Among the most serious problems encountered with the RCE we found the usage of questions to navigate without reading the questions. We also verified a problem in the ontology. The second user selected an equivalent question but the system opened a different option, the time series chart. This was not a good option to answer this question because the line was not very slanted (Fig. 4b).

Although the first user knew he already had an answer, he used the questions to try to find something better: "I understood they were many ways to show the information and I could filter sometimes. But I didn't want to filter. I wanted to find the better visualization. First I looked for a line chart. I found a chart that I didn't want (scatterplot)." He claimed to not have noticed the scores next to the visualizations and said they were useful because they opened the graphic to him.

The second user also used the questions and stated he accepted the first system recommendation and did not try other possibilities. He understood the questions and added that they were important to him: "They worked as a shortcut if you had something in mind to generate. I saw it was smart enough to see the data I wanted to analyze and match the questions with these data. For me it was helpful. I clicked here and I went straight to the answer. It just missed to improve the scale a little better, but it was just what I wanted. I thought it was important. It saved me a lot of time."

The third user did not interact with the questions because, according to him, there was too much text. When questioned about the influence of the language (English), he stated that if the questions were in his native language he probably would have read them.

4.3   Discussion

In task 1, we verified that the questions motivated the data analysis, and could also have promoted learning for two users. All the users of ViSC interacted with the questions and understood how they worked. Although it was not clear to them how the questions were generated, they noticed their changes and considered them an important functionality to achieve their results.

In task 2, the questions had an important value to the second user, even though the presented result was not very efficient. In this task, he was the only one who really understood how the questions work. The first user used them in an inadequate way and the third user did not use them.

In the interviews, users stated that the questions in ViSC and the way to filter charts make the task easier. Among ViSC difficulties, we found some HCI problems, but only one user mentioned the questions as potentially causing difficulties, because, in his opinion, they can create ambiguity.

All users understood that the questions are dynamically generated and help them to create efficient visualizations. However, the scores were not understood by everyone. We observed four different behaviors regarding interaction with the questions: (1) users who found in questions an opportunity to accomplish the task more quickly; (2) users who were not so satisfied or had doubts about the given solution and resorted to questions as a way to validate or to improve the result; (3) the user who used the questions as links to charts but who has not really read them; and (4) the user who did not interact with them.

Thus, we can answer how the questions influence the users' traversal through the charts. We observed that their influence was positive or neutral in all interactions. Regarding the task, we had some cases in which the questions sped up the process, working as a facilitator and, in other cases, they were important to check the result. Among the generated visualizations, users who used the questions created efficient graphs, except by the case in which we observed a problem with the ontology. Even in this case, the user understood the tool and performed the task quickly. We also verified one case which the user corrected the first generated graph with the recommended graph. In other two cases, the questions reinforced the option of the generated graph because they brought the same one. For those who examined the recommended options to choose from, we observed that recommendations have increased their confidence in the resulting chart and some learning may have taken place. Among those who did not use the question or used them as links to open the graph, their influence was neutral. None of them reported that the questions hindered the task performance.

5   Conclusions

The goal of this research was to create and evaluate a solution to support novice users to create efficient visualizations with statistical data.

Academic studies about information visualization, interactive graphs and evaluation with visualization tools were the bases to design and develop a visualization ontology and a knowledge-based chart recommender system called

ViSC, Visualization with Smart Charts. In ViSC, we sought to solve HCI issues we found in previously investigated tools. The most important point, however, was the inclusion of recommendations through common questions that users may want to answer about the data with efficient visualizations. The recommendations guide the user through charts related to the selected data during the interaction.

We evaluated ViSC using the Semiotic Inspection Method (SIM) and the Retrospective Communicability Evaluation (RCE). We explored how users understood the recommended questions and how the questions influenced users in performing the tasks and achieving their results. Five out of six users employed the questions, and four of them were able to obtain efficient results through their use and considered them important. Therefore we believe our main contribution to support efficient chart construction by novice users was achieved. In addition, some users analyzed more than one of the recommendations and compared them to the previous chart made by themselves, learning more about chart construction in the process.

Besides gathering some feedback for refining ViSC and its ontology, this research raised questions that require additional studies. First, we would like to conduct a longitudinal study to evaluate what kinds of learning take place. Second, we would like to better understand when and why users would not use the questions. Finally, we would like to evaluate how ViSC supports novice users who do not have a well-defined question and who want to check for new information through a process of knowledge discovery.

Acknowledgements. The authors thank the study participants for their valuable time and insights. Taissa Sousa thanks IBGE and Simone Barbosa thanks CNPq (process #308490/2012-6) for the support to her research work.

References

1. Amar, R., Eagan, J., Stasko, J.: Low-Level Components of Analytic Activity in Information Visualization. In: IEEE Symposium on Information Visualization 2005, USA (2005)
2. Bertin, J.: Semiology of Graphics: Diagrams, Networks, Maps (1918), ESRI 1st edn. (2011)
3. Bostock, M., Heer, J.: Protovis: A Graphical Toolkit for Visualization. IEEE Transactions on Visualization and Computer Graphics, InfoVis 2009 (2009)
4. Burke, R.: Knowledge-based recommender systems. Encyclopedia of Library and Information Science. Department of Information and Computer Science. U. of California, Irvine
5. Clement, J.: Misconceptions in Graphing. In: Proceeding of the 9th Annual Meeting of the International Group for the Psychology of Mathematics Education, pp. 369–375 (1985)
6. Cubrarnic, D.: Polstar: Assisted navigation for exploring multi-dimensional information spaces. In: Human-Computer Information Retrieval, HCIR (2008)
7. de Souza, C.S., Leitão, C.F., Prates, R.O., da Silva, E.J.: The Semiotic Inspection Method. In: Proceedings of the VII Simpósio Brasileiro de Fatores Humanos em Sistemas Computacionais, IHC 2006, pp. 148–157 (2006)

8. de Souza, C.S., Leitão, C.F.: Semiotic Engineering Methods for Scientific Research in HCI. Morgan & Claypool Publishers (2009)
9. de Souza, C.S., Leitão, C.F.: A method for evaluating the communicability of Users Interface. Morgan & Claypool Publishers (2009)
10. de Souza, C.S.: The semiotic engineering of human-computer interaction, Capítulos 1, 2 e 4. The MIT Press, Cambridge (2005)
11. Elias, M., Bezerianos, A.: Exploration Views: Understanding Dashboard Creation and Customization for Visualization Novices. In: Campos, P., Graham, N., Jorge, J., Nunes, N., Palanque, P., Winckler, M. (eds.) INTERACT 2011, Part IV. LNCS, vol. 6949, pp. 274–291. Springer, Heidelberg (2011)
12. Few, S.: Show me the numbers. Designing tables and graphs to enlighten. Analytics Press, Oakland (2004)
13. Goldenberg, E.P.: Mathematics, metaphors, and human factors: Mathematical, technical, and pedagogical challenges in the educational use of graphical representation of functions. The Journal of Mathematical Behavior 7(2), 135–173 (1988)
14. Gomes Ferreira, V.G.: Exploring Mathematical Functions Through Dynamic Microworlds, 353 f. Thesis (Education). Institute Education, Universidade de Londres (1997)
15. van den Haak, M.J., Jong, M.D.T., Schellens, P.J.: Retrospective vs. concurrent think-aloud protocols: testing the usability of an online library catalogue. Behaviour & Information Technology (2003)
16. Heer, J., Bostock, M., Ogievetsky, V.: A Tour Through the Visualization Zoo. Communications of the ACM (2010)
17. Heer, J., Shneiderman, B.: Interactive Dynamics for Visual Analysis. A taxonomy of tools that support the fluent and flexible use of visualizations. ACM Queue (2012)
18. Heer, J., Viégas, F.B., Wattenberg, M.: Voyagers and voyeurs: Supporting asynchronous collaborative information visualization. In: Proc. of the Conference on Human Factors in Computing Systems (CHI), pp. 1029–1038
19. Gao, L.: Latin Squares in Experimental Design. Michigan State University (2005), http://www.mth.msu.edu/~jhall/classes/mth880-05/projects/latin.pdf (last access in July 2013)
20. Mackinlay, J.D., Hanrahan, P., Stolte, C.: Show Me: Automatic Presentation for Visual Analysis. IEEE Trans. on Visualizations and Computer Graphics 13(6) (November/December 2007)
21. Mackinlay, J.D.: Automating the design of graphical presentations of relational information. ACM Trans. on Graphics 5(2), 110–141 (1986)
22. National e-Science Center. Visualization Ontologies, http://www.nesc.ac.uk/talks/393/vis_ontology_report.pdf (last access in November 2011)
23. Pinker, S.: A theory of graph comprehension. In: Freedle, R. (ed.) Artificial Intelligence and the Future Testing, pp. 73–126. Erlbaum, Hillsdale (1990)
24. Shah, P., Carpenter, P.A.: Conceptual limitations in comprehending line graphs. Journal of Experimental Psychology: General 124(1), 43–61 (1995)
25. Sousa, T.: Semantic characterization of visualization mechanisms. Tech. Report 16/12, PUC-Rio (2012)
26. Sousa, T.: How signification and communication systems influence the interpretation of statistical data by users with specific information needs. Tech. Report 15/12, PUC-Rio (2012)
27. Tory, M., Möller, T.: Rethinking Visualization: A High-Level Taxonomy. In: Proceedings of the IEEE Symposium on Information Visualization, INFOVIS 2004, pp. 151–158 (2004)
28. Tufte, E.R.: The Visual Display of Quantitative Information (2001)
29. Visko Visualization Knowledge, http://trust.utep.edu/visko/dl/ (last accessed in November 2011)

Deterministic Local Layouts
through High-Dimensional Layout Stitching

Martin Steiger[1,2], Hendrik Lücke-Tieke[1], Thorsten May[1], Arjan Kuijper[1,2],
and Jörn Kohlhammer[1,2]

[1] Fraunhofer IGD, Fraunhoferstr. 5, 64283 Darmstadt, Germany
[2] Department of Computer Science, Technische Universität Darmstadt,
Fraunhoferstrasse 5, 64283 Darmstadt, Germany
{martin.steiger,hendrik.luecke-tieke,thorsten.may,arjan.kuijper,
joern.kohlhammer}@igd.fraunhofer.de

Abstract. In this paper we present a layout technique for dynamic
views of large static graphs. It aims to minimize changes between two
consecutive frames and most importantly, it is deterministic. First, a set
of small layout patches is pre-computed. Then, depending on the users
view focus, a subset of these patches is selected and connected to generate the final layout. In contrast to the state-of-the-art approach that
operates in the 2D screen space only, we perform this process in high-
dimensional space before projecting the results into the 2D plane. This
gives additional degrees of freedom and consequently a smoother transition process between two consecutive frames. Whenever the user visits
an area of the graph for a second time, the layout will still look the same.
This enables the user to recognize areas that have already been explored
and thus preserve the mental map.

Keywords: dynamic graph, projection, explorative analysis, mental map.

1 Introduction

Among the most popular ones, graph analysis has gained strong interest due to
the fact that in contrast to tabular data, graphs also contain explicit links between data items. One type of visualizations for graphs is the node-link diagram
with its manifold variations. Despite their conceptual simplicity, they produce
pleasing drawings for small to medium-sized graphs. For large graphs, however,
they do no longer scale and the drawings become tangled up.

One idea to overcome this problem is to use *dynamic views*, in particular
for explorative tasks. Here, the focus of the data analyst is on local features
rather than on the global structure of the graph. Instead of trying to create a
complete picture of the entire structure, dynamic views work with a selected sub-
graph of the original data set. This implies that local structures are preserved
at the expense of global structures. The calculation of a dynamic view starts
with an initial start node (the *Focus*) in the graph which can be found, for
example, by a search query. Based on a degree-of-interest function, nodes from

M. Kurosu (Ed.): Human-Computer Interaction, Part I, HCII 2014, LNCS 8510, pp. 643–651, 2014.
© Springer International Publishing Switzerland 2014

the neighborhood are added to the visible sub-graph. For this initial data set, a layout is computed and displayed. The other parts of the graph can be explored from this sub-graph by changing the focus node.

Exploration is about creating and preserving a mental map of the displayed data. Lee et al. identified revisitation as one of the tasks of graph visualization [10]. We are convinced that the ability to recognize areas that have been visited before is an important factor in this process. However, conventional force-directed algorithms do not create identical layouts for the same set of nodes from different starting points. On the contrary, they are very sensitive even to small changes in the initial values. As a result, the computed layout of a sub-graph never looks the same. This makes it rather difficult for the user to decide whether an area has already been explored or not, because the visual shape of the topological structure appears to be different.

This problem has been addressed only recently by Steiger et al.[16] who work with a set a divide-and-conquer approach. They first partition the graph using an arbitrary clustering algorithm into a set of disjoint sub-graphs. Overlapping subgraphs are generated from the partitions by adding nodes from the 1-neighborhood. For each of them, an individual layout is computed. During runtime, the dynamic view is generated from a changing combination of subgraphs. The subgraphs are combined be merging node positions along the overlaps.

One major shortcoming of the original approach is that the merging operation is not very stable. The positions of the nodes that are used for the merging operation in one patch are often very different from those in the other subgraph. Due to the fact that only a two-dimensional affine transformation is used to bring them together, large divergences remain.

The claim of this paper is to improve the original work so that stable stitchings can be created that were unstable before. It goes beyond the original work by solving the stitching problem in high-dimensional space. The process involves the layout computation and the merging of two layout patches in order to get the aforementioned additional degrees of freedom. This stabilizes the stitching operation but also requires finding an appropriate measure to project the layout back into the 2D plane. We interpolate the points of two consecutive frames linearly to create a smooth transition between two exploration steps.

The rest of the paper is organized as follows: We will first discuss related work in Section 2 before we describe both the concept of the original paper and our contribution in Section 3. In Section 4 a proof of concept is presented before we conclude with an outlook in Section 5.

2   Related Work

We will first briefly discuss some important publications in the graph drawing domain before we present rather recent contributions on the preservation of the mental map.

Computing a layout for dynamic graphs has been first formalized by North[13]. Based on that, Huang and Eades brought up the idea to create a dynamic view of a static graph[8] that can be adjusted by user. We also use this metaphor to enable the user to navigate through the graph.

A major shortcoming of this is the missing context. There is no direct connection between the visible part and the entire graph. Some techniques use the fisheye concept to surround the current focus area with a distorted view on the neighborhood[4]. In contrast to that, other approaches show visual cues to support the user's orientation [12].

Most of these concepts are independent from the actual layout algorithm. Classical force-directed approaches have been researched but also used in practice for more than two decades now. Hierarchical layout algorithms use a divide and conquer scheme to first create a coarse layout which are refined in later steps[7], thus working in a top-down fashion. Using a bottom-up approach is also possible, calculating small layouts which are recursively combined until the whole graph can be drawn[14]. However, both approaches rely on certain properties of the division process while our approach is more flexible in regards to division levels.

Alternatively, multi-dimensional layouts like that of Gajer et al.[6] make use of additional dimensions to quickly create a robust layout before projecting it into two-dimensional screen space. Our approach goes in this direction, but it not restricted to a specific algorithm.

Yuan et al. propose an approach based on crowd sourcing. Users of the system manually create layouts of subgraphs, which are then automatically combined[18].

The memorability of structures in this drawing seems to be dependent on different cognitive factors such as symmetry and orthogonality[11]. Already in the early 90s, the concept of a mental map that should be preserved in dynamic graph views has been established by Eades et al[3]. According to Purchase et al.[15], one important criteria is that the movement during the transition from one view to another should be minimized. Also, different quality objectives for node movement have been introduced to enable the user to track the changes between two consecutive frames[5]. The shape matching approach we present pays respect to these findings: with the exception of stitched nodes, all nodes move uniformly during the transition process.

3   Concept

In this section we briefly outline the idea of 2D layout stitching and explain how we transfer this idea into high-dimensional space and project it back into the 2D plane (Figure 1). The basic idea stems from the image processing domain where overlapping images are stitched together creating a single, larger panorama image.

In panorama stitching, a set of feature points is first extracted from each image. The next step is about finding corresponding points across the different feature vector sets. After having identified the point pairs that match best, a transformation is computed that brings these points to a common location. Finally, the full images are transformed, creating a single, larger image. For additional details, the interested reader is referred to the work of Brown and Lowe[2].

Fig. 1. The original graph is first partitioned into clusters which are then used to create overlapping patches. For each pair of overlapping patches a linear transformation is computed that brings shared nodes together. They are then merged before they are projected into screen space.

3.1 Pre-processing

As already described in the original work of Steiger et al., we first cluster the graph dataset into smaller, overlapping patches. We decided to use Chinese Whispers, an algorithm whose only parameter is the number of iterations to run.[1] As most other clustering algorithms, it partitions the graph into non-overlapping clusters. Adding directly connected nodes from the border of a patch creates overlaps that are required for the stitching process (see Figure 2).

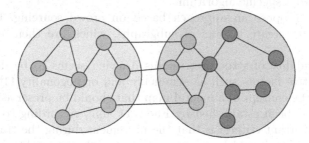

Fig. 2. Nodes that are directly connected to nodes from other patches are used to create overlapping patches

Two clusters are considered as being connected, if and only if at least one edge exists between the two. Up to this point, we follow the original version of the approach.

In the next step, an individual layout is computed for every patch in d dimensions. We use a straight-forward extension of the two-dimensional Fruchterman-Reingold algorithm to compute a high-dimensional position vector for every node. However, other methods such as that of Gajer et al.[6] should work at least equally well. The algorithm runtime does not play a major role here, as this can be precomputed.

3.2 Layout Stitching

Layout stitching defines the process of merging two overlapping layout sets. First, an optimal linear transformation between the node positions of overlapping patches is computed. We prefer linear over affine transformation as it preserves the shape better. We denote d as the number of dimensions that is used for the graph layout. To define a linear transformation between two patches in d dimensions, at least $d+1$ nodes which are shared among the patches are required. In that case, we consider these patches as overlapping. For two dimensions, three points are sufficient to derive a unique linear transformation. It brings the nodes that exist in both layout but with different position coordinates as close together as possible. If the patches share more than $d + 1$ nodes, we calculate the linear transformation which is optimal with respect to the given constraints.

This transformation is computed as follows: based on a least-square fitting method we define a target function that we want to minimize. This function measures the distances between the two corresponding positions of a node. We normalize both datasets by first moving the centroids of the two patches to the origin. As a side product, this already gives the translation vector of the transformation matrix. Then, a $d \times d$ cost matrix is created based on pair-wise distances. Variable p_i and p'_i denote the positions of node i, c_p and $c_{p'}$ represent the center of gravity of their respective patches.

$$H = \sum_i^n (p_i - c_p)(p'_i - c_{p'})^T$$

This matrix is then factorized by Singular Value Decomposition (SVD) so that the rotation component can be extracted. Applying the SVD splits the matrix into two rotation matrices U and V and a diagonal matrix. The rotation part R of the transformation is defined as VU^T. The original work of Steiger et al. contains a more detailed explanation of this computation.

As soon as the transformation matrix has been computed, two overlapping patches are stitched together by merging these duplicates into single positions. This is required, because nodes that exist in both layouts have a position in each of them and the linear transformation does not bring them to the exact same spot in general. We therefore use a linear interpolation of their weighted influence on the current view to derive a smooth transition between old and new node position.

3.3 Projection

In contrast to the original work, the node positions are still in high-dimensional space. Therefore, the dimensionality of the stitched point cloud must be reduced to the two most-relevant dimensions before it can be displayed on the screen.

We use non-linear multidimensional scaling (MDS) to achieve an optimal projection while preserving distances[17]. It uses a normalized stress function to define the difference in distance between the original and the projected space. This function is then minimized using optimization algorithms. From our practical experiments, the stress-based MDS (also referred to as SMACOF) achieves high-quality results. However, depending on the data set, other projection algorithms can perform better. A comparative overview of different dimensionality reduction methods can be found in the work of Joia et al.[9]. Since this step of our approach is transparent, it does not depend on any particular projection algorithm.

This projection is defined only up to rotation and scale, so additional constraints need to be added to keep these two constant across multiple operations. These free variables can be fixated by using the screen's display area. Based on the 2D screen coordinates, a principal component analysis (PCA) gives the two axes with the largest variances. Using rotation and scaling, they are aligned so that the larger goes from left to right, the smaller from bottom to top. This order is chosen to benefit from the fact that typical screen displays' width is larger than their height.

Nonetheless, the computed projection matrices for the old and new point cloud can be quite different. This causes strong sudden changes in the picture which makes it difficult to follow the transition process. We therefore interpolate the points of two consecutive frames linearly.

In this section, we outlined how we perform layout stitching based on only two overlapping patches. Creating a combined layout consisting of more than just two patches is not as straight-forward as it may appear, but we follow precisely the strategy of [16] here.

4   Proof of Concept

We conducted some tests to demonstrate the validity of our approach. For the purpose of the illustration, the individual layouts were projected into 2D. In the actual implementation, only the final, merged layout is projected. We performed the projection using classical MDS and a stress-based majorization algorithm. Projecting the points using stress majorization (SMACOF) methods is computationally more expensive, but yields a better spread between the nodes and thus a cleaner picture. This is why only the results of this approach are discussed. The first experiment was performed using an artificial graph (see Figure 3).

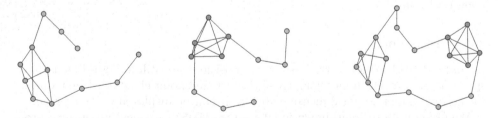

Fig. 3. The subgraph on the left side contains six unique nodes, the subgraph in the center contains a five-clique. Six nodes (in cyan) are in both layouts. The merged and projected results are depicted on the right side.

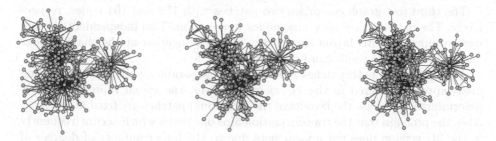

Fig. 4. Two subsets of the Diseasome network which share more than 90% of the nodes. The merged layout on the right integrates the purple nodes (center image) into the existing layout, preserving the general shape of the existing layout (depicted on the left).

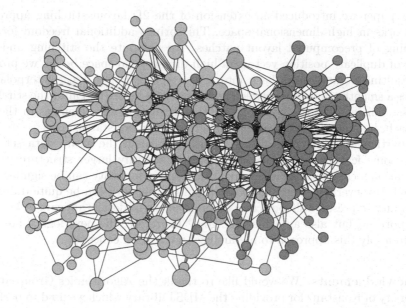

Fig. 5. Two overlapping patches, stitched in 5D space and projected with MDS. While the structures are still separable, some visual clutters appear in the area of the intersection. Using a smaller number of points for the stitching process and adding an offset to one of the patches mitigate the problem.

The other tests were performed based on the Diseasome[1] network data set. The second test was based on two patches with significant overlap. Most nodes were part of both layouts, which lead to highly similar shapes. As can be seen in Figure 4, the projection of the merged layout preserved the similarity in the new, integrated layout.

---

[1] http://diseasome.eu/

The third test graph comprises two patches with 152 and 104 nodes, respectively. The patches have only nine nodes in common. Two independent layouts were computed in 5D layout space, then stitched together at the shared nodes and projected. The result can be seen in Figure 5.

A large part of both patches remain clearly separable, while the overlapping areas appear cluttered in the 2D view. However, the visual representation is deterministic, because the layouts of the individual patches are fixed at runtime. Also, the problem that the transformation flips one patch which occurs frequently in the 2D version does not appear here due to the larger number of degrees of freedom.

5 Conclusion

In this paper we introduced an extension of the 2D layout stitching approach that works in high-dimensional space. This brings additional freedom for the matching of precomputed layout patches. We compute the stitching and the merge of duplicate position vectors in high-dimensional space before we project the resulting point vectors back into screen space. Using linear interpolation ensures a smooth transition between node positions before and after the stitching process. This enables the user to trace the changes in the layout as in the 2D approach, but the algorithm in the background is more stable.

In particular for large graphs, navigating through the entire data set is a cumbersome feature and makes it difficult to identify larger structure. Using aggregation techniques like clustering, the graph complexity can be significantly reduced. However, the overall appearance of the network can be quite different. The ability to preserve shape across different levels-of-details appears to be both an important, but also an achievable goal. Therefore, the next logical step for us is to apply this approach to hierarchical navigation concepts.

Acknowledgements. We would like to thank the Algorithmics Group at the University of Konstanz for providing the MDSJ library which we used to perform the projection operations. We would also like to thank the anonymous reviewers of a earlier version of this paper for their constructive feedback.

References

1. Biemann, C.: Chinese Whispers: an Efficient Graph Clustering Algorithm and its Application to Natural Language Processing Problems. In: Proceedings of the First Workshop on Graph Based Methods for Natural Language Processing, TextGraphs-1, pp. 73–80. Association for Computational Linguistics, Stroudsburg (2006)
2. Brown, M., Lowe, D.G.: Automatic Panoramic Image Stitching using Invariant Features. International Journal of Computer Vision 74, 59–73 (2007)
3. Eades, P., Lai, W., Misue, K., Sugiyama, K.: Preserving the mental map of a diagram. Proceedings of Compugraphics 91(9), 24–33 (1991)

4. Formella, A., Keller, J.: Generalized fisheye views of graphs. In: Brandenburg, F.J. (ed.) GD 1995. LNCS, vol. 1027, pp. 242–253. Springer, Heidelberg (1996)
5. Frishman, Y., Tal, A.: Online Dynamic Graph Drawing. IEEE Transactions on Visualization and Computer Graphics 14(4), 727–740 (2008)
6. Gajer, P., Goodrich, M., Kobourov, S.: A multi-dimensional approach to force-directed layouts of large graphs. In: Marks, J. (ed.) GD 2000. LNCS, vol. 1984, pp. 211–221. Springer, Heidelberg (2001)
7. Harel, D., Koren, Y.: A fast multi-scale method for drawing large graphs. In: Marks, J. (ed.) GD 2000. LNCS, vol. 1984, pp. 183–196. Springer, Heidelberg (2001)
8. Huang, M.L., Eades, P.: A Fully Animated Interactive System for Clustering and Navigating Huge Graphs. In: Whitesides, S.H. (ed.) GD 1998. LNCS, vol. 1547, pp. 374–383. Springer, Heidelberg (1999)
9. Joia, P., Paulovich, F., Coimbra, D., Cuminato, J., Nonato, L.: Local affine multi-dimensional projection. IEEE Transactions on Visualization and Computer Graphics 17(12), 2563–2571 (2011)
10. Lee, B., Plaisant, C., Parr, C.S., Fekete, J.D., Henry, N.: Task taxonomy for graph visualization. In: Proceedings of the 2006 AVI Workshop on Beyond Time and Errors, BELIV 2006, pp. 1–5. ACM, New York (2006)
11. Marriott, K., Purchase, H., Wybrow, M., Goncu, C.: Memorability of Visual Features in Network Diagrams. IEEE Transactions on Visualization and Computer Graphics 18(12), 2477–2485 (2012)
12. May, T., Steiger, M., Davey, J., Kohlhammer, J.: Using Signposts for Navigation in Large Graphs. Computer Graphics Forum 31(3 pt. 2), 985–994 (2012)
13. North, S.C.: Incremental layout in dynadag. In: Brandenburg, F.J. (ed.) GD 1995. LNCS, vol. 1027, pp. 409–418. Springer, Heidelberg (1996)
14. Papadopoulos, C., Voglis, C.: Drawing graphs using modular decomposition. In: Healy, P., Nikolov, N.S. (eds.) GD 2005. LNCS, vol. 3843, pp. 343–354. Springer, Heidelberg (2006)
15. Purchase, H.C., Samra, A.: Extremes are better: Investigating mental map preservation in dynamic graphs. In: Stapleton, G., Howse, J., Lee, J. (eds.) Diagrams 2008. LNCS (LNAI), vol. 5223, pp. 60–73. Springer, Heidelberg (2008)
16. Steiger, M., Lücke-Tieke, H., May, T., Kuijper, A., Kohlhammer, J.: Using layout stitching to create deterministic local graph layouts. In: WSCG 2013, pp. 1–9 (June 2013)
17. Torgerson, W.S.: Multidimensional scaling: I. Theory and Method. Psychometrika 17(4), 401–419 (1952)
18. Yuan, X., Che, L., Hu, Y., Zhang, X.: Intelligent graph layout using many users' input. IEEE Transactions on Visualization and Computer Graphics 18(12), 2699–2708 (2012)

SyncBox - Synchronizer and Interface for High-Speed Macro Photography

Krzysztof Szklanny, Armand Stańczak, Paweł Wojtków, Sergio Cosentino, and Alicja Wieczorkowska

Polish-Japanese Institute of Information Technology, Koszykowa 86,
02-008 Warsaw, Poland
{kszklanny,armand.stanczak,pawel.wojtkow,sergio.consentino}@pjwstk.edu.pl,
alicja@poljap.edu.pl

Abstract. The goal of this work was to create a fully automated synchronizer for macro photography, dedicated to water drop photography [2], [11]. An open-source electronics prototyping platform called Arduino was used for this purpose. The elaborated system includes a water system, a drop kit, and the synchronizer itself, attached to a digital photo camera. This system, named SyncBox, is simple, easy to use and fairly inexpensive. SyncBox can be operated using Dripper (the application interface) by a single mouse click, the pictures taken can be downloaded to a computer, and uploaded to the Internet. The proposed solution can be used as an interface for high-speed photography for water drop pictures, suitable for both amateur and professional purposes. The construction of the device, the interface, and exemplary pictures taken are shown in this paper. We conclude the paper with the proposed future works to make the entire system even more user friendly.

Keywords: Macro Photography, High-Speed Photography, Water Drop Photography.

1 Introduction

Phenomena that are too fast to see, if photographed, give very interesting results, admired in arts, and often used in advertising. Water drop photography is one of examples of events that could not be seen at all without a camera. High speed photography allows capturing such fast and amazing phenomena. There exist tools for high speed photography and, in particular, dedicated tools to photograph droplets of water, or milk, or other liquids. Tools available on the market include the photography trigger Camera Axe [5], the high-speed photography controller StopShot [7], and the SplashArt kit [8], However, such tools cost a few hundred dollars and are expensive for amateurs. CameraAxe, which is the least expensive and best solution for amateurs, allows connecting a camera, flash lamps, and sensors. However, even such a simple device is not so easy to use, as it's software requires adjustment of various values and settings, which can be difficult to a user. Therefore, we decided to build a system at a fraction of this

M. Kurosu (Ed.): Human-Computer Interaction, Part I, HCII 2014, LNCS 8510, pp. 652–661, 2014.

cost, to make water drop photography available to anyone interested in capturing water splashes, without investing into a professional studio. This solution can also be used by professional photographers.

The system presented in this paper is named SyncBox. It is a synchronizer for high speed macro photography, which can work with virtually any digital camera available in the market, provided the appropriate cable is used to connect the camera with SyncBox. This solution is based on Arduino [1], [3], [4], [9], [10], an open-source electronic prototyping platform, which can be connected to a computer with Windows, Mac OS X or Linux system, and it costs only about 20 Euros. It allows control over electric signals. The device build in the described work is a synchronizer, taking a picture when a water drop hits water surface, series of pictures can also be taken. The complete system also includes a water container, piping, a valve for releasing drops, a water pump, and altogether it costs about 50 Euros. The settings of the elaborated software allow choosing the desired effect in the picture. The details of the system are given in Section 2, and the interface is described in Section 3. Exemplary pictures taken using SyncBox are shown in Section 4. The paper is summarized and concluded in Section 5.

2 Construction of SyncBox

The SyncBox synchronizer for high-speed macro photography is based on Arduino Uno microcontroller [1], see Figure 1. The Arduino board was connected to a personal computer with Windows operating system. Utmost care was taken to assure repetitiveness of the resulting photographs, and full control over the pictures taken. Control with LCD Shield, manipulated with joystick, was also considered in the planning phase, but it would require making this project in Nokia environment and changing the entire architecture. Therefore, this solution was discarded.

Our synchronizer (Figure 2) consists of three removable parts that are removable for easy access, upgrade and repair. It consists of:

- central processing unit (CPU), powered from Arduino without the need for external power source;
- relay unit, created from scratch for the SyncBox system, to control AC 230V operated devices; and
- power adapter unit, to provide up to 4 water valves with DC 12V power.

The controller triggers electric impulses of the desired pulse length and frequency, at the precisely defined instant. Initially, a laser system consisting of a laser emitter and a photoresistor was used for triggering impulses sent to the peripheral devices. However, it required precise positioning of the emitter and the photoresistor, dark working conditions and it introduced delay to the entire macro-photography system. Therefore, the laser system was discarded.

The Arduino board has analog and digital inputs and outputs, and it is connected to the host computer via USB connector. The computer was applied for programming integrated circuits. Although Arduino cannot handle multithread

Fig. 1. Arduino Uno R3 board, front view [6]

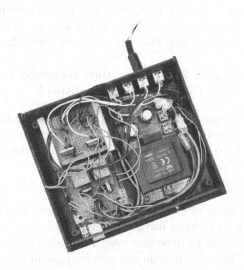

Fig. 2. The SyncBox synchronizer box

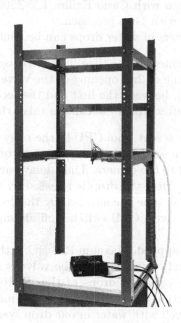

Fig. 3. The SyncBox main equipment. Devices shown on the shelf, the synchronizer box (black) and the pump (gray, partly behind framing) are normally placed aside, as a water container is placed here instead. In the middle part of the framing, the valve can be seen.

tasks, it can control potentially unlimited number of devices, since basic digital outputs can be extended using simple integrated circuits.

The synchronizer can be connected to any digital camera; the main equipment is shown in Figure 3. The camera is then connected to the system (placed on a tripod), and two flashes can be attached to this system. Fast flashes were used when taking photographs presented in this paper; when set to 1/320 s and 1/64 flash power, clear and sharp pictures were obtained.

The drop kit consists of a rectangular 1 liter water container, piping mounted on aluminum framing, a water pump to maintain pressure in rubber ducts, and a solenoid valve. The position of the camera is important, since it must be close enough to water in order to get high quality picture, but if it is really close, it should be protected from water drops.

2.1   Controlling Water Drops

The heart of the system is Dripper - the application for steering the synchronizer. This software allows changing the parameter settings. The user can control the size and number of drops, which allows creating desired shapes (see Section 3). On the mouse click, the drop is released, and the picture is taken when the drop contacts the water surface. The time of this contact was found on the basis of the 1000 FPS movie taken with Casio Exilim EX-Z200 camera, which allowed finding the contact time with 1-ms precision.

The following parameters of water drops can be controlled:

- 1st drop size: represented as the time [ms] of 1st opening of the valve;
- 2nd drop size: the time of 2nd opening of the valve, in [ms];
- time interval, in [ms], between the first and the second drop release;
- time delay, in [ms], after which the camera takes the picture.

The electrical impulse is sent from CPU to the relay unit, which first triggers the water pump, and then sends impulses, passing through SyncBox main board to the solenoid valve and to the camera. Time delay parameter controls the time between these impulses. After the drop is released by the valve, the impulse is switched off; the switch off time is controlled by the drop size parameters. After the picture is taken and saved, CPU switches off all impulses and waits for next commands.

The solenoid valve we applied, Magnum 12V DC, is the main device producing water drops. Opening and closing time of the valve is controlled, and since the drops are automatically released, drops of the desired and constant size are obtained. Minimum reaction time of our valve is 13 ms. Although this solenoid is a gas valve, it works well with water in our drop system.

The last stage of the system design was to test the quality and performance of SyncBox. The system successfully handled over 3.000 individual photographs in our tests.

3   Interface of the SyncBox

The existing solutions are usually based on Java technology. On the contrary, our interface is based on HTML5 and jQuerry. This solution allows designing user-oriented, ergonomic interface. Most of the existing solutions require additional steps to run the application, and setting appropriate configuration of at each run of the device. This usually is not easy for a user.

The graphical interface of SyncBox, i.e. Dripper, was designed using HTML5 and CSS3. This allowed dynamic change of settings without additional configuration of Arduino or restarting the system. This functionality was achieved through separating the interface from the main program code. Settings changes, if needed, are simple and intuitive to do by the user. The interface is user friendly, works well, and was easy to implement. The graphical user interface of our application is shown in Figure 4. The interface was implemented in Polish, with the following options:

- LISTA KONFIGURACJI - list of configurations,
- USTAWIENIA DODATKOWE - additional settings,
- URUCHOM POMPKE - run water pump,
- ZDJECIE JEDNEJ KROPLI - 1 drop photo,
- ZDJECIE DWOCH KROPLI - 2 drops photo,

- ROZMIAR KROPLI - 1st drop size,
- ROZMIAR DRUGIEJ KROPLI - 2nd drop size,
- OPOZNIENIE APARATU - time delay.

The list of configurations allows adding and editing of predefined settings (profiles) which can be used while working with SyncBox. Additional settings allow running the device in a loop, i.e. repeating drops, for 1-drop or 2-drop setting. Running the water pump might be needed in the case of the pressure decrease.

Fig. 4. Dripper - graphical user interface of our application. The interface was prepared in Polish. Available settings: LISTA KONFIGURACJI - list of configurations, USTAWIENIA DODATKOWE - additional settings, URUCHOM POMPKE - run water pump, ZDJECIE JEDNEJ KROPLI - 1 drop photo, ZDJECIE DWOCH KROPLI - 2 drops photo, ROZMIAR KROPLI - 1st drop size, ROZMIAR DRUGIEJ KROPLI - 2nd drop size, OPOZNIENIE APARATU - time delay.

Before the system is used, Arduino must be connected to the computer (and to the application). This is done by a single click on the button, see Figure 5.

4   Taking Pictures with SyncBox

Three basic water drop shapes can be photographed using SyncBox:

1. Shape 1, resembling a column, see Figure 6;
2. Shape 2, resembling an umbrella, see Figure 7;
3. Shape 3, resembling a crown, see Figure 8.

Fig. 5. The screenshot of the interface for connecting Arduino with SyncBox; POD-LACZ SYNBOXA - connect SyncBox. The user can start using the system by clicking one button, POLACZ (connect).

The shapes are controlled by means of parameters presented in Section 2.1. During works on the described system, the obtained photographs were also placed in an Internet gallery, see Figure 9. No sophisticated equipment is needed to taking such pictures. The presented photographs were taken using inexpensive digital cameras, like Canon 400D, Canon 450D and Nikon D5100, and second hand 10-Euro lenses.

In further works, we would like to prepare a new gallery, with a selection of best pictures available to show the capabilities of the SyncBox system.

5   Summary and Future Works

The goal of the presented work was to create the system for high-speed macro photography, dedicated to water drop pictures, and to make the system as simple as possible. The system is inexpensive, and can be extended according to users' needs. It can be utilized by both amateurs and professional studios.

The elaborated system, called SyncBox, is based on Arduino board and open-source environment, which can be used with all commonly used computer systems. SyncBox can be operated by a single mouse click. The elaborated interface, called Dripper, is simple and easy to use.

The quality of the work depends on cameras and lenses used, but inexpensive ones can also be successfully applied. The presented photos were taken in most cases using inexpensive digital cameras, and second hand 10-Euro lenses.

Fig. 6. Water drop, shape 1, resembling a column; picture taken using SyncBox

Fig. 7. Water drop, shape 2, resembling an umbrella; picture taken using SyncBox

Fig. 8. Water drop, shape 3, resembling a crown; picture taken using SyncBox

Fig. 9. Pictures taken using SyncBox, shown in the Internet gallery

Further works are planned on SyncBox. First of all, we would like to minimize the entire system, in order to make it easily portable. Additionally, we would like to obtain multi-color shapes, by adding another solenoid valve (or valves), to draw colored water from another container (or containers). The next step will be to make the project wireless, with peripherals controlled over the Internet, thus making it available worldwide.

Acknowledgments. This project was partially supported by the Research Center of PJIIT, supported by the Ministry of Science and Higher Education in Poland.

References

1. Arduino, http://www.arduino.cc/
2. Gorham, D.A., Field, J.E.: High-Speed Photography of Liquid Jets. In: Rolls, P.J. (ed.) High Speed Photography, pp. 442–447. Springer US (1975)
3. Kelly, J.F., Timmis, H.: Arduino Adventures. Escape from Gemini Station (2013) ISBN: 978-1-4302-4606-0 (Online)
4. McRoberts, M.: Beginning Arduino (2013) ISBN: 978-1-4302-5017-3 (Online)
5. CameraAxe, http://www.cameraaxe.com/
6. Chalkley, A.: The Absolute Beginner's Guide to Arduino, http://forefront.io/a/beginners-guide-to-arduino
7. Cognisys Inc.: StopShot - High Speed Photography Controller, http://www.cognisys-inc.com/stopshot/stopshot.php
8. High Speed Photography UK: SplashArt and Phototrigger products and demos, http://www.phototrigger.co.uk/
9. Oxer, J., Blemings, H.: Practical Arduino. Cool Projects for Open Source Hardware (2010) ISBN: 978-1-4302-2477-8 (Print) 978-1-4302-2478-5 (Online)
10. Shaikh, M.H.: Study of Arduino for Creative and Interactive Artwork Installations. In: Chowdhry, B.S., Shaikh, F.K., Hussain, D.M.A., Uqaili, M.A. (eds.) IMTIC 2012. CCIS, vol. 281, pp. 478–488. Springer, Heidelberg (2012)
11. Sakharov, A.A.: On New Elaborations in International Terminology of High-Speed Photography and Cinematography. In: Rolls, P.J. (ed.) High Speed Photography, pp. 592–593. Springer US (1975)

Author Index